HERITAGE STUDIES 5

Teacher's Edition

Fourth Edition

bju press®

Greenville, South Carolina

FREE
Lesson Plan
Overview
now available at
bjupress.com/resources

Note

The fact that materials produced by other publishers may be referred to in this volume does not constitute an endorsement of the content or theological position of materials produced by such publishers. Any references and ancillary materials are listed as an aid to the student or the teacher and in an attempt to maintain the accepted academic standards of the publishing industry.

HERITAGE STUDIES 5 Teacher's Edition
Fourth Edition

Writers
Carol Arrington Ardt, MEd
Annittia Jackson
Kathy Hynicka
Ann Larson, MEd

Consultant
L. Michelle Rosier

Bible Integration
Brian Collins, PhD

Project Editors
Elizabeth Turner, MA
Kaitlyn Chisholm

Page Layout
Bonnijean Marley

Permissions
Tatiana Bento
Sylvia Gass
Ashley Hobbs
Meg Jones
Carrie Walker

Designer
Michael Asire

Cover Design
Elly Kalagayan

Cover Art
Ben Schipper

Cover Photography
Craig Oesterling

Project Coordinators
Heather Chisholm
Michele White

Photo credits appear on page 469.

Some Background information in this Teacher's Edition and Teacher's Toolkit CD is adapted from material in the following BJU Press textbooks:
AMERICAN GOVERNMENT Teacher's Edition, Third Edition
AMERICAN REPUBLIC, Third and Fourth Editions
AMERICAN REPUBLIC Teacher's Edition, Third and Fourth Editions
HERITAGE STUDIES 4, Third Edition
HERITAGE STUDIES 4 Teacher's Edition, Third Edition
UNITED STATES HISTORY, Fourth Edition
UNITED STATES HISTORY Teacher's Edition, Fourth Edition
WORLD HISTORY, Fourth Edition
WORLD HISTORY Teacher's Edition, Fourth Edition
BIBLICAL WORLDVIEW

© 2016 BJU Press
Greenville, South Carolina 29609
First Edition © 1986 BJU Press
Second Edition © 1998 BJU Press
Third Edition © 2010 BJU Press

Printed in the United States of America

ISBN 978-1-60682-949-3 (Teacher's Edition with CD)

15 14 13 12 11 10 9 8 7 6 5 4 3

Contents

Teacher's Toolkit CD

Activity Manual Answer Key
Background Information
Instructional Aids
Instructional Aids Answer Key
Interactive Visual

Visuals
Quizzes
Quizzes Answer Key
Materials List
Rubrics

Goals

Strengthen knowledge of God and encourage Christian growth

- Reveal God's wisdom, omnipotence, sovereignty, and benevolence through the study of the history of the world (Psalm 19:1; Romans 1:20).
- Encourage evaluation and rejection of false philosophies.
- Promote discipline in the student's approach to and performance of responsibilities.
- Reinforce that all people need to trust Christ for salvation (John 3:16–18).

Develop interest in history, geography, citizenship, economics, and culture

- Emphasize God's plan for the individual, the family, and the nation.
- Emphasize the student's role in his expanding environment: family, community, state, country, and world.
- Encourage the student to make wise decisions and to become a responsible Christian citizen.
- Teach practical skills, such as reading maps and charts, sequencing events, and working with timelines.
- Develop an understanding of how people use resources to meet their needs.

Present a balanced overview of American heritage

- **American history**: the study of America's past
  - Develop an appreciation and comprehension of the past as it relates to the present and the future.
  - Recognize the significance of events.
  - Distinguish God's leading in historical events.
  - Examine the record of God's dealing with humanity.
  - Recognize the political views held by America's early leaders.
  - Teach the use of the Bible to evaluate events in American history.
- **Geography**: the study of the earth's surface and how it is used
  - Teach the reading and interpreting of maps and other geographic representations and tools to acquire and report information.
  - Demonstrate the wise use of natural resources to God's glory (Genesis 1:28).
  - Relate that God is worthy to be praised for creating all things (Genesis 1:1; Revalation 4:11).

- **Citizenship**: the study of government and civic responsibilities
  - Identify and examine the responsibility of the community, state, and country to their citizens.
  - Examine the Christian's responsibility to the government.
  - Identify the Christian's responsibility toward his community, state, and country.
- **Economics**: the study of how people use resources to meet their needs
  - Help students recognize that people everywhere have needs and wants.
  - Acknowledge that the physical environment affects the way people live and work.
- **Culture**: the study of the way of life of a group of people
  - Demonstrate how historians rely on primary sources to learn about the past.
  - Explain that landforms, climate, and resources influence the way of life of a group of people.
  - Express the need for worldwide missions (Acts 1:8).

Promote an understanding of and an ability to discern connections between events

- Develop skills such as making decisions and inferring relationships.
- Teach cause-and-effect relationships to explain historical events.

Explain how to organize information in chronological order

- Teach how daily life has changed over time.
- Explore events in historical order to see progression and connections between events.

Build silent and oral reading habits to further fluency

- Practice silent and oral reading habits so the student can read text independently.
- Use a variety of techniques before, during, and after reading similar to those used in a guided reading lesson.
- Give the student a purpose for reading before assigning pages to read silently.

Heritage Studies 5 from a Christian Worldview

God wrote a completely accurate history in the Bible. The Bible presents us with a perspective that guides our examination of history. This biblical perspective is called a **Christian worldview**.

What Is Our Place in God's World?

God made humans to declare His glory by being like Him. He has made each of us in His image (Genesis 1:26–27). In the **Creation Mandate** (the first command of God, found in Genesis 1:28), God called us to imitate His deeds. God is the infinite ruler of the universe, and people are to be finite rulers of His earth. As people have attempted to live out the Creation Mandate, they have created a way of living that includes language, religion, government, customs, and the arts. This way of living is a people's culture.

Tragically, shortly after Creation, people sinned. Adam and Eve disobeyed and failed to exercise the dominion given to them (Genesis 3:6). However, God did not abandon His image bearers. At that time, God promised to redeem the world to Himself by sending His own Son into the world to save His people from sin (Genesis 3:15). The story of humanity is the story of God's redemptive acts to rescue His people and to restore them to rule over the earth to His glory (Revelation 5:9–10). God has called His people to serve Him by living lives of good works (Matthew 5:16). God wants believers to help others by meeting their needs and showing them mercy.

Why Teach Heritage Studies 5?

Heritage Studies 5 is part of a developmental social studies program used to teach history, geography, government, economics, and culture skills, as well as a knowledge of God and Christian character. History is the record of the past acts of God and of humans from Creation to the present. It records mankind's attempts to live out the Creation Mandate in a fallen world. *Heritage Studies 5* focuses on a small but important part of this study—the United States and the country's interaction in world events. History is an account of good and evil, of great advances for God's work of redemption, and of human sin and suffering.

Why should fifth graders be taught about the accounts of evil in history? We believe there are at least three important reasons for studying the good as well as the evil.

Lessons for Life

In studying events from the past, the student can see the consequences of right and wrong choices. The main lesson to be learned from these choices is that people should trust God and obey His Word. As the student studies and applies lessons from these events, he gains not only knowledge but more importantly wisdom. This wisdom can then be used as he attempts to guide others toward right choices. Many of these choices are individual and personal. Others, however, are cultural and societal.

Cultural Identity

Studying *Heritage Studies 5* will help the student understand who he is as an American. Many Americans possess very little knowledge of their country's past. Therefore, they do not understand the values that have shaped our nation's story. They also lack the ability to critically evaluate the current conditions of our nation.

As this course is taught, special attention should be given to how Americans have valued freedom. Freedom in America allows people to make their own choices without fear of harm. Freedom can be a good thing (1 Corinthians 7:21, 23; Romans 6:17–22). But the kind of freedom that a Christian should value is guided by God's Word (Genesis 2:16–17; Psalm 2:10–12; 9:17). A good society protects the people's freedom to live according to God's commands, and it resists the selfish use of freedom. As students come to understand freedom in American culture, they become better prepared to speak for God in an increasingly secular society.

In the teaching of this course, attention should also be given to what Americans have thought about justice. All people have certain rights because all are made in God's image (Genesis 1:26–27). Americans have always valued the idea of justice. They have defended equal standing before the law and fought for the right of all citizens to vote, to own property, and to have access to education. But this view of justice has also been conflicted. African Americans, for example, have been denied these rights for much of American history. If students are to understand the past—and if they are to know how to live as Christians today—they will need to know about justice and injustice in the story of America.

Civics and the Christian

Civics is the study of rights and responsibilities of citizenship. The Christian understands that citizenship is a biblical concept. Citizenship has to do with civilization and the importance of being in a society. The Bible teaches that God made humans to make civilizations, to organize themselves into societies, and to develop various cultures (Genesis 1:28). The Bible also teaches that our most basic obligation is to love and serve God and people (Mark 12:30–31).

When these ideas are put together, a Christian view of civics begins to emerge. God expects Christians to love their neighbors and to show that love by being good citizens. Christians should obey the laws of their community. They should work hard in their vocations in order to help people, and they should give generously to meet the needs of others. They should also volunteer in their communities in various ways, such as serving in soup kitchens and helping the elderly. Above all, Christians should be active in the ministries of their church to help the gospel advance in their communities.

Instructional Materials

Student Text

The student text is a colorful, age-appropriate presentation of social studies that integrates civics, culture, economics, geography, government, and history through a biblical worldview. Students will chronologically traverse United States history, starting with America's earliest people and concluding with the Obama administration. Eye-catching artwork, maps, graphs, historical photos, short biographies, activities, and quick-check questions enhance learning. A Resource Treasury in the back of the book includes an atlas, a gazetteer, a biographical dictionary, a glossary, and an index.

Activity Manual

The *Heritage Studies 5 Activity Manual* contains full-color pages to review and enrich the lessons, including reinforcements, map skills, Primary Sources, expansion pages, sections for comparing worldviews, study guides, and chapter reviews. The main project will be designing a lap book of the Civil War. The Activity Manual's Answer Key is available on the Teacher's Toolkit CD.

Teacher's Edition

The *Heritage Studies 5 Teacher's Edition* contains 180 lessons and coordinates all the instructions and activities. Each lesson includes a lesson focus, identifies objectives and vocabulary, and gives ideas for discussion. Many lessons offer collaborative learning suggestions, and some include the use of graphic organizers that train students to organize informational text. Reduced student text pages appear with each lesson. Review games help prepare students for assessments.

Vocabulary Words

Introduce unfamiliar words before reading a section. Display and pronounce the words for the students. As the text is read, remind them to look for the vocabulary words in bold print. The students should demonstrate an understanding of the vocabulary words using context, text definitions, and Resource Treasury entries as needed.

Online Resources

Visit bjupress.com/resources for links to enhance the lessons. (*Note:* Although these links have been carefully selected, evaluate all material before presentation.)

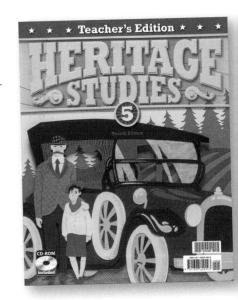

Teacher's Toolkit CD

The *Teacher's Toolkit CD*, located inside the back cover of this Teacher's Edition, includes the Activity Manual Answer Key, a materials list, quizzes, teaching visuals, additional Background information, rubrics, and instructional aids. The instructional aids include graphic organizers, charts, and creative activities that provide opportunities for students to work together in small groups.

Tests

The *Heritage Studies 5 Test Packet* provides one age-appropriate test per chapter, covering the most important concepts taught in the lessons. These tests can serve as the objective part of an evaluation of a student's progress. The most effective tests are an outgrowth of the teaching process. Accordingly, these tests should not replace the teacher's individual assessment of a student's understanding and application. The tests can be adjusted in accordance with the teaching emphasis and direction as well as the student's academic ability. An Answer Key is available separately.

United States of America

Because these materials emphasize United States history and citizenship, the readers in most cases are addressed as though they are in the context of the United States. If you are using these materials in a country other than the United States, you may choose to adapt as necessary. One possible adaptation would be to compare United States culture, symbols, and traditions with those of the area where you live.

Lesson Features

Chapter Opener
Discuss the chapter focus that introduces the chapter topic.

Art
Prepare students for chapter content by analyzing the corresponding art.

Objectives
Understand the outcome of instruction in terms of the students' behavior.

Timeline
Encourage history awareness and build sequencing skills by organizing and sequencing historical events using timelines.

Vocabulary Words
Develop understanding of new words.

Materials
Determine which materials need to be prepared for the lesson.

JourneyForth Books
Suggest books with a biblical worldview for readers of varying abilities and interests.

Chapter 7

Introduction

The history of slavery stretches back to the founding of the United States. Southern states based their economy on slavery. Slavery also provided money for the North.

Many Americans opposed slavery. This issue divided the nation. Southern states seceded after Abraham Lincoln was elected president. The Civil War began in South Carolina and continued on the eastern and western fronts. The cost of war was great. Many Confederate and Union soldiers lost their lives.

President Lincoln issued the Emancipation Proclamation that promised to free all enslaved people in rebellious states once a Union victory was achieved. General Robert E. Lee and his men surrendered at Appomattox Courthouse. The South had lost the war. Slavery ended in the United States. After years of working to save the nation from disunion, Lincoln was assassinated. The nation would need time to heal and rebuild.

Chapter Focus

Slavery caused much disagreement in the United States, eventually breaking the nation apart.

Chapter 7 Overview

Lesson	Student Text	Activity Manual	Content		Vocabulary	
55	138–42	99–101	Activity: Create a Lap Book		Dred Scott case	states' rights
56	143–46	102–3	Biography box: Sarah & Angelina Grimké Republican Party Abraham Lincoln	Stephen Douglas	abolitionist	secede
57	147–49	104–6	Ulysses S. Grant Jefferson Davis Robert E. Lee	Richmond, Virginia General Thomas Jackson	Anaconda Plan Bull Run	Confederates Union
58	150–52	107	General George McClellan Antietam Creek	Admiral David Farragut		
59	153–55		How It Was: Hardships of War President Jefferson Davis	President Abraham Lincoln	Emancipation Proclamation munition	negotiate
60	156–58	108–9	General George Meade Gettysburg Primary Source: The Battle Hymn of the Republic	Chattanooga	scouting siege	
61	159–61	110	Atlanta Appomattox Courthouse	Reconstruction	siegework	
62		111–12	Chapter Review	Visit bjupress.com/resources for links to enhance the lessons.		
63			Chapter Test			

Heritage Studies 5

140

---

7 The Civil War

Attack on Fort Sumter April 12
Lee Surrenders at Appomattox Courthouse April 9

1861 | 1862 | 1863 July Northern Victories at Gettysburg and Vicksburg | 1864 | 1865 April 14 Lincoln Assassinated by John Wilkes Booth | 1866

Focus
Slavery caused much disagreement in the United States, eventually breaking the nation apart.

What Caused the War

During the first decades of its history, the United States faced many challenges and opportunities. The nation explored the continent and fought wars. It built roads, canals, and railways to connect its citizens. But during these decades a division grew. The Northern states and the Southern states viewed themselves as different from each other. When they could no longer compromise, conflict erupted. The history of the American Civil War stretches back before the nation's founding and continues to influence American culture to the present day.

Slavery

History

Slavery began early in the history of the thirteen colonies. The earliest recorded African slaves arrived in Jamestown in 1619. John Rolfe, a tobacco planter who married Pocahontas, bought twenty Africans from a Dutch ship. For much of the colonial period, Africans were sold into slavery along the Chesapeake Bay in order to harvest tobacco. But colonists from Georgia to Massachusetts purchased slaves also. Sometimes enslaved people were able to gain their freedom. The freed slaves often lived alongside white colonists. However, by 1776 slavery was firmly established in the United States.

During the first decades of independence, white Americans disagreed about slavery. Many wanted to end slavery altogether. In the Northern states, slavery slowly faded away. Slave owners found that it was cheaper to hire workers than to keep slaves. Some preachers opposed slavery. But in the South, slavery grew. Crops, especially cotton, needed much labor. Plantation owners planned on enslaved people having children. These children would grow up and continue working in the fields.

Slavery and Money

The Southern states based their economy on slavery. Slaves harvested much cotton, tobacco, and rice. Many

139

JourneyForth

Avery's Battlefield and *Avery's Crossroad* by Deanna K. Klingel are available from JourneyForth Books, a division of BJU Press, at journeyforth.com.
Set during the Civil War, these historical fiction novels follow Avery and his dog Gunner through the period. Avery's skills as a doctor become useful to the soldiers in Civil War hospitals, and he develops special friendships along the way.

Chapter 7: The Civil War

Lesson 55

Student Text pages 138–42
Activity Manual pages 99–101

Lesson Focus
• The issues of slavery and states' rights divided the United States.

Objectives
• Identify the history of slavery in the United States
• Examine how slavery affected the economy
• Explain the controversy surrounding states' rights

Teacher's Toolkit CD
• Instructional Aid 37: *Slavery and the Civil War*

Materials
• Manila or colored file folders (three per student)
• Sources for information needed to complete the pieces of a lap book

Introduction
• Invite a student to read aloud the title of the chapter and predict what the chapter will be about. It will be about the Civil War in the United States.
• Why do you think this war was called the Civil War? Answers could include that it was a war between the citizens of the country.
• Explain that the Civil War is also referred to as the War Between the States.
• Invite a student to read the chapter focus aloud.
What do you think you will learn in this chapter? How disagreement over slavery divided the nation.
• Direct attention to the picture of the ships the *Merrimac* and the *Monitor*. Explain that the *Merrimac* was built in the North but salvaged from the Norfolk navy yard and rechristened by the Confederates as the *Virginia*. The *Monitor* was built and used by the Union. Explain that the battle at Hampton Roads in the harbor of the James River, Virginia, was the first battle in history between ironclad warships.
• Direct attention to the timeline.
Where did the first major event of the Civil War take place? Fort Sumter
When did General Lee surrender at Appomattox Courthouse? April 9, 1865
According to the dates on the timeline, how long did the Civil War last? about four years

Preparation for Reading
• Generate interest as you direct the students to read the titles and examine the images on pages 138–42.
• Guide pronunciation of any unfamiliar words in the lesson.
• Direct the students to read the pages silently and complete Instructional Aid 37 in small groups.

Lesson 55 • 141

The gear (⚙) indicates a higher-order question. These questions are based on information gathered from the text but require some analysis, synthesis, or evaluation of the text. Supply any prompts or background as needed to guide the students to the answer.

Other Features

Promote higher-order thinking skills through interactive learning strategies such as questioning, demonstrations, discussion, and hands-on activities.

Enhance students' curiosity and awareness by using pictures, graphs, and maps.

Apply integrated Bible truths and principles.

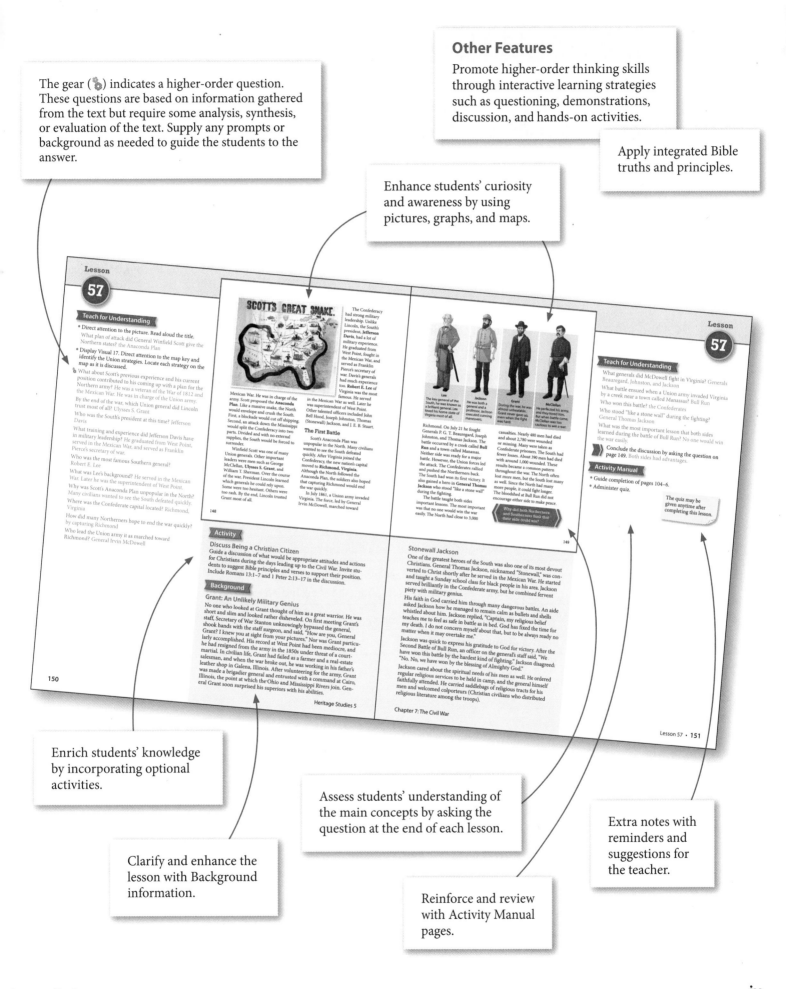

Enrich students' knowledge by incorporating optional activities.

Clarify and enhance the lesson with Background information.

Assess students' understanding of the main concepts by asking the question at the end of each lesson.

Reinforce and review with Activity Manual pages.

Extra notes with reminders and suggestions for the teacher.

Lesson Plan Overview

Chapter 1: America's First People

Lesson	Teacher's Edition	Student Text	Activity Manual	Content Objectives and Christian Worldview
1	2–6	2–6	1–4	• Identify what the earliest American artifacts suggest • Examine how Native Americans fulfilled the Creation Mandate • Locate the early Native American cultural groups
2	7–9	7–9	5	• Examine the culture of the Pueblos and their ancestors • Describe the Navajo way of life • Identify characteristics of the Chumash culture • Complete an organizer about the food, shelter, and crafts of the Pueblo, Navajo, and Chumash people
3	10–12	10–12	6–8	• Examine the culture of the Makah tribe • Identify customs of the Inuit people • Compare the cultures of the Makah and Inuit people
4	13–15	13–15	9–10	• Identify characteristics of the Nez Perces • Examine the culture of the Sioux • Compare the cultures of the Nez Perces and the Sioux
5	16–18	16–18	11–13	• Recognize the geographic area of the Northeast Woodland Indians and the Southeast Woodland Indians • Identify the culture of the Iroquois people • Examine Cherokee traditions and way of life
6	19–21	19–21	14	• Identify beliefs of several Indian culture groups • Describe shamans and shamanism • Use God's Word to draw a biblical conclusion about spirits
7	22			• Complete an organizer for an Indian tribe • Make a creative presentation about an Indian cultural group
8	23		15–16	**Chapter Review**
9	23			**Chapter Test**

Chapter 2: European Exploration and Settlement

Lesson	Teacher's Edition	Student Text	Activity Manual	Content Objectives and Christian Worldview
10	24–27	22–25	17–19	• Identify the changes, challenges, and pressures that made Europeans want to explore the world • Name some of the inventions and how they helped sailors navigate the new ships • Identify the countries that could have explored but chose not to
11	28–30	26–28	20	• Explain how Prince Henry of Portugal helped his nation become skilled at exploration • Recognize the accomplishments of explorers like Bartolomeu Dias and Vasco da Gama • State Christopher Columbus's idea about how to reach Asia • Explain how Columbus was able to find the Americas
12	31–33	29–31	21–23	• State the ways Christopher Columbus did not understand true Christianity • Explain how the Spanish treated the American Indians • Recognize that Bartolomé de Las Casas opposed the sinful treatment of the Indians
13	34–37	32–35	24–25	• Name the things that Peter Stuyvesant thought were important for New Amsterdam • List the reasons Roanoke failed • Compare the first settlements in North America
14	38–40	36–38	26	• List reasons the English began to start new colonies in America • Name several things Jamestown did right and wrong • Explain what John Smith did to help the colony • Compare and contrast what the colonial governors and the Virginia Company wanted for the colony
15	41–44	39–42	27	• Explain why the Separatists left England • List the reasons the Pilgrims believed they had to leave the Netherlands • Describe the Pilgrims' voyage across the Atlantic • Explain how the Lord provided for the Pilgrims at Plymouth
16	45–46	43–45	28–30	• Recognize John Winthrop's vision for the Massachusetts Bay Colony • Describe how the Puritans ran their churches in the New World • Compare and contrast Virginia and the Massachusetts Bay Colony
17	47		31–32	**Chapter Review**
18	47			**Chapter Test**

Chapter 3: The Thirteen Colonies

Lesson	Teacher's Edition	Student Text	Activity Manual	Content Objectives and Christian Worldview
19	48–51	46–49	33–36	• List reasons why Europeans came to America • Name the three regions of the thirteen colonies • Explain how some of the New England and middle colonies began
20	52–54	50–52	37	• Relate how Pennsylvania, Delaware, and the southern colonies started • Identify Virginia's House of Burgesses as the first representative government in America • Explain how Charles I helped Catholics • Recognize James Oglethorpe as the person who wanted to establish a colony for English people who could not pay their debts
21	55–57	53–55	38–40	• Describe local governments in the thirteen colonies • Compare the social classes in the colonies • Describe colonial family life
22	58–60	56–58	41–42	• Describe religion in the New England colonies • Explain why Anne Hutchinson was expelled from Massachusetts • Describe the education of the Puritan children • Name the industries in the New England colonies
23	61–63	59–61	43	• Identify the many cultures that made up the middle colonies • Name some industries of the middle colonies • Describe education in the middle colonies • Relate Benjamin Franklin's influence on education
24	64–66	62–64	44–45	• Explain religion in the southern colonies • Discuss education in the southern colonies • Explain farming in the southern colonies
25	67–69	65–67	46	• Explain why people in the colonies began to turn away from God • Name two leaders of the Great Awakening and what they did to bring revival to the colonies • List the effects of the Great Awakening
26	69		47–48	**Chapter Review**
27	69			**Chapter Test**

Chapter 4: American Independence

Lesson	Teacher's Edition	Student Text	Activity Manual	Content Objectives and Christian Worldview
28	70–75	68–73	49–51	• Identify the three groups that wanted to keep or expand their lands around the Ohio River • Describe how the French and Indian War began • Explain the consequences of the Proclamation of 1763
29	76–78	74–76	52–53	• Evaluate how colonists responded to Parliament's laws • Explain people's reactions to the Townshend Acts in Massachusetts
30	79–81	77–79	54–56	• Identify decisions made by the Continental Congress • Examine events leading to the Revolutionary War • Recognize military leaders in the war
31	82–84	80–82	57–58	• Understand the purpose of the Declaration of Independence • Identify British gains and losses in the North
32	85–87	83–85	59	• Examine how the war was supported financially • Identify the role of foreign soldiers in the war • Describe the impact of the war on civilian life
33	88–90	86–88	60–61	• Describe Revolutionary War fighting in different parts of the nation • Examine how Patriots persisted in fighting for independence
34	91–93	89–91	62	• Describe the final conflict of the Revolutionary War • Examine agreements after the war
35	93		63–64	**Chapter Review**
36	93			**Chapter Test**

Chapter 5: The Early National Period

Lesson	Teacher's Edition	Student Text	Activity Manual	Content Objectives and Christian Worldview
37	94–97	92–95	65–67	• Assess the problems in American life after the revolution • Detect the value of virtue and Christian principles • Determine how Shays' Rebellion confirmed the need for a more effective American government • Explain the weaknesses of the Articles of Confederation
38	98–101	96–99	68–69	• State the goal of the the Constitutional Convention • Explain compromises made during the convention • Name the three branches of government and what each branch consists of • Explain the process of ratifying the Constitution and the purpose of the Bill of Rights
39	102–4	100–102	70–72	• Describe the Electoral College and its purpose • Identify precedents set by President Washington • State the purpose of the president's cabinet • Summarize the conflict between American Indians and Americans moving westward
40	105–7	103–5	73–75	• Identify John Adams as the second president of the United States • Compare and contrast the views of the two political parties that formed during Adams's presidency • Describe the events that almost brought the United States to the point of war with France
41	108–11	106–9	76–77	• Identify Thomas Jefferson as the third president of the United States • Tell why Jefferson took action against the Barbary pirates • Explain the significance of purchasing the Louisiana Territory • Explain the significance of the Lewis and Clark expedition
42	112–14	110–12	78	• Identify James Madison as the fourth president of the United States • State reasons for the War of 1812 • Explain why the United States and Great Britain were not ready for war • Explain the reasons Madison adopted Federalist ideas after the war
43	115–17	113–15	79–80	• Identify James Monroe as the fifth president of the United States • List the four points of the Monroe Doctrine • Explain why the United States wanted to buy Florida • Explain how the Missouri Compromise solved the argument between the free states and the slave states
44	117		81–82	**Chapter Review**
45	117			**Chapter Test**

Chapter 6: The Young Nation Grows

Lesson	Teacher's Edition	Student Text	Activity Manual	Content Objectives and Christian Worldview
46	118–21	116–19	83–86	• Recognize how the Electoral College was put to the test in the election of 1824 • Identify characteristics of Andrew Jackson, John Quincy Adams, and Henry Clay • Examine the presidency of John Quincy Adams
47	122–24	120–22	87	• Identify the political party that Andrew Jackson and his followers created • Examine problems of Jackson's presidency
48	125–27	123–25	88–89	• Identify what right the Indian Removal Act gave to the US military • Examine events leading up to the Trail of Tears
49	128–30	126–28	90–91	• Define rationalism • Identify what Christians did in response to rationalism • Recognize aspects of the Second Great Awakening • Identify problems that occurred along with revival
50	131–33	129–31	92–93	• Examine changes in transportation • Identify changes in communication • Compare historical maps
51	134–36	132–34	94	• Describe the factory system in America • Identify inventions that changed American farming
52	137–39	135–37	95–96	• Examine events that led to the Mexican War • Explain how the war ended • Identify what America gained under the treaty as part of the Mexican Cession • Recognize that not everyone agreed with how America gained land
53	139		97–98	**Chapter Review**
54	139			**Chapter Test**

Chapter 7: The Civil War

Lesson	Teacher's Edition	Student Text	Activity Manual	Content Objectives and Christian Worldview
55	140–44	138–42	99–101	• Identify the history of slavery in the United States • Examine how slavery affected the economy • Explain the controversy surrounding states' rights
56	145–49	143–46	102–3	• Identify the candidates and the results of the election of 1860 • Examine secession in the South • Describe how the Civil War began
57	149–51	147–49	104–6	• Recognize strengths and weaknesses of the Confederacy and the Union • Identify generals of the Confederacy and the Union • Examine lessons the North and the South learned at Bull Run
58	152–54	150–52	107	• Relate the military advances on the eastern front and their results • Identify the military advances on the western front and their results
59	155–57	153–55		• Explain Union advantages in supplying food and goods • Relate how the South suffered great hardship during the war • Discuss politics in the North and the South
60	158–60	156–58	108–9	• Recognize generals and battles on the eastern front • Recognize generals and battles on the western front
61	161–63	159–61	110	• Examine Union campaigns in the East • Identify the roles of Grant and Lee at the end of the war • Relate how President Lincoln died
62	163		111–12	**Chapter Review**
63	163			**Chapter Test**

Chapter 8: Reconstruction and the West

Lesson	Teacher's Edition	Student Text	Activity Manual	Content Objectives and Christian Worldview
64	164–66	162–64	113–15	• List three things Southern states would have to do under Reconstruction • Identify the response Southerners had to the requirements placed on them • Describe the Black Codes
65	167–69	165–67	116–19	• Identify the purpose of the Freedmen's Bureau • Understand the purpose of the Fourteenth Amendment • Describe the Reconstruction Act of 1867 • Explain the impeachment of President Johnson
66	170–73	168–71	120–21	• Define *carpetbagger* and *scalawag* • Relate what the Fifteenth Amendment did for black people • Identify challenges black Americans faced
67	174–76	172–74	122	• Examine opposition to Reconstruction • Relate the meaning of Southern "redemption"
68	177–79	175–77	123	• Identify the tribes that make up the Five Civilized Tribes • Explain the impact of miners on the West • Examine sodbusters and how they changed the Great Plains
69	180–82	178–80	124–25	• Describe the work of a cowboy • Examine the role of railroads
70	183–85	181–83	126	• Identify the Indian conflicts that resulted as Americans moved west • State the role of Christians during the Indian Wars • Examine other kinds of conflict in the West
71	185		127–28	**Chapter Review**
72	185			**Chapter Test**

Chapter 9: The Gilded Age

Lesson	Teacher's Edition	Student Text	Activity Manual	Content Objectives and Christian Worldview
73	186–89	184–87	129–32	• Explain why the late 1800s in America were called the Gilded Age • Identify industries that experienced growth • Identify important leaders in industry • Explain why industry grew
74	190–93	188–91	133–34	• Identify new inventions and their inventors • Examine how new inventions affected life in America
75	194–96	192–94	135–36	• Explain social Darwinism and why it is a dangerous belief • Explain responses to problems created by social Darwinism • Evaluate how wealthy Americans managed their money
76	197–99	195–97	137–39	• Explain why and how cities experienced growth • Examine problems created by the urbanization of America • Write an imaginative journal entry
77	200–202	198–200	140	• Identify social reforms that began during the Gilded Age • Explain why social reform was needed
78	203–5	201–3	141	• Explain why Americans had more leisure time during the Gilded Age • Identify forms of entertainment and the arts • Evaluate the problems with newspapers
79	206–7	204–5	142–44	• Explain the two main problems that arose among Christians • Describe the ministries of Christians who met spiritual needs
80	208		145–46	**Chapter Review**
81	209			**Chapter Test**

Chapter 10: America's Influence Spreads Abroad

Lesson	Teacher's Edition	Student Text	Activity Manual	Content Objectives and Christian Worldview
82	210–13	206–9	147–49	• Examine American involvement in foreign countries • Analyze William Jennings Bryan's and William McKinley's 1896 campaign
83	214–16	210–12	150–51	• Describe events leading to the Spanish-American War • Examine the course of the war • Analyze the consequences of the war
84	217–19	213–15	152–53	• Examine changes that Roosevelt made during his presidency
85	220–23	216–19	154–55	• Discuss changes in the cities during the Progressive Era • Identify changes in voting
86	224–26	220–22	156–57	• Examine William Taft's presidency • Identify the importance of the Panama Canal
87	227–29	223–25	158	• Recognize problems related to American workers during the Progressive Era • Examine the struggle for equality by black Americans
88	230–33	226–29	159–60	• Examine education in the Progressive Era • Evaluate Woodrow Wilson's Progressive policies
89	233		161–62	**Chapter Review**
90	233			**Chapter Test**

Chapter 11: The First World War

Lesson	Teacher's Edition	Student Text	Activity Manual	Content Objectives and Christian Worldview
91	234–37	230–33	163–65	• Identify the nations that made up the Triple Entente • Recognize nations in the Triple Alliance • Recognize events that led to war in Europe
92	238–40	234–36	166	• Identify the original plan of the Central Powers to conquer the Allies • Recognize the significance of the Battle of the Marne • Define the *western front* • Relate what living and fighting from trenches was like
93	241–43	237–39	167–69	• Examine the war on the eastern front • Describe weapons of World War I • Evaluate Germany's unrestricted submarine warfare
94	244–46	240–42	170–71	• Describe important European battles of World War I • Recognize events that led to America's declaration of war • State what the United States did to get ready for war
95	247–49	243–45	172	• Identify the American Expeditionary Force (AEF) • Recognize Allied military commanders • Examine European battles
96	250–52	246–48	173–74	• Define the Committee on Public Information • Examine ways that Americans supported the war • Recognize the work of the Fuel Administration and the Food Administration • Identify jobs American women filled
97	253–55	249–51	175–76	• Recognize November 11, 1918, as Armistice Day • Examine the circumstances that led to the Treaty of Versailles • Define the "lost generation"
98	255		177–78	**Chapter Review**
99	255			**Chapter Test**

Chapter 12: Roaring '20s and Depressing '30s

Lesson	Teacher's Edition	Student Text	Activity Manual	Content Objectives and Christian Worldview
100	256–59	252–55	179–81	• Describe America's consumer culture in the 1920s • Explain the effects new technology had on American entertainment in the 1920s
101	260–62	256–58	182–83	• Examine challenges Christians faced in the 1920s • Analyze the significance of the Scopes Trial • Contrast Fundamentalists and modernists • Write about kinds of entertainment that are personally acceptable based on Scripture
102	263–65	259–61	184–86	• Identify Warren Harding and Calvin Coolidge as America's presidents in the 1920s • Explain Andrew Mellon's tax plan
103	266–68	262–64	187–88	• Identify Herbert Hoover and Franklin D. Roosevelt as the next two presidents of the United States after Calvin Coolidge • Explain why the stock market crashed in 1929 • Explain why banks failed at the end of 1930 • Describe Hoover's solutions to the Depression and their effects
104	269–71	265–67	189–90	• Recognize that the New Deal was proposed by Franklin D. Roosevelt • Explain the purpose of the New Deal • Identify the Civilian Conservation Corps and the National Recovery Administration as two jobs programs begun during Roosevelt's term
105	272–74	268–70		• Examine the strategies Roosevelt used to get reelected to a second term • Explain the purpose of the Social Security Act
106	275–77	271–73	191–92	• Examine the strategies Roosevelt used for keeping the New Deal in place • Explain the effects of Roosevelt's strategies
107	277		193–94	**Chapter Review**
108	277			**Chapter Test**

Chapter 13: Rulers with Iron Fists

Lesson	Teacher's Edition	Student Text	Activity Manual	Content Objectives and Christian Worldview
109	278–81	274–77	195–98	• Examine Joseph Stalin's early life • Describe Stalin's rise to power • State characteristics of Stalin's rule in the Soviet Union
110	282–84	278–80	199–201	• Examine collective farming under Joseph Stalin • Identify restrictions Stalin placed on citizens • Recognize how Stalin treated anyone who disagreed with him • Examine Communism in light of what the Bible says
111	285–87	281–83	202–3	• Describe Benito Mussolini's early life • Examine Mussolini's involvement in Socialism • Relate Mussolini's actions as the dictator of Italy
112	288–90	284–86	204	• Examine events leading to Hitler's rise to power in Germany • Recognize Hitler's hatred of Jews and Communists • Relate Hitler's actions as chancellor of Germany • Identify the treatment of the Jews after Hitler became the dictator of Germany
113	291–93	287–89	205–6	• Identify when it is right to have pride in one's nation • Realize that it is wrong to hate people of another nation • Relate why Hitler's hatred of the Jews was especially wicked
114	294	290	207	• Examine how the Japanese people treated Hirohito • Identify what Hirohito was like
115	295	291	208	• Compare how the Japanese worshiped the Showa to what the Bible says about worshiping one God • Tell why this period of history was a dark time for many people
116	295		209–10	**Chapter Review**
117	295			**Chapter Test**

Chapter 14: The Second World War

Lesson	Teacher's Edition	Student Text	Activity Manual	Content Objectives and Christian Worldview
118	296–99	292–95	211–14	• Explain the state of countries around the world before World War II • Identify the dictators of Russia, Germany, and Italy • Analyze Germany's aggression toward other nations
119	300–302	296–98	215–16	• Analyze efforts by the United States to remain neutral • Identify the countries that formed the Axis Powers • Explain why the United States declared war on Japan
120	303–5	299–301	217–18	• Describe what the United States did to mobilize for the war • Analyze Roosevelt's decision to make fighting Hitler the priority • Explain how German troops were pushed out of North Africa and the USSR
121	306–8	302–4		• Recognize that Allied forces were simultaneously fighting the Axis powers in Europe and in the Pacific • Analyze Japan's dominance in the Pacific • Explain the significance of the Allied victory at the Battle of Midway • Analyze the Allied strategy for winning in the Pacific
122	309–12	305–8	219	• List ways in which Americans at home supported the war • Explain why certain products were rationed • Describe the role entertainment had in supporting the war • Plan a victory garden
123	313–16	309–12	220–21	• Explain Eisenhower's strategy for winning the war in Europe • Explain how the Allied Powers defeated Hitler and Mussolini • Analyze the Holocaust
124	317–19	313–15	222	• Explain the Allies' strategy for fighting against Japan • State reasons that the atomic bomb was developed • Describe how the United States helped Japan and Europe after World War II ended
125	319		223–24	**Chapter Review**
126	319			**Chapter Test**

Chapter 15: Postwar America

Lesson	Teacher's Edition	Student Text	Activity Manual	Content Objectives and Christian Worldview
127	320–23	316–19	225–27	• Explain postwar changes in America • Analyze materialism • Explain Truman's Fair Deal
128	324–26	320–22	228	• Demonstrate an understanding of civil rights • Relate acts of discrimination • Explain how some Americans worked for civil rights
129	327–29	323–25	229–30	• Discuss the purpose of the United Nations • Explain what the Cold War was and the reason for it • Differentiate America's foreign policy before and after Congress approved the Truman Doctrine • Explain America's involvement in the Korean War
130	330–32	326–28	231–32	• State benefits of the Saint Lawrence Seaway and the Federal Aid Highway Act • Recognize that civil rights and the fight against Communism were ongoing struggles • Identify Alaska and Hawaii as the states admitted to the United States during Eisenhower's presidency • Explain why the United States became involved in the Vietnam War • Report on a state capital
131	333–35	329–31	233	• Explain how the space race was one way of fighting the Cold War • Recognize changes in American culture during the 1950s • Examine the role of Christianity in American culture in the 1950s
132	336–38	332–34	234	• Recognize that the election of 1960 was historically significant • Identify the Peace Corps as a program to help people in other countries • Identify the building of the Berlin Wall and the Cuban Missile Crisis as Cold War conflicts
133	339–41	335–37	235–36	• Identify Martin Luther King Jr. as a leader in the civil rights movement • Explain why there were protests in Birmingham • Describe Kennedy's assassination and America's reaction to it
134	341		237–38	**Chapter Review**
135	341			**Chapter Test**

Chapter 16: The Rise of the Counterculture

Lesson	Teacher's Edition	Student Text	Activity Manual	Content Objectives and Christian Worldview
136	342–45	338–41	239–42	• Understand the meaning of the Civil Rights Act of 1964 • Examine the meaning of the Voting Rights Act of 1965
137	346–48	342–44	243	• Identify the national program led by President Johnson to eliminate poverty • Recognize the informal name for Johnson's program to end poverty • Identify the name of the failed attack by the North Vietnamese on South Vietnam
138	349–51	345–47	244–45	• Identify groups that the liberals split between during the 1960s • Identify who said that black people should use force to gain power over white people • Identify how the New Left protested the establishment • Identify the founder of the feminist movement
139	352–55	348–51	246–47	• Describe the economy under President Nixon • Identify the purpose for the Environmental Protection Agency • Evaluate the *Roe v. Wade* Supreme Court ruling • Determine whether Nixon's presidency was conservative
140	356–59	352–55	248	• Examine events that led to the end of the Vietnam War • Identify the circumstances of the Cold War • Relate events leading to Watergate and the end of Nixon's presidency
141	360–62	356–58	249	• Relate how Gerald Ford became president • Describe the economic challenges Ford faced as president • Examine the Communist takeover of Vietnam and Cambodia • Create a budget
142	363–65	359–61	250	• Identify who won the presidency in 1976 • Relate Carter's handling of foreign affairs • Recognize that Americans struggled with discouragement about their nation
143	365		251–52	**Chapter Review**
144	365			**Chapter Test**

Chapter 17: A Time of Strength and Challenge

Lesson	Teacher's Edition	Student Text	Activity Manual	Content Objectives and Christian Worldview
145	366–69	362–65	253–56	• Recognize Soviet agression • Name Ronald Reagan as the winner of the 1980 presidential election • Identify the country that took Americans hostage
146	370–72	366–68	257	• Identify the name for Reagan's economic goals • Analyze whether Sandra Day O'Connor was a conservative • Recognize who made the assassination attempt on President Reagan
147	373–75	369–71	258–59	• Identify President Reagan's strategy for helping anti–Communist movements in other countries • Examine the United States' involvement with other countries • Participate in a mock summit
148	376–78	372–74	260	• Recognize why the United States bombed Libya • Examine the Iran-Contra Affair • Identify ways Reagan supported Christians on moral issues
149	379–81	375–77	261	• Recognize the space shuttle program • Acknowledge advances in medicine
150	382–83	378–79	262	• Identify what Reagan wanted Gorbachev to do when Reagan went to West Germany • Explain what the Intermediate-Range Nuclear Forces (INF) Treaty did
151	383		263–64	**Chapter Review**
152	383			**Chapter Test**

Chapter 18: Leader of the Free World

Lesson	Teacher's Edition	Student Text	Activity Manual	Content Objectives and Christian Worldview
153	384–87	380–83	265–67	• Identify experiences that prepared George H. W. Bush for the White House • Examine legislation Congress passed
154	388–91	384–86	268–70	• Identify the leader in Panama who surrendered to US forces • Recognize who opposed a Communist coup in the USSR • Analyze the crisis in the Middle East and the US involvement
155	391–93	387–89	271	• Identify the meaning of NAFTA • Recognize that Bill Clinton defeated Bush and Ross Perot in the presidential race
156	394–96	390–92	272–73	• Recognize the Republican leader who fought Clinton's ideas • Examine how Clinton promoted peace abroad
157	397–400	393–96	274–75	• Identify improvements in technology • Evaluate the economy and crime during the 1990s
158	401–3	397–99	276–77	• Recognize scandals involving President Clinton • Examine Clinton's foreign accomplishments • Relate how international trade grew during Clinton's time in office
159	404–7	400–403	278	• Recognize the Clinton administration's attitude toward the environment • Relate domestic and international terrorist acts
160	407		279–80	**Chapter Review**
161	407			**Chapter Test**

Chapter 19: A New Millennium

Lesson	Teacher's Edition	Student Text	Activity Manual	Content Objectives and Christian Worldview
162	408–11	404–7	281–83	• Identify who won the 2000 presidential election • Recognize the issues of compassionate conservatism
163	412–13	408–9	284	• Examine Bush's policies regarding embryonic stem cell research
164	414	410	285	• Identify Bush's attitude toward faith-based initiatives
165	415–18	411–14	286–87	• Examine events of September 11, 2001 • Identify the forces behind the attacks on September 11
166	419–21	415–17	288	• Recognize why the United States dropped bombs in Afghanistan • Examine events of the war in Afghanistan • Identify a major goal President Bush achieved in regard to Afghanistan
167	422–24	418–20	289	• Understand events leading to the invasion of Iraq • Recognize mistakes American leaders made while overseeing Iraq • Identify the major groups of people in Iraq • Examine opposition to the war in Iraq
168	425–27	421–23	290–91	• Recognize what caused the Iraqi people to give their support to the United States • Explain the problem with Social Security and how Congress responded to the problem • Identify what Bush wanted for Africa • Make an infograph
169	428–29	424–25	292	• Recognize factors that hurt the American economy • Explain Bush's response to the financial crisis
170	429		293–94	**Chapter Review**
171	429			**Chapter Test**

Chapter 20: Change Sweeps the Nation

Lesson	Teacher's Edition	Student Text	Activity Manual	Content Objectives and Christian Worldview
172	430–34	426–30	295–99	• Name the presidential candidates in the 2008 general election • Examine the political strengths of Barack Obama and John McCain • State campaign promises made by Barack Obama • Explain why the 2008 general election was historic
173	435–37	431–33	300	• Recognize that the economy was the most immediate domestic problem when Barack Obama assumed the presidency • Describe government programs intended to improve the economy • Explain why some Americans opposed Obama's programs
174	438–41	434–37	301–2	• Relate Obama's actions in Iraq and Afghanistan to promises he made while campaigning for president • Recognize that Osama bin Laden's death was a major victory for the United States • Explain the Arab Spring and why Obama chose to support it
175	442–44	438–40	303	• Identify gun violence and racism as domestic issues during Obama's presidency • Explain why Americans could not agree on a solution for gun violence • Recognize that African Americans suffered more disadvantages than other racial groups • Relate that President Obama was reelected in 2012
176	445–47	441–43	304	• Explain the secularization of American life • Relate positive and negative effects of the changing digital world • Recognize information as possibly the most valuable resource in the early twenty-first century
177	448–51	444–47	305	• Identify the Middle East and Eastern Europe as regions where Obama faced serious problems • Explain why the Middle East was important to the United States • Describe the Islamic State • Explain the problem Obama faced with Russia in Ukraine
178	452–55	448–51	306	• Recognize the environment, gay rights, and abortion as moral issues that separated Americans • Evaluate environmental issues, gay rights, and abortion in light of God's Word • Present a speech about a moral issue
179	455		307–8	**Chapter Review**
180	455			**Chapter Test**

Chapter 1

1 America's First People

Introduction

The earliest Americans were descendants of the people God scattered during the building of the tower of Babel. They possibly found their way to North America by crossing a land bridge at the Bering Strait.

Artifacts found across the North American continent suggest that these early people were hunters. Most native people also farmed and gathered food. American Indian groups settled in different areas, creating cultural groups.

Some of these early people held beliefs with similarities to some truths found in God's Word. In their belief of a supreme Great Spirit, we can see a faint similarity to the biblical truth that there is only one true God. It may be that some tribes remembered fragments of truth about God that their ancestors from the tower of Babel had once known. But most Native Americans also believed in spirits and shamanism. Students will be asked to come to a conclusion about their own view of spirits and shamanism after comparing those beliefs to the Christian worldview found in Scripture.

Native Americans filled North America and ruled over the earth as God commanded. Some of their descendants have come to Christ. Many more Native Americans need to hear that Christ died for them. People can be free from the fear of spirits when they accept God's gift of salvation.

Chapter 1 Overview				
Lesson	Student Text	Activity Manual	Content	Vocabulary
1	2–6	1–4	Tower of Babel Ancestral Pueblo people Bering Strait Creation Mandate Clovis points	archaeologist Creation Mandate artifact culture
2	7–9	5	The Pueblos The Navajos Four Corners The Chumash	hogan kiva tomol kachina pueblo
3	10–12	6–8	The Makahs The Inuits	harpoon migrate totem pole igloo potlatch
4	13–15	9–10	How It Was: A Day at Snake River People of the plateau The Sioux The Nez Perces Primary Source: Lakota Winter Count People of the plains	buckskin cradleboard tanning
5	16–18	11–13	Iroquois of the Northeast Woodlands Biography Box: Squanto Cherokees of the Southeast Woodlands	longhouse wampum wattle and daub
6	19–21	14	Native American beliefs and shamanism Activity: Presenting a Culture Part 1	oral shaman
7			Activity: Presenting a Culture Part 2	
8		15–16	Chapter Review	
9			Chapter Test	

Timeline

Olmec civilization
ca. 1500–400

many cultural groups
exist in North America
ca. 1400

first European contact
with North America
1492

500 — ‹BC 0 AD› — 500 — 1000 — ca. 1200 — 1500 — 2000

Ancestral Pueblos
move south

Student Text pages 2–6
Activity Manual pages 1–4

The Story of America Begins

The history of America is a fascinating story. It is a story of courage, loyalty, love, and faith. It is also a story of sin and suffering. It is a story about people. And as is true of all history, it is a story about God. God is the one who causes governments and nations to rise and fall. He works all things together to bring about His plans. God often accomplishes His work through people—not always great people, but ordinary people too.

The story of America begins with its earliest people. The ancestors of these early people were part of the civilization that tried to build the tower of Babel. God scattered the builders by confusing their languages. Each language group moved away from the others. Slowly the groups spread out to fill the earth as God had planned. Some descendants of these people found their way to America.

These earliest Americans did not call their land America. It did not look like the America we know today. It did not have cities and towns bustling with activity. It did not have road systems or railroads. The land that the earliest Americans found was filled with mountains and rivers and wide, open spaces. It had forests and treeless plains where wild animals roamed freely. The first people developed their own way of life in this new and untamed land. Today we refer to these earliest people as Native Americans or Indians.

The Earliest Americans
How Did They Come?

Historians have various ways to explain how the first people came to America from the continent of Asia. One popular view is that people crossed the Bering Strait between Russia and Alaska. Christians can agree with this view based on the Bible's account of the Flood.

The Flood produced many changes in the earth and its climate. These changes caused ice to form in various parts of the world. The ice sheets took

3

Chapter Focus

The Native Americans can be grouped into several cultural areas with a wide variety of traditions and beliefs.

JourneyForth

Mik-Shrok by Gloria Repp is available from JourneyForth Books, a division of BJU Press, at journeyforth.com.

With a sled team led by a dog named Mik-Shrok, Steve and Liz Bailey begin missionary work with the Inuit people in Koyalik, Alaska. Other books in the Arctic Missionary Series include *Charlie* and *77 Zebra*.

Visit bjupress.com/resources for links to enhance the lessons. (*Note:* Although these links have been carefully selected, check to ensure that the links are current and evaluate all material before presentation.)

Lesson Focus

- The earliest Americans helped fulfill the Creation Mandate that God gave to man.

Objectives
- Identify what the earliest American artifacts suggest
- Examine how Native Americans fulfilled the Creation Mandate
- Locate the early Native American cultural groups

Teacher's Toolkit CD
- Instructional Aids 1–2: *Reading Timeline Dates*; *Features of the Globe*

Materials
- map of Alaska and Russia
- world globe
- three-inch foam ball for each student

Introduction

- Invite a student to read aloud the title of the chapter and predict what the chapter will be about. the first people who lived in America
- Invite a student to read aloud the chapter focus.

  What do you think you will learn in this chapter? where Indian groups lived and what some of their traditions and beliefs were

- Display Instructional Aid 1. Direct attention to the first date on the timeline. Write the answers for display as you discuss the page.

  What letters come before the date? *ca*

  The letters stand for the word *circa*, which means "around."

  The dash between the years can be read as the word "to."

  What do the letters *BC* stand for? before the birth of Christ

- Point out that the farther away the date is from the birth of Christ, the larger the number is. Explain that the closer to the birth of Christ a year is, the smaller the number becomes.

- Explain that *AD* stands for the Latin words *anno Domini*, or "the year of our Lord." It denotes a time in Christian history referring to the time after Christ's birth.

- Read together the dates and events on the timeline.

Preparation for Reading

- Generate interest as you direct the students to read the titles and examine the pictures and maps on pages 2–6.
- Guide pronunciation of any unfamiliar words in the lesson.

Lesson

1

What is depicted in the picture at the beginning of this chapter? Native Americans coming to a new land

- Direct the students to read the pages silently to learn the name of the sharp stone points that were found across the North American continent. Clovis points

Teach for Understanding

How does God play a part in the history of America? God is the one who causes governments and nations to rise and fall. He works all things together to bring about His plans.

Who were the ancestors of America's earliest people? people who were part of the civilization that tried to build the tower of Babel

What happened to scatter people so that some found their way to America? God confused the languages.

- Direct attention to the world globe. Explain that the students will review information found on a globe.

- Distribute a copy of Instructional Aid 2 to each student. Direct the students to use the illustration of the globe to complete the page. Choose volunteers to read and answer each question. Direct the students to keep the instructional aid in their notebook or folder for future review.

What is a popular view of how the first people came to America from the continent of Asia? People crossed the Bering Strait between Russia and Alaska.

- Direct attention to the map of the Bering Strait on page 4 and the route people may have taken to America. Guide a discussion of how early Americans came to America by crossing the Bering Strait from the continent of Asia. Explain why Christians can agree with this view.

What do archaeologists do? They look for man-made objects called artifacts and study them to learn about the way ancient people lived.

What findings suggest that early Americans were hunters? sharp stone points called Clovis points

- Guide a discussion of the dirt mounds found in the eastern and midwestern United States.

The Bering Strait

Clovis point

many years to melt. Because so much water had frozen, the water level in the Bering Sea may have been low after the Flood. People might have been able to cross the Bering Strait on dry land. Historians who hold this view call the dry land the Bering Land Bridge or Beringia.

How Did They Live?

We know where some of the earliest people settled because their artifacts have been found. **Artifacts** are man-made objects left behind by people of the past. **Archaeologists** are people who look for artifacts. They study what they find to learn about the way ancient people lived. We refer to a people's way of life as its **culture**. A culture includes

such things as beliefs, customs, and creative arts.

Some of the early people in North America lived in what is now the United States. Archaeologists have found sharp stone points from spears and knives all across the continent. Archaeologists call these findings Clovis points. The first ones were found near the city of Clovis, New Mexico. These Clovis points suggest that early Americans hunted animals for food. Some people may have lived as nomads, going wherever they could find good hunting and moving often.

Huge mounds of dirt have been found in the eastern and midwestern United States. Archaeologists believe the Mound Builders had a religion connected with their mounds. They

4

Background

Early People

While various Europeans were discovering and exploring oceans and lands unknown to them, other non-Europeans were living in their own developed civilizations in South, Central, and North America. In South America lived the Incas. In Central America the Mayas and the Aztecs developed civilizations, and across North America were numerous thriving groups of American Indians. These civilizations are examples of the blessing of the Creation Mandate being lived out. Christians think that early people built impressive civilizations, in contrast to the evolutionists' assumption that early people were primitive.

Where had these early people come from? In the far north, near the Arctic Circle, the massive continents of Asia and North America each taper into slender fingers of land that rest just short of touching. Some historians think that sometime after the Flood, the ancestors of the American Indians entered the Western Hemisphere there. Some historians think they crossed the narrow Bering Sea in small boats or on foot over a bridge of ice. Other historians believe that a land bridge, which they call Beringia, connected the two continents and that the people simply walked over it.

> Clarify and enhance the lesson with information from the Background sections.

may have been used as burial places or religious centers.

Some other early people settled farther south. The Olmecs left many artifacts in Mexico along the Gulf Coast. They built cities with drainage systems. They carved huge stone heads with lifelike faces. These findings show that the Olmecs were intelligent and skilled.

The Mayas in Central America also left city ruins behind. Some of these cities have magnificent pyramids and palaces. The Mayas also left written records. These early Americans were advanced in art, literature, math, and science.

One ancient group lasted until more recent times. The Ancestral Pueblo people lived in the southwestern United States. They are also known as the Anasazi. The Ancestral Pueblos thrived until about AD 1400. They grew corn, which they called maize. They built homes of stone blocks and mud. Some of them built their homes in cliffs. They left behind beautiful pottery and baskets.

Artifacts help us learn about some of the earliest cultures in America. There is still much that we do not know about the early ways of life. But we know that in

God's perfect plan, these people began the story of America. They were the first to fill this land and to rule over it. We also know that the people who developed these cultures were made in God's image. God gave all people the command to rule over the earth. This command is called the **Creation Mandate**. When people work together to rule over their earth, they create cultures. It is not surprising that these early Americans had great ability and creative skills. They, like all people, are gifted by God to develop cultures.

By the 1400s, the Native Americans had grown into hundreds of groups, or tribes. Often tribes in the same region had similar cultures. In this chapter we will study several of these cultural groups. We will see how each of the groups used the resources and skills God gave them in unique ways.

Coastal

Arctic

Plains

Woodland

5

What do artifacts teach us about the Olmecs? They built cities with drainage systems. They carved huge stone heads with lifelike faces. The Olmecs were intelligent and skilled.

- Guide a discussion of the Mayan culture in Central America.

Which ancient group of people lived in the southwestern United States until more recent times? the Ancestral Pueblo people, or Anasazi

What is known about their culture? They grew corn, which they called maize. They built homes of stone blocks and mud. Some of them built their homes in cliffs. They left behind beautiful pottery and baskets.

- Direct attention to the picture on page 5. Read the labels aloud.

- How did the earliest people fulfill the Creation Mandate in America? They filled and ruled over the land by building cities with drainage systems, developing writing, growing maize, and making beautiful pottery.

What are Native American groups called? tribes

What was often true of the tribes living in the same region? They often had similar cultures.

The gear icon (⚙) indicates a higher-order question. These questions are based on information gathered from the text but require some analysis, synthesis, or evaluation of the text. Supply prompts or background to guide the students to the answer.

However they came, the Asian immigrants moved slowly southward. Eventually, their descendants settled the entire hemisphere down to the tip of South America. When the European explorers arrived in the New World, they found it already teeming with humans living in developed civilizations. Historians estimate that as many as several million American Indians were living in North America before Columbus made his discovery.

Historians of American Indians usually group them into tribes (several families sharing common customs) and culture areas (several tribes living near each other that share similar customs, means of livelihood, and level of civilization). When the Europeans arrived in the New World, it was already inhabited by several major groups, each in its own culture area. For example, in the Southwest was the Pueblo civilization. In the Midwest developed first the Adena, or Hopewell, civilization followed by the Mississippian civilization. In the Middle Atlantic region and the Northeast was the Woodlands civilization. These groups of peoples shared certain common characteristics. Yet each of them was different from the others in many ways.

1

Teach for Understanding

- Direct attention to the Native American Cultures map on page 6. Explain that the map organizes Indian groups by geography and culture.

- Direct the students to name and locate each Indian culture area shown on the map.

➤ Conclude the discussion by naming some artifacts that have helped us learn about early cultures in America. Clovis points, pottery, baskets

Activity Manual

- Introduce *Chapter 1 Looking Ahead* on page 3. Read the page together.

- Guide completion of pages 1–4.

Invite students to use information from *Chapter 1 Looking Ahead* in the Activity Manual to create flashcards to use for review.

The Activity Manual Answer Key is included on the Teacher's Toolkit CD.

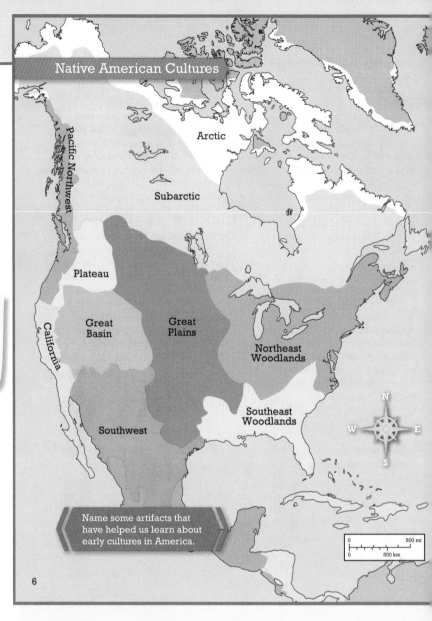

Native American Cultures

Arctic

Subarctic

Pacific Northwest

Plateau

California

Great Basin

Great Plains

Northeast Woodlands

Southeast Woodlands

Southwest

Name some artifacts that have helped us learn about early cultures in America.

0   800 mi
0   800 km

6

Cover Art

The art on the cover of HERITAGE STUDIES 5 was created using artistic paper manipulation called paper sculpture. It illustrates how the invention of the automobile changed American life by allowing people to live in the country and travel to the city. The concept was drawn as if it were going to be painted. The various shapes that make up the drawing were then cut out of colored paper. These shapes were reassembled to form the image. During this step of the paper-sculpture process, the shapes were layered or cut through to add interest. Paper sculpture may include painted patterns to give additional texture. To create the idea of depth, some of the paper shapes have been supported off the background surface using foam or cardboard. You may want to provide an opportunity for the students to create their own paper sculpture.

People of the Southwest

Much of the southwestern United States is desert. This region has rugged mountains, mesas, and canyons. Little rain falls there. Because of the dry weather, the Southwest does not have as many trees, plants, or animals as other regions. It was not an easy place for Native Americans to live.

The southwestern Indians learned to make the most of the resources they had. They developed their skills as farmers. Even in the sandy soil, they were able to grow enough crops to feed whole villages. They used resources in nature to make shelters and useful works of art. The Pueblos and the Navajos are two of the best-known groups of southwestern Indians.

The Pueblos

Sometime between AD 1200 and 1300, the Ancestral Pueblos left their homes. They had lived mainly in the area that is today called Four Corners. Four Corners is located where the borders of Utah, Colorado, Arizona, and New Mexico meet. The Ancestral Pueblos may have left because of famine. They may have had to flee because of danger from enemies. The only thing we know for certain is that they moved south and never returned to Four Corners.

The descendants of these Ancestral Pueblos lived in New Mexico and Arizona. We call them the Pueblo people. Some of them still live on reservations there. Several different tribes make up the Pueblos. The Hopis and the Zunis are examples of Pueblo tribes.

The Pueblos kept many of the traditions of their ancestors. They continued to grow their own food. They grew corn, beans, and squash in the dry southwestern desert.

The shelters the Pueblos made were also called **pueblos**. These shelters had many units like apartment buildings do. Each pueblo housed several families. The families in a pueblo were often closely related. Sometimes the people at one pueblo spoke a different language from the people at another. Each pueblo also had a kiva. **Kivas** were special rooms set aside for religious activities.

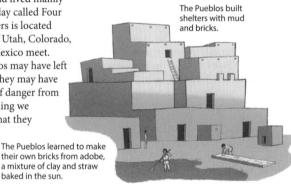

The Pueblos built shelters with mud and bricks.

The Pueblos learned to make their own bricks from adobe, a mixture of clay and straw baked in the sun.

7

Lesson 2

Student Text pages 7–9
Activity Manual page 5

Lesson Focus

- The Pueblos, Navajos, and Chumash had distinct cultures.

Objectives

- Examine the culture of the Pueblos and their ancestors
- Describe the Navajo way of life
- Identify characteristics of the Chumash culture
- Complete an organizer about the food, shelter, and crafts of the Pueblo, Navajo, and Chumash people

Teacher's Toolkit CD

- Instructional Aid 3: *People of the Southwest and California*

Review

- Choose a volunteer to state ways that God shaped American history.
- Choose a volunteer to tell what caused people to scatter over the earth and

Guide a review of important terms, maps, places, and people from each previous lesson. Direct the students to find and read the corresponding entries from the Resource Treasury.

---

how the earliest people fulfilled the Creation Mandate in America.

Preparation for Reading

- Generate interest as you direct the students to read the titles and examine the pictures on pages 7–9.
- Guide pronunciation of any unfamiliar words in the lesson.
- Direct the students to read the pages and complete Instructional Aid 3 in small groups.

Select one of the prepared rubrics from the Teacher's Toolkit CD or design a rubric to include your chosen criteria.

Teach for Understanding

What are the two southwestern Indian tribes in this lesson? Pueblos and Navajos

Where did the Ancestral Pueblos make their home? in Four Corners, located where the borders of Utah, Colorado, Arizona, and New Mexico meet

Where did the Pueblos move when they left their homes between AD 1200 and 1300? south

What are two examples of Pueblo tribes? the Hopis and the Zunis

- Choose one group to answer the following questions.

What are some crops the Pueblos grew? corn, beans, squash

What type of shelter did Pueblos make? They built shelters with mud and bricks called pueblos. These pueblos had many units like apartment buildings do.

Who lived in a pueblo? several families that were often closely related

Which room in a pueblo was set aside for religious activities? a kiva

- Direct attention to the picture on page 7. Read aloud the captions.

Assessments will include information from caption content in the student text.

Lesson

2

Teach for Understanding

- Direct attention to the pictures on page 8. Choose a volunteer to read the captions aloud.

- Choose a group to answer the following questions:

  What were some crafts that the Pueblo people made? baskets, fabric, pottery, dolls

  What did the dolls represent? kachinas, or spirits that were believed to control objects in nature

  How did the people think they could cause the kachinas to bring favorable weather, good health, and happiness? by pleasing the kachinas

  Which tribe in the Southwest all spoke a form of the same language? the Navajos

  How did the Navajos get their food? hunting, gathering plants, and farming

  What was the relationship between the Navajos and the Pueblos like? Sometimes there was fighting between them. At other times, they helped each other and traded with one another.

- Select another group to answer the following question:

  How did the Navajos build their hogans? Hogans were made of logs and poles covered with mud. They were round at the bottom and narrow at the top with an opening in the roof to let out the smoke from the cooking fire.

- Ask a volunteer to describe sand painting and what the Navajos believed the paintings would do.

- Where does true healing come from? God

  Where do many Navajos live today? on land in Utah, Arizona, and New Mexico

  How does the Navajo Nation compare in size to other Indian reservations in the United States? It is the largest reservation in the United States today.

The Pueblos believed that pleasing the kachinas would bring favorable weather, good health, and happiness.

The Pueblo people made baskets, wove fabric, and shaped pottery from clay. They also made dolls to represent kachinas. **Kachinas** were spirits that the Pueblos believed in. The Pueblo people believed that kachinas controlled objects in nature.

The Navajos

Another large tribe in the Southwest was the Navajo people. The Navajos all spoke a form of the same language. When they first came to the region, they hunted animals and gathered plants for food. Later they learned to farm. The Navajos built hogans as shelters. **Hogans** were made of logs and poles covered with mud.

Sometimes there was fighting between the Navajos and the Pueblos. At other times, they helped each other and traded with one

another. Some historians believe that the Pueblos taught the Navajos farming and weaving.

The Navajos were known for a special art called sand painting. They gathered materials from the desert to make the colors. Crushed stone could make brown, red, or gold. Pollen or cornmeal could make yellow. By sprinkling the colors over an area of sand, the Navajos could create pictures. Sand paintings were used in religious ceremonies. The Navajos believed these paintings would help heal sick people. We cannot find sand paintings today because the Navajos did not leave them in place after finishing the healing ceremonies.

Many Navajos today live on land in Utah, Arizona, and New Mexico. They still keep many of their traditions. The Navajo Nation is the largest reservation in the United States today.

Most hogans were round at the bottom and narrow at the top. An opening in the roof let out the smoke from the cooking fire.

8

Activity

Navajo Fry Bread

Find a recipe to make Navajo fry bread. Allow students to sprinkle the fry bread with powdered sugar or drizzle it with honey and enjoy.

Optional activities are provided in some lessons.

People of California

Many different Native American tribes lived in what is now California. They lived all along the California coast, and some lived farther inland. They all shared a similar culture. The Chumash people of southern California are just one example.

The Chumash

The Chumash lived in what is now the city of Santa Barbara. Some of them also lived on the Channel Islands off the coast. There were once more than one hundred Chumash villages in this part of California.

Like the Pueblos and Navajos, the Chumash learned to use materials they found in nature. They built snug, watertight homes from trees and plants. First they built a dome-shaped framework out of willow branches. Then they added a thatched roof made from tall coastal grasses.

They also used the plants around them for food. They collected acorns, mashed them into flour, and prepared soups and breads from them. Many Chumash families also had granaries where they stored acorns, nuts, and seeds during the winter months. Other food came from fishing and hunting small animals.

The Chumash were unique among the California tribes in one way. They learned to build boats from wooden planks. They cut cedar and redwood logs into boards. To smooth the lumber, they used shells, stones, and animal skins. They tied the smooth planks together with plant fibers. Then they sealed the planks with asphalt. These wooden canoes were called **tomols**. The Chumash used tomols to fish and to visit other villages to trade.

Shell beads were the Chumash form of money.

The Chumash were skilled basket weavers. Some baskets were woven tightly enough to hold water. The Chumash also cooked in baskets with heated rocks in them.

Historians have found colorful Chumash paintings on the walls of caves. The Chumash probably made these works of art for religious reasons. Like most other American Indians, they worshiped nature's objects such as the sun, animals, and sea creatures instead of the God who created these things.

> How were Pueblo, Navajo, and Chumash shelters different from each other?

9

Teach for Understanding

- Direct attention to the pictures on page 9. Read the captions aloud.

  Which Native American tribe lived in California and on the Channel Islands off the coast? the Chumash

- Choose a volunteer to describe the materials the Chumash used to build their homes and how the homes were constructed.

  What did the Chumash use as sources of food? plants, acorns, nuts, seeds, and food from fishing and hunting small animals

  What types of arts and crafts did the Chumash make? tomols, tightly woven baskets, paintings

  How were the baskets used? to hold water; to cook

  What was unique about the tomols, or canoes, the Chumash built? They were made from cedar and redwood logs cut into boards or planks.

- How do you think other Indians may have built their boats or canoes? Possible answers could include by hollowing out or digging out logs or by covering a frame of wood with tree bark.

  Where have Chumash paintings been found? on the walls of caves

  Why did the Chumash make these paintings? for religious reasons

  What did the Chumash and other Indians worship instead of the God who created all things? nature's objects such as the sun, animals, and sea creatures

>> Conclude the discussion by asking the question on page 9. Answers should include the idea that the shelters were built in different styles and from different materials. The pueblo was built of adobe brick and had many units like apartment buildings do. The hogan was made of logs and poles covered with mud. It was round at the bottom and narrow at the top. The Chumash shelter was a dome-shaped framework of willow branches with a thatched roof made from tall coastal grasses.

Activity Manual

- Guide completion of page 5.

Background

Chumash Tomol Crossing

In 1996 the Chumash Maritime Association was founded. The members built and continue to take care of the community's Chumash tomol, the 'Elye'wun, which means "swordfish of Santa Barbara."

Tribal members and descendants from the Chumash nation serve as crew members in an annual tomol crossing of the Santa Barbara Channel. The annual trip began in 2001 to retrace a historic Chumash trade route. The twenty-one-mile trip can take as long as thirteen hours. Sometimes the annual crossing is canceled due to turbulent ocean currents, wind, or heavy fog. On September 7, 2014, Chumash paddlers of tomols 'Elye'wun and Kalawashaq made the ninth crossing by tomol to Santa Cruz Island in 150 years.

Activity

Weave an Indian Basket

Use a basket-weaving kit to demonstrate basket weaving similar to what American Indians practiced.

3

Student Text pages 10–12
Activity Manual pages 6–8

Lesson Focus

- The early people of the Pacific Northwest and Arctic had diverse cultures.

Objectives

- Examine the culture of the Makah tribe
- Identify customs of the Inuit people
- Compare the cultures of the Makah and Inuit people

Teacher's Toolkit CD

- Interactive Visual: *Map of Indian Culture Areas*
- Instructional Aid 4: *People of the Pacific Northwest and Arctic Regions*

Review

- Display the interactive visual. Choose volunteers to place the symbol for each of the following tribes in the correct cultural area on the map: the Chumash, the Navajos, and the Pueblos.

Preparation for Reading

- Generate interest as you direct the students to read the titles and examine the pictures on pages 10–12.
- Guide pronunciation of any unfamiliar words in the lesson.
- Direct the students to read the pages and complete Instructional Aid 4 in small groups.

Teach for Understanding

- Direct attention to the picture on page 10. Have a volunteer read the caption aloud.

  What did totem poles look like? a series of carved faces, often of animals or birds, stacked on top of one another

  How did the Makahs bring in food from the Pacific Ocean? by making cedar canoes to take out on the open sea

- Choose a volunteer to explain the process the Makahs used to make their canoes.

  What are some animals the Makahs used for food? salmon, seals, sea otters, whales

  How did Makah men prepare in the months before a whale hunt? They would watch the sky and sea for signs about the weather. Each hunter would go alone into the forest to seek the help of the spirits the Makahs worshiped.

- 🕯 What can a Christian do when he needs help to get a job done? He can go to the Lord in prayer and ask for help.

People of the Pacific Northwest

The people of the Pacific Northwest lived along the coasts of Oregon, Washington, and British Columbia, Canada. Each tribe settled in a particular area along the coastline. These Indians built sturdy homes and stayed mainly in one place. The people of the Pacific Northwest depended on the sea, the forests, and the rivers for survival.

The Makahs

The Makahs settled in the northwestern tip of what is now Washington State. They built their houses out of cedar planks. A Makah home usually held more than a father, a mother, and their children. Often many relatives lived together in one large house.

The Makahs and the other Pacific Northwest tribes were known for their woodcarving skills. Many homes had large wooden statues or **totem poles** in front of them. The Makahs brought in much of their food from the Pacific Ocean. They made cedar canoes to take out on the open sea. This type of canoe had to be large and strong. Once a large enough tree was found, the Makahs hollowed out the inside. Then they steamed the tree using water and hot rocks. This process softened the wood so that the sides of the canoe could be shaped. When the canoe was finished, the Makahs painted colorful designs on the outside.

The Makahs fished for salmon and hunted seals and sea otters. But they were best known for their whale hunting. Hunting a whale was a difficult task. Makah men prepared months ahead of time. They watched the sky and the sea for signs about the weather. Each hunter went alone into the forest to seek the help of the spirits the Makahs worshiped.

Totem poles were a series of carved faces stacked on top of one another. The faces were often of animals or birds. These creatures were meant to be symbols of the family ancestors.

Activity

Totem Poles

Display pictures of Makah totem poles. Guide a discussion of their purpose. Choose volunteers to tell why they believe most people in America do not have totem poles in front of their homes.

When the time for the whale hunt came, eight to ten men went out in a canoe. They watched the water's surface. Whales do not breathe underwater and must come up for air regularly. When a whale was sighted, the men studied its breathing pattern. Soon they could predict the spot where it would rise next. They rowed the canoe near that spot to wait.

The Makahs threw **harpoons**, long-handled spears, to kill a whale. Makah hunters had to be very careful. Even a wounded whale was strong enough to overturn a canoe. Once the whale was dead, they had the difficult task of pulling it to shore. The men would sing traditional whaling songs as they paddled through the waves, towing the whale behind them.

The Makahs used every part of the whale. They ate the meat and the skin. They used the tendons to make rope. They used the blubber, or fat, for oil.

The Makahs and other Pacific Northwest tribes held events called potlatches. A **potlatch** was a feast that often lasted several days. During a potlatch, the host gave gifts to his guests. A gift might be anything from whale meat to a valuable woodcarving. Potlatches had different purposes. Sometimes the Indians at a potlatch celebrated a wedding or mourned a death. Sometimes they took care of business. Sometimes two different tribes would meet at a potlatch to trade with each other. The potlatch was an important way to preserve the culture of the people who lived in the Pacific Northwest.

People of the Arctic

Even farther north than the Pacific Northwest tribes lived the people of the Arctic. The Arctic tribes lived in what is now Alaska and northern Canada. The Arctic region has short summers and long frozen winters. On winter days the ground is covered with snow and ice, and in the far north the sky stays almost dark. Few plants can grow in these harsh conditions. Native Americans in the Arctic learned how to live in this cold, snowy wilderness.

Makah whale hunt

11

Teach for Understanding

- Direct attention to the picture on page 11. Choose a group to describe a Makah whale hunt.

What do you think was the message of the Makah whaling songs? Possible answers could include that the Makahs were asking the spirits to help them harpoon a whale, or the words might convey that the Makahs were skillful hunters.

What did the Makahs do with the whale after they harpooned it and brought it to shore? They used every part of the whale. They ate the meat and the skin. They used the tendons to make rope. They used the blubber, or fat, for oil.

What special events did Makahs and other Pacific Northwest tribes hold? potlatches

- Choose a group to describe potlatches.

Which region is even farther north than the Pacific Northwest? the Arctic

Background

A Buried Makah Village

A seaside village at the tip of Cape Flattery, Washington, suffered a terrible tragedy five hundred years ago. Ozette, a village that perfectly preserved Makah homes and artifacts, was buried by a mudslide. A storm in the winter of 1969–1970 caused the village to be exposed in a bank. A hiker told the Makah tribe about the discovery of the buried village. The tribe notified Washington State University, and the site began to be excavated two months later. Some fifty thousand artifacts were found at Ozette, including baskets, harpoons, various utensils, and sculptures. Visitors can see these artifacts at the Makah Museum in Neah Bay, Washington, on the Makah reservation. The village at Ozette provided a wealth of information about the Makah culture that dates back two thousand years.

Teach for Understanding

- Direct attention to the picture on page 12. Read aloud the caption.

  Which tribe is the best known of the Arctic peoples? the Inuits

  What were important food sources for the Inuits? seals, walruses, caribou, musk oxen, polar bears, fish

- Choose a group to describe the Inuit summer igloo.

- Select a different group to describe the Inuit winter igloo.

  What type of clothing and equipment did the Inuits make to protect themselves during the Arctic winters? warm coats, pants, mittens, boots, and goggles

  What did the Inuits bring with them when they came to North America? dogs called huskies

  What were huskies used for? pulling sleds over the ice for travel and hunting

  What types of boats did the Inuits use? kayaks and umiaks

- Choose a volunteer to describe kayaks and umiaks.

  ▶▶ Conclude the discussion by asking the question on page 12. Makahs fished for salmon and hunted seals, sea otters, and whales. The Inuits hunted seals, walruses, caribou, musk oxen, and polar bears and caught fish.

Activity Manual

- Guide completion of pages 6–8.

Assessment

- Administer quiz.

The quiz may be given anytime after completing this lesson.

The Inuits

The Inuits are the best known of the Arctic peoples. In their language the word *Inuit* means "people." For their food, the Inuits hunted sea animals such as seals and walruses. They also hunted land animals like caribou, musk oxen, and polar bears. They made holes in the ice for catching fish. They moved often, or **migrated**, to any place where they could find good hunting or fishing.

The Inuits built several types of homes. Because they were nomadic, the Inuits did not need to build homes that would last. They called each type of home an **igloo**. They made summer

The Inuits needed warm clothing. They made coats, pants, mittens, and boots out of animal skins and furs. They even made goggles to shield their eyes from bright sunlight on the snow.

tents out of caribou hides and poles carved from driftwood. Sometimes they built sod homes, packing sod over a framework of driftwood or whale ribs.

But the most unusual type of igloo was the snow house. This type of house is what we think of when we hear the word *igloo*. Snow houses were built only in winter. The Inuits cut blocks out of ice and stacked them in a dome shape. Handfuls of soft snow filled in the cracks. Most snow igloos included a block of clear ice for a window. An opening at the top allowed the Inuits to burn oil for cooking.

One small family group usually lived in each igloo. But several families stayed together when migrating. The men hunted together and helped protect each other and their families.

When the Inuits came to North America, they brought with them dogs called huskies. The Inuits trained the huskies to pull sleds over the ice. They used sleds for travel and hunting. The Inuits also went out on the sea in lightweight boats called kayaks. When hunting larger sea mammals, the Inuits used sturdier canoes called umiaks.

Although the Inuits had a harsh climate to call home, they learned to survive. They passed their ways on to their children and grandchildren. Inuits still live in Alaska and Canada today.

▶ How did the Makahs and the Inuits get their food? ▶

12

Activities

Dogsledding

Use resources for students to research dogsledding in Alaska today. Choose volunteers to share what they learn.

Make an Igloo

Find directions to make a winter igloo out of gallon plastic milk cartons. Compile pictures and information about the Inuits to display alongside the winter igloo.

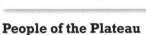

How It Was

A tall boy crouched on a rock overlooking the Snake River. Water droplets clung to his dark hair. The roar of the river filled his ears. He glanced over at his father standing on a nearby rock. He clutched his long spear in one hand, just as his father was doing, and shaded his eyes with the other. Like a hawk he watched the current rushing past beneath his perch.

Suddenly a flash of silver glinted beneath the water. He paused for a split second to take aim. Whoosh! His spear found its mark. He lifted the spear with a large salmon still thrashing about on the end of it. "Father!" he yelled. "I caught one."

"Very good, son." His father smiled at him. "We will eat well tonight."

People of the Plateau

Between the Cascade Mountains and the Rocky Mountains is an area of land called the Columbia Plateau. The first people who lived in this region are known as the Plateau Indians. The Plateau Indians lived mainly in Washington, Oregon, Idaho, Montana, and a small portion of Canada.

The Nez Perces

One tribe that lived on the Columbia Plateau was the Nez Perce people. The name Nez Perce was given to them by French settlers because some members of the tribe wore nose ornaments. In French, *Nez Perce* means "pierced nose." Most Nez Perces, however, did not pierce their noses.

The Nez Perces hunted, gathered, and fished for their food. One important food was salmon. Salmon swam from the ocean to freshwater rivers to lay eggs. The Nez Perces caught salmon in the rivers with spears, nets, or traps. During salmon season, the Nez Perces built shelters of wooden poles and grass mats. They lived along the banks of the rivers so they could fish more easily.

The Nez Perces also hunted animals such as deer, elk, and mountain sheep. They often used the skins of deer, called **buckskin**, to make clothing. They gathered roots, berries, and nuts in the forests.

During the winter, the Nez Perces sometimes made a different type of

13

Lesson 4

Student Text pages 13–15
Activity Manual pages 9–10

Lesson Focus

• The Plateau Indians and the Plains Indians each had distinct ways of living.

Objectives

• Identify characteristics of the Nez Perces
• Examine the culture of the Sioux
• Compare the cultures of the Nez Perces and the Sioux

Teacher's Toolkit CD

• Visual 1: *The Nez Perces*
• Interactive Visual 1: *Map of Indian Culture Areas*
• Instructional Aid 5: *People of the Plateau and Plains*

Review

• Display the interactive visual. Choose volunteers to place the symbol for each of the following tribes in the correct culture area on the map: the Chumash, the Inuits, the Makahs, the Navajos, and the Pueblos.

Preparation for Reading

• Generate interest as you direct the students to read the titles and examine the pictures on pages 13–15.
• Guide pronunciation of any unfamiliar words in the lesson.
• Direct the students to read the pages and complete Instructional Aid 5 in small groups.

Teach for Understanding

• Direct attention to the picture on page 13 and the How It Was box. Read the story aloud.

What does this story reveal about the Nez Perces? The Nez Perce men used spears to hunt salmon for food.

What was the geography of the area where the Nez Perces lived? They lived in an area of land called the Columbia Plateau between two mountain ranges.

In which locations did the Plateau Indians live? mainly in Washington, Oregon, Idaho, Montana, and a small portion of Canada

Why did the French give one tribe a name that meant "pierced nose"? Some members of the tribe wore nose ornaments.

• Choose a group to name foods the Nez Perces ate.

How did the Nez Perces catch salmon? with spears, nets, or traps

What did the Nez Perces use to build their shelters during salmon season? wooden poles and grass mats

What is deerskin called that was used to make clothing? buckskin

• Display Visual 1. Guide a discussion of the pictures of the Nez Perces.

Lesson

4

What type of shelter did the Nez Perces sometimes make during the winter months? an earth house

- Choose a group to explain how an earth house was built. The Nez Perces dug a large round pit and made a framework of poles around the pit. They covered the roof poles with bark, grass, and earth.

What was the name of the spotted horses that the Nez Perces bred? Appaloosas

Why were the Appaloosas valuable to the Nez Perces? The Appaloosas became important as a way for the Nez Perces to travel and hunt. Trading Appaloosas with people outside the tribe brought wealth to the Nez Perce people.

Where did the Plains Indians live? They lived on the Great Plains in what is now the Midwest. Their culture's region reached into Canada in the North and into Texas in the South.

Which Plains Indians were also known by the names Lakota, Dakota, and Nakota? the Sioux

What do these three names for the Sioux mean? "friends" or "allies"

What was the main source of food for the Sioux? bison, or the buffalo

Why did the Sioux become migratory? They followed the buffalo herds from place to place.

- Select a group to tell what the Sioux used buffalo for, besides eating the meat.

Primary Source: Lakota Winter Count

- Direct attention to Activity Manual page 9.
- Direct attention to the picture of the winter count.
- Read aloud the information about Lakota winter counts. Guide a discussion of the winter count as a historical record.

How did the Sioux hunt buffalo before horses were common? on foot

What changed the way they hunted buffalo? After Europeans brought horses to the continent, the Indians began hunting on horseback.

---

shelter called an earth house. First they dug large round pits. Then they made a framework of poles around the pit. They covered the roof poles with bark, grass, and earth. Earth houses held several families.

In time the Nez Perces became known for breeding horses. By the 1700s they were raising spotted horses called Appaloosas. Appaloosas were swift, strong, and intelligent. The Appaloosa horse became important as a way for the Nez Perces to travel and hunt. Trading Appaloosas with people outside the tribe brought wealth to the Nez Perce people.

People of the Plains

Many native peoples lived on the Great Plains in what are now the states of the Midwest. Their culture's region also reached into Canada in the North and into Texas in the South. We know these tribes as the Plains Indians.

Many people today know more about the culture of the Plains Indians than they do any other Native American group. The Plains Indians have often been portrayed in art, movies, and television programs. It is important to remember that they are just one of the many different cultural groups that lived in North America long ago.

The Sioux

One large group of Plains Indians was called the Sioux. The Sioux

migrated west to the plains from their original home, fleeing from an enemy tribe. The Sioux also went by the names Lakota, Dakota, and Nakota. These three names mean "friends" or "allies" in the Sioux language. Several different tribal groups made up the Sioux. Members of these smaller groups usually stayed in the same area.

The American bison, or the buffalo, was the main source of food for the Sioux people. Before Europeans came to North America, millions of buffalo roamed and grazed on the plains. The Sioux followed these buffalo herds, migrating from place to place as the buffalo moved.

Before horses were common in North America, the Plains Indians had to hunt buffalo on foot. After Europeans brought horses to the continent, the Indians began hunting on horseback. This was a much easier way to hunt the strong, fast-moving buffalo. Hunters learned to ride a galloping horse with their hands free to use a bow and arrow.

The Sioux used every part of the buffalo. They ate buffalo meat. They tanned the hides to make their clothing and homes. **Tanning** was a process of soaking, drying, and stretching the hides to preserve them. The Sioux made cups, spoons, and arrows out of buffalo horns. They made knives, tools, and pipes out of the bones. They lined moccasins with buffalo hair. They used

14

Appaloosas

The Spanish introduced horses to Mexico in the 1500s. Horses eventually spread through North America. Over time horses became part of the lives of Indians in the Northwest. The term *Appaloosa* was used in reference to the spotted horses of the Palouse region of Idaho and Washington, an area where the water drains into the Palouse River.

Appaloosas changed the lives of the Nez Perces. These spotted horses enabled the Nez Perces to become expert horsemen and hunters. The Nez Perces were probably some of the first Indians to breed horses for characteristics, such as the white- or black-spotted patterns on the horses' coats.

The Appaloosas are known for their beauty, intelligence, and strength. Breeding and trading the Appaloosas to other tribes, settlers, and western shows brought wealth to the Nez Perces. Appaloosas are still popular as riding horses for pleasure and for show.

the fat to make soap, and they even used buffalo manure for fuel.

The Sioux learned to preserve buffalo meat by drying it. The dried meat was similar to beef jerky. The Sioux could eat the dried meat even in winter when buffalo hunting was harder.

Because the Sioux followed the buffalo herds, they had to have homes that were easy to move. The tepee was the perfect home for them. It could be carried from place to place and was easily put together. Tepees had a framework of three or four poles forming a cone. The Sioux sewed buffalo skins together to make coverings for this framework. They often decorated these coverings with beautiful artwork. The symbols on tepees usually represented spirits or the family ancestors.

The Sioux wore clothing made from buffalo, deer, or elk skins. The women wore dresses with fringe around the sleeves and skirt hem. The men wore fringed shirts and leggings. All the Sioux wore moccasins. The Sioux men were also famous for their headdresses. Chiefs or great warriors wore war bonnets decorated with many long eagle feathers.

Sioux men and older boys did most of the hunting. Sioux women cooked, made clothing, tanned hides, and assembled the tepees. Sioux women carried their babies on **cradleboards** while they worked.

> Which animals were important to the Nez Perces and to the Sioux and why?

Sioux buffalo hunt

15

Teach for Understanding

- Direct attention to the pictures on page 15.

  How did the Sioux preserve buffalo meat? by drying it

  How was the tepee suited to the migratory life of the Sioux? It could be carried from place to place and was easily put together.

  How was the tepee made? It had a framework of three or four poles forming a cone. The Sioux sewed buffalo skins together to make coverings for this framework.

  What did the symbols that the Sioux decorated the tepee with usually represent? spirits or family ancestors

- Choose a group to describe what the Sioux wore. The Sioux wore clothing made from buffalo, deer, or elk skins. The women wore dresses with fringe around the sleeves and skirt hem. The men wore fringed shirts and leggings. All the Sioux wore moccasins. The Sioux men wore headdresses. Chiefs or great warriors wore war bonnets decorated with many long eagle feathers.

  What did the men and older boys do? most of the hunting

  What work did the Sioux women do? cooked, made clothing, tanned hides, assembled the tepees

  How did the women care for their babies while they worked? They carried their babies on cradleboards.

> Conclude the discussion by asking the question on page 15. The Nez Perces caught salmon in the rivers. They hunted deer, elk, and mountain sheep for food. The skins of deer were used for clothing. The Appaloosas were important as a way for the Nez Perces to travel and hunt and to trade with people outside the tribe.

Bison, or the buffalo, were important to the Sioux as the main source of food. The hide was tanned for making clothes and tepees. Every part of the buffalo was used for things the Sioux needed. Horses became important for hunting on horseback.

Activity Manual

- Guide completion of pages 9–10.

Activities

Make a Winter Count

Materials: paint, paintbrushes, pictures of Lakota winter counts

Direct the students to recall important or meaningful events that have happened from one winter to the next winter for the past several years. Instruct them to choose an event for each year to record on their winter count and to decide what symbol they will use. Direct the students to paint their pictographs in chronological order on a piece of paper. Choose volunteers to explain their winter counts. Encourage the students to keep their winter counts and continue adding a symbol each year.

Sioux Culture Display: Crafts

Use pictures and items to represent the Sioux culture. Include a tepee, clothing made from hide, fringed shirts and leggings, moccasins, items made from buffalo horn, a picture of a bow and arrows, a war bonnet, and a cradleboard in the display.

Lesson Focus

- There are two major groups of Woodland Indians.

Objectives
- Recognize the geographic area of the Northeast Woodland Indians and the Southeast Woodland Indians
- Identify the culture of the Iroquois people
- Examine Cherokee traditions and way of life

Teacher's Toolkit CD
- Interactive Visual: *Map of Indian Culture Areas*
- Instructional Aid 6: *Woodland Indians*

Review

- Display the interactive visual. Choose volunteers to place the symbol for each of the following tribes in the correct cultural area on the map: the Chumash, the Inuits, the Makahs, the Navajos, the Nez Perces, the Pueblos, and the Sioux.

- Ask questions such as the following to review the previous lesson.

  What is the name of a tribe that lived on the plateau? the Nez Perces

  Which American Indian people were Plains Indians? the Sioux

Preparation for Reading

- Generate interest as you direct the students to read the titles and examine the pictures on pages 16–18.
- Guide pronunciation of any unfamiliar words in the lesson.
- Direct the students to read the pages and complete Instructional Aid 6 in small groups.

Teach for Understanding

Which parts of the United States were home to the Woodland Indians? They lived throughout the region east of the Mississippi River. Some lived as far west as Illinois. Some also lived in Canada.

How can the Woodland Indians be divided into two major groups? They can be divided by language. One group spoke the Algonquian language. The other group spoke various forms of the Iroquoian language.

When did five tribes form the Iroquois Confederacy? during the 1500s

People of the Northeast Woodlands

The Northeast region of the United States was once filled with forests. The early people who lived in this area are often referred to as Woodland Indians. Woodland Indians lived throughout the region east of the Mississippi River. Some lived as far west as Illinois. Some also lived in Canada.

Many tribes were part of the Woodland Indians, including those who lived farther south. They can be divided into two major groups by language. One group spoke the Algonquian language. The other group spoke various forms of the Iroquoian language.

Iroquois longhouse

The Iroquois

The Iroquois people were primarily made up of five tribes, or nations. These tribes formed an alliance, or league, during the 1500s called the Iroquois Confederacy. The five nations in the league were the Mohawks, Oneidas, Onondagas, Cayugas, and Senecas.

Later in the 1700s, a sixth tribe, the Tuscaroras, joined them.

The Iroquois built **longhouses** as shelters. A longhouse was shaped like a rectangle. Its width and height were narrow compared with its long walls. The Iroquois used wooden poles as a framework and covered them with sheets of bark.

Many small family units shared one longhouse with their relatives. When a girl married, her husband came to live in her longhouse. There were sometimes as many as twenty related families living in one longhouse.

A group of Iroquois men met to make important decisions for all the Iroquois people. These men were called the Great Council. Although women could not serve on the Great Council, they elected the men to represent them. Each nation also had its own council to decide smaller matters. This form of leadership was one of the models that later influenced the way Americans set up their government.

The Iroquois were farmers. They grew corn, beans, and squash. They called these three important crops the Three Sisters. Iroquois women had a special method of planting these crops close together to gain the most benefit

16

- Direct attention to the picture of the Iroquois shelter on page 16.

  What type of shelter did the Iroquois build? longhouses

  What materials were used to build the longhouses? wooden poles and sheets of bark

  Who made important decisions for all the Iroquois people? the Great Council

  How did each nation decide smaller matters? Each nation had its own council to decide smaller matters.

  How did the model of the Great Council later influence America? in the way Americans set up their government

  Which crops were grown by Iroquois farmers? corn, beans, and squash

Squanto

Who: Patuxet man
When: the 1600s
Where: near Plymouth Colony

Tisquantum, better known as Squanto, belonged to the Patuxet tribe of the Northeast Woodlands. He was living near Plymouth when the Pilgrims first arrived in the New World from England. Earlier in his life Squanto had been captured and taken to Spain. From there he had gone to England. He lived with an Englishman and learned his language. Squanto later returned to his homeland. The Pilgrims believed God had prepared him, an English-speaking Indian, to be of help to them during their first difficult years in North America.

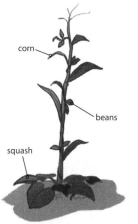

corn

beans

squash

The climbing bean plants used the cornstalks for support. The leaves of the squash kept the soil moist for all the plants.

from each. The Iroquois made good use of the resources around them. They made sugar and syrup from maple trees. They hunted and trapped animals in the forests and mountains. The deer was an important animal not only for its meat but also for its skin. The Iroquois wore deerskin shirts, leggings, skirts, and moccasins.

The Iroquois used beads called **wampum** for several purposes. They sewed the beads together to make belts that displayed symbols and pictures. A wampum belt could communicate a message or summon someone to a council meeting. It could record a decision or the terms of a treaty. Wampum beads were also used as money.

17

Teach for Understanding

- Direct attention to the pictures on page 17. Read the caption aloud.
- Choose a student to read aloud the Biography Box on page 17. Use the information to guide a discussion about Squanto.
- Use the Background information about Samoset and Squanto to show how they used their God-given abilities to help the settlers.

How did planting the Three Sisters close together benefit each type of plant? The climbing bean plants used the cornstalks for support. The leaves of the squash kept the soil moist for all the plants.

How did the Iroquois make good use of the resources around them? They made sugar and syrup from maple trees. They hunted and trapped animals. They used deer meat for food and the skin to make shirts, leggings, skirts, and moccasins.

What were some of the ways that the Iroquois used beads called wampum? The Iroquois sewed the beads together to make belts that displayed symbols and pictures. A wampum belt could communicate a message, summon someone to a council meeting, record a decision or the terms of a treaty, or be used as money.

Activities

Build a Longhouse
Find directions to build a model of the Iroquois longhouse using sticks and bark.

American Indians' Winter Food
Make and label a display of dried corn and beans, pumpkins or winter squash, nuts, pumpkin or sunflower seeds, dried berries, jerky, and smoked fish.

Make Succotash
Guide a discussion of whether the students have eaten succotash. Explain that succotash was a dish created by the Northeast Woodland Indians. People still eat succotash today. Combine cooked sweet corn and lima beans. Season with butter, and add stewed tomatoes or a little chopped and cooked sweet red pepper for color. Invite the students to try the succotash.

Background

Samoset and Squanto
In mid-March 1621 the settlers in Plymouth received a surprise visit from an Indian named Samoset. They were probably stunned when he greeted them in the broken English he had learned from contact with English fishermen. A few days later Samoset returned to Plymouth with another Indian named Squanto. Squanto had been in contact with the English since 1605 and had lived in England for a few years. In 1619 he had returned to his homeland and discovered that his tribe and neighboring tribes had been wiped out by a plague.

Squanto provided the settlers with lifesaving information about crop fertilization in order to increase food production. He also led them to areas where they could catch fish and eels to supplement their diet.

In addition, Squanto worked to establish peace between the settlers and the neighboring Wampanoag tribe. His efforts led to a peace that endured for nearly fifty years.

Teach for Understanding

- Direct attention to the picture on page 18. Read the caption aloud.

  What is the geography of the Southeast Woodlands? This region has mountains, coastal plains, forests, rivers, swamps, and marshes.

  What was one of the most significant Southeast Woodland tribes? the Cherokees

  Where in the Southeast did the Cherokees live? in the southern portion of the Appalachian Mountains, mainly in what is now the Carolinas, Georgia, and Tennessee

  What sources of food did the Cherokees have? They grew crops, hunted, fished, and gathered nuts and berries.

  What did they make for hunting animals? blowguns

- Choose a volunteer to describe how the Cherokees made blowguns. They hollowed out thick stalks from cane plants. The Cherokees placed darts inside the stalk and blew through the other end to shoot.

  What was stickball? Stickball was a Cherokee game similar to lacrosse. It was sometimes used to settle arguments. Often it had important religious purposes as well.

  ▶ Conclude the discussion by describing Iroquois and Cherokee methods of settling problems. Decisions for all the Iroquois people were made by a group of men called the Great Council. Each nation also had its own council to decide smaller matters.

  Stickball was sometimes used by the Cherokees to settle arguments between villages or tribes.

Activity Manual

- Guide completion of pages 11–13.

People of the Southeast Woodlands

The Southeast region of the United States is a place of great variety. This region has mountains, coastal plains, forests, rivers, swamps, and marshes. Many different types of trees, plants, and flowers grow there, and it is home to various kinds of animals, birds, and fish. The Indians who lived in the Southeast had abundant natural resources. Like the people of the Northeast, they are considered Woodland Indians.

The Cherokees

The Cherokees were one of many tribes in the Southeast. They were, however, one of the largest tribes and one of the most significant in the history of southeastern America. The

A dart from a blowgun could hit a target as far as sixty feet away.

Cherokees lived in the southern portion of the Appalachian Mountains, mainly in what is now the Carolinas, Georgia, and Tennessee.

The Cherokees grew crops, hunted, fished, and gathered nuts and berries. For hunting they made blowguns from cane plants that grew along the rivers. These plants had thick stalks that could be hollowed out like a gun barrel. The Cherokees placed darts inside the stalk and blew through the other end to shoot.

Most Cherokee homes were built in a style called **wattle and daub**. These shelters were small huts made of sticks or river cane plastered with mud. Often the Cherokees wove thatched roofs out of brush. At other times they made shingled roofs out of bark.

One interesting Cherokee tradition was the game of stickball. Stickball was similar to the game of lacrosse. Players used two sticks to move a ball from one end of the court to another. A team scored points when one of its players threw the ball against a wooden pole or through a goal. Sometimes stickball was more than a game to the Cherokees. It was sometimes used to settle arguments between villages or tribes. Often it had important religious purposes as well.

▶ Describe Iroquois and Cherokee methods of settling problems.

18

Background

River Cane

As a result of its great need for water, river cane grows in swamps and on creek banks. The Cherokees used river cane to make pipe stems and chairs. They used river cane to craft double-woven waterproof baskets, which are considered to be valuable works of art today. The Cherokees also hollowed out river cane to make blowguns for hunting.

Few Cherokees make crafts with river cane today. River cane is less abundant now because of the clearing of land, grazing of animals, and variable water levels. River cane grows outside the North Carolina Museum of History at the "History of the Harvest" exhibit that traces agriculture back to early native species.

Native American Beliefs

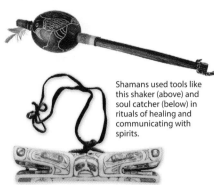

This chapter has highlighted several unique cultures among America's first people. But the most important part of a culture is not its food, language, or traditions. The most important part of a culture is what its people believe.

Religion is a person's belief about where he came from, how to worship, and how to live. Each cultural group that we have studied in this chapter had its own religious beliefs. Usually a tribe's religion affected every part of life. For Native Americans, religion was closely connected to stories, dances, art, music, traditions, and nature.

There is much we do not know about the religion of America's first people. Scholars have found great variety among the beliefs of different Indian groups. But most groups had certain features of their beliefs in common.

Belief in Spirits

Nearly every Indian cultural group believed in spirits. Most believed that people, animals, and everything else in nature had spirits. Spirits were thought to control every force of nature and every event in life. The Pueblo Indians trusted in kachinas to help them grow crops in the dry Southwest. The Inuits believed in a sea goddess who provided them with seals and walruses. Most Indians believed the animals they hunted had spirits who could help them

Shamans used tools like this shaker (above) and soul catcher (below) in rituals of healing and communicating with spirits.

as well. The people tried to please the spirits in order to have good health, success, and happiness.

Some groups believed in one Great Spirit who was supreme over all the others. The Sioux called this being Wakan Tanka. Some Northeast Woodland tribes called him Manitou. Some thought of him as the creator. These tribes honored and feared many other spirits as well as the Great Spirit. Romans 1 tells us that one way people reject God is by worshiping His creation rather than Him. This was true of the Native Americans in their efforts to please the many spirits that they thought lived in the world around them. In their belief of a supreme Great Spirit, we can see a faint similarity to the biblical truth that there is only one true God. It may be that some tribes remembered fragments of truth about God that their ancestors from the tower of Babel had once known.

19

Lesson 6

Student Text pages 19–21
Activity Manual page 14

Lesson Focus

- Each American Indian culture group had its own beliefs, but nearly all believed in spirits.

Objectives

- Identify beliefs of several Indian culture groups
- Describe shamans and shamanism
- Use God's Word to draw a biblical conclusion about spirits

Teacher's Toolkit CD

- Interactive Visual: *Map of Indian Culture Areas*
- Instructional Aids 7–8: *Comparing Historic Worldviews; Presenting a Culture*

Materials

- A list of Indian cultural groups (not mentioned in this chapter) for each group of students
- Resources to research the Indian cultural groups on the list

Review

- Display the interactive visual. Choose volunteers to place the symbol for each of the following tribes in the correct cultural area on the map: the Cherokees, the Chumash, the Inuits, the Iroquois, the Makahs, the Navajos, the Nez Perces, the Pueblos, and the Sioux.

Preparation for Reading

- Generate interest as you direct the students to read the titles and examine the pictures on pages 19–21.
- Guide pronunciation of any unfamiliar words in the lesson.
- Direct the students to read the pages silently to discover the name the Sioux called the one Great Spirit. Wakan Tanka

Teach for Understanding

- Direct attention to the pictures on page 19. Read the caption aloud.

    Which part of culture is more important than the food, language, or traditions? what the people believe

    What did nearly every American Indian cultural group believe in? spirits

    What did most Indian cultural groups believe about spirits? They believed that people, animals, and everything else in nature had spirits. Spirits were thought to control every force of nature and every event in life.

    Why did many Indians try to please the spirits? in order to have good health, success, and happiness

    What did some Indians believe about the Great Spirit? They thought of him as the creator.

    What did American Indian cultural groups honor and fear in additon to the Great Spirit? other spirits

    What does Romans 1 say people worship instead of God? His creation

- How did many Native Americans reject God? They tried to please the many spirits that they thought lived in the world around them.

    What might be a reason that some tribes held beliefs similar to the truth about the God of the Bible? It may be that some tribes remembered fragments of truth about God that their ancestors from the tower of Babel had once known.

Teach for Understanding

- Direct attention to the picture on page 20. Read the caption aloud.

What were Indian religious leaders called? shamans

What did Indians believe about shamans? that they had special healing powers because of their contact with the spirits

What is the use of shamans to communicate with spirits called? shamanism

What were some ways shamans contacted spirits? rituals and visions

What was Navajo sand painting used for? It was an attempt to get rid of disease through the power of spirits.

How did Indians feel toward shamans? Shamans were both respected and feared because of their ability to contact spirits.

How can a Christian know how to think about spirits? by reading God's Word (Leviticus 19:31; 20:6; Deuteronomy 18:9–13; Isaiah 8:19–20)

What did God tell His people when He first gave them His law? He told them not to try to communicate with the spirit world.

Who can help a Christian with every need? God

Why is it that a shaman cannot have power over evil spiritual forces? Evil forces can be overcome only by the Lord's power.

How can a Christian stand against these evil forces? by wearing the whole armor of God

How were a tribe's stories about its beliefs passed down from parents to children? orally

What are some stories parents pass down orally to children today? stories about family, Bible stories, war stories, stories about famous people

Shamanism

Religious leaders among the Indians tried to get in touch with spirits. These leaders were called **shamans**. Indians believed shamans had special healing powers because of their contact with the spirits. Using shamans to communicate with spirits is called shamanism. Nearly every cultural group of Native Americans practiced shamanism.

Shamans had various ways of getting in touch with spirits. Sometimes they would go through rituals, such as sitting in a steamy hut called a sweat lodge, doing a special dance, or chanting a spell. At other times they would seek to receive messages from spirits through visions. Even the Navajo

This Inuit carving is thought to depict a shaman's spirit leaving his body.

art of sand painting was an attempt to get rid of disease through the power of spirits. Shamans were both respected and feared because of their ability to contact spirits.

Christians must use God's Word to guide their thinking about shamanism. When God first gave people His law, He told them not to try to communicate with the spirit world (Leviticus 19:31). God wants all people everywhere to trust in Him alone for the help that they need. The Bible tells us that there are evil spiritual forces that can be overcome only by the Lord's power. A shaman can have no real power over these spirits. But a Christian wearing the whole armor of God can stand against them (Ephesians 6:10–17).

Stories

Most tribes had stories about how the world and the people in it came into being. A tribe's stories told which spirits were most important to please. Stories also revealed a tribe's beliefs about what happened to a person after death. These stories were passed down from parents to children **orally**, or by telling aloud. Eventually many of the stories were written down. These stories help us learn more about the religious beliefs Native Americans have held for many generations.

Sadly, the true story of God's love for the world and of His Son, Jesus Christ, was unknown to these first

20

Activity

Present a Story Orally

Direct the students to think of a story their parents, grandparents, or other family members like to tell about the family's history. Invite volunteers to tell the story to the class.

Americans. Many Europeans who came to North America in the 1500s and 1600s wanted the Indians to know this story. But as we will see, Europeans did not always share the gospel story in a loving way. In some cases, their dealings with the Indians added to the suffering in the story of America.

America's first people were good examples for us in many ways. They filled North America and ruled over the earth as God had commanded. They used the resources He had given them. Many tribes had strong families. They valued marriage and took good care of their children.

Yet like everyone else in the world, the Native American people were sinners in need of God's salvation. They needed to understand that only Jesus Christ could free them from their fear of spirits and give them eternal life. Only then could their story have a truly happy ending.

> What were some common features of most Native American beliefs?

//// **Activity** ///

Presenting a Culture

Choose an Indian tribe not included in this chapter from the list provided by your teacher. Locate this tribe's cultural area on the map on page 6. Research to learn how the culture of this tribe was affected by its geographical area.

What kind of food did these people eat? How did they dress? What kinds of shelters did they build? What unique traditions did they practice? What did they believe? Report your findings in a creative presentation.

///

21

How did America's first people fulfill the Creation Mandate? They filled North America and ruled over the earth.

What were American Indians able to do with their God-given abilities as they fulfilled the Creation Mandate? They used the resources God had given them as they ruled over the earth. Many tribes had strong families. They valued marriage and took good care of their children.

How can Native American people be free from their fear of spirits? They need to understand that all spirits were created by God. Even though some rebelled, no spirit can act apart from God's permission (Job 1:10–12). Instead of worshiping spirits, God commands all men everywhere to worship Him by trusting in Christ's death alone for the forgiveness of their sins.

▷▷ Conclude the discussion by asking the question on page 21. Nearly every Indian cultural group believed in spirits. Some believed in one Great Spirit. Some thought the one Great Spirit was the creator.

Activity Manual

- Guide completion of page 14.

// **Activity** //

Presenting a Culture

- Generate excitement about presenting a culture as you read the Activity information on page 21 aloud.
- Divide the students into small groups.
- Distribute a list of Indian tribes to each group. Direct each group of students to choose an Indian tribe they would like to learn more about and to locate its culture area on the map on Student Text page 6.
- Distribute Instructional Aid 8. Direct each group to write the name of its tribe and the name of the tribe's cultural area on the organizer.
- Direct students to use the resources you provide to complete information on the organizer as time allows. Direct students to keep the organizer in their notebook or folder. Explain to the students that the organizer will be used in Lesson 7.

Teach for Understanding

- Direct attention to the picture on page 21.
- Display Instructional Aid 7. Explain that the students will be comparing a historic worldview with a Christian worldview to draw a conclusion.
- Choose a volunteer to read aloud the Native American point of view and the question.
- Write for display what Native Americans believed about spirits.
- Direct attention to "The Biblical Point of View" section on the organizer. Read Leviticus 19:31 aloud.

How are people exposed to evil forces today? by reading books and watching movies about wizards, witches, or fortune tellers who seek power from evil spirits

- Read Ephesians 6:10–11 aloud.
- Guide a discussion as you write for display concerning God's warning about contacting spirits or seeking those who contact spirits and how a Christian can stand against evil spirits.
- Direct attention to the last section of the organizer. Explain that the students will be drawing a conclusion regarding Indian beliefs about spirits and what the Bible teaches. Guide a discussion as you write for display.

Lesson

7

Lesson Focus

- Native American culture groups represent a wide variety of traditions and beliefs.

Objectives
- Complete an organizer for an Indian tribe
- Make a creative presentation about an Indian cultural group

Materials
- Resources to research the American Indian culture groups on the list

Teacher's Toolkit CD
- Instructional Aid 8: *Presenting a Culture*

Teach for Understanding

- Direct the groups to use the resources to complete Instructional Aid 8.

- Encourage each group to think of creative ways to present the information.

- Invite each group to give a creative presentation of its Indian tribe.

Chapter Review
Activity Manual pages 15–16

Objective
- Recall concepts and terms from Chapter 1

Teacher's Toolkit CD
- Interactive Visual: *Map of Indian Culture Areas*

Materials
- 30 plastic or wooden beads
- 12" length of string for each group
- a list of thirty prepared questions with the answers

Introduction

- Display the interactive visual. Choose volunteers to place the symbol for each of the following tribes in the correct cultural area on the map: the Cherokees, the Chumash, the Inuits, the Iroquois, the Makahs, the Navajos, the Nez Perces, the Pueblo people, and the Sioux.

- Concepts for the Chapter 1 Test will be taken from Activity Manual pages 1–16. You may review any or all of the concepts during this lesson. You may choose to review Chapter 1 by playing "Wampum."

Review

Game: Wampum

- Divide the students into several small groups. Distribute a length of string to each group. Explain that you will read a question aloud. The first student to stand and give the correct answer will receive one wampum for his group to put on the string. Continue asking questions until all the wampum have been awarded. The group with the most wampum at the end is the winner.

Activity Manual

- Guide completion of pages 15–16.

Chapter 1 Test

Objective
- Demonstrate knowledge of concepts from Chapter 1 by taking the test

Assessment

- Administer Test 1.

Chapter 2

2 European Exploration and Settlement

Focus

Europeans explored and settled in the Americas for both religious and non-religious reasons.

Introduction

Many changes, challenges, and pressures led to the exploration of the world by Europeans. Better ships and new inventions made exploration possible. The Portuguese were successful in establishing trade with India and East Africa by sea. Christopher Columbus believed that it would be possible to reach Asia by sailing west across the Atlantic Ocean. On October 12, 1492, Columbus and his men set foot on an island in the Americas. With the arrival of the Spanish began the institution of slavery. Bartolomé de Las Casas worked to change how American Indians were treated.

Some of the earlier settlements in America were New France, New Netherland, Roanoke, and Jamestown. The Puritans wanted to purify the Church of England, but the Separatists did not think the Church of England would change. The Pilgrims left England and spent ten years in the Netherlands. They eventually founded a colony in America so they would have the freedom to do right. After Charles I tried to end Puritanism in his kingdom, the Puritans founded the Massachusetts Bay Colony in America. It proved to be a success for the Puritans.

Chapter 2 Overview

Lesson	Student Text	Activity Manual	Content	Vocabulary	
10	22–25	17–19	Europe and exploration Inventions that helped exploration People who could have explored	caravan caravel compass Iberian Peninsula	latitude quadrant tacking
11	26–28	20	Exploration of Africa and India Christopher Columbus		
12	29–31	21–23	Treatment of American Indians Bartolomé de Las Casas		
13	32–35	24–25	The French, Dutch, and English in North America Peter Stuyvesant	Huguenot	
14	36–38	26	Jamestown, Powhatan, and John Smith	indentured servant	
15	39–42	27	New England Biography Box: William Bradford Plymouth	Puritan Separatist	
16	43–45	28–30	How It Was: Freedom to Worship Massachusetts Bay Colony John Winthrop Primary Source: A Model of Christian Charity Activity: Establishing a Colony		
17		31–32	Chapter Review		
18			Chapter Test		

Visit bjupress.com/resources for links to enhance the lessons.

Columbus sails
1492
Protestant
Reformation begins
1517
Jamestown is established
1607

1400   1500   1585 1600 1620   1700

Roanoke is
established
Plymouth is
established

Age of Exploration
Europe and Exploration

Europe was changing in the 1400s. The days of lords and ladies, knights and squires, and serfs and crusaders were drawing to an end. For hundreds of years, Europe had kept mainly to itself. But now Europeans learned more about the rest of the world by trading with people in the Middle East. Some of the goods they bought came from India and China.

Europeans faced many challenges. The goods they wanted from India and China were expensive. These goods were brought by **caravans** to the Middle East. Merchants from the Italian cities of Genoa and Venice brought these goods to Europe. The prices increased each time a merchant bought and resold the goods. Some Europeans wondered if there was a cheaper way to get goods from Asia to Europe.

Europe was also under pressure from the Islamic religion. In the late 1400s, the Ottoman Empire began to conquer parts of eastern Europe. By the 1530s the Ottoman Turks were at the gates of Vienna, Austria. The Muslims, people who followed Islam, had conquered much of Spain and Portugal hundreds of years earlier. These two countries make up the **Iberian Peninsula**. But the Spanish kingdoms were able to push the Muslim invaders back and retake the Iberian Peninsula.

These changes, challenges, and pressures made Europeans want to explore the world. They wanted to discover new trade routes to the East. They also wanted to find new allies and wealth that would help them fight against the Muslim threat. Additionally, they desired to spread Roman Catholicism around the world.

Inventions That Helped Exploration

The age of exploration became possible because of new tools that helped sailors navigate the new ships. Before the age of exploration, oars or large square sails powered European

23

Chapter Focus

Europeans explored and settled in the Americas for both religious and non-religious reasons.

JourneyForth

The Hawk That Dare Not Hunt by Day by Scott O'Dell is available from JourneyForth Books, a division of BJU Press, at journeyforth.com.

Set in Europe during the 1500s, this book tells the story of two smugglers whose lives change when William Tyndale asks them to carry English Bibles along with their usual cargo.

Lesson 10
Student Text pages 22–25
Activity Manual pages 17–19

Lesson Focus

- The age of exploration became possible with the invention of new tools and better ships.

Objectives
- Identify the changes, challenges, and pressures that made Europeans want to explore the world
- Name some of the inventions and how they helped sailors navigate the new ships
- Identify the countries that could have explored but chose not to

Teacher's Toolkit CD
- Visual 2: *The Feudal System*
- Instructional Aids 9–10: *Inventions* (Prepare a copy for each student in class); *Why They Did Not Explore*

Materials
- A compass
- A map of the United States

Introduction

- Invite a student to read aloud the title of the chapter. What does the title tell you about this chapter? Answers should include that the Europeans explored and made settlements.
- Invite a student to read the chapter focus aloud.
- Explain that the picture on page 22 depicts a Columbus-era explorer in the captain's cabin charting the ship's course.
- Direct attention to the timeline.

  What event happened in 1492? Columbus sailed to the Americas.

  When did the Protestant Reformation begin? 1517

  When was Jamestown established? 1607

Preparation for Reading

- Generate interest as you direct the students to read the titles and examine the pictures on pages 22–25.
- Guide pronunciation of any unfamiliar words in the lesson.
- Direct the students to cut apart the Instructional Aid 9 cards and write on the back of each card how the invention helped sailing.

Teach for Understanding

- Use Visual 2 to guide a discussion about the feudal system. Explain that the system was drawing to an end.

  What two countries made up the Iberian Peninsula? Spain and Portugal

  What two things challenged Europe in the 1400s? expensive goods from India and China and pressure from the Islamic religion

What did these challenges make Europeans want to do? explore the world

What powered European ships before the age of exploration? oars or large square sails

Teach for Understanding

What did Arab ships use that allowed them to travel in a direction different from the wind? small triangular sails

What did the Portuguese construct? a caravel

How did the sails on the caravel help it to travel better than other kinds of ships? A big square sail gave the ship power, and the triangular sails allowed the ship to maneuver.

- Display the compass. Guide a discussion about how a compass is used.

  What does latitude measure? distance from the equator

- Choose students to share the description they wrote about each invention from Instructional Aid 9.

- Direct attention to the illustration on page 24 and discuss how tacking works.

ships. These ships had trouble traveling on the Atlantic Ocean. Ships with many rowers needed to carry lots of food. Ships with large square sails had trouble sailing against the wind.

Arab ships used small triangular sails. These sails helped ships travel in a direction different from the wind. A ship with this kind of sail could even sail into the wind by **tacking**. When sailors tack a ship, they set the sail at an angle to the wind. The wind might blow the ship to the right for a distance. Then the sailors shift the angle of the sails, and the wind blows the ship to the left. By zigzagging, the ship is able to sail into the wind.

The Portuguese constructed a ship called the **caravel**. The caravel had large triangular sails. The Portuguese sometimes added a square sail to these ships. The big square sail gave the ship power, and the triangular sails allowed the ship to maneuver.

Other new inventions helped bring about the age of exploration. The **compass** was an important invention for explorers. A compass is basically a magnet. The compass is built so that one end of the magnet points north. The compass allowed sailors to know which direction they were sailing. Maps began to include compass directions showing sailors how to reach specific places around the Mediterranean Sea.

A tool called a **quadrant** was invented by the Arabs. A quadrant looked like a right triangle with one curved edge. A string with a weight at the end was attached to the triangle's point. A sailor would look along one edge of the quadrant to line it up with the sun. The weighted string hung straight down. On the side of the quadrant was a scale. The sailor would compare the measurement on the scale with a chart. The chart told him that on particular days at a particular latitude, the sun would be at a particular angle at noon. **Latitude** measures distance from the equator. The quadrant helped sailors know where they were on the ocean.

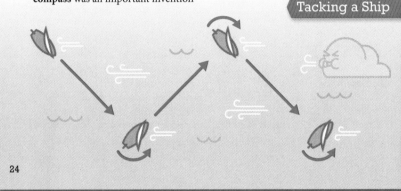

Tacking a Ship

24

Activities

Modern Ships

Direct the students to work in small groups to discover some of the latest advances and inventions that make sailing safer and faster today.

Virtual Field Trip

Show a video of sailing basics. Preview it for accuracy and appropriateness.

Exploring Your World

Encourage the students to think about how the explorers must have felt when they began to explore new lands. Discuss places in your community the students have never visited. Make a list of places to visit. Challenge the students to visit a new place, take notes about what they see and do, draw a map of the place, and share their experience with the class.

New Tools

Challenge the students to invent a new tool that would make something they do easier. Invite them to draw a sketch of the tool and explain how it would make work easier.

Make a Compass

Use resources to make and demonstrate a compass.

Background

Faster Ships

Before the mid-1400s, few Europeans ventured far out to sea because their ships could not handle the rough conditions away from the shore. This situation changed after the Portuguese adapted small fishing ships called caravels for long-distance travel. The caravels featured new sails that allowed the ships to sail directly into the wind and to turn quickly and easily. Two of Christopher Columbus's ships were caravels. Without these ships, the Europeans may not have reached the New World.

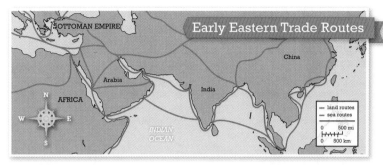

Early Eastern Trade Routes

People Who Could Have Explored

People other than Europeans could have explored the world. The Chinese had already invented the compass. Their ships were larger and stronger than the European ships. Their charts and instruments were precise, and they also made detailed maps.

In the early 1400s, the Chinese sailed to India, Arabia, and Africa. They explored those parts of the world for almost thirty years. Then the Chinese gave up exploration. The emperor did not allow more ships to be built.

Historians do not know the reason the Chinese stopped exploring. Some think that the Chinese did not need to sail to other countries for trade. All the people needed was in China. The Chinese may have believed that they had little to gain from exploring other countries. By the time the Portuguese reached the Indian Ocean, the Chinese had left.

The Arabs also had boats that often sailed the Indian Ocean on missions of trade. They too could produce charts and navigate by the stars. They could have built ships to sail around Africa to reach Europe. But they were busy trading on the Indian Ocean and in the Mediterranean. Since trade was already plentiful, there was little reason to go exploring.

The Mayas, who lived in America, used sturdy boats to travel on the Caribbean. Their boats did not have sails. But they could have found a way to sail across the Atlantic if they had wanted to. They could have used their knowledge about the stars for navigation. But instead of exploring, the Mayas built an impressive civilization in America. Perhaps they never felt a need to try to cross the Atlantic.

> Why did Europeans begin to explore the world?

25

By the time the Europeans discovered the Americas, they had better weapons and a more advanced civilization. They were able to conquer the Indians who lived in America. Later they would also conquer the East. In the nineteenth century, Europe exerted great power over China. But at various points in time, these other civilizations were more advanced than the Europeans. Some of the technological advances that enabled European exploration were learned through contact with the East. The Chinese had better ships long before the Europeans. Hundreds of years before European exploration, American Indians had built cities that were larger and more advanced than London of the same time.

None of these truths should surprise the Christian. All these people were created with God's image and blessed with the ability to rule over His world. They would all use these abilities for good and evil. We can marvel at the abilities God gave them and learn from their sins and errors the importance of seeking wisdom from God for how to live.

Teach for Understanding

- Direct attention to the map on page 25 and discuss trade between the Arab, Indian, and East Asian worlds.
- Divide the students into groups of three. Ask the students in each group to choose the Chinese, the Arabs, or the Mayas and complete that section of Instructional Aid 10.
- Guide a discussion about the countries that could have explored but chose not to.
- Explain that because all people are created in God's image, people of all cultures have the ability to do wonderful things. These abilities do not need to evolve over time. We should not be surprised to find remarkable accomplishments done by so-called primitive peoples.

> Conclude the discussion by asking the question on page 25. The goods they wanted from India and China were expensive. They were also under pressure from the Islamic religion.

Activity Manual

- Use the information at the top of page 17 as you explain cardinal and intermediate directions.
- Introduce the abbreviations of the directions.
- Practice finding cardinal and intermediate directions using a map of the United States. Point to a state and ask which direction you would go in order to get to another state.
- Guide completion of page 17.
- Explain that page 18 contains important terms, places, people, and concepts the students will learn in Chapter 2.
- Direct the students to look for familiar terms, places, people, or concepts on the page.
- Guide completion of pages 17–19.

Invite students to use information from *Chapter 2 Looking Ahead* to create flashcards to use for review.

Lesson

11

Student Text pages 26–28
Activity Manual page 20

Lesson Focus

- The Europeans began to explore routes to Africa and India.

Objectives

- Explain how Prince Henry of Portugal helped his nation become skilled at exploration
- Recognize the accomplishments of explorers like Bartolomeu Dias and Vasco da Gama
- State Christopher Columbus's idea about how to reach Asia
- Explain how Columbus was able to find the Americas

Teacher's Toolkit CD

- Instructional Aid 11: *Columbus Play* (Prepare one copy of each scene for each actor in the scene.)

Review

Why did Europe change in the 1400s? Europeans were trading with people in the Middle East.

> Guide a review of important terms, maps, places, and people from each previous lesson. Direct the students to find and read the corresponding entries from the Resource Treasury.

What were some of the inventions that helped exploration? small triangular sails, caravel, compass, quadrant

Preparation for Reading

- Generate interest as you direct the students to read the titles and examine the picture and maps on pages 26–28.
- Guide pronunciation of any unfamiliar words in the lesson.
- Direct the students to read the pages silently to find out who believed a person could sail west across the Atlantic Ocean to reach Asia. Christopher Columbus

Teach for Understanding

What area did the Portuguese begin to explore? the coast of Africa

What was Bartolomeu Dias (bahr to lo MEH oo DEE uhs) the first European to do? sail around Africa's southern tip

What did the king of Portugal call the tip of Africa? the Cape of Good Hope

Who was the first to sail from Europe to India? Vasco da Gama

How do you think Portugal benefited from da Gama's voyage to India? Answers could include that it opened India's spice trade to Portugal.

The First European Explorers
Exploration of Africa and India

Prince Henry of Portugal (1394–1460) helped his nation become skilled at exploration. In 1487 Bartolomeu Dias explored the coast of Africa for Portugal. He was the first European to sail around Africa's southern tip. Later, the king of Portugal called the tip the Cape of Good Hope. He had good hope that a water route to India had been found.

Ten years later Vasco da Gama set sail with four ships. He wanted to be the first to sail from Europe to India. He reached India after traveling for a year. Until this time only the Arabs had traded with India and East Africa. The only known route to these lands had been to sail from the Arabian Peninsula. The Portuguese were successful in establishing trade with India and East Africa by sea.

Telescopes helped explorers see long distances.

Christopher Columbus

Christopher Columbus had another idea for how to reach Asia. He thought that he could sail west across the Atlantic Ocean. His research had convinced him that Europe

Astrolabes, like quadrants, helped explorers find their position in the ocean.

and Asia were large. He believed the ocean between the two continents must not be large. Contrary to what some people think, Columbus did not need to convince anyone that the earth was a globe. This fact was well-known hundreds of years before Christ was born. However, Columbus did have to convince his supporters that the globe was really as small as he claimed. Columbus thought Japan was where Virginia and North Carolina are. He did not think that two continents and two oceans lay between Europe and Japan. Columbus was wrong, but his mistake led to a great discovery.

Columbus traveled to Spain to see whether the king and queen would pay for his voyage. The queen refused at first. Eventually, Columbus convinced Queen Isabella to support him.

Columbus wanted to lead this exploration westward to Asia for several reasons. Of course a voyage like this would bring fame and riches. If it proved to be a good trading route, both Columbus and the kingdom of Spain would become rich.

Columbus had specific ideas about

26

- Explain that the students will reinforce the information about Christopher Columbus by presenting a play. The first two scenes will need four students for each scene. The third scene will need five. Scene 4 will need three students.
- Distribute the scripts from Instructional Aid 11 to each group and direct the groups to practice their parts.
- Invite the students in Scenes 1 and 2 to perform their part of the play.
- Direct the students in Scene 3 to perform.

In what ways was Columbus wrong? He believed that Europe and Asia were large. He believed the ocean between the two continents must not be large. He thought the globe was smaller than most people thought. He did not think that two continents and two oceans lay between Europe and Japan.

- Explain that God in His providence uses even mistakes to work out His plan for the unfolding of history.

> Select one of the prepared rubrics from the Teacher's Toolkit CD or design a rubric to include your chosen criteria.

what should be done with the wealth his voyage brought. In 1492, the year that Columbus set sail, King Ferdinand and Queen Isabella had finally pushed the Muslims out of the Iberian Peninsula. But Columbus thought the war against the Muslims should continue. He especially wanted Christians to recapture Jerusalem. He thought the wealth from his voyage could pay for such a war. Columbus thought Christ would return soon. But he thought Jerusalem needed to be in Christian hands for Christ to return. Columbus wanted his voyage to prepare the way for the return of Christ.

Columbus set sail in August 1492 with three ships, the *Niña*, the *Pinta*, and the *Santa María*. Columbus sailed southwest along the coast of Africa for a month until he got to the Canary Islands. Columbus knew he could catch an easterly wind from the Canaries. An easterly wind blew from the east but pushed the sailing ships west.

Columbus left the Canaries in early September. Columbus and his ships sailed westward into little-known waters. Life on the ship was hard. The day was filled with watches, or periods of time in which sailors were on duty. During these watches, sailors were looking for land. Columbus varied activities by reading and singing prayers at certain hours. The men ate hard biscuits and salted meat. They drank water and wine (since the water tended to go bad). The men reported back to Spain that the food smelled and tasted bad, but Columbus reported that they all stayed healthy.

By the beginning of October, the men were restless. They wanted Columbus to find some westerly winds to ensure they made it home. Columbus persuaded them to persevere.

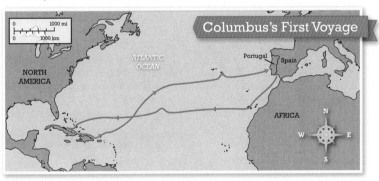

Columbus's First Voyage

27

What did Columbus plan to do with the wealth his voyage brought? make Spain wealthy; finance the war against the Muslims; help Christians recapture Jerusalem; prepare the way for the return of Christ

- Explain that the Bible does not teach that Christians must conquer Jerusalem for Christ to return. First Thessalonians 5 teaches that we should be prepared for the return of Christ at any time.
- Direct attention to the map on page 27 and ask the students to trace the route of Columbus's first voyage.

Geography

That people in the 1400s thought the earth was flat is now recognized to be a myth. There is no evidence that Columbus had to argue against the idea of a flat earth. There is abundant evidence that people knew the earth was a sphere. There also is no evidence that Columbus's crew thought the earth was flat.

The controversy was about the size of the earth. Though most geographers thought the earth was about 23,000 miles in circumference, Columbus thought it was about 18,000 miles in circumference. The circumference of the earth at the equator is actually 24,901.55 miles. Although Columbus's calculations were wrong, God used him to lead Europeans to a continent they had not previously known about. Columbus is just one example of a person God used, despite his many flaws, to accomplish His own greater purposes.

Activities

Difficulties at Sea

Direct the students to research some of the difficulties that Columbus's sailors experienced on their voyages, such as poor food, illnesses, and the amount of work.

News Reporter

Invite the students to pretend to be news reporters. Ask them to write five questions they would ask Columbus about his exploration. Then allow each student to ask one question and allow the other students to answer the questions.

Timeline

Direct the students to research the life of one of the explorers and develop a timeline of important events in his life.

Advertisement

Direct the students to design an advertisement that would attract sailors to sail with one of the explorers. Display the advertisements.

Teach for Understanding

- Direct attention to the map on page 28 and ask the students to identify some of the places Columbus may have visited in the Caribbean.

- Direct the students in Scene 4 of the play to perform their scene.

  What did Columbus do after he landed on San Salvador and declared it a possession of the king and queen of Spain? He met the people who lived on the island and began sailing to the various islands in the Caribbean.

  Where did Columbus think he was? in the Indies

- Why did Columbus think he was in the Indies? Answers could include that North and South America were not known to most Europeans.

  What mistakes had Columbus made? He was wrong about how large the earth was and where he landed; he was wrong to claim other people's land for his rulers.

  ▶ Conclude the discussion by asking the question on page 28. He discovered an island in the Americas that was previously unknown to Europeans.

Activity Manual

- Guide completion of page 20.

On October 11 Columbus and his men sighted land. The voyage had lasted longer than two months by this time. It had been more than one month since they had last seen land.

The next day, October 12, 1492, Columbus and his men set foot on an island in the Americas. Columbus named the island San Salvador, which means "Holy Savior." Columbus prayed a prayer of thanksgiving, set up a cross, and declared the island a possession of the king and queen of Spain.

Columbus met the people who lived on the island. He thought he had landed on one of the islands of Southeast Asia. That region of the world was called the Indies in Columbus's day so he called the Tainos people there Indians.

Columbus began sailing to the various islands in the Caribbean. He still thought he was in the Indies. He hoped to find mainland Asia and its large cities. Of course, he did not find these cities in the Caribbean.

In January Columbus finally decided to return to Spain. He had to sail north to find winds that would blow him east. After a month of sailing, including a fearsome Atlantic storm, Columbus reached the Azores, islands off the coast of Portugal. Once Columbus was back in Europe, he reported his travels to the king and queen. News spread throughout Europe of Columbus's travels.

Columbus made a number of mistakes. He was wrong about how large the earth was. He was wrong about where he landed. He was wrong to claim other people's land for his rulers. But God is in control of history even when people make mistakes or do wrong. Columbus's voyage was one of the most important discoveries Europeans ever made.

Columbus in the Caribbean

NORTH AMERICA · ATLANTIC OCEAN · Bahamas · San Salvador · Cuba · Santo Domingo · Jamaica · 500 mi · 500 km

Why is Columbus an important figure in history?

28

Activities

Life Today

Guide a discussion about what Columbus would think about life, travel, and exploration today. Invite the students to suggest some questions he might ask.

Letter

Encourage the students to write a letter from one of the sailors on Columbus's ships to his family back home. It could explain what it felt like to set sail, what life was like aboard ship, or how it felt to find the new land.

The Columbus Doors

Find a site that describes and shows pictures of the Columbus Doors, which are located at the main entrance to the United States Capitol Building. They tell the story of the life of Columbus in carvings sculpted by Randolph Rogers.

Background

The Label "Christian"

The label "Christian" is used in various ways in historical writings. Europeans are labeled as Christians in contrast to the Muslims of North Africa and the Middle East or to American Indians with their indigenous religions. As the Reformation made clear, there is a distinct difference between this Christianity of cultural influence and the Christianity brought about by the gospel received by faith.

Treatment of American Indians

Columbus wrote in his diary about his first meeting with Indians. He said he gave them gifts to encourage friendship. Columbus wrote that the Europeans should be friendly. Though he thought the Indians could be forced into Christianity, he thought it would be better for them to become Christians "by love." He also wrote that he thought they would make good slaves.

This diary entry highlights two major problems. First, the Spanish thought they could force people to become Christians. Second, they thought of Indians as slaves. Europeans did not think of them as equals. Columbus spoke often of making the Indians Christians. But he also kidnapped some of them. He wanted to take them back to Spain. He did not understand that these actions worked against each other.

Columbus returned to the Americas three more times. Other Spaniards followed. Some Spanish people began to live in America. They claimed America for the king of Spain.

The king of Spain wrote a document that explained why Spain had a right to the Indians' lands. It said that the Christian God had created the earth. It also said that all people were descended from Adam and Eve. But over the 5,000 years since Creation, people had divided into many kingdoms. This document might have led the Spanish to realize that the Indians should be allowed to rule the lands God gave them. The Spanish should have shared the gospel with the Indians. But they should not have tried to seize the lands.

Columbus kept a diary about his voyages. His diaries are a primary source that give historians important information about his explorations.

29

The King of Spain's Document

The document that the Spanish king had written contains one important truth: God created and rules over the earth and all its inhabitants. But it makes two large errors. First, the Bible nowhere teaches that God made Peter the ruler of all the world. Peter was an apostle who helped found the Christian church. But Jesus is the one that God made ruler over all the world (Psalm 2:6–8). Right now Jesus extends His reign through the preaching of the gospel. In the future He will judge those who resist His rule. This judgment is not delegated to Christians to execute. Second, God did not give the popes power to take land and give it to others. Acts 17:26 says that God is the one who sets the boundaries for the peoples of the world. The Spanish king violated the commandment against stealing by taking Indian land. He violated the commandment against taking God's name in vain by claiming that God gave him the right to do it.

Lesson Focus

- The Indians in America were not treated well by some of the Spanish.

Objectives

- State the ways Christopher Columbus did not understand true Christianity
- Explain how the Spanish treated the American Indians
- Recognize that Bartolomé de Las Casas opposed the sinful treatment of the Indians

Teacher's Toolkit CD

- Instructional Aid 12: *Treatment of American Indians*

Review

- Guide a discussion about the important events in the life of Christopher Columbus.

Preparation for Reading

- Generate interest as you direct the students to read the title and examine the pictures on pages 29–31.
- Guide pronunciation of any unfamiliar words in the lesson.
- Direct the students to read the pages and complete Instructional Aid 12 in small groups.

Teach for Understanding

What were the two major problems with the treatment of the Indians by the Spanish? The Spanish thought they could force people to become Christians, and they thought of Indians as slaves.

What was the problem with how Columbus treated the American Indians? Kidnapping them is the opposite of treating them with love.

Who claimed America? The Spanish claimed America for the king of Spain.

How was the document written by the king of Spain used to defend the Spanish right to claim the land? It said that God created the earth and that all people were descended from Adam and Eve. The document said that God made Saint Peter the ruler of the world so the entire world was his kingdom, and all peoples throughout the world must obey him and the popes that followed him. Since one of the popes had already given the land of the Indians to the king of Spain, the document said that the Indians should become Roman Catholics. If they did not, the soldiers of Spain could conquer their lands, take their property, and make them slaves.

- Explain that the name of the document is *Requerimiento* (reh keh ree MYEN toh), which means "requirement" or "demand" in Spanish.

Teach for Understanding

How were the Indians treated by the Spanish leaders who had control over them? They were treated like slaves.

What were Bartolomé de Las Casas's thoughts about the Indians? He opposed the sinful treatment of them.

What did he do with his slaves in America after he realized they were being mistreated? He freed them.

What else did he do to try to bring better treatment to the Indians? He traveled back to Spain and appealed to the king for better treatment for the slaves. He became a monk and wrote about the treatment of the Indians. He argued that the Indians should be treated as people and that no one could be forced to become a Christian.

- Direct attention to the picture of the horses on page 30. Read aloud the caption.

Cortés arrived on the coast of Mexico with sixteen horses. They had an intimidating effect on the Aztecs, who had never seen a horse.

But the document said that God made Saint Peter the ruler of the world. The entire world was his kingdom. All peoples throughout the world must obey him and the popes that followed him. One of the popes had already given the land of the Indians to the king of Spain. The document said that the Indians should become Roman Catholics. If they did not become Roman Catholics, the soldiers of Spain could conquer their lands. The Spanish could take their property and make them slaves.

Often the document from the Spanish king was read in Spanish to people who could not understand what it said. Sometimes it was read even when no Indians were around to hear.

But the Spanish soldiers thought that simply reading the document made it okay for them to conquer the Indians.

The Spanish government gave Spanish leaders control over Indian villages. The Indians who lived there were treated like slaves. Not all Spaniards approved of the treatment of the Indians. **Bartolomé de Las Casas** opposed the sinful treatment.

In 1502 Las Casas moved to America. He was given land and Indians to be his slaves. He became wealthy. But over time Las Casas realized the Indians were being mistreated. He freed his slaves.

Las Casas traveled back to Spain. He appealed to the king for better treatment for the slaves. Not much

30

Background

Slavery and the Mosaic Law

God placed strict restrictions on slavery in the Mosaic Law. Anyone who stole a person, transported a stolen person, or bought a stolen person faced the death penalty (Exodus 21:16). The death penalty was imposed because stealing a person was like taking his life. This is the kind of slavery that American Indians faced. God absolutely prohibited this kind of slavery.

Some people have noted that the Bible permitted certain kinds of slavery. This is true, but it was a very different kind of slavery. A person in debt could willingly sell himself as a slave to work for six years to pay off his debt. In his seventh year, he would be set free with a generous financial provision from his master (Deuteronomy 15:12–15). A person who preferred the security of working for a master and having his needs supplied by him could agree to become a bondservant for life (Deuteronomy 15:16–18). Day laborers who worked for a man for a set amount of money per day were sometimes referred to as slaves or servants.

changed after this meeting. Las Casas decided to become a monk. While in the monastery, he wrote about the treatment of the Indians. He argued that the Indians should be treated as people. He also argued that no one could be forced to become a Christian. People should convert to Christianity willingly and peacefully.

Eventually the pope declared that Indians were humans with souls. They were not to be treated like animals. They were not to be enslaved or stolen from. The Spanish king also passed new laws that were supposed to improve life for the Indians.

In 1544 Las Casas traveled to the Americas as a bishop. A bishop is a leader in the Roman Catholic Church. He found that the new laws were not being obeyed. It was difficult to get people to obey these new laws. The king was far away. People acted however they wanted.

The Roman Catholic Church attempted to convert the Indians peacefully. A group of monks called the Franciscans built missions. The missionaries did not go and live among the Indians. Instead, the Indians lived and worked at the missions. Sadly, the Indians were not always well treated at the missions. Sometimes their work at the missions was similar to their work for any Spanish landowner.

Men like Columbus talked much of spreading the Christian faith. But Columbus and many others in Europe did not understand true Christianity well. The Roman Catholic Church had become corrupt.

Many of its leaders were concerned about power and wealth. They were not concerned about people's salvation or about living holy lives. Europeans called themselves Christians, but many had little knowledge of the Bible. Few knew the gospel of salvation. Too many explorers saw the spread of Christianity as the spread of European empires. Few understood that Christianity spread when God's Word was preached. Few understood that the Holy Spirit had to work in a person's heart for him to become a Christian.

But times were changing. A German monk named Martin Luther began to study what the Bible really said about salvation. He proposed ninety-five theses for debate. Luther's proposal would bring to light truth that had been forgotten for years. He would convince many in Europe that the Roman Catholic Church had departed from the truth of the Bible. His preaching would begin a Reformation. The gospel would again be preached.

> **How should the Spanish have treated the Indians according to the Bible?**

31

Teach for Understanding

What did the pope decide about the Indians? Eventually, he declared that they were not to be treated like animals, be enslaved, or be stolen from.

 How do you think the taking of land from the Indians hindered evangelism? Answers could include that taking Indian land led to conflict, not evangelism; taking Indian land did not show the love of Christ.

What did the Spanish king do to help the Indians? He passed new laws that were supposed to improve life for the Indians.

What did the Franciscans build to work with the Indians? missions

How were the Indians involved at the missions? The Indians lived and worked at the missions.

How were the Indians treated by the Franciscans? They were not always treated well.

What had happened to the Roman Catholic Church over time? It had become corrupt.

What were the Roman Catholic leaders concerned about? power and wealth

How can we describe the Christianity of the Europeans and explorers? They had little knowledge of the Bible. Few knew the gospel of salvation. Too many explorers saw the spread of Christianity as the spread of European empires. Few understood that the Holy Spirit had to work in a person's heart for him to become a Christian.

- Invite a student to read Romans 10:9–10. Discuss the verse. Refer to Explaining the Gospel (p. 458) as you share the gospel with your students.
- Take this opportunity to share your testimony or invite a student to share his or her salvation testimony.

Who was about to bring change to the Roman Catholic Church? a German monk named Martin Luther

> Conclude the discussion by asking the question on page 31. with kindness and as equals

Activity Manual

- Guide completion of pages 21–23.

Only foreigners could be required to serve as slaves for life. Some would sell themselves to an Israelite because of their debts (Leviticus 25:45–46). Of course, the Israelites could not buy stolen foreigners. But even these foreigners could become Jews by being circumcised and worshiping the true God. They would then receive all the promised protections guaranteed to slaves.

Slavery of Indians or Africans in America cannot be justified by slavery as practiced by the Jews. Indian and African slaves did not sell themselves into slavery for a limited period of time in order to pay off debts. Instead, their lives were stolen. According to the Bible, those who traded and bought them were worthy of death for stealing lives.

Lesson

13

Student Text pages 32–35
Activity Manual pages 24–25

Lesson Focus

- The first settlements in North America were very different and varied in their successes.

Objectives

- Name the things that Peter Stuyvesant thought were important for New Amsterdam
- List the reasons Roanoke failed
- Compare the first settlements in North America

Teacher's Toolkit CD

- Instructional Aid 13: *Comparing the Settlements*

Materials

- World map

Review

- Ask questions such as the following to review the previous lesson.

  How were the Indians treated by the Spanish leaders who had control over them? They were treated like slaves.

  What did Bartolomé de Las Casas oppose? the sinful treatment of the Indians

  How can we describe the Christianity of the Europeans and explorers? They had little knowledge of the Bible. Few knew the gospel of salvation. Too many explorers saw the spread of Christianity as the spread of European empires. Few understood that the Holy Spirit had to work in a person's heart for him to become a Christian.

Preparation for Reading

- Generate interest as you direct the students to read the titles and examine the pictures and map on pages 32–35.
- Guide pronunciation of any unfamiliar words in the lesson.
- Direct the students to read the pages and complete Instructional Aid 13 in small groups.

Teach for Understanding

- Integrate information from Instructional Aid 13 and reinforce correct responses as you teach the lesson.
- Direct a student to find Newfoundland on the map on page 32.

First Settlements in North America

The French in North America

France was also interested in America. The French began to cross the Atlantic Ocean. They found good fishing grounds near what is now Newfoundland in Canada.

The French sent an Italian, Giovanni da Verrazzano, to explore this New World. Ten years later the French explorer Jacques Cartier did more exploration. Both men were looking for a Northwest Passage to the Pacific Ocean but did not find one. However, Cartier did find the Saint Lawrence River. This river was important because it was a path deep into North America.

A third explorer, Samuel de Champlain, explored the land around the Saint Lawrence River. He made agreements with some of the Iroquois and the Hurons. He also set up Quebec as a place to trade with them.

The French called their American settlements New France. The French wanted to establish colonies in North America. Spanish colonies brought wealth to Spain. The French wanted colonies that brought them wealth, but their colonies ended up being different from the Spanish colonies. The French were exploring land far to the north of the land Spain claimed. The northern part of America was cold. The land was not good for large plantations. Few French people wanted to move to America.

Some people were not allowed to go to America. France did not give religious freedom to French Protestants, called **Huguenots**. The Huguenots could have become colonists. If they

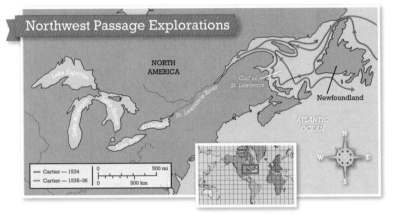

Northwest Passage Explorations

NORTH AMERICA

Gulf of St. Lawrence

Newfoundland

ATLANTIC OCEAN

Cartier — 1534
Cartier — 1535–36

0   500 mi
0   500 km

32

What did explorers find near Newfoundland? good fishing grounds

Who was looking for a Northwest Passage to the Pacific Ocean? Giovanni da Verrazzano and Jacques Cartier

What did Samuel de Champlain explore? the land around the Saint Lawrence River

Why was the Saint Lawrence River an important discovery? It was a path deep into North America.

- Direct a student to locate the Saint Lawrence River on the map on page 32.
- Direct a student to locate Quebec on the world map.

Why did the French want to establish colonies in North America? They saw that Spanish colonies brought wealth to Spain, and they wanted colonies to bring them wealth.

Who were the Huguenots? French Protestants

Trappers' hats were never made from valuable fur like beaver fur. This hat was made from badger fur.

Fur trappers did not have pockets in their pants so they carried bullets and other necessary items in a small bag called a "possibles bag."

Fringe on the coat sleeves helped shed rain from the trapper's skin.

had been granted the religious freedoms in America, they might have moved. Instead, they were forbidden to settle in America. Later the Huguenots would settle in England's colonies as productive citizens. The French sent Roman Catholic missionaries to New France. The French Catholics were different from Spanish Catholics. The French did not bring the Indians to work at missions. Instead French missionaries lived among the Indians. The missionaries learned Indian languages and customs. The work was slow and difficult. The leading French missionary was killed in a war between the Iroquois and the Hurons.

The French succeeded in creating fur-trading partnerships with the Indians. The Indians hunted and trapped animals. The French traded European goods for the furs. The Indians received copper kettles, metal tools, and French weapons in exchange. Sadly, the Indians received alcohol as well. Furs, especially beaver furs, were in high demand in Europe. The French could resell the furs for a great deal of money.

The Dutch and New Amsterdam

The Netherlands was a small nation. But it was a powerful force in trade. The Dutch already had a large trading operation in the East Indies. But they turned their eyes toward America in the 1600s. The Dutch founded New Netherland in America. Its governor, Peter Minuit, bought the use of Manhattan Island from the Lenape Indians in 1626.

The capital city was New Amsterdam. This city was built at a good trading spot. It had a good harbor for ships. The Hudson River also provided a way to travel inland. Dutch fur traders, shopkeepers, and farmers began to build the colony. But the colony had troubles. Its people were

33

Why did the Huguenots not become colonists? They were forbidden to settle in America.

How did the French Catholics differ from the Spanish Catholics? The French did not bring the Indians to work at missions. Instead French missionaries lived among the Indians and learned Indian languages and customs.

- Draw a word web for display with the words *Fur Trading* in the center oval. Guide the students as they think of facts to add to the web, such as the French and Indians trapped animals; the French traded furs for European goods; Indians received copper kettles, metal tools, alcohol, and French weapons; and beaver furs were in high demand.

- Direct attention to the picture on page 33. Read the captions and guide a discussion of how a fur trapper dressed.

What was the name of the colony founded by the Dutch? New Netherland

What was the name of New Netherland's capital city? New Amsterdam

What made New Amsterdam a good place for trading? It had a good harbor for ships, and the Hudson River provided a way to travel inland.

Who began to build the colony? Dutch fur traders, shopkeepers, and farmers

What troubles were found in the colony? Its people were disorderly, and they fought with the Indians.

Dutch Rule in New Netherland

Peter Minuit was the third director-general for the New Netherland Colony. He is commonly known for buying Manhattan Island from the Indians with about twenty-four dollars' worth of trinkets. The last director-general of New Netherland was Peter Stuyvesant, who served from 1647 to 1664. Directors-general were appointed by the Dutch West India Company from the Netherlands and gave the colonists no representation in their government. In his efforts to control the colony, Stuyvesant tried to enforce morality in the colony and failed. The Dutch settlers and some English settlers who had come into the area quickly tired of his political and religious demands. Therefore, they welcomed English conquest.

- Guide a discussion about Stuyvesant, who wanted a godly colony, and the people and the leaders back in the Netherlands, who had very different ideas for the colony.

Was Stuyvesant's vision for New Amsterdam realized? No, it became a center of trade and an important city.

- Direct attention to New Amsterdam in 1600 and 2000. Guide a comparison of the two pictures.

Develop in students an expectation of supporting their responses.

How did the Protestant Reformation delay English exploration? After Martin Luther convinced many people of the errors of the Roman Catholic Church, many people in Europe began to study their Bibles. They began reading writings by people who had studied the Bible. The teachings of the Reformation spread. The kingdoms of Europe became divided between Catholic and Protestant kingdoms.

New Amsterdam

ca. 1600

ca. 2000

disorderly. They also fought with the Indians.

Peter Stuyvesant came to New Amsterdam in 1647 to serve as its governor. Stuyvesant was the son of a pastor. He wanted New Netherland to be a godly colony. He wanted all the people to attend the Dutch Reformed Church. He did not want people to get drunk or fight and insisted that they treat the Indians fairly. If they wronged the Indians, they had to make it right.

But the leaders back in the Netherlands did not support these ideas. They wanted New Amsterdam to be a city that made money by trade. They said that anyone could live there no matter what his religion was. There

were many people in New Amsterdam who did not want to attend the Dutch Reformed Church. They did not like Stuyvesant telling them how they ought to live. His vision of a godly society would not come to pass. But New Amsterdam would become a center of trade and an important city.

The First English Colony

English exploration was delayed by the Protestant Reformation. After Martin Luther convinced many people of the errors of the Roman Catholic Church, many people in Europe began to study their Bibles. They began reading writings by people who had studied the Bible. The teachings of the

34

Reformation spread. The kingdoms of Europe became divided between Catholic and Protestant kingdoms.

King Henry VIII removed England from the pope's authority. But after Henry's death, his daughter Mary made it a Roman Catholic kingdom. After Mary died, England became Protestant. These changes created conflict in England and kept England from exploring America.

But things changed under Queen Elizabeth. Two men, Humphrey Gilbert and Walter Raleigh, warned Elizabeth that Spain was becoming powerful. Spain was an empire with colonies overseas. These Englishmen did not want Spain's power to keep growing. They thought Spain might force Protestant countries to become Roman Catholic.

Gilbert and Raleigh persuaded Elizabeth that England needed a colony in America. A colony would give England American land. It also might bring wealth and power. A colony meant living near Indians. Living near Indians would give the English opportunities to share the gospel.

The English colony, named Roanoke, started off well. The land where the English settled had plenty of fruit and animals that could be used for food. The Indians were friendly. But fighting broke out between the English and the Indians. The English failed to work hard enough at growing food. Ships that were taking supplies to America were delayed by war with Spain. When the ships did finally come, all the colonists had disappeared. No one knows what happened to them. Some think they were killed by Indians; others think they began living with the Indians.

Early Colonies

How were the French, Dutch, and English colonies different?

35

Background

The Lost Colony

Although he did not go to the New World himself, Sir Walter Raleigh, an English nobleman and favorite of the queen, organized several colonizing expeditions to Roanoke Island off the coast of North Carolina. The first attempt, made in 1585, failed because of famine, Indian attacks, and poor leadership. After one year the settlers returned home.

In 1587 Raleigh tried again. A man named John White was placed in charge of the new group sent to found a colony. Shortly after the group landed, White returned to England for supplies, but his return to America was delayed for three years by war with Spain. When he finally returned, the colony had disappeared. White's daughter and baby granddaughter were missing. The baby, Virginia Dare, was the first English baby born in the New World. The only clue to the colony's disappearance was the word "Croatoan" carved in the fort's gatepost. It was thought that the nearby Indians had taken the people captive, but to this day no one knows what happened to the "Lost Colony" of Roanoke Island.

Teach for Understanding

Why did the changes between being a Roman Catholic kingdom and a Protestant kingdom keep England from exploring America? The changes created conflict.

When did this conflict change? when Elizabeth became queen

Who persuaded Queen Elizabeth that England needed a colony in America? Humphrey Gilbert and Walter Raleigh

What were some of the advantages of having a colony in America? It would give American land to England. It might bring wealth and power. It would give the English opportunities to share the gospel.

What do you think life would be like for settlers in a new land? Answers could include that it would be a lot of work to build houses and provide food.

- Direct the students to locate Roanoke and Jamestown on the map on page 35.

What good things helped Roanoke start well? The land where the English settled had plenty of fruit and animals that could be used for food. The Indians were friendly.

What things went wrong? Fighting broke out between the English and the Indians. The English failed to work hard enough at growing food. Ships that were taking supplies to America were delayed by war with Spain.

When the ships did finally come, what did the passengers discover? All the colonists had disappeared.

What do you think happened to the colonists? Answers could include that they got sick and died; they were killed by Indians; they starved to death; or they moved to live with an Indian tribe.

Conclude the discussion by asking the question on page 35. New France had good fishing and fur trading, but few French people wanted to move there. Peter Stuyvesant wanted New Netherland to be a godly colony, but the leaders back in the Netherlands wanted New Amsterdam to be a city that made money by trade. Roanoke was founded in a good location but failed when fighting broke out between the English and the Indians; the English failed to work hard enough at growing food, and the ships that were taking supplies to America were delayed.

Activity Manual

- Guide completion of pages 24–25.

Assessment

- Administer quiz.

The quiz may be given anytime after completing this lesson.

Lesson Focus

- Jamestown struggled in many ways until the colonial governors took control.

Objectives

- List reasons the English began to start new colonies in America
- Name several things Jamestown did right and wrong
- Explain what John Smith did to help the colony
- Compare and contrast what the colonial governors and the Virginia Company wanted for the colony

Teacher's Toolkit CD

- Instructional Aids 14–17: *Jamestown: Planting Colonies*; *Jamestown: Indians*; *Jamestown: Problems*; *Jamestown: Colonial Governors*

Review

- Use questions such as the following to review the previous lesson.

What were the names of the early settlements in North America? New France, New Netherland, and Roanoke

What did Peter Stuyvesant want for New Netherland? He wanted it to be a godly colony. He wanted all the people to attend the Dutch Reformed Church. He did not want people to get drunk or fight. He insisted that the Indians be treated fairly.

What contributed to the failure of Roanoke? Fighting broke out between the English and the Indians. The English failed to work hard enough at growing food. Ships that were taking supplies to America were delayed by war with Spain.

Preparation for Reading

- Generate interest as you direct the students to read the title and examine the pictures on pages 36–38.
- Guide pronunciation of any unfamiliar words in the lesson.
- Direct the students to read the pages and complete Instructional Aids 14–17 in four small groups. Assign each group one page of Instructional Aids 14–17.

Teach for Understanding

- After the students have completed their Instructional Aids, ask the group with *Jamestown: Planting Colonies* to share what it wrote. Integrate information from Instructional Aid 14 and reinforce correct responses as you teach the lesson.

Jamestown

The English had good reasons for trying to start other colonies in America. The number of people living in England was growing. Available land was scarce. In wealthy families the oldest son would inherit the land. But younger sons would have to find their own land. Also, many Englishmen were having trouble finding work. Others received lower pay. Several were thrown into prison for not paying their debts. Many Englishmen thought they could find a better life elsewhere.

Merchants also wanted people to become colonists. America had lumber, furs, fish, and other resources. The merchants needed these items, but they had to buy them from the Dutch or the French. They wanted to buy these goods from English colonists. These raw materials would cost less money if they could be bought from English colonists.

People also wanted to start colonies for religious reasons. England's cities had become wicked. People believed that the temptations of the city would not be found in the New World. They said Spain's colonies spread the Roman Catholic religion. England's colonies would be Protestant. Spreading the gospel to the Indian people was another reason for becoming a colonist.

In 1607 the English tried to found another colony. James I had given permission for a Virginia Company of London to be formed. The Virginia Company gave instructions for setting up the new colony.

This colony was started in Virginia on the Chesapeake Bay. It would be called Jamestown to honor the king. This land was already occupied by several Woodland Indian tribes. These tribes were ruled over by a chief named **Powhatan**. Powhatan and his people had met Europeans before. They had traded with both Spanish and English ships. Some of Powhatan's people had been killed or captured. They were not sure that they wanted the English to start living on their land.

The colony did not begin well. Six men formed a council that was to lead the colony. But they quarreled instead of leading. They chose a poor spot on which to build their colony. Bad water and diseases made many sick. Many of the men who came were gentlemen and were not skilled at living in a wilderness. Because they were wealthy, they had not worked at a trade or business in England. The colony needed more carpenters, farmers, fishermen, and blacksmiths.

Many of the colonists would not work. They would not even plant and harvest food for themselves. For a while Captain **John Smith** made the colonists work in the fields. But then the people forced him out of the colony. They went back to enjoying their games and doing whatever pleased them. They did not

36

What did the English do in 1607? They tried to found another colony.

What was the name of the company that was given permission by James I to found the colony? the Virginia Company of London

Where was the colony started? in Virginia on the Chesapeake Bay

What did the English name the colony? They named it Jamestown to honor the king.

Who ruled over the Woodland Indian tribes? Powhatan

What did Captain John Smith make the colonists do? work in the fields

- Read 2 Thessalonians 3:10 aloud.

- What does this verse teach about the importance of work? If a person does not work, he should not eat.

- What kind of leader was John Smith? Answers could include that Smith was a good leader because he knew the importance of work.

- Why is it important to have good leadership in government? Answers could include that good leaders do what is best for the people.

plant enough food. The winter that followed was known as the starving time.

The colonists also fought with Powhatan's people. They did not share the gospel with the Indians. The English tried to rule over them. Powhatan did not want the English at Jamestown. He captured and almost killed John Smith early on. His daughter, Pocahontas, pleaded for and saved Smith's life. Powhatan was willing to make peace with the colonists. He was willing to trade with them. He knew the English had more powerful weapons. The English knew they could destroy Indian villages and take food supplies if they wanted to.

In 1609 John Smith returned to England. He told the Virginia Company about the problems at Jamestown. The Company appointed a governor who would carry the king's authority.

The colonial governor made laws for the colonists to obey. One of the laws said that people must attend church two times every day. Another law placed the governor in charge of trade with the Indians. The people were required to work for their food. Stealing food could be punished by death. The people were also required to take care of their houses and the land around them.

The Virginia Company wanted the colonists to start producing something to be sent back to England. The company existed to make money. The colonists chose to grow tobacco. This plant brought them the most money. People then did not know all the dangers of smoking that are known today. But they did know that smoking was not healthy. King James wrote that smoking was a danger to the body and a sin against God. He called it "a custom loathsome to the eye, hateful to the nose, harmful to the brain, dangerous to the lungs."

Under the colonial governors Jamestown began to do better. The colonists established good relations with the Powhatan Indians. The Virginia Company worked to see families come to Jamestown. And the colony grew. Eventually the people began to choose their own leaders.

John Smith started out as a farmer but became an accomplished soldier well before he sailed to Virginia. He was the victor of three duels and escaped slavery by killing his captor. His experiences helped him ascend to the leadership of Jamestown, and his maps of Virginia helped promote colonization. The Puritans used copies of his books and maps when they crossed the Atlantic.

37

Teach for Understanding

- Choose a volunteer from the group with *Jamestown: Indians* to present orally the answers to the questions.
- Invite the group with *Jamestown: Problems* to talk about what it wrote.
- Invite the group with *Jamestown: Colonial Governors* to tell about what it wrote.
- Direct attention to the picture of John Smith on page 37. Read aloud the caption.

Background

Powhatan Indians

The Powhatan Indians, a group of Woodland Indians, inhabited the part of Virginia where the English decided to settle. Like other Woodland Indians, the Powhatan lived in villages along rivers where they fished, hunted, and planted vegetables. They owed allegiance to one chief, who was also called Powhatan. In return for tribute of food or trinkets, Powhatan provided his tribes with protection. Almost from the start, he viewed the often violent English colonists with suspicion.

Indians of the Powhatan Confederacy complicated the existence at Jamestown. At first, relations between the two peoples were friendly enough, but as the colonists began to clear more land, the Indian chief Wahunsonacock, or Powhatan, ordered war parties to attack the colony. Not until 1614, with the marriage of his daughter Pocahontas to the Englishman John Rolfe, did a shaky peace come to the area.

John Smith

Captain John Smith joined the Virginia Company as an adventurer in colonizing the New World. Smith sailed on the *Susan Constant* to America. He was not originally the captain of the ship; he had been made a captain while fighting in Hungary for Austria. Smith was chosen by King James I to be one of the leaders in Jamestown. The weak leadership in the colony caused discontentment. The settlement was failing. Food was scarce, and there was no protection from the hostile Indians. Although he was not well liked, Smith was elected governor of the colony. Under his forceful leadership, all men were made to work. John Smith demanded that everyone work no matter what his background. He knew the importance of work. Laws were passed requiring all the men to work and pray daily. They were expected to listen to sermons. The laws prohibited the men from stealing and blaspheming.

Relationships with the Indians eased as they respected Smith's daring and determined personality. He told Chief Powhatan, "I have but one God, I honour but one king; and I live not here as your subject, but as your friend."

The strong leadership of John Smith and the religious character of his laws saved the Jamestown settlement.

Lesson

14

Teach for Understanding

What happened in 1619? A Dutch ship stopped at Jamestown. It sold the colonists some African indentured servants.

What was an indentured servant? It was someone who agreed to work for a period of time to pay off a debt. After his time of work was finished, he was free.

What changed about the American system after twenty years? Making money from growing tobacco required many inexpensive workers. Black slaves became these workers. Black servants were no longer set free like white servants. Instead they were enslaved because of the color of their skin. Their children were considered slaves too. They were no longer allowed to marry white people. They were not given equal treatment in the courts.

- Direct attention to the pictures of Jamestown and the artifact and guide a discussion of them both.

> Conclude the discussion by asking the question on page 38. For a while he made the colonists work in the fields. In 1609 he returned to England and told the Virginia Company about the problems at Jamestown. The Virginia Company appointed a governor who would carry the king's authority in the colony.

Activity Manual

- Guide completion of page 26.

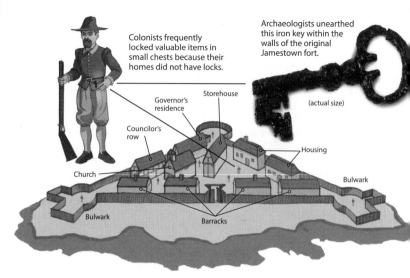

Colonists frequently locked valuable items in small chests because their homes did not have locks.

Archaeologists unearthed this iron key within the walls of the original Jamestown fort.

(actual size)

Governor's residence

Storehouse

Councilor's row

Housing

Church

Bulwark

Bulwark

Barracks

In 1619 something happened that no one at the time thought important. But it would have consequences for the United States later. A Dutch ship stopped at Jamestown. It sold the colonists some African **indentured servants**. An indentured servant agreed to work for a period of time to pay off a debt. Many people who came to America worked as indentured servants to pay for their ocean voyage. These first Africans in America were no different from European servants. After their time of work was finished, they were free. Many of the Africans made friends with or married Europeans in the colony. But within twenty years, the system changed. Making money from growing tobacco required many inexpensive workers. Black slaves became these workers. Black servants were no longer set free like white servants. Instead they were enslaved because of the color of their skin. Their children were considered slaves too. They were no longer allowed to marry white people. They were not given equal treatment in the courts. Hundreds of years would pass before these sins against black people would begin to be addressed.

> How did John Smith help Jamestown survive?

38

Activity

Online Field Trip
Use the official Jamestown site to take a virtual field trip of Jamestown.

Cornbread
Discuss the importance of corn for the colonists. Supervise the making of cornbread in small groups.

New England

Background

England had become a Protestant nation. It did not want Catholics to take over all of America. But the kings and queens of England did not necessarily believe the teachings of the Reformation. They were interested in being free from the power of the Roman Catholic Church. They were not as interested in reforming the Church of England.

Some of the English did want to purify the Church of England. They wanted to remove false teachings and practices. They thought that people should do only what the Bible told them to do. They were called **Puritans**.

The Church of England appointed bishops and priests. The Puritans said that the Bible did not teach this type of church government. The Bible did not say bishops should appoint priests. The Puritans believed that God's people should choose their own pastors. The Puritans did not think priests should read their prayers out of a book. They thought that prayers should come from the heart.

The Puritans thought they could change the Church of England. Another group did not think the Church of England would change. This group was called the Separating Puritans, or **Separatists**.

The Separatists thought that only Christians should be church members. The laws of England said that all Englishmen were members of the Church of England. The entire country was divided up into parishes. The law required everyone to go to the church in his parish.

The Separatists said that these laws were against what the Bible taught. The Separatists did not go to the Church of England. Instead they started their own churches and kept themselves separate from the Church of England.

From Scrooby to Plymouth

The people that we call the Pilgrims were a group of Separatists who lived in the English town of Scrooby. They were breaking the law by having their own church. But they believed they must break the law to obey God. Many of them were taken to prison.

Some Separatists wanted to leave England. Leaving England was a problem too. Staying and worshiping according to the Bible was against the law, but leaving was too. The Scrooby Separatists tried to leave. One time they were captured and imprisoned. After several attempts, many made it to the Netherlands.

The Separatists from Scrooby lived in the Netherlands for around ten years. While in the Netherlands, they had the freedom to worship God as the Bible taught, but they had concerns.

39

Lesson Focus

- The Pilgrims started a new colony in America so they could worship the Lord according to the Bible.

Objectives

- Explain why the Separatists left England
- List the reasons the Pilgrims believed they had to leave the Netherlands
- Describe the Pilgrims' voyage across the Atlantic
- Explain how the Lord provided for the Pilgrims at Plymouth

Teacher's Toolkit CD

- Instructional Aid 18: *From Scrooby to Plymouth*

Review

- Guide a review of the colony at Jamestown.

Preparation for Reading

- Generate interest as you direct the students to read the titles and examine the pictures on pages 39–42.
- Guide pronunciation of any unfamiliar words in the lesson.
- Direct the students to read the pages and complete Instructional Aid 18 in small groups.

Teach for Understanding

What did the kings and queens of England want to be free from? the power of the Roman Catholic Church

What did the Puritans want? They wanted to remove false teachings and practices from the Church of England.

What did the Puritans think when the Church of England appointed bishops and priests? The Puritans said that the Bible did not teach this type of church government. The Bible did not say bishops should appoint priests. The Puritans believed that God's people should choose their own pastors. The Puritans did not think priests should read their prayers out of a book. They thought that prayers should come from the heart.

What was the name of the group that did not think the Church of England would change? the Separating Puritans, or Separatists

Background

Separatists

Americans are used to choosing their own churches to attend. But the English could not choose in the time of the Pilgrims. The land of England was divided up into parishes. Each parish had its own church, which was part of the Church of England. Everyone was expected to attend the church in his or her parish every Sunday. People who skipped church had to pay a fine for every day they skipped.

The men and women we call Pilgrims today were called Separatists when they lived in England. They received this name because they separated themselves from their parish churches. They did not think that the church should be made up of everyone who lived in a particular location. They thought the church should be made up of Christians. Christians should gather together each Sunday to worship God together. So the Separatists met together to have their own worship services. Their meetings were against the law. The Separatists faced fines and even prison for worshiping together rather than at their parish churches.

Teach for Understanding

- Guide a discussion about why the Pilgrims left Scrooby, England, and what their concerns were about being in the Netherlands.

- Explain that even though the Pilgrims wanted to escape the temptations of the city, they would still encounter temptations in the new colony because people carry their wicked hearts with them and still do wicked things.

  What did the Pilgrims need to plan their trip to America? They needed to get permission from the king to start a colony. They needed permission to practice their religion. They needed money to hire ships and to buy supplies. They worked together with businessmen who saw the colony as a way to make money. They also needed other people to help them establish the colony.

- Choose a volunteer to read the Biography box aloud. Guide a discussion about William Bradford.

William Bradford

Who: William Bradford
When: 1590–1657
Where: Plymouth Colony

William Bradford grew up in England with his uncles. His father died when William was young. When he was twelve years old, he began to attend church with the Separatists at Scrooby. He had become a Christian, and he was convinced that the Separatists were serious about following God. When he was eighteen, Bradford moved to the Netherlands with the Scrooby church. He married his wife Dorothy while in the Netherlands. When Bradford was thirty, he was part of the group of Separatists who decided to move to America. Bradford was given responsibilities for arranging the journey. When he arrived in America, Bradford was one of the men responsible for picking the place where they would build the town of Plymouth. Sadly, while he was exploring the land, his wife fell off the *Mayflower* and drowned. Bradford was saddened by his wife's death. But he worked hard to help build the colony. Bradford became the second governor of Plymouth Colony. He served as governor for a total of thirty years.

They were in a foreign land. They had to learn to speak Dutch. They had to find a way to make a living. Many of them remained poor. Most important, they worried that their children would become like the Dutch. The Pilgrims did not think that the Dutch culture was good for their children. They thought the Dutch allowed too much sin. Children were allowed to do what they liked rather than follow God. The Lord's Day was not set apart as a special day for worship. The Separatists began to think about starting a colony in North America.

Starting a new colony was a huge undertaking. The Separatists needed to get permission from the king to start a colony. They needed permission to practice their religion. They needed money to hire ships and to buy supplies. In order to make this venture work, they worked together with businessmen who saw the colony as a way to make money. They also needed other people to help them establish the colony. About half the people who started this new colony were not Separatists. The Separatists called them strangers.

40

Background

The *Mayflower*

The *Mayflower* was a ninety-foot merchant or cargo ship. It used wind power from six sails to cross the Atlantic Ocean. The ship had three decks. The crew lived and worked on the main deck. The passengers lived in the middle deck. The bottom deck, or cargo hold, was used to store supplies and barrels. The captain of the *Mayflower* was Christopher Jones. He was in charge of navigating the ship. Simple tools such as the quadrant and the cross staff were used to locate the position of the stars against the horizon and to chart the route to the New World. On the voyage, the ship was crowded. It carried over one hundred passengers and a thirty-man crew. Living on the ship for sixty-six days was difficult for the Pilgrims. They ate biscuits, salted meat, and other foods that could be stored for long periods of time. Their belongings—tools, seeds, blankets, clothing, cookware, weapons, and Bibles—were kept in trunks. Rarely were the Pilgrims allowed to get fresh air or exercise on the main deck. Most of the passengers became seasick. At first the sailors were not friendly to the Pilgrims. They made fun of them for saying prayers, singing hymns, and reading the Bible. However, by the end of the voyage, the sailors respected the Pilgrims for their strong faith in God.

The voyage across the Atlantic was difficult. The Pilgrims had hired two ships, the *Mayflower* and the *Speedwell*. But the *Speedwell* had sprung leaks. The passengers on the *Speedwell* had to crowd onto the *Mayflower* or be left behind. The crossing itself was stormy. The Pilgrims were glad when their two-month voyage was over and they finally reached land. But their troubles were not over. They had landed farther north than they had expected. Since they were outside the land given to them by the king, the men signed the Mayflower Compact to set up a government under the king. Winter would come soon. Half of them would die during the winter.

The place where they landed was largely uninhabited. The Patuxet Indians who had lived there had died of a great sickness. But they had cleared the land for farming. The Pilgrims also discovered some corn that they had stored. One Patuxet survivor named Squanto taught the Pilgrims how to grow new kinds of food in the New World. Squanto also knew English. He served as a translator with the nearby Wampanoag Indians. The Pilgrims were able to make peace with them for a time.

crossed the Atlantic Ocean aboard the *Mayflower*: **102**

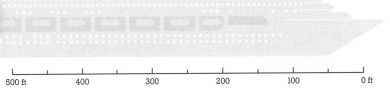

motorboat capacity: **6**

cruise-ship capacity: **4,000+**

submarine crew members: **132**

500 ft	400	300	200	100	0 ft

41

The Mayflower Compact

If the *Mayflower* had not been blown off course, the Pilgrims probably would not have written the Mayflower Compact. If they had landed farther south, they would have been under the authority of England. That was part of the agreement made between the king of England and the joint-stock company that transported them to America. This agreement was called a charter. Under the charter, the Pilgrims would have all the same rights and restrictions as the people who lived in England. But they could not have established an independent government. The Pilgrims decided that since they were outside the jurisdiction of the Virginia Company, they had the right to make their own laws and set up their own government. In 1692 the colony merged with the Massachusetts Bay Colony because the king refused to grant the Plymouth Plantation a legal charter.

Teach for Understanding

What were the names of the two ships the Pilgrims hired? the *Mayflower* and the *Speedwell*

What happened to the *Speedwell*? It sprung leaks.

What did the Pilgrims onboard the *Speedwell* do? They crowded onto the *Mayflower* or were left behind.

What did the Pilgrims have to do since they landed outside the land given to them by the king? The men signed the Mayflower Compact to set up a government under the king.

What happened the first winter? Half of the people died.

- Guide a discussion about how God provided for the Pilgrims at Plymouth and what the colony was like.
- Direct attention to the graph on page 41 and compare the size of the *Mayflower* to modern ships and boats.

15

Teach for Understanding

- Guide a discussion about how successful the Pilgrims of Plymouth were in creating a community where people lived to please God.
- Direct attention to the scene on page 42. Read each caption aloud.

▶▶ Conclude the discussion by asking the question on page 42. They wanted to live in a place where people had the freedom to do what was right.

Activity Manual

- Guide completion of page 27.

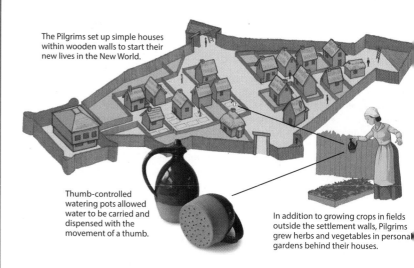

The Pilgrims set up simple houses within wooden walls to start their new lives in the New World.

Thumb-controlled watering pots allowed water to be carried and dispensed with the movement of a thumb.

In addition to growing crops in fields outside the settlement walls, Pilgrims grew herbs and vegetables in personal gardens behind their houses.

The Pilgrims named their colony Plymouth. They were grateful they now had a place to live and worship God as the Bible taught. They did not believe that unsaved people should be part of the church. In Plymouth, only Christians were members of the church. But everyone was required to attend church on Sunday.

The Pilgrims did not allow people to practice false religion or false worship in their colony. They also thought people should live moral lives. Immorality was punished. They had laws against drunkenness. Rules like these have caused some people to say the Pilgrims were hypocrites. They say that the Pilgrims came to America for freedom, but once they arrived they took people's freedoms away. However, the Pilgrims never wanted freedom for people to do whatever they wanted. The Pilgrims wanted to live in a place where people had the freedom to do what was right.

If people wanted to do what was wrong, they could live anywhere else in the world. The Plymouth Colony was to be a special place. This does not mean that the Pilgrims always did what was right. Like all humans, they were sinners. But their attempt to create a community where people lived to please God is one that every Christian should honor.

Why did the Pilgrims want to come to America?

42

How It Was

William sat up as straight as he could on the wooden bench in the meetinghouse in Salem. "Let us pray," said William's father. Just before William bowed his head, he noticed how happy his father looked today. The lines of sadness around his eyes were gone. His voice sounded strong, clear, and confident as he talked with God.

William remembered how many times he had heard his father pray since he had lost his church back in England. Time after time Father had clutched his Bible and pleaded, "Gracious Lord, if it be Thy will, grant us a place where we are free to worship Thee rightly. Grant me the freedom to read Thy scriptures and preach their precious truths to the people Thou hast given me." Now at last, here in America, William had seen God answer this prayer.

It was time to stand and sing a psalm. William stood and sang the words from his heart. "Thy word for ever is, O Lord, in heaven settled fast . . ." His eyes met his father's, and they smiled as they sang.

Massachusetts Bay Colony

England crowned Charles I king five years after the Pilgrims landed at Plymouth. The new king was determined to put an end to Puritanism in his kingdom.

The Puritans stayed in the English churches and tried to purify the worship, but Charles sent his bishops to these churches. He was going to make the Puritans obey the rules of the Church of England. Pastors who did not obey Charles's rules were removed from their churches. Some were put in prison. Some were fined large amounts of money. They were not allowed to work other jobs that would pay them more money. But the Puritans said they must obey the Bible. They could not obey the king when he disagreed with the Bible.

Some of the Puritans decided to move to America. They could begin a new England there. They would have freedom to purify the church there.

The Puritans had more wealthy men than the Pilgrims did. These men formed a company. The company

43

Lesson Focus

- The Massachusetts Bay Colony proved to be a success for the Puritans.

Objectives
- Recognize John Winthrop's vision for the Massachusetts Bay Colony
- Describe how the Puritans ran their churches in the New World
- Compare and contrast Virginia and the Massachusetts Bay Colony

Review

- Guide the reading of How It Was and contrast religion in England with religion in the English colonies. Discuss how the colonists must have felt to be allowed to worship God freely.

Preparation for Reading

- Generate interest as you direct the students to read the title and examine the pictures and map on pages 43–45.
- Guide pronunciation of any unfamiliar words in the lesson.
- Display a K-W-L chart with the title "Massachusetts Bay Colony." Elicit students' prior knowledge of the topic. Write the facts the students already know under *K* (know).
- Ask the students what they would like to learn about the topic. Enter the students' ideas as questions under the *W* (want to learn) column.
- Direct the students to read the pages to find out new facts about the Massachusetts Bay Colony.

Teach for Understanding

What did Charles I do to try to end Puritanism in his kingdom? Charles sent his bishops to the churches where the Puritans were trying to purify the worship. He was going to make the Puritans obey the rules of the Church of England. Pastors who did not obey Charles's rules were removed from their churches. Some were put in prison, and some were fined large amounts of money. They were not allowed to work other jobs that would pay them more money.

What did some of the Puritans decide to do? move to America Why? to begin a new England and purify the church

Teach for Understanding

- Guide a discussion about the company that would pay for setting up the colony.

  What position would Winthrop hold in the colony for many years? governor

  What did John Winthrop want the new colony to be like? a model of Christian love, different from communities of sinners

  What were the Puritan churches in Massachusetts Bay like? They were run the way the Puritans thought the Church of England should be run. They did not have bishops. Instead each church had its own leaders. Each church ran its own affairs.

  What was this type of church government called? congregational church government

  How did the churches remain united? The ministers would meet together and talk about how the churches were doing. They wanted to agree with one another about how to handle problems.

- Direct attention to the picture on page 44. Explain that it depicts Winthrop preaching to a group of Puritans getting ready to sail to America.

would pay for setting up the colony. This was common for all the English colonies started at this time. But the Puritans did something different with their company. The company leaders usually stayed in England to direct the colony. But the Puritan company leaders moved to America. All the leaders of the colony moved to America. They could have greater freedom from England and greater freedom in their churches.

In 1630 **John Winthrop** preached to a group of Puritans sailing for New England. He told them that their community must be a model of Christian love. They should be just and merciful in all their dealings with each other. Winthrop explained, "For we must consider that we shall be as a city upon a hill; the eyes of all people are upon us."

People in England and Europe knew the Puritans were serious Christians. Winthrop was telling them that their community needed to be different from communities of sinners. Other people should be able to see the difference God makes in a community of Christians. Winthrop would become the governor of the Puritans in the new Massachusetts Bay Colony for many years.

The Puritans did not separate from the Church of England. They did run their churches in the New World the way they thought the Church of England should be run. They did not have bishops. Instead each church had its own leaders. Each church ran its own affairs. This type of government was called congregational church government. But the churches stayed united because the ministers would

44

Background

What the Puritans Believed

The Puritans were originally part of the Church of England. Unlike the Separatists, they did not want to leave the church. They wanted to stay in the church and help it change its religious practices of worship and personal devotion. The Puritans believed that the Bible should be the guide for church government. They believed that each congregation should have independent control of its own affairs. The Puritans emphasized Bible reading, personal prayer, and preaching. The Puritans thought that their beliefs should guide the way they conducted their daily lives. They emphasized grace, devotion, prayer, and self-examination in order to live a virtuous life. Strict morals and rules of conduct were established, and believers were expected to hold each other accountable for keeping them.

Teach for Understanding

- Direct attention to the map on page 45. Invite a student to name the towns the Puritans started.

  What was the first town in the Massachusetts Bay Colony? Salem

  How was Massachusetts Bay different from the colony in Virginia? In Virginia, life was built around the plantation. People earned money in Virginia by growing crops like tobacco and sending them back to England. In Massachusetts Bay many people had small farms or worked in different types of trade.

  How was Massachusetts Bay Colony a success? The Puritans were able to establish a community where they could live and worship as they believed God wanted them to.

- Do you think God was pleased that the Massachusetts Bay Colony chose to live life and worship the way God wanted them to? yes

- Complete the K-W-L chart by writing what the students learned in the *L* column.

  Conclude the discussion by asking the question on page 45. The Puritans wanted to remove false teachings and practices from the Church of England. The Separatists, or Pilgrims, thought they could not change the Church of England.

meet together and talk about how the churches were doing. They wanted to agree with one another about how to handle problems.

Salem was the first town that the Puritans started. As more people arrived, the Puritans started many other towns near to one another. These many small towns made Massachusetts Bay different from the colonies in Virginia. In Virginia, life was built around the plantation. People earned money in Virginia by growing crops like tobacco and sending them back to England. In Massachusetts Bay many people had small farms or worked in different types of trade.

The Massachusetts Bay Colony proved to be a success for the Puritans. They were able to establish a community where they could live and worship as they believed God wanted them to. But they also knew they were sinners, despite their desire to be made more like Christ. They knew there was no guarantee that their children would continue to follow God. There would be times in the coming years when the light of their city would burn low. However, their effort to be a light to the world has inspired American Christians ever since.

> **How were the Puritans different from the Pilgrims?**

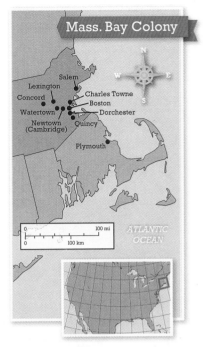

Mass. Bay Colony

Salem
Lexington
Concord
Charles Towne
Boston
Watertown
Dorchester
Newtown (Cambridge)
Quincy
Plymouth

ATLANTIC OCEAN

///// **Activity** ////////////////////////

Establishing a Colony

Suppose you were part of a group of people who wanted to form a new Christian colony. What would you name the colony? What rules would you establish?

//

45

Primary Source: A Model of Christian Charity

- Direct attention to Activity Manual page 29.
- Explain that the document is part of one of John Winthrop's sermons. Direct the students to listen for what John Winthrop believed would make the colony pleasing to God.
- Discuss what John Winthrop believed would happen if the people did not follow the Lord.

Activity Manual

- Guide completion of pages 28–30.

Activity //

Establishing a Colony

- Guide a discussion about what it would be like to be with a group of people who wanted to form a new colony.
- Divide the students into small groups and direct them to use Activity Manual page 30 as they plan a new colony.
- Direct the students to think of a name for their colony, draw a map of their colony, and write the rules for it.

Chapter Review
Activity Manual pages 31–32

Objective
- Recall concepts and terms from Chapter 2

Teacher's Toolkit CD
- Instructional Aid 19: *Supply Cards* (Prepare two sets of each card and cut them apart.)

Introduction

- Concepts for the Chapter 2 Test will be taken from Activity Manual pages 17–32. You may review any or all of the concepts during this lesson. You may choose to review Chapter 2 by playing "Supplying a Colony."

Review

Game: Supplying a Colony

Divide the students into two teams. Give each team turns answering review questions, one student at a time. When a student gets an answer correct, give him a supply card from Instructional Aid 19. The team with the most cards at the end of the game wins.

Activity Manual

- Guide completion of pages 31–32.

Lesson **18** **Chapter 2 Test**

Objective
- Demonstrate knowledge of concepts from Chapter 2 by taking the test

Assessment

- Administer Test 2.

Chapter 3

3 The Thirteen Colonies

Focus
The thirteen British colonies in America grew and thrived in the 1600s and 1700s.

Introduction

By the mid-1700s, thirteen colonies had been founded along the East Coast of America. These colonies were divided into three regions: the New England colonies, the middle colonies, and the southern colonies. This chapter begins with facts about the founding and founders of each colony.

Government by the people was an important idea in the New World. Most colonies had assemblies that met to make decisions and justices of the peace to settle problems, hold trials, and collect taxes. Colonial society had an upper, a middle, and a lower class. Some people were indentured servants or slaves. Slaves were often separated from family members when they were brought to America. Each group of colonies had its own religions, forms of education, and industries. The Great Awakening turned many people back to God and had several lasting effects on the colonists.

Chapter Focus

The thirteen British colonies in America grew and thrived in the 1600s and 1700s.

Lesson	Student Text	Activity Manual	Content	Vocabulary
			Chapter 3 Overview	
19	46–49	33–36	The founding of the colonies Thomas Hooker Roger Williams Boston Hartford Providence	separation of church and state
20	50–52	37	The founding of the colonies (continued) William Penn Lord Baltimore James Oglethorpe Philadelphia Cecilius Calvert Savannah Williamsburg Charles Towne	House of Burgesses Quaker representative government
21	53–55	38–40	Local governments Family life Social classes	justice of the peace royal colony proprietary colony town meeting
22	56–58	41–42	The New England colonies: religion, education, and industries Anne Hutchinson Yale College Harvard College	dame school meetinghouse grammar school *New England Primer* heresy
23	59–61	43	The middle colonies: cultures, religions, industries, and education Benjamin Franklin	diverse pamphlet journeyman
24	62–64	44–45	How It Was: Growing Indigo The southern colonies: religion, education, and economy Olaudah Equiano Primary Source: *The Interesting Narrative of the Life of Olaudah Equiano* Activity: Participating in Trade	Anglican cash crop
25	65–67	46	Revival: The Great Awakening George Whitefield Biography Box: Jonathan Edwards	revival
26		47–48	Chapter Review	
27			Chapter Test	

Visit bjupress.com/resources for links to enhance the lessons.

Harvard College founded
1636

Great Awakening peaks
1741

| 1600 | 1619 | 1650 | 1700 | 1732 | 1750 |

House of Burgesses formed

Georgia Colony founded

Colonists in America

A great migration to America's shores had begun. Jamestown, Plymouth, and Massachusetts Bay were only the beginning. As the seventeenth century went on, more and more Europeans came to America.

Some came for religious reasons. They wanted to escape persecution and worship more freely. Some came for new opportunities to work or to own land. Many came to the colonies as indentured servants. After working for a master for several years, indentured servants were freed and given a piece of land. Some colonists came hoping to discover gold or silver and get rich quickly. Not all who came were Europeans. Thousands of Africans were brought to the colonies as slaves. Between 1630 and 1750, America's population increased by hundreds of thousands.

By the mid-1700s, thirteen colonies had been founded along the East Coast of America. More than a million people lived in these colonies. Although the colonists came from many European countries, all thirteen colonies eventually belonged to Great Britain. They were under the rule of the English king or queen.

These colonies can be divided into three regions. The four northeastern colonies were called the New England colonies. The four colonies from New York to Delaware were known as the middle colonies. The five remaining colonies were called the southern colonies.

Thirteen Colonies

☐ New England
☐ Middle
☐ Southern

Massachusetts
New Hampshire
New York
Rhode Island
Connecticut
Pennsylvania
New Jersey
Delaware
Maryland
Virginia
North Carolina
South Carolina
Georgia

ATLANTIC OCEAN

0   250 mi
0   250 km

47

JourneyForth

Songbird by Nancy Lohr is available from JourneyForth Books, a division of BJU Press, at journeyforth.com.

In this historical-fiction book, Truxton Pilcher works in his father's pewter foundry in the colonial city of Williamsburg. When Mr. Scrivner is seriously wounded in an accident at the foundry, Truxton's father is declared guilty of a hanging offense, and Truxton may be the only one who can ask the Governor for a pardon.

SONGBIRD
NANCY LOHR

Lesson 19

Student Text pages 46–49
Activity Manual pages 33–36

Lesson Focus

- By the mid-1700s, thirteen colonies had been founded along the East Coast of America.

Objectives

- List reasons why Europeans came to America
- Name the three regions of the thirteen colonies
- Explain how some of the New England and middle colonies began

---

Teacher's Toolkit CD
- Visual 3: *Thirteen Colonies*

Materials
- A map of the United States
- A map with a map key (to use with Activity Manual page 33)

Introduction

- Invite a student to read aloud the title of the chapter and predict what the chapter will be about. the thirteen colonies

- Invite a student to read the chapter focus aloud.

  What do you think you will learn in this chapter? facts about the thirteen British colonies in America

- Direct the students to think of a caption for the picture on page 46. Allow some of them to share their captions with the class.

- Direct attention to the timeline.

  What year was Harvard College founded? 1636

  When did the Great Awakening reach its peak? 1741

  Was the colony of Georgia founded before or after the House of Burgesses was formed? after

Preparation for Reading

- Generate interest as you direct the students to read the titles and examine the map and pictures on pages 46–49.

- Guide pronunciation of any unfamiliar words in the lesson.

- Divide the students into six groups and assign one colony to each group: Massachusetts, Connecticut, Rhode Island, New Hampshire, New York, and New Jersey.

- Direct the students to read pages 46–49 and write facts about their assigned colony to share with the class.

Teach for Understanding

Why did more and more Europeans come to America? for religious reasons; to escape persecution; to worship more freely; for new opportunities to work or to own land; to become indentured servants; to discover gold or silver and get rich quickly

What other ethnic group came to America besides Europeans? Africans

How many people lived in the thirteen colonies by the mid-1700s? more than a million

Which country did the thirteen colonies eventually belong to? Great Britain

What are the three regions the colonies can be divided into? New England, middle, and southern colonies

Lesson

19

Teach for Understanding

- Display a map of the United States and point out Massachusetts, Connecticut, and Rhode Island.

- Use Visual 3 to locate each colony as it is discussed.

- Point out that the Massachusetts Bay Colony was a much bigger area than the state of Massachusetts is today.

- Direct each of the following groups to take a turn sharing its facts with the class: Massachusetts, Connecticut, and Rhode Island

---

The Founding of the Colonies

Massachusetts

Plymouth was never as large a colony as Massachusetts Bay. However, it continued for seventy years. In 1691 it finally joined with Massachusetts Bay to form one colony. By this time Massachusetts Bay had become very large, and some of its people had settled in the territory of Maine. This territory too became part of the colony. This colony came to be known simply as Massachusetts.

The city of **Boston** was the center of the Massachusetts Colony. Its good location as a port helped it quickly become the colony's largest, wealthiest city. Boston would play an important part in America's history in years to come.

Connecticut

Three years after it was founded in 1630, Massachusetts Bay was already becoming too crowded for some people. Some of the Puritans moved west. They formed two towns in the Connecticut River Valley. In 1636 the Puritan minister **Thomas Hooker** moved to this area along with about one hundred members of his church. They founded a third town called **Hartford**. Soon the three settlements joined to form the colony of Connecticut.

Connecticut was the first colony to write a constitution. This plan of government stated that the people's agreement was needed in setting up leaders. It also said that laws would be made on the basis of God's Word.

Rhode Island

Another pastor in Massachusetts, **Roger Williams**, had a large church. He spoke out against the Puritan leadership

Puritans of the 1600s are often shown in black. However, black dye was expensive and faded in the sun. Black clothing was usually reserved for special occasions or for the wealthy. Those who wanted more sober dress often wore brown or earth-toned clothing. But daily dress also included brighter colors such as red, blue, violet, and green.

Roger Williams was an English preacher who bought land from the Narragansetts and started the colony of Rhode Island.

48

Activities

Interests

Direct the students to write down several of their interests. Group the students who have common interests together. Ask them to discuss their mutual interests. Guide a discussion about how having similar interests, cultures, and traditions could help build a new society.

Jobs

Guide a discussion about which jobs would be important in a new colony. Discuss how different job skills would help the colony.

Background

Roger Williams

Roger Williams believed that government should not make laws regarding religion. Williams believed that the government should make laws about honoring parents and against adultery. But it should not make laws against public blasphemy of God or teaching false doctrine or false religion.

Williams's views were new and controversial. At the time most people believed that a society that did not outlaw false religion would soon descend into confusion and anarchy. Disappointed in the Puritans' unwillingness to change, Williams decided to move to Plymouth Colony. At first Williams's ministry was well received. But as he pressed the people to change their view of religion and government, the Pilgrims became concerned that he had been carried away with strange teachings. For instance, he did not allow families to pray with their unsaved children. He did not let unsaved people come to church. He thought they should hear the gospel outside of church. Prayer and preaching were only for Christians.

Eventually, Williams accepted a church post in Salem, north of Boston. There he gathered a congregation that accepted his beliefs. But controversy continued to follow him. Williams began to publicly denounce the king, saying that the king had no right to provide land to the English for the settling of Massachusetts. Williams did not agree with the Puritan leaders about how much control they should have over the religious life of the colony. He believed that the government should not meddle in church matters. This belief is called **separation of church and state**.

The Puritans, however, were trying to establish a colony that followed God in all of life. Those who lived in Massachusetts were expected to obey the Bible willingly. The leaders thought that anyone who did not want to worship God as the Bible taught should not be part of the colony.

Williams continued to stir up trouble. Finally the leaders asked him to leave. He left Massachusetts in 1635. It was winter, and he needed a place to live. The Narragansett Indians let him live with them for the winter. He bought land from them and founded a town. He named the town **Providence**, believing that God had provided for him. The town grew and became the colony of Rhode Island.

New Hampshire

Crowded conditions continued to be a problem in Massachusetts. People began to move north. King James had planned that land in this area be cleared for fishing villages. Colonists moved into the region, and the small villages grew. In the late 1600s, this group of settlements became the colony of New Hampshire.

New York and New Jersey

New York and New Jersey began as the Dutch colony of New Netherland. New Netherland's first settlement, New Amsterdam, had begun in 1626. The colony prospered and several more settlements were formed.

England saw the colony's wealth and wanted this land. The English king decided to say that the land was rightfully his. An English explorer named John Cabot had sailed along the Atlantic coast in the 1400s. He had claimed the entire coast for England. England sent warships to capture New Netherland from the Dutch in 1664. At this time many Dutch settlers were unhappy with the leadership of their governor, Peter Stuyvesant. Many thought his rules for the colony were too harsh. The Dutch decided to surrender to the English. The land passed peacefully to the Duke of York, who named it New York. Later he gave the southern portion of the land to two of his friends. They named their colony New Jersey after Jersey Island in the English Channel.

> Name some reasons colonists came to America.

49

- Direct the group assigned *New Hampshire* to share its facts with the class.
- Explain that New York and New Jersey are in the middle colonies.
- Direct the group assigned *New York* to share its facts with the class.
- Direct the group assigned *New Jersey* to share its facts with the class.

> Conclude the discussion by naming some reasons colonists came to America. for religious reasons; to escape persecution; to worship more freely; for new opportunities to work or to own land; to become indentured servants; to discover gold or silver and get rich quickly

Activity Manual

- Use the information at the top of page 33 as you explain map symbols and keys. Display a map. Direct a student to explain what the symbols represent. Use the symbols to read the map together.
- Guide completion of page 33.
- Explain that page 34 contains important terms, places, people, and concepts the students will learn in Chapter 3. Direct the students to look for familiar terms, places, people, or concepts on the page.
- Guide completion of pages 33–36.

Encourage students to use information from *Chapter 3 Looking Ahead* to create flashcards to use for review.

of their colonies. The authorities in Massachusetts Bay charged him not to make such statements. Initially he agreed, but later he broke his promise. Eventually, Williams even called into question the right of the authorities to govern the colony.

In October 1635, the General Court of the Massachusetts Bay Colony banished Williams, ordering him to leave the colony within six weeks. He made his way south to Narragansett Bay and chose a site on a cove. He bought the land from the Narragansett Indians and called the place Providence. Some of his followers from Salem joined him there. Williams began to realize that they were in need of some form of government. He decided to draft a political compact. The most important aspect of the compact was that he left out a purpose to build a model of God's kingdom on the earth. It also did not claim to advance God's will.

Politically, Williams helped to change the course of American history. Before Williams, it was generally accepted that government needed to support true religion by protecting it from heresy and sin. After Williams, however, the door was opened to questioning this view. Eventually, Americans came to see religion as a private matter. And instead of viewing obedience to God as the purpose of a civilization, Americans have come to see freedom as the supreme civic value.

Lesson Focus

- Pennsylvania, Delaware, Virginia, Maryland, the Carolinas, and Georgia grew and thrived in the 1600s and 1700s.

Objectives

- Relate how Pennsylvania, Delaware, and the southern colonies started
- Identify Virginia's House of Burgesses as the first representative government in America
- Explain how Charles I helped Catholics
- Recognize James Oglethorpe as the person who wanted to establish a colony for English people who could not pay their debts

Teacher's Toolkit CD

- Visual 3: *Thirteen Colonies*

Materials

- A map of the United States

Review

Why did Boston become the largest and wealthiest city in the Massachusetts Bay Colony? its good location as a port

> Guide a review of important terms, maps, places, and people from each previous lesson. Direct the students to find and read the corresponding entries from the Resource Treasury.

Which Puritan minister moved with about one hundred of his church members and founded a town called Hartford? Thomas Hooker

Who spoke out against the Puritan leadership of Massachusetts and founded a town which became the colony of Rhode Island? Roger Williams

What circumstances brought on the founding of New Hampshire? Crowded conditions in Massachusetts caused people to move north to the small fishing villages.

Which two colonies began as the Dutch colony of New Netherland? New York and New Jersey

Preparation for Reading

- Generate interest as you direct the students to examine the pictures on pages 50–52.
- Guide pronunciation of any unfamiliar words in the lesson.
- Divide the students into six groups and assign one colony to each group: Pennsylvania, Delaware, Virginia, Maryland, the Carolinas, and Georgia. Direct the students to read pages 50–52 and write facts about their assigned colony to share with the class.

Pennsylvania

The colony of Pennsylvania was started by **William Penn**. Penn was a Quaker who lived in England. **Quakers**, or the Society of Friends, did not agree with either the Church of England or the Puritans. The Quakers believed that people have an "inner light" to guide them. This inner light was more important to them than God's Word.

Quakers were not well treated in England. Many were put in prison for their beliefs. Penn was troubled as he

Quakers refused to swear an oath of loyalty to the crown. They also refused to bow to other men or even to take off their hats.

"I expect to pass through this world but once. Any good therefore that I can do, or any kindness or abilities that I can show to any fellow creature, let me do it now. Let me not defer it or neglect it, for I shall not pass this way again."

–William Penn

saw the persecution of Quakers around him. He became a spokesperson for persecuted Quakers. He held meetings and wrote about religious freedom. At last he formed a plan to start a colony for Quakers in America. In this colony, not only Quakers but people of any religion would be free to worship as they chose.

Penn founded his colony in 1681. It was called Pennsylvania, meaning "Penn's Woods." Although the king granted him the land, Penn paid the Indians to use it. This thoughtful act helped him make friends with the Indians and avoid problems with them in the future. Penn also drew up plans for a capital city named **Philadelphia**. *Philadelphia* means "city of brotherly love."

People from several European countries came to settle in Pennsylvania. Many were Quakers, but people of other religious groups came too. They found Pennsylvania to be a place of freedom where they would not be persecuted for their beliefs.

Delaware

Part of Penn's land had already been settled by Swedes. They lived along the Delaware River, and their colony was called New Sweden. The Swedish colony remained small, and for a number of years, it struggled to survive. Finally it passed into Dutch hands and was part of the land surrendered to the

50

Teach for Understanding

- Locate Pennsylvania on the map of the United States.
- Display Visual 3. Choose a student to find Pennsylvania on the map.
- Direct the group assigned *Pennsylvania* to share its facts with the class.
- Choose a student to find Delaware on the map.
- Locate the colony of Delaware on Visual 3.
- Direct the group assigned *Delaware* to share its facts with the class.

Duke of York. William Penn received the land in 1682, and Delaware finally became a separate colony in 1776.

Virginia

Virginia was the oldest of the colonies. Jamestown, the first permanent settlement in the New

World, was the beginning of the Virginia Colony. Jamestown began to profit from growing and selling tobacco. Like Massachusetts Bay, Jamestown became crowded as more and more colonists came. People spread out to form new towns. One of these towns was called **Williamsburg**.

Virginia developed a governing body of lawmakers called the **House of Burgesses**. The House of Burgesses first met in Jamestown. The people in Virginia elected men to represent them in the government. It was the first **representative government** in America.

In 1698 a fire destroyed much of Jamestown. The capital was moved to Williamsburg. The House of Burgesses began meeting there, and the city became a center of arts, trades, and culture. Williamsburg was one of the most important cities in the thirteen colonies. People can still visit Williamsburg today to find out what life was like in the colonies.

Maryland

The colony of Maryland was founded to help another religious group that suffered persecution in England. Roman Catholics were mistreated under the reigns of some of the English kings. In 1625 King Charles I took the throne. He decided to help Catholics. He granted land in America to his friend George Calvert to begin a colony for Catholics. Calvert's title was **Lord Baltimore**. The colony would be named Maryland after the queen. Later, its largest city would be named Baltimore.

But George Calvert died. His son, **Cecilius Calvert**, led the first group of settlers to Maryland. They established a settlement called Saint Mary's. Later, Protestants also began coming to Maryland. The people decided to make the colony a place of religious freedom for both Protestants and Catholics.

51

Teach for Understanding

- Continue to use Visual 3 to locate each colony as it is discussed.
- Invite a student to find Virginia on the map of the United States.
- Direct the group assigned *Virginia* to share its facts with the class.
- Choose a volunteer to find Maryland on the map.
- Direct the group assigned *Maryland* to share its facts with the class.
- Point out that Catholics, like Puritans, Baptists, and Quakers, were persecuted in England because society at the time thought that a stable country had only one religion. In England that religion was the Church of England.
- Tell the students that Charles I wanted to help Catholics who lived in his country. Charles's wife was a French Catholic. He was sympathetic to people of her religion.
- Explain why Charles's solution to helping Catholics in America was to create a colony for Roman Catholics. This solution was consistent with the thinking that only one religion could exist under a stable government. For Catholics to be able to practice their religion under Charles, they needed to live somewhere else under their own local colonial government.
- Point out that religious toleration began to be practiced in Maryland because many people who settled there were Protestants.

Background

Quakers

The Quaker religion was originally called the Society of Friends. The founder was George Fox, and his followers believed that God guided them through an inner light. The inner light had to agree with the Bible but was more important than the Bible. Quakers traveled to America to escape religious persecution in Europe. They established several colonies in Rhode Island, New Jersey, and Pennsylvania. They actively participated in government but did not believe in war and refused to support the military.

Friction between the Quakers and the monarchs of England existed for several reasons. The Quakers rejected the Church of England and its teachings, refused to serve in wars, and refused to give allegiance to the king. Because of their strong beliefs, they were often imprisoned. Over three-fourths of the Quaker men who migrated to America had spent time in prison. In America they refused to establish a state-supported church, allowed religious freedom, and allowed women to participate in some religious and political practices.

William Penn

William Penn was born into an Anglican family but became a Quaker when he was twenty-two. He is best known for founding the Pennsylvania Colony based on liberty and equal rights, which he called his "Holy Experiment."

Penn inherited his father's wealthy English estate. Since the king owed money to his father, William was awarded land in America as payment. The prospects of a better life for Quakers in the New World became a reality. Penn dreamed of "a civil society of men enjoying the highest possible degree of freedom and happiness."

Penn's ideas of freedom and good relations with Native Americans were key factors in fulfilling his dream. Penn planned that the city of Philadelphia would be far superior to the crowded and depressed cities of England. He designed a city with wider streets and enough land for family gardens. The last years of his life were disappointing to him. He suffered from debt, false legal accusations, and colonial dissatisfaction. Penn died on July 30, 1718.

Lesson

20

Teach for Understanding

- Direct a student to find the Carolinas on the US map.
- Locate the colonies of North and South Carolina on Visual 3.
- Direct the group assigned *Carolinas* to share its facts with the class.
- Direct a student to find Georgia on the map of the United States and on Visual 3.
- Direct the group assigned *Georgia* to share its facts with the class.
- Explain that the colony of Georgia provided a security buffer between the English colonies and Florida, which belonged to the Spanish.

> Conclude the discussion by asking the question on page 52. Virginia

Activity Manual

- Guide completion of page 37.

The Carolinas

The next king after Charles I was Charles II. When he came to power in 1660, England had just been through a civil war. Charles II wanted to reward the men who had supported him in the war. He granted land in America to eight of these men. They named it Carolina after the Latin word for Charles, *Carolus*.

The southern part of Carolina attracted many settlers from England. One of the settlements was positioned on a beautiful harbor. It was called **Charles Towne**. This town later became the important city of Charleston, South Carolina.

The settlements in the northern part of Carolina also grew. Many of these colonists had moved south from the colony of Virginia. Northern and southern Carolina were more like two separate colonies than one. In 1712 the colony was divided into two colonies, North Carolina and South Carolina.

Georgia

The last colony in the New World was founded for a different purpose from the others. **James Oglethorpe** wanted to establish a colony for English people who could not pay their debts. In his colony the debtors could work and earn money to repay what they owed. He also wanted his colony to be a place that did not allow slavery or drinking alcohol.

James Oglethorpe was a member of British Parliament and founded Savannah, Georgia.

Oglethorpe was the only colonial founder that lived to see his colony gain independence.

Oglethorpe is remembered for his kindness to America's first ambassador to England, John Adams. Though many in the British court looked down on Adams, Oglethorpe welcomed him warmly.

King George gave Oglethorpe the land south of the Carolinas. Oglethorpe took the first settlers to this colony, Georgia, in 1733. The colony did not turn out as he had planned. Most of the people who settled there were not debtors, and some did not want to follow his rules. But Oglethorpe did succeed in starting a city called **Savannah**. Savannah had neatly planned streets and squares. Over time it became a major shipping center.

> Which colony was the first to elect its own lawmakers?

52

Background

James Oglethorpe

During his service in the English Parliament, James Oglethorpe defended the rights of colonists and opposed slavery. His Christian beliefs made him the driving force behind the idea of creating a colony for poor people. Using his connections with the king, Oglethorpe was able to obtain a charter for Georgia. After landing in South Carolina, several of the leaders explored the land and decided to set up the colony in the area that we know today as Savannah, Georgia. As the leader of the colony, Oglethorpe developed a reputation as a strong disciplinarian. He banned rum and slavery because he did not want the colony to be a place full of sin and vice. He was influential in introducing John Wesley and George Whitefield to the colony. After being replaced by a new leader, Oglethorpe returned to England.

Life in the Colonies

The thirteen colonies were started for a variety of reasons. Some colonies were settled by people of one religion. Others drew people from many different backgrounds. Because each colony was different, colonial America was not really like one country. The colonies were more like thirteen little countries along the Atlantic coast. But all the colonies did have certain things in common.

Local Governments

All thirteen colonies were under the English king. In some colonies, the king of England had direct control. These were called **royal colonies**. Other colonies were **proprietary colonies**. They had the king's permission to choose their own governor.

But because the king lived far away across the ocean, he could not be involved in all the colonies' decisions. The colonies also needed local governments. Virginia's House of Burgesses was one type of local government. Most colonies had local assemblies that met to make decisions. In some colonies, landholders voted for men to represent them in these assemblies. In New England all men who owned property and were church members attended **town meetings**. In a town meeting any of the men could have a say in decisions. A vote would be taken, and the majority would win.

Each colony also appointed **justices of the peace**. These justices would settle problems, hold trials for people accused of crimes, and collect taxes. The most common tax was a tax on property. Anyone who owned land or a home had to pay the tax. These taxes paid the salaries of government workers. They also provided money to carry out decisions.

The colonists liked having a voice in their own government. Government by the people was an important idea in the New World. It would later become the basis for the American system of government when the colonies formed a country.

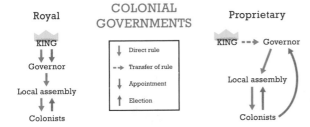

53

Student Text pages 53–55
Activity Manual pages 38–40

Lesson Focus

- The colonies were alike in local government, social classes, and family life.

Objectives
- Describe local governments in the thirteen colonies
- Compare the social classes in the colonies
- Describe colonial family life

Materials
- US map with cities of Philadelphia, Williamsburg, Charleston, and Savannah labeled

Review

- Display the following terms: *Cecilius Calvert*, *House of Burgesses*, *James Oglethorpe*, *Lord Baltimore*, *Quaker*, *representative government*, and *William Penn*.
- Direct the students to look up the people and terms in the Resource Treasury and read the entries aloud.
- Direct the students to find the following cities on the US map: Philadelphia, Williamsburg, Charleston, and Savannah.

Preparation for Reading

- Generate interest as you direct the students to examine the graph and pictures on pages 53–55.
- Guide pronunciation of any unfamiliar words in the lesson.
- Direct the students to read the pages silently to find out the names of the three social classes in the colonies. upper class, middle class, lower class

Teach for Understanding

- Direct attention to the graph on page 53, and guide a discussion about the difference between the two kinds of colonies.
- Draw an oval for display and write the words *local government* in it.
- Add facts about colonial local government in ovals extending out from the title of the web.
- The following facts should be included: local assemblies met to make decisions; landholders voted for men to represent them in the assemblies; justices of the peace would settle problems, hold trials for people accused of crimes, and collect taxes; and government by the people was an important idea in the New World.

Lesson

21

Teach for Understanding

Why was social class important to the colonists? A person's lifestyle, friendships, and marriage opportunities depended on his wealth and position.

- Explain that in colonial times, those in the upper classes thought they should set good moral examples for those in lower classes. People in these cultures believed that pastors, elected officials, and others in authority should be respected. These ideals are good as long as people can move from the lower class to the upper class. Class becomes a problem when people in the upper class take advantage of people in lower class and do not allow them to rise.

- Divide the students into three groups. Assign the groups *upper class*, *middle class*, or *lower class*. Direct the students to learn what life was like in their assigned social class.

- Direct each group to share what it learned about the social class with the other students.

Social Classes

To the colonists, social class was very important. A person's lifestyle, friendships, and marriage opportunities depended on his wealth and position.

Sometimes social class even determined where a colonist sat in church. Colonial society had an upper, a middle, and a lower class.

The Upper Class

The upper class was made up of the wealthiest people in the colonies. Merchants and people with large landholdings were part of the upper class. Some ministers were wealthy enough to be part of this class too. People of the upper class usually had large homes and kept servants or slaves. They were able to have the best clothing and goods from overseas. They could afford to give their children a good education.

As the colonies grew, those who worked hard sometimes gained enough wealth to move into the upper class. Others married into it. But in the early years of the colonies, the upper class was a small group of a few wealthy families.

The Middle Class

The middle class was made up of those with an average income. Tradesmen, farmers, shopkeepers, and ship captains were part of the middle class. Most people in the middle class were able to own some land. Not as many kept servants or slaves. Through hard work, people in the middle class earned enough to provide for their families. But they were not wealthy. The majority of people in the colonies belonged to the middle class.

The Lower Class

The lower class was made up mainly of servants and slaves. People in the lower class worked for others and usually could not afford to have their own homes. Most depended on their masters for their daily needs such as food and clothing.

Indentured servants could work their way into the middle class once they were freed. However, enslaved people were hardly ever freed. They were purchased by colonists and served as household slaves or field workers for life.

54

Activity

Social Classes of the Colonial Period

Direct the students to find more information about the social classes during the colonial period. This research could include hairstyles, clothing, housing, leisure pursuits, education, and religion.

Background

The Upper Class

All three colonial regions had an upper class made up of aristocrats. These people had refined tastes and manners. These families enjoyed more comforts and luxuries than the lower class. Usually the upper class imported much of its fabric and clothing, furniture, and other goods from Europe. Sons received good educations. Servants helped perform family household chores.

The Middle Class

The middle class included those colonists who were neither wealthy nor poor. Unlike Europe, America had plenty of land, and it was available to almost everyone. A good effort at farming would usually feed and clothe a family. Many in the middle class had gradually made their way up the social ladder in the New World. They generally owned some land and had a reasonably comfortable home, but they lacked the servants and the luxuries that the aristocrats could afford. The middle classes included farmers, clergymen, shopkeepers, ship captains, carpenters, and blacksmiths. These people formed the core of colonial society.

Plantation owner — Lady — Son — Nurse — Slaves — Servant — Apprentice

Family Life

Among the upper- and middle-class colonists, a family included a father, a mother, and children. But the household income often supported more than just the family members. Servants or slaves working for the family were the responsibility of that family as well. A household might even include a boy from another family. Sometimes young boys became apprentices to learn a trade. An apprentice usually lived in the home of the tradesman who was teaching him.

Most colonists expected the father to earn an income and support the family. Many colonists, especially Puritans, also believed the father should be the spiritual leader in the family. He should read the Bible in the home and lead the family in prayer.

The mother was expected to manage the house. If she had servants, she would assign them their duties and oversee their work. If she had no servants, she was in charge of cooking, cleaning, and sometimes making the family's clothing. She also took care of the children.

Children helped with the household chores too. If the family had animals, the children often fed and cared for them. Girls helped with indoor housework while boys helped outside in the gardens or fields. Like today's children, most colonial children went to school or learned at home.

Enslaved people were not able to have the same family relationships as the white colonists. When they were brought to America, they were often separated from family members. Even if a husband and wife worked for the same master, one of them might suddenly be sold to another master. The children of slaves worked as their parents did. They were not able to go to school.

> How were the three social classes in the colonies different from one another?

55

The Lower Class

Those who were poor tended to be servants and slaves. The servants owned no land and had few material possessions. At the very bottom of the social scale was the growing number of slaves.

Many of the servants had willingly entered a lifetime of servitude in order to make a living or to get to America. Other servants were called redemptioners and indentured servants. Redemptioners usually came from continental Europe and brought their families and possessions. Because they could not pay for all of their passage, they hoped to find a relative or friend to pay the remaining fees after they arrived. If they did not, the fees were paid by some wealthy colonist who required several years of service as repayment.

Indentured servants gained their passage to America in return for four to seven years' labor. They were usually single men from ages eighteen to thirty. When his service was completed, the indentured servant received land and his "freedom dues"—a new suit, an ax, a hoe, and even cash. Most of these people moved quickly into the middle classes. Although other people could move up the social ladder, slaves and free blacks could not. Most slaves worked six days a week, fifteen to sixteen hours a day in the summer, and fourteen hours a day the rest of the year. Black people had few chances to own land, vote, choose their jobs and religion, or get an education.

Teach for Understanding

- Direct attention to the picture on page 55.

  What constituted a family in the upper and middle classes? The family included a father, a mother, children, servants or slaves, and possibly an apprentice.

- Guide a discussion about the members of the colonial family and their responsibilities, and compare the colonial family to members of families today. Include a discussion of how the father in a Puritan family read the Bible in the home and led the family in prayer. Invite students to share how their family does Bible reading in the home.

- Invite volunteers to share why keeping people and their descendants as slaves is wrong. Include that God created all people equally as His image bearers (Genesis 1:26–28). God said that we should love others and not take advantage of them (Matthew 22:39). We should look out for what is best for others and not just what is best for ourselves (Philippians 2:4).

> Conclude the discussion by asking the question on page 55. The upper class was made up of the wealthiest people in the colonies; it was made up of merchants and people with large landholdings and homes who kept servants or slaves. The middle class was made up of those with an average income; it was made up of tradesmen, farmers, shopkeepers, and ship captains. They owned some land and maybe a few servants or slaves. The lower class was made up mainly of servants and slaves who worked for others and usually could not afford to have their own homes. Most depended on their masters for their daily needs such as food and clothing.

Activity Manual

- Guide completion of pages 38–40.

Assessment

- Administer quiz.

> The quiz may be given anytime after completing this lesson.

Lesson Focus

- The New England colonies were settled mainly by English Puritans who wanted a safe place to practice their own religion.

Objectives

- Describe religion in the New England colonies
- Explain why Anne Hutchinson was expelled from Massachusetts
- Describe the education of the Puritan children
- Name the industries in the New England colonies

Materials

- A map of the United States

Review

- Guide a discussion about local governments, social classes, and family life in the colonies.

Preparation for Reading

- Generate interest as you direct the students to read the titles and examine the pictures on pages 56–58.
- Guide pronunciation of any unfamiliar words in the lesson.
- Explain that the lesson will cover the religion, education, and industries of the New England colonies. Divide the students into three groups. Assign one of the topics to each group, and direct the students to take notes about their topic to share with the class.

Teach for Understanding

- Direct attention to the United States map and point out the names and locations of Massachusetts, New Hampshire, Connecticut, and Rhode Island.

  Which religious group mainly settled the New England colonies? the English Puritans

  Why did the Puritans not welcome people of other religions to their colonies? They wanted their colonies to be a safe place to practice their own religion.

- Guide a discussion about problems that might arise when people of many different religions live side by side with one another. Include what a Christian's responsibility is in such a situation.
- Direct the group with the topic *religion* to explain religion in the New England colonies.

The New England Colonies
Religion

The four New England colonies were Massachusetts, New Hampshire, Connecticut, and Rhode Island. These colonies were settled mainly by English Puritans. The Puritans wanted their colonies to be a safe place to practice their own religion. For this reason, they did not welcome people of other religions to their colonies.

The Puritans carefully trained their children to worship God as they did. Parents baptized their children as babies. Baptizing an infant meant that the child was now part of a Christian community. Parents taught their children God's Word and expected them to trust Christ for salvation. Older children who showed evidence of being true believers could join the church.

Puritans were required to attend church on Sundays. Church was held in buildings called **meetinghouses**. Puritan church services were different from those in the Church of England. There were no altars or statues in the meetinghouse. The ministers prayed in their own words and preached from the Bible rather than reading prayers and sermons from a book. The congregation sang the words of the psalms together without any musical instruments playing along.

Sunday was the most important day of the week for the Puritans. Most Puritans considered it wrong to work on Sundays. When not in church, they spent the free hours of the day resting, praying, or talking about spiritual topics. Children even had special toys to play with on Sundays. They often played with toys that

Puritan meetinghouse

56

Background

Anne Hutchinson

Anne Marbury was born on July 20, 1591. After she married William Hutchinson, they followed the Puritan preacher John Cotton to New England. Anne Hutchinson started having women's meetings in her home to encourage discussions about sermons and theological views. Hutchinson taught the women her beliefs and criticized the Puritan preachers for not preaching the gospel. Hutchinson and the Puritans both believed that a person is justified by the righteousness of Christ alone apart from human works. But they disagreed about the process of sanctification. The Puritans believed that the Holy Spirit worked in the hearts of Christians to transform the way they lived. Good works were the fruit or the evidence of justification. Hutchinson believed that any good works a Christian did were actually directly done by Christ or the Spirit. If the Christian did not do good works, that was not his responsibility but Christ's. Good works were not necessary evidence of justification. This belief is known as antinomianism. The Puritans convicted Anne Hutchinson of heresy and excommunicated her. Hutchinson established a settlement on Aquidneck Island in 1638. She then moved to New York and continued to teach her beliefs until she was killed by Indians in 1643.

Heritage Studies 5

reminded them of Bible stories, such as a Noah's ark toy.

The Puritans wanted to guard the New England colonies from false teaching. There were strict penalties for anyone they believed to be teaching falsehood. In the 1630s a woman in Boston named **Anne Hutchinson** began meeting with women in her home to discuss the Sunday sermons. After a while a large number of townspeople, including men, came to the meetings. Hutchinson began to express disagreement with the Puritan ministers. The Puritans taught that our good works are evidence of our salvation. Anne Hutchinson had a different view. She did not believe obedience is necessary to show our relationship to God. She taught that people can be Christians whether they obey God or not. This view is a **heresy**, a belief contrary to Scripture. The book of James deals with the relationship between a Christian's faith and works (James 2). Hutchinson was tried in court and expelled from the colony. She went to Rhode Island for a while and later lived in New York.

It was not until the 1690s that Massachusetts came under more direct control of the English king. At this time Puritanism in New England began to weaken. The colony could no longer require everyone to follow Puritanism. The Puritan influence remained strong for many more years. But people in

New England gradually drifted from their Puritan heritage.

Education

The Puritans believed that every person needed to be able to read the Bible for himself. Because they placed great importance on reading, they wanted their children to have a good education. Massachusetts even passed a law that parents must teach their children to read.

In some New England towns, one woman took on the task of educating the neighborhood children in her home. This type of school was called a **dame school**. Another type of school in New England was the **grammar school**. Larger towns hired teachers to teach subjects such as Greek, Latin, math, and writing. Grammar school took seven years to complete. Only boys attended grammar school. In 1647 a law was passed in New England that said towns with fifty or more families had to have a school.

Children first learned to read from hornbooks. A hornbook looked like a wooden paddle and was often hung from a string around the neck. Fastened to the paddle was a paper printed with the alphabet. The paper might list vowels, consonants, and the Lord's Prayer as well. The page was covered with a transparent layer of animal horn to protect it.

57

- Direct the group with the topic *education* to explain the education of the children in the New England colonies to the class. Explain that one of the basic teachings of the Reformation included the "priesthood of all believers." This belief means that everyone could approach God as an individual without going through a priest. The Puritans believed that every person needed to be able to read the Bible for himself so he could interpret Scripture and know what God wanted him to do.

Although salvation cannot be earned by good works (Ephesians 2:8–9), a true Christian will live a life that is characterized by doing good works (Ephesians 2:10; James 2:14–26). Christians will still sin, and those sins will not cause them to lose their salvation (1 John 1:10-2:2). But people who claim to be Christians and live in sin without repentance should evaluate whether they have truly trusted God for salvation from sin (1 John 1:6–10).

Hornbook

The hornbook was used by schoolchildren for several centuries, starting in the mid-fifteenth century in Europe and then in America. The hornbook consisted of a wooden paddle with a handle. Lessons were tacked to the paddle and then covered by a piece of transparent horn. A hole was made in the handle with a leather thong tied to it so the child could carry the hornbook on his belt or around his neck. The lessons consisted of different combinations of the following things: the alphabet, vowel and consonant combinations, the Lord's Prayer, a form of a cross, and a praise of the Trinity. These lessons were handwritten on a piece of parchment and then tacked to the wooden paddle. The horn placed over the lessons was used to keep the lessons from being soiled.

A horn was left in cold water for several weeks, separating the usable part from the bone. The usable part was then heated, first in boiling water and then by fire, and pressed by plates and machines to make it smooth and

transparent. As time went on, hornbooks began to be made of a variety of other materials such as ivory, metal, leather, and cardboard. Hornbooks came in a wide range of styles: plain, whittled, carved, tooled, embossed, and engraved.

Timeline

Direct the students to work together to make a timeline of education in America from 1751–1801. Assign small groups certain decades to research.

Teach for Understanding

- Direct the group with the topic *industries* to explain industries in the New England colonies to the class.

▶▶ Conclude the discussion by asking the question on page 58. The New England colonies were settled mainly by English Puritans, and they did not welcome people of other religions to their colonies.

Activity Manual

- Guide a discussion about Anne Hutchinson's beliefs, and guide completion of pages 41–42.

Benjamin Harris published the *New England Primer* about 1690. By 1830, several million copies had been sold.

In 1690 the first textbook was printed in the colonies. It was called the **New England Primer**. The book had pictures and short poems to help teach the alphabet. Many of the rhymes came from stories in the Bible. Puritan children could learn both reading and Bible truths at the same time.

Eventually the first college in America was begun in New England. **Harvard College** opened in Cambridge, Massachusetts, in 1636. It was named after John Harvard, a minister who willed all his books to the college. For many years young men who wanted to be ministers received biblical training at Harvard.

A second college was founded in New England in 1701. This college came to be known as **Yale College**. When Harvard College began promoting new ideas that were not biblical, Yale continued to teach biblical views.

Industries

Many New England colonists were farmers. Because New England did not have very good soil for farming, most farms were small. The colonists used the crops they grew to feed their families but did not sell many crops for profit. Farmers also kept animals such as sheep, cattle, hogs, and chickens.

The New England forests provided resources for a much larger industry than farming. The colonists cut down trees to build ships. New England led the colonies in the shipbuilding industry. The region supplied ships to both the colonies and England.

Another important industry was fishing. Codfish were plentiful off the New England coast. Cod could be salted and preserved and then shipped around the world. The New England colonists also hunted whales. Whales provided oil and bone for making products like candles and tools. The fishing and whaling industries expanded as better and stronger ships were built.

> Why was Puritanism the main religion of the New England colonies?

58

Activity

Moby Dick

For a good description of whaling, read an excerpt from *Moby Dick* by Herman Melville. Read a portion of Chapter 61, "Stubb Kills a Whale." Young-reader versions may be available.

Background

Whaling

In the fall of 1712, a whaler named Christopher Hussey set out along the Nantucket coast to hunt baleen whales. However, he and his crew found more than they anticipated. In the midst of a storm, they came upon a herd of whales unfamiliar to them. Hussey managed to harpoon one of the beasts, lash it to his ship, and bring it back to Nantucket. The whalers had killed a sperm whale. It was larger than a baleen whale and proved to be more valuable. The sperm whale produced higher-quality oil. Eventually, other whalers were sailing farther into the ocean to hunt these large whales. Before this time, whales had been brought back to shore for processing, but now whalers were farther away from home. They started processing the oil onboard, storing it in barrels, and carrying it directly to England for sale.

The Middle Colonies

Diversity

New York, New Jersey, Pennsylvania, and Delaware were called the middle colonies. The middle colonies were the most diverse of the three regions. Being **diverse** means that there was variety in their colonies. Unlike in New England, people from many different countries settled in these colonies. The result was that the middle colonies were home to many different cultures and religious beliefs.

Many Cultures

New York and New Jersey had both Dutch and English settlers. Delaware had a large Swedish population. Nearly a third of Pennsylvania's settlers were Germans. Scots-Irish and French colonists lived in the middle colonies. There were also a number of Africans, most of whom were slaves. Of course, Native Americans still lived in some parts of these colonies too.

Each of these groups had different cultures. They spoke different languages. They ate different foods. They built their homes in different styles. They practiced various customs and traditions. The middle colonies became a blend of many cultures.

Many Religions

Many different religious groups existed in the middle colonies. We have already learned that Quakers settled in Pennsylvania. Many of the French who came were Huguenots. These Protestants had come to the colonies to flee persecution by Roman Catholics in Europe. A large number of Germans were Lutherans. Others were part of smaller religious groups like the Amish and the Mennonites. There were Dutch Reformed, Baptist, and Anglican colonists as well. The middle colonies were filled with many different kinds of churches. New York even allowed Jews to open a synagogue.

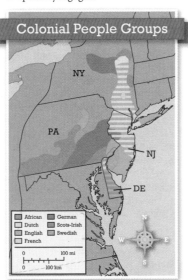

Colonial People Groups

NY

PA

NJ

DE

African — German
Dutch — Scots-Irish
English — Swedish
French

0   100 mi
0   100 km

59

Student Text pages 59–61
Activity Manual page 43

Lesson Focus

- The middle colonies were home to many different cultures and religious beliefs.

Objectives

- Identify the many cultures that made up the middle colonies
- Name some industries of the middle colonies
- Describe education in the middle colonies
- Relate Benjamin Franklin's influence on education

Teacher's Toolkit CD

- Visual 4: The *Pennsylvania Gazette*
- Instructional Aid 20: *The Middle Colonies*

Review

- Guide a discussion about religion, education, and industries in the New England colonies.

Preparation for Reading

- Generate interest as you direct the students to read the titles and examine the map and pictures on pages 59–61.
- Guide pronunciation of any unfamiliar words in the lesson.
- Direct the students to read the pages and complete Instructional Aid 20 in small groups.

Teach for Understanding

- Which colonies made up the middle colonies? New York, New Jersey, Pennsylvania, and Delaware
- What does *diverse* mean? having variety
- Guide a discussion about the diverse culture of the middle colonies. Integrate information from Instructional Aid 20, and reinforce correct responses as you teach the lesson.
- Display a list of the religious groups in the middle colonies.

Teach for Understanding

Why was farming a major industry in the middle colonies? The soil was especially fertile in these colonies because of their many rivers.

What were some of the crops grown? wheat, barley, oats, and corn

Why were the middle colonies nicknamed the Breadbasket Colonies? They supplied flour for making bread to all the other colonies. They also shipped some flour to England.

Which Indian group traded with the colonists? the Iroquois

What did the Iroquois trade animal fur for? goods they needed

Why was beaver fur popular? It could be made into felt, which was used in hats. As more and more beaver furs were traded, hat prices came down, and more people from the middle class could wear beaver hats.

- Direct attention to the chart of colonial trades. Guide a discussion about what some of the tradesmen did.
- Ask several students to choose a trade from the list that they would like to learn about and to explain why they would like to learn that trade.
- Direct attention to the process of making a tricornered beaver hat.

Industries

Farming was a major industry in the middle colonies. The soil was especially fertile in these colonies because of their many rivers. The colonists were able to grow large crops of wheat, barley, oats, and corn. After these grains were harvested, they could be ground into flour in mills. The middle colonies supplied flour for making bread to all the other colonies. They also shipped some flour to England. These colonies were nicknamed the Breadbasket Colonies.

Fur trading was another important industry in the middle colonies. In New York and Pennsylvania, the colonists had made friends with the nearby Iroquois. The Iroquois were expert trappers. They supplied fur traders with animal fur in exchange for goods they needed.

One of the most popular furs was beaver. Beaver fur could be made into felt, and this felt was used in hats. At first only the wealthy could afford to wear hats made of beaver felt. But as more and more beaver furs were traded, hat prices came down. More people from the middle class could wear beaver hats.

The colonists practiced many kinds of trades in the middle colonies. A

Colonial Trades	
apothecary	made and prescribed medicines
blacksmith	made iron products such as horseshoes and tools
cabinetmaker	built furniture from wood
chandler	made candles
cooper	made barrels
gunsmith	made guns
milliner	made cloaks, hats, gloves, etc.
printer	printed books and newspapers
silversmith	made silver objects such as spoons and buttons
tailor	made and altered clothing
wheelwright	made wagon wheels
wig maker	made wigs worn for fashion; cut and styled hair

pelt   shaved fur   felt   hat

60

Activities

Tradesmen

Direct the students to research one of the colonial trades and prepare a presentation for the class.

A Small Business

Invite the owner of a small business to visit your class and tell about how his business was started. Direct the students to think of questions to ask the owner.

Tricornered Hat

Use online sources to find a pattern and directions for making a tricornered hat. Guide the students as they work together to make their hats.

Advertising

Explain that Benjamin Franklin used newspapers, letters, and pamphlets to sell his ideas and products. Direct the students to gather samples of some of the advertising methods used today, and use them to make a display.

Timeline

Direct the students to research the life of Benjamin Franklin and make a timeline of his life and accomplishments.

Background

Benjamin Franklin

Benjamin Franklin was born in Boston in 1706 to a chandler with ten older children. As a member of such a large family, Ben was apprenticed to his much older brother James, a printer. Occasionally Ben wrote letters to his brother's newspaper, the *New England Courant*, under the pen name "Silence Dogood." When James found out that the middle-aged "Silence" was in reality his younger brother, he became angry.

At age seventeen, Ben ran away from his apprenticeship and ended up in Philadelphia where he established himself as a printer. He published the *Pennsylvania Gazette* and *Poor Richard's Almanack*, which was known for its wise sayings and advice. Franklin was so successful as a printer that he was able to retire at an early age and pursue his varied interests. During this same time, he and his wife Deborah Read raised their two children.

trade was a job that required special training in a certain skill. Large cities like Philadelphia and New York City offered jobs for people with various skills.

The first step toward learning a trade was becoming an apprentice. Apprentices studied a trade with a master tradesman for several years. If he learned well, an apprentice might become a **journeyman**. A journeyman continued to work for the master but received pay for his work. Once a person mastered a trade, he could open his own business or shop.

Education

In the middle colonies, schools were often conducted by churches. Children were taught the religious beliefs of their church along with other school subjects. Since there were many kinds of churches in the middle colonies, there were also many kinds of schools.

Benjamin Franklin was a leader in the middle colonies who cared about education. Franklin had been an apprentice to his older brother, a printer in Boston. Franklin learned quickly. He read whatever books he could find and became a good writer. Franklin ran away before his apprenticeship was finished. He eventually settled in Philadelphia and started his own newspaper. He did his best to make books available to everyone. He opened the first public library in America.

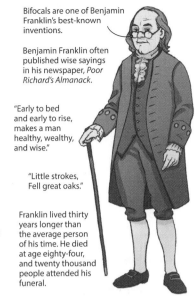

Bifocals are one of Benjamin Franklin's best-known inventions.

Benjamin Franklin often published wise sayings in his newspaper, *Poor Richard's Almanack*.

"Early to bed and early to rise, makes a man healthy, wealthy, and wise."

"Little strokes, Fell great oaks."

Franklin lived thirty years longer than the average person of his time. He died at age eighty-four, and twenty thousand people attended his funeral.

Franklin encouraged young people to get an education. He published a **pamphlet**, or short paper, on the subject. His pamphlet said that the aim of education should be to better serve one's country, friends, family, and all mankind. The pamphlet helped lead to the founding of the University of Pennsylvania. This college later opened the first medical school in the colonies.

> What were the most important industries in the middle colonies?

61

Ben was a thoroughly enlightened thinker. He hoped to improve himself and the world around him. In 1727 he organized the Junto, a club for improving society and its members. Part of the Junto's work was establishing a militia, a lending library, the University of Pennsylvania, and an insurance company. The club also founded Philadelphia's first volunteer fire department and its first public hospital.

Franklin earned fame in Europe and America for his scientific experiments. He was especially famous for his work with electricity. He invented the lightning rod, bifocals, a glass harmonica, the iron stove, and the odometer.

Franklin was also known for his diplomatic efforts. He was on the committee to write the Declaration of Independence. He was also the oldest member of the Constitutional Convention.

Franklin believed the highest good of man was in morality and integrity. He believed in a god, but he did not believe that Jesus was God. He also did not believe the Bible was God's Word. Despite all his efforts at improving himself and doing good to others, he fell short of his own goals. He also fell short of God's mark.

Teach for Understanding

What was a trade? a job that required special training in a certain skill

What was the first step toward learning a trade? becoming an apprentice

What happened if an apprentice learned well for several years? He might become a journeyman and continue to work for the master but receive pay for his work.

What happened once a person mastered a trade? He could open his own business or shop.

How do you think it would feel to open your own business? Answers could include excited, happy, and a little anxious.

Why were there many kinds of schools in the middle colonies? Schools were often conducted by churches. Since there were many kinds of churches in the middle colonies, there were also many kinds of schools.

Which leader in the middle colonies published pamphlets to encourage young people to get an education? Benjamin Franklin

- Draw a large oval for display to start a word web.
- Write *Benjamin Franklin* for display in the oval.
- Direct the students to name some facts about Benjamin Franklin. Write the facts under the oval. Answers may include the following facts:

He was apprenticed to his older brother.

He was a printer in Boston.

He read whatever books he could find.

He became a good writer.

He ran away before his apprenticeship was finished.

He settled in Philadelphia and started his own newspaper.

He did his best to make books available to everyone.

He opened the first public library in America.

He encouraged young people to get an education.

He published a pamphlet, or short paper, that helped lead to the founding of the University of Pennsylvania.

- Display Visual 4 and point out some of the interesting features on the newspaper page.

> Conclude the discussion by asking the question on page 61. farming, fur trading, and mastering colonial trades

Activity Manual

- Guide completion of page 43.

Student Text pages 62–64
Activity Manual pages 44–45

Lesson Focus

- The southern colonies did not place as much emphasis on religion as the other regions did and had a cash-crop economy.

Objectives

- Explain religion in the southern colonies
- Discuss education in the southern colonies
- Explain farming in the southern colonies

Teacher's Toolkit CD

- Instructional Aid 21: *The Southern Colonies*

Introduction

- Guide the reading of the How It Was box.
- Use the background information on indigo to explain its impact on the southern colonies.

Preparation for Reading

- Generate interest as you direct the students to read the titles and examine the pictures on pages 62–64.
- Guide pronunciation of any unfamiliar words in the lesson.
- Direct the students to read the pages and complete Instructional Aid 21 in small groups.

Teach for Understanding

What colonies made up the southern colonies? Virginia, Maryland, the Carolinas, and Georgia

- Guide a discussion about the religion in the southern colonies. Integrate information from Instructional Aid 21, and reinforce correct responses as you teach the lesson.
- Discuss education in the southern colonies.

How It Was

Eliza bent down to cup the purple flowers of a plant in her fingers. She tilted her head to let the wide brim of her hat shade her face from the hot sun. She loved the morning sounds of her father's South Carolina plantation. Insects buzzed, a wren chirped, and the breeze carried the voices of men at work in the rice fields.

"Indigo," Eliza murmured. "Father was right—it is a beautiful plant. Next time I write, I'll tell him how well the seeds he sent are growing."

She leaned closer to study the color of the flowers. Then she looked out over the fields. Her thoughts went back to the words in her father's letter. "He said indigo makes a lovely blue dye. I wonder if we could clear enough land to grow a whole field of these plants." She looked out across the nearest field, and a small smile played on her lips. "It might be worth a try. Who knows? In a few years all the ladies of the colonies might be wearing blue."

The Southern Colonies
Religion

Virginia, Maryland, the Carolinas, and Georgia were the five southern colonies. Like New England, these colonies were settled mainly by the English. However, the English who settled in the South were not Puritans. Most were members of the Church of England, or **Anglicans**. Maryland still had some Roman Catholics, but their freedoms were limited because of religious changes in England. There were also some Huguenots from France who settled in the southern colonies.

However, the southern colonies as a whole did not place as much emphasis on religion as the other regions did.

Education

Many families in the southern colonies did not send their children to school. Because the South had many farms, homes were spread out. It was difficult to have a community school that would be close to everyone. Instead many parents taught their own children or hired tutors to educate them at home. Tutors were especially common among the upper classes.

62

Background

Indigo

Indigo has been grown for thousands of years. In biblical times, only the wealthy could afford to wear the purple color of cloth dyed from indigo. Eliza Lucas Pinckney introduced indigo to the South. Her father, who was governor of Antigua, sent her seeds of various plants that he thought might be suited to the growing conditions in the Carolinas. Extracting the dye from the indigo plant was a long and exhausting process. After the dye hardened, it was cut into squares for export. The indigo plant produces a deep, rich, blue-purple dye. Indigo became a staple crop for the Carolinas. It was so valuable that, between rice and indigo, Charleston became one of the richest cities in the colonies.

Some young men of the upper class went to England for college. The colony of Virginia started one of the early colleges in colonial America. It was named the College of William and Mary after an English king and queen. This college was the first in the colonies to have a law school.

Cash-Crop Economy

The most important industry in the southern colonies was farming. The warm climate made these colonies a good place for growing tobacco and rice. Tobacco was the most common crop in Virginia, Maryland, and North Carolina. Rice was more common in South Carolina and Georgia.

A young woman in South Carolina named Eliza Pinckney grew a new crop called indigo. Her father had sent her indigo seeds from the West Indies. Eliza shared the new plant with her neighbors. Soon indigo had become a third popular crop in the southern colonies. It was in high demand for its use in making dye for cloth.

Tobacco, rice, and indigo became known as the three **cash crops** of the southern colonies. These three crops grew well and brought in a profit. The whole economy of these colonies came to depend on these crops.

Farms in the southern colonies were often small. Many farmers did their work with only the help of their families. Others kept a few Africans as slaves to help with farming. Larger southern farms were known as plantations. A plantation owner needed more help to produce his crops. Many plantations used enslaved Africans to work in the fields. The only pay the slaves received was food, clothing, and shelter. The largest plantations had hundreds of slaves.

Some large plantations were like small communities with many buildings. In addition to field slaves, these plantations used slaves to cook, help with housework, and care for farm animals. Plantations with a large number of slaves often housed them in cabins on the property.

Plantations were often located along rivers. From these rivers planters could ship crops to port cities. Tobacco, rice, and indigo were sold within the colonies. They were also shipped overseas to England.

The Triangular Trade

Before long, a system of trade developed between the colonies, England, and West Africa. The goods produced in the colonies traveled by ships to England. These goods included such things as whale oil, lumber, furs, fish, tobacco, rice, and indigo. England also shipped goods to America for the colonists to purchase. Many of these goods were luxury items not found in the colonies. Tea, spices, cloth, and tools were a few of these goods.

63

Teach for Understanding

- Guide a discussion about the cash-crop economy in the southern colonies. Integrate information from Instructional Aid 21, and reinforce correct responses as you teach the lesson.

- Draw two columns for display and label them "farms" and "plantations." Guide the students as they compare and contrast the two.

- Divide the students into small groups. Direct each group to draw a large triangle on a sheet of paper and label the points "colonies," "England," and "West Africa." Direct the groups to write by each point which goods were produced and traded and to draw arrows showing where the goods were shipped.

- Why did slavery thrive in the southern colonies? The answer could include that plantation owners needed slaves to grow and harvest the cash crops.

Activities

Religions

Guide the students as they research and make a list of religions in their area.

Economy

Direct the students to research industries and jobs in their area.

Teach for Understanding

- Guide a discussion about the slave trade.

- Explain that slavery thrived in the South because of greater secularism. While the South purported to be Christian, the Bible did not support the South's form of slavery.

- Do you think slavery would have thrived in a Puritan colony? The answer could include that the soil in New England was not good so the farms were small, and laborers were not needed in the fields like they were in the South.

- Point out that the first Puritans had laws against slavery. However, later they did allow for slaves.

  Who wrote a book about his life as an enslaved person? Olaudah Equiano

- Explain that the accuracy of Equiano's book has been questioned. Some people believe he falsified parts of the account. Others still think it is accurate.

  What did Equiano's book do? It made many people think seriously about the evils of slavery.

- Direct attention to the picture of Olaudah Equiano on page 64.

Activity

Primary Source
- Direct attention to Activity Manual page 44.
- Read aloud the excerpt.
- Guide a discussion of Equiano's account.

Participating in Trade
- Direct the students to decide what goods they would like to make available for trade and how they want the goods to be traded.

- Each student will design a poster to advertise his goods.

- After the posters are complete, the students will examine the other posters and choose which goods they would like to trade for. They will work with the other "traders" to negotiate several exchanges of goods. No money or actual goods should be used.

- After the mock trading is complete, ask the students what they learned from the activity, which goods seemed the most popular, which were the most expensive, and why.

  » Conclude the discussion by asking the question on page 64. tobacco, rice, indigo

Activity Manual

- Guide completion of pages 44–45.

The sad part of the triangular trade was that goods were not the only items traded. People were traded too. European and African traders kidnapped African men, women, and children from their homes. These traders placed them on ships and took them to the West Indies and America to be sold as slaves. The African people were crowded tightly into the ships' holds. Often they were laid on their backs and chained together. Many did not survive the voyage.

Scholars estimate that more than ten million Africans were sold into slavery from the 1400s to the 1800s. **Olaudah Equiano** was sold to a master who put him to work on ships. During his travels Equiano witnessed many of the slave trade's horrors. He also learned to read and write. Later he was sold to another master who allowed him to earn money. In time Equiano saved enough to buy his freedom. Equiano spent his later life in England. He wrote a book about his life as an enslaved person. The book made many people think seriously about the evils of slavery.

"I was soon put down under the decks, and there I received such a salutation in my nostrils as I had never experienced in my life."
–Olaudah Equiano

Equiano had the dangerous job of carrying gunpowder from the ship's hold to the cannons.

The proceeds from his book, *The Interesting Narrative of the Life of Olaudah Equiano*, allowed him to leave his children a generous inheritance.

> What were the three main cash crops in the southern colonies?

Activity

Participating in Trade

Decide what goods you will make available for trade. Design a poster that advertises your goods.

Examine the other posters and choose goods that you would like to trade for. Work with the other "traders" to negotiate several exchanges of goods.

When you have finished trading, discuss what you learned from your experience. Which goods seemed the most popular? Which goods were the most expensive? What might be some reasons for this?

64

Revival in the Colonies
The Great Awakening

As the eighteenth century went on, more and more people in the colonies turned away from God. The colonies were gaining wealth from trade. Some people became more interested in the things money could buy than in living for God. Colleges in the colonies changed. A number of them had begun with a spiritual focus. Now most of these colleges had drifted from the truth of God's Word. People still went to church. But many attended church only because everyone else did. They wanted others to think well of them. Many churchgoers had never experienced Christ's saving work in their hearts.

It was almost as if the Christian faith of the colonies had fallen asleep. The colonists needed a **revival**. A revival is a work that only God can do. It is when God works in the hearts of many people to wake them up to their spiritual needs. A revival did come to the colonies in the 1730s and '40s. This revival came to be known as the Great Awakening.

One of the leaders of the Great Awakening was a minister in Massachusetts named **Jonathan Edwards**. The Puritan churches in New England were now called congregational churches. Edwards had spent two years helping his grandfather, the pastor of one of these churches. When his grandfather died, Edwards became the pastor.

Edwards was still a young man, but he was a gifted preacher. He soon realized that many people in his church were not truly converted. He saw ungodly living all around him. The people needed to know that when a person is truly saved, his life changes. Edwards preached about the need for repentance from sin and faith in Jesus Christ. During the late 1730s, more than three hundred people came to Christ through his ministry.

The Great Awakening spread throughout the colonies. Another pastor God used during this time was an English minister named **George Whitefield**. Whitefield had become a traveling evangelist. His travels brought him across the ocean to America. He preached in all three regions of the colonies. God had given Whitefield a powerful voice. Often he held meetings outdoors in open fields. There were no microphones in those days. But Whitefield could speak loudly enough for thousands of people to hear him all at one time.

65

Lesson Focus

- A revival called the Great Awakening came to the colonies in the 1730s and '40s.

Objectives

- Explain why people in the colonies began to turn away from God
- Name two leaders of the Great Awakening and what they did to bring revival to the colonies
- List the effects of the Great Awakening

Teacher's Toolkit CD

- Instructional Aid 22: *The Great Awakening*

Review

- Guide a review of the religion, education, and cash-crop economy in the southern colonies.
- Review what was involved in the triangular trade.

Preparation for Reading

- Generate interest as you direct the students to read the titles and examine the pictures on pages 65–67.
- Guide pronunciation of any unfamiliar words in the lesson.
- Direct the students to read the pages and complete Instructional Aid 22 in small groups.

Teach for Understanding

- Guide a discussion about revival and why the colonies needed it. Integrate information from Instructional Aid 22, and reinforce correct responses as you teach the lesson.
- Choose a volunteer to explain George Whitefield's role in the Great Awakening.
- Why would there need to be a revival in colonies planted by Christians who wanted a place to worship God as the Bible taught? Their children were not born Christians. Each child must decide for himself to follow God.

  How do we know that the Great Awakening was a special work of God? Only God can work in the hearts of many people so that they wake up to their spiritual needs.

Lesson

25

Teach for Understanding

- Read aloud the Biography box. Guide a discussion about Jonathan Edwards's role in the Great Awakening.

  Why would the Great Awakening cause people to become interested in taking the gospel to American Indians? Once people realized that they were sinners who needed the gospel, they started to see other people as sinners who needed the gospel of salvation.

- Explain that revival is a work God does. He often uses willing servants, however, such as Edwards and Whitefield.

Jonathan Edwards

Who: congregational minister
When: 1703–1758
Where: Massachusetts

Jonathan Edwards was one of the preachers God used to begin the Great Awakening in New England. Edwards was born in Connecticut and attended Yale College. He began pastoring a congregational church in Northampton, Massachusetts, in 1729. His preaching on justification by faith caused many people to see their need for Christ. His most famous sermon was "Sinners in the Hands of an Angry God." During this sermon, God used His Word to bring many people to repentance of sin.

George Whitefield, like Jonathan Edwards, preached about the need for true conversion. He too saw that many people claimed to be Christians, but they did not live godly lives. As a result of his preaching, many people were awakened to their spiritual needs. Many people became true believers, and their lives changed.

Effects of the Great Awakening

The Great Awakening had several lasting effects on the colonies. First, it led to a greater emphasis on evangelism. More Christians became concerned for the souls of the people around them. Many Africans and Indians in the colonies had never heard the gospel preached before. Most colonists feared the Indians. Disputes over land sometimes led to fighting with Indian tribes. But now some colonists began to see the Indians as people with spiritual needs. Missionaries such as David Brainerd and Samuel Kirkland went to live among Indian tribes. They spent their lives obeying God's command to take the gospel to every human being. A number of Indians and Africans became true followers of Christ during this time.

The Great Awakening also led to the founding of new colleges. Princeton was started in New Jersey.

66

Activity

Revivals

Provide resources for the students to research some of the great revivals of the past to find out how they started, the names of some of the leaders, and how society changed as a result.

Background

The Great Awakening

The moral and spiritual conditions in America gradually began to decline. Churches accepted people and ministers who were not true believers. Signs of revival began to appear under the preaching of Jonathan Edwards and George Whitefield. Edwards preached for about ten years in the New England colonies. He proclaimed that people were guilty before God and that they must seek His gracious forgiveness. Edwards's most famous sermon was "Sinners in the Hands of an Angry God." In this sermon he made it clear that salvation was by faith alone and could not be attained by works or church membership. The Great Awakening brought significant changes to New England. Much of the sin and insincerity was swept away by this remarkable work of God. But there were political changes as well. People had seen the wisdom and character of church leaders called into question by the revival. They therefore felt bolder about doubting the opinions of their authorities. In this way the Great Awakening helped to pave the way for the American Revolution.

It had a special focus on the training of preachers. Dartmouth was founded in New Hampshire. Its purpose was to give Indians a Christian education.

The Great Awakening had another effect that would be important in America's future. It made people think more about freedom and equality. The gospel was for everyone, not just for people of European descent or for the upper class. People realized that they must find the truth in the Bible. They must answer to God alone for what they believed, not to their government. More churches began to value independence.

New churches were formed. Church members chose their pastors. They used their own money to support themselves. At times, however, churches misused these freedoms. Sometimes churches did not honor their pastor's God-given authority. Sometimes false teachers started churches that misled people. Yet the Great Awakening's emphasis on independence was important. It would help pave the way for the next great event in American history.

What were the effects of the Great Awakening?

67

Chapter Review
Activity Manual pages 47–48

Objective
- Recall concepts and terms from Chapter 3

Introduction

- Concepts for the Chapter 3 Test will be taken from Activity Manual pages 33–48. You may review any or all of the concepts during this lesson. You may choose to review Chapter 3 by playing "Q and A."

Review

Review Game: "Q and A"

- Divide the students into two teams. Direct the teams to write down questions from the chapter to ask the other team. Alternate having one team ask the other team a question. Award points for correct answers. The team with the most points at the end of the game wins.

Activity Manual

- Guide completion of pages 47–48.

Teach for Understanding

- Guide a discussion about the effects of the Great Awakening.

Why was increased independence of churches good? New churches were formed. Church members chose their pastors. They used their own money to support themselves.

Why was increased independence of churches bad? Sometimes churches did not honor their pastor's God-given authority. Sometimes false teachers started churches that misled people.

Conclude the discussion by asking the question on page 67. The Great Awakening led to a greater emphasis on evangelism. It led to the founding of new colleges. It made people think more about freedom and equality.

Activity Manual

- Guide completion of page 46.

Lesson **27**   **Chapter 3 Test**

Objective
- Demonstrate knowledge of concepts from Chapter 3 by taking the test

Assessment

- Administer Test 3.

American Independence

Focus

From 1754 to '83 the colonists came to view themselves as a unique nation that should be independent, and they fought to prove that they were right.

Introduction

This chapter is about conflict. The French and Indian War began when the English, the French, and the American Indians confronted each other over land in the Ohio River valley. The British won a great victory, but the English colonists were not completely happy with the results. They were especially bothered by the Proclamation of 1763, which reserved land west of the Appalachians as solely for the Indians. Colonists also disliked the Stamp Act, which taxed some purchases. The Townshend Acts also raised money for Britain by taxing certain goods. Tensions between colonists and the British government led to the Boston Massacre and the Boston Tea Party. The Battles of Lexington and Concord were just the beginning of the Revolutionary War. Colonists were divided between being loyal to King George or loyal to the fight for independence. The Declaration of Independence was passed by the Continental Congress. Colonists continued to fight in order to gain freedom from British rule. They finally defeated the British at Yorktown in 1781. Independence was officially achieved in 1783 when the last British troops left New York. The war was over.

Chapter 4 Overview

Lesson	Student Text	Activity Manual	Content	Vocabulary
28	68–73	49–51	Iroquois Confederacy Fort Duquesne Ohio River valley James Wolfe George Washington Proclamation of 1763	militia pacifism Parliament
29	74–76	52–53	King George III Townshend Acts Intolerable Acts Stamp Act Boston Massacre Patrick Henry John Adams Sons of Liberty Boston Tea Party	coerce prime minister customs agent repeal Loyalist smuggling Patriot
30	77–79	54–56	Battles of Lexington and Concord Battle of Bunker Hill	besiege Continental Congress boycott Continentals commander in chief minuteman
31	80–82	57–58	George Washington July 4, 1776 Valley Forge Thomas Jefferson Delaware River Horatio Gates Biography Box: Nathan Hale Saratoga Primary Source: The Declaration of Independence	Declaration of Independence
32	83–85	59	Marquis de Lafayette How It Was: Completing the mission	Continental dollar mercenary envoy
33	86–88	60–61	George Rogers Clark Charles Cornwallis Thomas Sumter Joseph Brant Francis Marion Nathanael Greene	
34	89–91	62	Chesapeake Bay Activity: Creating a Timeline Yorktown	
35		63–64	Chapter Review	
36			Chapter Test	

Visit bjupress.com/resources for links to enhance the lessons.

French & Indian War
1754–63

Declaration of
Independence
1776

Yorktown
1781

1750 1760 1770 1775 1777 1780 1783 1790

April 19 Saratoga Treaty of Paris
Lexington & Concord

The French and Indian War Begins

As England's colonies in North America prospered, they spread north, south, and west. The colonists often ran into Indian tribes. Sometimes they ran into other Europeans. In 1754 a war began in North America and traveled back to Europe.

Three groups wanted to keep or expand their lands around the Ohio River. Native Americans, French trappers, and English settlers all wanted the region. It was unclear which parts of the land belonged to each group. The French needed land for fur trade.

Their main goal was to keep the English out of lands where the French trapped and hunted. The English colonists wanted to spread west. Virginians and Pennsylvanians in particular believed that what is now western Pennsylvania around the start of the Ohio River was their land. Many English colonists wanted land to farm. The Six Nations of the **Iroquois Confederacy** controlled many Indian tribes in the Northeast. They also believed all the Indians in this region were under their control. The Iroquois had alliances with both

English colonists wanted the Ohio River valley to farm.

The French wanted the Ohio River valley to trap and to supply their fur industry.

The Iroquois wanted to live in the Ohio River valley. They wanted both the French and the English out of the area.

69

Chapter Focus

From 1754 to 1783 the colonists came to view themselves as a unique nation that should be independent, and they fought to prove that they were right.

JourneyForth

Regina Silsby's Secret War and *Regina Silsby's Phantom Militia* by Thomas J. Brodeur are available from JourneyForth Books, a division of BJU Press, at journeyforth.com.

Rachel Winslow is willing to go to great lengths to help the Sons of Liberty, even changing her identity when necessary. Join this daring young woman in her exciting adventures during the American Revolution.

Lesson 28 Student Text pages 68–73
Activity Manual pages 49–51

Lesson Focus

- The French and Indian War was a conflict between the English colonial militia, the French, and the Native Americans.

Objectives

- Identify the three groups that wanted to keep or expand their lands around the Ohio River
- Describe how the French and Indian War began
- Explain the consequences of the Proclamation of 1763

Teacher's Toolkit CD

- Visuals 5–6: *The Ohio River Valley in 1754*; *Nova Scotia*
- Instructional Aid 23: *The French and Indian War*

Materials

- An inch ruler for each student

Introduction

- Invite a student to read aloud the title of the chapter and predict what the chapter will be about. American independence
- Invite a student to read the chapter focus aloud.

  What do you think you will learn in this chapter? how colonists fought to be independent

- Direct attention to the timeline.

  Which war began in 1754? the French and Indian War

  What are some other battles that occurred from 1775 to 1781? Lexington and Concord, Saratoga, and Yorktown

Preparation for Reading

- Generate interest as you direct the students to read the titles and examine the pictures on pages 68–73.
- Guide pronunciation of any unfamiliar words in the lesson.
- Direct the students to read the pages silently and complete Instructional Aid 23 in small groups.

Teach for Understanding

In what directions did the English colonies in North America spread? north, south, and west

What other people did the colonists run into? Native Americans and other Europeans

- Direct attention to Visual 5. Choose a volunteer to find the Ohio River valley area on the map.

  Who wanted to keep or expand land around the Ohio River? Native Americans, French trappers, and English settlers

  Why did the French need the land? for fur trade

  What did the English colonists want to do with the land? farm it

- Direct attention to the pictures at the bottom of page 69. Invite a student to read aloud the captions.
- Choose a volunteer to explain the role of the Iroquois Confederacy.

Lesson

28

Teach for Understanding

- Invite a group to name the three groups that finally confronted each other over land in the Ohio River valley. Native Americans, French trappers, and English settlers

  What did Virginia do since it also claimed land around the Ohio River? This colony sent George Washington with colonial militia soldiers to set up its own fort.

- Direct attention to the picture on page 70. Read the captions aloud.

- Choose a group to tell what happened in the Ohio River valley on May 28, 1754. George Washington and his American Indian allies met and fought some French soldiers.

  What did this confrontation begin? the French and Indian War

  What sides developed during the continuing war? The British and French fought each other, and the Indian tribes changed sides.

  What did the Indian tribes hope would be the outcome of the war? They hoped that neither European power would win a great victory. They hoped to keep the lands.

- Invite a group to tell about the British plans to attack the French and how successful they were. The British planned to attack the French in four places. First, General Edward Braddock would march west and fight the French at the Forks of the Ohio. At the same time, three armies would travel north from New England and attack French Canada. One attack was successful; a French fort in Nova Scotia fell to British forces.

  During his approach to Fort Duquesne, what did General Edward Braddock do that caused many of his soldiers to be killed? He made his soldiers march in straight lines and in red coats.

- Guide a discussion of how fighting like European soldiers was not a good strategy. Include the idea that British troops were easy targets because they could be seen easily.

  What approach did the French and Indians use? They fought from the woods, hiding and shooting.

  Who led the British retreat after General Braddock and many of his soldiers were killed in an ambush? Washington

- What do you think Washington learned from the British army being defeated in this way? to use a different strategy in warfare, such as not allowing troops to be visible to the enemy

---

the British and the French. These Indians preferred that few Europeans move to the Ohio area.

In 1754 all three groups finally confronted each other in the **Ohio River valley**. The French in North America set up forts south of the Great Lakes. But Virginia also claimed these lands. This colony sent **George Washington** with colonial soldiers called a **militia** to set up its own fort. On May 28, 1754, Washington and his American Indian allies met and fought some French soldiers. The French and Indian War had begun. During the war the British and French fought each other. Indian tribes casually changed sides, often

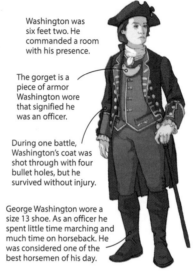

Washington was six feet two. He commanded a room with his presence.

The gorget is a piece of armor Washington wore that signified he was an officer.

During one battle, Washington's coat was shot through with four bullet holes, but he survived without injury.

George Washington wore a size 13 shoe. As an officer he spent little time marching and much time on horseback. He was considered one of the best horsemen of his day.

70

misleading both the British and French with inaccurate information. The Indians hoped that neither European power would win a great victory. If all Europeans would stay outside the lands in the Ohio River basin, then the Indians could keep the lands.

British Losses

In 1755 the British planned to attack the French in four places. First, General Edward Braddock would march west and fight the French at the forks of the Ohio. At the same time, three armies would travel north from New England and attack French Canada.

Only one attack succeeded. A French fort in Nova Scotia fell to British forces. A battle in the northern Hudson River valley was a draw. The planned attack of French Fort Niagara never even occurred because the British forces did not have a good leader.

Farther south of Canada, Braddock led his troops toward **Fort Duquesne**. He brought Washington along as an aide. Braddock wanted his men to fight like European soldiers by marching in straight lines and in red coats. British troops were easy targets. But the French adapted more easily to the changed environment of North America. The French and Indians fought from the woods, hiding and shooting. Braddock and many of his soldiers were killed in an ambush. Washington helped organize the British retreat. This defeat helped train him for later warfare.

Background

Militia vs. Regulars

Militia were "citizen soldiers," part-time fighters who left their farms and businesses to fight in emergencies. The famous "minutemen" of the War for Independence (citizens supposedly ready to fight at a minute's notice) are an example of American militia. Although militia units might serve for months or even years at a time, they remained non-professionals, serving only as long as the emergency lasted.

Regulars, on the other hand, were professional, full-time soldiers who made the military their career. The British army in the War for Independence consisted entirely of regulars, although some Loyalist militia units fought alongside them. The Continentals were America's regulars in the war, serving as the veteran core of Washington's army. Although militiamen often performed valiantly in battle, most generals—including Washington—preferred regulars. These seasoned professional soldiers often proved more dependable in battle.

Disputed Lands

Two More Years of British Defeats

During 1756–57 the British continued to suffer defeats against the French and their American Indian allies. Although the Iroquois had an alliance with the British, they preferred to remain neutral. French allies, such as the Huron and Abenaki, launched raids on colonial frontiers.

The European approach to battle was not effective against guerilla warfare tactics.

Virginia and Pennsylvania suffered much from Indian attacks. As the Virginians had pushed west during the 1700s, they drove out Indian tribes from the woodlands. Now that war was official, the Indians repeatedly attacked English settlements. Virginians were either killed or sold as slaves to the French. Women and children were often captured and forced to live with the Indian tribes. Some joined and began to live like the tribes that captured them.

The war was especially troubling for Pennsylvania. The Quakers who founded the colony believed in Christian **pacifism**. They thought no Christian should ever fight. For over seventy years, their colony had fought no wars. Instead of taking lands from the neighboring tribes, Pennsylvania's

71

The Outbreak of the French and Indian War

In the spring of 1754, Lieutenant Colonel George Washington led his men toward the Forks of the Ohio River (the site of modern Pittsburgh). Governor Dinwiddie of Virginia had ordered Washington to clear the territory of the French who, according to the English, had illegally entered the area. On the way, Washington and his troops surprised a small group of French soldiers. In the ensuing skirmish, ten Frenchmen were killed and the rest captured—although Britain and France were officially at peace.

A much larger force of French soldiers and Indian warriors, however, was waiting at the Forks of the Ohio at the newly constructed Fort Duquesne (doo KANE). Realizing that he was outnumbered, Washington retreated and hastily threw up defenses. Aptly named Fort Necessity, the structure showed Washington's inexperience. Located in a low area, the fort allowed the French to fire directly into it from nearby heights. Washington was soon forced to surrender, but the French were surprisingly gracious. They allowed the Virginians to march home after Washington naively signed a note of surrender that put the blame for the whole affair on the British. The government repudiated Washington's note, and Britain and France went to war.

Teach for Understanding

What did Quakers do to acquire land from neighboring tribes? They bought land from the Indians.

- Point out that it was right for the Quakers to buy land rather than just take it from neighboring Indian tribes.

What caused Indian bands to take revenge on colonists in the 1700s? William Penn's sons did not follow their father's practice of buying land, and they unfairly took land from the Delaware Indians.

Which man did King George II appoint as a new leader for Parliament in an effort to change the course of the war? William Pitt

What strategy did Pitt use to change the war? He sent much money to British generals in North America and Britain's allies in Europe.

What else helped change the way the war was going? the persistence of British generals and colonists

- Choose a group to tell which major campaigns the British forces won in 1758. The French abandoned the Ohio River valley and Fort Duquesne. In Nova Scotia, Fort Louisbourg also fell.

- Explain that the French controlled some areas in parts of what is now Canada. Direct attention to Visual 6. Select a volunteer to find Nova Scotia and Fort Louisbourg.

What was happening throughout the world that helped turn the tide of the war? Britain's ally Prussia fought France and its ally Austria. The British navy defeated French fleets.

What were two major British victories over the next several years? the capture of Fort Ticonderoga and the fall of Quebec

- Guide a discussion of how General James Wolfe led the British to claim Quebec.

What events followed the fall of Quebec and led up to the Treaty of Paris? French forces were defeated in Canada, in the Caribbean, and in India. The British defeated France's ally Spain in Cuba and the Philippines.

---

leaders bought land from them. But William Penn's sons did not follow this practice. They unfairly took land from the Delaware Indians in the early 1700s. When war broke out, Indian bands took their revenge. The Pennsylvania colonists were surprised at the cruelty of the raids. The colony survived but suffered greatly.

By late 1757 the English government was tired of losing the war. King George II chose a new leader for **Parliament**, William Pitt. Pitt sent much money to British generals in North America and Britain's allies in Europe. This money, along with the persistence of British generals and colonists, helped change the course of the war.

Winning Battles

In 1758 British forces won two major campaigns in North America. The French abandoned the Ohio River valley and Fort Duquesne. The fort was renamed in honor of William Pitt. In Nova Scotia, Fort Louisbourg also fell.

The war spread throughout the rest of the world. In Europe, Britain's ally Prussia fought France and France's ally Austria. The British navy defeated French fleets as well. The tide of the war seemed to be turning.

For the next several years, the British continued to win victories. They captured Fort Ticonderoga far north of

New York City. Later, the fortress city of Quebec fell. The British capture of this city was perhaps the most famous battle of the war.

Quebec sits high above the Saint Lawrence River. The French general Louis Joseph de Montcalm directed its defense. Thousands of French troops guarded the city on all sides—all except one. Directly to the southwest of the city lay a flat area called the Plains of Abraham. Steep cliffs dropped from the plains to the river. In the middle of a fall night, British general **James Wolfe** told his troops to scale the cliffs. When the morning sun rose, the French found a British army sitting at their front door. In the battle that followed, Generals Montcalm and Wolfe both died. But at the end of the day, the British claimed Quebec.

The war dragged on for several years after this battle, but the French were losing the fight. Their forces were defeated in Canada, in the Caribbean, and in India. The British defeated France's ally Spain in Cuba and the Philippines. In early 1763 the Treaty of Paris showed the extent of Britain's victory. All of Canada except two tiny islands became Great Britain's. The French left India.

72

Activity

Research the French and Indian War
Invite the students to do research to learn another name for the French and Indian War.

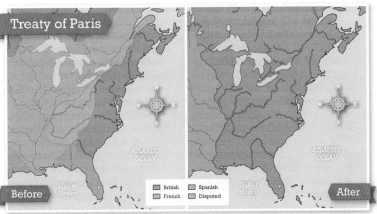

Treaty of Paris

Before

After

British   Spanish
French   Disputed

The Spanish surrendered Florida to Britain. A great British victory had been won.

Consequences for the Colonies

Although the colonies supported the British war effort, the final results did not completely please them. The colonies had fought to expand west into the Ohio River valley. They had feared the American Indians and the Catholic French. With the war over, the colonists felt that Britain had forgotten about their help. The British left many French Catholics in Canada. Most remained in Quebec. But the colonists were bothered more by the

Proclamation of 1763. This document drew an imaginary line across the frontier. The line marked land west of the Appalachians as solely for the Indians. In addition, when the British insisted on leaving an army in the colonies, they expected that the colonists would help pay for it. These decisions caused disagreements between the colonies and Britain.

Why were British colonists disappointed with the results of the French and Indian War?

73

Teach for Understanding

What lands did Britain acquire after its victory in the French and Indian War? Britain acquired all of Canada except two tiny islands. The French left India. The Spanish surrendered Florida to Britain.

- Invite a group to explain the Proclamation of 1763.
- Direct attention to the maps on page 73 showing the results of the French and Indian War. Guide a discussion of what the land was like before and after the war.
- Choose a volunteer to explain the picture showing the response of a colonist to the Proclamation of 1763.

Conclude the discussion by asking the question on page 73. At the end of the war, the colonists felt that Britain had forgotten about their help. The Proclamation of 1763 marked land west of the Appalachians as solely for the Indians. In addition, the British expected the colonists to help pay for a British army in the colonies.

Activity Manual

- Guide completion of pages 49–51.

Background

The Proclamation of 1763

After the French and Indian War, the colonists desired to resume their expansion into the western frontier. Consequently, some trappers and settlers moved into the region. But Pontiac, an Ottawa Indian chief, wanted to stop the entrance of the white man. He organized the tribes from Canada almost to the Gulf of Mexico. The Indians captured British forts and terrorized settlers along the frontier. The British, who finally put down Pontiac's revolt, took steps to prevent further problems in the West.

The king issued the Proclamation of 1763, which banned colonists from going west of the Appalachians. The British did not want traders or settlers stirring up unrest among the Indians. Settlers already there were asked to leave. Trappers and traders were allowed into the region only with official licenses. Such actions angered the colonists. They had fought to open the frontier to expansion during the war. And Britain was violating the charters that promised the colonies the land from the Atlantic to the Pacific.

Lesson

29

Student Text pages 74–76
Activity Manual pages 52–53

Lesson Focus

- Colonists resisted taxation because they had no say in Parliament.

Objectives

- Evaluate how colonists responded to Parliament's laws
- Explain people's reactions to the Townshend Acts in Massachusetts

Review

- Choose a volunteer to re-view what happened when three groups confronted each other in the Ohio River valley in 1754.

> Guide a review of important terms, maps, places, and people from each previous lesson. Direct the students to find and read the corresponding entries from the Resource Treasury.

- Invite a student to explain what contributed to the British defeat near Fort Duquesne.

  What did William Pitt do that helped change the course of the French and Indian War? Pitt sent much money to British generals in North America and Britain's allies in Europe.

- Choose a student to describe the capture of Quebec.

Preparation for Reading

- Generate interest as you direct the students to read the titles and examine the pictures on pages 74–76.
- Guide pronunciation of any unfamiliar words in the lesson.
- Instruct the students to read the pages silently to discover who the Sons of Liberty were. secret organizations that were set up to oppose the Stamp Act

Teach for Understanding

After King George III became the British king, which man did he choose as a new leader for Parliament? George Grenville

What did Britain attempt to do under these new leaders that caused new difficulties in the colonies? pay for the cost of the war

What act did Grenville lead Parliament to pass? the Stamp Act

What did the Stamp Act require of the colonists? Under this law, the thirteen colonies helped pay for stationing British troops in their colonies by buying stamps.

- Direct attention to the pictures of the British stamps on page 74.

  What items required stamps? certain legal documents, playing cards, dice, and newspapers or pamphlets

---

Leading in Another War
The Stamp Act

Soon after the peace treaty was signed in Paris, the British king chose a new leader for Parliament, George Grenville. King **George III** had become king in 1760. The new leaders created new difficulties between Britain and the colonies. Under these new leaders Britain tried to pay for the cost of the war.

Grenville became Britain's **prime minister**. He led Parliament to pass a law called the **Stamp Act**. Under this law, the thirteen colonies helped pay for stationing British troops in their colonies by buying stamps. The law made people pay for small stamps with some purchases. Items such as certain legal documents, playing cards, dice, and newspapers or pamphlets required stamps. For most purchases the stamps cost little. Parliament hoped to raise money in small amounts. The British did not think this law would trouble the colonists.

One-penny stamps bought by colonists

74

But the colonists did not react the way Parliament thought. They opposed the tax. In Virginia, a young lawyer named **Patrick Henry** led the House of Burgesses in opposing the law. Nine colonies sent representatives to New York City. In a meeting called the Stamp Act Congress, they wrote a petition to the king. They demanded that he **repeal** the law. Some colonies set up secret organizations called the **Sons of Liberty** to oppose the Stamp Act. In Boston and other cities, citizens formed angry mobs. They made dummies of tax collectors to burn. Sometimes the mobs damaged houses and property. Throughout the colonies, merchants refused to buy and sell British-made goods. People who opposed the British government called themselves **Patriots** or Whigs. Those who chose the king were called **Loyalists** or Tories.

These reactions had one complaint in common. The colonists believed that no free man should be taxed without having a say. If colonies did not send representatives to Parliament, then Parliament must not tax them.

Finally Parliament backed down. Britain did not agree that it could not tax the colonies. However, British merchants feared losing money. Many colonists would not buy their goods. Grenville resigned as prime minister, and the Stamp Act was repealed. But Parliament also passed the Declaratory Act, stating that Britain could legally tax the colonists whenever it wanted.

Why did the British not think this law would trouble the colonists? For most purchases the stamp cost little.

Who led the House of Burgesses in opposing the law? Patrick Henry

How did representatives from nine colonies express their displeasure in a meeting called the Stamp Act Congress? They wrote a petition to the king and demanded that he repeal the law.

Who were the Sons of Liberty? secret organizations set up to oppose the Stamp Act

- Invite several students to describe the actions of colonists who opposed the Stamp Act.

How did many colonists feel about Parliament taxing them? If colonies did not send representatives to Parliament, then Parliament must not tax them.

How did Parliament respond to the actions the colonists took? Parliament backed down. The Stamp Act was repealed.

What was the Declaratory Act? a law stating that Britain could legally tax the colonists whenever it wanted

The Townshend Acts

Parliament still wanted tax money from the colonies and formed a new plan. Charles Townshend was in charge of British taxes. In 1767 he proposed several laws. These laws, the **Townshend Acts**, raised taxes on paper, paint, lead, glass, and tea. The laws also attempted to stop **smuggling**. Smuggling is illegally bringing goods into a place. These laws sent British **customs agents** to the colonies to stop the smuggling. Parliament also made a law stating that accused smugglers could be tried without a jury.

The colonists became increasingly angry with Parliament and its laws. They still believed that only people who had representatives in Parliament should be taxed. They thought every English citizen deserved a jury trial. Many even supported smugglers. They bought smuggled goods, such as Dutch tea.

The colonies tried to protest the Townshend Acts much like they had the Stamp Act. Some refused to buy British goods. The colonial legislature in Massachusetts wrote a letter to all the other colonies asking them to oppose the Townshend Acts. Despite the opposition, Parliament refused to change the law.

Massachusetts showed more anger about the laws than any other colony.

The people of Boston protested, mobbed in the streets, and bought goods from smugglers. Finally in October 1768 the British government sent soldiers to Boston to be sure the laws were obeyed. This action made the situation worse. Many people in Boston complained that they were being treated like enemies, not citizens. The colonists mocked the soldiers and made their lives unpleasant.

Finally on March 5, 1770, violence broke out in Boston. That evening a mob surrounded a company of British soldiers. The mob threw snowballs, ice chunks, and paving stones. The soldiers were in danger of serious injury. In the confusion one soldier fired into the crowd. Then all the soldiers fired. Five colonists died, and six more were injured. This disturbing event was called the **Boston Massacre**.

Although one Boston man named **John Adams** defended the soldiers in court, most colonists were enraged with the British. They thought the soldiers meant to kill people. Britain moved its soldiers from the city to an island in the harbor. Over the next few months, news reached the colonies that the Townshend taxes were

75

Background

The Sons of Liberty

The Sons of Liberty were secret groups begun in 1765 in reaction to the Stamp Act. Their actions were directed against the symbols and representatives of British authority, including the property of customs agents and Loyalists. They burned officials in effigy, tarred and feathered tax collectors, dumped the tea into Boston Harbor, and intimidated those who seemed to support the Crown's rule, policies, and agents.

The Sons of Liberty were not officially or formally organized. Their leaders tended to come from the middle and upper levels of society; the regular members came from all social levels. Almost all the colonies had some such group, but Boston's was probably the most prominent. The leader of the Boston Sons of Liberty was Samuel Adams.

Some American leaders did not approve of the Sons of Liberty breaking the law by abusing tax collectors and destroying tea. They believed that opposition to unjust policies needed to be done lawfully.

Teach for Understanding

What did Charles Townshend do to raise taxes that Parliament wanted? He proposed the Townshend Acts.

What did the Townshend Acts try to prevent? smuggling

- Invite a student to explain the meaning of smuggling and tell how the Townshend Acts affected this activity. Explain that customs agents were sent to the colonies, and discuss what could happen to smugglers.

What were ways colonies tried to protest the Townshend Acts? Some refused to buy British goods. The colonial legislature in Massachusetts wrote a letter to all the other colonies asking them to oppose the Townshend Acts.

How did Parliament respond to opposition to the Townshend Acts? Parliament refused to change the law.

Where in the colonies was the most anger shown against Parliament and its laws? Boston, Massachussetts

Why did the British government send soldiers to Boston? to be sure the laws were obeyed

How did the people of Boston treat the soldiers? The colonists mocked them and made their lives unpleasant.

- Guide a discussion of which of the colonists' actions were appropriate and which actions were wrong (Romans 13:1–7; 1 Peter 2:13–17). Writing a petition to the king was not wrong. The colonists could refuse to buy or sell British goods. But the unruly actions by the mobs were wrong. Buying goods from smugglers was wrong because smuggling is illegal. Mocking the British soldiers and making their lives miserable was unkind and wrong.

How did the Boston Massacre happen? A mob surrounded a company of British soldiers and threw snowballs, ice chunks, and paving stones at them. In the confusion one soldier fired into the crowd, and then all the soldiers fired.

How did most colonists feel about the Boston Massacre? They thought the soldiers meant to kill people.

- What might be a reason that the British government moved its soldiers to an island? possibly to prevent provoking the colonists any more and to protect the soldiers from harassment; to stop another confrontation

Teach for Understanding

After the Townshend Acts were repealed, what was the only tax that still remained? **the tax on tea**

What was a concern that the colonists had for the next few years even though everything seemed calm? **They were concerned that Parliament and King George III were planning new attacks on the colonies' freedoms.**

Why did the colonies suspect Parliament of trickery when it allowed the British East India Company to sell tea directly to the colonies? **They thought Parliament was trying to get them to buy taxed tea.**

Why was the British East India Company unable to unload its wares? **The major port cities refused to give the tea ships permission to unload their wares.**

How did this matter become a problem for Boston? **Governor Thomas Hutchinson refused to allow the tea ships to sail from port without paying a fee; citizens refused to let the ships unload their tea; without selling the tea, the captains could not pay the fee; and a band of citizens boarded the ships and threw the tea overboard.**

How did the British government feel about the Boston Tea Party? **The British government was angry.**

How did Parliament try to coerce Boston to behave? **It passed a number of new laws.**

How did the laws threaten to destroy Boston? **They closed Boston's port to ships.**

What did colonists call these harsh new laws? **the Intolerable Acts**

How did the new laws affect the situation in Boston? **The situation grew worse and worse.**

Conclude the discussion by asking the question on page 76. **Colonists thought that they should not be taxed when they could not send representatives to Parliament.**

Activity Manual

- Guide completion of pages 52–53.

repealed. Only the tax on tea remained. Colonists were happy with that news. However, they remained concerned that British soldiers might show up in their towns and cities. For the next decade, Bostonians remembered each March 5 as Massacre Day.

The Tea Party

For the next few years, the colonies seemed calm. But in each colony some were concerned that Parliament and even King George III were planning new attacks on the colonies' freedoms. In 1773 conflict arose again.

Parliament feared that the British East India Company might go bankrupt. The company had many debts. Few colonists bought its tea. To help the company, Parliament allowed it to sell tea directly to the colonies. The tea tax still applied, but the cost would be less than the normal price for British tea. Maybe both the company and the colonists could be happy.

But the colonies suspected Parliament of trickery. They thought Parliament was trying to get them to buy taxed tea. The major port cities refused to give the tea ships permission to unload their wares.

In Boston, the matter became a problem. Governor Thomas Hutchinson refused to allow the tea ships to sail from port without paying a fee. The citizens refused to let the ships unload their tea. Without selling the tea, the captains could not pay the fee. On the night of December 16, 1773, Samuel Adams called together a band of citizens. Adams was a politician who organized the Sons of Liberty in Boston. Angered by the tea tax and by the Loyalist governor, the crowd marched to the docks. The people boarded the ships, threw the tea overboard, swept the decks clean, and left.

The consequences were severe. No people were hurt in the **Boston Tea Party**, but the British government was now angry. Laws stated that no one could destroy another person's property. Parliament passed a number of new laws to **coerce**, or force, Boston to behave. These laws were so harsh that the colonists did not believe they could accept them. The colonists believed the laws reduced their freedom beyond what was acceptable. The laws also threatened to destroy Boston. They even closed Boston's port to ships. The colonists called these laws the **Intolerable Acts**. The situation in Boston grew worse and worse.

> Why did some colonists think they should not have to obey the Stamp and Townshend Acts?

76

Background

Tea in Other Ports

Boston was not the only colonial port that faced an unwanted supply of tea. That city's "tea party" was copied in New York. Charleston stored its tea until the war broke out and then sold it at auction to help pay for colonial forces. Philadelphia let its tea rot in warehouses.

Minutemen

In rural towns surrounding Boston, the colonists began storing arms and ammunition in case armed resistance against the British became necessary. They also prepared their local militia. The youngest and most energetic militiamen were chosen to be minutemen. These men were to be ready to fight at a moment's notice.

War Begins

First Continental Congress

After Parliament passed the Intolerable Acts, the colonies were concerned for their future. Because the laws closed Boston's port, the merchants who brought money to Boston could not conduct their business. Perhaps all food would have to be delivered by land. Parliament's punishment might then affect all the colonies. If Parliament could close one city, other cities were threatened too.

In the fall of 1774, the thirteen colonies sent representatives to Philadelphia. These men met as a **Continental Congress** to discuss the situation in Boston. Their goal was to decide how all the colonies should deal with Parliament and King George.

The Continental Congress made several decisions. First, all the colonies agreed to **boycott** British goods. They thought boycotting might encourage Parliament to repeal the Intolerable Acts. Second, they wrote a letter to King George. They hoped that a respectful request for justice would receive a friendly response. Finally, they agreed to meet again the next year. Whether or not things went well, the colonies could talk matters over in May 1775.

The Battles of Lexington and Concord

While the Congress worked in Philadelphia, matters only got worse

Northeastern Battles

in Massachusetts. The British army under General Thomas Gage forced obedience to the new laws. Throughout the colony, militia forces trained as **minutemen**. They would be ready to fight at a minute's notice. Men opposed to Parliament, its taxes, and the king met outside Boston. They called their meeting a Provincial Congress of Massachusetts. Its two most important leaders were Samuel Adams and John Hancock. Adams helped lead the Sons of Liberty. Hancock was a successful businessman.

By spring 1775 General Gage had to act. He feared that the people of Massachusetts might rebel and attack him. He asked Parliament to send more soldiers, but Parliament refused. On April 14, 1775, Gage received detailed instructions. He was to capture the leaders of the rebellious colonists and seize their weapons and gunpowder.

77

Lesson **30**

 Lesson **30**

Student Text pages 77–79
Activity Manual pages 54–56

Lesson Focus

• Patriots continued to fight for independence from King George of Britain.

Objectives

• Identify decisions made by the Continental Congress
• Examine events leading to the Revolutionary War
• Recognize military leaders in the war

Teacher's Toolkit CD

• Visual 7: *Paul Revere's Ride*
• Instructional Aid 24: *Events Leading to War*

Review

• Review the previous lesson by writing the following dates for display. Invite volunteers to identify the event that happened on each date.

1767: Charles Townshend proposed new tax laws called the Townshend Acts.

March 5, 1770: Violence broke out in Boston called the Boston Massacre.

December 16, 1773: Citizens boarded ships and threw tea overboard in an event called the Boston Tea Party.

Preparation for Reading

• Generate interest as you direct the students to read the titles and examine the pictures on pages 77–79.
• Guide pronunciation of any unfamiliar words in the lesson.
• Direct the students to read the pages silently and complete Instructional Aid 24 in small groups.

Teach for Understanding

What was the meeting called that was held in Philadelphia to discuss the situation in Boston? the Continental Congress

• Guide a discussion of the decisions the Continental Congress made regarding Parliament and King George. Include that all the colonies agreed to boycott British goods; the representatives wrote a letter to King George hoping he would repeal the Intolerable Acts. They agreed to meet again the next year.

As the Congress worked in Philadelphia, did matters get better or worse in Massachusetts? worse

Who forced obedience to the new laws? the British army under General Thomas Gage

What characterized the minutemen who trained in the colonies? They would be ready to fight at a minute's notice.

What was the Provincial Congress of Massachusetts opposed to? Parliament, its taxes, and the British king

What fear did General Gage have about the people of Massachusetts? They might rebel and attack him.

What request of Gage's did Parliament disagree with? to send more soldiers

What detailed instructions did Gage receive from Parliament when he was denied more British soldiers? He was to capture leaders of the rebellious colonists and seize their weapons and gunpowder.

• Direct attention to the map on page 77. Point out several battles of the Revolutionary War.

Teach for Understanding

As British soldiers took small boats toward the road leading to Concord, who were the three Patriots who set out to warn Massachusetts of the coming troops? Paul Revere, William Dawes, and Samuel Prescott

- Display Visual 7. Guide a discussion of the picture and whether the picture is historically accurate since William Dawes and Samuel Prescott also warned of the British approach.

What did British troops find when they marched into Lexington, just outside Concord? the local militia assembled against them

What was the shot that was fired in the confusion there called? "the shot heard round the world"

What did the British do after winning the skirmish but realizing that the Patriot leaders had escaped? They marched on to Concord.

Under what conditions did the British soldiers march back to Boston? They were under constant attack by militiamen.

What did the British soldiers do in frustration? They burned and looted farmhouses along the road.

After the British soldiers reached Boston, how did they become trapped? News spread from Boston through Massachusetts and the rest of the colonies. Soon thousands of militiamen surrounded Boston, trapping the British in the city.

- Choose a volunteer to explain how the Patriots captured Fort Ticonderoga. Point out that the capture of the fort proved that Americans were determined to fight.

Activities

Read a Poem

Read aloud portions of Henry Wadsworth Longfellow's poem, "Paul Revere's Ride."

Learn About Paul Revere

Provide information about Paul Revere. Direct students to work in small groups to learn more about his life. Invite students to share what they learn about Paul Revere.

Choose Sides

Choose volunteers to pretend to be Loyalists, and choose volunteers to pretend to be Patriots. Invite students to explain why they decided to be a Loyalist or a Patriot during the Revolutionary War.

Gage tried to fulfill his command. Late in the evening of April 18, British soldiers left Boston. They took small boats toward the road leading to Concord. In Boston, Patriots heard of the boats. Three men, Paul Revere, William Dawes, and Samuel Prescott, set out to warn Massachusetts of the coming troops. The Patriots hoped to prevent the British from seizing Samuel Adams and John Hancock in Lexington and the military supplies in Concord.

British troops marched into the town of Lexington, just outside Concord. There they found the local militia assembled against them. British major John Pitcairn commanded the militia to leave. Then events became confused. Some turned to leave, but no American colonist was willing to give up his weapons. Someone, either a British soldier or a militiaman, fired. That shot became known as "the shot heard round the world." Soon both sides were firing. The British won the skirmish, but they did not find Adams and Hancock. The leaders had escaped. Unhappy, the British marched on to Concord.

The British arrival in Concord caused more problems. The soldiers discovered a stash of musket balls but little else. The surrounding countryside had heard of the British arrival. Minutemen from all over eastern Massachusetts poured into Concord. The British soldiers marched back to Boston under constant attack by militiamen. In frustration, the soldiers burned and looted farmhouses along the road. By the time they reached Boston, about 275 redcoats were dead or injured.

The First Battles

The **Battles of Lexington and Concord** were just the beginning of the conflict. News spread from Boston through Massachusetts and the rest of the colonies. Soon thousands of militiamen surrounded Boston. The British were trapped in the city.

Northwest of Massachusetts, in the region between New Hampshire and New York, another battle occurred. Ethan Allen, a well-educated farmer, and Benedict Arnold, a Connecticut merchant, led militias to capture Fort Ticonderoga. Allen's Green Mountain Boys and the Connecticut soldiers won without a battle. The British soldiers in the fort were caught asleep. Now the fort and its cannons were in Patriot hands. The capture of Ticonderoga proved that the Americans were determined to fight. Lexington and Concord were not just a mistake.

Battles for Boston

With British troops settled in Boston, Patriot forces moved toward

78

Background

The British Are Coming

The British commander, General Thomas Gage, learned of a stockpile of arms and ammunition in nearby Concord. He ordered a detachment of British soldiers to destroy it. He also gave orders to arrest two colonial leaders in nearby Lexington: Samuel Adams and John Hancock, who had left Boston seeking safety.

On the night of April 18, 1775, British troops left Boston and began their march toward Lexington and Concord. They hoped to surprise the colonists, but their departure did not go unnoticed. Samuel Prescott, William Dawes, and Paul Revere rode through the countryside warning colonists that the British were coming. As the soldiers marched, the alarm was spread. Bells rang and guns fired. Early the next morning the soldiers reached Lexington. In the middle of the town square, they encountered about seventy colonial minutemen. No one knows who fired first, but shots rang out. Eight colonists lay dead; ten more were wounded. The rest of the militiamen scattered. The British continued to Concord. There was a skirmish at North Bridge. As the British began their retreat to Boston, colonial minutemen fired at them from behind trees, stone walls, and buildings. The British made it back to Boston but suffered heavy losses.

the city. Since Boston was almost an island, troops easily **besieged** the city. The British navy sent reinforcements to Gage.

Citizens of Massachusetts had an important decision to make. Should they remain loyal to King George or join the revolution? Those who chose the king were called Loyalists. Those fighting for more freedoms were called Patriots. Most Patriots left Boston. Many Loyalists from the countryside moved to the city.

In June 1775 Patriot forces fought an important battle north of Boston. They tried to hold Breed's Hill against the British. This hill could house cannons. Today the battle is called the **Battle of Bunker Hill**. Although the Patriots lost the battle, they lost fewer men overall. The British began to wonder how much complete victory would cost. The Patriots would be hard to defeat.

Soon after the battle a new general arrived to lead the Patriot troops. George Washington of Virginia was the **commander in chief** of the Continental armies. By choosing a southerner to command a northern army, the Continental Congress showed that the war was for all Americans. Northerners and southerners would fight together for freedom. The soldiers were called **Continentals**. They would fight for all thirteen colonies, not just their own.

For the next several months, Washington and his army kept the British holed up in Boston. Finally in March 1776, the British gave up. They sailed out of Boston Harbor. Although the British would fight in other colonies, Massachusetts enjoyed its liberty.

Washington wore a coat sewn by a servant back at Mount Vernon. Although the colors of the coat were those of the Fairfax militia, Washington wore it throughout the Revolutionary War.

Washington was appointed commander in chief by unanimous vote. Despite his many accomplishments, George Washington entered the role with deep humility. Washington said to the delegates, "I do not think myself equal to the command I am honored with." In a letter to his wife he remarked, "So far from seeking this appointment I have used every endeavour in my power to avoid it, not only from my unwillingness to part with you and the Family, but from a consciousness of its being a trust too great for my Capacity."

Why did other colonies support Massachusetts after the Battles of Lexington and Concord?

79

The Battle of Bunker Hill

Back in Boston, the conflict continued to grow. While the Second Continental Congress debated the issues, the Boston Patriots took possession of Bunker and Breed's Hills on the Charleston peninsula, just across the bay from the city. Colonel William Prescott then ordered his men to build trenches in case of attack.

The British general Gage wanted to force the Americans from these hilltop positions. Reinforced by William Howe and his three thousand men, Gage ordered Howe to capture the hills. The first two assaults were driven back. On the third attempt, the colonists ran out of ammunition and were forced to retreat. Howe had won, but his casualties were heavy.

Teach for Understanding

Why was it easy for Patriots to besiege the city of Boston? It is almost an island and is easy to surround.

What was the battle where Patriots tried to hold Breed's Hill against the British in 1775? Battle of Bunker Hill

Who was the new southern general who would lead the Patriots as the commander in chief? George Washington

What did choosing a southern general to command a northern army show? that the war was for all Americans

What were the northern and southern soldiers called? Continentals

What happened in March 1776 after Washington and his army kept the British holed up in Boston? The British gave up and sailed out of Boston Harbor.

- Direct attention to the picture on page 79. Choose volunteers to read aloud the information.

▶▶ Conclude the discussion by asking the question on page 79. The other colonies saw that the Americans were determined to fight. The other colonies heard about the British soldiers burning and looting farmhouses along the road on their way to Boston.

Activity Manual

- Guide the students in locating the Biographical Dictionary and Gazateer in the Resource Treasury in the Student Text. These resources will be used in addition to the Glossary for Activity Manual page 55.

The quiz may be given any time after completing this lesson.

- Guide completion of pages 54–56.

Assessment

- Administer quiz.

Lesson Focus

- Colonists continued to fight the British as Patriots celebrated the birth of a new nation.

Objectives

- Understand the purpose of the Declaration of Independence
- Identify British gains and losses in the North

Teacher's Toolkit CD

- Visuals 8–10: *Washington Crossing the Delaware*; *Valley Forge*; *George Washington's Camp Chest*
- Instructional Aid 25: *Declaring Independence*

Review

What group of men met to decide how all the colonies should deal with Parliament and King George? the Continental Congress

What militia forces trained to be ready to fight at a minute's notice? minutemen

What happened after news spread throughout the colonies about the Battles of Lexington and Concord? Thousands of militiamen surrounded Boston. The British were trapped in the city.

Which southern general became the commander in chief of the Continental armies? George Washington

- Choose a volunteer to describe the result of Washington and his army keeping the British holed up in Boston. The British gave up and sailed out of Boston Harbor.

Preparation for Reading

- Generate interest as you direct the students to read the titles and examine the pictures on pages 80–82.
- Guide pronunciation of any unfamiliar words in the lesson.
- Direct the students to read the pages silently and complete Instructional Aid 25 in small groups.

Teach for Understanding

- Choose a group to tell what the Second Continental Congress continued working on after meeting on May 10, 1775.
- Select a group to tell the result of the vote by the Continental Congress to support the declaration.

What did the Declaration of Independence declare? "These United Colonies are, and of Right ought to be Free and Independent States."

- Invite a group to explain how the declaration created the birth of a new nation.

The First Years of War: Fighting in the North
Declaring Independence

While Washington and the Continentals kept the British confined in Boston, the Continental Congress stayed busy. The Second Continental Congress began meeting on May 10, 1775, and continued throughout the war. The delegates tried to raise money for the war. Robert Morris of Pennsylvania helped run the finances. He spent much of his own money to pay for Washington's soldiers. The Congress also sent men to request help from foreign countries. If a nation agreed to a treaty, the Congress reviewed and signed it. In addition, only the Congress could appoint men to positions as army officers. All these responsibilities kept them busy. Perhaps the most famous work of the Continental Congress was writing a document to define why the war was being fought. The result was the **Declaration of Independence**.

Thomas Jefferson of Virginia is known as the author of the declaration. Several other delegates gave Jefferson advice on his draft. Jefferson put together the final proposal. His words form the foundation of the declaration.

Every colony took part in voting on the declaration. Some delegates wanted more time. John Adams, cousin of Samuel Adams, encouraged the Congress to vote. After much discussing, editing, and voting, the Continental Congress voted unanimously to support the document. The congressmen did not think that signing the document made them free. It simply declared a fact that existed. "These United Colonies are, and of Right ought to be Free and Independent States." Hereafter they no longer thought of themselves as colonies. They were states.

Twelve of the thirteen states adopted the declaration on July 2, 1776. After Congress made some changes to the Declaration of Independence, it was officially adopted on **July 4, 1776**. Bells rang throughout Philadelphia. As the news spread to each state, Patriots celebrated the birth of a new nation.

The British in New York

But 1776 had defeats as well as triumphs. After the British left Boston, they sailed for New York City. George Washington traveled by land to set up a defense, but no one knew whether or not he could save the city.

During the summer and fall, the British army and navy fought in and around New York. They seized the major islands and marched inland. Although Washington fought several battles, he was unable to stop the British troops. By November the British held New York City.

80

- Direct attention to Instructional Aid 25. Read aloud the paragraph about the first reading of the Declaration of Independence. Guide a discussion about Independence Hall and the Liberty Bell.

What was the outcome of Washington fighting the British to save New York City? By November the British held New York City.

Nathan Hale

Who: a schoolteacher
When: June 6, 1755–September 22, 1776
Where: Connecticut and New York

Nathan Hale grew up in Connecticut and went to Yale College at age fourteen. After graduating, Hale became a teacher and militiaman. In July 1775 he joined the Continental army and was eventually promoted to captain. In September 1776 Hale accepted a dangerous mission. He became a spy. He dressed as a civilian and went behind enemy lines on Long Island, New York. Hale was soon caught. Because the British found him as a spy and not a soldier, he was hanged. But Nathan Hale's short life is remembered in what are recorded as his last words. "I only regret that I have but one life to lose for my country."

Christmas in New Jersey

Although he had lost New York City, Washington did not lose hope. He and his men settled in Pennsylvania for the winter. Some soldiers gave up and went back to their homes. On Christmas Day, Washington took a dangerous chance. Across the **Delaware River** in Trenton, New Jersey, a group of Hessians, German soldiers hired by the British, were celebrating Christmas. Hoping that they would be unprepared, Washington sneaked his men over the river. Although threatened by ice in the river and snow and wind in the air, his army marched against the Hessians. Surprising them, the Continentals captured one thousand men and many supplies. After recrossing the river, Washington's army settled with hope that the new year would bring more victories.

1777: Gains and Losses

After losing Boston and gaining New York City, the British needed to make more gains. In 1777 they tried two major northern campaigns.

Philadelphia

Philadelphia was the next major city the British wanted to capture. Not only was it large, but it also housed the Continental Congress.

In late August a British army commanded by General William Howe landed south of Philadelphia. He marched up toward the city. Washington stationed troops on the Brandywine Creek to stop the British advance. On September 11, 1777,

81

Teach for Understanding

- Choose a student to read aloud the Biography box on page 81. Use the information to guide a discussion about Nathan Hale.

  What did Washington and his men do on Christmas Day in New Jersey? They sneaked across the Delaware and were victorious against the Hessians.

- Direct attention to Visual 8. Guide a discussion of how Washington and his men may have felt as they took a dangerous chance in crossing the Delaware River and facing the Hessians.

  What did the Continentals capture from the Hessians? 1,000 men and many supplies

  How did this victory make Washington and his men feel? It gave them hope that the new year would bring more victories.

  What was the next major city the British wanted to capture after gaining New York City? Philadelphia

  What was housed in Philadelphia? the Continental Congress

  What British general landed south of Philadelphia and marched up toward the city? General William Howe

  Where did Washington station his troops? on the Brandywine Creek

Nathan Hale: The Schoolmaster Who Gave His Life

One problem Washington faced in New York was the desperate need for information about British plans and troops on Long Island. When officers were asked to volunteer for this dangerous task, there was only one volunteer. He was a schoolteacher from East Haddam, Connecticut, named Nathan Hale. Hale is considered to be the first spy for the United States.

Hale had no special training for such a mission. He did have his Yale diploma, however, which enabled him to travel as a schoolmaster. He was thus able to work his way south from Connecticut to Long Island in a few days.

But Hale had no sooner gotten information on Long Island when William Howe forced the Continental army across to Manhattan. Because his information about Long Island would now be of less value, Hale pursued the British army up Manhattan Island. There, on the night of September 21, he was captured. The information he was carrying implicated him, and Howe ordered him hanged the next morning without even a trial.

Captain Frederick Mackenzie, a British officer who described Hale's death, wrote, "He behaved with great composure and resolution." He added that some of Hale's last words were, "It is the duty of every good officer to obey any orders given him by his commander-in-chief."

Lesson

31

Teach for Understanding

- Direct attention to the picture on page 82. Choose volunteers to read aloud the captions.

  What happened on September 11, 1777? Howe defeated Washington, and the British advanced into Philadelphia.

  What did the members of the Continental Congress do? They fled to neighboring cities.

  After Washington lost the battle at Germantown, where did he spend the winter? at Valley Forge

- Display Visual 9 and lead a discussion of the hardships Washington and his men would have faced during the long, cold winter at Valley Forge.

- Display Visual 10. Invite students to name some things that George Washington carried in his camp chest.

  Where else was the British army advancing besides Pennsylvania? New York State

  Which British general recaptured Fort Ticonderoga and then proceeded toward New York City? General John Burgoyne

  Who commanded the American forces as they fought the British at Saratoga? General Horatio Gates

  What was the outcome of the Battle at Saratoga? On October 7 the Americans won the battle. On October 17 Burgoyne surrendered to Gates.

  How was this victory a turning point in the war? For the first time a British army surrendered. Washington and his men were encouraged. The French decided to help the Americans.

   Conclude the discussion by asking the question on page 82. Saratoga

Activity Manual

- Guide completion of pages 57–58.

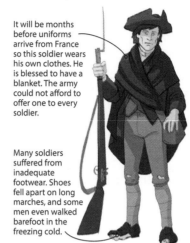

This soldier is an immigrant from Ireland. Irish immigrants made up a large portion of the American troops.

It will be months before uniforms arrive from France so this soldier wears his own clothes. He is blessed to have a blanket. The army could not afford to offer one to every soldier.

Many soldiers suffered from inadequate footwear. Shoes fell apart on long marches, and some men even walked barefoot in the freezing cold.

Howe's army defeated Washington. After a few minor skirmishes, the British advanced into Philadelphia.

The capture of the city did not end the war. The congressmen fled to neighboring cities. Washington kept fighting. He lost a battle at Germantown in early October, but he did not give up. The commander in chief spent a long cold winter at **Valley Forge**, about twenty miles from Philadelphia.

Saratoga

As one British army advanced into Pennsylvania, another marched into New York State. Led by General John Burgoyne, this force came down from Canada. The British hoped this army would be able to separate New England from the other states.

Burgoyne's march south began with success. He recaptured Fort Ticonderoga. Then he proceeded toward New York City.

American forces under the command of General **Horatio Gates** did their best to stop the British. The two sides first fought at **Saratoga**, New York, on September 19. The Patriot forces did not defeat the British. The battle left both sides wounded, and the British waited for reinforcements that never came. On October 7 the two sides fought again, and the Americans won the battle. On October 17 Burgoyne surrendered to Gates.

The American victory at Saratoga is remembered as the turning point of the war. For the first time a British army surrendered. The news traveled to Pennsylvania. Washington and his men were encouraged. News of the victory also traveled to Europe. The French, longtime enemies of the British, decided to help the Americans. They resolved to send money and military support. Anyone who could defeat the British was a friend of the French.

> What battle encouraged France to support the United States in fighting for independence?

82

Background

Valley Forge

Word of the French alliance did not reach America until the spring of 1778. Meanwhile, Washington and his army went through perhaps the darkest period of the war. With the British controlling Philadelphia, the American army made its headquarters for the winter of 1777–78 some twenty-five miles away at Valley Forge. The army had to build its camp from scratch. A city of wooden barracks and huts soon sprouted in Valley Forge, but its citizens were hungry and ill clothed. Few men had whole uniforms, and even fewer had shoes. Washington grimly observed that "you might have tracked the army from White Marsh to Valley Forge by the blood of their feet."

Washington could do little to relieve the suffering of his men. For one thing, the general had only the worthless paper currency of the Continental Congress to buy supplies. Farmers and merchants found it far more profitable to sell their goods to the British in Philadelphia who paid in gold and silver. Despite the hardships, Washington's men bore up surprisingly well. Some even joked about their ragged condition. A group of officers, for example, held a party to which no one was admitted who had a whole pair of pants.

The War and American Life
Paying for the War

The cost of the war created problems in the thirteen states. The Continental Congress first paid its bills by printing paper money. By 1780 it had printed well over two hundred million dollars. Before the war the colonists usually used gold or silver money. Most people preferred gold or silver to paper. People often would not accept paper money for face value. A merchant selling cloth might accept one dollar in gold or silver or else fifteen paper dollars. Each state charged taxes that paper **Continental dollars** could pay. These taxes made Americans angry. The problem of paper money lasted throughout the war.

Loans from foreign countries helped pay for the war. France loaned the United States millions of dollars. France also encouraged the Netherlands to loan money to the states. This money helped pay for military equipment and other supplies. France hoped that the states would win their independence. If not, this money would all be lost.

In order to raise money and foreign support, the Continental Congress sent **envoys** to Europe. An envoy is a representative of one country to another. These envoys tried to persuade other countries to recognize the states as a new nation. Later they worked to raise money. Perhaps the most important was Benjamin Franklin, who served in France during the war. When the war broke out, Franklin was already famous as an inventor, printer, and scientist. His missions to France gained much sympathy for the Revolution. John Adams also served as an envoy. He distrusted the French. By the end of the war, he preferred to deal directly with the British.

Each of the thirteen states tried to raise money. They taxed their citizens. They also issued paper money. States borrowed much money to help pay for the war. As time went on, they slowly repaid their debts. Some hoped that the national government would pay all the debts once the war ended.

83

Lesson Focus

- Foreign countries and United States civilians played a role in the Revolutionary War.

Objectives
- Examine how the war was supported financially
- Identify the role of foreign soldiers in the war
- Describe the impact of the war on civilian life

Review

- Use questions such as the following to review the previous lesson.

  What document created the birth of a new nation? the Declaration of Independence

  Who is considered to be the author of the Declaration of Independence? Thomas Jefferson

  When did Americans learn that Congress had passed the declaration? July 4, 1776

  Why did Washington cross the Delaware River on Christmas Day? to march against the Hessians

  Why was the Battle of Saratoga significant? It was the turning point of the war. For the first time a British army surrendered. The French decided to help the Americans.

Preparation for Reading

- Generate interest as you direct the students to read the titles and examine the pictures on pages 83–85.
- Guide pronunciation of any unfamiliar words in the lesson.
- Instruct the students to find out the term for representatives that the Continental Congress sent to Europe to raise money and foreign support. envoys

Teach for Understanding

  What did the Continental Congress first use to pay its bills? paper money

  Before the war what had colonists usually used for money? gold or silver

  What were Continental dollars? paper money printed by the Continental Congress to fund the war

- Direct attention to the picture on page 83.

  What problem did using Continental dollars present? People often would not accept paper money for face value.

  Who was an important envoy to France who gained much sympathy for the revolution? Benjamin Franklin

  How did states try to raise money for the war? They taxed their citizens. They issued paper money. They borrowed money.

Teach for Understanding

How did the British government meet the need for more soldiers? It hired mercenaries.

What was the reaction of Americans to Britain sending the Hessians to fight against them? They were displeased. Hessians were believed to have bad morals. Americans thought that no free people should be oppressed by hired soldiers.

What was the attitude of some German mercenaries? They often did not like their job. Many Hessians deserted the British fight and settled themselves in America.

What French nobleman joined the cause for American independence when he was nineteen? the Marquis de Lafayette

How did the Prussian nobleman Baron von Steuben help the fight for American independence? He drilled and trained the Continentals into a more professional force.

How did Thaddeus Kosciuszko from Poland help defeat the British? He served as an engineer who designed and built fortifications.

Foreigners in America

Hessians

In order to have enough soldiers, the British government hired **mercenaries**. Most of these men were from German states. They were usually called Hessians, although not all came from Hesse.

Americans were displeased that the king sent foreigners to fight them. The Hessians were believed to have bad morals. Americans thought that no free people should be oppressed by hired soldiers.

German mercenaries often did not like their jobs. Poor German princes sometimes sent unwilling men to fight in order to earn money. Many Hessians deserted the British fight and settled themselves in America.

Supporters

The colonists received help from foreign soldiers who knew how European warfare worked. Perhaps the most famous was the **Marquis de Lafayette**. This French nobleman joined the cause for American independence when he was only nineteen. For the remainder of the war, he worked tirelessly to support the Continental army. He and Washington had a close friendship. When Lafayette's wife had a son, he was named Georges Washington de Lafayette.

After a brief return to France in 1779, Lafayette rejoined the war and promised French military support.

He continued to lead Continental forces until the end of the war. When Washington planned his final campaign, he relied on Lafayette. The French officer kept the British busy until Washington could arrive himself. Probably more than any other non-American, Lafayette helped the thirteen states win their independence.

Other men also helped. Baron von Steuben was a Prussian nobleman. He drilled and trained the Continentals into a far more professional force. Thaddeus Kosciuszko from Poland served as an engineer. He designed and built fortifications. From Vermont to South Carolina, his work helped defeat the British.

Lafayette was a celebrated French aristocrat. Congress gave him an officer rank in the Continental army. The title was to be only an honorary one, but after Lafayette was wounded in the Battle of Brandywine, Congress voted to give him command of a division. Washington and Lafayette became lifelong friends, and Lafayette was a great asset to the Revolution.

84

Activity

Create a Timeline Map

Materials: large white sheet of construction paper for each student

Invite the students to draw a map and to label the major battles, events, and dates of events. Remind the students to include a title, a compass rose, and a map key.

How It Was

Not far away Andrew heard troops marching. The cicadas buzzed in the oaks above. Patches of sunlight dappled the forest. He tried to lie still, ignore the sweat dripping in his eyes, and think. The message from the wounded Patriot scout seemed to burn in his fingers like a hot coal. He knew the words by heart. *Attack on border farms planned tonight.* If he could just get the information through to the Patriot militia, perhaps it could stop the British troops. But if he moved too fast, the enemy might hear. If he were discovered, his courier mission would fail. All would be lost.

Andrew lay thinking of his mother and family. The British troops might be marching to Patriot homes. He had seen what the British did at other farms. They took the animals. They forced old men to fight. Who would keep the farms going? Andrew stuffed the message deep in his pocket near his pounding heart. Slowly he drew himself upright and began his cautious trip to the Patriot forces. *Keep clear of the British. And keep a clear head—till the mission is done.*

Civilian Life

Never during the war did all thirteen states face much warfare. Until the evacuation of Boston in 1776, Massachusetts dealt with many British troops in the East. Virginia had no military threats until the end of the war. Other states had long periods of fighting. South Carolina suffered through many Revolutionary War battles. Troops remained in New York until the end of the war.

But even when armies were not ranging across fields or settled in cities, the war made civilian life difficult.

Many men left their homes and farms to fight. Men from Delaware left to fight in the Carolinas. Women, old men, and young boys often took up the work left behind. The states tried to support the Continental army with supplies. Food, clothing, horses, and wagons could all help the army. Despite the heavy cost of the war, many Americans were Patriots. They wanted to see their country free.

> Which inventor and scientist worked hard to raise support for the United States?

85

Teach for Understanding

- Direct attention to the picture on page 85 and the How It Was box. Read the story aloud.

  What is Andrew attempting to do in this story? warn the Patriot militia of the approaching British troops

  What did he fear the British troops might do if they reached the homes of Patriots? They might take the farm animals or force the old men to fight.

  How did Andrew proceed after stuffing the message deep in his pocket? cautiously; slowly

- Invite a volunteer to suggest what it may have been like for American children during the Revolutionary War.

  How did the Revolutionary War impact civilian life? The war made civilian life difficult. Many men left their homes and farms to fight. Women, old men, and young boys often took up the work left behind. States tried to support the Continental army with supplies.

  How did Americans feel about the war? Many were Patriots. They wanted to see their country free.

   Conclude the discussion by asking the question on page 85. Benjamin Franklin

Activity Manual

- Guide completion of page 59.

Lesson

33

Student Text pages 86–88
Activity Manual pages 60–61

Lesson Focus

- Revolutionary War battles were fought in the North, South, East, and West.

Objectives

- Describe Revolutionary War fighting in different parts of the nation
- Examine how Patriots persisted in fighting for independence

Teacher's Toolkit CD

- Instructional Aid 26: *The West and the South*

Review

- Use questions such as the following to review the previous lesson.

What is an envoy? An envoy is a representative of one country to another.

What was the job of the envoys the Continental Congress sent to Europe? They tried to persuade other countries to recognize the states as a new nation. Later they worked to raise money.

Who was an important envoy who served in France during the war? Benjamin Franklin

Who were the mercenaries? soldiers hired by the British government, usually from Germany

Who was a French nobleman who helped the Continental army from the time he was nineteen until the end of the war? the Marquis de Lafayette

Preparation for Reading

- Generate interest as you direct the students to read the titles and examine the pictures and map on pages 86–88.
- Guide pronunciation of any unfamiliar words in the lesson.
- Direct the students to read the pages silently and complete Instructional Aid 26 in small groups.

Teach for Understanding

Where did the British hold some frontier forts? in the West, although most were in the upper Mississippi River basin

- Choose a group to tell why George Rogers Clark is considered to be a hero of the frontier.
- Select a group to explain why American Indians sided with the British in the Revolutionary War.
- Invite a volunteer from one of the groups to explain Joseph Brant's role in the war.

The West and the South
Frontier Fighting

Not every battle of the Revolution took place in the East. The British held some frontier forts in the West, although most were in the upper Mississippi River basin.

George Rogers Clark was the hero of the frontier. He fought British troops in several battles. When the British regained territory, Clark came back to fight again. He then defeated a new British force. Clark's battles gave the new nation a strong claim to the frontier. The lands he won formed the basis of five midwestern states.

American Indians

In addition to British troops, Clark fought against American Indians. Many Indians sided with the French in the French and Indian War. During the Revolution, the Indians usually favored the British. The British had two advantages. They offered better rewards to tribes that allied with them. Controlling trade allowed the British to give valuable goods to friendly tribes. More importantly, most tribes knew that the Americans wanted to spread farther west and south. If the British won, perhaps Indian lands would be left alone.

In the North, the Iroquois mainly supported the British. This confederation of tribes had supported the British during the French and Indian War as well. **Joseph Brant** was one of the most important chiefs. He fought in many battles against the American forces. Brant tried to get other tribes to support the British as well. At one point, he went west and helped defeat George Rogers Clark. After the war Brant and many Loyalist Iroquois moved to Canada.

In the South, the British tried to raise local Indian support against the states. Members of the Creek and Seminole tribes helped fight in Georgia and South Carolina. After the war, the people of these states continued to be angry with tribes that had fought against them.

During the Revolutionary War, young Andrew Jackson refused to shine the muddy boots of a British officer and received a saber cut across his hand and forehead. These marks stayed with him his entire life.

86

After the war, where did Brant and many Loyalist Iroquois move? to Canada

What Indian support did the British have in the South? Members of the Creek and Seminole tribes helped fight in Georgia and South Carolina.

How did the people of these states feel toward these tribes after the war? They continued to be angry with tribes that had fought against them.

- Direct attention to the picture on page 86. Read the caption aloud.

British soldier
The British military was well trained and had much more experience than the Continentals.

Hessian mercenary
Britain hired thousands of these mercenaries, professional foreign soldiers, to serve in almost every major battle.

Continental regular
Baron von Steuben trained these inexperienced and ill-equipped soldiers to fight respectably against European soldiers.

Minuteman
These men could be ready at a moment's notice. They were excellent marksmen and kept their guns nearby at all times.

The South

After giving up Philadelphia in 1778, the British moved south. They hoped to have more success there than in the North. Many in Britain believed that the South was full of Loyalists. They thought that a British army's arrival would change the course of the war. If Britain could gain the South, it would have a secure base to fight the northern rebels.

At first the British proved successful. In December 1778 they claimed Savannah, Georgia. This port city was a gateway to the South. Despite this victory, British troops had little control away from Savannah. In late 1779 more troops left New York to capture the South's largest city, Charleston, South Carolina. In May 1780 the city and over four thousand Patriot troops surrendered. General **Charles Cornwallis**, a British nobleman, was left to lead the British into the interior of the southern states. The British hoped he would unify the South as Loyalist colonies.

Patriot Persistence

Although its biggest cities fell, the South was not conquered. It was also not completely Loyalist. Militias and a portion of the Continental army continued to resist the British. Many southerners rejoined the Patriot forces when the British demanded that they fight against fellow Americans. Men such as **Francis Marion** and **Thomas**

87

- Choose a group to explain why the British thought they would have more success in the South after giving up Philadelphia in 1778.

  As the British advanced to the South, which two port cities did they take control of? Savannah, Georgia; Charleston, South Carolina

- Select a group to tell what the British hoped General Charles Cornwallis would be able to do in the southern states.

  Why was the South not conquered? It was not completely Loyalist. Militias and a portion of the Continental army resisted the British. Many southerners rejoined the Patriot forces when the British demanded that they fight against fellow Americans.

- Direct attention to the picture on page 87. Read aloud the captions. Guide a discussion of the differences between the types of soldiers and their uniforms.

  Who gathered militias to harass British troops? Francis Marion and Thomas Sumter

Flags of the Revolutionary War

Materials: construction paper

Direct the students to research flags used by the colonists during the Revolutionary War. Invite each student to make one of the flags out of construction paper. Display the flags.

Lesson

33

Teach for Understanding

- Direct attention to the map on page 88. Invite volunteers to point out several battle locations.

Who won the battle when General Gates met Cornwallis in Camden, South Carolina? the British

What happened at the Battle of Kings Mountain? Patriot forces trapped and defeated a Loyalist army.

How did the British respond to this defeat? They responded with cruelty to many civilians in the Carolinas. Houses and farms were looted and burned. Civilians were sometimes killed.

Who was the new Quaker general sent to the Continental army in the South? Nathanael Greene

What happened when Greene fought Cornwallis at Guilford Courthouse? The British won this battle but lost far more men than Greene lost.

Why did Cornwallis think that Greene would win in the Carolinas and Georgia? Greene was persistent.

▶ Conclude the discussion by asking the question on page 88. They gathered militias to harass British troops. They ducked into the wilderness to avoid losing a fight. Then they would return to skirmish again.

Activity Manual

- Guide completion of pages 60–61.

Southeastern Battles

Sumter gathered militias to harass British troops. Often unable to fight major battles, they ducked into the wilderness to avoid losing a fight. Then they would return to skirmish again. The British found these tactics hard to defeat.

During the summer of 1780, Congress sent General Gates, the hero of Saratoga, to fight for the Patriot cause in the South. He rushed his army to meet Cornwallis in battle. In Camden, South Carolina, the British won a crushing victory. Almost two thousand of Gates's five thousand men were killed, wounded, or captured. Gates headed north in disgrace. The British seemed ready to conquer.

Even without a famous general, the Patriots of the South refused to give up. Patriot forces trapped and defeated a Loyalist army at the Battle of Kings Mountain in October 1780. While no British bases were lost, their army had lost an advantage. The British responded with cruelty to many civilians in the Carolinas. Houses and farms were looted and burned. Civilians were sometimes killed.

George Washington advised Congress to send a new general to the Continental army in the South. **Nathanael Greene** was from a Quaker family in Rhode Island. His task of bringing victory and peace to the South was challenging. His army was from Maryland and Delaware and was unfamiliar with the land. Local militias were fighting diligently against British and Loyalist forces. Although Greene strengthened his forces, he was unable to decisively defeat Cornwallis. But Greene persisted in fighting when he could. He wanted to prevent the British from gaining control of the interior of the South. Finally, Greene fought Cornwallis at Guilford Courthouse in western North Carolina. The British won this battle in March 1781 but lost far more men than Greene. Cornwallis realized that Greene's persistent strategy would win in the Carolinas and Georgia.

> What tactics did Patriot militias use to defeat the British in the South?

88

Background

Swamp Surprises

One small band of South Carolinians kept the war alive in the British-occupied low country of South Carolina. The group was "distinguished by small black leather caps and the wretchedness of their attire; their number did not exceed twenty men and boys, some white, some black, and all mounted, but most of them miserably equipped." The leader of this motley assortment of guerrillas was the elusive General Francis Marion, who soon earned the nickname "Swamp Fox."

Marion and his men would slip out of the swamps and sand flats to attack British outposts and supply lines. Such small guerrilla bands, of course, could not beat a British army in open battle. Their strategic importance lay in pressuring the enemy. Marion's successful hit-and-run operations pinned down British troops, kept them from joining the main British force, and forced Cornwallis to keep looking over his shoulder. Banastre Tarleton gave begrudging respect to the "Swamp Fox" when he declared that "the devil himself could not catch" Marion.

The Last Battle and Peace
Yorktown

Rather than fight small battles again and again, Cornwallis decided to move the war to Virginia. Major Patriot leaders such as Washington and Jefferson were from that state. It provided supplies to the Continental forces. Cornwallis hoped that by controlling Virginia, the British could gain the victory against all thirteen states.

After arriving, Cornwallis led his troops into eastern Virginia where he marched on the city of Charlottesville. Few Patriot forces were in the state. Washington and his army still planned on retaking New York City. Late in the summer of 1781, Washington moved his troops down to Virginia.

The American strategy was risky. If enough troops could gather to trap Cornwallis and his army on a peninsula, a French fleet might be able to block British supplies. Washington had a poor record of defeating British armies in battle. The French had a poor record of defeating the British at sea. Despite this history, Washington and his French allies had no choice but to try for a victory.

The plans began to fall into place. The British fleet doubted that the French could block **Chesapeake Bay**. When the British ships arrived in early September, they realized that they were outnumbered. Aided by the French, Washington set up artillery outside the British lines in **Yorktown**. On October 9 the guns began firing. The outnumbered British troops had no hope of victory.

On the afternoon of October 19, 1781, Cornwallis sent his second in command to

Surrender of Lord Cornwallis by John Trumbull
As a child, John Trumbull lost the use of one eye, but that loss did not prevent him from becoming a famous painter later in life. Trumbull painted scenes of the American Revolution with the encouragement of his tutor, Benjamin West. Trumbull had served as a personal aide to George Washington and observed the Battle of Bunker Hill firsthand.

89

Lesson 34

Student Text pages 89–91
Activity Manual page 62

Lesson Focus

- Americans fought one more battle before signing a peace treaty with Britain.

Objectives
- Describe the final conflict of the Revolutionary War
- Examine agreements after the war

Materials
- A large timeline with important dates from the chapter. (*Note*: A timeline may be made using white construction paper.)
- Sources for information about each date you choose for the timeline activity
- Items or clothing to represent the colonial Revolutionary War period

Review

- Use questions such as the following to review the previous lesson.

  Who was the hero of the frontier? George Rogers Clark

Who was Joseph Brant? He was an important Iroquois chief who fought in many battles against the American forces.

What ports in the South were taken by the British? Savannah, Georgia; Charleston, South Carolina

Who led British troops into the southern states to unify the South as Loyalist colonies? General Charles Cornwallis

What men gathered militias to harass British troops? Francis Marion and Thomas Sumter

What American general led forces against Cornwallis in the South at Guilford Courthouse? Nathanael Greene

Preparation for Reading

- Generate interest as you direct the students to read the titles and examine the pictures on pages 89–91.
- Guide pronunciation of any unfamiliar words in the lesson.
- Direct the students to read the pages silently to find out the name of the last battle of the Revolutionary War. Yorktown

Teach for Understanding

What was the American strategy to defeat the British in Virginia? If enough troops could gather to trap Cornwallis and his army on a peninsula, a French fleet might be able to block British supplies.

What is the name of the bay that the French blocked? Chesapeake Bay

When the British ships arrived in early September, what did they realize? They were outnumbered.

With the help of the French, where did Washington set up artillery outside the British lines? Yorktown

What happened on October 19, 1781? Cornwallis sent his second in command to surrender.

- Read aloud the information about the artist John Trumbull's painting at the bottom of the page.

Activity

Illustrate the Revolutionary War
Materials: white paper

Explain that pictures help people understand history. Direct the students to illustrate a famous person, fort, or event from the Revolutionary War. Remind the students to include a title with their drawing. Invite students to share and explain their drawings.

Teach for Understanding

What made the British realize it was time to agree that the thirteen colonies were now independent states? The Continental army had triumphed over the major forces, and few members of Parliament wanted to send more soldiers to North America. Battles against French and Spanish forces were also expensive.

What country gained the most benefits from the Treaty of Paris? the United States

What did the United States receive? It received land south of the Great Lakes and all land east of the Mississippi except for Florida. American fishermen could fish from the Grand Banks off Canada.

What benefits did France receive? It regained fishing rights off the coast of Canada. Two small islands were returned to France.

What did Britain lose in North America after the war? It lost its thirteen main colonies.

What did Britain realize it would gain by staying on friendly terms with the United States? Much valuable trade would continue.

Activity

The Peace of Paris
Guide a discussion of the treaty. Invite students to decide whether the treaty was fair and to state reasons for their decision.

Background

Religion in America After the War
The Revolutionary War changed American religion. Independence from Britain assured freedom from the Anglican Church, although some states still had officially recognized churches. But Americans after the war began to question state-supported religious authorities. Congregational churches became less popular. The decline of these churches gave new groups, such as the Baptists and Methodists, space to grow. The Baptists and Methodists were better prepared than the older churches to reach out to the people. They were zealous in spreading the gospel, and their churches had a more flexible structure. They allowed unpaid laymen to pastor churches—helping end a shortage of ministers—while other denominations did not. Their emphasis on liberty also appealed to the common people of the young republic.

---

surrender. The second-to-last major British army in the thirteen states had lost. British troops still held New York City, portions of the southern coast, and scattered forts, but the Continental army had triumphed over the major forces. Back in Britain few members of Parliament wanted to send more soldiers to North America. Battles against French and Spanish forces were also expensive. It was time to agree that the thirteen colonies were now independent states. The only matter left to settle was how much Britain had lost.

The Peace of Paris

After Yorktown, Americans in Europe began to work out a peace treaty with Britain. There were some major questions. Would the new nation gain land west of the Proclamation Line of 1763? Could Americans still fish off the coast of Canada? What would happen to Loyalists? Other nations were involved too. France was fighting Britain as an ally of the United States. Spain was fighting Britain as France's ally. Even the Netherlands had joined in fighting Britain. No politician in Britain wanted to be the person to surrender valuable possessions.

Despite these problems the nations made agreements. The United States gained more benefits than any other nation. The land south of the Great Lakes would go to the states. Except for Florida, the states also received all land east of the Mississippi River. American fishermen could fish from the Grand Banks off Canada.

France received some benefits from defeating Britain. It regained fishing rights off the coast of Canada. Additionally, two small islands were returned to France. France had lost Saint Pierre and Miquelon to Britain during the course of the revolution.

The other two countries received less. The Netherlands gained nothing. Spain received part of Florida from Britain, but it did not regain Gibraltar. This tiny peninsula juts from Spain's southern coast and guards the entrance of the Mediterranean. Since Spain had not captured it during the war, Britain refused to give it up.

Overall, Britain lost much. Here and there around the world it lost small possessions. In North America it lost its thirteen main colonies. But as time went on, Britain realized that by staying on friendly terms with the new nation, much valuable trade would continue. From 1607 until the 1760s, Britain and the colonies had close ties. Two decades of unrest and then warfare did not completely destroy their relationship.

America Independent

During the months between Yorktown and the treaty, Americans worked diligently on their new nation.

Teach for Understanding

When did the last British troops leave New York City? in 1783

What did Americans look forward to independence bringing? good governments, new constitutions for their states, new prosperity, settling lands west of the Appalachians, more trade

 How did the colonists prove that they had the right to be independent states and a unique nation? by fighting hard in the Revolutionary War

Conclude the discussion by asking the question on page 91. Yorktown

Activity Manual

- Guide completion of page 62.

All thirteen states worked together in the new government. Finally, in 1783 independence was achieved. The last British troops left New York City. The war was over.

Americans looked forward to what independence would bring. They wanted to have good government. They wrote new constitutions for their states. They planned on new prosperity. Lands west of the Appalachians could be settled. More farms and towns could trade. Americans knew that independence would not be easy. Winning the war had been hard. Running a country would be hard too. But Americans looked forward to the rewards of living in a free land.

> Which battle ended the Revolutionary War?

Chapter Review
Activity Manual pages 63–64

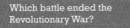

Activity

Creating a Timeline

Make a timeline that is exciting and instructive. List events and dates in a horizontal or vertical style. Create a circular or rambling timeline for a journey. Make parallel timelines. Record events in a person's life on one timeline with events of that time period on a second one. Take part in a living timeline. Choose an event from a large timeline on display. Dress for the time period and report on that event as you stand by the date. Create a timeline that interests and teaches.

91

Activity

Creating a Timeline

- Generate excitement about creating a timeline as you read the Activity information aloud.

- Display a timeline with important dates relating to the chapter in the Student Text.

- Explain that the students will participate in a living timeline. Divide the students into small groups. Assign a date to each group.

- Allow each small group to use the Student Text to identify the major event that happened on the date and research the event in the Student Text and in other sources you provide.

- Invite each group to choose someone to participate in the living timeline.

- Allow each participant to stand by his date. The student may hold an object or wear clothing that represents the time period or event as he tells about what happened on that date.

Objective
- Recall concepts and terms from Chapter 4

Materials
- Questions written on strips of paper and corresponding answers written on strips of paper (one set of questions and answers for each team)

Introduction

- Concepts for the Chapter 4 Test will be taken from Activity Manual pages 49–64. You may review any or all of the concepts during this lesson. You may choose to review Chapter 4 by playing "Puzzling Questions."

Review

Game: Puzzling Questions

- Divide the class into teams. Mix each set of questions and answers. At a given signal, each team should start organizing its papers and matching the questions with the correct answers. The first team to display all the questions and answers correctly wins.

Activity Manual

- Guide completion of pages 63–64.

Lesson **36** **Chapter 4 Test**

Objective
- Demonstrate knowledge of concepts from Chapter 4 by taking the test

Assessment

- Administer Test 4.

Chapter 5

Introduction

After the Revolutionary War, Americans were faced with the challenges of establishing a government for the new nation. Originally, each state was a republic. However, under the Articles of Confederation, the states often did not work together. Representatives from each state gathered for the Constitutional Convention. After much debate, compromises were made and the states ratified the Constitution. Later, the first Congress under the Constitution passed the ten amendments known as the Bill of Rights. The Electoral College chose George Washington to be America's first president. Washington set many precedents and encountered problems as Americans moved westward.

Successive presidents also set precedents and faced problems. John Adams faced the possibility of war with France, and political parties formally developed during his presidency. Thomas Jefferson stood up to the Barbary pirates and purchased the Louisiana Territory. James Madison was president during the War of 1812. James Monroe helped develop the Monroe Doctrine and the Missouri Compromise, which was designed to end debates about slavery. Each of these presidents set precedents for America's future.

5 The Early National Period

Focus

The American founders established a strong but limited national government.

Lesson	Student Text	Activity Manual	Content		Vocabulary
			Chapter 5 Overview		
37	92–95	65–67	Life after the revolution Shays' Rebellion	The Articles of Confederation	faction veteran
38	96–99	68–69	Constitutional Convention Branches of government	Bill of Rights	Anti-Federalists sovereignty
39	100–102	70–72	George Washington Electoral College	Westward expansion and Indian relations	cabinet
40	103–5	73–75	John Adams Political parties Primary Source: Thoughts on Relations with France and Great Britain Biography Box: Timothy Dwight		Democratic-Republicans Federalists
41	106–9	76–77	Thomas Jefferson How It Was: Mission in Tripoli	Activity: Planning an Expedition	
42	110–12	78	James Madison	The War of 1812	
43	113–15	79–80	James Monroe The Monroe Doctrine	The Missouri Compromise	
44		81–82	Chapter Review		
45			Chapter Test		

Visit bjupress.com/resources for links to enhance the lessons.

George Washington
becomes president
1789

Thomas Jefferson
becomes president   War of 1812
1801   **1812**

1780   **1788 1790**   **1797 1800**   **1810**   **1820**
Ratification of   John Adams
the Constitution   becomes president

Life After the Revolution

The Americans had won the Revolutionary War. Now they set out on a bold experiment. They were going to see if they could make republican government work. A republican government has no king. The people choose their leaders. After the revolution, each state was its own republic. But the states formed a confederation. In a confederation, states join with one another. They agree to act together on issues such as defense and trade with other nations.

Problems in American Life

Equality became more valued to Americans after the American Revolution. Equality is often good, but it can be used to justify sinful actions. In the years following the revolution, certain sins became more common. More people began to disrespect authority. More children began to disrespect their parents. Some students rebelled against the authority of their teachers. More wives rejected the authority of their husbands. More Americans were unfaithful to their spouses. Many younger people did not respect older people as they should have. More people disregarded the authority of godly pastors. And violence became more common. These sins existed before the revolution. Even after the revolution, these sins did not describe most Americans. But these sins became so much more common that wise Americans became worried. Some began to write books that warned Americans against their sins.

A republic must have a moral people in order to have a moral government. In a republic, the people choose the government leaders. If the people are wicked, they are more likely to choose wicked leaders. They may choose leaders who do special favors for friends. These leaders do not rule for the good of all the people.

Americans had gotten rid of their king. A good king can make sure that the laws of the land are good laws. He can see that the laws encourage people

93

Chapter Focus

The American founders established a strong but limited national government.

Lesson Focus

- Americans faced problems as they strove to create a government for their new nation.

Objectives
- Assess the problems in American life after the revolution
- Detect the value of virtue and Christian principles
- Determine how Shays' Rebellion confirmed the need for a more effective American government
- Explain the weaknesses of the Articles of Confederation

Teacher's Toolkit CD
- Instructional Aid 27: *Weaknesses & Solutions*

Introduction

- Invite a student to read aloud the title of the chapter and predict what the chapter will be about. America's early years as a nation
- Invite a student to read the chapter focus aloud.

  What do you think you will learn about in this chapter? the establishment of America's national government

- Explain that the picture on page 92 is an illustration of George Washington being escorted across New York Harbor in a specially made barge to his inauguration. Thirteen sailors dressed in white rowed the barge. Three newly appointed senators and representatives for the House were also onboard.

- Direct attention to the timeline.

  In which year was the Constitution ratified? 1788

  Identify the first three American presidents in the order they were elected. George Washington, John Adams, and Thomas Jefferson

  What happened in the year 1812? The War of 1812 began.

Preparation for Reading

- Generate interest as you direct the students to read the titles and examine the pictures and the infograph on pages 92–95.
- Guide pronunciation of any unfamiliar words in the lesson.
- Instruct the students to read the pages silently to discover what life in America was like after the Revolutionary War.

Teach for Understanding

What task did the Americans face after they won the Revolutionary War? They needed to establish a national government.

What kind of government did the Americans want? Why? They wanted a republican government; it had no king, and the people could choose their leaders.

What kind of republican government did the states actually form? a confederation

- Invite a student to explain how the confederation worked. Answers should include that each state was its own republic. The states joined with one another to act together on certain issues.

- Explain that although the thirteen states agreed to work together under a set of laws called the Articles of Confederation, the states were given many rights.

What happened when equality was used to justify sinful actions? Answers may include that certain sins became more common.

- Choose students to read aloud examples of these sins. Guide a discussion about rules at home and at school. Include the purpose of the rules and what life would be like without them.

How do you think rules were enforced when people disrespected authority and did not obey rules? Answers should include the idea that rules could not be enforced because people thought they were free to do whatever they wanted.

> Encourage students to support their responses to higher-order questions. Provide prompts or background as needed to guide the students to the answer.

Overall, whom are we disobeying when we do not respect or obey authority? We are disobeying God; He rules over all people.

What character trait must people living in a republic have in order to have a moral government? They must be moral.

- Explain that a moral person is able to judge between right and wrong. He makes righteous choices and behaves in a right way.

What would the government of a republic be like if the people were immoral? The government would be immoral. The people would be more likely to choose wicked leaders who would not rule for the good of all the people. If the majority of the people were wicked, they could become tyrants over other people.

Why did some Americans begin to consider how they could change American government? The best men were not being elected to the state legislatures.

---

to be moral. If the people are bad, a good king can restrain their wickedness. But Americans did not want another king. A bad king can be a tyrant. He can do evil. And it is hard to stop him. Americans did not want a king.

But anyone can do evil actions. Sinful people can become tyrants over other people. Americans had to make sure that they were righteous and virtuous themselves.

But the best men were not being elected to state legislatures. Often men would propose laws that would personally help them. To get votes, a legislator would promise to vote for the other man's law if that man would vote for his. Some Americans began to think about how they could change American government. They wanted the best men to govern. Men like James Madison thought that if the size of the country grew from thirteen small republics to one large republic, no one **faction** could seize control of the government. Then the best men from across the country could be selected to be part of the national government.

Madison's original idea for the national government would have allowed it to veto state laws. A veto stops a bill from becoming law. He thought the wiser men elected to serve in the national government could serve as a check on the state governments.

In Madison's plan, the national government would not be large. Its job would be that of a referee between the states. Other American leaders shared Madison's concerns about the weak national government.

Then Shays' Rebellion broke out in western Massachusetts. The people revolted because their money was worth less each year. Some people were placed in jail for their debts. States raised taxes because they needed money to run the government. But the people found it hard to pay these taxes. Revolutionary War **veteran** Daniel Shays raised an army of 2,000 men in protest. They attacked a

Shays' Rebellion confirmed that a more effective American government was needed.

94

- Invite a student to explain James Madison's plan for the national government. Guide the explanation to include the word *faction* and its meaning.

Who led a rebellion in Massachusetts? Daniel Shays

Why did the people rebel? Their money was worth less each year; people were placed in jail for their debts; the people found it hard to pay the taxes that were raised by the states.

- Direct attention to the picture on page 94. Choose a student to read the caption aloud.

Although Shays' Rebellion confirmed that a change was needed in the government, was it right for the people to rebel against the authority of the state? Answers should include that the Bible teaches people to obey authority.

- Explain that Christians may need to disobey an authority in order to obey God, but the Bible does not give Christians permission to rebel against their leaders.

courthouse and an armory where weapons were stored. Though the rebellion was defeated, the attacks concerned many Americans.

Problems with the Articles of Confederation

The Articles of Confederation gave Congress the responsibility to pay off United States debt. These debts were gained during the Revolutionary War. But there was a problem. Congress did not have money to pay the debts. Governments make money with taxes. The legislatures in every state had to agree to any tax Congress proposed before it could become law. Congress tried to pass a tax, but it failed. Congress asked the states to give money to the government. But the states were not willing to help. Without the ability to tax, the confederation government could not afford to carry out the most basic functions.

Congress could make laws. But there was another problem. It did not have the power to make sure people obeyed the laws. It did not have the power to punish people who disobeyed the laws. Of course, without enforcement or punishment people often ignored Congress's laws.

Under the Articles of Confederation, the states often did not work together. This individualism was a third major problem. The states placed tariffs on

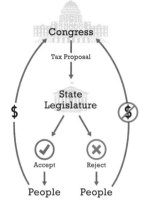

PASSING A TAX
UNDER THE ARTICLES
OF CONFEDERATION

Congress

Tax Proposal

State Legislature

$ / $

✓ Accept / ✗ Reject

People / People

goods moved from state to state. The states could not agree on trade treaties with other nations. Each state printed its own money. Often this money lost value quickly.

Americans came to believe that a change was necessary. In 1787 Congress approved a convention with representatives from the states. These representatives met to talk about amending, or changing, the Articles of Confederation.

> Why do republics need to have a moral people in order to succeed?

95

> Additional Background information for this lesson is on the Teacher's Toolkit CD.

What responsibility did the Articles of Confederation give Congress? to pay the debts that the United States gained during the Revolutionary War

Did Congress have the money to pay the debts? no

How do governments make money? They tax the people.

- Select a student to use the infograph on page 95 to explain the process of passing a tax under the Articles of Confederation.

Was Congress able to raise the money to pay the debts? Why? No, the legislatures did not agree to the tax, and the states were not willing to give money to Congress.

- Display Instructional Aid 27. Invite students to list weaknesses of the Articles of Confederation as you write for display. (*Note:* The Instructional Aid will be completed in the next lesson.)

Why do you think money printed by the individual states often lost value quickly? Answers should include that with different types of currency between states, people could not know if their money would be accepted so they lost trust in it.

Why did Congress approve a convention with representatives from the states? Americans believed that the Articles of Confederation needed to be amended, or changed.

> Conclude the discussion by asking the question on page 95. The people need to be moral in order for a republic to have a moral government. Moral people are more likely to choose the best men to rule for the good of all the people.

Activity Manual

- Guide completion of pages 65–67.

Background

Shays' Rebellion

At the end of the Revolutionary War, money was in short supply. Farmers were affected the most. In Massachusetts, farmers were taxed one-third of their income. The government insisted on payment in silver. Many lost their farms and equipment. Some were imprisoned when they could not pay. The farmers pleaded with the authorities to accept payment in farm products, to lower taxes, and to stop jailing debtors.

Daniel Shays, a former Revolutionary War captain, led a group of rebels against their government. The group tried to keep the government from meeting. The rebels also attacked an ammunitions storehouse. Soldiers paid by wealthy merchants broke up the storehouse attack, killed some of Shays' followers, and captured several rebel leaders. Although Shays' Rebellion failed in its original purpose, it did cause American leaders to realize the need for a stronger national government.

Activity

Write an Opinion

Direct the students to decide which weakness in the Articles of Confederation was the most important to be changed. Then encourage them to write their opinion, telling why it should be changed and how.

Lesson Focus

- Delegates at the Constitutional Convention penned the Constitution, forming a strong, but limited, government.

Objectives

- State the goal of the the Constitutional Convention
- Explain compromises made during the convention
- Name the three branches of government and what each branch consists of
- Explain the process of ratifying the Constitution and the purpose of the Bill of Rights

Teacher's Toolkit CD

- Visual 11: *Two Plans for Congress*
- Instructional Aids 27–28: *Weaknesses and Solutions; Delegate Views*

Materials

- A copy of the Constitution of the United States

Review

What kind of government did the Americans have immediately after the Revolutionary War? a republican government

What kind of republican government did the states form? a confederation

- Invite students to explain problems that existed in American life at this time.

Why is it important for the people living in a republic to be moral people? The people must be moral in order for the government to be moral. Moral people are more likely to choose the best men to rule for the good of all the people.

Why did some Americans start thinking of ways to change American government? The best men were not being elected to state legislatures, and if the states grew to one large republic, Americans did not want one faction taking control of the government.

Guide a review of important terms, maps, places, and people from each previous lesson. Direct the students to find and read the corresponding entries from the Resource Treasury.

- Choose students to explain weaknesses in the Articles of Confederation.

Preparation for Reading

- Generate interest as you direct the students to read the titles and examine the pictures on pages 96–99.
- Guide pronunciation of any unfamiliar words in the lesson.
- Direct the students to read the pages silently and complete Instructional Aid 28 in small groups.

The Constitutional Convention

Americans had gained their independence from the British king through the Revolutionary War. Some of the men at the Constitutional Convention had fought in that war. Others had served in the Congress that declared independence. Americans did not want a tyrannical government, but they knew a weak government was just as much a problem. They wanted to form a strong, but limited, government.

Important Men at the Convention

The Constitutional Convention brought important Americans to Philadelphia. George Washington was persuaded to come out of his retirement at Mount Vernon to attend. Americans respected Washington. The convention's supporters believed Washington needed to be present for the convention to succeed. Washington knew the strengths and weaknesses of Congress. He had worked with Congress during the Revolutionary War. Washington desired a strong, but limited, national government.

James Madison was one of the most important men at the convention. He came with well-researched ideas. Madison was worried about too much democracy. He thought majorities could be just as tyrannical as kings. But he wanted to make sure the government also protected people's liberties. He wanted a national government strong enough to lead and help the states work together. But he did not want a government so strong that it took over the responsibilities of the states. Madison took careful notes of the discussions. Much of what we know about the convention comes from his pen.

James Wilson of Pennsylvania was another important delegate to the

George Washington

James Madison

James Wilson

Roger Sherman

96

Teach for Understanding

- Choose a student to tell the name of the convention that had been approved by Congress. the Constitutional Convention

What was the goal of the men attending the convention? to form a strong, but limited, government

Where did the convention take place? Philadelphia

Who were some of the men representing their states at the convention? George Washington, James Madison, James Wilson, Roger Sherman, Alexander Hamilton, and Benjamin Franklin

Why did people think it was important for George Washington to attend the convention? Americans respected him; supporters of the convention believed he needed to be present for the convention to succeed; he knew the strengths and weaknesses of Congress; he had worked with Congress during the Revolutionary War.

- Why do you think Madison was one of the most important men at the convention? Answers may include that Madison came to the convention with well-researched ideas and that he took careful notes during the convention.

convention. He was on a committee that began to write the Constitution based on the convention's discussions. He thought that all men had common sense. Common sense made them able to make right and wise decisions. He was less worried than some of the other founders were about democracy. He wanted the people to have a strong voice in government.

Roger Sherman of Connecticut offered an important compromise that allowed the convention to succeed. A compromise happens when two sides give up part of what they want in order to both get part of what they want. Without Sherman's plan the large states and the small states would not have agreed on the Constitution. Sherman was less confident than Wilson about the wisdom of the people. He wanted them to have a role, but he was also concerned that they were often too ill-informed to make wise decisions.

Other important men at the convention included Alexander Hamilton and Benjamin Franklin. Some men are not well known today. But they were important leaders in their states at that time.

Debates at the Convention

The men at the convention agreed that the government of the United States needed to change, but they did not always agree about what those changes should be. Madison suggested that the number of congressmen be set by state population. This idea made the congressmen representatives of the people. But larger states would have more representatives.

Smaller states wanted to keep this part of the government the same. They wanted each state to have one vote in Congress, making the small states equal to the large states. The small states did not want to be ruled by the large states in the new government.

But one vote for each state gave the people of the small states more power than the people in the large states. Fewer people lived in Delaware than in Virginia. But the few people in Delaware would have as much say in Congress as all the people in Virginia.

This issue divided the delegates for a long time. Finally, Roger Sherman proposed a compromise. There would be two parts to the national lawmaking body, the House of Representatives and the Senate. The number of representatives in the House would be set according to population. And each state would have two senators appointed by the state legislatures. In this way the people and the states had a voice in the government.

97

Additional Background information for this lesson is on the Teacher's Toolkit CD.

Background

Constitutional Convention

To guarantee secrecy during the Constitutional Convention, delegates took an oath not to speak about, publish, or print anything said during the meetings. In addition, the windows of the state house were nailed shut and guards were posted. James Madison said later that the Constitution would never have been developed had the convention not been held in private. What we know today about the happenings inside the state house is due to Madison's diary.

James Madison

James Madison was the most influential member of the Constitutional Convention. He has been called "America's first political scientist" and the "Father of the Constitution." He was a lawyer and a student of government. The journal he kept during the convention is the most accurate source of information about the private event.

Teach for Understanding

What was Madison worried about? too much democracy

- Guide a discussion about what a democracy is. Include that in a democracy, the government is ruled directly by the people. A faction or a majority of the people could force their views on others. The rules for governing could change whenever the views or wishes of the majority changed.

- Do you think Madison was wise to be concerned about too much democracy? Answers may include that he was wise because a strong government would not change its rules just because a group of people changed their minds.

- Invite the groups to explain the delegates' views of a national government. Compare and contrast the views.

  Who offered an important compromise? Roger Sherman

  What is a compromise? Two opposing sides each give up part of what they want in order to both get part of what they want.

  What did the men at the convention agree on? The United States government needed to change.

  What was a main issue that divided the men at the convention? how the states should be represented in Congress

- Display Visual 11. Choose a student to explain the two opposing views.

- Direct attention to the infograph on page 98. Invite a student to explain Sherman's compromise. Answers should include that the national government would have two parts in the national lawmaking body. The number of representatives in the House would be based on state population, and each state would have two senators in the Senate.

- Why did both sides agree to the compromise? Answers should include that the compromise provided a way for the people to have a voice in the government by having the House of Representatives based on state population. The compromise also prevented the larger states from having more power than the smaller states by allowing the same number of senators from each state.

Lesson

38

Teach for Understanding

What other compromise resulted from Sherman's compromise? Slaves would be counted as three-fifths of a person for determining representation in Congress.

🔊 Why was the Three-Fifths Compromise made? Answers should include that Sherman's first compromise raised the question of who should be counted toward the population. People did not agree on slaves being included in the population because slave states would have more power in Congress than others.

● Invite five students to stand. Point out that *three-fifths* means three out of a group of five. Select a student to tell how many people the group of five students would represent based on the Three-Fifths Compromise. three

● Point out that one way to understand the Three-Fifths Compromise is to think that for every group of five slaves, three people would count toward the population.

What other agreements were reached regarding slaves? The slave trade could not be cut off before 1808, and runaway slaves were to be returned to their masters.

🔊 Why do you think the delegates thought a compromise regarding slaves was necessary? Answers may include that they wanted to ensure the union of all the states.

● Guide the students in evaluating the compromises and determining whether Christians should vote in favor of them.

● Direct attention to the infograph on page 99. Invite students to identify the three branches of government and tell who or what makes up each branch.

What is the responsibility of Congress? to make the laws

What is the president's responsibility? to be sure the laws are carried out

🔊 What do you think the responsibility of the Supreme Court is? Answers may include the responsibility to decide if laws have been broken.

● Invite a student to tell why the next section in the text is called "Ratification."

🔊 Do you think it would have been a problem if only nine states approved the Constitution? Answers may include that it would have been a problem. Any states that did not approve the Constitution would not have to obey it.

SHERMAN'S COMPROMISE

House of Representatives
(based on population)

Senate
(same for each state)

This compromise raised a new question. Who would count toward the population? All people? Only those who paid taxes? Only those who could vote? What about slaves, who could not vote? If slaves were counted, then states with slaves would have more power in Congress than others. Rewarding slave states for a practice many saw as wrong did not seem right. In the end another compromise was reached. Slaves would be counted as three-fifths of a person for determining representation in Congress.

Georgia, North Carolina, and South Carolina wanted to make sure that the slave trade would not be forbidden. As a result, the Constitution did not allow the slave trade to be cut off before 1808. In addition, the Constitution guaranteed that runaway slaves would be returned to their masters. Luther Martin of Maryland objected that the Constitution was based on the Americans' claims to freedom from Great Britain's tyranny. How could America deny freedom to slaves in the Constitution? George Mason warned that slavery would "bring the judgment of heaven."

Nonetheless, the delegates concluded that the union of all the states was important. So a compromise was necessary on this point. But the judgment that Mason warned about did come when the Civil War broke out.

In the end the delegates proposed a government with three branches. The legislative branch, Congress, would make laws. It would have two parts: the House of Representatives and the Senate. The executive branch would be led by a president. He would ensure that the laws were carried out. The judicial branch would be led by the Supreme Court.

Ratification

The delegates agreed on the Constitution, but it was not yet law. The Constitution had to be approved by the states. Nine states had to approve the Constitution for it to become law. And it would be law only for the states that approved it.

98

Background

Bill of Rights

James Madison proposed nineteen amendments to the states for approval in 1789. In 1791 three-fourths of the states ratified ten of those amendments. This set of ten amendments became known as the Bill of Rights. These amendments restricted the power of the national government and protected individual rights.

The First Amendment protects the freedoms of religion, speech, press, assembly, and petition. The Second through Fourth Amendments protect security rights by guaranteeing the right to bear arms, prohibiting the forced quartering of troops in private homes during peacetime, and protecting against unreasonable searches and seizures. The Fifth through Eighth Amendments guarantee fair judicial procedures for the accused. The Ninth and Tenth Amendments place restrictions on the extent of national power by limiting its constitutional bounds and by guaranteeing that freedoms not specified in the Bill of Rights nor restricted by the states belong to the people.

THREE BRANCHES OF GOVERNMENT

Legislative (Congress)	Executive (President)	Judicial (Supreme Court)
makes the laws	carries out the laws	decides if laws have been broken

Some people did not want the Constitution to become law. The **Anti-Federalists** argued that the Constitution took away the **sovereignty** of the states. The Constitution gave the national government power to tax people. It could declare war. It could make laws about trade between states. It could make treaties with foreign countries. A state could not declare war. A state could not make treaties with other countries. A state could not place a tariff on goods from other states. The Anti-Federalists wanted the states to have these powers.

Many Americans came to believe that it was best for a national government, not a state government, to exercise these rights. But they also wanted promises that the national government would limit itself. They wanted the states and people to keep the other rights they had enjoyed previously.

The Anti-Federalists said the Constitution did not protect these rights. The Constitution said nothing about protecting freedom of speech or freedom of religion. It did not promise the right to carry weapons or to a trial by jury.

The Federalists supported the Constitution. They said that these rights were protected. After all, the Constitution did not give the national government the right to violate their freedoms. The national government could do only what the Constitution permitted.

In the end the people in each of the states ratified the Constitution. Most agreed that the country needed the new Constitution. But the Anti-Federalists' concerns were also heard. The first Congress under the new Constitution passed ten constitutional amendments. These amendments are known as the Bill of Rights. The Bill of Rights protects the rights that the Anti-Federalists wanted protected.

> Why should government be both strong and limited?

99

Activities

Compromise

Materials: a 3 × 5 card for each group of students

Divide the students into groups. Give each group a 3 × 5 card. Explain that some students want to have hot dogs for a class party, but others want to have pizza. Instruct each group to discuss whether the class should have hot dogs or pizza and to write its decision on the card. Read the cards aloud after each group has made its decision. If there is a difference of opinion, ask if anyone has an idea about how to solve the problem in a way that will satisfy all the groups. Allow the students to vote on the best compromise. Ask appropriate questions to help the students find a good compromise. Explain that many times settling a disagreement is not easy. Often, both sides must give up something in order to reach a compromise.

Illustrate the Bill of Rights

Materials: a copy of the Bill of Rights, a sheet of drawing paper for each group of students

Guide the students in reading the Bill of Rights. Divide the students into small groups. Instruct each group to choose one of the amendments and discuss how the amendment protects the rights of the American people. Then direct the groups to illustrate the amendment and write a caption for their illustration.

Teach for Understanding

Who did not want the Constitution to become law? the Anti-Federalists

Why did the Anti-Federalists not want the Constitution to become law? Answers should include that the Anti-Federalists believed that the Constitution took away the sovereignty of the states and that it did not protect the rights previously enjoyed by the people.

- Display Instructional Aid 27. Invite students to tell how the Constitution solved some of the weaknesses of the Articles of Confederation as you write for display.

- Display the Constitution. Point out the Preamble, articles, sections, and clauses. Explain that Article I addresses the powers of Congress, and Section 8, Clause 5 allowed Congress to print money and regulate its value.

- Ask a volunteer to explain the Federalists' argument in support of the Constitution. Answers should include that the Federalists believed that the people's rights were protected by the Constitution because it did not give the national government the right to violate their freedoms. The Federalists said that the government could do only what the Constitution allowed it to do.

How many states ratified the Constitution? all thirteen

Do you think it was good that all the states ratified the Constitution? Answers could include that it was good. If any states did not ratify the Constitution, they would not have to obey it. Those states would be like separate nations with their own rules.

What did the first Congress under the Constitution do in order to protect the rights of the American people? Answers should include that it passed ten amendments known as the Bill of Rights.

Conclude the discussion by asking the question on page 99. Government should be strong so that it can lead the country and help the states work together. It should be limited so that it does not become tyrannical, violating the rights of the states and the people.

Activity Manual

- Guide completion of pages 68–69.

Lesson

39

Student Text pages 100–102
Activity Manual pages 70–72

Lesson Focus

- As America's first president, George Washington set precedents for those who would become president after him.

Objectives

- Describe the Electoral College and its purpose
- Identify precedents set by President Washington
- State the purpose of the president's cabinet
- Summarize the conflict between American Indians and Americans moving westward

Teacher's Toolkit CD

- Instructional Aid 28: *Delegate Views*

Materials

- A copy of the Constitution of the United States
- A map of the United States

Review

What was the goal of the delegates at the Constitutional Convention? to form a strong, but limited, government

- Display Instructional Aid 28 without answers. Invite students to briefly summarize each delegate's view for a national government.
- Choose volunteers to explain the need for Sherman's compromise and why the Three-Fifths Compromise was made.

Who or what makes up each branch of the national government? The president leads the executive branch, the House of Representatives and the Senate make up the legislative branch, and the Supreme Court makes up the judicial branch.

Why was the Bill of Rights passed by Congress? to protect the rights of the American people and states

Preparation for Reading

- Generate interest as you direct the students to read the titles and examine the picture and infograph on pages 100–102.
- Guide pronunciation of any unfamiliar words in the lesson.
- Direct the students to read the pages silently and write a list of the precedents set by George Washington while he was president.

George Washington was aware of the example his actions would set. Instead of a suit of fancy foreign-made material, Washington wore a simple suit of brown cloth made in Connecticut.

Washington wore a ceremonial sword to his inauguration. It was the same sword that he wore in a 1772 portrait by Charles Wilson Peale.

George Washington

Everyone knew that George Washington would be the first president chosen under the new Constitution. Americans all over the new nation admired him. Washington led the Americans to victory in the Revolutionary War. He also resigned as general after the war. In many revolutions the triumphant general will place himself in charge of the new government. All too often he becomes a tyrant. Often, life is worse after a revolution than before. But Washington believed that those in government should always act with the common good in mind. He did not think leaders in government should act for their own personal good. For this reason Americans trusted him.

Election and Precedents

The Electoral College unanimously chose Washington as president. Americans do not vote for the president directly. Instead, each state is given electors. The number of a state's US representatives and senators is the number of electors a state gets. In the early days, the state legislatures often chose the state's electors. The founders did not want the people to choose the president directly. They knew a man could be popular and yet not be a good and wise leader. They wanted a check on the people's choice for president.

Washington was a good and wise leader. He knew that his actions as the first president would set precedents. A precedent is an example that is followed by others. Washington was very careful about the example he set. He always wore a dark suit while president to show that the office deserved respect.

Washington also tried to prevent Americans from splitting into political parties. He thought that leaders should always act for the good of the nation. They should not act merely for the good of their party. He also did not

100

Teach for Understanding

Why did Americans trust George Washington? He believed that people in government should act for the good of the people, not their own personal good.

- What is the Electoral College? a group of electors or men who are responsible for choosing the president

How is the number of electors for each state determined? The number of a state's representatives and senators is the number of electors a state gets.

- Explain that today electors are chosen when people vote for a presidential candidate.

Why did America's founders not want the people to choose the president directly? They knew that people could be influenced to vote for a man who was popular even if he was not a good and wise leader.

- Why do you think Washington was always careful about the example he set? He knew that the example he set as the first president would set a precedent followed by presidents after him.

Heritage Studies 5

ELECTORAL COLLEGE

| Voters 👤 | Electors 👤 |

People vote for their candidate.

States choose electors based on how the people vote.

Electors from each state vote on who the president will be.

want parties to fight for control of the government. He thought political parties would make life in the United States unstable.

Washington's Cabinet

Washington appointed a **cabinet** when he became president. *Cabinet* is the term for people who help the president see the laws of the land carried out.

Washington did not like political parties. He did not appoint men of all one viewpoint to his cabinet. He appointed men with different ideas about how the country should be run. Washington trusted these men. He was willing to hear their different viewpoints.

Two men on Washington's cabinet had very different views. These men were Thomas Jefferson and Alexander Hamilton. One important debate shows their difference of opinion. Hamilton thought the national government should create a national bank. This bank would help both trade and American cities. Jefferson rejected this plan. Jefferson reminded Washington that the Constitution did not say anything about banks. The Tenth Amendment says Congress can do only what the Constitution says it can do. Jefferson also believed that governments and cities corrupted people. He wanted as little of both as possible.

Hamilton pointed to Article I, Section 8 of the Constitution. It said that Congress could make laws that "were necessary and proper" for carrying out the powers that the Constitution gives. Hamilton also pointed out that banks were a tried, tested way of managing a nation's money. He and his supporters wanted to do what they already knew would work. They were suspicious of Jefferson's new ideas about government.

Washington sided with Hamilton and signed the bill setting up the bank. Washington wanted the national government to be strong enough to fulfill its obligations. But he also wanted to keep the obligations of the government limited by the Constitution.

101

- Ask volunteers to identify precedents that were set by Washington. Discuss why they were good precedents. He always wore a dark suit; he appointed men to his cabinet that he trusted but that had different viewpoints; he listened to different viewpoints; he stepped down from being president after serving two terms.

- Which branch of government is the cabinet part of? How do you know? The cabinet is part of the executive branch; the people in the cabinet help the president see that the laws of the land are carried out.

- Divide the students into pairs. Encourage each student to explain to his partner why he thinks Washington's listening to different viewpoints was good or bad.

  What significant difference of opinion existed between Thomas Jefferson and Alexander Hamilton? They disagreed on whether the national government should create a national bank.

- Invite students to explain Jefferson's and Hamilton's views about creating a national bank.

- Display Article I, Section 8 of the Constitution. Point out that Article I addresses the powers of Congress, and Section 8, Clause 1 gives Congress the power to pay the nation's debts. Read aloud Clause 18 and discuss the powers it refers to. The discussion should include that Congress has the power to legislate and collect taxes in order to defend the United States and to provide for the country's general welfare.

  Why did Washington side with Hamilton? Washington wanted the national government to be strong enough to fulfill its obligations, but he also wanted to keep the government's obligations limited by the Constitution.

- Why do you think it is important for a government to manage its money well? Answers may include that when a government manages its money, it can pay its obligations. By staying within a budget, the government will not increase the national debt. There would be less chance of raising the taxes that people pay.

- Use the parable of the talents in Matthew 25 to guide a discussion about stewardship.

George Washington Biography

Encourage the students to read a biography about George Washington. Direct them to write a brief report and include something about Washington's life that was not mentioned in the lessons. Allow time for the students to present their findings to the class.

George Washington Timeline

Challenge groups of students to research important events in Washington's life. Direct each group to write the date of an event and either write a brief statement about the event or illustrate it. Guide the students as they plot the events on a timeline.

Lesson

39

Teach for Understanding

How did the United States government treat the Indians who lived in the West? **as Indian nations living within the borders of the United States**

🖋 Why do you think the United States made treaties with the Indians? **Answers may include that the treaties would prevent Americans from moving westward too quickly and trampling on the rights of the Indians.**

Did Americans obey the national government? **No, Georgia refused to keep the treaties and sold land that belonged to the Creek Indians; settlers refused to stay out of Indian land.**

• Guide the students in completing Activity Manual page 70. Point out on the map of the United States where the Battle of Fallen Timbers took place. Explain that the battle was along the Maumee River near present-day Toledo, Ohio. Use Background information to guide a discussion about the battle. Point out the area of land that was ceded to the United States.

🖋 What were Americans doing when they violated the treaties and took land from the Indians? **stealing**

🖋 Was it right for settlers and states to steal land that belonged to the Indians? **No, answers should include that God commands people not to steal.**

🖋 How long is one presidential term? **four years**

What precedent did Washington set after serving two terms? **He stepped down from being president.**

🖋 Why do you think Washington set this precedent?

▶▶ Conclude the discussion by asking the question on page 102. Washington believed leaders in government should always put the good of the people ahead of their own. He believed that political parties would cause government leaders to act for the good of their own party rather than for the good of the nation. He also believed that the political parties would fight for control of the government.

• Point out that Washington's stepping down after two terms and his opposition to political parties are examples of Christian-influenced virtues.

Activity Manual

• Guide completion of pages 70–72.

Assessment

• Administer quiz.

> The quiz may be given any time after completing this lesson.

American Indian Relations

Many Americans moved westward while Washington was president. But American Indians already lived on much of this land. The United States government treated the Indian groups as nations, but they were a special kind of nation because they were within the borders of the United States. The United States made treaties with the Indian nations. These treaties promised that the national government would pay for lands the Indians gave up. The treaties also promised that the national government would protect Indian lands. Washington wanted Americans to move westward in a slow and ordered manner. He did not want American settlers trampling on the rights of the Indians.

But people and states disobeyed the national government. Georgia refused to acknowledge the treaties that the national government made with the Creek Indians. Instead the state sold Creek land. Settlers who moved west did not obey the government's demand to stay out of Indian land. Fighting broke out between American settlers and the Indians.

Fighting broke out in other places as well. Washington sent the US Army west to fight the Delaware, Shawnee, Chippewa, and Miami tribes that had united against American settlers. The army was led by General Anthony Wayne. Wayne defeated the Indians in the Battle of Fallen Timbers.

The effects of this battle were important. The defeated tribes signed another treaty. It gave much of Ohio and part of Indiana to the United States. Also, the British finally left their forts in this part of the country. Even though the Revolutionary War had ended, the British had kept forts in the United States. They now left the United States entirely.

The Spanish grew worried that the British and Americans might become allies. They did not want to fight both the Americans and the British. The Spanish agreed that Americans could use New Orleans for trade. The Spanish controlled New Orleans. Americans who wanted to ship goods down the Mississippi River to the ocean had to pass through New Orleans. This agreement opened new opportunities for Americans in the West.

George Washington was elected as president twice. Some people thought that every four years a president would be reelected for as long as he lived if he was a good man. But George Washington set another precedent. He stepped down after his second term. Only one president has served more than two terms.

> Why did George Washington oppose political parties?

102

> Additional Background information for this lesson is on the Teacher's Toolkit CD.

Background

Battle of Fallen Timbers

The Battle of Fallen Timbers was the third attempt of the United States to put down the resistance by the Northwest Indian Confederation. The confederation included the Miami, Potawatomi, Shawnee, Delaware, Ottawa, Chippewa, Iroquois, and other tribes. More than two thousand warriors gathered near Fort Miami in Ohio. Anthony Wayne and his army of more than a thousand soldiers used strategy and went against a group of Indians gathered behind some fallen timbers. The army was successful. The Indians lasted less than two hours before they fled. The Indians' morale was affected by the lack of promised help from the British. In the Treaty of Fort Greenville, the confederation ceded to the United States most of Ohio and parts of Indiana, Illinois, and Michigan.

John Adams was educated and well spoken, and he let others know it. In his diary, Adams described pride as his chief problem. Throughout his life, he sought to improve himself in this area.

John and Abigail Adams moved into the White House before it was finished. Abigail Adams hung laundry in the East room. This room is now used for concerts, dances, and receptions.

Despite his education, John Adams had the rough hands of a farmer. When his presidency was completed, he returned to his New England farm, Peace Field, where he lived the rest of his life.

John Adams
The Party System

In his farewell address George Washington gave advice to the nation. He warned against dividing into political parties. In a political party, people work together for common goals. But different parties have different goals. Parties would divide Americans. But Americans continued to separate into **Federalists** and **Democratic-Republicans**.

John Adams and the Federalists were conservatives who wanted to follow tested paths. The United States was different from European kingdoms. But the Federalists did not want to be too different. They wanted to learn wisdom from the past.

The Federalists distrusted human nature. They did not trust the majority of people to make wise decisions. They wanted men of proven character to be those who ran governments. The Federalists also thought the United States needed a strong government. It needed to support trade and banking. They wanted their strong government to have strict limits set on it.

The Federalists also believed that the state governments should support churches. Federalist leaders like John Adams did not believe everything the Bible teaches about Christ and salvation. But they thought that the churches were important for making people moral. And they thought moral people were important for good government. Some Christians supported the Federalists because they thought the Federalists would help keep the churches strong.

Thomas Jefferson was the leader of the Democratic-Republicans. He thought old traditions held people back. He thought people needed to use reason to come up with the best ideas for the future.

Jefferson trusted in human goodness and wisdom. He thought government and cities corrupted people. If the governments were small and did not have an army, then the world would be at peace. He thought

103

Lesson 40

Student Text pages 103–5
Activity Manual pages 73–75

Lesson Focus

- The presidency of John Adams proved to be more turbulent than Washington's as Adams faced growing political differences among the people, disagreements with Thomas Jefferson, and the threat of war.

Objectives

- Identify John Adams as the second president of the United States
- Compare and contrast the views of the two political parties that formed during Adams's presidency
- Describe the events that almost brought the United States to the point of war with France

Teacher's Toolkit CD

- Instructional Aid 29: *Comparing Political Parties*

Review

Who actually chose George Washington to be the first president of the United States? the Electoral College

---

Why did America's founders establish the Electoral College? They did not want the people to directly choose the president, and they wanted a check on the people's choice because a man who is popular might not be a good and wise leader.

What was Washington's view of political parties? He did not like political parties. He thought that government leaders should act for the good of the nation, not the good of their own party. He also thought that political parties would fight to control the government.

- Choose volunteers to explain precedents set by Washington during his presidency. He always wore a dark suit; he appointed to his cabinet men that he trusted but that had different viewpoints; he listened to different viewpoints; he stepped down from being president after serving two terms.

Preparation for Reading

- Guide the students in reading Activity Manual page 73. Instruct them to determine how Adams defines happiness. A man is happy when he is virtuous.

> Activity Manual page 73 will be completed in this Preparation for Reading section.

- Point out that Psalm 1 and Matthew 5 indicate that this definition for happiness is biblical.
- Do you think Adams is correct in saying that happiness is the end, or the proper goal, of government? Answers could include that Adams was not correct because happiness is only one end of government. Justice is a more important end.
- Guide a discussion about the need to elect wise and good men, and about the requirements for justice and the importance of justice. Explain that virtue is necessary for justice.
- Generate interest as you direct the students to read the titles and examine the pictures on pages 103–5.
- Guide pronunciation of any unfamiliar words in the lesson.
- Direct the students to read the pages silently and complete Instructional Aid 29 in small groups.

Teach for Understanding

What advice did George Washington give in his farewell address? He warned the nation against dividing into political parties.

What two political parties were being formed? the Federalists and the Democratic-Republicans

Which group was John Adams a part of? the Federalists

- Invite groups to state Federalist views.

  Why did the Federalists think that the state governments should support churches? They thought that churches were important for making people moral and that moral people were important for good government.

- Do you agree with the Federalists' belief about the importance of churches?

- Explain that Federalists were right to be concerned about morality, but God is concerned about more than morality. He wants people to trust Christ for salvation and then obey Christ with their lives.

  Why did some Christians support the Federalists? They thought the Federalists would keep the churches strong.

  Who led the Democratic-Republicans? Thomas Jefferson

- Invite groups to state Democratic-Republican views.

- Did Jefferson think that religion was good for America? Why? Answers may include that he did not think religion was good for America because he thought that religion trampled on people's freedoms. It also tied them to ideas of the past rather than encourage them to think of new ideas for the future.

- Do you agree with Jefferson's belief about religion?

  Why did some Christians support Jefferson? Their states did not support their churches, and they thought Jefferson's approach would give them more freedom of worship.

- Guide the students in comparing and contrasting the views of both political parties.

- Do you think freedom was important to both parties? Answers may include that it was important because the United States had fought the Revolutionary War to be free from England.

  How was the vice president chosen in 1796? The man with the second-most votes became the vice president.

- Choose a volunteer to explain why this method for electing the vice president was a problem. Answers should include that Adams's and Jefferson's disagreements on important issues caused much conflict during Adams's presidency.

  What difficulties did the United States have with France when Adams was president? The French were at war with Britain. They boarded American ships and seized goods because they did not like that the Americans were trading with the British.

that if Americans lived on farms and were independent, they would be better than people who lived in cities and traded. Freedom was very important to Jefferson, and he thought that farmers were freer than merchants because farmers could provide for their own needs. Merchants often had to borrow money from banks. They needed people to buy their goods. They were more dependent on others. Jefferson also thought that religion trampled on people's freedoms. It tied them to ideas of the past.

Jefferson led the Democratic-Republicans, but they did not always agree with his religious beliefs. Some Christians supported Jefferson because their churches were not supported by their states. They thought his approach would give them more freedom of worship.

At this time the president and vice president did not have to be part of the same party. The man with the second-most votes became vice president. In the election of 1796, the man who won the most votes was John Adams, and the man with the second-most votes was Thomas Jefferson. Since these men disagreed on some of the most important issues facing the young nation, much conflict loomed ahead.

Almost at War

John Adams faced important problems as president. The United States now faced troubles with France. France had helped the Americans in the Revolutionary War. But now the Americans had begun to trade again with Great Britain. France was at war with Britain. The French did not like the Americans trading with the British. The French began to board American ships and seize the goods they carried.

The Democratic-Republicans favored the French in their fight against the British. The French had just fought a revolution. They got rid of their king. They said the people were now in control. Democratic-Republicans thought that Americans should support revolutions.

The Federalists, however, said the French Revolution was very different from the American Revolution. The French placed liberty above law. They even placed it above God. The Federalists wanted to remain close with Great Britain. They said Americans shared an important heritage with the British. Trade with Great Britain was also important to Federalist merchants.

The Federalists wanted to go to war with France for stopping American ships. The Democratic-Republicans wanted peace with France. John Adams steered a middle course. He asked Congress to give him the power to begin building an American navy. The navy gave him the power to go to war. But he did not go to war. Instead he sent three men to France. He wanted them to

104

Additional Background information for this lesson is on the Teacher's Toolkit CD.

Democratic-Republican Party

The Democratic-Republican Party arose in the early 1790s to counter Alexander Hamilton's programs of Federalism. Key proponents included Thomas Jefferson, James Madison, and James Monroe. As a whole, Democratic-Republicans supported individual and states' rights and felt that a central bank system was unconstitutional. They held a strong belief in the people and favored farmers, whom they believed to be the backbone of America, over bankers, industrialists, merchants, and investors. Democratic-Republicans feared that Federalism might lead to monarchy because of its mistrust of the general public and its support of England. In foreign affairs, the Democratic-Republican Party favored France because of France's support of the United States during the revolution. Also, France was itself going through a revolution, which reinforced democracy and countered the despised monarchy of England. Democratic-Republicans dominated the southern states and came to power in 1800 alongside Jefferson's landslide victory in the presidential election. They held the presidency through 1824, at which time the Democratic-Republican Party broke down and formed two separate parties.

Timothy Dwight

What: President of Yale University
When: 1752–1817
Where: Connecticut

Timothy Dwight became president of Yale in 1795. Many in the colleges were unbelievers. Dwight wrote books and preached sermons that defended the accuracy of the Bible. He also showed the problems with unbelieving philosophies. Dwight was the leader of the Federalist Party in Connecticut. He encouraged Christians to remain active in public life. Dwight also wrote hymns, many of them based on Psalms. His most famous hymn is "I Love Thy Kingdom, Lord."

work out an agreement with the French. But the French proposed harsh terms. Even the Democratic-Republicans were embarrassed and angry when the French terms were revealed. The terms gave Adams the support he needed at home to stand up to France.

Life in the Party System

Like Washington, Adams was not in favor of political parties. Adams thought every leader in government should do what is best for the whole country. He should not do what is best for his political party.

But political parties developed during Adams's presidency. Each party had its own newspapers. These papers attacked the idea that the men of the best character and ability should be elected. They mocked and even told lies about men holding office. These papers were mostly Democratic-Republican.

They were the exact opposite of what the Federalists wanted. The Federalists did not want society run by the loudest voices. The newspapers also made the Federalists unpopular.

The Federalists in Congress passed a law, and Adams signed it. The law made it a crime to tell lies about officials in the national government. The law protected Federalists in government from Democratic-Republican attacks. By signing it John Adams appeared to be putting his party's good above the country's. This law concerned Democratic-Republicans and even some Federalists. The law undid the free speech protection promised in the Bill of Rights.

> Why did the Federalists not trust people to make wise decisions?

105

Federalist Party

Washington hoped that the United States could avoid dividing into differing political parties. But after the Democratic-Republican Party formed in opposition to the policies of Washington and Hamilton, the Federalists formed to support those policies. Federalists wanted a government filled with people of virtue and skill, but worried that most people did not have the wisdom to make the best decisions for government. The Federalists also recognized that if the new country was to succeed, it needed to pay its debts to other nations. Under the influence of Alexander Hamilton, the government set up a central bank, began paying the national and state debts, and established tax laws. These monetary measures most likely saved the newly formed republic. The Federalists understood that strong nations need to have strong trade, industries, and financial systems. In foreign affairs, the Federalists supported Great Britain. Great Britain was an important trading partner, and the Federalists thought the shared culture between the two nations was important. The Federalists did not approve of the French Revolution and were concerned that the Democratic-Republicans would bring chaos to the United States. After Jefferson became president in 1800, the Federalists never again secured the presidency. The party faded away after the War of 1812.

Teach for Understanding

- Choose a volunteer to contrast the Federalists' and the Democratic-Republicans' views regarding this difficulty with France. The Democratic-Republicans favored France in its fight against the British and wanted peace with France. The Federalists favored the British because of their shared heritage and because trade with Great Britain was important. Federalists wanted to go to war with France.

What did Adams do to try to settle the difficulty with France? Answers should include that although Congress gave Adams the power to build a navy in order to go to war with France, he chose not to go to war. Instead, he sent men to France to work out an agreement.

What was the result of Adams's attempt to reach an agreement with France? The French proposed harsh terms that gave Adams the support he needed at home to stand up to France.

Was Adams in favor of the party system? No, he believed that every government leader should do what is best for the country, not what is best for his political party.

- Guide a discussion about the appropriateness of political newspapers.

Why did Adams sign the law that made it a crime to tell lies about officials in the national government? to protect Federalists in government from being mocked and lied about in the Democratic-Republican newspapers

- Do you think Adams made a wise decision when he signed the law? Answers may include that it was not a wise decision because it appeared that Adams was doing what was best for his political party, and the law violated the Constitution.

- Why do you think Timothy Dwight encouraged Christians to remain active in public life? Answers may include that he knew the problems of unbelieving philosophies and the influence Christians would be in having a moral government.

> Conclude the discussion by asking the question on page 105. The Federalists distrusted human nature

Primary Source: From "Thoughts on Government"

- Direct the students to silently read along as you read aloud the excerpt of John Adams's "Thoughts on Government." Discuss Adams's views on government.

Activity Manual

- Guide completion of pages 73–75.

Student Text pages 106–9
Activity Manual pages 76–77

Lesson Focus

- During Jefferson's presidency, precedents continued to be set, and the United States grew larger.

Objectives

- Identify Thomas Jefferson as the third president of the United States
- Tell why Jefferson took action against the Barbary pirates
- Explain the significance of purchasing the Louisiana Territory
- Explain the significance of the Lewis and Clark expedition

Teacher's Toolkit CD

- Visuals 12–13: *Barbary Coast; Lewis & Clark Expedition, 1804–1806*

Review

What two political parties developed during Adams's presidency? Federalists and Democratic-Republicans

- Choose volunteers to explain the differing views of Adams and the Federalists and Jefferson and the Democratic-Republicans.

Why did the United States almost go to war with France? The French were at war with Great Britain and did not like that the Americans were trading with the British. The French would board American ships and seize the goods.

What happened when Adams tried to reach an agreement with the French? The French proposed harsh terms, and Adams received the support he needed at home to stand up to France.

- Invite a student to explain the negative effects of political newspapers.

Preparation for Reading

- Generate interest as you direct the students to read the titles and examine the pictures and map on pages 106–9.
- Guide pronunciation of any unfamiliar words in the lesson.
- Direct the students to read the pages silently to find out what significant events occurred during Jefferson's presidency. The Supreme Court set a precedent; the Barbary pirates were defeated; the Louisiana Territory was purchased; and Lewis and Clark explored the Louisiana Territory.

Teach for Understanding

- Select a student to read aloud Jefferson's quote about religion.
- What does Jefferson's quote tell you about his view of God? Answers should include that Jefferson did not think

Jefferson was both thin and tall. He earned the nickname "Long Tom."

Thomas Jefferson dressed carelessly and surprised several guests by receiving them at the White House in casual clothes and house slippers.

He refused to wear buckles on his shoes at his 1801 inauguration, preferring leather laces instead. Jefferson avoided extravagant dress to make a point about democracy.

Thomas Jefferson

John Adams and Thomas Jefferson faced each other in the election in 1800. Neither Adams nor Jefferson believed all that the Bible taught. But Jefferson had publicly written, "It does me no injury for my neighbor to say there are twenty gods, or no god. It neither picks my pocket nor breaks my leg." The Federalists believed that a lack of religion did do them injury. They believed Americans needed to be moral. Immoral people would destroy the nation. They did not think that all religions led to good morals.

Christians responded to Jefferson in different ways. Some people buried their Bibles when they heard Jefferson was elected president. They were afraid that Jefferson would burn their Bibles. On the other hand, some Christians supported him. They did not think the official churches in their states treated other Christians well. They thought Jefferson might push for more freedom of worship.

When Jefferson won the election, Baptists in New England sent him a giant cheese in celebration. Jefferson wrote a letter in reply and gave a generous donation to the congregation. He said that the First Amendment created "a wall of separation between church and state." The rest of the letter made Jefferson's meaning clear. He meant that the national government should not interfere with churches.

Supreme-Court Precedent

The Supreme Court also set an important precedent while Jefferson was president. Before leaving office John Adams appointed William Marbury to be a judge. The secretary of state was supposed to give Marbury his commission. This didn't happen. James Madison, the new secretary of state, refused to give Marbury his commission. Marbury took Madison to court. He said that a law passed in 1789 required Madison to give Marbury his commission. The Supreme Court ruled that the 1789 law violated the Constitution. This case set the precedent that the Supreme Court could declare laws unconstitutional.

106

a person's view of God was important and that it did not affect his life.

Why did the Federalists not agree with Jefferson's view of God? The Federalists believed that Americans needed to be moral and that not all religions led to good morals.

- Guide a discussion of how Christians responded to Jefferson's election. Include the students' views of some people burying their Bibles.

What did Jefferson think the First Amendment meant? The national government should not interfere with churches.

- Explain that when Jefferson wrote that the First Amendment created "a wall of separation between church and state" in a letter, the rest of his letter clarified what he meant. The national government should not interfere with churches. But in the 1940s the Supreme Court interpreted Jefferson's comment to mean that the First Amendment created a wall that kept religion out of government. The Supreme Court's interpretation is not what the First Amendment says. But it is how many people now understand it.

What precedent regarding the Supreme Court was set during Jefferson's presidency? The Supreme Court could declare laws unconstitutional.

Barbary Pirates

A problem developed in foreign waters during Jefferson's term as president. American ships that traded on the Mediterranean Sea were attacked by the Barbary pirates. These pirates came from small kingdoms on the southern edge of the sea. France or Britain could have put an end to the piracy. They had strong navies. Instead they paid for the pirates to leave them alone. And they allowed the pirates to attack ships from small countries. The small countries could not afford to pay the pirates. France and Britain used the conflict with the pirates to help their merchants. Their merchants were safe while those of other countries were attacked.

How It Was

Stephen Decatur carefully guided his ship into the harbor of Tripoli. His mission: to recapture or destroy the USS *Philadelphia*. The pirates had captured the ship. And the Americans did not want them to use the ship to fight against America.

He thought through his plan again. His ship was captured from Tripoli. It looked natural. He had hired a crew that could speak Arabic. The men should be able to fool the harbor master. Stephen and his men were disguised as Arab sailors.

As they sailed into the harbor at Tripoli, sailors who spoke Arabic called out to the harbor master, "We lost our anchors. Can we come into your harbor for repairs?"

Permission granted, Decatur maneuvered his ship alongside the *Philadelphia*. "I don't want to raise their suspicions," he thought. "Let's make this look natural." Since they had said they had no anchor, the sailors tied their ship to the *Philadelphia*.

Decatur gave the signal. He and his men leapt from their ship and began to board the *Philadelphia*. Swords glinted in the evening light. Shouts rang out. The surprised pirates dove into the harbor and swam for shore.

Stephen Decatur quickly surveyed the *Philadelphia*. The ship was too damaged to sail away. He ordered his men to set fire to the ship. By now the guns from Tripoli had opened up on them. Cannonballs splashed around them. Decatur and his sailors scrambled back onto their ship and slipped out of the harbor as the darkness gathered about them. They had just participated in one of the most daring naval actions of the time.

107

Background

First Barbary War

The Barbary pirates came from the North African states of Tripoli, Tunis, Morocco, and Algiers, which made up the area called the Barbary Coast. The pirates plundered merchant ships, held crews for ransom, and demanded tribute. Wealthy countries, including England and France, were willing to buy protection from pirate attacks. During the Revolutionary War, the American colonies were no longer under England's protection but benefited from France's protection. Once America became an independent country, however, the new government had to fend for itself against the demands of the pirates. Thomas Jefferson was the US minister to France at the time and disagreed with paying the pirates tribute. However, the nation's leaders believed that paying the annual tributes and ransoms for crews was less expensive than starting a war. When Jefferson became president in 1801 and refused to pay the tribute, the pirate countries declared war on the United States, leading to the First Barbary War. Although Jefferson's navy made key attacks on the pirates and a treaty was signed in 1805, the United States was not totally free from the tribute payments until 1815. England and France continued to pay tributes until 1830. One significant reason Jefferson fought the pirates was to earn respect for the United States from European nations.

Teach for Understanding

What problem developed on the Mediterranean Sea? The Barbary pirates attacked American trade ships.

- Direct attention to Visual 12. Explain that it is a political map showing the borders of several countries during the early 1800s.

- Choose two volunteers. Direct one to locate the United States on the map and identify the continent it is on. Instruct the other to trace the Barbary Coast and identify the continent it is on.

How did France and Britain choose to deal with the pirates? They paid the pirates to leave their ships alone.

Why did France and Britain pay the pirates to leave their ships alone? Since small countries could not afford to pay the pirates, France and Britain used the conflict to help their merchants by paying to keep them safe while other countries were attacked.

- Use Background information to guide a discussion about how Jefferson handled the situation with the Barbary pirates.

- Direct attention to the How It Was box.

What was Stephen Decatur's mission? to recapture or destroy the USS *Philadelphia*

Why did Stephen Decatur need to recapture or destroy the USS *Philadelphia*? The pirates had captured the ship. The Americans did not want them to use it to fight against America.

- Invite a student to explain Stephen Decatur's plan for completing the mission.

Why did Stephen Decatur decide to set fire to the USS *Philadelphia*? It was too damaged to sail away.

- Why do you think Decatur's mission is considered to be one of the most daring naval actions of that time? Answers may include that the mission was dangerous. Decatur and his crew had to go into the harbor of Tripoli, which was controlled by the pirates. Decatur could not be sure that his plan would fool the harbor master. There were pirates on the USS *Philadelphia*. When the pirates realized what was happening, they opened fire on Decatur and his men.

Teach for Understanding

Who owned New Orleans when Jefferson became president? **the French**

Why did Jefferson want to buy New Orleans? **Jefferson wanted to be sure American farmers in the West could continue to ship goods down the Mississippi River; he did not want the French to decide that American goods could no longer pass through the city.**

Who gave Jefferson permission to buy New Orleans? **Congress**

How did the French reply to Jefferson's offer to buy New Orleans? **They wanted to sell all the land called Louisiana, not just New Orleans.**

How much money did the French want in exchange for all the Louisiana Territory? **$15 million**

Do you think that $15 million was a good price for the Louisiana Territory? **Answers may include that it was a good price because the Louisiana Territory would give the United States a lot of good farmland.**

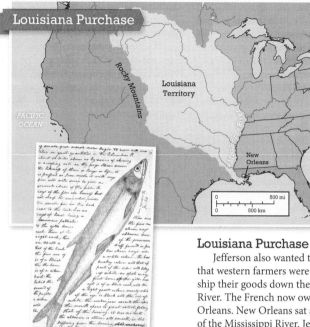

Louisiana Purchase

Jefferson refused to pay the pirates. Jefferson also refused to allow the pirates to attack Americans. John Adams had begun to build an American navy. Jefferson decided to put it to good use. The US Navy cruised the southern Mediterranean. American sailors and marines defeated the pirates in several battles. The pirate kingdoms agreed to leave American ships alone.

Louisiana Purchase

Jefferson also wanted to make sure that western farmers were allowed to ship their goods down the Mississippi River. The French now owned New Orleans. New Orleans sat at the mouth of the Mississippi River. Jefferson did not want the French to decide that American goods could no longer pass through the city.

Congress gave Jefferson permission to buy New Orleans for up to two million dollars. The French wanted to sell much more than New Orleans. They were willing to sell a large portion of land, called Louisiana, for fifteen million dollars. This land included New Orleans, but it stretched far to the west of the Mississippi. This offer looked

108

Additional Background information for this lesson is on the Teacher's Toolkit CD.

Background

Louisiana Purchase

The land west of the Mississippi was known as the Louisiana Territory. It comprised about 828,000 acres, making it larger than the existing United States. This land originally belonged to France, which lost it to Spain after the French and Indian War. As the United States was pushing farther west and needed the port of New Orleans for trade purposes, conflict between America and Spain was resolved with a treaty granting the United States the right to use both the Mississippi River and New Orleans for commerce. When Napoleon Bonaparte became emperor of France, he wanted to restore France's territories in North America. He reclaimed the Louisiana Territory, creating an urgent need for the United States to buy the city for itself. By the time Jefferson sent a representative to France with a proposal, however, Napoleon's plans for a French empire were starting to crumble, making it more desirable for France to sell the whole territory than to try to protect it and most likely lose it again. Thus the United States spent more than what was originally allotted for the purchase of New Orleans but came away with the entire Louisiana Territory, a purchase that is often called the greatest real-estate deal in history.

like a lot of land for a little amount of money. By buying Louisiana, the United States would also get New Orleans. The purchase would also give the United States lots of farmland. Jefferson wanted America to be a nation of farmers.

The Federalists did not want to buy the land. They gave two reasons. First, the people who lived there practiced a different religion from Americans. Their government was also different. The Federalists thought Americans should share the same values. Second, the Federalists said slavery would spread into the new land. They did not want to see slavery spread any farther.

Jefferson faced another problem. The Constitution did not say the national government could buy territory. Jefferson wanted a constitutional amendment that gave him this permission. But his advisors said the process would take a long time. He would lose the sale. So Jefferson sent the treaty to Congress. The Congressmen debated the constitutional issue. Once again they discussed the Constitution's statement that Congress could make "necessary and proper" laws. The Democratic-Republicans now appealed to it. Article II Section 2 of the Constitution permitted the president to make treaties as long as two-thirds of the Senate agreed. It did not say what treaties could or could not be made. Congress decided that the president could make a treaty that purchased land.

The United States bought the Louisiana Territory. Jefferson appointed two men to lead a group to explore the new land. Meriwether Lewis was Jefferson's secretary. William Clark was a retired soldier. He knew about surveying land and making maps. Along the way they met Sacagawea, an American Indian woman who helped translate for them. The explorers traveled all the way to the Pacific Ocean and back. The trip lasted almost two and a half years. They made contact with several Native American peoples. They also recorded 178 new plants and 122 different animals.

Why did some Christians support Jefferson?

//// **Activity** ////////////////////////

Planning an Expedition

Plan an expedition to an area that your teacher gives you. You will explore the area and draw maps of the land. You will also take notes and make sketches of what you find. What will you need to prepare for? Make a list of the provisions you will need.

//

109

good trails to travel on; she might have shown them what plants were good for food; she might have helped them trade with Indian tribes.

- Select a volunteer to locate on Visual 13 where Lewis and Clark began their expedition and to trace the route they traveled.

  Did Lewis and Clark explore only the Louisiana Territory? No, they traveled all the way to the Pacific Ocean.

- What kinds of land did Lewis and Clark travel over? Answers may include plains, hills, forests, mountains, and rivers.

- How do you think Lewis and Clark traveled over the territory? Answers may include by foot, by boat or canoe, by wagon, by horse

  How long did the trip take Lewis and Clark? two and a half years

  What did Lewis and Clark discover on the trip? several Native American peoples, new plants, different animals

  Conclude the discussion by asking the question on page 109. Some Christians did not think the official churches in their states treated them well, and they thought Jefferson might push for more freedom of worship.

Activity Manual

- Guide completion of pages 76–77.

// **Activity** ///

Planning an Expedition

- Generate excitement about planning an expedition as you read the Activity information aloud.

- Tell the students the location you have chosen for them to explore, such as a playground, a zoo, a local park, or a state park. Discuss what they might look for and write notes about.

- Invite students to list items that might be needed for the expedition.

- Divide the students into small groups. Assign each group one of the following tasks: plan a schedule for the day; make a list of food to bring along; and make a list of other items that will be needed, such as hand sanitizer, a first-aid kit, notebooks, and pencils.

- Invite groups to share their plans.

Teach for Understanding

Who opposed buying the Louisiana Territory? the Federalists

- Choose volunteers to explain why the Federalists did not want to purchase the Louisiana Territory.

  What was another problem that Jefferson faced when trying to purchase the Louisiana Territory? The Constitution did not say that the national government could buy territory.

  Why was Jefferson advised not to request a constitutional amendment that would give him permission to buy the Louisiana Territory? The process for passing an amendment would take too long.

  What did Congress finally decide Jefferson could do to purchase the territory? make a treaty

  Which men did Jefferson send to explore the Louisiana Territory? Meriwether Lewis and William Clark

- Why do you think Jefferson chose Lewis and Clark to explore the Louisiana Territory? Answers may include that Lewis would be good at taking notes and Clark could survey the land and draw maps.

  Which woman did Lewis and Clark meet who was able to help them communicate with American Indians? Sacagawea

- In what other ways do you think Sacagawea was able to help the explorers? Answers could include that she might have shown them

42

Student Text pages 110–12
Activity Manual page 78

Lesson Focus

- The United States and Great Britain engaged in another war.

Objectives

- Identify James Madison as the fourth president of the United States
- State reasons for the War of 1812
- Explain why the United States and Great Britain were not ready for war
- Explain the reasons Madison adopted Federalist ideas after the war

Teacher's Toolkit CD

- Visual 14: The USS *Constitution*
- Instructional Aid 30: The USS *Constitution*

Review

Who was the third president of the United States? Thomas Jefferson

What were two important challenges Jefferson faced during his presidency? conflict with the Barbary pirates and buying the Louisiana Territory

- Invite a student to summarize the conflict with the Barbary pirates. Instruct the student to include the cause of the conflict and how Jefferson handled the situation.

Why did Jefferson want to purchase New Orleans? to make sure that western farmers could ship their goods down the Mississippi River

- Choose a volunteer to explain why Jefferson was unable to buy only New Orleans from the French.

What did Congress say Jefferson could do in order to buy the Louisiana Territory? make a treaty

What important information did Lewis and Clark bring back from their expedition? They made contact with several Native American peoples and recorded many new plants and animals.

Preparation for Reading

- Generate interest as you direct the students to read the titles and examine the pictures and map on pages 110–12.
- Guide pronunciation of any unfamiliar words in the lesson.
- Direct the students to read the pages silently to find out what countries fought in the War of 1812. the United States and Great Britain

Teach for Understanding

Which of George Washington's precedents did Jefferson follow? He did not seek a third term.

James Madison dressed in black and is said to have had only one suit of clothes at a time. However, he liked horses more than clothes and never had fewer than seven while he was president.

Standing 5'6" tall and weighing only 100 pounds, Madison is the smallest American president. However, his legacy is large. His arguments in the Federalist papers influenced the division of our government into three branches.

James Madison

Thomas Jefferson was a popular president, but he followed the precedent set by George Washington. Jefferson did not seek a third term. James Madison became the fourth president. Madison is often called the Father of the Constitution. He played an important role in the Constitutional Convention. Madison had also served in Congress. He and Jefferson worked closely together.

Great Britain and France were at war when Madison became president. The United States tried to stay neutral. But France objected when the United States traded with Britain. Britain objected when the United States traded with France. Both the French and the British stopped American ships on the ocean.

The British forced sailors on American ships to join the British navy. When accused of doing this, the British claimed they did not force American citizens to join their navy. They claimed they captured only British deserters. But the Americans did not believe the British claims. The Americans also said that the British were giving weapons to American Indians in the United States.

In June of 1812 the United States declared war on Great Britain. But the United States was not ready for war. The army and navy were small. Democratic-Republicans thought that having an army at all times threatened American liberty. Armies also cost money. The Democratic-Republicans disliked taxes. They would not raise taxes to pay for a larger army and navy. Democratic-Republicans also disliked banks. They had put an end to the Bank of the United States in 1811. It was difficult for Congress to borrow the money needed to fight the war.

The War of 1812

At first the war was fought against the Indians in the West. William Henry Harrison attacked the tribe of Tecumseh. Tecumseh was an Indian leader who tried to stop Americans from moving west. The Americans lost

110

Who was chosen to be the fourth president of the United States? James Madison

Why is Madison often called the Father of the Constitution? He played an important role in the Constitutional Convention.

Which countries were at war when Madison became president? Great Britain and France

What was the result of the United States trying to remain neutral in the war between Great Britain and France? Both Great Britain and France objected when the United States traded with the opposing country; both the British and the French stopped American ships.

- Choose a volunteer to explain why the United States declared war on Great Britain.

Was the United States ready to fight another war? No, the army and navy were small, and the Democratic-Republicans would not raise taxes to pay for a larger army and navy; it was difficult for Congress to borrow the money needed to fight a war because the Democratic-Republicans had put an end to the Bank of the United States in 1811.

- Why do you think the United States first fought against the Indians in the West during the War of 1812? Answers may include that the Indians wanted to stop Americans from moving west; the Indians sided with the British who gave them weapons.

112

twice as many men as the Indians. But Harrison burned Tecumseh's village.

The Americans then invaded Canada. They hoped the Canadians would fight for freedom from Britain. But the Canadians did not want independence from Great Britain. Instead the British and Canadians invaded the United States. The Americans lost Michigan.

The American navy performed better than the army. The British navy had more ships than the Americans. But their ships were spread out around the world. The American ships were also sturdier. The USS *Constitution* was nicknamed "Old Ironsides." British cannonballs bounced off her sides during battle. But by 1813 the British were able to bring more ships to American waters. The British then regained control of the seas.

The US Navy also fought the British on the Great Lakes. Captain Oliver Hazard Perry destroyed the British fleet there. The Americans were now able to push the British back into Canada.

But the war was not over. The British sailed up the Chesapeake Bay. They marched into Washington, DC, and burned the White House and many other government buildings. The British then attacked

Baltimore, but Fort McHenry stood fast. The British withdrew. It was during this battle that Francis Scott Key wrote "The Star-Spangled Banner," which became the American national anthem. Then the British came down from Canada to attack the Americans at Plattsburgh, New York. But the Americans were prepared for the attack and defeated the British.

By this time both the Americans and the British were tired of the war. They were ready to sign a peace treaty. The treaty set everything back the way it had been before the war. Land or ships captured by either side would be returned. All prisoners of war would be returned.

News of the treaty traveled slowly. The final battle actually took place after the treaty was signed. The British attacked the Americans at New Orleans. Andrew Jackson defeated the British attack and became a popular American hero.

War of 1812

★ American victory
✦ British victory

111

Background

USS *Constitution*

President George Washington signed the Naval Armament Act in 1794. It called for six frigates to be built. On October 21, 1797, the USS *Constitution* was launched. The ship had forty-four guns. The *Constitution* won battles in the Quasi War with France (1798–1801) and the Barbary Wars (1801–1805).

During the War of 1812, the *Constitution* defeated four English warships. Each of its three captains earned a congressional gold medal. The ship's victories had little effect on the outcome of the war, but they did uplift American morale. The *Constitution* was taken out of active service in 1855.

Teach for Understanding

Why did the Americans invade Canada? They hoped the Canadians would fight for freedom from Britain.

What was the result of the Americans invading Canada? The British and Canadians invaded the United States, and the Americans lost Michigan.

In what way were the American ships better than the British ships? The American ships were sturdier.

Why was the USS *Constitution* given the name "Old Ironsides"? British cannonballs bounced off its sides during battle.

- Direct attention to Visual 14. Guide a discussion about interesting features of the USS *Constitution*. Use Background information to discuss the ship's history.

Where did the American navy fight the British? on the sea and on the Great Lakes

What was the result of Captain Oliver Hazard Perry destroying the British fleet on the Great Lakes? The Americans pushed the British back into Canada.

What did the British do when they marched into Washington, DC? They burned the White House and other government buildings.

Who won the battle for Baltimore? the Americans

- Invite a student to read aloud the text that tells who won the battle for Baltimore.

What did Francis Scott Key do during the battle? He wrote "The Star-Spangled Banner."

What was the location of the battle that occurred immediately before the peace treaty was signed? Plattsburgh, New York

Do you think the war changed anything? Answers may include that the treaty set everything back the way it had been before the war, so nothing changed.

- Invite a student to read aloud the text that tells that the war did not change anything.

Why did the battle at New Orleans take place after the treaty was signed? News of the treaty traveled slowly.

- Guide a discussion about the major engagements shown on the map on page 111.

Lesson

42

Teach for Understanding

Although Andrew Jackson was a war hero, did he always do what was right? No, he did not honor the peace treaty or obey President Madison by returning Indian lands that the Americans had captured.

Why was President Madison not able to force Jackson to obey the law? Jackson was too popular.

What caused the Federalist Party to lose power after the war? The Federalists had opposed the war, so they lost the support of many Americans.

- Choose volunteers to explain the Federalist ideas that Madison adopted after the War of 1812.

- Why do you think the issues adopted by Madison remained matters of political debate? Answers may include that people do not always agree on different issues.

- Use Background information to guide a discussion about the good results the war brought to the United States.

▶ Conclude the discussion by asking the question on page 112. Jackson was allowed to break the law because of his popularity.

Activity Manual

- Guide completion of page 78.

Quick to take offense, Jackson fought in many duels. He was shot twice and the bullet fragments remained in his body throughout the rest of his life.

As a boy young Andrew Jackson was wiry and tough. He fought other boys often and loved to wrestle. One schoolmate said, "I could throw him three times out of four, but he never would stay thrown. He . . . never would give up." Jackson's habit of fighting, along with his quick temper and will of iron, stayed with him his entire life.

After the War

Jackson was a war hero. But not all of his actions were right. The peace treaty said that the Indians should receive back the lands the Americans captured from them. But Jackson had used his victories in the war to take land away, even from the Indians who fought with the Americans. President Madison ordered Jackson to return the land to the Indians. Jackson refused. He was too popular for Madison to force him to obey the law. The founders had warned against allowing popular heroes to break the law.

The war also changed the political parties. The Federalists would never again be a powerful party. They had opposed the war, so they lost the support of many Americans.

But the war led Madison to adopt some Federalist ideas. He asked Congress to reopen the Bank of the United States. Then the country could borrow money in times of crisis. Madison still did not want a permanent army. But he wanted permanent leaders so an army could be raised quickly. He asked for new ships to be built for the navy. Madison also realized the importance of American manufacturing. American-made cannons had helped lead to victory in the battle of New Orleans. Madison asked Congress for a tariff or a tax on imported goods to protect American manufacturers from more powerful British ones. Finally, Madison asked Congress to pass a constitutional amendment that would allow the national government to build internal improvements such as roads and canals. Without good roads, the army had difficulty moving about the country during the war. Congress agreed that internal improvements were a good idea, but it did not think an amendment was necessary. Many of these issues would remain matters of political debate over the coming decades.

How does Andrew Jackson show one of the dangers of democracy?

112

Activities

Research Facts

Materials: sources for researching the USS *Constitution*

Distribute copies of Instructional Aid 30. Instruct the students to research facts about the USS *Constitution* and write the fact they think is the most interesting on the hull of the ship. Encourage the students to look for facts that were not discussed in the lesson.

Memorize "The Star-Spangled Banner"

Use Background information on the Teacher's Toolkit CD to guide a discussion about the history of "The Star-Spangled Banner." Point out that "The Star-Spangled Banner" was written as a poem and later set to music. Read the poem aloud. Then discuss how the poem describes the British attack on Fort McHenry and discuss the meaning of the last verse. Guide the students in memorizing one verse a week.

Background

Importance of the War of 1812

Some of the results of the war with Britain were good for the United States. As a result of the war, American leaders realized the importance of having a military to protect the nation. Americans felt unified after the War of 1812. The people realized that America could now handle foreign threats. The War of 1812 aided the growth of manufacturing because trade was disrupted during the war. The war also revealed the need for another national bank. The Second Bank of the United States was chartered in 1816.

Additional Background information for this lesson is on the Teacher's Toolkit CD.

Eighteen-year-old James Monroe was wounded in his left shoulder at the Battle of Trenton during the Revolutionary War.

He was the last of the Presidents to have fought in the Revolutionary War. This is why the people nicknamed him "The Last Cocked Hat." Cocked hats, also known as tricorns, were worn during the Revolutionary War.

These knee-breeches were unfashionable by the time Monroe was in office, but they helped to cement his connection to the Nation's founding era.

James Monroe

James Monroe won the election of 1816 as the Democratic-Republican candidate.

The Monroe Doctrine

South American nations had been declaring independence from Spain. The United States supported this revolution. Americans had won their independence from Great Britain. They wanted other countries to become independent too. The United States did not want European nations to try to take lands in North or South America.

James Monroe worked with his secretary of state, John Quincy Adams, to develop the Monroe Doctrine. The Monroe Doctrine stated four things. First, European nations should not create any more colonies in North or South America. Second, European nations must not meddle in the affairs of any independent country in North or South America. The United States would take the meddling as a threat to itself. Third, the United States promised not to meddle in the affairs of Europe. Fourth, the United States said Spain should not give any land it owned in America to another European nation. If Spain gave up lands, they should be given to a nation in North or South America.

Florida

When Monroe became president, Florida belonged to Spain. Because the US government had no authority over Florida, it had become a place for refugees. Black Americans would flee slavery and hide in Florida. American Indians who lost their lands could flee to Florida. These Indians were called Seminoles. Sometimes the Seminoles would raid over the border into the United States.

Before the United States could purchase Florida, the Spanish would have to be willing to sell. But Spain did not want to sell because of Andrew Jackson. President Monroe had sent

113

Lesson 43

Student Text pages 113–15
Activity Manual pages 79–80

Lesson Focus

- During James Monroe's presidency, America supported the revolutions in South American nations and began to divide into slave and free states.

Objectives

- Identify James Monroe as the fifth president of the United States
- List the four points of the Monroe Doctrine
- Explain why the United States wanted to buy Florida
- Explain how the Missouri Compromise solved the argument between the free states and the slave states

Teacher's Toolkit CD

- Instructional Aid 31: *The Monroe Doctrine & Missouri Compromise*

Review

Who was elected president after Thomas Jefferson? James Madison

What war did the United States fight during Madison's presidency? the War of 1812

Why did the United States declare war on Great Britain? The Americans did not believe the British claims that they did not force Americans to join their navy, and the Americans said that the British were giving weapons to American Indians.

- Choose a volunteer to explain why the United States was not ready for the war. The army and navy were small, and the Democratic-Republicans would not raise taxes to pay for a larger army and navy; it was difficult for Congress to borrow the money needed to fight a war because the Democratic-Republicans had put an end to the Bank of the United States in 1811.

- Who do you think won the War of 1812? Answers may include that neither country won because the treaty set everything back the way it had been before the war.

- Choose volunteers to tell what Federalist ideas Madison adopted after the war. He wanted Congress to reopen the Bank of the United States; he wanted permanent leaders so an army could be raised quickly; he asked for new ships to be built for the navy; he asked Congress for a tariff or tax on imported goods; he wanted the national government to build internal improvements.

Preparation for Reading

- Generate interest as you direct the students to read the titles and examine the picture and maps on pages 113–15.
- Guide pronunciation of any unfamiliar words in the lesson.
- Direct the students to read the pages silently and complete Instructional Aid 31 in small groups.

Teach for Understanding

Who was elected president immediately after James Madison? James Monroe

Who developed the Monroe Doctrine? James Monroe and John Quincy Adams

Why did James Monroe and John Quincy Adams develop the Monroe Doctrine? The United States supported South American nations declaring their independence from Spain and did not want European nations to try to take lands in North or South America.

- Select groups to tell the four points stated in the Monroe Doctrine.

How would the United States treat the meddling of a European nation in the affairs of an independent North or South American country? as a threat to the United States

- Ask a student to explain why the United States wanted to buy Florida from the Spanish. Black Americans fleeing from slavery hid from their masters in Florida; American Indians who lost their lands would flee there; these Indians, or Seminoles, would raid over the border into the United States.

Teach for Understanding

Why did the Spanish not want to sell Florida at first? They were angry that Jackson destroyed many Seminole villages and captured a Spanish fort and Pensacola, the capital of Spanish Florida, when Monroe sent him to Florida to track down the Seminole raiders.

Did Monroe order Jackson to attack the Spanish? No, Jackson disobeyed Monroe's orders.

What else did Americans argue about during Monroe's presidency? territory within the United States

- Direct attention to the map on page 114.

Why is Missouri colored orange? It is a territory.

What do you know about the number of free states and the number of slave states before the Missouri Compromise? Elicit that they were equal.

- Guide a discussion about how granting Missouri statehood as a slave state or a free state would upset the balance of the country.

- Invite groups to tell what people on each side argued to support their belief that their way of life was better.

Why did neither side want the other to gain more representatives in Congress? Neither side wanted Congress to help the other side's way of life spread.

Jackson to Florida to track down the Seminole raiders. President Monroe ordered Jackson not to attack the Spanish. However, Jackson disobeyed the order. He destroyed many Seminole villages. Then he captured a Spanish fort. He even captured Pensacola, the capital of Spanish Florida. Secretary of War John Calhoun wanted Jackson arrested. The Spanish were also angered. But they eventually sold Florida to the United States.

Missouri Compromise

Americans also argued about territory within the United States. In 1819 Missouri asked to become a state. At this time the United States had eleven states that permitted slavery. The other eleven states were free.

The free states and the slave states both thought their way of life was better. Some people in the slave states argued that the institution of slavery allowed owners to develop the virtues of culture, honor, courage, and chivalry. They said people in the North were just concerned about making money. Southerners claimed they treated their slaves better than Northerners treated their factory workers. Some people in the northern states argued that slavery was wrong. It did not build virtue. It corrupted the owners. It did not treat slaves as human beings made in God's image.

Neither side wanted the other to gain more representatives in Congress. Neither wanted Congress to help the

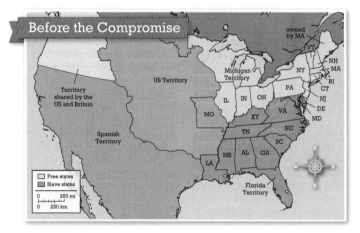

Before the Compromise

114

Background

James Monroe

James Monroe had been Madison's secretary of state during the War of 1812. Several governors and congressmen signed a petition asking Monroe to run for president, but he was hesitant. He finally agreed to run, but only if he would not be tied to a single political party and would not have to wage an active campaign. He wanted to run on his own record. Monroe won the election during a unique time in American politics. During Monroe's two terms in office, the major parties did not clash on the national level. Monroe's terms in office came to be known as the "Era of Good Feelings."

Monroe was the fourth Virginian to become president. Rather than give the usual inaugural address, he just said he would do his best. He chose good men for his cabinet. He listened to the varied ideas that developed within the Republican Party. During his presidency Mississippi and Alabama gained statehood. Monroe also championed American interests abroad. One of his greatest accomplishments was the Monroe Doctrine.

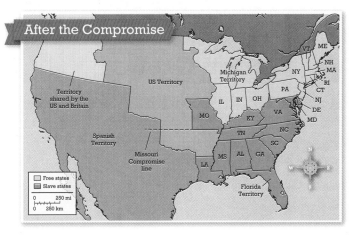

After the Compromise

US Territory

Territory shared by the US and Britain

Spanish Territory

Michigan Territory

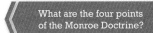

Missouri Compromise line

Free states
Slave states

0   250 mi
0   250 km

ME
VT NH
NY MA
MI RI
PA CT
IL IN OH NJ
DE
MO KY VA MD
TN NC
MS AL GA SC
LA

Florida Territory

other side's way of life spread. Those in the South also did not want Congress to pass high tariffs. High tariffs hurt their sale of cotton overseas. Northerners preferred high tariffs. Tariffs protected northern businesses from competition overseas.

The solution was a compromise. Maine was part of Massachusetts at this time. Massachusetts was willing for Maine to become its own state. Maine would enter the United States as a free state. Missouri would enter as a slave state. This solution would keep the number of senators balanced evenly.

In addition, Congress decided that future states above the southern border of Missouri would be free states.

Future states below the border could be slave states. The goal of the Missouri Compromise was to end debates about slavery. When new states were added to the Union, everybody would already know whether those states would be free or slave.

Conclusion

The United States was a young nation. But it had fashioned a Constitution that would stand the test of time. Its first presidents also set wise precedents for the future.

> What are the four points of the Monroe Doctrine?

115

Teach for Understanding

- Choose a volunteer to explain the opposing views Southerners and Northerners had about tariffs. Southerners did not want high tariffs because they hurt the sale of cotton overseas. Northerners preferred high tariffs because they protected northern businesses from competition overseas.

How did the Missouri Compromise solve the debate between the free states and the slave states? Two new states would enter the United States. Maine would enter as a free state, and Missouri would enter as a slave state. This solution would keep the number of senators balanced evenly.

- Direct the students to locate Maine and Missouri on the map on page 115.

What did Congress decide about states being added in the future? Future states above the southern border of Missouri would be free states, and future states below the border could be slave states.

- Direct the students to trace the line that would divide future free and future slave states.

What was the goal of the Missouri Compromise? to end debates about slavery

- Do you think that the Missouri Compromise ended debates about slavery? Why?

Conclude the discussion by asking the question on page 115. European nations would not create any more colonies in North or South America; European nations must not meddle in the affairs of any independent country in North or South America; the United States promised not to meddle in the affairs of Europe; Spain should not give any land it owned in America to another European nation but could give land to a nation in North or South America.

Lesson **44**

Chapter Review
Activity Manual pages 81–82

Objective
- Recall concepts and terms from Chapter 5

Introduction

- Concepts for the Chapter 5 Test will be taken from Activity Manual pages 65–82. You may review any or all of the concepts during this lesson. You may choose to review Chapter 5 by playing "Jump Start."

Review

Game: Jump Start

- Divide the class into teams. Provide a "jump" chair in the front of the room for each team. Instruct one student from each team to sit in his team's chair. After the question is read, the students should jump to their feet and remain standing when they know the answer. The first student to stand and give the correct answer receives a point for his team.

Activity Manual

- Guide completion of pages 81–82.

Lesson **45**

Chapter 5 Test

Objective
- Demonstrate knowledge of concepts from Chapter 5 by taking the test

Assessment

- Administer Test 5.

Introduction

As a new nation, America experienced many different kinds of growth. It needed to grow in its knowledge of how to govern itself wisely. America had room to grow in geographical size and in population. Americans were seeking new, better ways to travel, communicate, and get work done. God raised up leaders who helped many Americans grow spiritually.

Some growth came at a great cost. America had conflict with the American Indians and with Mexico as it struggled to gain land in the West. Sadly, as Americans expanded their land westward, the problem of slavery also increased.

Chapter Focus

As a new nation, America experienced many different kinds of growth.

6 The Young Nation Grows

Focus

As a new nation, America experienced many different kinds of growth.

Chapter 6 Overview

Lesson	Student Text	Activity Manual	Content		Vocabulary
46	116–19	83–86	Election of 1824 Andrew Jackson	John Quincy Adams	
47	120–22	87	Democrats	Whigs	nullify
48	123–25	88–89	Biography Box: Sequoyah	Trail of Tears	Indian Removal Act
49	126–28	90–91	The Second Great Awakening Asahel Nettleton	Charles Finney Primary Source: Good News from Yale	rationalism transcendentalism
50	129–31	92–93	Robert Fulton Peter Cooper	Samuel Morse Activity: Comparing Historical Maps	
51	132–34	94	How It Was: Mill Village Girls Samuel Slater Francis Cabot Lowell Elias Howe	Eli Whitney Cyrus McCormick John Deere	Industrial Revolution interchangeable parts
52	135–37	95–96	James Polk Zachary Taylor	Mexican Cession	
53		97–98	Chapter Review		
54			Chapter Test		

Visit bjupress.com/resources for links to enhance the lessons.

Peter Cooper's locomotive
1830

First telegraph message
1844

Mexican Cession
1848

1830   1838 1840   1846   1850

Cherokees go west
on the Trail of Tears

Mexican War
begins

Room to Grow

The United States of America had finally become an independent nation. It had written its own constitution and set up its own government. God had blessed the United States. From its founding, it had enjoyed gifted leaders such as George Washington, John Adams, and James Madison.

The United States was a growing nation. But compared to other nations in the world, it was still young. As a young nation, the United States had much to learn. The American people were still learning how the Constitution worked. The writers of the Constitution had tried to make sure that everyone's rights were respected. They wanted the Constitution to ensure justice for everyone. But the writers had not been able to think about every possible situation ahead of time. Everyone would not always be treated fairly. And

not everyone would always agree on what the Constitution allowed and did not allow. America had room to grow in its knowledge of how to govern itself wisely and well.

America also had room to grow in geographical size. Now that new lands had been explored in the West, people began to move and spread out. In addition, America was growing in population. Immigrants continued to arrive on America's shores. Growth almost always results in change. Americans began seeking new, better ways to travel, communicate, and get work done.

God also raised up leaders who helped many Americans grow spiritually. During the early part of the nineteenth century, a revival swept through the United States. God was at work in exciting ways in the young, growing nation.

117

JourneyForth

Captive Treasure by Milly Howard is available from JourneyForth Books, a division of BJU Press, at journeyforth.com.

In this historical novel set in Wyoming in the 1850s, the Talbot family travels west to help with a mission to the Indians. Near Fort Laramie, their daughter Carrie is kidnapped by raiding Cheyennes and taken to their camp. She has only the family Bible and her faith in God to guide her through her difficult yet rewarding experience.

Lesson Focus

- The United States grew in its understanding of how to govern itself.

Objectives

- Recognize how the Electoral College was put to the test in the election of 1824
- Identify characteristics of Andrew Jackson, John Quincy Adams, and Henry Clay
- Examine the presidency of John Quincy Adams

Teacher's Toolkit CD

- Instructional Aids 32–33: *Room to Grow*; *The Election of 1824*

Introduction

- Invite a student to read aloud the title of the chapter.

  What do you think this chapter will be about? growth in America

- Invite a student to read the chapter focus aloud.

  What do you think you will learn about in this chapter? the many types of growth that America experienced

- Direct attention to the timeline.

  What two inventions are shown on the timeline? the locomotive and telegraph

  When did the Cherokees go west? 1838

  What country did America go to war with in 1846? Mexico

Preparation for Reading

- Generate interest as you direct the students to read the titles and examine the pictures on pages 116–19.
- Guide pronunciation of any unfamiliar words in the lesson.
- Direct the students to read the pages silently to learn the name of the man who won the election of 1824. John Quincy Adams

Teach for Understanding

- Display Instructional Aid 32. Choose groups to state the kinds of growth America experienced as you complete the word web. Select volunteers to answer the questions as you write for display.

Teach for Understanding

- Direct the students to complete Instructional Aid 33 in small groups.
- Write answers for display as Instructional Aid 33 is discussed.
- Invite a group to tell what it learned about Andrew Jackson.
- Invite another group to state what it learned about John Quincy Adams.
- Direct the following questions to different groups:

How many candidates were in the election of 1824? four

What did the Constitution require in order to have a clear winner in an election? a majority of the electoral votes

When there was no clear winner in the election, who did the US Constitution say would elect the president? the House of Representatives

How was the House of Representatives influenced to elect John Quincy Adams as president? Henry Clay was the Speaker of the House, and he knew that Jackson did not always respect the law. Clay had influence among the other representatives. He influenced them to support Adams.

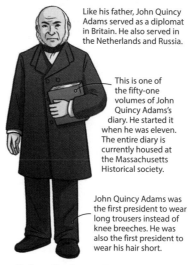

Like his father, John Quincy Adams served as a diplomat in Britain. He also served in the Netherlands and Russia.

This is one of the fifty-one volumes of John Quincy Adams's diary. He started it when he was eleven. The entire diary is currently housed at the Massachusetts Historical society.

John Quincy Adams was the first president to wear long trousers instead of knee breeches. He was also the first president to wear his hair short.

John Quincy Adams
The Election of 1824

The presidential election of 1824 had Americans on the edge of their seats. Four men, all Republicans, were running for president. The top two candidates were **Andrew Jackson** and **John Quincy Adams**.

Jackson and Adams were different in personality. Jackson enjoyed great popularity with the American people. He had served in Congress and had been a hero in the War of 1812. Many people saw him as a down-to-earth leader who understood the problems of the common man. Adams had been a foreign minister, a senator, and a secretary of state. He had a record of doing what he believed was right no matter what others thought of him. He was reserved, and some people saw him as cold and distant. However, many Americans believed that he was a man of principle who would lead the country well.

Jackson won more votes from the people than Adams. He also won more Electoral College votes. But the two other candidates received some votes from electors too. Jackson did not win enough support to have a majority of the electoral votes. The Constitution required a majority in order to have a clear winner.

A situation like this had never happened before. The Constitution said that if the Electoral College did not elect a president by a majority, there had to be another vote. This time the vote would go to the House of Representatives. Each state would have one vote, and it could choose any of the top three candidates.

Henry Clay had been one of the four candidates. He had come in last in the Electoral College vote, so he was no longer in the running. Clay was concerned. He knew that Jackson did not always respect the law. As Speaker of the House, Clay held the most important position in the House of Representatives. He had influence among the other representatives. He used his influence to gain support for

118

Background

The President Who Never Retired

John Quincy Adams's career continued after he left the White House. In 1830 he ran for Congress for his home district in Massachusetts. He had the attitude of a servant. The position did not matter, nor did the pay. (He received $8.00 a day for his services.) Serving the people, however, did matter. He wrote, "No person could be degraded by serving the people. . . . If the people elected me town selectman [a member of a board of town officers that helped oversee local affairs], I would consider it an honor."

In Congress he was highly respected for his many accomplishments. His speechmaking was so skilled, he was soon nicknamed "old man eloquent." In 1832 he led the fight to revise the tariff downward (lower the rates). The new tariff has sometimes been called "the Adams tariff."

A lifelong foe of slavery, he forced the House to repeal the gag rule, which had forbidden antislavery petitions to be submitted to the House. He predicted correctly that wars would be fought if the country did not settle the issue of slavery. He introduced a constitutional amendment to abolish slavery in 1839. His antislavery speeches were not just idle talk. When a freed slave named Nathan Jones saw his family sold into slavery, Adams gave him money and the names of friends to contact to raise the funds needed to secure their freedom.

his choice, John Quincy Adams. In the end, Adams won the election.

Some Americans thought that the election had been unfair. When Adams appointed Clay as the new secretary of state, Jackson's supporters were angry. They accused Adams of making a deal with Clay ahead of time to gain his support. They called it a "corrupt bargain." Adams and Clay, however, insisted that no bargain had been made.

The election of 1824 showed why the Constitution was so important. The process for electing a president had been decided long before this election. The Constitution provided a map to guide the nation through a difficult contest. The majority is not always right. The Constitution's process was meant to protect the country from a leader who was popular but would not uphold the law. In the end, no one could really argue with the election's outcome. The election had been handled just as the Constitution said.

A President with Principle

John Quincy Adams served as America's sixth president. He was not a popular president. Yet he continued to act as he always had—with honesty, courage, and principle.

One of the first things Adams did was seek to set up Henry Clay's national program, the American System. This was the same program James Madison

had wanted. It called for a national bank, a high tariff on imported goods, and more roads and canals. The program was meant to help America become more self-supporting and less dependent on trade with Britain.

THE AMERICAN SYSTEM

High Import Tariffs

National Bank · Roads & Canals

Adams had other plans besides the American System. He wanted to build a university. He wanted more support for the arts and sciences. And he wanted to end slavery.

But not everyone liked Adams's plans. Some Americans believed that the government was trying to take too much control. Some did not like the idea of high tariffs. Many feared giving up the slaves. Jackson's supporters in Congress worked to defeat Adams's plans. With so little support, Adams did not enjoy much success as president.

> Why was the Constitution important in the election of 1824?

Teach for Understanding

How did some Americans feel about the way the election was handled? They thought the election had been unfair.

- Guide a discussion of the importance of the Constitution in the election of 1824.
- Point out that Adams sought to set up Henry Clay's national program, the American System.
- Direct attention to the illustration of the American System on page 119. Choose a volunteer to state what the American System called for.

What besides the American System characterized the presidency of John Quincy Adams? He was not popular. Yet he continued to act with honesty, courage, and principle. He wanted to build a university. He wanted more support for the arts and sciences. He wanted to end slavery. He did not enjoy much success as president.

> Conclude the discussion by asking the question on page 119. It guided the nation through a difficult contest (election). It protected the country from a leader who was popular but who would not uphold the law.

Activity Manual

- Guide completion of pages 83–86.

He also helped establish the United States Naval Academy at Severn, Maryland, and he led an eleven-year drive to found a national museum, the Smithsonian. James Smithson, a British chemist, had willed one-half million dollars to the United States for such a purpose, but Congress had wanted to divert the money to other causes.

In 1846 a tall, slim Whig congressman from Illinois was elected to the House. In his initial meeting with Adams, Abraham Lincoln praised the veteran congressman for what he had done to repeal the gag rule. The old patriarch looked at Lincoln and slowly said, "There is much yet to be done."

On February 21, 1848, when Adams rose for a roll call vote in Congress, he collapsed from a stroke. He was carried into the cloakroom. Too sick to be moved, he died there two days later. Abraham Lincoln represented the House and rode the funeral train back to Massachusetts. John C. Calhoun, who often opposed Adams, served as a pallbearer. Daniel Webster wrote his epitaph. Adams had devoted fifty-eight years of his life to serving his nation. He has been called "the president who never retired."

Activity

Create a Word Web

Use background information to create a word web of terms that describe John Quincy Adams.

Lesson Focus

- During his years in office, Andrew Jackson did some good but also much harm.

Objectives
- Identify the political party that Andrew Jackson and his followers created
- Examine problems of Jackson's presidency

Review

- Invite a volunteer to state the ways America had room to grow.
- Choose a student to state the problem that occurred with the election of 1824.
- Invite a volunteer to state how the Constitution gave the solution to the problem of the election of 1824.

> Guide a review of important terms, maps, places, and people from each previous lesson. Direct the students to find and read the corresponding entries from the Resource Treasury.

Preparation for Reading

- Generate interest as you direct the students to read the titles and examine the pictures on pages 120–22.
- Guide pronunciation of any unfamiliar words in the lesson.
- Direct the students to read the pages silently to discover what opponents of Andrew Jackson nicknamed his advisors. his "Kitchen Cabinet"

Teach for Understanding

- Direct attention to the picture on page 120 and read the captions aloud.

In what way was Andrew Jackson's background different from previous presidents? He came from a poor family.

What traits was he known for before he began to take responsibility for his life? for his quick temper and for being wild

---

Andrew Jackson's nickname was "Old Hickory." The name helped portray him as tough and determined.

For eighteen years, Jackson had the remnants of a lead bullet in his arm. The discomfort increased until Jackson called a surgeon to the White House. The surgeon removed the bullet without any anesthetic.

Jackson was not an easy man to like. He made enemies easily and was the first president to face an attempted assassination.

Andrew Jackson

Andrew Jackson won the election of 1828. He became the seventh president of the United States. Jackson began his presidency in a time of great personal grief. His wife, Rachel, died only a few weeks after he was elected. Jackson settled into the White House alone to begin his first term. He remained in office for the next eight years.

Jackson's background was different from the presidents before him. He was the first president to have come from a poor family. He had grown up in South Carolina and later moved to Tennessee. As a boy, he was known for his quick temper and for being wild.

But as a young man, he began to take more responsibility for his life. He became educated and held respectable jobs. People began to notice his leadership skills. Eventually he became a politician, a military general, and a wealthy man. However, sometimes he still acted in a lawless manner. Even as a military officer, there had been times when he refused to obey his authorities. Some Americans worried that he would not respect the law as president.

A New Political Party

Jackson and his followers had created a new political party. They now called themselves the Democratic Party, or **Democrats**. The other party took the name National Republican Party. This party came to be known as the **Whig Party**.

When Jackson became president, he began giving government jobs to people in his party who had supported him. Some of the people Jackson replaced had been dishonest. They had used their positions to steal money from the United States treasury. But many capable, honest men were replaced simply because they were not Democrats. In some cases, the men who replaced them were not as qualified to do the job.

120

What positive changes were seen in Jackson after he took more responsibility for his life? He became educated. He held respectable jobs. He had noticeable leadership skills. He became a politician, a military general, and a wealthy man.

What negative trait did he still possess? He sometimes acted in a lawless manner.

What do you think God wants a leader to be like (2 Samuel 23:3)? Answers may include that God wants a leader to be just, ruling in the fear of God.

What was the name of the new political party that Jackson and his followers created? the Democratic Party, or Democrats

What was the name of the other political party? the Whigs

What were the advantages and disadvantages of Jackson replacing people in government jobs with Democrats? Some of the people he replaced had been dishonest, but many capable, honest men were replaced simply because they were not Democrats. In some cases, the men who replaced them were not as qualified to do the job.

Jackson's actions as president pleased some Americans. But others did not believe Jackson was doing what was best for the American people. Jackson's opponents nicknamed his advisors his "Kitchen Cabinet." The Whigs thought he was trying to take too much control.

Tariff Trouble

One problem during Jackson's presidency had to do with the high tariff on goods imported from Britain. James Madison had asked for this tariff to protect American businesses. If people had to pay a high price for imported goods, they would be more likely to buy American-made goods instead. But people in the southern states did not like this tariff. The South did not have as many factories as the North did. Southern people could not produce as many of their own goods. They had to rely on foreign goods or goods made in the North. They also relied on foreign trade for income from their cash crops. If they did not buy foreign products, other countries would not buy the crops the South produced.

The vice president was John C. Calhoun from South Carolina. Calhoun tried to defend his home state. He said that the tariff was hurting South Carolina. Calhoun said that South Carolina had the right to **nullify**, or refuse to obey, the tariff law. Jackson did not agree. He said that one state

The South needed imports more than the North.

121

Teach for Understanding

Who thought that Andrew Jackson was trying to take too much control as president? the Whigs

- Direct attention to the political cartoon on page 121. Guide a discussion of the effects of the high import tariffs on the North and the South.

What did Jackson's vice president say about the tariff hurting South Carolina? He said that South Carolina had the right to nullify, or refuse to obey, the tariff law.

Background

Old Hickory

The democratic movement that won Jackson the presidency was underway before Old Hickory became its popular hero. Some people argue that had there not been an Andrew Jackson, it would have been necessary to invent one. Jackson had a remarkable life.

Jackson was born in the Carolina backcountry in 1767. Frontier life then was crude and perilous. Andrew Jackson Sr. died in an accident while clearing his fields for spring planting. A few days later, Andrew was born and was given the name of his father.

Young Andrew's early life was as rough-and-tumble as the land on which he lived. At thirteen he joined Patriot forces against the British, serving as a messenger. In April 1781, Andrew and his brother Robert were captured by British cavalry. When one of the officers ordered Andrew to clean his boots, Jackson refused. The angry officer slashed the boy on his head with a saber and hacked at his raised arm. Jackson would bear the scars of his defiance the rest of his life.

After the war, Jackson studied law in Salisbury, North Carolina, and became a young lawyer. He later became a public prosecutor in Tennessee and a state judge. In 1796 Jackson was elected to a term in Congress where he gained some respect for his straightforward, though roughshod, manner.

Jackson's reputation was not made in Washington; it was forged on the frontier, fighting Indians and redcoats. General Jackson drove his men hard, but he drove himself harder. His grit earned him the admiration of his ranks. "He's tough as hickory," they would say, and so he was.

As president, Andrew Jackson was not an innovator. His success was as a symbol of what America had become. His life mirrored the life of the young republic. With Jackson in the White House, America offered ordinary people extraordinary opportunity.

Activity

Discuss Nicknames

Explain that a nickname often represents an obvious characteristic of something or someone. A nickname should not be something that is negative or hurtful.

Refer to Background information in Lessons 46–47 to guide a discussion of why John Quincy Adams was called "old man eloquent" and why Andrew Jackson was called "Old Hickory."

Invite students to think of nicknames for their pets or a friend's pet and share the meaning.

Teach for Understanding

How did Andrew Jackson respond to what John C. Calhoun said about the tariff in South Carolina? He said that one state could not decide that a law was unconstitutional.

What did South Carolina begin to talk about doing? leaving the Union

What did Jackson do to reach a compromise in regard to the tariff? Henry Clay worked to develop a new tariff that would gradually lower people's costs.

What did Andrew Jackson believe about the national bank? The bank was owned by a few wealthy men who profited from it.

Why did Andrew Jackson fire the secretary of the treasury? He refused to obey Jackson's orders to stop putting money in the national bank and to put it in state banks instead.

Why did several state banks run out of money and close? The national bank required the state banks to pay back their loans.

▶ **Conclude the discussion by asking the question on page 122.** It was a positive action when Jackson replaced some people in government who had been dishonest. A negative result was that some people Jackson put in government were not as qualified to do the job as the people that were replaced.

It was a negative action when Jackson asked the secretary of the treasury to break the law by depositing money in state banks. When the secretary of the treasury refused to break the law, Jackson fired him.

Activity Manual

• Guide completion of page 87.

---

could not decide that a law was unconstitutional. The state of South Carolina began to talk about leaving the Union. Jackson sent soldiers to the port of Charleston to make South Carolina obey the law and pay the tariff.

Thankfully, Congress was able to reach a compromise in 1833. Henry Clay worked to develop a new tariff. This tariff would gradually lower the people's cost. For now, the Union would stay together.

Bank Battles

Another problem during Jackson's presidency concerned the national bank. Jackson thought the national bank had too much power. He claimed that the bank was owned by a few wealthy men and that they were the ones who profited from it. Jackson believed the bank helped only the rich, not the common people.

Jackson wanted to get rid of the national bank. He ordered the secretary of the treasury to stop putting funds in the national bank. He was to deposit money in the state banks instead. The secretary knew that Jackson was asking him to do something against the law. He refused to obey Jackson's orders, so the president fired him. Jackson hired a new secretary who would carry out his plan.

But then serious problems arose. The national bank had loaned money to the state banks. Now it began requiring these banks to pay back their loans. Several state banks ran out of money and had to close. Thousands of Americans lost the money they had been saving in these banks.

America began to struggle with economic problems that would increase during Martin Van Buren's presidency. Jackson had used his power to make a decision without fully counting the cost for the American people. His choice would create problems for years to come.

During his years in office, Andrew Jackson did some good but also much harm. In some ways he demonstrated a belief in the rights of all Americans. He cared about the problems of the poor because he had come from poverty himself. Yet the results of his actions did not always help the common man. Furthermore, he did not always respect the freedom of others, particularly those who were not white Americans. He owned more than a hundred slaves. He also placed the rights of white Americans above those of Native Americans. This prejudice showed itself in one of the most hurtful actions of his presidency.

> What positive and negative actions of Jackson have we studied so far?

122

Activity

Banking

Materials: resources about banking and finance

Use resources to discuss the value of money, checking, budgeting, saving, building credit, investing, or starting a business.

The Indian Removal
Broken Promises

Ever since the first white settlements in the New World, white Americans had clashed with American Indians. Things were no different in the early 1800s. White Americans were beginning to move farther west. They saw that the Indians lived and hunted on land that would be good for farming. They wanted this land for themselves.

Many Indians resented white people for taking over their lands. Sometimes violence broke out on both sides during land disputes. Many white Americans lived in fear of Indian attacks. They thought Indians were wild and uncivilized because they had a different way of life. They did not understand that the Indians were people just like them—people made in God's image with feelings, needs, and desires. The Indians wanted a safe, peaceful place to live with their families, just as the white people did.

Some Christians tried to take the gospel to the Indians. God used His Word to bring some of the Indians to Christ. But often the missionaries had trouble earning the trust of the tribes they wanted to reach.

The United States had made peace treaties with some of the Indians. Jackson decided that the government would not honor these treaties. He wanted the Indians to move. He said that if the Indians moved west of the Mississippi River, they could keep their way of life. Jackson signed a bill called the **Indian Removal Act**. This bill gave the US military the right to forcefully move the Indians.

The Indians did not want to leave the land their people had lived on for centuries. But they also wanted to be able to live the way they always had. A few tribes, such as the Sauk and Fox Indians, went to war with American soldiers and lost. The Seminoles had escaped into the Florida Everglades to avoid moving west. But most of the Indians were weary of fighting. Their peace treaties had been broken. So they did as the government ordered and moved west.

Indian Removal

123

**Student Text pages 123–25
Activity Manual pages 88–89**

Lesson Focus

- Andrew Jackson decided he would not honor treaties that the United States had made with some Indians.

Objectives
- Identify what right the Indian Removal Act gave to the US military
- Examine events leading up to the Trail of Tears

Review

- Guide a review of the type of man Andrew Jackson was and what he did during his presidency.

Preparation for Reading

- Generate interest as you direct the students to read the titles and examine the pictures and map on pages 123–25.
- Guide pronunciation of any unfamiliar words in the lesson.
- Direct the students to read the pages silently to discover the name of the bill that Andrew Jackson signed, giving the US military the right to forcefully move the Indians. the Indian Removal Act

Teach for Understanding

Why had the US government made treaties with the Indians? White Americans had clashed with the Indians over land. Sometimes violence broke out.

What made it difficult for missionaries to give tribes the gospel? They often had trouble earning the trust of the tribes they wanted to reach.

Why did most of the Indians move west as the government ordered after President Jackson signed the Indian Removal Act? Most of the Indians were weary of fighting. Their peace treaties had been broken, so they did as the government ordered.

What did the US government do that was wrong? It broke the treaties that it had made with the Indians and took their land.

What is it called when we take something that belongs to someone else? stealing

- Direct attention to the map on page 123. Explain that the land west of the Mississippi was designated as Indian territory.

Background

Indian Resistance

Not all the Indians gave in meekly to being moved westward and opening Indian lands in the East to white settlers. In 1832 a group of Sauk and Fox Indians under Chief Black Hawk crossed the Mississippi River back into northern Illinois to reclaim their land. A force of regular soldiers and Illinois militia moved to intercept the Indians. The resulting Black Hawk War was brief but bloody. As with most United States and Indian conflicts, the Indians suffered more and lost the war.

More challenging was the Seminole War (1835–42). The Seminoles, led by the canny Osceola, also resisted efforts to move them west. They hid in swamp lands and marshes of Florida as American troops tried in vain to track them down. Over 1,500 Americans and an unknown number of Indians died in the conflict. Most Seminoles were rounded up and sent west, but some held out in Florida until the government gave up and left them to live in peace.

Teach for Understanding

Where did members of the Cherokee tribe live? Georgia, Tennessee, North Carolina

- Choose a volunteer to explain how the Cherokees were like white Americans in many ways.

How did the Cherokees feel when the Georgia legislature decided that the Cherokees had to obey its state laws? They wanted to continue making their own laws.

What did the Cherokees do to protest the Indian Removal Act? They took their case to the Supreme Court.

Why did Chief Justice John Marshall rule in the Cherokees' favor? They had kept their side of the peace treaty. Marshall said that the Indians had a right to own their own lands and make their own laws.

- Direct attention to the picture on page 124. Choose a student to read aloud the Biography box. Use the information to guide a discussion about Sequoyah.

One of the tribes that had a treaty with the US government was the Cherokees. The Cherokee people lived in Georgia, Tennessee, and North Carolina. The Cherokees had a highly developed civilization. They had a constitution. They published materials in their own written language. They had schools and large farms. They used the same farming methods as their white neighbors. They had helped the United States during the War of 1812. A number of Cherokees had even become Christians.

But then in 1829, miners discovered gold on Cherokee land in Georgia. Many more white Americans moved there. The Cherokees had governed themselves for hundreds of years. Now the Georgia legislature decided that the Cherokees had to obey the state laws. The Cherokees, however, wanted to continue to make their own laws.

The Cherokees protested against the Indian Removal Act. Christian missionaries who worked among them also defended them. But President Jackson did not offer the Cherokees any help. The Cherokees took their case to the Supreme Court. Chief Justice John Marshall ruled in their favor. He reminded Americans that the Cherokees had kept their side of the peace treaty. He said that the Indians had a right to own their own lands and to make their own laws. He said it was

Sequoyah

What: Cherokee scholar

When: ca. 1770–1843

Where: Tennessee and Indian Territory (Oklahoma)

Sequoyah lived his early life in Cherokee territory in Tennessee. When he grew up, he became a silversmith. He also became interested in the Cherokee language. He developed an alphabet so that his language could be written down. Using this alphabet, he taught other Cherokees to read.

Sequoyah's Cherokee alphabet allowed literature to be published in his own language for the first time. Cherokee Christians helped translate and print the Bible. Cherokees also printed a weekly newspaper.

Sequoyah often acted as a diplomat on behalf of his people. He eventually moved west with them to Oklahoma.

124

Activity

The Cherokee Alphabet

Materials: resources about the Cherokee alphabet

Divide the students into groups. Direct the students to use sources to learn about the development of the Cherokee alphabet and how Sequoyah and other Cherokees used it. Display a picture of the Cherokee alphabet. Invite volunteers to tell what they learned.

Background

Christians and the Indian Removal Act

Many Christians thought that the removal plan was wrong. Some Christians wrote newspaper articles and tracts about American Indian rights. Missionaries to the Cherokees defended the Indians' right to stay in their homelands. Some even walked with the Indians through the Trail of Tears.

against the law for the United States government to force the Cherokees and other tribes from their lands.

Jackson, however, refused to uphold the law. The Cherokees continued to argue against the removal. They sent representatives to appeal to the government. But Jackson did not listen. He said the Cherokees would have to move.

The Trail of Tears

In the end, the Cherokees had to leave. Thousands of Cherokees joined the march to the West. Some went west on their own. The US Army forced others from their homes at gunpoint. The long westward journey of the Cherokees was one of the saddest events in their history. It came to be called the Trail of Tears.

The Cherokees began their journey in the summer of 1838. But many months passed before they reached the Oklahoma Territory, where the government was sending them. As the weather grew colder, many Cherokees became sick. Sometimes they had little food or water. Heavy rains fell, and then winter brought ice and snow. About four thousand Cherokees died before the end of the journey.

Some government leaders believed Jackson's Indian Removal Act was wrong. John Quincy Adams, now serving in the House of Representatives, was one of these. He wrote that the nation's actions against the Indians were sins for which it would be judged. But he did not have the influence to change the situation. As time went on, United States citizens would take lands from the Indians again and again.

> How did Jackson and Adams differ in opinion on the Indian Removal Act?

125

Teach for Understanding

How did Jackson react when the Cherokees sent representatives to appeal to the government? Jackson did not listen. He said the Cherokees would have to move.

What was the Trail of Tears? the long westward journey of the Cherokees

What was the condition of the Cherokee people as they journeyed to the Oklahoma Territory? As the weather grew colder, many Cherokees became sick. Sometimes they had little food or water. Heavy rains fell, and then winter brought ice and snow. About four thousand Cherokees died before the end of the journey.

> Conclude the discussion by asking the question on page 125. Jackson thought the US government did not have to honor its treaties. He said that if the Indians moved west of the Mississippi, they could keep their way of life. John Quincy Adams believed the Indian Removal Act was wrong. He wrote that the nation's actions against the Indians were sins for which it would be judged.

Activity Manual

- Guide completion of pages 88–89.

Assessment

- Administer quiz.

> The quiz may be given any time after completing this lesson.

"The Trail Where They Cried"

Perhaps the saddest event in the Indian resettlement process was the Trail of Tears that forced the removal of more than ten thousand Cherokees from North Carolina to the Indian Territory (now known as Oklahoma) from 1838 to 1839. The name comes from a Cherokee phrase describing it: *Nunna-da-ul-tsun-yi*, "the trail where they cried." Beginning in virtual prison camps in the Carolinas, the Cherokees were herded like cattle by the US Army through freezing winter weather without adequate food, shelter, or even blankets. Many of them died along the way. The sick, the aged, and the very young suffered the most.

A handful of Cherokees escaped the army roundup and hid in the Smoky Mountains. They eventually emerged from hiding and were allowed to legally reclaim about fifty thousand of the seven million acres of Cherokee land the government had seized. This grant was an extremely small reparation to a people who had suffered so much and so unjustly.

Lesson

49

Student Text pages 126–28
Activity Manual pages 90–91

Lesson Focus

- True Christians were concerned about rationalism and prayed for America to turn back to a biblical faith.

Objectives

- Define rationalism
- Identify what Christians did in response to rationalism
- Recognize aspects of the Second Great Awakening
- Identify problems that occurred along with revival

Teacher's Toolkit CD

- Instructional Aid 34: *Religion*

Review

- Guide a review of the events and people related to the Indian Removal Act.

Preparation for Reading

- Generate interest as you direct the students to read the titles and examine the images on pages 126–28.
- Guide pronunciation of any unfamiliar words in the lesson.
- Direct the students to read the pages silently and complete Instructional Aid 34 in small groups.

Teach for Understanding

- Direct attention to the illustration of rationalism on page 126. Invite a student to explain the meaning.
- Display Instructional Aid 34. Write for display as each section is discussed.
- Choose a group to tell what rationalism is.
- Choose another group to explain how Christians reacted to rationalism.
- Explain that Christians are not opposed to reason. God gave humans the ability to reason as a tool to understand Scripture and the world God made. But when humans take the tool of reasoning and make it an authority above God, they become rationalists. Likewise, help students to see that feelings are not bad. God gave people feelings. People's feelings are supposed to delight in God and in the world He made. But feelings should never be an authority above God and His Word.

Religion in Early America
Rationalism

Since the first Great Awakening, religious beliefs in the United States had been slowly changing. Some people had adopted an attitude called **rationalism**. Rationalism placed man's reason above the truth of God's Word.

Some rationalists denied important doctrines of the Christian faith. For example, many of them did not believe in the doctrine of the Trinity. Harvard College adopted this position in the early 1800s. The college no longer taught that Jesus was God. Many Americans were influenced by the Harvard position. They thought they could trust scholars to have wise ideas. The problem was that some scholars were not getting their ideas from the Bible. Rationalistic thinking spread, even among those who had claimed to be Christians.

Many American pastors were greatly disturbed. True Christians began to pray for America to turn back to a biblical faith. God answered by sending a widespread revival through the United States. It was the **Second Great Awakening**.

The Second Great Awakening

One man God used in the Second Great Awakening was Timothy Dwight. Dwight was the president of Yale in the early 1800s. He was also the grandson of a pastor God had used in the First Great Awakening, Jonathan Edwards.

When Dwight became president of Yale, students at the college were already questioning the truth of Christianity. Dwight was concerned for the souls of these students. He began to preach messages to the students at Yale about the Bible and its teachings. God used his faithful preaching. After a period of several years, God brought

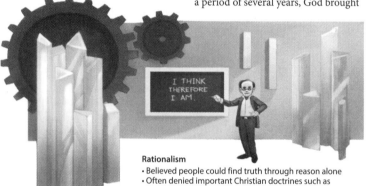

Rationalism
- Believed people could find truth through reason alone
- Often denied important Christian doctrines such as the Trinity and the deity of Christ

126

Primary Source: Good News from Yale

- Direct attention to Activity Manual page 91.
- Divide the students into groups. Assign paragraphs from the excerpt to the groups to read together and discuss. Guide the students in understanding difficult words and concepts.
- Ask each group to tell what it learned.
- Point out that many of the students at Yale had repented of their sins and asked God to forgive them. God sent Jesus Christ to die for our sins. When we repent of our sins and ask Jesus to be our Savior, we receive salvation (John 3:16). The Bible says we become a new creation (2 Corinthians 5:17).
- Share your testimony of salvation or invite a student to share his testimony of salvation.
- Choose a volunteer to read John 3:16 and 2 Corinthians 5:17. Refer to Explaining the Gospel on page 458 for help in leading a child to Christ.
- Invite students to identify characteristics of Yale students after receiving salvation during the revival as you write for display.

revival to the students at Yale. Student after student trusted Christ as Savior. In June of 1802, Dwight wrote that more than eighty students had come to faith in Christ. The changes in the students' lives were real and lasting.

God used some of these students to continue the revival. In 1809 a student named **Asahel Nettleton** graduated from Yale. Under the ministry of Timothy Dwight, Nettleton had grown in his faith and developed a passion for the salvation of his friends. He often helped counsel other students during the revival at Yale.

After college, Nettleton spent some time studying under a minister in Connecticut. Then he began a ministry as a traveling evangelist. Nettleton felt burdened that the Second Great Awakening be a work of God's Spirit. He wanted his preaching of God's Word to lead to true spiritual change and not just emotional responses. He also did

not want his ministry to take people away from their local churches and faithful pastors.

God used Nettleton's humble spirit and faithful preaching. For many years he traveled the United States, preaching from New England to Virginia and South Carolina. After becoming sick with typhus fever, he spent a period of time in Great Britain for rest. God gave him opportunities to preach there too. When he returned to America, he helped found an institute to train young men to be preachers.

Problems Along with Revival

God was working, and America was experiencing revival. But at the same time, certain problems were developing. Not every pastor was preaching the biblical gospel message. One of these pastors was **Charles Finney**.

Finney preached mainly in the state of New York. Although he called

Christianity
- Believe people can find truth through God's Word
- View Jesus as God's Son
- Understand that Jesus Christ brings reason and mystery together in harmony

127

- Direct attention to the illustration about Christianity on page 127. Read aloud the information.
- Invite a group to tell about the Second Great Awakening.

calm in its tone. The spiritual fervor of the revivals in the East was deep but quiet, and the results were profound.

Results of the Awakening

Like the colonial Great Awakening, the Second Great Awakening produced dramatic results. First and most important, thousands of people accepted Christ and joined churches. American Methodists, for example, numbered 15,000 in 1785. By 1840 their numbers had grown to 850,000, and Methodism had become the largest denomination in the United States. Second was the birth and growth of America's foreign missions movement. Third, moral sins declined in the wake of the revival; for example, drunkenness declined. Also, the revival fueled the drive for moral reform. Many of the leaders in the Prohibition and abolition movements were zealous converts of the revival. Fourth, new methods of evangelism resulted from the revival. The Second Great Awakening touched and transformed the lives of a large segment of the American people.

Background

Revival in the East

The Second Great Awakening began in the East. There the revivals centered in the churches and colleges, where Christian zeal had lapsed into apathy and even into open sin. Yale, founded in 1701 to train ministers, was an example of how low spirituality had fallen. One minister recalled his student days at Yale in the years before the awakening:

The College was in a most ungodly state. The college church was almost extinct. Most of the students were skeptical, and rowdies were plenty. Wine and liquors were kept in many rooms; intemperance, profanity, [and] gambling . . . were common.

Into this situation at Yale came Timothy Dwight, a grandson of Jonathan Edwards. Elected president of Yale in 1795, Dwight confronted the problem of a rebellious student body. He openly challenged all comers in public debates on the truths of the Christian faith. Dwight also preached a series of sermons in chapel on basic Christian theology. The fruit of Dwight's labors was a series of revivals in which at least a third of Yale's students were converted.

Revival in the other schools and churches of the East followed the pattern of Yale. The Second Great Awakening was characterized by the faithful work of local pastors and laymen rather than prominent leaders like Edwards and Whitefield. The awakening endured for sixty years and influenced the nation for several generations. The preaching was urgent in its message but

Activity

Discuss the Results of the Second Great Awakening

Present the work of the Christian missionary Adoniram Judson, who was influenced by the Second Great Awakening. Use the Background information to guide a discussion of the results of the Second Great Awakening, such as the growth of churches, evangelism, and missions.

49

Teach for Understanding

- Select a group to explain how Charles Finney was part of a problem that happened during the Great Awakening.

- Direct attention to the illustration of transcendentalism on page 128. Read aloud the information.

- Invite another group to explain how transcendentalism was a problem during the Second Great Awakening.

- Read aloud the question at the bottom of Instructional Aid 34. Choose volunteers to answer the question. Allow any reasonable answer.

- Remind the students that rationalists claimed to value reason and transcendentalists claimed to value feeling. Christians should value all that God created humans to experience, including both reason and feeling.

▶▶ Conclude the discussion by asking the question on page 128. Nettleton felt burdened that the Second Great Awakening be a work of God's Spirit. He wanted his preaching of God's Word to lead to true spiritual change and not just emotional responses. He also did not want his ministry to take people away from their local churches and faithful pastors.

Activity Manual

- Guide completion of pages 90–91.

himself a Presbyterian, he soon began to deny key doctrines. He did not believe that people were born sinners because of Adam's sin. He denied that Christ died in the place of sinners. He did not believe people are justified by faith alone. He did not depend on God to do the work of revival in his preaching services. Instead, he taught that following certain rules would bring revival.

Finney not only preached these ideas, but he also wrote a theology book about them. His ministry looked successful to many Christians. Large crowds came to hear him speak, and many people made decisions at his meetings. But his teachings and writings brought confusion and harmed the cause of Christ. Many faithful preachers such as Asahel Nettleton publicly opposed Finney's teachings.

Another problem that arose during the Second Great Awakening was a new philosophy. This philosophy was called **transcendentalism**. Transcendentalism was a reaction against the rationalism of America's colleges. But transcendentalism was also in error. A transcendentalist believed that he could find truth through his feelings and senses rather than in God's Word.

This philosophy became popular. Several important writers of this time period were transcendentalists. The most famous of these writers were Ralph Waldo Emerson and Henry David Thoreau. These writers wrote thoughtful essays and beautiful poetry. They often expressed appreciation for nature. They emphasized morality and goodness. But the transcendentalists also influenced many people to rely on their own understanding rather than on God. Transcendentalism was another problem that drew many people away from the truth of God's Word in the early 1800s.

What were Asahel Nettleton's desires for revival?

Transcendentalism
- Believed people could find truth through feelings and senses
- Often wrote beautiful poetry and essays expressing appreciation for nature

128

America Becomes More Connected

As America grew, the citizens' needs changed. People were moving west and settling new lands. Roads to the West were scarce, and travel was difficult, especially in winter. Americans needed better forms of transportation to reach faraway places. They needed better ways to ship goods from one part of the country to another. People also needed easier ways to communicate over such great distances. News took months to travel from the cities near the coast to settlements farther west. As needs changed, new ideas helped America become more connected.

Transportation
Roads and Stagecoaches

The first road to reach from the East Coast to the Midwest was called the National Road. Traveling the National Road by stagecoach was much faster than driving a wagon and walking beside it. But roads like this one were expensive to build. Keeping up the roads was another expense. The stones that paved the roads broke as heavy wheels traveled over them.

Canals and Steamboats

Many people believed that canals were a better way to travel. Canals could connect rivers and lakes and provide a good way to transport goods from place to place. While President Monroe was in office, the Erie Canal had been built. The Erie Canal connected the Great Lakes with the Hudson River, which flowed to the Atlantic Ocean. People began to build more canals. Cities grew near them.

Along with canals came a new invention that made traveling by water even faster. Up until now, boats had needed wind, water currents, or man-power to propel them forward. **Robert Fulton** built on the ideas of others to make the steamboat a reality. A steam engine gave a boat enough power to travel against the wind and the current. Soon steamboats were churning up and down America's rivers. Steamboat travel had become common by 1825.

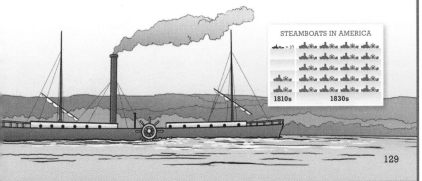

STEAMBOATS IN AMERICA

= 10

1810s   1830s

129

The National Road

Despite reluctance to use government funds, Congress approved the first federally funded highway in 1806. Construction began in 1811 at Cumberland, Maryland. The first section of the road, reaching to Wheeling (now in West Virginia), opened in August 1818. Because of the need for drainage, the road was raised with ten-foot shoulders and ditches sloping from each side. The twenty-foot-wide roadbed was a foot deep on the sides and a foot and a half deep in the middle. All stones for the bottom layer were to be about seven inches in diameter while those for the surface were to be about three. The original National Road, or Cumberland Road as it was sometimes called, cost $1.7 million or about $13,000 a mile. Later the road extended westward to Vandalia, Illinois.

Background

The National Road

Despite reluctance to use government funds, Congress approved the first federally funded highway in 1806. Construction began in 1811 at Cumberland, Maryland. The first section of the road, reaching to Wheeling (now in West Virginia), opened in August 1818. Because of the need for drainage, the road was raised with ten-foot shoulders and ditches sloping from each side. The twenty-foot-wide roadbed was a foot deep on the sides and a foot and a half deep in the middle. All stones for the bottom layer were to be about seven inches in diameter while those for the surface were to be about three. The original National Road, or Cumberland Road as it was sometimes called, cost $1.7 million or about $13,000 a mile. Later the road extended westward to Vandalia, Illinois.

River Transportation

Several Americans had been trying since 1763 to develop a steam-powered ship. The idea was finally perfected by a talented, imaginative inventor from Philadelphia, Robert Fulton. In 1807, Fulton unveiled his steamboat, the *Clermont*, on the Hudson River. Critics called it "Fulton's Folly," but it successfully sailed upstream to Albany. The steamboat soon revolutionized river traffic.

Lesson Focus

- America became more connected.

Objectives
- Examine changes in transportation
- Identify changes in communication
- Compare historical maps

Teacher's Toolkit CD
- Instructional Aid 35: *US Canals and Railroads*

Materials
- Sources about Morse code and today's communication for use with Activity Manual page 93

Review

- Guide a review of rationalism, the Second Great Awakening, Charles Finney, and transcendentalism.

Preparation for Reading

- Generate interest as you direct the students to read the titles and examine the pictures and graphs on pages 129–31.
- Guide pronunciation of any unfamiliar words in the lesson.
- Direct the students to read the pages silently to learn the name of the first American-built engine to run on an American railroad. the Tom Thumb

Teach for Understanding

What was the first road to reach from the East Coast to the Midwest? the National Road

What did many people believe was a better way to travel than traveling on the National Road? traveling by canals

What invention made traveling by water even faster? the steamboat

Who built on the ideas of others to make the steamboat a reality? Robert Fulton

Activity

Research the *Nautilus*

Use resources to learn about the *Nautilus* that Robert Fulton built in 1800 under a grant from Napoleon.

What was a disadvantage of traveling by canal in the winter? The water might freeze and make canal travel impossible.

What changed railroads from being used only by horse-drawn rail cars? the steam-powered locomotive

What was the Tom Thumb? the first American-built steam engine to run on an American railroad

What caused the Tom Thumb to lose a race against a stagecoach? A part in the engine came loose.

How do we know that travel by steam-powered trains became the wave of the future? Twenty years after Cooper invented his steam locomotive, there were almost 10,000 miles of railroad track in America.

What had changed about the number of post offices in the United States by the 1820s? The nation had only about seventy-five post offices until the 1820s when nearly every town had its own post office.

Why did postal service become more efficient? Roads, canals, and railroads were built so that letters could be sent to faraway places by stagecoach, steamboat, or train.

- Direct attention to the picture and the graph. Choose a volunteer to comment on the meaning of each.

Railroads and Locomotives

Canals had some disadvantages. One problem was that they were not dependable in winter. The water might freeze and make canal travel impossible. Like roads, canals were also costly to build and to keep up.

With the invention of the steam engine, railroads had new possibilities. Up until now, railroads had been used only by horse-drawn rail cars. But what if a steam-powered locomotive could be invented? An inventor named **Peter Cooper** wanted to try.

Cooper's steam locomotive was not the first, but it was the first American-built engine to run on an American railroad. Cooper named it the Tom Thumb because it was small. Cooper ran the Tom Thumb on a Maryland railroad from Baltimore to Ellicott's Mills. The journey took just over an hour. A stagecoach company challenged the Tom Thumb to a race on the way back to Baltimore. A part in the engine came loose, and the Tom Thumb lost the race to the stagecoach. But it was clear that steam-powered trains were the wave of the future.

Now that there was a faster way to travel by railroad, Americans began laying more railroad track. Twenty years after Cooper designed and built his steam locomotive, there were almost 10,000 miles of railroad track in America. In 1833 President Andrew Jackson became the first president to travel by train.

Communication
The Postal Service

Benjamin Franklin had helped organize the nation's postal service. At the time the Constitution was written, the nation had about seventy-five post offices. But by the 1820s, nearly every town had its own post office. As roads, canals, and railroads were built, the postal service became more efficient. Now letters could be sent to faraway places by stagecoach, steamboat, and train. Even people living in remote settlements could receive mail and feel more connected to the rest of the country.

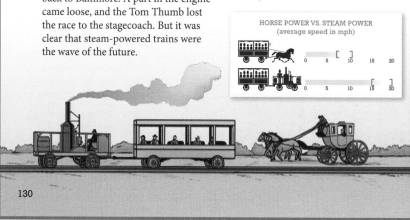

HORSE POWER VS. STEAM POWER
(average speed in mph)

130

Visit a Railroad Museum
Visit the B&O Railroad Museum in Baltimore, Maryland, or visit the museum website.

Railroads
Nineteenth-century American transportation climaxed with the development of the railroad, which combined the flexibility of canals and roads with the dependable power of steam. The first economically successful railroad in America was the Baltimore & Ohio (B&O) Railroad. Originally, the B&O consisted of horse-drawn carriages on metal rails. Inventor Peter Cooper believed that the line could develop a steam-driven engine, like the ones British companies were using. Working mostly with scrap metal, Cooper constructed the Tom Thumb. This small but powerful steam engine was well designed to handle the sharp curves and steep climbs of the B&O rail line. To display the engine's capabilities, Cooper agreed to run the Tom Thumb in a thirteen-mile race against a horse-drawn car. Although the horse-drawn car won narrowly because the engine had a mechanical problem, the future of American transportation was clearly with steam power. South Carolina's Charleston-to-Hamburg line opened in 1833, and its 137-mile length made it the longest line in the world. Other lines, usually local in service, grew around major cities.

The Telegraph

An important invention of this era made communication even faster. **Samuel Morse** discovered a way to send messages along a wire by means of electrical pulses. The machine he invented to send and receive these messages was called a telegraph. When his telegraph received a message, it placed dots and dashes on a piece of paper. A telegraph operator could then translate this code and read the message. Samuel Morse's first successful message read, "What hath God wrought!" This statement from Numbers 23:23 expresses wonder at God's work. It was a way of giving credit to God for the new invention.

Later, telegraphs sent their coded messages as long and short clicking sounds. The operators could write down the message by simply listening to the lengths of the sounds. This code became known as Morse code, and it is still used today.

In order for the telegraph to work, wires had to be strung across the

The telegraph became a popular way to send brief messages.

country. The telegraph needed these wires to transmit the electrical signals. At first only a few key cities had wires hung between them. But gradually more and more telegraph poles and wires went up. The railroads were able to use telegraph signals. As railroad station workers received messages from other cities, they could help keep the trains running on schedule. Advances in transportation and communication were working together.

> Why were changes in transportation and communication needed?

Activity

Comparing Historical Maps

The two maps your teacher will give you show the northeastern United States in two different years. How has the network of canals changed from the earlier year to the later one? How has the railroad system changed? Use your knowledge of this period in history to discuss why these changes took place.

131

Canals

The canal era began in 1817, when New York, at the urging of Governor DeWitt Clinton, began building a canal from Albany to Lake Erie. With the backbreaking labor required for the task, the idea of a 363-mile canal seemed, as Thomas Jefferson said, "little short of madness." Costing about six million dollars, the canal was a gamble for the state. Critics called it "Clinton's Big Ditch." Yet the Erie Canal proved such a success that it had paid for itself in tolls in fewer than ten years. Furthermore, the cost of shipping goods plunged. Before the canal opened, it cost twenty cents a pound to ship goods from Buffalo to New York City. After the canal opened, the price dropped to less than a penny a pound. In 1827, the governor of Georgia complained that wheat from upstate New York was selling more cheaply in Savannah than wheat from central Georgia.

The success story of the Erie Canal encouraged other efforts. The Wabash and Erie Canal in Indiana and the Miami and Erie Canal in Ohio connected Lake Erie to the Ohio River. The Illinois and Michigan Canal connected Lake Michigan to the Mississippi River by way of Chicago. By the 1830s, one could travel from New York City to New Orleans completely by inland waterways.

Teach for Understanding

What important discovery did Samuel Morse make? a way to send messages along a wire by means of electrical pulses

- Explain that Samuel Morse did not invent the telegraph. He improved the design methods of other inventors in order to send messages by means of electrical impulses.

When the telegraph received a message, how did the machine record the message? The machine placed dots and dashes on a piece of paper.

What did the telegraph operator do with the dots and dashes? translate this code and read the message

What did Samuel Morse's first successful message say? "What hath God wrought!"

Why do you think Morse sent a statement from the Bible? He was giving credit to God.

What is Morse code? Telegraphs send their coded messages as long and short clicking sounds. Operators can write down the message by simply listening to the lengths of the sounds.

As more telegraph wires and poles went up, how did railroads use the telegraph signals? As railroad station workers received messages from other cities, they could help keep the trains running on schedule.

- Direct attention to the picture on page 131.

> Conclude the discussion by asking the question on page 131. As people moved west there was a need for better transportation to reach faraway places and to ship goods. People needed easier ways to communicate over such great distances.

Activity Manual

- Guide completion of pages 92–93.

Activity

Comparing Historical Maps

- Generate excitement about comparing historical maps as you read the Activity information aloud.

- Explain that the students will participate in a group discussion. Divide the students into small groups. Distribute a copy of Instructional Aid 35 to each group.

- Allow each small group to compare and discuss the two maps on the instructional aid. Direct the groups to choose a student to record what they observe about the expansion of canals and railroads from the two maps. Remind them to include why the expansion was necessary.

- Invite each group to tell what it observed when it compared the maps. Remind the groups to include the reasons for expansion of canals and railroads.

Lesson

51

Lesson Focus

- The United States advanced in industry and inventions.

Objectives
- Describe the factory system in America
- Identify inventions that changed American farming

Teacher's Toolkit CD
- Visual 15: *Old Slater Mill*

Review

- Guide a review of transportation and communication expansion in the United States. Include a review of the important men who helped make this expansion possible.

Preparation for Reading

- Generate interest as you direct the students to read the titles and examine the pictures and chart on pages 132–34.
- Guide pronunciation of any unfamiliar words in the lesson.
- Direct the students to read the pages silently to discover what invention made the production process in factories even faster. interchangeable parts

Teach for Understanding

- Direct attention to the picture on page 132 and the How It Was box. Read the story aloud.
- Invite a student to explain the meaning of the story.
- Guide a discussion of what it may have been like to live in a boarding house away from family and to work in a factory as a child or young person.

  In what country had factories become common? England

  How was work done in a factory? Many of a certain kind of item were produced quickly by having each factory worker focus on one step in the production process.

  What was the first successful American factory? a mill producing cotton thread that was opened in the 1790s in Rhode Island

- Display Visual 15. Point out that the mill was built near water. The water was necessary to drive the water wheels that powered the machinery.

How It Was

It was dark when Rachel and Caroline left the mill to walk home to the boarding house. Rachel could barely see the coins in her hand, but she counted them with her finger once again.

Caroline skipped for a few steps. "Just one more day's wages, and I'll have enough money, Rachel. I can buy some new shoes. No more wet feet on rainy days. What about you? What will you do with your wages?"

"I'm saving them." Rachel smiled in the darkness. "Every penny. I want to help send my brother James to college." She had kept a pouch under her pillow for months, adding coins to it each day. She loved to imagine the joy on her brother's face when she handed him the pouch. He would be the first one in her family to go to college.

Industries and Inventions

Along with the changes in transportation and communication came changes in how Americans worked. Until 1800 most American farms were small. Many farmers grew just enough produce to feed their families. Most American goods were manufactured in small quantities by tradesmen. Tradesmen made goods mainly for people in their own towns.

But now the United States began making advances in industry. Businessmen began to dream of producing goods in large quantities and shipping them across the country by boat or train. Business owners could make large profits if they had many workers in one place producing large quantities of goods.

The Factory System

Americans had heard that factories were becoming more and more common in England. Factories were buildings where workers produced many of a certain kind of item quickly. Each factory worker focused on one step in the production process. Workers received a salary from the factory owner. The owner received the profit from the goods produced in his factory.

The first successful American factory opened in the 1790s in Rhode Island. It was a mill that produced cotton thread. **Samuel Slater** was hired to manage the factory. Slater had come

132

Background

Textile Manufacturing

Great Britain was the world's leader in manufacturing, and the British intended to keep it that way. The British government carefully guarded not only all machinery relating to Britain's textile industry but also the blueprints for the machinery. Laws prevented skilled workers in the textile industry from emigrating. But that law did not deter Samuel Slater. Although a successful apprentice in an English textile mill, Slater saw greater economic opportunities for himself in America. Slater carefully memorized the construction of the textile machines, disguised himself as a farm hand, and escaped to the United States in 1789.

In Providence, Rhode Island, Slater—working entirely from memory—constructed an English-style mill with the financial support of American inventors. This mill proved to be the first of a series of mills that sprouted across New England. The region, with its numerous streams and rivers to drive the water wheels used to power the machinery, was a natural site for the textile industry. The factory system was critical in the establishment and growth of the fledgling American economy. It spread throughout New England and the rest of the North. An interesting example of American industry in this period is the textile mills of Lowell, Massachusetts. Textiles became America's first major industry.

to America from England. He knew how to build and operate the machines used in British mills. Slater hired people of all ages to work in his factory. Even children as young as seven years old worked alongside their parents or older siblings. Years later the nation would make laws against hiring children to do this kind of work. But at the time, factory work was viewed as a way that children could help earn money for their families.

Factories also allowed many women to earn an income. A mill owner named **Francis Cabot Lowell** organized a village for young female factory workers. These "mill girls" lived in boarding houses and ate their meals together. Factory wages provided these girls with the means to support themselves or other family members.

In the 1830s and 1840s, various inventors were working to develop a sewing machine. **Elias Howe** was the first to patent a sewing machine in 1846. The sewing machine was an important invention for the factory system. Now cloth and thread produced in factories could be quickly turned into clothing. Long hours spent hand sewing a dress or a shirt would soon be a thing of the past.

Another important idea improved the quality of factories. **Eli Whitney** and other men developed the idea of making products such as guns and clocks with **interchangeable parts**. Factories could produce large numbers of each part. Workers could then quickly assemble the parts rather than make each product separately. This idea made the production process in factories even faster.

133

Teach for Understanding

What characteristics did Samuel Slater have that suited him to manage the mill? He had come to America from England, and he knew how to build and operate the machines used in British mills.

What kind of people did Slater hire to work in his factory? people of all ages, even children as young as seven years old

Why did people at that time allow children to work alongside their parents or older siblings? They viewed factory work as a way that children could help earn money for their families.

What did Francis Cabot Lowell organize for young female factory workers? a village

Which inventor was the first to patent a sewing machine? Elias Howe

Why was the sewing machine an important invention for the factory system? Cloth and thread produced in factories could be quickly turned into clothing.

What invention of Eli Whitney's made the production process in factories even faster? interchangeable parts

- Direct attention to the picture on page 133.
- Choose a volunteer to explain how interchangeable parts sped up the production process.

Activity

Learning about a Sewing Machine

Use a video clip to point out the various parts of a sewing machine and how it works.

Lesson

51

Teach for Understanding

- Direct attention to the chart on page 134. Invite a student to explain the meaning of the chart.

What did Eli Whitney invent that allowed cotton to quickly become the largest cash crop in the South? the cotton gin

What did the cotton gin do? removed seeds from cotton

How did Cyrus McCormick's reaper help farmers? It allowed the farmer to cut as much grain in one hour as the average farmer could cut in one day.

How was John Deere's plow different from previous plows? It had steel blades that could cut more smoothly through the soil than iron plows could.

What do we call the period of history when new inventions and methods made work, communication, and travel faster and easier? the Industrial Revolution

▶ Conclude the discussion by asking the question on page 134. sewing machines, interchangeable parts, the cotton gin, the reaper, the steel plow

Activity Manual

- Guide completion of page 94.

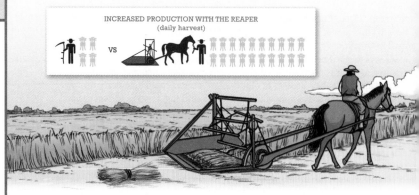

INCREASED PRODUCTION WITH THE REAPER
(daily harvest)

vs

Changes in Farming

Changes in technology affected not only factories, but farms as well. During the 1800s, new machines began replacing the simple tools farmers had used for centuries. In 1793 Eli Whitney invented the cotton gin, a machine for removing seeds from cotton. With the help of the cotton gin, cotton quickly became the largest cash crop in the South.

In the 1830s, **Cyrus McCormick** invented the reaper. His reaper could cut as much grain in one hour as the average farmer could cut in a whole day. Sales of the reaper took off in the 1840s when McCormick moved west. He opened a factory in Chicago, close to the nation's best region for growing grain. By the 1850s, he was selling thousands of reapers a year.

Another important invention for farmers was the steel plow. **John Deere** created the plow in the late 1830s. The steel blades of his plow could cut more smoothly through the soil than iron plows could. The steel plow became a valuable tool for farmers working in the sticky soil of the Midwest.

These three inventions changed American farming. Now farms could produce more crops in a shorter time. Farmers could make greater profits from the sales of their crops.

The era from the Revolutionary War to the Civil War was a time of great progress in American life. Many new inventions and methods made work, communication, and travel faster and easier. The changes that took place during this period of American history are often called the **Industrial Revolution**.

▶ What new inventions improved factories and farms?

134

Activity

Learning About Modern Farming Equipment
Visit a local farm. Ask the farmer to identify the equipment he uses. Invite him to tell what each piece of equipment is used for and how it helps him get his work done faster.

The Mexican War
Texas

In 1845 **James Polk** became president of the United States. At that time, Texas was an independent country. Americans had helped fight for Texas in its war for independence from Mexico. Texas wanted to become part of the United States. But the US government knew that Mexico would declare war on America if Texas became a state. The United States did not want to go to war with Mexico. It also did not want to upset the balance of slave states and free states. So from 1836 to 1845, Texas remained independent and called itself "The Lone Star Republic."

James Polk wanted Texas to be part of the United States. During his election campaign, he had promised to help the nation gain both Texas and the Oregon Territory. Texas became a state after Polk took office.

President Polk believed in the idea of "Manifest Destiny." This idea was that God wanted the United States to possess all the land westward to the Pacific coast. Polk's presidency was a time when many settlers, miners, and missionaries headed west. Some Americans believed God really had destined the United States to have the lands of the West. Many Christians, however, could not justify this idea. God had made no such promise to America in the Bible.

Now that Texas was part of the United States, Polk was ready to gain even more land from Mexico. He wanted California as well. California would bring with it new resources, such as minerals and good natural ports.

But Mexico did not agree with Manifest Destiny. The Mexican government still owned land in the southern part of Texas. And the Mexicans did not want to give up California. They refused to sell this land to the United States.

James Polk gave serious thought to the art of the handshake. In his diary he wrote that a man should "shake and not be shaken, grip and not be gripped, taking care always to squeeze the hand of his adversary as hard as he squeezed him."

Despite growing up in a hardy pioneer environment, Polk was a weak child and often ill. As an adult, he studied law so diligently that his health suffered. He worked so hard as president that at the end of his term, his health was spent. He died only 103 days into his retirement.

135

Lesson **52**

Student Text pages 135–37
Activity Manual pages 95–96

Lesson Focus

- President Polk's belief in Manifest Destiny led to war with Mexico.

Objectives

- Examine events that led to the Mexican War
- Explain how the war ended
- Identify what America gained under the treaty as part of the Mexican Cession
- Recognize that not everyone agreed with how America gained land

Teacher's Toolkit CD

- Instructional Aid 36: *War with Mexico*

Review

- Guide a review of Samuel Slater and the factory system. Review the inventors and inventions that improved factories and farms.

Preparation for Reading

- Generate interest as you direct the students to read the titles and examine the picture and map on pages 135–37.
- Guide pronunciation of any unfamiliar words on the page.
- Direct the students to read the pages silently and complete Instructional Aid 36 in small groups.

Teach for Understanding

- Invite a student to read aloud the title of the lesson and predict what the lesson will be about. the war with Mexico

Who became president of the United States in 1845? James Polk

What did Texas call itself while it remained independent? "The Lone Star Republic"

What was the meaning of "Manifest Destiny"? that God wanted America to possess all the land westward to the Pacific coast

Why could many Christians not justify this idea? God had made no such promise to America in the Bible.

After Texas became part of the United States, what other land did Polk want from Mexico? California

What part of Texas still belonged to Mexico? land in the southern part

How did Mexico feel about Manifest Destiny? It was not in agreement with Manifest Destiny.

- What is it called when land is taken unlawfully from another person or country? Answers should include that it is called stealing

Activity

Research the State Flag of Texas

Provide resources for the students to research the history of the Texas state flag. Guide a discussion about why the flag has only one star.

Under whose command did President Polk send soldiers to the Texas border? Zachary Taylor

Why were the soldiers camping along the Rio Grande? This river was where they thought the Texas border should be.

Where did Mexicans think the border should be? farther north

When the Mexicans told the Americans to leave, what did the Americans do instead? set up a blockade, keeping Mexican supplies from being shipped along the river

What happened after the Mexicans fired at the Americans? President Polk pressed for Congress to declare war.

- Guide a discussion of the various opinions Americans held about the Mexican War.

What was the outcome of Zachary Taylor's and Santa Anna's forces meeting at the village of Buena Vista? After a hard-fought battle, Taylor defeated the Mexicans.

What did Captain John C. Frémont do in California? He occupied San Francisco with the help of American warships.

What would the United States need to do as a last step in its battle strategy? take control of the Mexican capital, Mexico City

War Begins

President Polk sent soldiers to the Texas border under the command of **Zachary Taylor**. Taylor and his men camped along the Rio Grande. This river was where they thought the Texas border should be. The Mexicans thought it should be farther north. They told the Americans to leave. But Taylor and his men would not leave. They set up a blockade, keeping Mexican supplies from being shipped along the river. Eventually the Mexicans fired at the Americans. President Polk pressed for Congress to declare war. Congress declared war against Mexico in May of 1846. The war would last for nearly two years.

One of America's new inventions made this war different from earlier ones. Now news about the war could be quickly sent across the country by telegraph. Americans far away from the fighting could follow the war news.

Americans had various opinions about the war. Some Americans supported it. They wanted to see their country expand by gaining more land. But others believed that the war was not justified. They believed President Polk had started a war in hopes of taking Mexican land by force. Some worried that adding new lands to the United States would result in more slave states. These Americans did not believe it was right to own slaves. They were saddened to see slavery spread to new territories.

American Victory

Taylor's forces captured the city of Monterrey a few months after the war began. The Mexican ruler Santa Anna and his forces met Taylor at the village of Buena Vista. Santa Anna had about three times as many men as Taylor had. However, Taylor had a valuable resource in Captain Benjamin McCulloch. McCulloch led a company of Texas Rangers on spy missions. The Texas Rangers were tough men, familiar with the Texas frontier. Their missions uncovered valuable information and gave Taylor an advantage in the conflict. After a hard-fought battle, Taylor defeated the Mexicans.

Meanwhile another American soldier, Colonel Stephen Kearny, led an army farther west and captured Santa Fe, New Mexico. His plan was to press on and capture California. But when he got there, he found that Americans had already taken it. Captain John C. Frémont, with the help of American warships, had occupied San Francisco.

The last step in America's battle strategy was to take control of the Mexican capital, Mexico City. President Polk placed General Winfield Scott in charge of this campaign. Scott traveled by steamship to capture the port city of Veracruz. From there he marched

136

Missions to the Northwest

One of the more positive aspects of westward expansion was an increased interest in missions. In fact, the great spur to the settlement of Oregon came from American missionaries to the Indians. In 1833, an Indian convert to Christianity published an appeal for Christians to reach the Indians of the Northwest with the gospel. Many eagerly responded, the most famous of whom were two missionary couples: Marcus Whitman and his wife, Narcissa, and Henry Spalding and his wife, Eliza. The Spaldings settled in what is today northern Idaho. They enjoyed some success among the Nez Perce Indians. They were able to establish both a church for the Nez Perces and a school for children. Eliza hand painted visual aids, such as charts, to present the gospel pictorially to the Indians.

American Slavery

Slavery was a national problem. Attitudes toward slavery began to change in the last half of the 1700s. Often the moral offense was an argument against slavery. It was difficult to reconcile the practice with the admonition to "love thy neighbor as thyself" (Matthew 22:39). It was also difficult to reconcile slavery with the principles of American government in the Declaration of Independence ("inalienable rights," including liberty).

Yet many times people discarded moral arguments in favor of economic and political motives for keeping or ending slavery. As northern states became more mercantile and less agricultural, slavery became less desirable and was eventually abolished (though New England merchants still participated in the slave trade). In the South, slavery increasingly became a vital part of the economy.

The institution of slavery had consequences that reached across society and far into the future. Slavery resulted in untold suffering. It led to the division of a nation and a bloody war to reunite it. And it brought tension and bitterness between blacks and whites in the United States.

Mexican Cession

against Mexico City. The capital fell to the Americans in September of 1847.

Under the treaty that ended the war, the United States gained a large amount of territory in the West. All or parts of California, Nevada, Utah, Wyoming, Colorado, Arizona, and New Mexico were part of the **Mexican Cession**. The Rio Grande became the southern border of Texas.

By the end of his presidency, James Polk had added more than one million square miles of land to the United States. Although Polk still wanted more land, he was glad to have achieved the dream of Manifest Destiny.

But not all Americans believed that the way he had gained this land was right. One such person was Nicholas Trist, the diplomat who worked out the treaty. Because he disagreed with Polk, he did not ask Mexico for as much land

as the president wanted. Congress accepted the treaty, but Polk later fired Trist.

The United States had grown in many ways since becoming a nation. It had developed new ways to travel, communicate, and work. It was learning how to interpret and apply its Constitution to different situations. Above all, it had experienced a Second Great Awakening that brought about spiritual growth in many individuals.

The nation had also grown in geographical size. It now claimed territory from the Atlantic Ocean to the Pacific Ocean. However, this growth had come at a price. Indians, Mexicans, and Americans had lost their lives in the struggle to expand. But the greatest cost was one that the young nation could not estimate at this time. Expanding its territory had also expanded its problem of slavery. The resulting conflict would threaten to rip the nation apart permanently. Only God could determine whether America would stand or fall.

> Why were there mixed feelings in America about the Mexican War?

137

Teach for Understanding

When did Mexico City fall to the Americans? September of 1847

What did America gain from the treaty that ended the war? It gained a large amount of territory in the West: all or parts of California, Nevada, Utah, Wyoming, Colorado, Arizona, and New Mexico.

What term is used for the land Mexico gave up to the United States? Mexican Cession

• Direct attention to the map on page 137 showing the territory the United States gained in the Mexican Cession.

What did Nicholas Trist do when he worked out the treaty? He did not ask Mexico for as much land as the president wanted.

Why do you think Trist did not ask for as much land as Polk wanted? Trist believed the United States was unjust in fighting Mexico.

What problem expanded as US territory expanded? the problem of slavery

>> Conclude the discussion by asking the question on page 137. Texas wanted to become part of the United States, but the US government thought that Mexico would declare war on America if Texas became a state. The United States did not want to go to war with Mexico. It did not want to upset the balance of slave states and free states. James Polk wanted Texas to be part of the United States. Polk believed in the idea of "Manifest

Destiny." Some Americans agreed with Polk while others could not justify this idea.

Activity Manual

• Guide completion of pages 95–96.

Lesson 53 **Chapter Review**
Activity Manual pages 97–98

Objective
• Recall concepts and terms from Chapter 6

Materials
• One set of 3 × 5 cards with questions and one set with the answers for each team

Introduction

• Concepts for the Chapter 6 Test will be taken from Activity Manual pages 83–98. You may review any or all of the concepts during this lesson. You may choose to review Chapter 6 by playing "Match the Cards."

Review

Game: Match the Cards

• Divide the students into teams. The teams should sit at tables if possible. Place a set of question cards and a set of answer cards face-down on each table. (*Note:* Answer cards should be in a different order than the questions.) At a given signal, each team should turn over the cards and match the questions with the answers on the table. The first team to match the cards correctly is the winner.

Activity Manual

• Guide completion of pages 97–98.

Lesson 54 **Chapter 6 Test**

Objective
• Demonstrate knowledge of concepts from Chapter 6 by taking the test

Assessment

• Administer Test 6.

Chapter 7

Introduction

The history of slavery stretches back to the founding of the United States. Southern states based their economy on slavery. Slavery also provided money for the North.

Many Americans opposed slavery. This issue divided the nation. Southern states seceded after Abraham Lincoln was elected president. The Civil War began in South Carolina and continued on the eastern and western fronts. The cost of war was great. Many Confederate and Union soldiers lost their lives.

President Lincoln issued the Emancipation Proclamation that promised to free all enslaved people in rebellious states once a Union victory was achieved. General Robert E. Lee and his men surrendered at Appomattox Courthouse. The South had lost the war. Slavery ended in the United States. After years of working to save the nation from disunion, Lincoln was assassinated. The nation would need time to heal and rebuild.

Chapter Focus

Slavery caused much disagreement in the United States, eventually breaking the nation apart.

7 The Civil War

Focus
Slavery caused much disagreement in the United States, eventually breaking the nation apart.

Chapter 7 Overview				
Lesson	Student Text	Activity Manual	Content	Vocabulary
55	138–42	99–101	Activity: Create a Lap Book	Dred Scott case states' rights
56	143–46	102–3	Biography box: Sarah & Angelina Grimké Republican Party Stephen Douglas Abraham Lincoln	abolitionist secede
57	147–49	104–6	Ulysses S. Grant Richmond, Virginia Jefferson Davis General Thomas Jackson Robert E. Lee	Anaconda Plan Confederates Bull Run Union
58	150–52	107	General George McClellan Admiral David Farragut Antietam Creek	
59	153–55		How It Was: Hardships of War President Abraham Lincoln President Jefferson Davis	Emancipation Proclamation munition negotiate
60	156–58	108–9	General George Meade Chattanooga Gettysburg Primary Source: The Battle Hymn of the Republic	scouting siege
61	159–61	110	Atlanta Reconstruction Appomattox Courthouse	siegework
62		111–12	Chapter Review	
63			Chapter Test	

Visit bjupress.com/resources for links to enhance the lessons.

What Caused the War

During the first decades of its history, the United States faced many challenges and opportunities. The nation explored the continent and fought wars. It built roads, canals, and railways to connect its citizens. But during these decades a division grew. The Northern states and the Southern states viewed themselves as different from each other. When they could no longer compromise, conflict erupted. The history of the American Civil War stretches back before the nation's founding and continues to influence American culture to the present day.

Slavery

History

Slavery began early in the history of the thirteen colonies. The earliest recorded African slaves arrived in Jamestown in 1619. John Rolfe, a tobacco planter who married Pocahontas, bought twenty Africans from a Dutch ship. For much of the colonial period, Africans were sold into slavery along the Chesapeake Bay in order to harvest tobacco. But colonists from Georgia to Massachusetts purchased slaves also. Sometimes enslaved people were able to gain their freedom. The freed slaves often lived alongside white colonists. However, by 1776 slavery was firmly established in the United States.

During the first decades of independence, white Americans disagreed about slavery. Many wanted to end slavery altogether. In the Northern states, slavery slowly faded away. Slave owners found that it was cheaper to hire workers than to keep slaves. Some preachers opposed slavery. But in the South, slavery grew. Crops, especially cotton, needed much labor. Plantation owners planned on enslaved people having children. These children would grow up and continue working in the fields.

Slavery and Money

The Southern states based their economy on slavery. Slaves harvested much cotton, tobacco, and rice. Many

139

JourneyForth

Avery's Battlefield and *Avery's Crossroad* by Deanna K. Klingel are available from JourneyForth Books, a division of BJU Press, at journeyforth.com.

Set during the Civil War, these historical fiction novels follow Avery and his dog Gunner through the period. Avery's skills as a doctor become useful to the soldiers in Civil War hospitals, and he develops special friendships along the way.

Lesson Focus

- The issues of slavery and states' rights divided the United States.

Objectives

- Identify the history of slavery in the United States
- Examine how slavery affected the economy
- Explain the controversy surrounding states' rights

Teacher's Toolkit CD

- Instructional Aid 37: *Slavery and the Civil War*

Materials

- Manila or colored file folders (three per student)
- Sources for information needed to complete the pieces of a lap book

Introduction

- Invite a student to read aloud the title of the chapter and predict what the chapter will be about. It will be about the Civil War in the United States.

- Why do you think this war was called the Civil War? Answers could include that it was a war between the citizens of the country.

- Explain that the Civil War is also referred to as the War Between the States.

- Invite a student to read the chapter focus aloud.

  What do you think you will learn in this chapter? How disagreement over slavery divided the nation.

- Direct attention to the picture of the ships the *Merrimac* and the *Monitor*. Explain that the *Merrimac* was built in the North but salvaged from the Norfolk navy yard and rechristened by the Confederates as the *Virginia*. The *Monitor* was built and used by the Union. Explain that the battle at Hampton Roads in the harbor of the James River, Virginia, was the first battle in history between ironclad warships.

- Direct attention to the timeline.

  Where did the first major event of the Civil War take place? Fort Sumter

  When did General Lee surrender at Appomattox Courthouse? April 9, 1865

  According to the dates on the timeline, how long did the Civil War last? about four years

Preparation for Reading

- Generate interest as you direct the students to read the titles and examine the images on pages 138–42.

- Guide pronunciation of any unfamiliar words in the lesson.

- Direct the students to read the pages silently and complete Instructional Aid 37 in small groups.

Teach for Understanding

- Ask a small group to identify how slavery was not a new occurrence in the 1860s. The earliest recorded African slaves arrived in Jamestown in 1619. John Rolfe bought twenty slaves. Colonists from Georgia to Massachusetts purchased slaves also. By 1776 slavery was firmly established in the United States.

   How did white Americans view slavery? They disagreed about slavery. Many wanted to end slavery. In the Northern states, slavery slowly faded away. Some preachers opposed slavery. Plantation owners in the South planned on enslaved people having children who would grow up and continue working in the fields.

- Direct attention to the map on page 140.

- Choose a volunteer to explain what the map illustrates.

- Invite a group to explain the relationship between slavery and money in the South.

- Ask a group to explain the relationship between slavery and money in the North.

- Choose volunteers to state the different types of opposition to slavery.

- What do you think would have allowed cotton to support the US economy without using slaves? hiring workers who were paid and who received benefits for their work

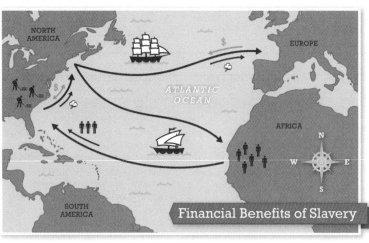

Financial Benefits of Slavery

Southerners feared that without slavery they could not produce crops. Slavery provided money for the South.

Slavery also provided money for the North. Until 1808 many ships sailed from New England to Africa and brought slaves to the Americas. Even after the international slave trade ended, slavery made money for the North. Much Southern cotton traveled to England on ships from New York City. Selling cotton grown by enslaved people made many Northern merchants rich.

Opposition to Slavery

Not all Americans supported slavery. Many, especially in the North, opposed it. Some argued that slavery was unchristian. Since God made all people in His own image, all were brothers and sisters. Christians believed that Jesus died to save people from the slavery of sin. Many slaves had become Christians. Some Americans asked how people could enslave their fellow Christians. The Second Great Awakening helped raise antislavery feelings.

Some Americans opposed slavery for financial reasons. They said slaves did not work as hard as they would if they were free. They did not blame the slaves for this. According to the idea of the free market, people work hard if they will get a reward. Slaves got little reward for working hard. The crops they grew benefited their masters. If slaves were free, they would work more.

140

Activity

Discuss John Jasper

Use sources to present information about John Jasper's rise from fifty years of slavery to national prominence as a preacher. Display a picture of John Jasper. Guide a discussion of how people can overcome past circumstances with God's help to live a life of service to the Lord and others.

Background

Dred Scott

Dred Scott was the slave of John Emerson, an army surgeon from Missouri. During the 1830s, Emerson had taken Scott to the free state of Illinois and the unorganized free territory of the Louisiana Purchase. Emerson later returned to Missouri, a slave state, with Scott. After Emerson's death in 1843, Scott sought to gain his freedom on the grounds that he had become free by entering free territory and could not be reenslaved. The Missouri Supreme Court had ruled in 1824 that if a slave owner moved to a free state and lived there, his slaves would be free based on the Northwest Ordinance (1787), which banned slavery north and west of the Ohio River. Scott won in a lower court but lost the appeals. The case eventually found its way to the Supreme Court.

A famous book also raised antislavery feelings among Americans. *Uncle Tom's Cabin* by Harriet Beecher Stowe told a story of slaves. It pointed out how badly they could be treated. When Northerners read the book, they felt that something must be done to help the slaves.

Northerners also grew angry because of the **Dred Scott case**. Dred Scott was a slave who lived in the free state of Illinois. He sued his owners to receive his freedom. The Supreme Court under Chief Justice Roger Taney ruled against Scott. Taney said that slaves were only property. He said that a man could take his property wherever he wanted without it being taken away from him. The Supreme Court seemed to be saying that all states could be slave states.

States' Rights

Another issue also divided the Northern and Southern states. They understood the idea of states' rights differently. **States' rights** is the principle that the federal government has only limited authority over each state. Southern states usually supported more states' rights. Southerners reminded Northerners of what the Constitution said. The Tenth Amendment in the Bill of Rights states that any powers not given to the federal government belong to the states. The Constitution also permitted slavery. Sometimes the federal government took actions that Southern states thought did not follow the Constitution. The Southern states tried to demand states' rights.

South Carolina's battle over nullification happened many years before the Civil War. President Andrew Jackson had forced South Carolina to pay a tariff, and Southerners remembered this lost argument. The national government could force states to obey. A state would lose the fight if it fought the president.

Southerners feared that their states' rights might be lost. They especially worried about their right to keep slaves. If too many antislavery men were elected to Congress, the Constitution could change. The slave states needed to make sure that new slave states were created. In some cases they succeeded. Missouri and Texas both joined the Union as slave states. But many states joined as free states. When Kansas became a state, the decision process was violent.

From 1854 to 1861, people for and against slavery fought to control Kansas. The territory was about to become a state. Whoever chose the legislators would decide whether the state was free or slave. Men on both sides of the issue fought each other. Some of them even murdered their opponents. Both sides wanted their men elected to Congress.

Northerners sometimes argued for states' rights as well. They were

141

How did Harriet Beecher Stowe's book affect readers in the North? They felt something must be done to help slaves.

What did the Supreme Court seem to be saying when it denied Scott his freedom when he lived in a free state? that all states could be slave states

What issue along with slavery divided the Northern and Southern states? states' rights

● Invite a volunteer to read the sentence that defines the principle of states' rights.

What part of the country usually supported more states' rights? the Southern states

What does the Tenth Amendment to the Constitution say about states' rights? Any powers not given to the federal government belong to the states.

What did the Constitution say about slavery? It permitted slavery.

What action did Southern states take when they thought the federal government did not follow the Constitution? They demanded states' rights.

Why did Southerners especially fear losing their right to keep slaves? They would lose their way of life.

What might happen if too many antislavery men were elected to Congress? The Constitution could change.

What was happening in Kansas from 1854 to 1861? People for and against slavery fought to control Kansas.

The Bible and Slavery

Some Christians defended slavery by claiming that the Bible permitted it. But they failed to recognize that God made selling stolen people a capital crime (Exodus 21:16). All American slaves were stolen or were offspring of people who had been stolen. In general, God permitted those in debt to work off that debt for six years as slaves. In the seventh year, the person they worked for was to give them enough money to help them start an independent life again (Deuteronomy 15:12–14). The Bible even says that these six-year slaves were not to be treated like slaves (Leviticus 25:39). The slavery permitted by God was designed to help people out of debt. It was not designed to keep a race of people as perpetual servants. Americans could not justify their enslavement of African Americans from the Bible.

Additional Background information for this lesson is on the Teacher's Toolkit CD.

Teach for Understanding

What concerned Northerners about states' rights? the issue of runaway slaves

What was the Fugitive Slave Act of 1850? It required Americans to help return runaway slaves to their owners.

What deepened the divide between the North and the South? the issues of slavery and states' rights

Which antislavery political parties mainly existed in the North? the Free Soil Party and the Republican Party

What did Southern Whigs often become? Democrats

▶▶ Conclude the discussion by asking the question on page 142. Selling cotton grown by enslaved people made many Northern merchants rich.

Activity Manual

- Guide completion of pages 99–101.

///// Activity ///

Create a Lap Book

- Develop a plan for how you will have the students prepare their lap books throughout the chapter. You may choose to have the students use all or some of the lap book materials on Activity manual pages 309–49, or you may provide alternate materials.

- Generate excitement about making a lap book as you read the Activity information on page 142 aloud.

- Explain that the students will be working on a Civil War lap book in Chapter 7.

- Direct Attention to Activity Manual pages 309–10. Read the directions together for how to make a lap book.

- Distribute two or three folders to each student. Guide the students as they assemble the lap book.

> Completing each section of the lap book may take more than one class period. Students may work on the lap book as seatwork or during free time.

---

concerned about the issue of runaway slaves. The Fugitive Slave Act of 1850 required Americans to help return runaway slaves to their owners. However, some Northern states had laws to protect enslaved people who escaped. People who argued in favor of slavery said that the Northern states had no grounds to argue. The Constitution demanded that every state support laws passed by Congress.

The issues of slavery and states' rights helped deepen the divide between the North and the South. Both sides thought that they were right. Both sides became convinced that the other was not just making a mistake, but was purposely trying to harm them. This feeling grew during the election of 1860.

Political Parties

Political parties also divided the United States. By the mid-1850s, almost all Southerners and many Northerners were Democrats. This party supported slavery. Some Democrats believed that states should be allowed to choose whether to be slave or free. Others said that owners should be allowed to take their slaves anywhere. The other political parties were smaller. From the 1830s to the 1850s, the Whig Party slowly lost supporters. Some joined antislavery parties such as the Free Soil Party or the Republican Party. These parties existed mainly in the North. Southern Whigs often became Democrats.

> How did the North benefit from slavery in the South?

///// Activity ///

Create a Lap Book

Use sources to find information about the topic you will use for your lap book. Attach two or three manila or colored file folders together to make the foldable lap book.

Glue a title, a picture, and topic information to the cover. Inside the lap book, display information in an interesting way. Use papers that fold

out, pockets that hold slips of paper, booklets that open, timelines, maps, pictures, puzzles, or other activities. Add fabric or other items where appropriate.

By making a lap book, you will reinforce and expand your knowledge of the topic. Share your lap book with others.

//

142

Background

The Republican Party

By 1852 the Whigs had split into two factions over slavery: the Cotton Whigs and the Conscience Whigs. After the Kansas-Nebraska Act passed, which allowed settlers in the West to decide the slavery issue for themselves, the Cotton Whigs, the smaller of the factions, joined the Southern Democrats in supporting slavery. The Kansas-Nebraska Act angered Conscience Whigs and Northern Democrats. They joined Free Soilers to oppose the spread of slavery.

In 1854 the antislavery groups formed a new political party: the Republican Party. It grew with startling speed. It elected congressmen in its first year. Two years later, it ran its first candidate for president, John C. Frémont. Although Democrat James Buchanan defeated Frémont, the Republicans gained national attention and laid the groundwork for the next campaign in 1860.

Student Text pages 143–46
Activity Manual pages 102–3

Sarah & Angelina Grimké

When: 1792–1873 and 1805–1879
Where: Charleston, SC

The Grimké sisters grew up in Charleston, South Carolina, where their father was a politician and owned a large estate. He kept many slaves. In 1819 Sarah visited Philadelphia and eventually decided to become a Quaker. In 1821 she moved to Philadelphia, and eight years later her younger sister joined her. Over the next decade, the Grimké sisters' work brought much attention to the abolitionist cause.

Election and Secession
The Election of 1860
The Candidates

The election of 1860 divided the people of the United States. Most elections had two major candidates for president. In 1860 there were four. The rise of a new political party helped cause this division.

The **Republican Party** was founded in 1854. Its members opposed slavery. Some wanted to end slavery immediately. These people were called **abolitionists**. Some members wanted to stop the spread of slavery. They believed that if slavery could not spread, it would die off.

In 1860 the Republican candidate for president was **Abraham Lincoln**. He was a lawyer and former member of Congress. Although he was born in the slave state of Kentucky, Lincoln grew up in the North. Both in Congress and the Illinois legislature, Lincoln opposed slavery. The Republicans wanted a man who would fight to stop slavery's spread.

The Democrats could not decide on one candidate to oppose Lincoln. They chose two. The Northern Democrats' choice was **Stephen Douglas**. Like Lincoln, he lived in Illinois. He did not oppose slavery. But Douglas believed that states could exclude slavery from their land. The Southern Democrats would not accept a candidate who did not believe that slavery should be nationwide. Instead, they chose John Breckinridge of Kentucky as their candidate. Breckinridge supported slavery throughout the country.

The final candidate was John Bell of Tennessee. The Constitutional Union

143

The Election of 1860

The presidential campaign was really two sectional races: Lincoln and Douglas competing in the Northern states and Bell and Breckinridge in the Southern and border states. Douglas became the first presidential candidate to make a nationwide campaign tour, including the South even thought he did not expect many votes from the Southern states. With the Democrats hopelessly divided, Lincoln won by a plurality with just under 40 percent of the popular vote. Since his sectional strength was confined to the more populous North, however, he gained a strong majority in the Electoral College.

The election of 1860 was a critical contest in American politics. The outcome of the campaign would shatter the last truly national institution tying the sections together—the Democratic Party—and serve as a catalyst for the dissolution of the Union.

Lesson Focus

- Some states seceded from the Union after the election of an antislavery president.

Objectives
- Identify the candidates and the results of the election of 1860
- Examine secession in the South
- Describe how the Civil War began

Teacher's Toolkit CD
- Visual 16: *The First Flag of the Confederacy*
- Instructional Aid 38: *Election and Secession*

Review

- Guide a review of the history of slavery in the United States.
- Invite a volunteer to explain how slavery impacted the economy in the South and the North.
- Choose several students to name the types of opposition to slavery that existed.
- Guide a review of how states' rights divided the North and the South.
- Invite a student to name the political parties that Northern and Southern Whigs joined or became.

> Guide a review of important terms, maps, places, and people from each previous lesson. Direct the students to find and read the corresponding entries from the Resource Treasury.

Preparation for Reading

- Generate interest as you direct the students to read the titles and examine the pictures and map on pages 143–46.
- Guide pronunciation of any unfamiliar words in the lesson.
- Direct the students to read the pages silently and complete Instructional Aid 38 in small groups.

Teach for Understanding

- Choose a student to read aloud the Biography box on page 143. Use the information to guide a discussion about Sarah and Angelina Grimké.

  What attitude did the Republican Party have toward slavery? Some wanted to end slavery immediately. Some members wanted to stop the spread of slavery. They believed that if slavery could not spread, it would die off.

- Choose a group to name the political parties in the election of 1860 and their candidates.

Lesson

56

Teach for Understanding

- Direct attention to the pictures. Read aloud the information.

  What was the position of the Constitutional Union Party in regard to slavery? The party would not try to make slavery legal in the North or try to end slavery. Bell and his party pointed out that the Constitution already protected slavery.

  In what way did the election of 1860 show the deep divide in America? Southern voters mainly picked either Breckinridge or Bell. Northern voters chose between Lincoln and Douglas. When the votes were counted, almost no one voted for Abraham Lincoln in the South. In the North, almost fifty-two of every one hundred voters chose him.

  What fears did the South have about Abraham Lincoln? Perhaps he would make slavery illegal. At the very least, he would prevent slavery's spread west. Eventually slavery would be destroyed. This election would end the South's way of life.

- Invite volunteers to suggest how life in the South would change once slavery was abolished.

  What action did South Carolina take on December 20? It voted to secede from the union.

Abraham Lincoln and Stephen Douglas participated in seven debates about slavery, which were later compiled in a book. Douglas was appointed to the Senate over Lincoln, but Lincoln's performance in the debates paved his way to the presidency.

Lincoln described Douglas as "the least man I ever saw." Stephen Douglas was a foot shorter than Lincoln and weighed only ninety pounds as a young man.

Lincoln and Douglas both courted Mary Todd. She married Lincoln.

Party chose him. These men hoped to save the Union by changing nothing. Unlike many Democrats, they would not try to make slavery legal in the North. Unlike the Republicans, they would not try to end slavery. Bell and his party pointed out that the Constitution already protected slavery.

The Election

When the election took place in November 1860, the United States seemed to be two countries. In the South, voters mainly picked either Breckinridge or Bell. In the North, they chose between Lincoln and Douglas. No one thought that any candidate would win more than half the votes. But if a candidate could win enough votes in enough states, he could win the election.

When the votes were counted, they showed America's deep divide. In the South almost no one voted for Lincoln. But in the North almost fifty-two of every one hundred voters chose him. Lincoln won enough votes to win the election. An antislavery man would be president.

Secession

The South was not happy, and Southerners feared what Lincoln would do. Perhaps he would make slavery illegal. They knew the Constitution protected slavery, but they did not trust the Republicans. Many Republicans already disobeyed the Constitution by refusing to return runaway slaves. At the least, Lincoln would prevent slavery's spread west. Eventually slavery would be destroyed. For many Southerners this election meant the end of their way of life. They did not know how to live without slaves. Like most white Americans, they did not want former slaves to be considered equal to white Americans.

The states of the Deep South took action first. On December 20, South

144

Background

A History of Secession

Talk of secession had occurred at various times for various reasons in both the North and the South since the earliest years of the Republic. The foundational argument was that the individual sovereign states had voluntarily united with other sovereign states to form a union for the purpose of guiding foreign relations and easing relations among the various states. They voluntarily gave up some specified (enumerated) rights and authority to the national union. In so doing, however, they retained all other rights and authority, even if unspecified, and in no way surrendered any of their sovereignty. Having entered the Union, they could at any time leave the Union voluntarily.

Those taking an opposing view pointed to Article V of the Constitution and noted that it does not recognize the states as independently sovereign in terms of amending the Constitution. An individual state may object to an amendment but is nonetheless bound by it if it meets the stipulations of Article V. This position insisted that ratification of the Constitution entailed the surrender of state sovereignty. The states had also given up the privileges of sovereignty, such as the ability to coin money, enter into treaties, create standing armies, declare war, and more; in addition, many of the states were created out of territories overseen by the national government.

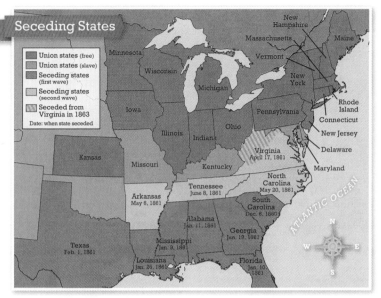

Seceding States

Carolina voted to **secede** from the Union. Secession means that the state would withdraw from the Union and become an independent nation. Over the next months other states took the same action. Mississippi, Florida, Alabama, Georgia, Louisiana, and Texas did not want President Lincoln. These seven states decided to form a new union. They called it the Confederate States of America.

Not all Southerners wanted to leave the Union. Some slave states were next to free states. They did not want to form a new country. However, they believed that slavery was legal. They also believed that states had a right to secede. States such as Virginia waited to see how the president would respond to secession.

At first not much happened. President-elect Lincoln did not take over until March 4, 1861. President James Buchanan said that secession was illegal. He also said that he could not stop the states' leaving. Lincoln said little. Until March he could do nothing. He let the Southern states know that he did not want to forcibly end slavery. The Confederate states continued to set up their government.

145

Lesson 56

Teach for Understanding

- Choose a volunteer to read the sentence that tells the meaning of secession.

What other states took the same action as South Carolina? Mississippi, Florida, Alabama, Georgia, Louisiana, and Texas

What was the new union that the seven Southern states decided to form called? the Confederate States of America

- Direct attention to Virginia on the map.

When did Virginia secede? April 17, 1861

What did part of the state do in 1863? It seceded from Virginia.

What was President Buchanan's response to secession? He said secession was illegal. He said he could not stop the states from leaving.

What did the Confederate states continue to do? set up their government

Additional Background information for this lesson is on the Teacher's Toolkit CD.

Teach for Understanding

- Direct attention to picture on page 146. Read aloud the caption.

When Abraham Lincoln was sworn in as president, what promise did he make to the South? to leave slavery alone

What did Lincoln promise in regard to federal property, federal laws, and the Union? He promised to guard federal property and enforce federal laws. He would not let the Union disintegrate.

Who controlled the federal property in South Carolina after it seceded? South Carolina had taken over most federal property after it seceded. One federal fort was left in Charleston Harbor under the command of Major Robert Anderson.

What happened when Lincoln informed the governor of South Carolina that the federal government would send food but not weapons to Fort Sumter? Confederate forces attacked the fort and began the Civil War.

- Display Visual 16. Explain that the Confederate forces took control of Fort Sumter after the Union forces surrendered. The picture shows the Confederate flag flying over the fort.

> Conclude the discussion by asking the question on page 146. The election divided the people of the United States over the issue of slavery. The creation of a new political party also contributed to the division. The Republican Party wanted a man who would fight to stop slavery's spread. Abraham Lincoln opposed slavery, so the Republican Party chose Lincoln as its candidate. The Democrats could not decide on one candidate to oppose Lincoln. They chose two. The Northern Democrats' choice was Stephen Douglas. He did not oppose slavery but believed that states could exclude slavery from their land. The Southern Democrats chose John Breckenridge who supported slavery throughout the country. The final candidate was John Bell of Tennessee. The Constitutional Union Party chose him. Bell and his party pointed out that the Constitution already protected slavery.

Activity Manual

- Guide completion of pages 102–3.

The Confederate forces firing upon Fort Sumter

War Begins

On March 4, 1861, Abraham Lincoln was sworn in as the sixteenth president of the United States of America. He promised to leave slavery alone in the South. He assured the South he meant it no ill will. But Lincoln also promised to guard federal property and enforce federal laws. He would not let the Union disintegrate.

Lincoln had a problem in South Carolina. The state had taken over most federal property after it seceded. One federal fort was left in Charleston Harbor. Fort Sumter was under the command of Major Robert Anderson. He needed supplies in order to hold the fort. Lincoln knew that if he sent supplies, the Confederate military might attack. If he sent nothing, then the fort must surrender.

After talking with his cabinet, Lincoln resolved to hold the fort. He informed the governor of South Carolina that the federal government would send food but not weapons to Fort Sumter. Rather than let that happen, Confederate forces attacked the fort on April 12. The Civil War had begun.

> Why were there four major candidates for president in 1860?

146

Background

First Fire

Only a spark was needed to bring the country to war. Fear in the South of Northern aggression combined with frustration and anger in the North to put neither side in the mood for reconciliation. The spark came through the issue of federal forts in the South, particularly Fort Sumter, strategically centered in the mouth of Charleston Harbor.

In March the Confederacy sent three peace commissioners to Washington to resolve the problem of federal forts. Both Lincoln and Secretary of State Seward refused to meet the commissioners personally, since to do so would be, in effect, to recognize the Confederate government. Seward, however, sent word that Fort Sumter would be evacuated and on April 7 confirmed his promise in writing—although it is unclear whether Lincoln knew of Seward's actions. On April 9, when the commissioners learned that a squadron of ships had been sent to take supplies to the garrison at Sumter, they could only conclude that they had been deceived. Although Lincoln notified the governor of South Carolina of his intentions, Confederate leaders interpreted his actions as a declaration of war and advised capturing the fort if necessary.

Strategies and Opening Battles

Strengths and Weaknesses

Once the war began, both sides needed a strategy to win. The South, or the **Confederates**, only needed to keep the Northern, or **Union**, forces out. The North needed to conquer a large and populous country. The weeks following the attack on Fort Sumter saw the Confederacy grow even larger. Once Lincoln called out troops to reverse the secession, four more states joined the Confederacy. Virginia, Arkansas, Tennessee, and North Carolina would not fight against their fellow Southerners. Many people in the border states of Missouri, Kentucky, Maryland, and Delaware also supported the Confederacy. However, using persuasion and force, Lincoln kept them in the Union.

Despite these losses, the North had some clear advantages. First, far more people lived in the North. There were twenty-two million people there but only around nine million in the Confederacy. The North also had far more railroads and factories. It could produce more weapons and uniforms. It could also ship troops and supplies more easily. Even without railroads, the North could move supplies. It had far more mules and horses. Finally, the North had a navy. Although it was not massive, it was better than nothing.

But the South had advantages too. Reaching battles took less travel for Southern troops. The soldiers of the Confederacy were fighting for their homeland. They knew the land well. The South also had more formally trained military leaders. The Union generals had good training, but the South had encouraged military careers for many men. Southerners had championed the Mexican War and had received much experience there. Although Northern officers might learn quickly, many Southern officers were already prepared for battle.

One last advantage was not yet known in 1861. Which group would Britain and France side with? The South hoped that it could gain their friendship. British mills relied on Southern cotton. If one or both of these European powers would help the South, the outcome of the war could change. Confederates remembered how with France's help the thirteen colonies defeated Britain. Northerners hoped to keep Europe neutral. Britain fought the slave trade on the Atlantic. The North hoped that the country would see the South as a poor ally.

Strategy and Generals

The North needed more than England's neutrality. It needed a good plan of attack. General Winfield Scott gave the Northern states one. Scott was a veteran of the War of 1812 and the

147

When Lincoln's heavily armed naval expedition neared Charleston on April 12, 1861, Confederate general Pierre G. T. Beauregard opened fire on Fort Sumter, which was commanded by Major Robert Anderson. When Beauregard was a cadet at West Point, his artillery instructor was the same Robert Anderson. Now Beauregard had a chance to show his old teacher just how well he had learned his lessons. After a two-day bombardment, Anderson surrendered the garrison.

Remarkably, no one on either side had been killed in the two-day fight. However, two men were killed accidentally after the battle during the surrender ceremony. Union troops were permitted to leave for New York on steamships.

Activity

Create a Poster

Materials: a large sheet of construction paper for each student

Encourage the students to make a poster showing the strengths of both the North and the South in 1860.

Lesson Focus

- Neither the Confederates nor the Union would win the war easily.

Objectives
- Recognize strengths and weaknesses of the Confederacy and the Union
- Identify generals of the Confederacy and the Union
- Examine lessons the North and the South learned at Bull Run

Teacher's Toolkit CD
- Visual 17: *The Anaconda Plan*
- Instructional Aid 39: *The North and the South at War*

Review

- Choose a volunteer to identify the political parties and candidates relating to the election of 1860.
- Invite a student to explain the concerns of the people in the South when Abraham Lincoln was elected president.
- Guide a review of the actions that led to the beginning of the Civil War.

Preparation for Reading

- Generate interest as you direct the students to read the titles and examine the pictures on pages 147–49.
- Guide pronunciation of any unfamiliar words in the lesson.
- Direct the students to read the pages silently and complete Instructional Aid 39 in small groups.

Teach for Understanding

- Select a group to state the strengths that the North had when the Civil War began.
- Invite a group to state the strengths that the South had when the war began.

Teach for Understanding

- Direct attention to the picture. Read aloud the title.

  What plan of attack did General Winfield Scott give the Northern states? the Anaconda Plan

- Display Visual 17. Direct attention to the map key and identify the Union strategies. Locate each strategy on the map as it is discussed.

What about Scott's previous experience and his current position contributed to his coming up with a plan for the Northern army? He was a veteran of the War of 1812 and the Mexican War. He was in charge of the Union army.

By the end of the war, which Union general did Lincoln trust most of all? Ulysses S. Grant

Who was the South's president at this time? Jefferson Davis

What training and experience did Jefferson Davis have in military leadership? He graduated from West Point, served in the Mexican War, and served as Franklin Pierce's secretary of war.

Who was the most famous Southern general? Robert E. Lee

What was Lee's background? He served in the Mexican War. Later he was the superintendent of West Point.

Why was Scott's Anaconda Plan unpopular in the North? Many civilians wanted to see the South defeated quickly.

Where was the Confederate capital located? Richmond, Virginia

How did many Northerners hope to end the war quickly? by capturing Richmond

Who lead the Union army it as marched toward Richmond? General Irvin McDowell

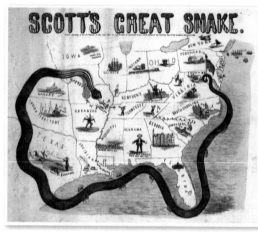

Mexican War. He was in charge of the army. Scott proposed the **Anaconda Plan**. Like a massive snake, the North would envelope and crush the South. First, a blockade would cut off shipping. Second, an attack down the Mississippi would split the Confederacy into two parts. Divided and with no external supplies, the South would be forced to surrender.

Winfield Scott was one of many Union generals. Other important leaders were men such as George McClellan, **Ulysses S. Grant**, and William T. Sherman. Over the course of the war, President Lincoln learned which generals he could rely upon. Some were too hesitant. Others were too rash. By the end, Lincoln trusted Grant most of all.

The Confederacy had strong military leadership. Unlike Lincoln, the South's president, **Jefferson Davis**, had a lot of military experience. He graduated from West Point, fought in the Mexican War, and served as Franklin Pierce's secretary of war. Davis's generals had much experience too. **Robert E. Lee** of Virginia was the most famous. He served in the Mexican War as well. Later he was superintendent of West Point. Other talented officers included John Bell Hood, Joseph Johnston, Thomas (Stonewall) Jackson, and J. E. B. Stuart.

The First Battle

Scott's Anaconda Plan was unpopular in the North. Many civilians wanted to see the South defeated quickly. After Virginia joined the Confederacy, the new nation's capital moved to **Richmond, Virginia**. Although the North followed the Anaconda Plan, the soldiers also hoped that capturing Richmond would end the war quickly.

In July 1861, a Union army invaded Virginia. The force, led by General Irvin McDowell, marched toward

148

Lee
The key general of the South, he was known as a brilliant general. Lee loved his home state of Virginia most of all.

Jackson
He was both a general and a professor. Jackson executed cunning maneuvers.

Grant
During the war, he was almost unbeatable. Grant never gave up, even when the fight was hard.

McClellan
He perfected his army, and they loved him. But when battle came, McClellan was too cautious to win a war.

Richmond. On July 21 he fought Generals P. G. T. Beauregard, Joseph Johnston, and Thomas Jackson. The battle occurred by a creek called **Bull Run** and a town called Manassas. Neither side was ready for a major battle. However, the Union forces led the attack. The Confederates rallied and pushed the Northerners back. The South had won its first victory. It also gained a hero in **General Thomas Jackson** who stood "like a stone wall" during the fighting.

The battle taught both sides important lessons. The most important was that no one would win the war easily. The North had close to 3,000 casualties. Nearly 480 men had died and about 2,780 were wounded or missing. Many were taken as Confederate prisoners. The South had fewer losses. About 390 men had died with around 1,000 wounded. These results became a common pattern throughout the war. The North often lost more men, but the South lost many as well. Since the North had many more people, it could fight longer. The bloodshed at Bull Run did not encourage either side to make peace.

> Why did both Northerners and Southerners think that their side could win?

149

Teach for Understanding

What generals did McDowell fight in Virginia? Generals Beauregard, Johnston, and Jackson

What battle ensued when a Union army invaded Virginia by a creek near a town called Manassas? Bull Run

Who won this battle? the Confederates

Who stood "like a stone wall" during the fighting? General Thomas Jackson

What was the most important lesson that both sides learned during the battle of Bull Run? No one would win the war easily.

> Conclude the discussion by asking the question on page 149. Both sides had advantages.

Activity Manual

- Guide completion of pages 104–6.
- Administer quiz.

> The quiz may be given anytime after completing this lesson.

Stonewall Jackson

One of the greatest heroes of the South was also one of its most devout Christians. General Thomas Jackson, nicknamed "Stonewall," was converted to Christ shortly after he served in the Mexican War. He started and taught a Sunday school class for black people in his area. Jackson served brilliantly in the Confederate army, but he combined fervent piety with military genius.

His faith in God carried him through many dangerous battles. An aide asked Jackson how he managed to remain calm as bullets and shells whistled about him. Jackson replied, "Captain, my religious belief teaches me to feel as safe in battle as in bed. God has fixed the time for my death. I do not concern myself about that, but to be always ready no matter when it may overtake me."

Jackson was quick to express his gratitude to God for victory. After the Second Battle of Bull Run, an officer on the general's staff said, "We have won this battle by the hardest kind of fighting." Jackson disagreed: "No. No, we have won by the blessing of Almighty God."

Jackson cared about the spiritual needs of his men as well. He ordered regular religious services to be held in camp, and the general himself faithfully attended. He carried saddlebags of religious tracts for his men and welcomed colporteurs (Christian civilians who distributed religious literature among the troops).

Chapter 7: The Civil War

- Confederate and Union forces fought on the eastern front and on the western front.

Objectives
- Relate the military advances on the eastern front and their results
- Identify the military advances on the western front and their results

- Guide a review of the strengths and weaknesses of the South and the North when the Civil War started.
- Choose a volunteer to explain the Anaconda Plan.
- Guide a review of Confederate and Union generals.
- Invite a student to explain the battle of Bull Run.

- Generate interest as you direct the students to read the titles and examine the maps on pages 150–52.
- Guide pronunciation of any unfamiliar words in the lesson.
- Direct the students to read the pages silently to find out where Union and Confederate forces met in the bloodiest single-day battle of the Civil War. by Antietam Creek in Maryland

Who stopped repeated Union attacks on Richmond? General Robert E. Lee with the Army of Northern Virginia

Who led the Peninsular Campaign in an effort to take Richmond? General George McClellan

Why was Richmond able to remain the capital of the Confederacy after the Peninsular Campaign? After seven days of Union and Confederate forces fighting, McClellan withdrew.

Who was the next Union general to attempt defeating Lee and his army? General John Pope

What enabled the Confederates to be victorious at the second battle at Bull Run? During the battle Lee was assisted by Stonewall Jackson and James Longstreet. Together they managed to soundly defeat Pope.

What did Lee do immediately after the second battle of Bull Run? He marched north.

Fighting in Earnest
The Eastern Front

Following the First Battle of Bull Run, Union goals focused on Richmond. If only the Confederate capital were defeated, then the secession would be over. But capturing Richmond was no easy task. Between any Union army and the city stood Robert E. Lee. With the Army of Northern Virginia, Lee stopped repeated Union attempts to reach Richmond.

The next Union attempt was the Peninsular Campaign. **General George McClellan** led this attack. Rather than march south from Washington, DC, he brought his troops to Virginia's coast. After landing on the Virginia Peninsula, they marched northwest toward Richmond. Unfortunately for his career, McClellan had a major weakness: he was timid. McClellan would not push quickly toward the Confederate capital. As he inched forward, the Union general met some Southern resistance. Although his forces were far larger, McClellan hesitated to attack. Finally in late June 1862, Union troops arrived within five miles of Richmond. By then Confederate reinforcements had arrived. Union forces numbered about 100,000 men. The Confederates had 90,000. For seven days Lee and McClellan sent their forces at each other. At the end, McClellan withdrew. Richmond remained the capital of the Confederacy.

Union general John Pope next attempted to defeat Lee and his army. Lincoln chose Pope because he had been successful fighting in Tennessee. Pope's army marched into Virginia in late August 1862. From August 28 through August 30, they fought a second battle at Bull Run. This time both sides knew that the war would be long and hard.

The Confederates wanted to thoroughly defeat Pope. He had said that he would take civilian property such as horses and food if his army needed them. Most Southerners did not approve of such a ruthless method of fighting. During the battle, Lee was assisted by Stonewall Jackson and James Longstreet. Together they managed to soundly defeat Pope. He had more men, but he also had more casualties. After the battle, Pope was sent to Minnesota to fight the Dakota, or Sioux, Indians.

Lee was encouraged and hopeful. He had defeated large Union armies twice in a row. The best generals that Lincoln could find were not good enough. If Lee could successfully invade the North, perhaps the South would win the war. Immediately after the Second Battle of Bull Run, Lee marched north. His advantages were clear. This attack was unexpected, his strategies had proved unbeatable against Union generals, and he was facing McClellan again.

150

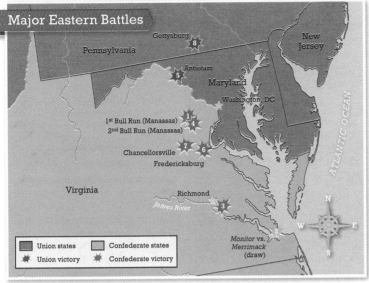

Major Eastern Battles

Gettysburg 8

Pennsylvania

New Jersey

Antietam 5

Maryland

Washington, DC

1st Bull Run (Manassas) 1 4
2nd Bull Run (Manassas)

Chancellorsville 7 6
Fredericksburg

Virginia

Richmond
James River 3

ATLANTIC OCEAN

Monitor vs. 2
Merrimack
(draw)

| Union states | Confederate states |
| Union victory | Confederate victory |

The battle did not happen as Lee planned. He split the invading army into five parts with plans to reunite them. But a Confederate officer lost his copy of the invasion plans. McClellan got them. Despite gaining this key to Lee's campaign, McClellan still hesitated to push his advantage. He feared that Lee had far more troops than he actually had. On September 17, 1862, the two armies met by **Antietam Creek** in Maryland.

The course of the battle also failed to meet Lee's hopes. McClellan's army outnumbered Lee's two to one. Union forces repeatedly stopped Confederate advances. A few Union assaults seemed to defeat Lee's forces. However, McClellan did not let his forces deliver a uniform attack. Lee was able to adjust his troops and avoid a disaster. At the end of the day, the wounded and outnumbered Confederate army held its ground. The next day McClellan left the Confederates alone, and Lee headed south. McClellan failed to seize his advantage. The bloodiest single-day battle of the war had not changed the military situation in the East.

151

Teach for Understanding

● Direct attention to the map. Invite a student to identify Confederate and Union victories.

What strategy did Lee use with his army as he sought to attack the North? He split the invading army into five parts with plans to reunite them.

What went wrong with Lee's plan? A Confederate officer lost his copy of the invasion plans. McClellan got them.

Where did Lee and McClellan's armies meet? by Antietam Creek in Maryland

How did the Confederate army respond to McClellan's attacks? Lee adjusted his troops to avoid disaster. The Confederate army held its ground.

What did McClellan and Lee do the next day? McClellan left the Confederate army alone, and Lee headed south.

Teach for Understanding

- Direct attention to the map. Choose a volunteer to identify Confederate and Union victories.

What was the main Union goal in the West? to control the Mississippi River

What Confederate forts fell to Union general Ulysses S. Grant? Forts Henry and Donelson

What did Grant's victories enable the Union to do? sail Tennessee's major interior rivers

What key city was vital for the Union to capture in order to control the Mississippi River? Memphis, Tennessee

What happened on June 6? Union ships defeated the Confederate ships defending Memphis. The city then surrendered.

What major city in Tennessee did Confederate forces still control in late 1862? Chattanooga

Why was it important for the Confederacy to control Chattanooga? This city linked railroads throughout the South. As long as it had its railroads, the Confederacy could transport men and supplies to meet Union advances.

▶▶ Conclude the discussion by asking the question on page 152. If the Confederate capital were defeated, then the secession would be over.

Activity Manual

- Guide completion of page 107.

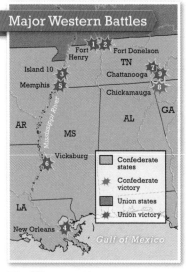

Major Western Battles

The Western Front

War in the West gave the Union more hope. The main Union goal was to control the Mississippi River. To do that, Tennessee and its rivers needed to fall to the North. Despite strong Confederate resistance, Union forces made steady progress.

General Ulysses S. Grant had early success. In the winter and spring of 1862, he moved against two Confederate forts. Forts Henry and Donelson guarded tributary rivers of the Mississippi. Once they fell, the Union could sail Tennessee's major interior rivers.

The capture of Memphis, Tennessee, was vital to control the Mississippi. From February to April, General John Pope worked at capturing Island Number 10 just north of Memphis. On April 8, 1862, the fort and Confederate army were in Pope's control.

Union control of the Mississippi continued to advance. On May 1, Union troops occupied New Orleans. **Admiral David Farragut** had risked sailing his fleet past the city's defensive battery of guns. Once past the defenses, the Union fleet and soldiers easily took the city. Several weeks later Memphis fell. On June 6, Union ships defeated the Confederate ships defending the city. Memphis then surrendered. Only the fortified city of Vicksburg, Mississippi, still held a stretch of the Mississippi under the Confederate flag.

Union armies in the West had other less spectacular victories than the Mississippi triumphs. They fought many times in Tennessee. Slowly the Union gained control of the state. However, not everything fell. In late 1862, Confederate forces still controlled Chattanooga. This city in the east of the state linked railroads throughout the South. As long as it had its railroads, the Confederacy could transport men and supplies to meet Union advances.

> Why did the North keep invading Virginia?

152

Background

East Tennesseans and the Draft

Because East Tennesseans were so badly divided in their sentiments, they suffered drafts from both sides, depending on which side happened to be in control. Many Unionists were drafted into Confederate service, but such men were usually assigned to posts deep inside the South, where they could do less harm and not escape so easily. Men on both sides who were drafted contrary to their beliefs often deserted, hid in the rugged hills and mountains, or became bushwhackers. Many Unionists fled to Kentucky and joined Union armies there.

How It Was

"I wish Father were here." Ellen gazed out toward the last flaming rays of the January sunset above the pasture. Another day ending—without Father. "Mother, when do you think he'll be home? Why doesn't President Davis trade him for a Yankee prisoner? How can we plant without him? Now that Tom's gone off to fight, it's frightening with just us at night."

"Now, Ellen, stop fretting. We have your father's letter from Johnson's Island. He says he's well. You know God takes care of His children, and we must trust Him. When Sherman marched through, we lost only the slaves, not our buildings or seed."

Ellen sighed. "But I wish we could *do* something."

"We can." Mother's voice was quiet but firm. "We can pray. Let's ask God to send Father back in time for planting. Even better, let's pray that this war will end soon. Then Tom will come home too."

Life During the War
Civilian Life

Supplying food during the war was not a problem for the North. Both civilians and soldiers needed food. Although many men fought in the war, production never failed. Older men, women, and boys stepped in to work in the fields. Improvements in farm machinery made the task easier. The North managed to raise enough food to feed civilians and soldiers and sell extra to Europe.

Factories also stayed busy in the North. Any raw materials the country lacked could be supplied from overseas. The loss of Southern cotton was the hardest blow. Supplying uniforms and shoes for the Union army kept many factories busy. It also led to the development of better sewing machines.

During the war, women filled in for men. Both on the field and in the factory, they took up the missing men's work. Women even worked in **munitions** factories. They usually earned lower wages than men, often because they had less experience or could not work as swiftly or accurately. After the war, most traditionally male jobs were filled by men once again.

The South experienced far greater hardship during the war. Initially it

153

Lesson Focus

- The Civil War cost both the Union and the Confederacy, but the South experienced greater hardships.

Objectives
- Explain Union advantages in supplying food and goods
- Relate how the South suffered great hardship during the war
- Discuss politics in the North and the South

Teacher's Toolkit CD
- Visual 18: *Confederate and Union Paper Money*
- Instructional Aid 40: *Supplying Food and Goods*

Review

- Choose a volunteer to tell why the Union wanted to capture Richmond, Virginia.
- Guide a review of Union and Confederate generals.
- Invite a student to review the battle at Antietam Creek.
- Guide a discussion of the importance of Chattanooga to the Confederates.

Preparation for Reading

- Generate interest as you direct the students to read the titles and examine the pictures on pages 153–55.
- Guide pronunciation of any unfamiliar words in the lesson.
- Direct the students to read the pages silently and complete Instructional Aid 40 in small groups.

Teach for Understanding

- Direct attention to the picture on page 153 and the How It Was box. Read the story aloud. Invite volunteers to discuss the hardships Southerners experienced as a result of the Civil War.
- Invite a group to explain what supplying food in the North was like during the Civil War.
- Choose a group to describe factory production in the North during the war.

Teach for Understanding

What was the easiest means used by both the Union and Confederate governments to pay for the war? issuing paper money

- Display Visual 18. Direct attention to the paper money used by the Union and the paper money used by the Confederacy.

Was issuing paper money successful? In the North this system worked well. In the South paper money failed.

What else provided money for the governments during the Civil War? Both governments raised taxes and borrowed money.

What was the center of the political confusion in the South? Answers could include that a key idea for the Confederacy was states' rights. But in order to run the war efficiently, the central government needed control. The forces of national unity and states' rights troubled the South.

Who tried to keep the government together in the South? President Jefferson Davis

What was Davis accused of as he tried to run the government and the war? having too much power

- Invite a student to explain politics in the North regarding secession.

---

suffered little. Much agricultural work was done by slaves before 1861. Even if the white men went to war, slaves would remain behind to work. Over time, though, several factors disrupted the South's economy. In areas such as Tennessee and Virginia, battles raged across fertile fields. Newly sprouted crops might be trodden down by the boots of soldiers. A second factor was the flight of slaves. Slaves might leave their owners' fields to try to gain their freedom. Transport of troops and the Northern invasion disrupted both rail and river transportation. Even when surplus food was grown, it might not reach the troops or cities that needed it. By the end of the war, many Southerners suffered from food shortages.

Factory production also suffered in the South. Before the war, the South had far fewer factories than the North. After the war began, almost all supplies had to be made in the Confederacy. The Union blockade stopped many foreign shipments to the South. Although the region was rich in cotton, little could be woven into cloth. Uniforms and shoes were hard to obtain. Civilians patched and repatched their clothing.

Paying for the War

Both Union and Confederate governments paid for the war in similar ways. The easiest means was issuing paper money. In the North this system worked well. People trusted that the

government would make sure their money was accepted. In the South paper money failed. By the end of the war, few people trusted that the Confederacy would win. If it lost, perhaps no one would accept its money. Prices for goods rose higher and higher. Both governments also raised taxes and borrowed money.

Politics

The South suffered from political confusion. A key idea for the Confederacy was states' rights. But in order to run the war efficiently, the central government needed control. The forces of national unity and states' rights troubled the South.

President Jefferson Davis tried to keep the country together. His experience in the United States Army and Senate proved valuable. But as he tried to run the nation and the war, he was accused of having too much power. State politicians often opposed Davis's policies. However, they supported the war and left him in power until the end.

Politics were more complicated in the North. Not everyone supported the war. Some Northerners believed that the South should be allowed to go in peace. Some opposed secession but supported slavery. President Lincoln had to **negotiate** with many different viewpoints. In order to keep running the war as he wanted, Lincoln also had to fight for two elections.

154

Background

The Emancipation Proclamation

Lincoln said that it was his "personal wish that all men everywhere could be free," but as president he had no power to free slaves. As the war progressed, Lincoln's official duty to restore the Union and his personal desire to see slaves freed could come together. In September 1862, after Antietam, he issued the Emancipation Proclamation. It would take effect January 1, 1863. As commander in chief, Lincoln had the power to free slaves only in Confederate-held states. Slaves in the border states or any other areas then under federal control could not be freed.

Lincoln hoped the proclamation would convince people that this war was worth the blood of thousands of Americans. The proclamation also hurt the South's war efforts. As word spread that slaves who reached Northern lines would be free, thousands of slaves fled from their masters. The proclamation ended all Southern hopes of recognition from Britain, since most of the British opposed slavery.

Black soldiers had asked to fight for the Union since the beginning of the war, but prejudice kept them from being accepted into the army. After the Emancipation Proclamation, black regiments began to form. Black Union soldiers were not treated the same as white Union

President Lincoln presenting the Emancipation Proclamation to his Cabinet

Lincoln's biggest opponents were the Democrats. Some opposed the war altogether. They believed that the secession was legal. Other Democrats wanted to fight for the Union. However, they disliked Lincoln and abolitionism. Some people feared that freeing slaves would disrupt the economy. Irish immigrants worried that freed slaves would move north. They could provide cheaper labor than the Irish, so many Irish feared losing their jobs.

Lincoln also faced some challenges from his own party. Most Republicans supported the president. But some thought that he should free the slaves once the war began. They wanted him to take more action against slavery.

During the war the North had two elections. Shortly before the first election, Lincoln decided that he was strong enough politically to issue the **Emancipation Proclamation**. This notice promised to free all enslaved people in rebellious states. Then in November 1862, Americans elected members of Congress. Lincoln believed that despite the antislavery move of the Emancipation Proclamation, Republicans would stay in control of Congress. The Republicans lost seats, but they did keep control. Lincoln's announcement ensured that a Union victory would bring about the end of slavery.

Two years later Lincoln fought for reelection. His first opponent was from his own cabinet. The secretary of the treasury, Samuel Chase, wanted to become the Republican nominee for president. However, the party wanted Lincoln. In the general election, Lincoln faced a Democrat. His former chief general, George McClellan, opposed him. All but three states gave Lincoln more votes.

In both North and South, politics threatened to disrupt the war. Both sides focused enough to keep fighting. Most Southerners were more concerned with secession than a strong president. Northerners believed that Lincoln would lead them to a reunited nation.

Why did the South struggle so much to feed and clothe its people?

Teach for Understanding

• Direct attention to the picture. Read aloud the caption.

Who were Lincoln's biggest opponents? the Democrats

Why were Democrats against abolition, or the freeing of slaves? It might disrupt the economy.

What concerned Irish workers? Freed slaves might move north. They could provide cheaper labor than the Irish, so many Irish feared losing their jobs.

What did Lincoln do to ensure that a Union victory would bring about the end of slavery? He issued the Emancipation Proclamation.

Conclude the discussion by asking the question on page 155. In areas such as Tennessee and Virginia, battles raged across fertile fields. A second factor was the flight of slaves. Additionally, food was scarce. Even when surplus food was grown, it might not reach the troops or cities that needed it. The Union blockade stopped many foreign shipments to the South. Although the South was rich in cotton, it was poor in factories; little cotton could be woven into cloth.

soldiers. Until 1864, black soldiers were paid less and received less medical care. As a result, the death toll for black soldiers ran 37 percent higher than that for white soldiers. Black soldiers also were assigned the most mundane tasks, and none were appointed as officers. To be captured in a Union uniform would mean almost certain enslavement. Nevertheless, more than 190,000 black Americans fought on the Union side. Their performance in battle demonstrated that black Americans were as capable as white Americans, and their service for their country ended talk of sending freed black people to colonies in Africa or South America.

Black Soldiers in the Confederate Armies

Black men served in the Confederate armies in noncombatant (non-fighting) jobs, such as cooks, wagon drivers, laborers, and personal servants to officers. The Confederate Congress ignored advice from commanders such as General Patrick Cleburne that black men be used in the Southern armies. By March 1865, however, when the South experienced a severe manpower shortage, the Confederate Congress passed a bill to draft 300,000 black men. The first two black companies astounded white soldiers with their skill at arms. But black soldiers did not fight for the Confederacy because the war ended before black companies could take the field.

Lesson Focus

- The Civil War continued on the eastern and western fronts.

Objectives

- Recognize generals and battles on the eastern front
- Recognize generals and battles on the western front

Teacher's Toolkit CD

- Instructional Aid 41: *The War Continues*

Introduction

- Invite a student to explain how supplying food during the war was not hard in the North.
- Choose a volunteer to describe manufacturing in the North during the war.
- Guide a review of why the South experienced greater hardship concerning agriculture and manufacturing goods than the North did during the war.

What methods did the governments use to pay for the war? issuing paper money, raising taxes, and borrowing money

Who was the Confederate president? Jefferson Davis

Who was the Union president? Abraham Lincoln

What did Lincoln do to ensure that a Union victory would end slavery? He issued the Emancipation Proclamation.

Preparation for Reading

- Generate interest as you direct the students to read the titles and examine the pictures on pages 156–58.
- Guide pronunciation of any unfamiliar words in the lesson.
- Direct the students to read the pages silently and complete Instructional Aid 41 in small groups.

Teach for Understanding

- Choose a group to give the names of the Union and Confederate generals and the outcome of the battle at Fredericksburg.
- Choose a group to give the names of the Union and Confederate generals and the outcome of the battle at Chancellorsville.

Why did General Lee cross into the North? He wanted to win on Northern territory. He wanted the North to feel the burden of war as much as the South did.

The War Continues

Eastern Front

The war continued despite the election. A new Union commander fought in Virginia. Ambrose Burnside planned to succeed where many generals had failed. Once again the North had far more troops. Burnside's 113,000 men faced 74,000 of Lee's. The two armies met near Fredericksburg in December 1862.

The battle was as unsuccessful as previous Union invasions. Burnside's commanders could not defeat Lee's. Half of the Union army never managed to fully engage in battle. Northern forces suffered more than double the Confederate casualties. One more commander had failed to defeat Lee.

Burnside had time to improve. However, over the winter he failed to strengthen his army. In late January he attempted another invasion of the South. By then his troops had no confidence in him. A drenching rain turned the roads into a muddy challenge. Burnside returned with his troops to Washington, and Lincoln accepted his resignation. The Army of the Potomac needed another leader.

General Joseph Hooker had a promising start. He was energetic and popular with the men. He improved their conditions and their morale. His boasts of capturing Richmond inspired the men with confidence. By late spring 1863, Hooker was ready to try to defeat the Confederate army.

But the Battle of Chancellorsville proved that Lee was a truly great general. Hooker had nearly double Lee's 60,000 men. The two forces met in a forested region near Fredericksburg. Lee dared to split his smaller army and to attack Hooker. The Union general hesitated and held back some troops. The Confederates hit hard. At the end of the battle, Union forces headed home in defeat once again.

Chancellorsville cost both sides. As was often the case, the North suffered greater casualties. The energized Army of the Potomac lost again. But the South lost a great general. Stonewall Jackson was injured by his own men. Not recognizing their general, they shot him as he rode by in the dark. In battle after battle, he had carried out Lee's commands. His faithful service enabled Lee to execute daring plans. Several days later, Jackson died. Although Lee had won Chancellorsville, the cost was heavy.

Despite this loss, Lee wanted to push ahead. Time and again he had defeated Union armies. Each victory occurred in Virginia. If he could only win on Northern territory, Lee hoped to end the war. He wanted the North to feel the burden of war as much as the South did. In June 1863, Lee's forces crossed into the North.

The resulting battle tested both armies and commanders. As Lee

156

Background

Civil Religion in America

Civil religion is the use of religion for political purposes. For instance, some political leaders may think that belief in a god and in the moral teachings of the Bible will make the country a better place. These people may not believe in the deity of Christ, the Trinity, or salvation by grace through faith alone. They are not interested in people becoming Christians. They just want to use parts of Christianity to help the country.

Civil religion also links piety and patriotism. It teaches that its nation is God's special chosen nation. And it teaches that the success of the nation is God's will. Some people speak of those who die in service of the nation as if they are therefore expected to receive a place in heaven because of their service to the nation.

During the Civil War, civil religion was often intertwined with promotion of the war effort. This can be seen in "The Battle Hymn of the Republic." In that hymn, the cause of the nation is the cause of God.

> "I have seen Him in the watchfires of a hundred circling camps;
> They have builded Him an altar in the evening dews and damps;
> I can read His righteous sentence by the dim and flaring lamps,
> His day is marching on."

The Battle of Gettysburg proved to be one of the bloodiest battles of the Civil War as two ill-prepared armies fought for three days.

marched north into Pennsylvania, Union forces hunted his army. Hooker suggested marching on Richmond. Then he worried that he needed more soldiers. Lincoln realized that Hooker could not do the job and replaced him with **General George Meade**. Three days after receiving the command, Meade's army joined the battle in **Gettysburg**, Pennsylvania.

Neither side was ready for battle. Meade had just learned that he would command the army. Lee's cavalry was **scouting**. The battle began on July 1, 1863, when Confederate soldiers ran into Union troops. Both sides moved to reinforce their positions.

The Battle of Gettysburg lasted three days. Lee performed poorly compared to his usual brilliance. Not having Jackson hurt his command.

Union forces staunchly defended their positions against waves of gray-clad soldiers. The slaughter was immense. Almost 8,000 dead men covered the hills and fields of Gettysburg. On July 4, Lee led his men in retreat. Despite his advantage, Meade hesitantly pursued the defeated army. Lee and his army escaped into Virginia.

The Battle of Gettysburg had a profound influence on the Civil War. Never again did Lee invade the North. Although the North had suffered heavy casualties, the battle was proclaimed a victory. Lee was defeated, and the invasion was repelled. The site of the battle became a military cemetery. Several months later, President Lincoln spoke at its opening ceremony. His brief speech helps explain the struggles of the Civil War.

157

Teach for Understanding

- Direct attention to the picture. Invite a student to read aloud the caption.
- Choose a group to give the names of the Union and Confederate generals and the outcome of the battle at Gettysburg.

Primary Source: "The Battle Hymn of the Republic"

- Direct attention to Activity Manual page 108.
- Read aloud the introduction.
- Invite a student to explain what inspired Julia Ward Howe to write the words to "The Battle Hymn of the Republic."
- Sing the song together.

Lesson

60

Teach for Understanding

- Choose a group to give the names of the Union and Confederate generals and the outcome of the battle at Vicksburg.

- Choose a group to give the names of the Union and Confederate generals and the outcome of the battle at Chattanooga.

▶ Conclude the discussion by asking the question on page 158. to gain control of the Mississippi River

Activity Manual

- Guide completion of pages 108–9.

The Shirley House in Vicksburg was caught in the crossfire between the two armies.

Western Front

While Lee battled in the East, the Union slowly progressed in the West. Grant worked on his goal of taking Vicksburg. Confederate and Union forces both tried to control parts of Tennessee.

Grant's long campaign toward Vicksburg showed his talents. The city sat on the eastern bank of the Mississippi. Confederate guns defended it from the river and threatened Union shipping. On the land side, strong defenses prevented an easy victory. Grant needed to bring his entire army to **siege** the city. Taking a great risk, Grant crossed the Mississippi downstream of Vicksburg and left his supply line behind. Grant's army added the supplies it found in Mississippi to those the men had brought with them. After swinging east into the state, Grant returned to Vicksburg's land side. Unable to force a decisive battle, he

settled down to a siege in May. As Lee's forces marched through Pennsylvania, the Vicksburg campaign finally wore down. Finally, after weeks of siege, the defending army surrendered on July 4. Grant captured 30,000 men and gained control of the Mississippi.

Union forces had difficulty in Tennessee. Controlling the railroad hub of **Chattanooga** was a key objective. Union general William Rosecrans outfought and outmaneuvered General Braxton Bragg and the Confederate army. On September 9, Rosecrans gained the city. But Bragg refused to give up. He tricked Rosecrans into advancing against him. At the Battle of Chickamauga, only the heroic stand of General George Thomas saved Rosecrans's army from a complete disaster. Rosecrans still kept control of the city. Bragg then besieged Rosecrans at Chattanooga.

But the later autumn proved better for the Union. After capturing Vicksburg, Grant was able to relieve Rosecrans and help fight for Chattanooga. In late November 1863, Grant and Bragg fought for the city. During the Battle of Chattanooga, the Union defeated the Confederates. Chattanooga and its railway were firmly in Northern hands. From there the road to Atlanta stretched ahead.

> Why did the North need to capture Vicksburg?

158

Background

Hardship in Vicksburg

General Grant laid siege to Vicksburg to starve it into submission. Conditions inside the besieged city worsened. Life in Vicksburg during the siege was so dangerous that civilians began living in caves they dug into the hillsides around the city. Conditions became so desperate that horses, cats, dogs, and even rats disappeared as the starving populace sought food.

Victory and Defeat

The remainder of the war offered little hope to the South. Confederate armies managed only to slow Union advances. Two eastern campaigns caused the most damage. The leaders there were Generals Grant and Sherman. After the victory of Chattanooga, Lincoln brought Grant to the East. Lincoln placed him in charge of all the Union armies. Most of all, Lincoln hoped that Grant could defeat Lee in Virginia. Grant appointed Sherman to replace him in carrying on the campaign that secured Chattanooga.

Union Campaigns in the East

Atlanta

Following the fall of Chattanooga, Union forces advanced southeast into Georgia. The goal was **Atlanta**. This young city was an important rail hub for the Confederacy. From May to July, Sherman advanced toward Atlanta, pushing Confederate general Joseph Johnston backwards. In July, Davis, the Confederate president, replaced Johnston with John Bell Hood. Sherman's success continued against the new general. Finally, on September 1, Atlanta fell to the Union forces. Much of the city burned as the retreating Confederate army tried to make sure that nothing of value fell into Union hands.

To Petersburg

Up in Virginia, Grant was less immediately successful. In May and June he led his army through eastern Virginia. Grant's goal was the city of Petersburg. Although it was not as important as Richmond, Petersburg helped supply the capital. Beginning in May 1864, Union forces built **siegeworks** near Petersburg. Grant planned to move steadily toward Richmond.

Atlanta after Sherman's march

Sherman Marches

After capturing Atlanta, Sherman made a bold decision. He would not hunt Confederate armies. Instead, he would leave his supply line behind and march to the sea. Georgia's rich farmland promised to supply his men. In the process, he could crush support for Confederate troops. Sherman commanded his men to seize supplies

159

Lesson Focus

- As the Civil War drew to a close, President Lincoln was assassinated.

Objectives
- Examine Union campaigns in the East
- Identify the roles of Grant and Lee at the end of the war
- Relate how President Lincoln died

Introduction

- Guide a review of the generals and outcomes of the battles at Fredericksburg, Chancellorsville, Gettysburg, Vicksburg, and Chattanooga.

Preparation for Reading

- Generate interest as you direct the students to read the titles and examine the pictures on pages 159–61.
- Guide pronunciation of any unfamiliar words.
- Direct the students to read the pages silently to find out why much of Atlanta burned after it fell to Union forces. The retreating Confederate army tried to make sure that nothing of value fell into Union hands.

Teach for Understanding

- Direct attention to the picture. Read aloud the caption.

  Why did Union forces want to take control of Atlanta, Georgia? It was an important rail hub for the Confederacy.

  What Confederate generals fought against Sherman and the Union soldiers to keep control of Atlanta? Joseph Johnston and his replacement, John Bell Hood

  Where was Grant leading his army? in eastern Virginia

  Why did the Union forces build siegeworks near Petersburg? Grant's goal was to take control of Petersburg because it helped supply the capital.

- Invite a student to look up *siegework* in the Glossary and read aloud the definition.

  What city did Grant plan to move toward next? Richmond

  Why did Sherman decide he would not hunt Confederate troops but would instead leave his supply line behind and march to the sea? Georgia's rich farmland promised to supply his men. In the process, he could crush support for Confederate troops.

Teach for Understanding

What did Sherman do to crush support for Confederate troops? He commanded his men to seize supplies and to destroy railroads that might help the Confederacy.

What did Union troops do that harmed civilians? They burned houses and devastated much of Georgia from Atlanta to Savannah.

Where did Sherman march after capturing Savannah? into the Carolinas

What major cities fell in South Carolina? Charleston and Columbia

When Sherman reached North Carolina, why did he warn his soldiers to be kinder to the civilians there? North Carolina was the last to secede, so he thought it did not deserve harsh punishment.

After the Union sieged Petersburg and Richmond fell, what did Lee and his army do? They fled.

What major event happened at the Appomattox Courthouse? Lee surrendered.

- Direct attention to the picture. Choose a volunteer to read aloud the caption.

- Why do you think Grant allowed Lee and his officers to keep their swords and horses? Answers could include that by allowing the officers to keep their swords and horses, Lee and his army were agreeing not to fight anymore and that they would obey the laws. It is also possible that Grant allowed the officers to keep their swords and horses to respect them rather than to shame them.

In an act of honor during the Confederate surrender, Grant "permitted Lee and his officers to keep their swords and horses."

and destroy railroads that might help the Confederacy. Civilians were to be left alone. Before leaving Atlanta, Sherman set on fire anything of military use in the city. Much that had escaped the earlier fire was burned. Atlanta lay in ruins.

Much of Georgia shared Atlanta's fate. Union soldiers were not careful about civilian property. They considered all Southerners to be rebels. If a rebel house burned, few Northern soldiers were bothered. From Atlanta to Savannah, a wide swath of Georgia was devastated. Four days before Christmas 1864, Sherman captured Savannah.

Sherman then marched north into the Carolinas. South Carolina received harsh treatment. Charleston and Columbia both fell. Following Columbia's fall, the city burned. Although no one is certain who caused the fire, Southerners blamed Sherman. Many Northerners were pleased that the capital of the first seceding state suffered from the war. When Sherman reached North Carolina, he warned his soldiers to be kinder to the civilians there. He felt that since North Carolina was the last to secede, it did not deserve harsh punishment.

Grant and Lee

In Virginia, Grant stuck to the siege of Petersburg. After months of fighting, the city fell on April 3. Confederate authorities in Richmond knew that they would fall next. By the morning of April 3, the Confederates had burned anything of value in the city. Lee and his army also fled.

Lee surrendered less than a week later. His troops had been chased to the **Appomattox Courthouse** in Virginia. On April 9, Grant and Lee

160

Background

The "Bummers"

Worse than the regular Union troops were the "bummers," an ugly collection of renegades on the fringes of Sherman's army. Most of the bummers were Union deserters. Under no discipline whatsoever, the bummers committed the worst atrocities of the march—robbery, assault, and murder. Sherman's inability or unwillingness to control these men left a bitter legacy long after the war was over.

met to discuss the terms of surrender that Grant proposed. He permitted Lee and his officers to keep their swords and horses. Although Lee surrendered only one army, the result was clear. The South had lost the war.

Fully ending the war would take some time. Other Southern armies still had to surrender. Jefferson Davis and other Confederate leaders would be captured. But those problems would be solved during the **Reconstruction**. In the days, months, and years after the Civil War, all Americans would have to work together to rebuild a united nation.

Lincoln's Death

With the war close to being over, President Lincoln could finally relax. Five days after the surrender at the Appomattox Courthouse, Lincoln and his wife visited a theater to watch a play. During the play, an actor from the slave state of Maryland attacked the president. John Wilkes Booth burst into Lincoln's box, shot the president, jumped to the stage, and escaped on a waiting horse. Despite immediate medical care, the shot was fatal. President Lincoln died early the next morning.

Lincoln had worked many years for his nation. He had fought slavery as a Whig and as a Republican. He had fought to save the nation from disunion. And he had a new plan for rebuilding the Union. After his death, Americans continued this work during the Reconstruction.

The surrender of which Confederate general showed the war was almost over?

After the war, soldiers were eager to return to their loved ones and get back to life as usual.

161

Teach for Understanding

- Direct attention to the picture. Read aloud the caption.

What was the period of time after the war when the nation rebuilt itself called? Reconstruction

What sad event happened five days after the surrender at Appomattox Courthouse? John Wilkes Booth shot Lincoln.

> Conclude the discussion by asking the question on page 161.
> General Lee

Activity Manual

- Guide completion of page 110.

Objective
- Recall concepts and terms from Chapter 7

Materials
- Lap books

Introduction

- Concepts for the Chapter 7 Test will be taken from Activity Manual pages 99–112. You may review any or all of the concepts during this lesson. You may choose to review Chapter 7 by having the students complete and review their lap books.

Review

- Direct the students to complete their lap books and use them for review.

Activity Manual

- Guide completion of pages 111–12.

Lesson **63** Chapter 7 Test

Objective
- Demonstrate knowledge of concepts from Chapter 7 by taking the test

Assessment

- Administer Test 7.

Chapter 8

Introduction

After the Civil War, much of the South needed to be rebuilt. Many Southern states resisted the requirements for Reconstruction placed on them by the US government. Congress passed laws and gave the army the responsibility of enforcing the laws in each of five military districts in the South.

Once the army was withdrawn, Southern states returned to their former Democratic rule. Some reactions to Reconstruction were unjust and violent. Civil rights for black Americans were hindered by Democrats passing Jim Crow laws that segregated black people again.

Farmers relocated to the Great Plains. Cowboys sent cattle east by train. Railroads spread across the country.

Conflict arose when white settlers trespassed on land in the West reserved for American Indians. Ranchers had land disputes in regard to grazing sheep and cattle. Outlaws stole cattle. Ranchers sometimes took the law into their own hands. The West needed government in order to promote good and restrain evil.

Chapter Focus

After the Civil War, the United States worked to rebuild and expand.

8 Reconstruction and the West

Focus
After the Civil War, the United States worked to rebuild and expand.

Lesson	Student Text	Activity Manual	Content			Vocabulary	
64	162–64	113–15	Presidential Reconstruction Thirteenth Amendment			Black Codes Thirteenth Amendment	
65	165–67	116–19	Civil rights bill Freedmen's Bureau Primary Source: Freedman's Rights	Fourteenth Amendment Reconstruction Act of 1867		Fourteenth Amendment impeach Reconstruction Act of 1867	
66	168–71	120–21	Biography Box: Robert Smalls Challenges of black Americans	Fifteenth Amendment		carpetbagger Fifteenth Amendment	scalawag segregate
67	172–74	122	Politics of Reconstruction Ku Klux Klan	Southern "redemption"		fraud Jim Crow laws	
68	175–77	123	American Indians of the West	Miners	Sodbusters	vigilante justice	
69	178–80	124–25	How it Was: Life on the Trail Cowboys	Railroads			
70	181–83	126	Sitting Bull and Crazy Horse defeat Custer Chief Joseph and the Nez Perce Activity: A Historical Exhibit			Battle of the Little Bighorn	
71		127–28	Chapter Review				
72			Chapter Test				

Chapter 8 Overview

Visit bjupress.com/resources for links to enhance the lessons.

Timeline

Reconstruction Act 1867

Battle of the Little Bighorn 1876

Reconstruction ends 1877

1860   1865   1868   1870   1880

Thirteenth Amendment ratified

Fourteenth Ammendment ratified

The Civil War was over, but the United States still needed to be put back together. The war had broken many things. The time period in which the country was put back together was called the Reconstruction.

Much in the South needed to be reconstructed. Many Southern cities had been burned. Farmland was ruined in much of Virginia. Railroads had been destroyed. Confederate money was worthless. Formerly wealthy Southerners were now poor. In addition, state governments needed to be reconstructed.

Presidential Reconstruction and Response

The Confederate army had surrendered, and many Southerners feared the worst. They knew that the United States government viewed them as rebels. Throughout history, the leaders of failed rebellions were often killed.

Abraham Lincoln's vice president, Andrew Johnson, became president after Lincoln died. At first people thought he would act harshly against the Southern states. He spoke of punishing those who rebelled against the United States. But instead Johnson pardoned most of the Confederate leaders. Only Jefferson Davis remained in prison. Johnson appointed governors over the Southern states. The governors placed leaders of the secession back into power.

Johnson had a simple plan for Reconstruction. The states had to hold a convention that did three things. First, the states had to approve the **Thirteenth Amendment**. This amendment to the Constitution outlawed slavery.

> Andrew Johnson was supposed to have been assassinated along with Lincoln, but his would-be assassin backed out.
>
> Johnson never went to school and did not learn to read until the age of seventeen.

163

JourneyForth

The following books are available from JourneyForth Books, a division of BJU Press, at journeyforth.com.

Beyond the Smoke by Terry Burns

When Bryan Wheeler's parents are killed by Comanche raiders, he sets out with a few supplies, two guns, and his mother's Bible to make a life for himself in America's Wild West.

Brave the Wild Trail by Milly Howard

Set in the post-Civil War era when many in the South were poverty-stricken, this is the story of twelve-year-old Josh Bramlett's dangerous journey as a Florida Cracker, helping his family drive a herd of cattle across the Florida wilderness.

Prairie Anna by Peggy House

This story about a family of Russian immigrants explores some of the adjustments they must make after settling in the American West.

Lesson Focus

- The Thirteenth Amendment freed the slaves, but the Southern states passed the Black Codes to treat them like slaves again.

Objectives

- List three things Southern states would have to do under Reconstruction
- Identify the response Southerners had to the requirements placed on them
- Describe the Black Codes

Teacher's Toolkit CD

- Instructional Aid 42: *Reconstruction*

Introduction

- Invite a student to read aloud the title of the chapter and predict what the chapter will be about. It will be about rebuilding the country and about the West.
- Invite a student to read the chapter focus aloud.

  What do you think you will learn in this chapter? what the United States did to rebuild and to expand

- Direct attention to the timeline.

  When was the Thirteenth Amendment ratified? 1865

  What event is given for 1867? the Reconstruction Act

  What battle occurred in 1876? the Battle of the Little Bighorn

Preparation for Reading

- Generate interest as you direct the students to read the titles and examine the pictures on pages 162–64.
- Guide pronunciation of any unfamiliar words in the lesson.
- Explain that the image on page 162 depicts Bass Reeves, a former slave, who became the first black US marshal west of the Mississippi. A marshal is an official who carries out the orders of a court in a particular district. His duties can be compared to the job of a sheriff.
- Direct the students to read the pages and complete Instructional Aid 42 in small groups.

Teach for Understanding

- Choose a volunteer to read aloud the paragraph that tells what the South was like after the Civil War.

  Who became the president of the United States after Abraham Lincoln died? the vice president, Andrew Johnson

- Direct attention to the image on page 163. Read aloud the caption.

Lesson

64

What was the first thing Southern states would be required to do under Johnson's plan for Reconstruction? approve the Thirteenth Amendment

What did the Thirteenth Amendment do? outlawed slavery

Teach for Understanding

- Choose a group to state the other requirements placed on Southern states under Johnson's plan for Reconstruction.

- Choose a group to identify the immediate response some states had to the requirements placed on them.

- Direct attention to the picture on page 164. Choose a volunteer to explain the meaning of the picture.

- Invite a group to describe the Black Codes.

> Conclude the discussion by asking the question on page 164. The purpose was to force black people to work for white people; black people were not able to become self-sufficient.

Activity Manual

- Introduce *Chapter 8 Looking Ahead* on page 114. Read the page together. Guide completion of pages 113–15.

Second, the states had to admit that secession was wrong. Third, the states had to cancel the debts they owed as a result of fighting against the Union. The United States did not want the people who loaned money or supplies to the Confederacy to be repaid.

Response

These conditions were much lighter than expected. But many states still resisted. Some refused to ratify the Thirteenth Amendment. And South Carolina insisted that it pay its war debts.

Some of these states also voted the leaders of the Confederacy back into power to their state houses and to Congress. For example, Georgia elected Alexander Stephens as a United States senator. Stephens had been the vice president of the Confederacy.

Most significantly, the Southern states passed **Black Codes**. Black Americans had been freed from slavery. But the Black Codes were laws that treated black Americans like slaves. Some laws did not let black people rent or buy property. They were prevented from starting their own farms. In some states, laws would not let black people live in towns or cities unless they were servants to white people. Black men had to get permission to preach the gospel.

Black people had to have a job contract for an entire year. If they switched jobs before the year was up, they would lose all the money they had earned. This law prevented black workers from moving to jobs that paid better. Some contracts said that black people had to live on plantations. They could not leave without permission. They had to refer to their employer as their master. Another law allowed the state to take children from their parents. The state could apprentice the children to work for white employers. Because the slaves were hired as apprentices, they were not paid for their work. Often they were "apprenticed" back to their former owners.

When they were slaves, black people had been allowed to graze animals, to fish in streams, and to hunt. Now it was a crime to do these things. All animals had to be fenced in. This law meant that only people with land could own animals. The goal was to force black people to work for white people. Black Americans were not able to become self-sufficient.

> What was the purpose of Black Codes?

164

Background

Christians' Opposition to Black Codes

Christianity played a significant role in the Radical Republican idea that black people are equal to white people. Historian Kenneth Stampp wrote:

> In the nineteenth century most white Americans, North and South, had reservations about the Negro's potentialities—doubted that he had the innate intellectual capacity and moral fiber of the white man and assumed that after emancipation he would be relegated to an inferior caste. But some of the Radical Republicans refused to believe that the Negroes were innately inferior and hoped passionately that they would confound their critics. The radicals had little empirical evidence and no scientific evidence to support their belief [because to this point black people had been kept in subservient positions]— nothing, in fact, but faith. Their faith was derived mostly from their religion: all men, they said, are the sons of Adam and equal in the sight of God. And if Negroes are equal to white men in the sight of God, it is morally wrong for white men to withhold from Negroes the liberties and rights that white men enjoy.

Stampp, Kenneth M, *The Era of Reconstruction 1865–1877* (New York: Knopf, 1965), 12.

(*Note:* Stampp wrote in 1965 when *Negro* was the common term used for black Americans; since the 1960s, the term *Negro* has fallen out of favor because of its associations with slavery and segregation.)

Congress Intervenes

These laws angered Republicans in Congress. Some of them had long opposed slavery. They saw the Civil War as a way to end the injustices of slavery. They believed that the Black Codes had to be outlawed. If they were left in place, then the Civil War was fought in vain.

Some went further than wanting to see black people freed from these unfair laws. They wanted to see black Americans treated equally with white Americans. This view was not popular at this time.

Those who supported the equality of black and white citizens were influenced by the Bible. The Bible says that all people descended from Adam. They are all equal before God as His creation made in His image. Therefore, they should be treated equally by the government too.

Congress had other concerns as well. Since black Southerners were now free, black people were counted as full persons for the purpose of representation in Congress. This change gave even more power to those who had supported slavery and secession. The former slave states would get more representatives in Congress. But black people still could not vote. Northern congressmen did not think that those who supported secession should be rewarded with more power than they had before the Civil War.

When Congress met in December 1865, the House of Representatives refused to recognize Southern representatives. Congress declared that the Constitution gave Congress, not the president, the right to admit states into the country. President Johnson said the Southern states had never left the Union because they had no right to leave. But his critics noted that just because someone doesn't have the right to murder a person doesn't mean he can't. They agreed that the Southern states did not have a legal right to leave. But the states did leave. They were now like territories that had to be readmitted by Congress. Congress would now set the requirements of Reconstruction.

The Civil Rights Bill and the Freedmen's Bureau

Congress passed bills that protected the civil rights of black Americans. One bill said that states could not take black people's citizenship away. Another bill protected black Americans' civil rights. It allowed the Freedmen's Bureau to oversee civil rights trials.

The Freedmen's Bureau had been set up to provide food and clothing to freed slaves and poor white Southerners. It tried to find jobs for the freedmen. It also set up schools for black people. But many Southerners accused the Bureau of corruption. In response, President Johnson ordered an investigation. The investigators found so little

165

The Freedmen's Bureau

One of the most important agencies in Southern Reconstruction was the Freedmen's Bureau, founded in 1865 to provide help to the newly freed slaves. When Congress took control of Reconstruction, the Bureau became a tool for protecting freedmen's legal rights as well. State courts in the South were not being fair to blacks so Congress set up "Freedman's United States Courts" administered by the Bureau. These Bureau courts protected the rights of the freedmen, but they also offended many Southerners by overriding local courts.

Activity

Plan a School

Explain that one of the jobs of the Freedmen's Bureau was to oversee the establishment of schools for black children. Divide the students into groups. Direct the students to plan a school. Ask them to determine a design for the school and grounds and what grades of students would attend there. Remind them to list subjects that would be taught and a daily schedule that includes other interesting activities. Encourage them to think of rules and guidelines that would help the school run effectively.

Lesson Focus

- Congress set the requirements for Reconstruction.

Objectives
- Identify the purpose of the Freedmen's Bureau
- Understand the purpose of the Fourteenth Amendment
- Describe the Reconstruction Act of 1867
- Explain the impeachment of President Johnson

Review

- Invite a student to tell what the Thirteenth Amendment did.
- Guide a review of how black Americans were treated under the Black Codes.

> Guide a review of important terms, maps, places, and people from each previous lesson. Direct the students to find and read the corresponding entries from the Resource Treasury.

Preparation for Reading

- Generate interest as you direct the students to read the titles and examine the map on pages 165–67.
- Guide pronunciation of any unfamiliar words in the lesson.
- Direct the students to read the pages silently to learn the name of the act that divided the former Confederacy into five military districts. the Reconstruction Act of 1867

Teach for Understanding

What was the response of Republicans to the Black Codes? These laws angered them.

What influenced those who supported the equality of black and white citizens? the Bible

Why was Congress concerned that freed black people were counted as full persons for representation in Congress? This change gave more power to those who had supported slavery and secession.

How did the House of Representatives act toward Southern representatives when Congress met in December 1865? The House refused to recognize the Southern representatives.

Who would now set the requirements for Southern states to be readmitted to the United States? Congress

What were some of the things the Freedmen's Bureau did? oversaw civil rights trials, provided food and clothing to freed slaves and poor white Southerners, found jobs for the freedmen, and set up schools for black people

Why did President Johnson order an investigation of the Freedmen's Bureau? Many Southerners accused the Bureau of corruption.

What did the investigation show? little corruption

Chapter 8: Reconstruction and the West

Primary Source: Freedmen's Rights

- Direct attention to Activity Manual page 117.
- Read aloud the introduction.
- Read the excerpt. Guide a discussion of the meaning of each sentence.

Teach for Understanding

What did the first part of the Fourteenth Amendment state? Any person born in the United States was a US citizen.

Why did the Fourteenth Amendment include this part? to make sure that male black Americans were included as citizens who could vote

What did the second part of the amendment say? People who fought against the United States could not hold office again unless Congress pardoned them.

What was the third requirement of the Fourteenth Amendment? The United States would not pay debts owed by the Confederacy. The states could not pay them either.

Why did Congress use the Reconstruction Act of 1867 to divide the former Confederacy into five military districts? to give the army the responsibility of enforcing the laws in each district

How do you think Southerners felt about the South being divided into military districts? Possible answers could include that Southerners may have resented being forced by the military to obey the laws.

- Direct attention to the map on page 166 and the dates that the states reentered the Union.

---

corruption that the investigation was an embarrassment to the accusers.

Fourteenth Amendment

The bills that Congress passed were a first step. But the Republicans knew that a future Congress could get rid of these bills. Republicans wanted the Constitution to defend civil rights with a constitutional amendment.

Certain Republicans proposed the **Fourteenth Amendment**. It had three major parts. First, any person born in the United States was a US citizen. He was also a citizen of the state where he lived. If a state did not let all male citizens vote, it would lose some of its representatives in Congress. This part was written to make sure that black Americans were included as citizens who could vote.

People who serve in a government office or in the military have to swear an oath. By reciting this oath, they promise to uphold the Constitution. Some people broke this oath by fighting against the United States. The second part of the Fourteenth Amendment said these people could not hold office again unless Congress pardoned them.

Third, debts owed by the Confederacy would not be paid by the United States. The states could not pay them either. Congress did not think that people or businesses who had helped the Confederacy should be paid.

Reconstruction Act of 1867

Congress had passed laws. But it needed to make sure those laws were obeyed. The **Reconstruction Act of 1867** enforced them. This act divided the former Confederacy into five military districts. Congress gave the army the responsibility of enforcing the laws in each district.

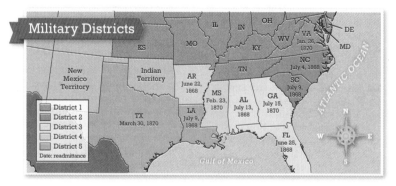

Military Districts

166

Background

Andrew Johnson

Andrew Johnson opposed Tennessee's vote to secede in 1861. He was the only Southern senator not to resign his Senate seat. When Nashville fell, Lincoln named Johnson military governor of Tennessee. Later, Lincoln chose Johnson to be his running mate. Johnson's public statements won him the support of Radical Republicans. He once said that Jefferson Davis and other leading Confederates should be hanged. He assured people that "treason must be made odious." But when Johnson became president upon Lincoln's death, he decided instead that Reconstruction should be quick and lenient.

Johnson seemed to lack the tact that the nation needed in leaders at that time. He was firm in his view that Reconstruction should be quick and easy for the Southern states. When Congress insisted on a Reconstruction program that would protect black Americans' civil rights, he refused to change. He lashed out at his opponents. His inflexibility often disheartened moderates, driving them into the radical camp. With most of Congress united against Johnson, the days of presidential Reconstruction were numbered.

The Reconstruction Act also laid out the plan for reconstructing Southern states. First, they had to write new state constitutions. These constitutions had to guarantee the rights of black men to vote. Second, the majority of voters had to approve these constitutions. Congress had to approve them too. Third, the states had to ratify the Fourteenth Amendment. When these requirements were met, the army would leave the state.

The Reconstruction Act had positive effects for black Southerners. They believed they could now resist injustice. Black Southerners served on juries. They now rode on public transportation with white people. They insisted that their employers treat them fairly.

Impeachment

President Johnson opposed Congress's plan for Reconstruction. He wanted the Southern states brought back into the Union quickly, but he was not interested in giving black Americans the right to vote. He removed some of the military men who were overseeing Reconstruction. He replaced them with men who opposed Reconstruction. He also removed Edwin Stanton from office. Stanton was the secretary of war. But Congress had passed a law in 1867 that did not allow Johnson to remove Stanton.

Republicans in Congress said that the president had broken the law and should be removed from office. The Constitution lays out the way to dismiss the president. First, the House of Representatives votes to **impeach** the president. To impeach means to make an accusation against someone—especially someone in authority. According to the Constitution, a president can be impeached only for "treason, bribery, or other high crimes and misdemeanors." But impeachment does not remove the president from office. After a president is impeached by the House, a trial takes place in the Senate. The chief justice of the Supreme Court oversees the trial. After evidence is presented, US senators vote to convict the president or leave him in office. Two-thirds of the Senate must vote for the conviction.

The House of Representatives voted to impeach President Johnson. The Senate had to decide what to do. Some did not think the law he broke was constitutional to begin with. Others did not think Johnson had broken the law. Many Congressmen clearly wanted to get rid of Johnson. Americans knew that impeaching a president because he caused some people trouble was not a good reason. The Senate found Johnson not guilty by one vote.

> How did the Bible influence support for racial equality?

167

Andrew Johnson's Impeachment

Even though Congress believed that Johnson was opposing good and necessary laws that would bring justice to black Southerners, it was wrong to impeach Johnson for political purposes. (The law Congress claimed he had broken was unconstitutional, and it was not even clear that he had broken it.) Such actions set a bad precedent that undermined the protections that the Constitution provides.

Teach for Understanding

What plans did the Reconstruction Act lay out for reconstructing Southern states? Southern states had to write new state constitutions to guarantee the rights of black men to vote. The majority of voters and Congress had to approve the constitutions. States had to ratify the Fourteenth Amendment.

When would the army leave a state? when the requirements of the Reconstruction Act were met

In what ways did President Johnson oppose Congress? Although he wanted Southern states brought back into the Union quickly, he was not interested in giving black Americans the right to vote. He removed some of the military men who were overseeing Reconstruction and replaced them with men who opposed Reconstruction. He removed Edwin Stanton from office in spite of a law Congress passed in 1867.

- Invite a student to read aloud the definition of *impeach* from the Glossary.

Why did Republicans in Congress say the president should be dismissed? They said he had broken the law.

What does the Constitution say a president can be impeached for? "treason, bribery, or other high crimes and misdemeanors"

What happens after the impeachment of a president by the House? A trial takes place in the Senate.

What happened in the Senate even though the House of Representatives voted to impeach President Johnson? The Senate found Johnson not guilty by one vote.

- Why do you think Johnson should or should not have been impeached?

▶ Conclude the discussion by asking the question on page 167. The Bible says that all people descended from Adam. They are all equal before God as His creation made in His image. They should be treated equally by the government too.

Activity Manual

- Guide completion of pages 116–19.

Lesson Focus

• Progress in Reconstruction met with opposition.

Objectives

• Define *carpetbagger* and *scalawag*
• Relate what the Fifteenth Amendment did for black people
• Identify challenges black Americans faced

Teacher's Toolkit CD

• Visual 19: *Carpetbaggers and Scalawags*

Materials

• Sources with information about Hiram H. Revels and Blanche K. Bruce to use with Activity Manual page 120

Review

• Guide a review of the three major parts of the Fourteenth Amendment.

What did the Reconstruction Act of 1867 do? This act divided the former Confederacy into five military districts to enforce laws that Congress passed. It also laid out the plan for reconstructing Southern states.

• Invite a student to define *impeach*.

What was the outcome of the impeachment trial of President Johnson? The Senate found him not guilty by one vote.

Preparation for Reading

• Generate interest as you direct the students to read the titles and examine the pictures on pages 168–71.
• Guide pronunciation of any unfamiliar words in the lesson.
• Direct the students to read the pages silently to find out what Southerners who supported Reconstruction were called. scalawags

Teach for Understanding

What are the names of some black men who were elected to Congress? Senators Hiram H. Revels and Blanche K. Bruce and South Carolina representative Robert Smalls

---

Progress and Opposition
Black Political Leaders, Carpetbaggers, and Scalawags

The delegates to the state conventions that wrote new state constitutions included black men. These black delegates tended to be well educated. They were pastors, teachers, and skilled workers. Some of them had spent their lives before the war in the North, and some already had political experience.

Some Southerners who had opposed secession tried to prevent former Confederates from voting and holding office in the reconstructed states. Black delegates and legislators opposed these efforts. Black people wanted to have the right to vote and to hold office. So they did not want to see those rights denied to others. Sadly, many white Southerners still tried to limit the opportunities of black people to vote or hold office.

White Southerners often said that black people were not educated enough to hold office. They also claimed that black legislators were corrupt. But many of these claims were not true. The black men who were elected to Congress were well educated. The Mississippi senators Hiram H. Revels and Blanche K. Bruce and South Carolina representative

Robert Smalls

What: US Congressman
When: 1839–1915
Where: Beaufort, SC

Robert Smalls was a slave hired out by his master to work on the docks and on ships in the coastal waters of South Carolina. During the Civil War, Smalls worked on the *Planter*, a ship used to supply Confederate forts. After the US Navy blockaded the coast, Smalls, his family, and other slaves sailed through the Confederate defenses and gave the *Planter* to the US Navy. Smalls continued to pilot the *Planter* for the Union. Eventually he was promoted to captain.

After the war, Robert returned to Beaufort where he bought the house of his old master. He helped write South Carolina's new constitution. He then served five terms in the US Congress as a representative from South Carolina.

168

• Direct attention to the picture on page 168, and read aloud the Biography box.

What was Robert Smalls hired out by his master to do? He worked on the docks and on ships in the coastal waters of South Carolina.

What did Smalls, his family, and other slaves do after they sailed the *Planter* through Confederate defenses? They gave the *Planter* to the US Navy.

What promotion did Smalls eventually receive? He was promoted to captain.

How did Smalls contribute to the government of South Carolina? He helped write the new constitution. He served five terms in the US Congress as a representative from South Carolina.

Blanche K. Bruce (MS)   John R. Lynch (MS)   Hiram H. Revels (MS)

John M. Langston (VA)   Joseph H. Rainey (SC)   Josiah T. Walls (FL)

Robert Smalls were men who represented their states with great ability. Black men who served in lower offices often had little education. When they were slaves, they had not been allowed to get an education. But as representatives they still did their jobs well. Accusations of corruption in black political leaders were usually found to be false.

Northerners came to help rebuild the South after the war. Those who came to help were businessmen, lawyers, Union army veterans, and pastors. They came for many reasons. Some came to help the freedmen build schools and other institutions. Others saw opportunities to build businesses, factories, and railroads. Northern women came south to teach. But many Southerners did not like Northerners

coming south. Southerners called them **carpetbaggers**. Carpetbags were small suitcases made of pieces of carpet. Southerners said the carpetbaggers were corrupt. Most of the Northern men who came south after the war were not corrupt, though corruption was true of some.

Not all white Southerners opposed Reconstruction. Southerners who supported Reconstruction were called **scalawags**. Some scalawags had opposed secession. They had not wanted to leave the Union. Other scalawags thought that Reconstruction was helping the South. Still other scalawags were just looking for opportunities to help themselves. Most white Southerners viewed scalawags as traitors.

169

Teach for Understanding

• Direct attention to the pictures on page 169. Invite a student to read the names of the pictured congressmen.

• Display Visual 19. Read aloud the captions.

What did Southerners call Northerners who came South to work during Reconstruction? carpetbaggers

Who was a scalawag? a Southerner who supported Reconstruction

Background

Thomas Nast

Thomas Nast used his cartoons to express his political views. He drew pictures of carpetbaggers and scalawags during Reconstruction. A die-hard Republican, Nast defended Grant during his presidential scandals. Nast drew and made popular the symbols of the two parties: the Republicans' elephant and the Democrats' donkey.

Teach for Understanding

Which man did the Republicans nominate as their candidate in 1868? Ulysses S. Grant

- Direct attention to the picture of Grant on page 170. Invite a volunteer to read aloud the caption.

  What did the Fifteenth Amendment do to protect the rights of black Americans? It did not allow states to deny black people the right to vote.

- Invite a student to locate the word *segregate* in the Glossary and read the definition aloud.

  What public place still remained segregated? schools

- Why do you think the freedmen did not press to end school segregation? Answers could include that they were pleased to have schools and that they wanted an education.

Grant and the Fifteenth Amendment

The Democrats did not nominate Johnson as their candidate in 1868. The Republicans nominated Ulysses S. Grant, the famous Civil War general. Grant won the election. He supported Congress's plan for Reconstruction. He also asked Congress to pass the **Fifteenth Amendment**. The Fifteenth Amendment did not allow states to deny black people the right to vote. It said that nobody could be denied the right to vote because of their race or skin color.

Ulysses S. Grant's middle initial does not stand for anything. The extra S was added to his name by mistake when he entered West Point. His classmates called him "Uncle Sam" Grant as a play on his initials.

After his presidency, Grant lost his fortune through a dishonest financial firm. Bankrupt and diagnosed with throat cancer, Grant set about writing his memoirs. The sales of this work paid his debts and left his wife some money to live on. He finished writing the memoirs four days before he died.

170

Some Republicans wanted black Northerners to have the right to vote. Black Americans had this right in the New England states. But several midwestern states did not allow black men to vote. These Republicans also wanted to make sure black citizens in the South could continue to vote in the future. The amendment was added to the Constitution in 1870.

Black Americans Rising to the Challenges

Black Americans still faced challenges. They hoped that they could work with Republican governments to meet those challenges. Black Americans wanted their children to receive a good education. This goal was one of the most important. They knew education was important for success. The laws in some states had not allowed slaves to learn to read. Now laws said that both black and white students had the opportunity for schooling.

Sadly, these schools remained **segregated**. The white children had their schools. Black children had their schools. The two groups could not go to school together. Black people did not press to end the segregation of schools. They just wanted to make sure the students were taught well.

Black Southerners did press to end segregation in other areas. They said that black people should be able to use the public places that white people used.

Background

Sharecropping

Sharecropping developed as an answer to the economic deprivations of the South. Several different arrangements existed under the sharecropping system. Some laborers leased the land, provided their own tools and seeds, grew what they wanted, and then paid their rent with cash or crops. Others provided only labor; the landowner provided land, tools, and other supplies. The landowner's share of the crop ranged from one-fourth to one-half of the harvest, depending on how much material he supplied. Because of the need for profits, landowners usually insisted that their tenants grow cash crops, such as tobacco or cotton. But those crops quickly depleted the soil of nutrients and provided nothing for the sharecroppers to eat. Low prices for cotton and tobacco only worsened the situation for both sharecroppers and landowners.

Sharecropping was not limited to black farmers. About three-fourths of the black farmers in the South and one-third of the white farmers were sharecroppers.

Segregation in schools in America during the late 1800s

During Reconstruction, segregation in public places stopped.

The freedmen also wanted to own land. They knew that owning land would give them opportunities to earn money. They could be more independent. But land was hard to get. The freedmen did not have much money. White lenders often refused to lend money to black borrowers. Some Republicans in Congress suggested dividing plantation land among the former slaves. The land would be repayment for all the years of working as a slave. But most Congressmen thought it would set a bad precedent for the government to take private property and give it to someone else.

Without some way of buying land, many of the freedmen were forced to work as sharecroppers. A sharecropper raised crops for the owner of the land and received some money from the sale of the crops as payment. Often the sharecropper borrowed money from the owner to buy tools or seed. He was often in debt to the owner.

> Why did black Americans want education and land?

171

Teach for Understanding

- Direct attention to the pictures on page 171. Choose a volunteer to compare the pictures.

  What prohibited freedmen from owning land? They did not have much money. White lenders often refused to lend money to black borrowers.

  What occupation did many freedmen have because they had no way to buy land? They worked as sharecroppers.

 Why was it difficult for a sharecropper to prosper? Although he received some money from the sale of the crops, the sharecropper often borrowed money from the landowner to buy tools and seed. He was often in debt to the owner.

> Conclude the discussion by asking the question on page 171. They knew education was important for success. They knew that owning land would give them opportunities to earn money and be more independent.

Activity Manual

- Use sources with information about Hiram H. Revels and Blanche K. Bruce to complete page 120. Guide completion of page 121.

Assessment

- Administer quiz.

The quiz may be given any time after completing this lesson.

Lesson Focus

- Reconstruction was very unpopular with many white Southerners.

Objectives

- Examine opposition to Reconstruction
- Relate the meaning of Southern "redemption"

Teacher's Toolkit CD

- Visual 20: *The Election of 1876*

Review

What were Northerners called who went south to work during Reconstruction? carpetbaggers

What term was used for Southerners who supported Reconstruction? scalawags

- Invite a student to explain what the Fifteenth Amendment did.
- Choose a volunteer to explain how segregation continued in education.

Preparation for Reading

- Generate interest as you direct the students to read the titles and examine the pictures on pages 172–74.
- Guide pronunciation of any unfamiliar words in the lesson.
- Instruct the students to read the pages silently to learn the name of the laws that Democrats passed to segregate black people again. Jim Crow laws

Teach for Understanding

Why would it be difficult for Republicans to attract white Southern voters? The Southern states had fought a war to leave the Union so that they could keep their slaves. They did not want the national government to interfere in their affairs. Now the national government had freed their slaves. The war also destroyed much of the South's wealth, affecting all of life. They believed they were being treated unjustly. They believed that their right to self-government had been taken away from them.

Reactions to Reconstruction

Reconstruction was very unpopular with many white Southerners. It is not hard to see why. The Southern States had fought a war to leave the Union so that they could keep their slaves. They did not want the national government to interfere in their affairs. Now the national government had freed their slaves. Laws made the former slaves voting citizens. The laws allowed black citizens to hold office.

The war also destroyed much of the South's wealth, affecting all of life. The war led to much suffering among Southern people. It was difficult to keep food on the table. It was hard to provide for a family's needs. Important institutions such as colleges had a hard time continuing. People in the South had little money to give to colleges. These people believed that they were being treated unjustly. They believed that their right to self-government had been taken away from them.

The Republicans knew that they would have to win these people over. Republicans allowed former Confederate leaders to vote again. Republicans also appointed Democrats to some government positions. They hoped these Democrats would become Republicans. Some Republicans stopped helping black citizens. These Republicans wanted to get more white votes. They thought black voters would vote for Republicans anyway. In Georgia, Democrats were joined by some Republicans to illegally remove black legislators from the state legislature.

These efforts did not cause many people to switch from the Democratic Party to the Republican Party. Southern Democrats still viewed Republicans as the party of carpetbaggers, black people, and scalawags. Democrats also accused Republican governments of being horribly corrupt. The Republicans were not more or less corrupt than the governments that came before and after them. But that standard of comparison was too low. Republicans claimed to be the party of good morals. They should not have allowed any corruption. But they did allow it.

Southern Democrats tried a number of strategies to regain power. A few said black Southerners should have the right to vote. These Democrats tried to earn black votes. But more often Democrats worked to prevent black people from voting. The Democrats worked hard to ensure that former Confederates were allowed to vote. And they attacked the corruption of Republican government officials.

Other opponents to Reconstruction pursued more violent methods. Groups like the **Ku Klux Klan** attacked Republican officeholders. Members would disguise themselves in white, hooded clothes. They would intimidate,

172

How did Republicans try to win over the Democrats in the South? They allowed former Confederate leaders to vote again. They appointed Democrats to some government positions. Some stopped helping black citizens. In Georgia, some joined with Democrats to illegally remove black legislators from the state legislature.

What strategies did Southern Democrats use to try to regain power? A few said black Southerners should have the right to vote, trying to earn black votes. More often Democrats worked to prevent black people from voting. Democrats worked hard to ensure that former Confederates were allowed to vote. They attacked the corruption of Republican governments. The Ku Klux Klan pursued more violent methods.

What did the Klan do to black Republican leaders? The Klan would intimidate, beat, and even murder them.

174

beat, and even murder people. They especially targeted black Republican leaders. Black men who participated in state constitutional conventions were killed or beaten. The Klan did the same to black men elected to office. Even voting made a black person a target. The violence made it difficult for Republicans to run for office. In some places, Republicans could not even vote.

Black churches and schools were also targeted by the Klan. The Klan wanted to prevent black people from gaining an education. The group did not want black Americans to become self-sufficient. Successful black people were special targets. Sometimes even dressing nicely made a black person a target. The Klan tried to drive the black people who owned land off their property. Klan members wanted to force them to work for white people. The Klan would also threaten violence against businesses. The secret group did not want white businesses to serve black customers. In 1868 alone, over a thousand black people were killed by the Klan.

The Klan was powerful because there were many important people in it. Some white Southerners hated the Klan's violence. But they did not speak out against it. If a person spoke against the Klan, that person also became a target of violence.

In 1870 and 1871, Congress passed two laws. These laws gave the US Army the authority to protect people who voted. The military also worked to put an end to Klan violence.

"Redemption" of the South

The various strategies employed by the Southern Democrats slowly paid off. By 1876 only South Carolina, Florida, and Louisiana still had Republican governments. Southern Democrats thought they could win these states in 1876.

They used armed men to keep black voters away from some polls. They stuffed ballot boxes. In some places, there were more votes cast for the Democratic candidate than there were people living in that county. They also printed misleading ballots that listed only Democratic candidates.

These state elections affected the presidential election. If the Republican candidate won South Carolina, Florida, and Louisiana, he would win in the Electoral College by one vote.

The Democrats claimed their party had won those states. But the Republicans said that there had been

173

Teach for Understanding

- Direct attention to the picture on page 173. Guide a discussion of the methods used by the Ku Klux Klan.

  Why did the Klan target black schools? It did not want black people to get an education.

  What would the Klan threaten against businesses that served black people? It would threaten violence.

  Why was the Klan so powerful? There were many important people in the Klan.

- What laws of God was the Klan violating? Answers could include that man is commanded to not kill. He is commanded to love his neighbor as himself (Exodus 20:13; Leviticus 19:18). The Klan violated God's laws against murder and violence. The members did not love their neighbors as themselves.

  What did the two laws passed in 1870 and 1871 do? They gave the US Army the authority to protect people who voted.

  How did the Southern Democrats try to win the three Southern states that still had Republican governments in 1876? They used armed men to keep black voters away from some polls, stuffed ballot boxes, and printed misleading ballots that listed only Democratic candidates.

- What do you think it means when a person stuffs a ballot box? Answers should include that he casts more than one ballot even though he is supposed to vote only once.

Lesson

67

Teach for Understanding

- Direct attention to the picture on page 174 and read the caption aloud.

- Display Visual 20. Read aloud the caption.

When fraud was suspected, who decided the results of the presidential election? an independent commission set up by Congress

What caused the Republican governments in the South to fall after Rutherford B. Hayes became the president? Hayes kept his promise and removed US troops from the South.

What did Southern Democrats call the end of Reconstruction? redemption

Why did they call it redemption? They had won back control of their states.

What did the Jim Crow laws do? They segregated black people once again.

How was the "redemption" of the South different from God's redemption in the Bible? "Redemption" in the South brought injustice. God's redemption refers to the restoration of God's good creation from all the effects of the Fall. God's redemption will bring justice to the world.

▶ Conclude the discussion by asking the question on page 174. These laws segregated black people once again. But the Bible teaches that all people were created equal.

Activity Manual

- Guide completion of page 122.

---

fraud. The Republicans said their party won.

Congress had to decide who really won the presidential election. Congress created an independent commission to investigate. The commission was made up of fifteen members. Five members were Republican congressmen. Five members were Democratic congressmen. Five members were Supreme Court justices. The commission decided that the Republican candidate won the election. Rutherford B. Hayes became the president.

Hayes had promised the commission that he would remove US troops from the South if he was elected. Hayes kept his promise. But without the protection of the military, the Republican governments fell.

Southern Democrats called the end of Reconstruction "redemption." They called it redemption because they had won back control of their states.

Sadly, these people did not think that black people were equal to white people. The Democrats worked to prevent black citizens from voting. The Fifteenth Amendment did not allow the Democrats to pass laws that denied black people the right to vote. Instead they used other methods. They might

Rutherford B. Hayes served as an officer in the Civil War, and he was the only president to have been wounded in that war. He was the sixth president to have lost his father when he was young. Nearly a third of our US presidents up to the present day grew up without a father.

require a poll tax be paid prior to voting. Someone who was poor would find the tax difficult to pay. Or the Democrats might require a literacy test. Since slaves had not been allowed to learn to read, this test excluded many former slaves. White voters who could not read were often still allowed to vote. The laws often said that people could vote if their grandfathers had been able to vote. This law kept black people from voting. Their grandfathers had been slaves and unable to vote.

The Democrats also passed **Jim Crow laws**. These laws segregated black people once again. They could not use the same public places that white people used. The public places they could use were often inferior to the ones the white people used.

In the Bible, redemption refers to the restoration of God's good creation from all the effects of the Fall. Sadly, the "redemption" of the South brought injustice. God's redemption, however, will bring justice to the world.

Why were Jim Crow laws unjust?

174

Background

The Hayes Presidency

Although the Republicans won the presidency in 1876, the election was the final blow to Reconstruction. Hayes had sought the support of Southern whites who favored his economic policies. To gain their support, he embraced policies that they liked. However, Hayes soon found that he had bargained away most of his presidential power. By the time he saw the real picture, it was too late to change his position.

In April 1877, a month after Hayes took office, he withdrew the last troops from the South. With troops no longer supervising elections, the Democrats soon replaced the Republicans in power. With the military gone and white Southern Democrats back in control in the South, Reconstruction effectively ended.

People of the West
American Indians

By the middle of the 1800s, the Cherokee, Choctaw, Creek, Chickasaw, and Seminole Indians who had lived east of the Mississippi were relocated to Indian Territory. That territory matches closely with the current state of Oklahoma. These tribes have been called the Five Civilized Tribes because they could read. They wrote constitutions for their governments. Also, many had adopted Christianity as their religion. The United States government promised that the Indian Territory would be kept for American Indians.

Other American Indian groups already lived west of the Mississippi. Different Indian peoples followed different customs. The Pueblo Indians lived in the Southwest. They lived in unique mud-brick houses. They grew crops to sustain themselves. Others, such as the Hopi people, were herders of sheep. On the Great Plains the Sioux, Cheyenne, Blackfeet, and other tribes hunted buffalo. These peoples lived in tepees made from buffalo hides.

In the years prior to the Civil War, this land had all become part of the United States. Americans were most interested in the lands along the Pacific coast. Settlements had long existed in Oregon. Gold was discovered in

California in 1848. Many moved west to take part in the gold rush.

The Americans called the Great Plains the "Great American Desert." They did not think the land was good for farming. It had little water. There were also few trees for building houses and fences. At first there was little conflict with the American Indians who lived on the Great Plains. The pioneers were just passing through. Often Indians served as guides for these wagon trains. But by the 1860s, American Indians were concerned about how many settlers were coming west.

175

Lesson Focus

- Different groups of people lived in the West.

Objectives
- Identify the tribes that make up the Five Civilized Tribes
- Explain the impact of miners on the West
- Examine sodbusters and how they changed the Great Plains

Teacher's Toolkit CD
- Visuals 21–23: *Prospecting and Mining*; *Windmills on the Plains*; *Turkey Red Wheat*
- Instructional Aid 43: *Life in the West*

Review

- Guide a review of why Reconstruction was unpopular with white Southerners.
- Invite volunteers to explain strategies the Democrats used to regain power.

  Which opponents of Reconstruction used violent methods? the Ku Klux Klan

  What did the Jim Crow laws do? They segregated black people again.

Preparation for Reading

- Generate interest as you direct the students to read the titles and examine the pictures on pages 175–77.
- Guide pronunciation of any unfamiliar words in the lesson.
- Direct the students to read the pages and complete Instructional Aid 43 in small groups.

Teach for Understanding

- Invite a group to state the names of the tribes that had been relocated to Indian Territory.

  Why were these tribes called the Five Civilized Tribes? They could read. They wrote constitutions for their governments. Many had adopted Christianity as their religion.

- Ask a group to identify some of the tribes that already lived west of the Mississippi. Pueblo, Hopi, Sioux, Cheyenne, Blackfeet

- Direct attention to the picture on page 175. Invite a student to identify the tribes that lived in teepees.

  What name did Americans give to the Great Plains? the "Great American Desert"

  Why did Americans think the land was not good for farming? It had little water.

  What was the relationship of Indians with the pioneers? At first there was little conflict. Often Indians served as guides for the wagon trains, but later they became concerned about how many settlers were coming west.

Teach for Understanding

- Direct attention to the picture of the miner on page 176.
- Display Visual 21. Read the captions aloud.

  How were mining towns built? *Often a rough town would be slapped together around a mining site.*

  What were ghost towns? *mining towns that people abandoned after the gold or silver was gone*

- Invite a group to explain how mining towns were governed.

- Why did mining towns need churches and missionaries to bring the gospel? *Wickedness abounded because people are born with a sinful nature. Jesus Christ redeems those who turn away from sin and trust Him for salvation.*

  Why did the first farmers build their houses out of sod? *There were few trees on the Great Plains.*

Miners

Miners pushed west first. Gold was discovered first in California. Later, miners found gold in Colorado, Nevada, Idaho, Montana, Wyoming, and South Dakota. Miners also discovered silver in the West. Many men thought that mining for gold and silver would be a way to get rich quickly. However, very few miners became wealthy. Usually, the shopkeepers who followed the miners benefited the most from the rush—while it lasted. Often a rough town would be slapped together around a

mining site. People abandoned these towns after the gold was gone. These abandoned towns are called ghost towns.

Mining towns were rough places. They did not have an organized government. Each individual looked out for himself. When someone committed a crime, men in the community would decide what the punishment would be. This system was called **vigilante justice.** Sometimes vigilante justice was just. Other times it was a mask for other crimes and injustices. Churches were usually built later rather than sooner in mining towns. But missionaries did travel to mining towns with the gospel. They knew the gospel was needed in places where wickedness abounded.

Sodbusters

Some people decided to give farming a chance in the Great American Desert. The US government said it would sell land for $1.25 an acre. Or a farmer could live and work on a plot of land for five years. Then he could have it for free.

There were few trees on the Great Plains. The first farmers built their houses out of sod. They cut thick strips of earth held together by the roots of prairie grass. Farmers fitted these pieces together to make walls and a roof. Some families added doors and put glass panes in the windows.

176

Activities

Pan for Gold

Materials: metal pie pans; sandbox sand; containers of water; tiny bits of rock painted gold to be used as "gold nuggets"; flat, shallow plastic containers; large spoons or plastic sand-pail shovels

Set up several centers with sand in the bottom of the plastic containers. Mix in the "gold nuggets." Pour water into the plastic container to about one inch above the sand. Divide the students into groups to work at the centers. Direct the students to put a scoop of sand in their pie pans, then tilt the pan, and dip the edge in the container of water. Explain that they will swirl the pan to wash away the sand and reveal the nuggets.

Learn About Wheat

Use resources to discover the six classes of wheat and what each type is best suited for. Display products made from different classes of wheat, and label what class of wheat they were made from.

Farming was hard work on the plains. Sometimes prairie fires, locust plagues, or drought would destroy months of hard work. Lack of water made farming on the Great Plains difficult.

New technologies made farming in the West possible. Water did exist deep below the prairie surface. Farmers learned that they could dig deep wells to get to the water. They used windmills to power the pumps to bring the water to the surface. Wind was a plentiful resource on the Great Plains.

Other inventions helped farmers plant and harvest their crops. Steel plows broke up the hard soil. Earlier inventions, such as the reaper, helped farmers bring in the harvest.

Many immigrants to the United States settled in the Great Plains. Often people from the same country would settle together. The immigrants who settled east of the Mississippi before the Civil War were typically British. Later, Irish and German immigrants came. The immigrants who settled the West were often from Scandinavia or eastern Europe. In some towns Swedish, German, or Polish might have been the main language spoken. These people also brought many traditions from Europe to America.

Black Southerners also saw the Great Plains as a land of opportunity. They had a hard time getting farmland in the South. Some decided to move west as sodbusters. Thousands began to move west. But this relocating worried Southerners who depended on black sharecroppers to work their land. As a result, Mississippi River crossings were closed to black Americans moving west.

Immigrants from Russia also brought a crop that made farming the Great Plains successful. They brought Turkey Red wheat. It grew well on the prairie even in the winter. The wheat could be ground into flour and turned into bread. It was a good crop to sell. As a result, the Great American Desert became "America's Breadbasket."

> Why did Americans call the Great Plains the "Great American Desert"?

Teach for Understanding

- Direct attention to the picture on page 177. Invite a student to tell why he thinks farmers were called sodbusters.

  What were some difficulties that farmers faced on the Great Plains? prairie fires, locust plagues, drought

- Choose a group to name the technology and inventions that made farming in the West possible.

- Display Visual 22. Read aloud the caption.

  What immigrants settled the West? immigrants from Scandinavia and eastern Europe

- Choose a group to explain why black Americans saw the Great Plains as a land of opportunity.

- Invite a group to tell why the Mississippi River crossings were closed to black Americans moving west.

  How did Russian farmers make farming in the Great Plains successful? They grew Turkey Red wheat, which grew well on the prairie even in the winter.

- Display Visual 23. Read aloud the captions as you discuss each picture.

▶ Conclude the discussion by asking the question on page 177. People did not think the land was good for farming. It had little water. There were few trees for building houses and fences.

Activity Manual

- Guide completion of page 123.

Lesson

69

Student Text pages 178–80
Activity Manual pages 124–25

Lesson Focus

- Cowboys drove cattle to the railroad for transport.

Objectives
- Describe the work of a cowboy
- Examine the role of railroads

Review

- Use questions such as the following to review the previous lesson.

What were characteristics of the Five Civilized Tribes? They were tribes that were relocated to Indian Territory from east of the Mississippi. They could read. They wrote constitutions for their governments, and many had adopted Christianity as their religion.

What were the prairie farmers called? sodbusters

What were two different names given to the Great Plains? the "Great American Desert" and "America's Breadbasket"

Preparation for Reading

- Generate interest as you direct the students to read the titles and examine the pictures and map on pages 178–80.
- Guide pronunciation of any unfamiliar words in the lesson.
- Direct the students to read the pages silently to learn the names for cowboys that kept cattle from wandering off. swing and flank riders

Teach for Understanding

- Direct attention to the picture on page 178 and the How It Was box. Read aloud the story.

What does the story say about the work of a cowboy? The work was hard. It was different from plantation work.

Why did Tom feel free for the first time in his life? He was a former slave. He was finally able to choose where to live and what job to work.

Once the cattle were rounded up on the Great Plains, where would they be sent? east

Why was being a cowboy an opportunity for black men? Many other opportunities were closed to black men, but working as a cowboy was open.

Who else became cowboys? immigrants from Mexico and Europe, easterners who moved west

How would a cowboy identify his cattle? by the brand

Tom shaded his eyes and peered northward as the sun began its evening descent. It was time to call the drive to a halt for the night. "Looking forward to some bread and beef tonight, Juan."

The cowboy riding beside him slapped his dusty chaps with his hand. "Yep. Long day in the saddle. I'm hungry."

When they got to camp, Tom set up his cot, laid some old blankets on it, and then put the sack with his clothes at the top for a pillow. He stretched his back and rubbed a sore muscle in his shoulder. Life on the trail was hard work. But it felt completely different from plantation work. Out here with the grass stretching out on every side and the endless sky above, he was free, truly free, for the first time in his life.

Cowboys

In Texas, at the southern portion of the Great Plains, millions of longhorn cattle roamed. These cattle were a good supply of beef and leather. They just needed to be rounded up and sent east.

Driving cattle for a living was a good opportunity for many men who moved west. In particular, it was a good opportunity for black men. While many other opportunities at this time were closed to black men, working as a cowboy was open. In some parts of the West, one in every four cowboys was black. Immigrants from Mexico and Europe, along with easterners who moved west, also worked as cowboys.

Cowboys have been made into an American symbol in many movies.

But life as a cowboy was not typically exciting. Most cowboys did not ride around with guns on their belts. They would not want to carry that extra weight most of the time. Their guns were probably in their saddle roll. Much of a cowboy's life was spent watching and waiting. The rest of it was hard work.

Before a cattle drive, the cowboys had to round up the herd. They had to find the cattle. They could tell which cattle were theirs and which belonged to others by brands. A brand was burned onto the cowhide with a hot iron.

During the drive some riders, called point riders, rode ahead of the herd. They looked for trouble ahead. Swing and flank riders rode on the sides of

178

---

the herd. They kept the cattle from wandering off. Drag riders rode in the rear. They kept the herd moving. The trail boss was in charge of the drive.

The drives led the cattle from Texas to the railroad. At first the cattle had to be driven all the way to Missouri. But settlers in Missouri did not like the cattle drives coming through their lands.

As railroads moved west, cowboys did not have to travel all the way to Missouri. Soon Abilene, Kansas, became the goal of cattle drives. The railroad ran through Abilene. Cowboys could drive their cattle straight north from Texas. And they would not upset the people who lived in Missouri. Later, other towns in Kansas sprang up along the railroad as destinations for cattle drives.

At first the cattle were loaded onto cattle railroad cars and shipped east. But cattle lost weight on the long journey, and there was less beef from each one.

In 1869 an inventor figured out how to refrigerate a train car. Now cattle were killed when they reached the railroad. The meat was then kept cold in the trains.

The cowboy's hat had many uses. Not only did it keep the sun off the cowboy's face, it could also be filled with water for his horse to drink.

horse blanket

This bandana covered the mouth and nose during dust storms.

Colt .45 and holster

"The singing was supposed to soothe the cattle and it did. . . . The two men on guard would circle around with their horses on a walk, if it was a clear night and the cattle was bedded down and quiet, and one man would sing a verse of a song, and his partner on the other side of the herd would sing another verse; and you'd go through a whole song that way. . . . I had a crackerjack of a partner in '79. I'd sing and he'd answer, and we'd keep it up like that for two hours."
—Montana cowboy Teddy Abbott

Many cowboys owned their saddle, but not their horse.

179

Teach for Understanding

- Direct attention to the picture on page 179 and discuss the captions.

What was the job of the point riders during a cattle drive? They rode in front of the herd and looked for trouble ahead.

Who rode on the sides of the herd to keep the cattle from wandering off? swing and flank riders

What was the job of the drag riders? They rode in the rear to keep the herd moving.

Who was in charge of the cattle drive? the trail boss

Why did cowboys not have to travel all the way to Missouri any longer? The railroads moved west.

What problem occurred when cattle were loaded onto railroad cars and shipped east? The cattle lost weight on the long journey, and there was less beef from each one.

How did an inventor change how beef was shipped? Train cars were refrigerated. Now cattle were killed when they reached the railroad, and the meat was then kept cold in the trains.

What are some ways beef is transported today? Answers may include by truck, train, plane, or ship.

Activity

Create a Cattle Brand

Materials: pictures of cattle brands, black markers, white paper

Encourage the students to design their own cattle brand based on their name or something they like. Display the cattle brands.

Lesson

69

Teach for Understanding

- Direct attention to the map on page 180.

  What are two achievements in relation to the railroad? standardized tracks, a transcontinental railroad

  Who worked on building the railroads? immigrants from Ireland and China

  What two railroads met at Promontory Summit, Utah, in 1869? the Central Pacific and Union Pacific

  ▶▶ Conclude the discussion by asking the question on page 180. They brought cattle or beef from the West to the East. The railroad also brought easterners to the West.

Activity Manual

- Guide completion of pages 124–25.

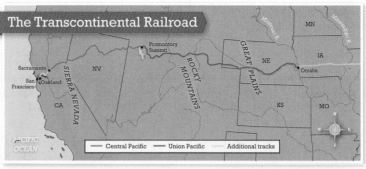

The Transcontinental Railroad

Central Pacific — Union Pacific — Additional tracks

Railroads

The railroad played a large role in the settling of the West. It brought cattle or beef from the West to the East. The railroad also brought easterners west.

Before the Civil War, different companies owned different stretches of track. Each company might have a different width of track for its trains. A single train could not travel along all the track. After the Civil War, the width of the railroad track was standardized. Trains could now travel on any of the track laid.

Another achievement was to build a railroad that stretched from one side of the continent to the other. This railroad was called a transcontinental railroad. The project began in two places. The Central Pacific Railroad Company began laying track in San Francisco and headed east. The Union Pacific Railroad Company began in Omaha, Nebraska, and headed west.

Many immigrants worked on building these railroads. Many of these immigrants came from Ireland. Chinese immigrants worked on the Central Pacific line. The Chinese immigrants were hard workers. They were also given some of the hardest jobs. They were often insulted simply because they were Chinese. But their hard work won them respect.

The Central Pacific and Union Pacific railroads met at Promontory Summit, Utah, in 1869. Now a train could travel across the entire continent. Travelers to California or Oregon did not have to sail around South America in a boat. Nor did they have to travel across the Great Plains in a wagon. They could travel by train. The transcontinental railroad was only the beginning. Other railroads spread out over other parts of the West.

> Why were railroads important to the West?

180

Indian Wars

As more miners, farmers, and cattlemen moved west, more American Indians saw their lands slipping away. Treaties with the United States government promised that American citizens would keep off the Indian lands. But prospectors looking for gold or silver often trespassed on Indian land. If gold or silver was discovered, the Indians often found their land overrun. More settlers traveled west. People continued to intrude onto Indian hunting grounds. Various tribes began to push back with raids on mining camps and wagon trains traveling west. The United States responded by assigning reservations to the Indians, moving them to lands that the American settlers were not interested in. For those that resisted moving to the reservations, the US cavalry sought to disrupt their lives. They kept the Indians on the move. The cavalry made it difficult for the Indian families to get food. It tried to make life difficult enough that the Indians would be willing to move to the reservations.

The US cavalry was up against a skilled enemy. The American Indians often won battles. The most spectacular of these was the defeat of George Custer by Sitting Bull and Crazy Horse. It was called the **Battle of the Little Bighorn**. Custer's much smaller force was overwhelmed by the Sioux Indians and wiped out.

Several years after Custer's defeat, conflict broke out in what is today Idaho. The Nez Perce Indians were a peaceful tribe. At one time they were open to the gospel. But as the land reserved for them shrank, they began to resist the US government.

General Oliver O. Howard was sent to move the Nez Perce to their reservation. Howard was known as "the Christian General" for his Christian testimony. He had fought for the Union during the Civil War. After the war he oversaw the Freedmen's Bureau. He had also conducted negotiations with various Indian groups before. He wanted to see peace and fairness between American Indians and US citizens.

Chief Joseph was one of the Nez Perce leaders. He would not let his men attack civilians. He did not let them scalp their opponents. He would not steal what his people needed. He bought supplies. For these actions he gained the respect of many Americans.

As he fought General Howard, he retreated 1,500 miles to Canada. But before he was able to lead his people across the border, he lost a final battle. He was reported to have said at the surrender, "Hear me, my chiefs! I am tired. My heart is sick and sad. From

181

Lesson 70

Student Text pages 181–83
Activity Manual page 126

Lesson Focus

- Conflicts erupted as people moved west.

Objectives

- Identify the Indian conflicts that resulted as Americans moved west
- State the role of Christians during the Indian Wars
- Examine other kinds of conflict in the West

Teacher's Toolkit CD

- Visuals 24–25: *Indian Removals; Seals of the Five Civilized Tribes*

Materials

- Prepared state outlines with location of the Five Civilized Tribes (use Visual 24 as a reference; use a different color for each tribe)
- Prepared outline of Indian Territory in the West with the reservations labeled (use Visual 24 as a reference; match reservation color to tribe's color before relocation)
- String or yarn (five colors corresponding to the tribes' colors)
- One set of cut-out seals from Visual 25.
- Objects or pictures representing each tribe

Review

- Review the role of cowboys and how cattle were sent east.
- Choose a volunteer to state two achievements that were made in regard to the railroads in the late 1800s.

Preparation for Reading

- Generate interest as you direct the students to read the titles and examine the picture and map on pages 181–83.
- Guide pronunciation of any unfamiliar words in the lesson.
- Direct the students to read the pages silently to find out the name of the battle where George Custer was defeated. the Battle of the Little Bighorn

Teach for Understanding

What prompted the Indian raids on mining camps and wagon trains traveling west? Prospectors and settlers trespassed on Indian lands and continued to intrude onto Indian hunting grounds.

How did the United States respond? by assigning reservations to the Indians, moving them to lands that the American settlers were not interested in

What happened to Indians who resisted moving to the reservations? The US cavalry sought to disrupt their lives.

Why were the Sioux Indians able to defeat General Custer? Custer's much smaller force was overwhelmed by the Sioux Indians and wiped out.

- Invite a student to read aloud the sentences that describe the kind of tribe the Nez Perce Indians were.

Why did the Nez Perce Indians begin to resist the US government? The land reserved for them shrank.

Who was sent to move all the Nez Perces to their reservation? General Oliver O. Howard

What did General Howard want when he negotiated between American Indians and US citizens? peace and fairness

Which Nez Perce leader gained the respect of many Americans? Chief Joseph

What caused Chief Joseph to gain this respect? He did not let his men attack civilians or scalp their opponents. He would not steal. Instead, he bought needed supplies.

What did Chief Joseph do as he retreated to Canada? He fought General Howard.

What was the outcome of Chief Joseph's final battle with Howard? Chief Joseph lost and surrendered.

70

Teach for Understanding

- Guide a discussion of the picture and the map on page 182.

What role did Christians play during the conflict with American Indians? Some Christian leaders spoke out against the injustices and broken promises faced by the Indians. Later, Christians would set up schools for Indian children. Christians tried to bring the gospel to Indian people.

What other conflicts were there in the West? There were disagreements over land for grazing animals. There were outlaws who stole cattle.

How did ranchers deal with cattle thieves? In some places the ranchers would get together and capture the people that they thought had done wrong and hang them. Sometimes they would hire gunmen to catch cattle thieves.

What were some of the difficulties America faced after the Civil War? Southern states had to rebuild. Black Americans struggled to establish themselves as American citizens. American Indians suffered many injustices.

What part did Christians play during these difficulties? Some white Christians were unjust toward other ethnicities. Others tried to end the injustices and help those being treated unjustly. Christians often showed the love of Christ to others.

⟫ Conclude the discussion by asking the question on page 183. Government promotes good and restrains evil.

Activity Manual

- Guide completion of page 126.

---

where the sun now stands, I will fight no more forever."

The conflict with American Indians was difficult for Christians. Some Christian leaders spoke out against the injustices and broken promises. Later, Christians would set up schools for Indian children. Christians tried to bring the gospel to Indian people. The mistreatment of many Indians by a nation that called itself Christian made this task difficult.

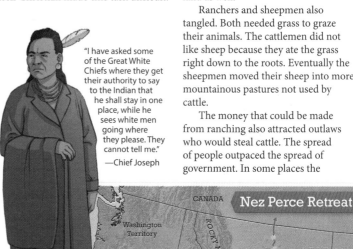

"I have asked some of the Great White Chiefs where they get their authority to say to the Indian that he shall stay in one place, while he sees white men going where they please. They cannot tell me."

—Chief Joseph

Nez Perce Retreat

CANADA

Washington Territory

Columbia River

ROCKY MOUNTAINS

Nez Perce

Oregon

Montana Territory

→ Nez Perce retreat
⚔ Battles

Idaho Territory

Wyoming Territory

N
W E
S

182

Conflict, Law, and Order

Other kinds of conflict abounded in the West. As more people began to raise cattle, land for grazing became an important resource. Some began to keep other people's cattle off their land by fencing it with barbed wire. Sometimes the land was public, and ranchers who owned only a little land would cut the barbed-wire fences. They believed that they had a right to the land as well.

Ranchers and sheepmen also tangled. Both needed grass to graze their animals. The cattlemen did not like sheep because they ate the grass right down to the roots. Eventually the sheepmen moved their sheep into more mountainous pastures not used by cattle.

The money that could be made from ranching also attracted outlaws who would steal cattle. The spread of people outpaced the spread of government. In some places the

---

ranchers would get together and capture the people that they thought had done wrong and hang them. Sometimes they would hire gunmen to catch cattle thieves. But trials were often not fair, and concern that justice truly be done was not always of the highest concern. The lawlessness in some western towns shows the wisdom of God in ordaining government to promote good and to restrain evil (Romans 13:3–4).

Conclusion

The years following the Civil War were difficult ones for the United States. The Southern states had to rebuild after the war. They saw the culture they loved slipping away from them.

Black Americans also struggled during this time to establish themselves as American citizens. They worked hard to ensure that they had equal rights and responsibilities with other Americans. Sadly, they saw many of

these gains slip away toward the end of the Reconstruction.

The movement west was a time of opportunity for many immigrants. They came to the United States looking for a better life. Through hard work, they were able to make a new life in the western United States. American Indians, however, suffered many injustices as they were pushed off their land.

Sometimes American Christians were influenced by the culture rather than by the Bible. For example, some white Christians were unjust in how they treated other ethnicities. But other Christians responded wisely to these injustices. They tried to end the injustices and help those being treated unjustly. As a result, these hard times were often opportunities for Christians to show the love of Christ to others.

> Why is God's institution of government important for a nation?

Activity

A Historical Exhibit

Display outlines of each state in the United States. Label the location of the Five Civilized Tribes: Cherokee, Choctaw, Creek, Chickasaw, and Seminole Indians. Include the names of the reservations in

Indian Territory after the Indian Removal Act. Show the routes the tribes took on their way to Indian Territory. Display the seal of each Indian nation. Exhibit objects that represent each tribe.

183

Activity

A Historical Exhibit

- Generate excitement about creating a historical exhibit as you read the activity information aloud.
- Display state outlines with the location of each of the Five Civilized Tribes before removal (reference Visual 24). Label the name of each tribe.
- Use the same color to show each tribe's reservation in Indian Territory after removal (similar to Visual 24).
- Use string or yarn of the tribe's color to trace the routes the Indians took to Indian Territory.
- Display the seal of each tribe from Visual 25 with objects or pictures representing the tribe.
- Invite a volunteer to choose a tribe, locate the tribe on the map, and locate the route the tribe took to its reservation in Indian Territory. Invite the student to describe the tribal seal and objects or pictures representing the tribe.

Objective
- Recall concepts and terms from Chapter 8

Materials
- Questions of varying difficulty with answers written on 3×5 cards (each card assigned a point written on the back according to the difficulty of the question)

Introduction

- Concepts for the Chapter 8 Test will be taken from Activity Manual pages 113–28. You may review any or all of the concepts during this lesson. You may choose to review Chapter 8 by playing "Point Cards."

Review

Game: Point Cards

- Divide the students into two teams. Explain that teams and players will alternate turns.
- Place the cards with the point side up. Invite the first player to select a card by the number of points he wants to earn for his team and to give the card to you.
- Read the question aloud. If the player answers correctly, record the points for his team. When an incorrect answer is given, no points are recorded and play switches to the other team.
- Continue the game until all questions have been answered. The team with the most points wins the game.

Activity Manual

- Guide completion of pages 127–28.

Lesson **72** **Chapter 8 Test**

Objective
- Demonstrate knowledge of concepts from Chapter 8 by taking the test

Assessment

- Administer Test 8.

Chapter 9

Introduction

The late 1800s in America are often called the Gilded Age. There was a growth in industry, and several inventions were developed. Some Americans had more wealth than before, and the average American had more leisure time for activities and entertainment, such as vaudeville shows, amusement parks, sporting events, and bicycling. Millions of immigrants came to the United States seeking a better life. Many settled in cities, contributing to urbanization.

This time of prosperity also presented Americans with new problems. Social Darwinism prompted some business leaders to make selfish decisions. Sometimes employees suffered from the greed of their employers. Many Americans were poor and lived in tenement houses. People began to see the need for social reform. Since true faith in God and the Bible was questioned during the Gilded Age, God raised up men like D. L. Moody to preach the truth.

Chapter Focus

The Gilded Age brought growth and prosperity, but also new problems, to America.

9 The Gilded Age

Focus
The Gilded Age brought growth and prosperity, but also new problems, to America.

Chapter 9 Overview

Lesson	Student Text	Activity Manual	Content		Vocabulary	
73	184–87	129–32	Growth of industry Steel, oil, and railroad industries Andrew Carnegie	John D. Rockefeller James J. Hill	corporation trust	
74	188–91	133–34	How It Was: Edison's new invention Inventions and inventors Alexander Graham Bell	Thomas Edison		
75	192–94	135–36	Problems created by social Darwinism Effects of capitalism on American society Cornelius Vanderbilt		capitalism social Darwinism labor union philanthropist Sherman Antitrust Act	
76	195–97	137–39	Growth of cities and its problems Activity: Writing a Journal Entry		urbanization	
77	198–200	140	Biography Box: Nellie Bly Jane Addams Social reform Salvation Army Jacob Riis Woman's Christian Temperance Union		campaign social reformer	
78	201–3	141	Entertainment Music Literature Newspapers Art		realism	
79	204–5	142–44	Religion Fanny Crosby B. B. Warfield Primary Source: Gospel Song Dwight L. Moody			
80		145–46	Chapter Review			
81			Chapter Test			

Visit bjupress.com/resources for links to enhance the lessons.

An Age of Glitter

With the Civil War and Reconstruction behind them, Americans enjoyed a period of freedom from war. The late 1800s were a time of growing prosperity in the United States. New cities were beginning to thrive. In some parts of America, the landscape was changing. Instead of long, unbroken views of trees and fields, skyscrapers could now be seen on the horizon. Immigrants were pouring into the country, steadily increasing the population. More people in America meant more people to get work done. Inventors and businessmen were developing new ways to work faster and better. And some Americans were wealthier than they had ever been before.

Although this period was a prosperous time, it presented Americans with new problems. On the surface, life in America seemed to glitter like gold. But beneath the surface, not everything was golden. The late 1800s in the United States is often called the Gilded Age.

The Growth of Industry

The Gilded Age was an era of growth and success in American business. From the colonial period on, Americans had made their living mainly from farming, small businesses, and trades. Before the Civil War there had been a limited number of factories, mostly in the North. But now more factories opened, and cities grew up around them. America still had farms, but these farms did not need as many workers. New machines could do much of the work that people had done before. Some people decided to move from farms to cities to find new work opportunities. The number of Americans who lived on farms was slowly decreasing. Many more Americans began to work in large industries.

(185)

JourneyForth

The following books are available from JourneyForth Books, a division of BJU Press, at journeyforth.com.

Ira Sankey: Singing the Gospel by Kelly Bruss

This is the biography of Ira Sankey, who sang the gospel to thousands of men and women while traveling with D. L. Moody's ministry team during the Gilded Age.

The Choctaw Code by Brent Ashabranner and Russell G. Davis

This historical fiction book is set in the Choctaw Nation in the 1890s. Tom and his family move to Indian Territory for his father's railroad job. Tom becomes friends with a Choctaw man, Jim Moshulatubee, who teaches him to hunt, fish, and respect the land. Jim also teaches Tom a difficult life lesson about the consequences of a man's actions.

Lesson Focus

- America experienced a growth of industry during the Gilded Age.

Objectives
- Explain why the late 1800s in America were called the Gilded Age
- Identify industries that experienced growth
- Identify important leaders in industry
- Explain why industry grew

Introduction

- Invite a student to read aloud the title of the chapter and predict what the chapter will be about. a time in America called the Gilded Age
- Invite a student to read the chapter focus aloud.

  What do you think you will learn about in this chapter? a time of growth, prosperity, and new problems in America
- Direct attention to the timeline.

  What book was published in 1873? *The Gilded Age*
- Explain that the book was a novel written by Mark Twain.

  What other book was published during the Gilded Age? *How the Other Half Lives*

  In what year was *How the Other Half Lives* published? 1890
- What do you think *How the Other Half Lives* was about?
- Explain that the students will learn more about Mark Twain and *How the Other Half Lives* as they learn about the Gilded Age.
- Choose students to identify other significant events on the timeline.
- Choose a student to describe the illustration on page 184. Guide the students in contrasting picnics they might have had with the one in the illustration. Explain that picnics were popular during the Gilded Age and were fancier than picnics today.

Preparation for Reading

- Generate interest as you direct the students to read the titles and examine the pictures and map on pages 184–87.
- Guide pronunciation of any unfamiliar words in the lesson.
- Instruct the students to read the pages silently to discover why the late 1800s in the United States is often called the Gilded Age. On the surface, life in America seemed to glitter like gold. New cities were beginning to thrive, immigrants were pouring into the country, inventors and businessmen were developing new ways to work faster and better, and some Americans were wealthier than they had ever been before.

Timeline:

Carnegie's steel plant opens 1875 — Salvation Army first organized in America 1880 — *How the Other Half Lives* published 1890

1870 *The Gilded Age* published — 1873 — 1876 Bell patents his telephone — 1880 — 1890

Teach for Understanding

How did many Americans make a living before the Civil War? farming, small businesses, trades

What happened to the number of factories after the Civil War? More factories opened.

What grew up around new factories? cities

What effect did the growth of industry have on the way Americans made a living? Some people moved from farms to cities to find new work opportunities, and many more Americans began to work in large industries.

Why did people decide to move from farms to cities and work in factories? Not as many farm workers were needed because new machines could do much of the work that people had done before.

- Guide a discussion about why farms were still needed in the United States.

What were three important industries during the Gilded Age? the steel industry, the oil industry, and the railroad industry

- Invite a student to read aloud the sentences that tell why the steel industry prospered.

Who became America's most important manufacturer of steel? Andrew Carnegie

Was Carnegie born in America? No, his family immigrated from Scotland.

Was the United States the only country to recognize Carnegie as an important manufacturer of steel? No, the world recognized him as a leading steel producer.

- How did Carnegie become the leading producer of steel? Answers should include that he worked hard.

- Choose a volunteer to read aloud the sentences that tell why the oil industry prospered.

- Explain that supplies of whale oil were decreasing in the late 1800s. Refined crude oil, also called petroleum, was superior to whale oil for lubricating mechanical parts to keep machines running smoothly. Petroleum could be further refined to make kerosene. Kerosene was cheaper than whale oil, and it burned cleaner and brighter, making it popular for use in lamps.

Who became America's leader in the oil industry? John D. Rockefeller

How was Rockefeller able to help Americans? He lowered the price of kerosene so that many more Americans could afford it.

- Invite a student to read aloud the sentences that tell how Rockefeller treated his employees.

Why were more people traveling west? to settle and farm or find jobs

- Choose a volunteer to read aloud the sentences that tell why the railroad industry grew during the Gilded Age.

188

Carnegie and the Steel Industry

One of the most important industries in this era was the steel industry. God had blessed the United States with abundant natural resources of iron ore. One English inventor had recently found an inexpensive way to produce steel from iron. The railroad and construction industries needed large amounts of steel. For all these reasons, the steel industry prospered in the United States.

Andrew Carnegie became America's most important manufacturer of steel. Carnegie came from a poor family that had immigrated from Scotland. But he worked hard at various jobs. He rose to a management position at the Pennsylvania Railroad. After the Civil War, he decided to invest in the steel industry. He opened his first steel plant near Pittsburgh, Pennsylvania, in 1875. Carnegie quickly became the leading steel producer in the world. His success eventually made him a millionaire.

Rockefeller and the Oil Industry

Another important industry during the Gilded Age was the production of oil. Up to the time of the Civil War, people had used oil from whales to light lamps and keep machines running smoothly. Now oil drilled from the ground was replacing whale oil. Oil from underground, or crude oil, could

be refined. Refined oil was useful for many different purposes. One of the most popular uses was making kerosene for lamps.

John D. Rockefeller was the nation's leader in the oil industry. He and two business partners opened an oil refinery in the 1860s. Rockefeller later became the president of his own oil company, Standard Oil. He was able to lower the price of kerosene so that many more Americans could afford it. Other oil companies could no longer compete with his prices. Standard Oil bought out other refineries until it controlled nearly all the oil production in the United States. The company employed hundreds of workers and paid good wages. It helped many families be able to enjoy a higher standard of living. It also made a fortune for the Rockefeller family.

The Railroad Industry

Along with the rise of steel and oil industries came the expanding of America's railroads. The more products Americans manufactured, the more they needed railroads to transport these goods around the country. More people were traveling west to settle and farm or find jobs. More railroads were needed to transport these people. The transcontinental railroad had been completed in 1869. By 1900 four more lines ran across the continent to cities on the West Coast.

186

Background

Andrew Carnegie

Carnegie spent his childhood in Scotland as a bobbin winder in a textile factory, earning only twelve and one-half cents a day, making $2.50 per week. In America he got a job as a railroad telegraph boy. Soon Carnegie was promoted to telegraph operator, making twenty dollars per month. Several years later, he earned thirty-five dollars each month working as a clerk to the divisional superintendant for the Pennsylvania Railroad.

Carnegie saved his money and looked for ways to invest it. He believed that steel would be needed to build America. Carnegie got his foot in the door of the steel industry when he invested in the Keystone Bridge Company, which built steel bridges.

Later Carnegie started his own steel company. Structural steel was soon used to build large buildings and even skyscrapers. Barbed wire replaced wooden fences. Wire nails took the place of forged nails. Railroads used steel for rails and railroad cars. These new uses for steel made his business boom.

Additional Background information for this lesson is on the Teacher's Toolkit CD.

Tracks Across America

Legend:
- Great Northern
- Northern Pacific
- Union Pacific
- Central Pacific
- Southern Pacific
- Additional tracks

James J. Hill

One of these, the Great Northern Railway, was the project of **James J. Hill**. Hill wanted to build a good-quality railroad while keeping costs down. Many railroads of the day relied on money from the government. But Hill was able to build his railroad without using government money. He not only built a railroad, but he also helped settle the surrounding land. He allowed immigrants to travel west on his railroad for a low price. The only condition was that they must agree to build settlements along the railroad.

Hill bought several other lines over the course of his life. He constantly worked to improve his railroads. His wise management earned him the nickname "Empire Builder."

Corporations

During the Gilded Age, a new way of doing business began. Many owners of large businesses decided to form **corporations**. When a business becomes a corporation, it is owned not by one person but by many. These owners are called investors, or stockholders. Becoming a corporation allows a business to raise funds quickly by selling stock. Banks can also invest in corporations.

John D. Rockefeller's Standard Oil corporation was called a **trust**. A trust combines several smaller companies into one gigantic corporation. Many other industries also formed trusts during the Gilded Age.

> Which industries experienced growth during the Gilded Age and why?

187

John D. Rockefeller

Rockefeller's first job was working on commission for merchants and produce shippers. He and a neighbor started a business as commission merchants in grain, hay, and meats. During the Civil War, Rockefeller put his money into a refinery. However, he believed that refineries employed wasteful business practices. In 1870 Rockefeller formed the Standard Oil Company by buying the refineries in his area. He promised the railroads larger shipments if they would charge him reduced rates. On paper the railroad charged him the public rate, but they gave him a rebate, or kickback, for each barrel of oil he shipped. Rockefeller's methods, though not illegal at the time, were unfair. Within two years Rockefeller had gained control of one-fourth of the refining industry. By 1910 the Standard Oil Company controlled 90 percent of the nation's refineries and 92 percent of the crude-oil supply from the Appalachians, the nation's major oil source at the time.

Teach for Understanding

Who built the Great Northern Railway? James J. Hill

What did Hill achieve in building the Great Northern Railway? He built the railroad without using government money, and he helped settle the surrounding land by allowing immigrants to travel west on his railroad if they agreed to build settlements.

- Direct attention to the map on page 187. Instruct the students to use the map key to identify each of the railroads.

Which cities did the Great Northern Railway connect? Chicago, Minneapolis, Seattle

What did Hill do to improve his railroads? He constantly worked and wisely managed them.

What new way of doing business began during the Gilded Age? Many owners of large businesses decided to form corporations.

- Guide a discussion about what a corporation is and why many business owners decided to form corporations.

Why was Rockefeller's Standard Oil corporation called a trust? Several smaller companies combined to form one gigantic corporation.

> Conclude the discussion by asking the question on page 187. The steel industry grew. The United States had an abundance of iron ore from which to produce steel inexpensively. The railroad and construction industries needed large amounts of steel. The oil industry grew. Whale oil was being replaced with crude oil, which was useful for many different purposes when refined. The railroad industry grew. Americans manufactured more products that needed to be transported around the country. More people who wanted to settle and farm or find jobs in the West needed transportation.

Activity Manual

- Guide completion of pages 129–32.

74

Student Text pages 188–91
Activity Manual pages 133–34

Lesson Focus

- New inventions changed the way Americans lived and worked.

Objectives
- Identify new inventions and their inventors
- Examine how new inventions affected life in America

Teacher's Toolkit CD
- Visual 26: *QWERTY Keyboard*
- Instructional Aid 44: *Inventions & Change*

Review

- Choose a volunteer to explain why the late 1800s in America are called the Gilded Age.

  What three important industries prospered during the Gilded Age? the steel industry, the oil industry, and the railroad industry

  Who was a leader in each of these industries? Andrew Carnegie in the steel industry, John D. Rockefeller in the oil industry, James J. Hill in the railroad industry

- Choose volunteers to explain why each of the three industries prospered.

Preparation for Reading

- Generate interest as you direct the students to read the titles and examine the pictures on pages 188–91.
- Guide pronunciation of any unfamiliar words in the lesson.
- Direct the students to read the pages silently and complete Instructional Aid 44 in small groups.

> Guide a review of important terms, maps, places, and people from each previous lesson. Direct the students to find and read the corresponding entries from the Resource Treasury.

How It Was

Peter stood next to his father, listening to the low murmur of the crowd around him. The city had just finished installing Mr. Edison's new invention—an electric lighting system. Any moment now, the mayor would flip a switch and . . .

Suddenly the nearby buildings burst into light. The city was brighter than Peter had ever seen it before. A cannon blasted, and all around, people gasped and shouted. Then the crowd exploded into deafening applause. A band began to play.

"It's like magic!" Peter shouted.

"It's not magic, son," said his father. "It's progress."

New Inventions

Another key to the progress in industry was new inventions. During the Gilded Age, God allowed several important scientific discoveries to be made. These advances in technology and communication changed the way Americans lived and worked.

Bell and the Telephone

Electricity was the focus of many experiments in the late 1800s. People had been growing in their understanding of electricity throughout the nineteenth century. But during the Gilded Age, some of the most practical uses for electricity were found.

The telegraph was already using electrical signals to send coded messages over a wire. But in the 1870s **Alexander Graham Bell** experimented with the use of electric currents to transmit spoken messages. Bell was a teacher of deaf children. He had researched the ear, the voice, and sound waves. The result of his study was the development of a working telephone. Although other inventors were experimenting with similar ideas, Bell was the first to get a patent for his invention.

As Bell and others improved the telephone, it became a valuable tool. By 1884, underground wires allowed people to talk over long distances by telephone. Few inventions have had as great an impact on the way people communicate as the telephone.

188

Teach for Understanding

Who allowed the scientific discoveries that resulted in advances in technology and communication? God

- Point out that God oversees and allows all that happens in the world. Explain that the Creation Mandate (Genesis 1:27–28) implies that people should make scientific discoveries and advances in technology that enable us to rule wisely over God's world. However, because people are sinful, not every invention is wise or is used for the best purpose.

  Who patented the telephone? Alexander Graham Bell

- Explain that a patent is issued by a government and specifies a number of years in which only the inventor can make or sell the invention.

  What did Bell do that helped him develop a working telephone? He experimented with the use of electric currents to transmit spoken messages, and he had researched the ear, the voice, and sound waves.

- Why do you think Bell was interested in studying the ear, the voice, and sound waves? Answers could include that he taught deaf children.

- Invite a group to tell how the invention of the telephone changed life in America. Direct attention to the picture of the early telephone. Guide a discussion contrasting it with phones used today.

Edison and Electric Light

Thomas Edison was one of several inventors to experiment with a light bulb. He was not the first to find a working design. But he was able to design a light bulb that was both practical and affordable. His light bulb lasted longer than others and was cheaper to produce. He also invented the system of power plants and wiring that would provide electricity for light bulbs.

The light bulb changed the way Americans lived. Electric lighting was more affordable than kerosene. Before electric lighting, families often gathered around one light source in their homes in the evenings to read or do needlework. Now families could put more lamps in their homes and spread out around the house at night.

Factories and stores could stay open in the evenings. People could stay later at dinner parties and evening events. The light bulb may seem like a small invention, but it had an enormous effect on American family life and culture.

Along with the light bulb, Edison invented the phonograph. This device recorded the human voice and played it back. Edison also did some early work with motion pictures.

Other Inventions

Not every invention created as much change as the telephone and electric lighting. And not every inventor was as well-known as Bell or Edison. But many other inventions improved everyday life for Americans during the Gilded Age.

Alexander Graham Bell   Thomas Edison

189

Was Thomas Edison the only inventor to experiment with a light bulb? No, he was one of several inventors to do so.

- Explain that inventions are often improvements of existing inventions.

What was significant about Edison's light bulb? It was both practical and affordable.

How would light bulbs get electricity? by a system of power plants and wiring that Edison also invented

- Invite a group to tell different ways in which the invention of the light bulb changed life in America.

- Guide the students in reading the How It Was box on page 188.

What do you think the mood of the crowd was as the people waited for the mayor to turn on the lights? Answers could include that there was excitement and anticipation.

Why do you think Peter thought that the buildings bursting into light was like magic?

What did Peter's father say the lights were? progress

What did Peter's father mean when he said, "It's progress"? Answers could include that Edison's electric lighting system was an improvement of the previous ways of lighting buildings.

- Direct attention to the picture on page 189. Guide a discussion contrasting Edison's light bulb with light bulbs used today.

What else did Edison invent? the phonograph

What did the phonograph do? It recorded the human voice and played it back.

Which two inventions changed American life more than others? the telephone and electric lighting

- Choose volunteers to name other inventions that had an effect on American life.

Alexander Graham Bell and the Telephone

Alexander Graham Bell thought it might be possible to transmit the human voice over a wire using electricity. He asked an electrician friend to assist him in his experiments. On June 2, 1875, the men transmitted a sound that sounded like a moving clock spring. The next day, Bell was able to transmit his voice to his assistant, Thomas A. Watson. A patent was issued for the first telephone on March 7, 1876. By the end of 1880, there were 47,900 telephones in the United States. Early telephones were sold in pairs. The owner had to put in wire to connect the phones. In 1889 the first pay phones were established, and the first cordless phones were available in the 1970s.

Thomas Edison

In 1878 Edison began experimenting to find a way to manufacture light bulbs. Edison applied his work ethic to inventing, saying, "There is no substitute for hard work." He also said, "Genius is 1 percent inspiration and 99 percent perspiration." By the time he died in 1931, he owned more than a thousand patents. These included the printing telegraph, electric printing machine, stencil pen, brake for electromagnetic motors, addressing machine, vacuum pump, electromagnetic railway, typewriter, junction box, locomotive for an electric railway, process for

nickel plating, rotary cement kiln, fluorescent electric lamp, device for grinding coal, and sprocket-chain drive. Most of his inventions were improvements on existing inventions or processes. But a few of them—for example, the alkaline storage battery, the movie projector, and the phonograph—were innovations that led to whole new industries.

Teach for Understanding

Who is credited with inventing the typewriter? Christopher Sholes

What was significant about Sholes's typewriter? It was the first typewriter to use the QWERTY keyboard.

- Invite a group to tell how Sholes's typewriter changed life in America.

- Display Visual 26. Guide a discussion about the similarities between the two keyboards and how technology has changed.

What did George Eastman invent? the Kodak camera and rolled film

- Invite a group to tell how the invention of the Kodak camera and rolled film changed life in America.

- Direct attention to the picture on page 190. Guide a discussion contrasting Eastman's Kodak camera with cameras used today.

How were George Westinghouse and Thomas Edison alike? They both experimented with electricity.

What did Westinghouse help to prove? Alternating current is a better electrical system than direct current.

What is Westinghouse best known for inventing? an air brake for trains

Why was the air-brake system for trains an important invention? It controlled trains in a safer way and prevented the problem of runaway trains.

What invention helped to make George Pullman famous? the Pullman sleeping car

- Invite a group to tell how the Pullman sleeping car changed life in America.

Christopher Sholes is credited with inventing the typewriter. His machine was the first to use the QWERTY keyboard that is still in use today. Sholes's invention resulted in great progress in the publishing industry.

George Eastman invented the Kodak camera. It was the first camera that was easy enough for nearly anyone to use. Eastman also invented rolled film. A roll of film took the place of heavy plates and could be easily loaded in a camera.

George Westinghouse, like Edison, experimented with electricity. He worked with two different kinds of electrical current. He helped prove that alternating current (AC) is a better electrical system than direct current (DC). But he is best known for inventing an air brake for trains in 1869. His brake invention controlled trains in a safer way and prevented the problem of runaway trains.

At the same time as the air-brake invention, George Pullman was also rising to fame in the railroad industry. His invention was the Pullman sleeping car. This comfortable train car allowed passengers to enjoy better sleep on long journeys. Some Pullman cars also had sitting rooms and dining areas.

Not all inventors were men. Margaret Knight was a factory worker who loved to observe the way machines worked. During the course of her life,

Christopher Sholes George Eastman

190

Background

The Sholes and Glidden Typewriter

Christopher Sholes was part of a group of inventors working at a machine shop in Milwaukee, Wisconsin, in 1868. A friend suggested he read an article in a magazine. It predicted that a typewriting machine might be one of the next useful inventions. Since Sholes liked the idea, he began to develop it. He mounted a telegraph key on a base. When he tapped it, a letter would hit the paper held against a glass to produce the letter. He continued to work until he had a typewriter that would print the entire alphabet. Sholes thought of a way of arranging letters on the keyboard, which came to be called the QWERTY keyboard. The Sholes and Glidden typewriter had only capital letters. The E. Remington Company produced it from 1874 to 1878. Although it was not a great success at first, Sholes's typewriter changed the printing industry forever.

she invented numerous machines. Her most famous invention was a machine for folding and gluing a flat-based paper bag. Knight also patented many other inventions. Among them were a numbering machine, a sewing-machine reel, and a shield for protecting skirts from rain and dirt.

New inventions helped give the Gilded Age its glitter. Few of these inventors gave glory to God for their accomplishments. Many of them rejected the Christian faith entirely. Yet it was God who gave them gifted minds and creative skills. God allowed them to exercise these gifts to improve life for people in many parts of His world.

Changes that came from new inventions were not always improvements. For example, the changes caused by electric lighting sometimes kept families apart more than they were together. The telephone sometimes kept friends from making personal visits and speaking face to face. Inventions brought a challenge to Americans. They had to learn how to move forward with new tools without despising the God-given wisdom of people of the past.

> Which inventions of this era brought the greatest changes to American life?

George Westinghouse   Margaret Knight

191

Teach for Understanding

- Guide a discussion about how Margaret Knight's inventions helped people.

  Did these inventors give glory to God for their accomplishments? No, many of them rejected the Christian faith entirely.

  Why should they have given glory to God for their accomplishments? It was God who gave them gifted minds and creative skills and allowed them to exercise their gifts to improve life for people.

- Guide a discussion about changes resulting from new inventions that were not always improvements. Encourage the students to examine how improvements in technology can have negative effects on their relationships with others.

  What challenge did inventions bring to Americans? They had to learn how to move forward with new tools without despising the God-given wisdom of people of the past.

- Use 1 Corinthians 3:19 and James 1:5 to guide a discussion about the importance of seeking wisdom from God and learning from the God-given wisdom of others.

  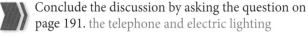 Conclude the discussion by asking the question on page 191. the telephone and electric lighting

Activity Manual

- Guide completion of pages 133–34.

Activities

Keyword Search

Direct pairs of students to do keyword searches. Instruct them to find facts and images for an invention, such as the phonograph or the Pullman sleeping car. Encourage the students to present their information with the class.

Never Invented

Instruct the students to choose an invention such as the light bulb, the telephone, the camera, or the computer. Direct them to write one or more paragraphs about what life would be like if the object they choose had never been invented.

Becoming an Inventor

Challenge the students to pretend to be inventors and to think of a product they can invent or improve. Instruct them to think about whether the product would make a person's life easier and whether it would be practical. Direct the students to write about the original invention or improved product and draw a picture of it. Invite them to present their product with the class.

75

Student Text pages 192–94
Activity Manual pages 135–36

Lesson Focus

- Capitalism made it possible for some Americans to be richer than others.

Objectives

- Explain social Darwinism and why it is a dangerous belief
- Explain responses to problems created by social Darwinism
- Evaluate how wealthy Americans managed their money

Teacher's Toolkit CD

- Instructional Aid 45: *Wealth & Work*

Review

- Invite volunteers to name an invention, tell who invented it, and how the invention changed life in America.

  Who gave these inventors their gifted minds and creative skills? God

  Did many of these inventors give glory to God for their accomplishments? No, many of them rejected the Christian faith entirely.

  Which two inventions brought the most change to American life during the Gilded Age? the telephone and electric lighting

- Invite volunteers to explain why changes that resulted from new inventions were not always improvements.

Preparation for Reading

- Generate interest as you direct the students to read the titles and examine the pictures on pages 192–94.
- Guide pronunciation of any unfamiliar words in the lesson.
- Direct the students to read the pages silently and complete Instructional Aid 45 in small groups.

Teach for Understanding

What was another reason that the late 1800s were called the Gilded Age? It was a time of wealth in America.

How did men like Carnegie, Rockefeller, and Hill earn their fortunes? from their industries

What made it possible for some people to be richer than others? America's system of capitalism

- Choose a volunteer to read aloud the glossary definition of *capitalism*.
- Invite a group to tell two things that capitalism encouraged.

Wealth and Work

Another source of the glitter of the Gilded Age was its wealth. Many wealthy businessmen had risen from poverty to riches in a fairly short time. In the past, most wealthy men had inherited wealth from their families. But men like Carnegie, Rockefeller, and Hill earned their fortunes from their industries. America's system of **capitalism** made it possible for some people to be richer than others. But it was also a system that encouraged hard work and competition among businesses. Competition often helped lower the prices of goods.

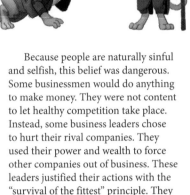

Social Darwinism

By this time in history, many Americans had accepted Charles Darwin's theory of evolution. This belief states that all the types of plants and animals developed on their own over millions of years. Evolution teaches that humans developed gradually from animals.

Herbert Spencer, another evolutionist, promoted an idea called "survival of the fittest." He said that only the fittest members of a species can survive the harsh conditions of nature. He applied this principle to many areas of society, including business. The idea that only the fittest people can survive in society is known as **social Darwinism**.

Because people are naturally sinful and selfish, this belief was dangerous. Some businessmen would do anything to make money. They were not content to let healthy competition take place. Instead, some business leaders chose to hurt their rival companies. They used their power and wealth to force other companies out of business. These leaders justified their actions with the "survival of the fittest" principle. They were not living by God's command to love their neighbors.

Another problem was that workers sometimes suffered from the greed of their employers. Sometimes employees had to work long hours for little pay. Employers might lower the wages of employees without sharing the loss themselves. Employees might even be suddenly let go if they were injured by a machine at work.

192

- Explain that by allowing for some people to be richer than others, America's system of capitalism grows the economy in such a way that both the rich and the poor are better off in the end.

  What theory did Charles Darwin develop? a theory of evolution

  How is the theory of evolution contrary to the Bible? The theory of evolution claims that all types of plants and animals developed on their own over millions of years, but the Bible states that God created all types of plants and animals during the six days of creation.

  What evolutionist idea did Herbert Spencer promote? survival of the fittest, in which only the fittest members of a species can survive the harsh conditions of nature

- Choose a student to tell what social Darwinism is.

  What do you think social Darwinists mean by "the fittest people"? Answers could include people who are smart, powerful, or wealthy.

- Direct attention to the political cartoon on page 192. Explain that the cartoon represents social Darwinism.

  What does the well-dressed lion represent? It represents the fittest people in society, the people who are smart, powerful, or wealthy. In addition to being well-dressed, the lion appears to be strong, healthy, and wealthy.

  What does the other lion represent? It represents needy people. It appears to be weak, sick, poor, and looking to the well-dressed lion for help.

Responses to the Problems

The United States government found ways to respond to some of these problems. Many businessmen did not want the government to step in and help. Social Darwinists believed government control would make people lose their freedom as individuals. But others pressured the government to make laws protecting workers and small businesses.

Many lawmakers thought it was unfair for one corporation to control an entire industry. When this happened, there was no competition to keep prices down for customers. Lawmakers were concerned that Standard Oil and other large corporations had too much control of their industries. Congress passed the **Sherman Antitrust Act** in 1890. This act sought to limit the power a corporation could have.

Factory workers also responded to problems in their own way. Workers began to organize groups called **labor unions**. They thought that if large numbers of workers joined together, they could force their employers to make changes.

Some of the labor unions organized strikes. During a strike, workers refused to work until their employers agreed to their demands. Some strikes were successful. The workers got the higher wages or the better conditions they had

asked for. However, some strikes ended in violence. Property was damaged or destroyed, and in some cases, people lost their lives.

Sometimes the courts took action against labor unions. They ordered the unions to stop strikes. However, these orders did not always result in justice for everyone. The tensions between workers and employers would continue into the next century.

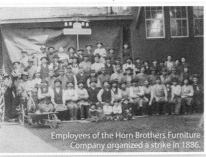
Employees of the Horn Brothers Furniture Company organized a strike in 1886.

Managing Millions

For the first time in its history, the United States had a very wealthy upper class. Many of the men who had made millions in industry built homes like palaces. They filled their homes with fine furnishings. They gave extravagant dinners and parties. They took expensive vacations. Becoming wealthy is not sinful, but making a show of wealth for selfish reasons is wrong.

America's wealthy people understood that riches can be a burden

193

🔧 What do you think the cartoon says about some people in society? Answers may include that some people do not care about the needy or those who are less fortunate. They do not care about hurting others so that they can have more or be wealthier. They are not content with what they have. They always want more.

🔧 Do you think the Bible allows for social Darwinism? Answers could include that the Bible teaches us to love others. Social Darwinism encourages people to act in an unloving way toward others.

🔧 Do you think social Darwinism encourages people to trust God to meet their needs? Answers may include that social Darwinism encourages people to place their faith in being one of the "fittest" rather than in trusting God to meet their needs.

- Choose a student to read aloud the sentences that tell why social Darwinism is a dangerous belief.

- Invite groups to tell what problems were created by social Darwinism.

Teach for Understanding

Who did not want the government to step in and help solve some of the problems created by social Darwinism? many businessmen and social Darwinists

🔧 Why do you think many businessmen did not want the government to step in and help? Answers could include that many businessmen wanted to continue in their sinful and selfish ways in order to make money.

Why did social Darwinists not want the government to step in and help? They believed government control would make people lose their freedom as individuals.

Why did some people pressure the government to step in and help solve some of the problems? They wanted the government to make laws protecting workers and small businesses.

- Explain that one of the biblical purposes of government is to ensure justice (Psalm 72:1–7, 11–14; Jeremiah 22:13–16).

- Invite a group to explain how the United States government responded to some of the problems created by social Darwinism.

- Invite another group to explain how factory workers responded to some of the problems.

- Choose a volunteer to read aloud the caption for the picture on page 193. Guide a discussion about the success of strikes and why courts sometimes took action against labor unions.

How did many of the men who had made millions in industry spend their money? They built homes like palaces and filled them with fine furnishings. They gave extravagant dinners and parties and took expensive vacations.

Is it a sin to become wealthy? It is not sinful, but making a show of wealth for selfish reasons is wrong.

Teach for Understanding

- Guide a discussion about how riches can be a burden as well as a blessing.

  What did Carnegie think a person should do with his wealth? He thought that it was better to give money away during one's life. It would be better to leave children only enough to live a comfortable life. The rest of one's wealth should be given away to help needy people and good causes.

  Why did Carnegie think it was better not to leave large sums of money to children? The money could be a burden to them, or they could choose to use the money unwisely.

- Do you think Carnegie felt strongly about what he wrote in "The Gospel of Wealth"? yes

- Choose a volunteer to read aloud the paragraph that indicates that Carnegie felt stongly about what he wrote.

  What is a person who gives large sums of money to help public causes called? a philanthropist

- Invite a student to read aloud the caption for the photograph on page 194.

- Invite groups to name other philanthropists and tell what they did with some of their wealth.

  Why was Vanderbilt able to give a large gift to found a university? He had made millions in the transportation industry.

  What is the best motive for giving away money? obedience to God's Word

- Do you think we should give money only to public causes? No, God's Word tells us to give to those in need. This command includes giving to individuals.

- Guide a discussion about how Christians can glorify God by giving to help people in need.

  >> Conclude the discussion by asking the question on page 194. Some business leaders used their power and wealth to force other companies out of business. Some employers made their employees work long hours for little pay, lowered the wages of employees without sharing the loss themselves, or let employees go if they were injured by a machine at work. Congress passed the Sherman Antitrust Act to limit the power a corporation could have. Workers began to organize groups called labor unions. Some of the labor unions organized strikes, and workers refused to work until their employers agreed to their demands.

Activity Manual

- Guide completion of pages 135–36.

Assessment
- Administer quiz.

The quiz may be given anytime after completing this lesson.

Andrew Carnegie, seated in the center of the front row, donated a large sum of money to Tuskegee Institute, a college for African Americans, in Alabama.

as well as a blessing. Andrew Carnegie wrote an essay called "The Gospel of Wealth." In it he taught that it was better to give money away during one's life than to leave it to others after death. Large sums of money left to children could be a burden to them, or they could choose to use the money unwisely. Carnegie stated that it would be better to leave children only enough to live a comfortable life. The rest of one's wealth should be given away to help needy people and good causes.

Carnegie applied this advice to his own fortune. He believed everyone should have opportunities to read and learn. During his lifetime, he gave millions of dollars to build libraries. He also gave money to support schools, colleges, and churches.

Other wealthy men chose to give money away while still living. **Cornelius Vanderbilt** was the first man to make millions in the transportation

industry. He gave a large gift to found a university that now bears his name. John D. Rockefeller also gave money to schools. He donated millions to open an institute for medical research. George Eastman used his fortune from Kodak to support colleges and technology institutes.

The giving of large sums of money to help public causes is called philanthropy. We call men like Carnegie, Vanderbilt, Rockefeller, and Eastman **philanthropists**. People can have various motives for giving away money. The best motive is obedience to God's Word. Ephesians 4:28 emphasizes the need to work hard so that we will have the means to give to those in need. Giving out of love for God and others is the kind of philanthropy that brings Him glory.

> What problems did social Darwinism create, and how were they handled?

194

Activity

Helping Others Project

Guide the students in helping someone who has a need. The project may include collecting and delivering groceries, doing yard work, shoveling snow, or writing a letter to someone who might be lonely.

Background

Vanderbilt's Wealth

Cornelius Vanderbilt's life and work made the name Vanderbilt synonymous with great wealth. However, he did not live in palatial homes or have an extravagant life style. Nor did he give away much of his wealth. The one million dollars he gave to found Vanderbilt University in Tennessee was his only significant philanthropic contribution. When he died in 1877, Vanderbilt left an estate estimated to be in excess of one hundred million dollars. The vast majority of this wealth was left to his son William. Cornelius's grandson George Washington Vanderbilt II was born into that wealth and built the now-famous Biltmore Estate in Asheville, North Carolina.

Expanding Cities
Causes of Growth

The Gilded Age was a time of growth for cities. New cities were springing up in many parts of the country. Existing cities were becoming even larger. By 1880 the population of New York City had reached more than one million. Chicago's population tripled during the last two decades of the century.

The growth of cities had two main causes. One was that more and more people from rural areas were moving to cities. Often the children of farmers chose city life rather than staying on the family farm. Many came to cities hoping for opportunities to find higher-paying jobs. Young Americans were often lured by the dream of going from "rags to riches" in the big cities as Andrew Carnegie had done. Many also came to enjoy the entertainment that cities had to offer, or they came simply to meet new people.

Another reason for the growth of cities was immigration. Between 1870 and 1900, more than ten million people came to America from other countries. They came seeking jobs, land, and a better life. Some came for greater freedom to practice their religion. Europeans usually came to the East Coast and Asians to the West Coast. Ellis Island in New York Harbor became America's first immigration station. The towering Statue of Liberty welcomed immigrants to America's shores.

Though some European immigrants went west to settle on farms, many more settled in cities. New York, Boston, Philadelphia, and Chicago were popular cities for immigrants. San Francisco, California, became home to thousands of Chinese immigrants. Immigrants were often willing to work for lower pay than other Americans. For some immigrants, any job in America was an improvement from life in their home countries. Many immigrants found low-paying factory or railroad jobs.

Not only did cities grow in population, but they actually grew taller. Before elevators were invented in the 1850s, tall buildings were not practical. But in the last half of the century, people began constructing taller buildings. The Home Insurance Building in Chicago was

195

Lesson **76**

Student Text pages 195–97
Activity Manual pages 137–39

Lesson Focus

- The urbanization of America during the Gilded Age brought a new set of problems.

Objectives
- Explain why and how cities experienced growth
- Examine problems created by the urbanization of America
- Write an imaginative journal entry

Materials
- Sources for researching the Statue of Liberty

Review

- Invite volunteers to explain social Darwinism and the problems it created.
- What were responses to some of the problems? Congress passed the Sherman Antitrust Act to limit the power a corporation could have. Workers began to organize groups called labor unions. Some of the labor unions organized strikes, and workers refused to work until their employers agreed to their demands.

—How did many wealthy Americans spend the millions of dollars they had made in industry? They built homes like palaces and filled them with fine furnishings. They gave extravagant dinners and parties and took expensive vacations.

— What does a philanthropist do? gives large sums of money to help public causes

- Choose volunteers to name some philanthropists who lived during the Gilded Age. Carnegie, Vanderbilt, Rockefeller, and Eastman

Preparation for Reading

- Generate interest as you direct the students to read the titles and examine the pictures on pages 195–97.
- Guide pronunciation of any unfamiliar words in the lesson.
- Direct the students to read the pages silently to discover how cities changed during the Gilded Age. New cities were springing up, and existing cities were becoming even larger. Cities also grew taller as taller buildings with elevators were constructed.

Teach for Understanding

What were the two main causes of city growth? People from rural areas were moving to cities, and more than ten million immigrants came to America.

- Choose a student to read aloud the sentences that tell why people moved from rural areas to cities.
- Choose another student to read aloud the sentences that tell why people came to America from other countries.

Where would immigrants who came to the East Coast usually come from? Europe

Where would immigrants who came to the West Coast usually come from? Asia

Where was America's first immigration station located? Ellis Island in New York Harbor

What welcomed immigrants as they sailed into New York Harbor? the Statue of Liberty

- Invite a volunteer to tell where European and Chinese immigrants settled. Some European immigrants went west to settle on farms, but many more settled in cities such as New York, Boston, Philadelphia, and Chicago. Thousands of Chinese immigrants settled in San Francisco, California.

Why were some immigrants often willing to work for lower pay than other Americans? For some immigrants, any job in America was an improvement from life in their home countries.

What kinds of jobs did many immigrants find? low-paying factory or railroad jobs

Teach for Understanding

Why could tall buildings and skyscrapers be constructed in American cities in the late 1800s? Answers could include that elevators were invented in the 1850s. Steel was lighter than brick but could support more weight and was used to construct the tall buildings.

What attractions did cities have that could not be found in rural areas? parks, museums, theaters, art galleries, and amusements parks

What do historians call this growth of American cities? the urbanization of America

What were the three main problems urbanization brought to American cities? The more crowded cities became, the harder it was to keep them clean. Providing housing for everyone was difficult. Many poor children worked to help support their families.

- Choose a student to read aloud the sentences that tell why it was difficult to keep cities clean.
- Read aloud the caption for the photograph on page 196.
- Invite a volunteer to read aloud the sentences that describe tenements.

What problems were caused by so many people living close together? Diseases spread quickly, and children born in tenements often did not survive to adulthood.

- Invite a volunteer to read aloud the sentences that tell why children were hired to work.

the first modern skyscraper. It had a framework of steel. Steel was lighter than brick but could support more weight. With steel it was possible to construct very tall buildings. By the early 1900s, New York also had several skyscrapers.

Cities had other attractions that could not be found in rural areas. Large cities developed parks where people could relax in a beautiful outdoor setting. Museums, theaters, and art galleries drew crowds of people interested in the arts. Some cities even opened amusement parks with shows and rides for people to enjoy.

It is not hard to imagine why so many people were drawn to America's cities in the late 1800s. Cities promised them things that country life could not. Historians call this growth of cities the **urbanization** of America.

Problems Along with Growth

Urbanization brought a new set of problems to America. The more crowded cities became, the harder it was to keep them clean. Horse traffic made the streets messy, and factory smoke polluted the air. Cities did not yet have modern sewer systems or workers who collected trash.

Providing housing for everyone was also difficult. Many city dwellers could not afford to buy houses. Poor families crowded into tenements. Tenements were buildings with small rooms and unhealthy living conditions. Most tenements had no running water or toilets and few windows to let in fresh air. With so many people living close together, diseases spread quickly. Many people in tenements suffered from tuberculosis, cholera, and typhoid. Children born in tenements often did not survive to adulthood.

Children who did survive were part of another problem. Among the poor, many children worked to help support their families. At this time, America had no laws against child labor. Many factories had jobs that children could

This photo by Jacob Riis shows an immigrant family in a tenement home.

196

Background

Ellis Island

The largest number of European immigrants came to America by way of New York Harbor at Ellis Island. The island served as a temporary stopover for incoming immigrants who used its beautifully designed great hall, dining room, and hospital. Those who looked healthy enough to hold a job and who could prove they had the means to reach distant destinations usually took the ferry to New Jersey and rode a train inland. Others entered New York City totally bewildered. Public Health Service doctors assisted the immigrants who were ill. If they could be cured, they were treated and sent on their way as soon as possible. The immigrant center at Ellis Island operated from 1892 to 1954 and handled the entry of more than seventeen million immigrants. The one-day record for immigrants processed occurred on April 17, 1907, when 11,747 went through the system. Most immigrants stayed at Ellis Island for an average of only three to five hours. About 20 percent of them encountered problems or questions that required them to

stay overnight in dormitory-like facilities until their cases could be resolved. Their accommodations were far better on Ellis Island than they had been on the ship. Often immigrants feared being turned back at Ellis Island, but of the millions who came, the number rejected was less than 2 percent.

The Statue of Liberty

The Statue of Liberty was given to the United States by the people of France in 1886. The statue holds her torch in one hand and a tablet representing the law in the other. She wears a seven-pronged crown. A broken chain lies at her feet. Because of the statue's closeness to Ellis Island, the statue has come to represent America's freedom to the oppressed around the world.

Additional Background information for this lesson is on the Teacher's Toolkit CD.

do. Employers hired children to work long hours with very little pay. Often the conditions in these factories were unsafe for the children. These children could not go to school or have much free time to play as wealthy children did. By the year 1900 more than one million children under the age of sixteen worked in America's factories.

Some of the cities' problems were the result of sinful human nature. Cities had bars and gambling halls that profited from people's weaknesses. People were tempted to forget their problems by getting drunk or wasting money on risky games. Certain parts of the cities also had a high crime rate. Immigrants from the same country tended to settle together. Sometimes tensions broke out between people of different ethnic groups.

During the Gilded Age, the leadership within the cities was weak. City governments were slow to deal with these kinds of problems. Cities did not make changes until concerned citizens saw these needs and spoke out about them. The miserable part of city life was one of the problems beneath the glittering surface of the Gilded Age.

> Name several problems that developed from the growth of cities.

Activity

Writing a Journal Entry

Create an imaginative journal entry. Pretend you are an immigrant coming to America for the first time. Or pretend that you are leaving America to live in another country. What hopes, dreams, or fears might you experience? Write your thoughts about leaving your homeland and preparing to live in a new country.

197

Teach for Understanding

- Direct attention to the picture on page 197. Guide a discussion about what kind of work the children are doing.

 Although they were helping to support their families, do you think it was wise for children to work in factories? Answers could include that it was not wise because factories were unsafe for children. These children could not go to school or have much free time to play.

What were some of the cities' problems a result of? sinful human nature

- Choose a student to read aloud the sentences that show sinful human nature in city life.

Why did concerned citizens need to speak out about changes needed in city life? Leadership within the cities was weak. City governments were slow to deal with the problems.

> Conclude the discussion by naming several problems that developed from the growth of cities. The more crowded cities became, the harder it was to keep them clean. Providing housing for everyone was difficult. Many poor children worked to help support their families.

Activity Manual

- Guide completion of pages 137–39.

Activity

Writing a Journal Entry

- Generate excitement about writing an imaginative journal entry as you read the Activity information aloud.
- Invite students to share their journal entries with the class.

Activities

Guest Speaker

Invite a relative of a student or another person who has immigrated to America or is an American who has lived in another country to speak to the class. Ask the speaker to share what it was like to leave his or her homeland and move to a new country.

Ethnic Foods

Plan a tasting party or a lunch using foods from foreign countries of your choosing. Then guide a discussion about what it would be like to move to a new country and eat foods that were very different from what you were used to eating.

Immigrating to America

Divide the students into small groups and direct them to research one of the following topics: the reasons people gave for coming to America, what ships were available, what people packed for the journey, what happened when they arrived at Ellis Island, where the immigrants settled, or what life was like for them in America. Set aside a time for the students to present their findings to the class.

- Social reform began during the Gilded Age.

Objectives
- Identify social reforms that began during the Gilded Age
- Explain why social reform was needed

Teacher's Toolkit CD
- Visual 27: *Jane Addams & Hull-House*

Review

- Choose volunteers to explain why cities grew during the Gilded Age.

  How did cities grow? New cities were springing up and existing cities were becoming even larger because their populations increased. Cities also became taller as taller buildings and skyscrapers were constructed.

- Guide a review of the three main problems urbanization brought to America.

Preparation for Reading

- Generate interest as you direct the students to read the titles and examine the pictures on pages 198–200.

- Guide pronunciation of any unfamiliar words in the lesson.

- Direct the students to read the pages silently to discover what changes to try to solve problems in society are called. social reforms

Teach for Understanding

  Why did changes often come about during the Gilded Age? Individuals cared enough to try to make a difference.

  What are people who try to solve problems in society called? social reformers

- Direct attention to the Biography box. Choose a volunteer to explain the information at the top of the box.

  What is a journalist? a newspaper reporter

- Explain that although Nellie Bly worked in New York and was living there when she died, she was born in Pennsylvania and had worked there also.

- Guide a discussion about how Bly helped to bring about social reform.

 Was Bly's work effective? Yes, her work convinced a grand jury to investigate the asylum. As a result, the asylum was given funds to make necessary changes in its care for the mentally ill. She reported on other injustices to bring about social reforms.

Nellie Bly

Who: journalist
When: 1864–1922
Where: New York

Nellie Bly was born Elizabeth Cochran but took her pen name from a popular song by Stephen Foster. As a young woman she became a newspaper reporter for the *New York World*. Bly accepted an unusual assignment. She was to pretend to be insane, enter a New York asylum, and write an article about the conditions she found there. She spent ten days in a mental institution on Blackwell's Island. After her release, she wrote about the poor living conditions and the cruelty to the patients. Her work convinced a grand jury to investigate the asylum. As a result, the asylum was given funds to make necessary changes in its care for the mentally ill. For many years, Bly continued to work undercover to report on various injustices and to bring about social reforms.

A Time for Change

During the Gilded Age, many people began to realize the need for changes. Some change did happen during this time. But it was not until the next century that change took place on a larger scale. Changes during the Gilded Age often came about because individuals cared enough to try to make a difference. People who try to solve problems in society are called **social reformers**.

Jacob Riis

Jacob Riis immigrated to America from Denmark in 1870. He spent his first few years living in tenement housing in New York City. He worked in a variety of jobs before he found more permanent work as a journalist. He began working as a police reporter in places where the crime rate was high. Riis saw firsthand the dirtiest and poorest parts of the city. He was saddened by what he saw. He wanted to help improve the lives of the city's poor. He decided that the best way to help would be to let as many people as possible know what life was like in New York's slums.

Riis taught himself photography so he could take pictures of the people and places he saw. He wrote articles and showed his pictures to middle- and

198

What other journalist was a social reformer? Jacob Riis

Where was Riis born? in Denmark

Where did Riis live during his first few years in America? in tenement housing in New York City

- Choose volunteers to review what tenement housing was like.

 Why do you think Riis wanted to help improve the lives of the city's poor? Answers could include that Riis had lived in tenement housing and knew what life was like for the poor who lived there. As a police reporter he saw firsthand the dirtiest and poorest parts of the city. He was saddened by what he saw.

What were these places with high crime rates in the dirtiest and poorest parts of New York City called? slums

How did Riis think he could best help the people who lived in New York's slums? by letting as many people as possible know what life was like there

- Guide a discussion about what Riis did to let others know what life was like for people living in the slums.

upper-class people. He finally decided to write a book about his findings.

In 1890 his book *How the Other Half Lives* was published. The book was a huge success. Many people were shocked at the horrible living conditions of the poor and wanted to help. As a result of Riis's work, some tenements were torn down, and others were improved.

Jane Addams

Jane Addams grew up in Illinois. As a young woman she became concerned

Jacob Riis worked to expose the problems of the lower class so others could help meet the needs.

about the immigrants living in the poor sections of Chicago. In 1889 she opened a settlement house for immigrant women. This home, called Hull-House, gave women practical help in adjusting to life in America. Hull-House offered medical care, English classes, lessons in art and music, a library, and childcare for working mothers.

More settlement houses opened in other large cities. Some were secular, and some were organized by churches. Many of these houses were for immigrants. Others focused on black Americans who had migrated from the South to find work and a better life.

The Temperance Movement

Many Americans, especially women, were concerned about the problem of alcoholism. Women noticed that families suffered when a father or mother drank too much. They wanted to protect their homes and their children from harm. The Temperance Movement had started earlier in the nineteenth century.

199

Additional Background information for this lesson is on the Teacher's Toolkit CD.

Jacob Riis

In 1890, a book titled *How the Other Half Lives* was published. In its pages, author Jacob Riis exposed the condition of inner-city tenements in New York. However, the book's popularity was not so much from its text but from its line drawings, which were based on photographs of the inner city taken by Riis.

Through his photographs, Riis captured scenes of families inside their cramped tenements, homeless children sleeping on the streets, and alleys full of people with laundry hanging from above. Readers were shocked by what they saw. Theodore Roosevelt, then the New York police commissioner, wrote Riis, "I have read your book, and I have come to help." Eventually, public reaction to the book brought about legislation to clean up New York slums.

Hull-House

One of the most common misconceptions about Hull-House was that the poor lived there. In reality, the residents were wealthy people who wanted to live among the poor and help them improve the neighborhood. Some of the more famous people who stayed at Hull-House included Gerard Swope, the future president of General Electric; Charles Beard, historian; and William Lyon Mackenzie King, the future prime minister of Canada.

Chapter 9: The Gilded Age

Teach for Understanding

- Direct attention to the pictures on page 199. Point out that the photographs were taken by Jacob Riis. Guide a discussion about what is pictured in the photographs.

- Was Riis's work effective? Yes, as a result of his work, some tenements were torn down, and others were improved.

- Display Visual 27. Invite a student to identify the woman who was concerned about the immigrants living in the poor sections of Chicago. Jane Addams

What did Addams do to help immigrant women? She opened a settlement house called Hull-House.

- Direct attention to the photograph of Hull-House on Visual 27. Guide a discussion about the kind of help immigrant women received there.

- Do you think that immigrant women were thankful for the help they received at Hull-House? Answers could include that they most likely were thankful. They were poor and would not have been able to pay for important things such as medical care, English classes, lessons in art and music, libraries, or childcare.

- Was Addams's work effective? Yes, more settlement houses opened in other large cities. Many of these houses were for immigrants. Others focused on black Americans who had migrated from the South to find work and a better life.

- What is meant by the phrase "black Americans who had migrated from the South?" Black Americans had moved from the South to another part of the country.

- Guide a discussion about what kind of help black Americans who had migrated from the South might have received at settlement houses.

What problem was the Temperance Movement concerned about? alcoholism

When did the Temperance Movement begin? earlier in the nineteenth century

Lesson

77

Teach for Understanding

- Choose a volunteer to explain the purpose of the Temperance Movement.

  What organization began in 1874 as a result of a new interest in making alcoholic drinks illegal? the Woman's Christian Temperance Union

- What was the main purpose of the Woman's Christian Temperance Union? Answers should include that the women wanted local bars to close, they wanted people to make pledges not to drink, and they wanted new laws banning the sale of liquor.

- Do you think that it is acceptable for Christians to have organizations whose main focus is something other than spreading the gospel? Answers could include that it is acceptable for Christians to have organizations whose main purpose is to provide for the needs of others. But Christians should be alert to opportunities for sharing the gospel in every situation.

- Explain that hearing the gospel and accepting Christ as their Savior from sin results in people turning away from their sinful lifestyles.

- Use the photograph to guide a discussion about a Salvation Army soup kitchen.

  How was the Salvation Army different from other relief efforts? Its workers openly preached the gospel and took care of physical needs.

- Choose volunteers to explain other kinds of reform that people wanted in addition to social reform.

  Conclude the discussion by asking the question on page 200. Tenements were torn down, and others were improved. Settlement houses were opened to help immigrants adjust to life in America and to help black Americans who had migrated from the South. Women were making their voices heard and were working for various social reforms. The Salvation Army preached the gospel to the needy and took care of physical needs.

Activity Manual

- Guide completion of page 140.

But now there was a new interest in making alcoholic drinks illegal. The Woman's Christian Temperance Union began in 1874. Many of the women who joined the union were Christians. However, the union was not very concerned with pointing people to Christ. Women met to pray and to visit local bars to demand that they close their doors. The women asked people to make pledges not to drink, and they **campaigned** for new laws banning the sale of liquor.

The WCTU quickly became the largest organization for women in the United States. Its most powerful leader was Frances Willard. Under Willard's leadership, the union began to involve itself in other issues as well. The members worked for laws banning child labor and the sale of tobacco. They tried to reform America's prison system. They also campaigned for women's suffrage, the right of women to vote. American women were making their voices heard as never before.

The Salvation Army

The Salvation Army had begun in London, England. By 1880 the organization had opened its first branch in the United States in the city of Philadephia. The Salvation Army was different from the other relief efforts because it openly preached the gospel to the needy. In addition, its workers took care of physical needs. They opened soup kitchens and provided shelters for the homeless.

Other Reforms

Social reform was not the only kind of reform people wanted. Many people wanted to reform the government too. They wanted to stop leaders from using power in unrighteous ways. Other people wanted changes in business and education. Many of America's farmers wanted to limit the power of the railroads. They wanted to have a say in the prices for transporting crops. Behind the scenes during the Gilded Age, people in all parts of America hoped and worked for change.

> What important social reforms began during the Gilded Age?

200

Activity

Stories of Local Ministries

Discuss rescue missions and other local ministries that are supported by the churches your students attend. Students whose families help with those ministries could share their experiences. If possible, invite a speaker to come and tell about the history of those ministries and share experiences of helping with them.

Entertainment and the Arts
New Ways to Play

During the Gilded Age, Americans had more leisure time than in the past. People on farms had often worked from dawn till dusk. But now more people worked industrial or office jobs. They had many new time-saving inventions to help them. As a result, middle- and upper-class Americans worked fewer hours. They had more free time in the evenings and on weekends. The average American also had more money to spend on entertainment than in the past. And the cities were filled with things to see and do. Americans were quick to find many new ways to play.

One popular form of entertainment was watching and playing sports. Baseball and basketball were newly invented games at this time. Crowds watched baseball and boxing matches. Tennis and golf were common sports to play. With the invention of the bicycle, cycling became a leisure activity. Even women rode bicycles. Some of them adopted a different style of dress for riding. Bloomers, women's trousers with wide, billowy legs, were safer than skirts for cycling. However, many people criticized bloomers as a symbol of the women's rights movement. They thought that women were trying to dress too much like men. Most American women continued wearing dresses and skirts for all activities.

Other forms of entertainment included going to plays and operas. Another popular kind of show called vaudeville developed around this time. Vaudeville shows were made up of a series of short acts. A show might contain acrobats, clowns, jugglers, and musical numbers. One type of vaudeville show was all about life in the West. It included cowboys on horseback, gunslinging, and staged fights between Indians and white settlers. Many of these shows were appropriate family entertainment. However, sometimes Christians objected to the content of these shows and chose not to attend.

Expressions of the Times
Literature

Perhaps the most famous author of the Gilded Age is Samuel Clemens. He is better known by his pen name, Mark Twain. The name "Gilded Age" comes from the title of a book he and another author wrote together. Their novel showed the problems of greed and corruption during this era. Twain is also famous for his works about two young boys, Tom Sawyer and Huckleberry Finn.

Twain's writing was more realistic than the literature of the past. The children in his books did not always behave well. They often got into trouble. The trend toward **realism** was true of many works of literature of this time.

201

Lesson **78** | **Student Text pages 201–3**
Activity Manual page 141

Lesson Focus

- The average American had more leisure time and money to spend on entertainment than in the past.

Objectives
- Explain why Americans had more leisure time during the Gilded Age
- Identify forms of entertainment and the arts
- Evaluate the problems with newspapers

Teacher's Toolkit CD
- Visuals 28–29: *Annie Londonderry*; *Tiffany Lamps*

Review

- Choose volunteers to name three social reformers during the Gilded Age.
  Nellie Bly, Jacob Riis, Jane Addams

  Why were Bly, Riis, and Addams called social reformers? They cared enough about others to try to solve problems in society.

- Choose volunteers to explain the kinds of social reform that Bly, Riis, and Addams worked for.

  What were two organizations that worked for social reform? the Woman's Christian Temperance Union and the Salvation Army

- Choose volunteers to explain the differences between the Woman's Christian Temperance Union and the Salvation Army.

Preparation for Reading

- Generate interest as you direct the students to read the titles and examine the pictures on pages 201–3.

- Guide pronunciation of any unfamiliar words in the lesson.

- Direct the students to read the pages silently. Instruct pairs of students to draw a T-chart and list the forms of entertainment during the Gilded Age on one side of the T-chart. List the forms of the arts on the other side.

Teach for Understanding

- Invite students to explain why Americans had more leisure time during the Gilded Age than in the past. Before the Gilded Age people on farms had often worked from dawn till dusk. But during the Gilded Age, more people worked industrial or office jobs. They had many new time-saving inventions to help them. As a result, middle- and upper-class Americans worked fewer hours and had more free time in the evenings and on weekends.

  What else allowed the average American to enjoy different kinds of entertainment? The average American had more money than in the past.

- Invite pairs of students to name forms of entertainment that Americans enjoyed. watching and playing sports, cycling, going to plays, operas, and vaudeville shows

  What style of clothing did some women adopt for cycling? bloomers

- Display Visual 28. Choose a volunteer to read aloud the caption. Explain that some bloomers were more billowy then the ones worn by Londonderry.

- Why do you think bloomers were safer than skirts for cycling? Answers could include that bloomers would not become caught as easily in a bicycle's wheels or chain.

  Why did some people criticize bloomers? They thought bloomers were a symbol of the women's rights movement. They thought that women were trying to dress too much like men.

  What style of clothing did most women continue to wear for all activities? dresses and skirts

- Choose volunteers to tell what kind of acts might be included in vaudeville shows. acrobats, clowns, jugglers, musical numbers, cowboys on horseback, gunslinging, and staged fights between Indians and white settlers

Why did Christians sometimes choose not to attend vaudeville shows? They objected to the content of the shows.

- **Invite pairs of students to name forms of the arts that Americans enjoyed.** literature, art, music

- Why do you think literature, art, and music are included in the section titled "Expressions of the Times"? Answers could include that people can express themselves through literature, art, and music.

Who was perhaps the most famous author of the Gilded Age? Samuel Clemens, or Mark Twain

- Why do you think authors might choose to use a pen name? Answers could include that authors often exposed the problems of the Gilded Age. A pen name may have protected the author from the readers' reactions to people being presented as weak and sinful.

What works about two young boys is Twain famous for? his stories about Tom Sawyer and Huckleberry Finn

How was Twain's writing different from literature of the past? Twain's writing was more realistic.

Teach for Understanding

- **Choose a volunteer to read aloud the sentences that describe realism.**

Who were some other well-known authors of this time? Louisa May Alcott, William Dean Howells, and Stephen Crane

- **Invite students to explain why American art began to come into its own during the Gilded Age.**

What kind of art was popular among wealthy families? portraits

Who was the best-known portrait painter of the day? John Singer Sargent

Who was another well-known painter? Mary Cassatt

- **Use the illustration on page 202 to guide a discussion about about Sargent's painting and Cassatt's painting. Include a comparison of the two paintings.**

What did Candace Wheeler become famous for painting? textiles

What media did Wheeler use? paint, fabric, and wallpaper

What media did Tiffany use? paint and glass

Authors sought to portray life just as it was. Everyday events were the subjects of stories. People were presented as weak and sinful. The difficult side of life was not glossed over. Some other well-known authors of this time were Louisa May Alcott, William Dean Howells, and Stephen Crane.

Art

American art began to come into its own during the Gilded Age. The first art galleries were built in American cities. People enjoyed going to see works of art. Many people were wealthy enough to buy and display expensive paintings in their homes. Several American artists made a name for themselves with their own styles.

In wealthy families of this time, portraits were popular. People paid to have themselves or a family member represented on canvas. Then they would hang the painting in their homes. John Singer Sargent was the best-known portrait painter of the day. He painted portraits of presidents, millionaires, and upper-class women. He also sometimes painted scenes from his travels. Mary Cassatt was also a well-known painter. She often portrayed women and children in her work.

Artists worked with other materials, or media, besides paint and canvas. Candace Wheeler became famous for painting textiles. Her fabrics and wallpapers decorated the furniture and walls of many homes. Louis Comfort Tiffany did much of his design work in glass. He often cut and painted pieces of glass to create mosaic designs.

John Singer Sargent

Mary Cassatt

202

Background

Mark Twain

Samuel Langhorne Clemens, known as Mark Twain (his pen name), was born on November 30, 1835, in Florida, Missouri. Clemens lived in Hannibal, right on the Mississippi River, from the age of four to seventeen. Steamboats arrived several times a day, and the town was filled with the hustle and bustle of people coming and going. His mother loved to tell stories. After his father died, Clemens had to quit school and find a job. His first jobs were with newspapers and magazines. Clemens fulfilled his dream of becoming a river pilot in 1858. This experience had a big influence on his writing.

His novels *The Adventures of Tom Sawyer* and *The Adventures of Huckleberry Finn* became American classics. He wrote more than thirty books. He also wrote hundreds of essays, speeches, articles, reviews, and short stories. He married Olivia Langdon in 1870, and they had four children. Clemens died on April 21, 1910.

Additional Background information for this lesson is on the Teacher's Toolkit CD.

The Tiffany style of lampshade is still popular today.

Music

Attending concerts was a favorite pastime during the Gilded Age. Cities had concert halls where local performers filled the orchestra seats. Not only European operas, but also new music by American composers drew crowds to music halls. Marches by John Philip Sousa had audiences tapping their feet. The songs of Stephen Foster, such as "Oh! Susanna" and "Beautiful Dreamer," were popular. Black composer Scott Joplin was famous for a new style of piano music called ragtime. A major work of that time was the *New World* Symphony by Antonín Dvořák. The Bohemian composer wrote the symphony while living in America.

In the music he tried to express his feelings about the new land.

Newspapers

The press took on a new importance during the Gilded Age. Newspapers competed with each other for readers. Joseph Pulitzer and William Randolph Hearst both published newspapers in New York. But not everything they published was truthful. They added details to news stories to make them more exciting, hoping to sell more papers. In years to come, Americans would realize just how much influence newspapers can have on public thought.

> Why did Americans have more free time during the Gilded Age?

Candace Wheeler

Louis Comfort Tiffany

203

Activities

Realistic Stories

Challenge the students to use realism to write a fictional story about an actual event. Allow the students to use this opportunity to write an impromptu story without focusing on the writing process.

Works of Art

Materials: art paper; a variety of media such as fabrics, paints, markers, and different weights of yarn or string

Instruct the students to use media of their choosing to create a work of art such as a portrait, an outdoor scene, or a mosaic. Use the works of art to create a classroom art gallery.

Music Appreciation

Play samples of music selections written by composers discussed in this lesson. Guide a discussion about the genre of music each sample represents. Use Background information located on the Teacher's Toolkit CD to share information about the composers.

Teach for Understanding

What did Tiffany make using paint and glass? lampshades

Display Visual 29. Guide a discussion about the mosaic designs created for each lamp.

What was a favorite musical pastime during the Gilded Age? attending concerts

What kind of music was performed in concert halls? European operas, new music by American composers, marches, ragtime, symphonies

- Choose volunteers to name popular composers during the Gilded Age. John Philip Sousa, Stephen Foster, Scott Joplin, Antonín Dvořák

- Why do you think Antonín Dvořák's symphony is called the *New World* Symphony? Answers could include that he was Bohemian and wrote the symphony while living in America. In the music he tried to express his feelings about the new land.

Who were two important newspaper publishers during the Gilded Age? Joseph Pulitzer and William Randolph Hearst

Why were published news stories not always truthful? Newspapers competed with each other for readers. Publishers added details to news stories to make them more exciting, hoping to sell more papers.

- Do you think it was right for publishers to add untruthful details to news stories? Answers could include that telling anything untruthful is lying, which is against God's Word. Since newspapers influence public thought, untruthful details could be used to sway public thought or opinion.

> Conclude the discussion by asking the question on page 203. More people worked industrial or office jobs. They had many new time-saving inventions to help them.

Activity Manual

- Guide completion of page 141.

79

Student Text pages 204–5
Activity Manual pages 142–44

Lesson Focus

- God raised up people to meet spiritual needs in the Gilded Age.

Objectives

- Explain the two main problems that arose among Christians
- Describe the ministries of Christians who met spiritual needs

Teacher's Toolkit CD

- Instructional Aid 46: *Meeting Spiritual Needs*

Review

What forms of entertainment and the arts did Americans enjoy during the Gilded Age? watching and playing sports, cycling, going to plays, operas, and vaudeville shows

Why were many Americans able to enjoy these activities? They had more leisure time, or free time, and more money to spend on entertainment than in the past.

- Choose volunteers to explain why Americans had more leisure time.
- Invite students to explain the problem with newspapers during the Gilded Age.

Preparation for Reading

- Generate interest as you direct the students to examine the picture and read the titles on pages 204–5.
- Guide pronunciation of any unfamiliar words in the lesson.
- Direct the students to read the pages silently and complete Instructional Aid 46 in small groups.

Teach for Understanding

Who attacked the Bible during the 1800s? many scholars in America's colleges

- Invite volunteers to explain why and how scholars attacked the Bible. They exalted their God-given reason above the Bible's authority rather than using reason as a tool for understanding the Bible. Some scholars did not believe the Bible was inspired by God. They rejected the Bible's accounts of miracles. They found fault with some of its most important doctrines. Some denied the deity of Christ.

How were Christians affected by what these scholars said? Christians struggled to know how to think. Some listened to the scholars. Some believers who were unsettled in their faith wanted to know if there was truth in what these men were saying.

- Choose a volunteer to read aloud the captions about B. B. Warfield. Discuss his character.
- Invite a group to explain how B. B. Warfield responded to scholars rejecting key doctrines of the Christian faith.

Religion in the Gilded Age
Defending the Bible

During the 1800s, the Bible came under attack by many scholars in America's colleges. These scholars did not use their God-given reason as a tool for understanding the Bible. Instead, they exalted their reason above the Bible's authority. Some scholars did not believe the Bible was inspired by God. They rejected the Bible's accounts of miracles. They found fault with some of its most important doctrines. Some denied the deity of Christ.

Christians struggled to know how to think about these matters. Some people in America's churches respected and listened to these highly educated scholars. Some believers were unsettled in their faith. They wanted to know if there was truth in what these men were saying.

B. B. Warfield was a teacher at Princeton Theological Seminary in New Jersey. He was one of the best scholars of his time. He saw that modern scholars were rejecting key doctrines of the Christian faith.

A volume on American birds and mammals is said to have been Warfield's chief treasure when he was young.

Benjamin Breckinridge Warfield was once described as "a gentleman to his fingertips" by the president of Princeton.

Warfield studied math and physics in college but later became one of the greatest Bible scholars of his day.

He was able to point out the weaknesses in the arguments of these scholars. He spoke out for the truth of the Bible and its doctrines. He wrote articles encouraging Christians to take the Bible at its word.

The Social Gospel

Another problem arose among Christians during the Gilded Age. Social reformers of the day were placing great emphasis on meeting people's physical needs. Many Christians wanted to improve people's living conditions. They tried to help people with both physical and spiritual needs. They sought to follow Christ's example of compassion. They hoped to make a difference in society along with sharing the gospel. But some Christians began to lose sight of what was most important. They thought that preventing problems like poverty and drunkenness was more important than telling people about Christ. These Christians had been influenced by the unbelieving scholars who had

204

What was greatly emphasized by social reformers during the Gilded Age? meeting people's physical needs

- Choose volunteers to explain how many Christians responded to meeting people's physical needs. Explanations should include that many Christians wanted to help and sought to follow Christ's example of compassion. They tried to help people with both physical and spiritual needs, hoping to make a difference in society along with sharing the gospel.

How were some Christians influenced by the unbelieving scholars? They began to lose sight of the gospel being the most important. They thought that preventing problems like poverty and drunkenness was more important than telling people about Christ.

Which movement placed social reform above the salvation of souls? the Social Gospel

- Do you think the Social Gospel continues to be a problem among Christians today? Answers could include that some who identify as Christians still think they can bring about a social salvation by Christianizing the nation. Although not opposed to individual salvation, they often confuse it with moral improvement.

- Use the Background information about the Social Gospel to impress on the students that telling people about Christ is more important than meeting physical needs.

denied key Bible doctrines. They emphasized doing good works above the gospel. The movement that placed social reform above the salvation of souls was called the Social Gospel. This movement had its beginning in the Gilded Age. But it became much larger as America moved into the twentieth century.

D. L. Moody

Dwight L. Moody trusted Jesus Christ after his Sunday school teacher shared the gospel with him. He then moved to Chicago. There he began a mission Sunday school for the youth of the city. He realized that more than anything, people needed Christ.

Because so many of America's people were city dwellers, Moody focused his ministry in cities. He began a church in Chicago. He later became a traveling evangelist. Eventually he opened Christian schools for young people. His ministry reached thousands of people, both in America and overseas, with the message of salvation in Christ.

Gospel Hymns

Along with Moody's ministry, a new style of hymn became common in America's churches. Ira Sankey traveled with Moody and sang at his meetings. He began writing songs that focused on the gospel. These new songs were often more personal than many well-known hymns. They helped people express their feelings about what Christ had done for

them. Many of these songs encouraged unbelievers to place their trust in Christ.

Perhaps the most famous writer of gospel hymns in America was **Fanny Crosby**. Blind from childhood, she taught for many years at a school for the blind in New York City. Later she spent most of her time writing hymns. She also visited the tenements and prisons of the city. She spoke to people she met about Christ. She is believed to have written thousands of hymns, although not all of them were published under her own name. Hymns such as "Blessed Assurance," "To God Be the Glory," and "Rescue the Perishing" have been loved and sung for more than a century.

Beneath the Glitter

In many ways America sparkled with wealth and progress during its Gilded Age. Cities flourished, industries grew, and people prospered. But beneath the glitter of America's Gilded Age were many problems and needs. God raised up people who saw these needs. Individuals tried in various ways to make life better for all Americans. Now the nation stood poised at the edge of a new century. The twentieth century would bring changes to America that people in the Gilded Age had only begun to imagine.

> Who were some of the people God used to meet spiritual needs in the Gilded Age?

205

> Additional Background information for this lesson is on the Teacher's Toolkit CD.

Teach for Understanding

Who shared the gospel with D. L. Moody? *his Sunday school teacher*

- Invite a group to explain what D. L. Moody did to spread the gospel.

What style of hymn became common in America's churches during the Gilded Age? *gospel hymns*

Who are two people who wrote gospel hymns during the Gilded Age? *Ira Sankey and Fanny Crosby*

- Invite groups to explain what Ira Sankey and Fanny Crosby did to meet spiritual needs.

- Choose a volunteer to read aloud the titles of some hymns written by Fanny Crosby.

How did America sparkle during its Gilded Age? *Cities flourished, industries grew, and people prospered.*

Who raised up people to see the needs during the Gilded Age? *God*

▶ Conclude the discussion by asking the question on page 205. *B. B. Warfield, D. L. Moody, Ira Sankey, Fanny Crosby*

Primary Source: Gospel Song

- Guide the students in reading "Blessed Assurance." Discuss what might have led Fanny Crosby to write the hymn.

Activity Manual

- Guide completion of pages 142–44.

Background

The Social Gospel

What makes the Social Gospel different from orthodox Christianity is not seeking social reforms that end true injustice or the providing of food, medical aid, and other care for those truly in need. Christians had done these kinds of good works long before the Social Gospel existed. The Social Gospel is different from orthodox Christianity because it sees these works as ways of saving society. Followers thought they could bring the kingdom of God about on the earth through their works. Though the early Social Gospelers did think that individuals needed to be saved from their sins, they did not believe that people were saved by trusting Jesus who died in their place. Eventually the need of individuals for salvation from sin became lost in the emphasis on social reform.

B. B. Warfield

B. B. Warfield was a Princeton-educated theologian who sought to uphold Princeton's demanding scholarship while actively resisting the spread of religious liberalism. He effectively used his pen to defend the authority and accuracy of Scripture against the assaults of various unscriptural philosophies, including those developed by Friedrich Schleiermacher and Immanuel Kant. Warfield also wrote to refute the growing influence of evolution. His writings helped to lay the foundation for Fundamentalism.

Activities

Read a Biography

Encourage the students to read a biography of B. B. Warfield, D. L. Moody, Ira Sankey, or Fanny Crosby. Direct them to write a brief report about the life of the person they choose. Allow time for the students to share their reports with the class.

Sing Gospel Hymns

Lead the students in singing a variety of gospel hymns written by Ira Sankey and Fanny Crosby.

80

Objective
- Recall concepts and terms from Chapter 9

Teacher's Toolkit CD
- Instructional Aid 47: *Build a Skyscraper*

Introduction

- Concepts for the Chapter 9 Test will be taken from Activity Manual pages 129–46. You may review any or all of the concepts during this lesson. You may choose to review Chapter 9 by playing "Build a Skyscraper."

Review Game: Build a Skyscraper

- Prepare a list of questions and answers to use for review. Make enough copies of Instructional Aid 47 to allow a section of skyscraper for each question, excluding the first (ground) floor and the roof.
- Cut out the skyscraper sections and write a question on the back of each. Stack the sections with the skyscraper side up.
- Divide the class into teams. Display the first floor of a skyscraper as the starting point for each team.
- Direct the first player to choose a question, read it aloud, and then give the answer. Attach a section of skyscraper to the corresponding team's display for each correct answer. Continue rotating teams and players until all the questions have been answered. The team whose skyscraper is the tallest wins the game.

Activity Manual

- Guide completion of pages 145–46.

Objective
- Demonstrate knowledge of concepts from Chapter 9 by taking the test

Assessment
- Administer Test 9.

Chapter 10

10 America's Influence Spreads Abroad

Introduction

America had made many improvements by the twentieth century. It was ready to be involved with other nations because of the growth of businesses, the desire to share the gospel, and the fear rooted in social Darwinism that European nations would dominate the world. America grew in its influence in foreign affairs. US forces fought to end Spanish oppression in Cuba. After a peace treaty ended the Spanish-American War, the United States gained Cuba, Puerto Rico, Guam, and the Philippines from Spain.

There were changes in voting in both urban and rural areas. President Roosevelt and President Taft ran a Progressive foreign policy. Progressives addressed problems related to workers in America. Black Americans struggled for equality. Progressives improved schools because they believed that knowledge would bring improvements to the nation. Progressivism continued as Congress passed reforms under President Woodrow Wilson. Progressive changes were set aside for a while due to a war in Europe. But in spite of all the changes that Progressives made, the United States still had problems.

Chapter Focus

The United States prospered and tried to improve itself and other nations.

Focus
The United States prospered and tried to improve itself and other nations.

Lesson	Student Text	Activity Manual	Content		Vocabulary	
82	206–9	147–49	Expanding US influence Election of 1896 Cuba	William Jennings Bryan William McKinley	annex coup	
83	210–12	150–51	Spanish-American War Theodore Roosevelt	George Dewey Anti-Imperialist League	Rough Riders USS *Maine*	yellow journalism
84	213–15	152–53	Progressive Era	Biography Box: Lincoln Steffens	conservation	trust busting
85	216–19	154–55	Progressivism in the Cities Voting Reform and Suffrage		initiative recall	referendum
86	220–22	156–57	Election of 1908 and William H. Taft		commercial Open Door Policy	Panama Canal
87	223–25	158	Progressivism in the workplace Primary Source: *Up from Slavery: An Autobiography* Booker T. Washington	W. E. B. Du Bois	Socialism	
88	226–29	159–60	How It Was: A new life in America Progressive education	Woodrow Wilson Activity: Public Participation		
89		161–62	Chapter Review			
90			Chapter Test			

Chapter 10 Overview

Visit bjupress.com/resources for links to enhance the lessons.

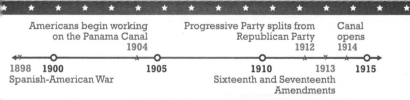

Americans begin working
on the Panama Canal
1904

Progressive Party splits from
Republican Party
1912

Canal
opens
1914

1898 **1900**   **1905**   **1910**   **1913**   **1915**
Spanish-American War   Sixteenth and Seventeenth
Amendments

At the turn of the century, America wanted improvement. The United States was doing well. Most people had jobs. Cities were growing. Farms were producing more food. But there were also problems. No one thought the Gilded Age was perfect. Dishonesty, sickness, and poverty threatened the life, liberty, and happiness of many Americans. Other countries suffered from worse conditions. Those who had enjoyed the improvements of the last century wanted more people to share in them.

US Expansion

In 1896 few Americans would have imagined their nation beginning an empire. They remembered that the United States had once been thirteen colonies. The Revolutionary War had freed them from the British Empire. Some nations still had empires. The British Empire stretched across the globe. France controlled large areas in Africa and Asia. Even Spain still owned a few colonies. One of these, **Cuba,**

lay just ninety miles south of Florida. Americans did not approve of empires.

However, Americans had several reasons to want to be involved with other nations. Growing businesses in America wanted more international trade. Some goods, such as ivory, could not be found in the United States. American factory owners needed new markets. They wanted to sell their goods around the world. Another reason for American involvement in other nations was the gospel. American missionaries shared the Bible around the world. Christians wanted to have more opportunities to bring the good news to people who had never heard it. Social Darwinism was a third reason for desiring more influence. This theory argued that people and nations were always competing. Whichever nation was stronger and faster would survive. Some Americans feared that European nations would take over the whole world. Americans wanted their power to prevent European domination. Even though these reasons influenced most

207

Lesson **82** **Student Text pages 206–9**
Activity Manual pages 147–49

Lesson Focus

• America had a growing influence in the world.

Objectives
• Examine American involvement with foreign countries
• Analyze William Jennings Bryan's and William McKinley's 1896 campaign

Teacher's Toolkit CD
• Visual 30: *A Victory for McKinley*

Introduction

• Invite a student to read aloud the title of the chapter and predict what the chapter will be about. the spread of American influence around the world

• Invite a student to read the chapter focus aloud.

What do you think you will learn in this chapter? how America grew and tried to make improvements at home and around the world

• Direct attention to the timeline.

What happened in 1898? the Spanish-American War

When did Americans begin working on the Panama Canal? 1904

When did the canal open? 1914

Preparation for Reading

• Generate interest as you direct the students to read the titles and examine the picture on pages 206–9.

• Guide pronunciation of any unfamiliar words in the lesson.

What do you see in the picture? men digging a large trench or ditch with water in the background

• Explain that the image depicts men working on the Panama Canal. Upon completion, the canal allowed ships to carry goods faster and cheaper between the Atlantic and Pacific Oceans.

• Direct the students to read the pages silently to discover the three reasons Americans wanted to be involved with other countries. growing businesses, the gospel, social Darwinism

Teach for Understanding

Why did America want more international trade? Some goods could not be found in the United States. American factory owners looked for new markets. They wanted to sell their goods around the world.

How did the gospel encourage some Americans to be involved with other nations? They wanted more opportunities to share the gospel around the world.

• Invite a student to explain how social Darwinism caused America to want more international influence. This theory argued that people and nations were always competing, and whichever nation was stronger and faster would survive. Americans wanted their power to prevent European domination.

Teach for Understanding

- Invite volunteers to locate *coup* and *annex* in the Glossary and read aloud the definitions.

  Who created a coup that overthrew Queen Liliuokalani of Hawaii? a group of rich landowners

  How did these landowners feel about the queen's policies? They felt that her policies were unjust and harmful.

  How did President Grover Cleveland feel about the land-owners overthrowing the queen? He questioned whether it was just.

- Why do you think the overthrow was unjust? The Bible tells us to obey and honor rulers.

- Guide a discussion of how rulers should be treated according to Romans 13:1–7 and 1 Peter 2:13–17.

  What was the relationship between the US and Hawaiian governments after President Cleveland refused to annex Hawaii? The two governments remained on friendly terms, and American ships continued to use Hawaii's Pearl Harbor.

  What was the central issue in the dispute between Britain and Venezuela? the border between Britain's colony and Venezuela

  What demand was made by President Cleveland that Britain agreed to? to allow other nations to help settle the dispute

  Between what countries did the United States intervene to settle a dispute? Britain and Venezuela

  Who were the candidates in the election of 1896? William Jennings Bryan and William McKinley

  What was the biggest debatable issue for the election? free silver

  What was McKinley's position on free silver? He opposed it. He wanted to keep the value of currency from changing.

Americans, the United States did not set out to build an empire.

The United States was not trying to gain colonies, but it was growing in international importance. Businessmen and missionaries traveled around the world. Wherever American citizens went, the United States tried to protect them. Two independent nations also asked for American involvement in their countries.

Growing American Influence

In 1893 a **coup** occurred in the kingdom of Hawaii. The queen was overthrown by a group of rich men. Many were of American descent. They felt that Queen Liliuokalani's policies were unjust and harmful. These men wanted the United States to **annex** Hawaii. President Grover Cleveland refused. He questioned whether over-throwing the queen was just. But the United States remained on friendly terms with the government set up by the coup and continued to use Hawaii's Pearl Harbor.

The United States also helped settle another international conflict. Britain owned a colony in South America called British Guiana. Its neighbor, Venezuela, was an independent nation. When Britain and Venezuela could not agree on the border, it seemed that Britain might use force to gain the land. President Cleveland demanded that Britain allow other nations to help decide the dispute. Eventually Britain agreed. The United States had gotten its way. But although the United States had some foreign involvement, most Americans were not concerned about foreign countries.

Election of 1896 and a New President

In 1896 Americans had two choices for a new president. The Democratic Party chose **William Jennings Bryan** as its candidate. Although he was only thirty-six, Bryan had already served two terms as a representative from Nebraska. Bryan was a good speaker. **William McKinley** was the candidate for the Republicans. He had experience as a politician, and he had been a Union officer in the Civil War. Later he was an Ohio congressman and then the state's governor.

The biggest debatable issue for the election was free silver. By the 1890s, American money was based on gold. The government allowed only some silver to be turned into coins. Any gold could be minted into coins. However, far more silver than gold was mined at this time. Bryan wanted the United States government to freely mint silver into coins. Having more government money would raise prices. Farmers

Background

Pacific Expansion

The most important Pacific addition to the United States was Hawaii (also known as the Sandwich Islands). The Hawaiian Islands had been an important supply point for whalers, merchant ships, and warships since the 1700s. In the early 1800s, American missionaries had come to the islands and had enjoyed remarkable success in winning many islanders to Christ. Unfortunately, many Americans who followed the missionaries—and sadly, the sons of the missionaries themselves—proved more interested in profit than in souls. American investors soon built a thriving sugar industry that dominated the economy of the islands and, indeed, helped the islands prosper.

Until 1891, Hawaii was ruled by native kings who usually went along with the sugarcane planters' wishes. In that year, however, Queen Liliuokalani (lih-lee-uh-wah-kah-lah-nee) took the throne. She tried to reestablish native control of the island and limit the power of the planters. In 1893, the planters revolted against "Queen Lil" and asked to be annexed to the United States. President Grover Cleveland, how-ever, refused to approve the uprising and blocked annexation of the islands. Like Texas after its war for independence, Hawaii was forced to exist for several years as an independent republic. In 1898, however,

McKinley did not go around the country campaigning, but spoke to crowds from his front porch.

He was the last president to have served in the Civil War. He served under Colonel Rutherford B. Hayes.

McKinley was shot by an anarchist. He died eight days later. The last words on his lips were from the hymn "Nearer, My God, to Thee." It was sung at his funeral and in churches all around the country.

would earn more money. William McKinley opposed free silver. He said that Republican ideas were best. These ideas included keeping the value of currency from changing. McKinley did not want prices to rise quickly. Rising prices would also mean that farmers paid more for goods.

Bryan received support from the Populist Party as well as from the

Democrats. Populists mainly lived in the South and West. They thought that big businesses did not care about farmers. They feared that rich businessmen might control the election of politicians. The Populists decided that Bryan's message for free silver might help them. In 1896 they supported the Democratic candidate as their own.

During the campaign both men argued this case differently. Bryan traveled the country by train. He gave exciting speeches on the topic of silver. Millions of Americans heard Bryan speak. McKinley did not travel at all because his wife was often ill. In addition, McKinley knew that he could not speak as often or as well as Bryan. Instead, McKinley had a front-porch campaign. Americans traveled to his home in Ohio, and he spoke to them from his porch. Of course, newspapers reported on both men. Even Americans who never heard them speak knew what Bryan and McKinley stood for.

In November 1896, Americans finally voted. McKinley won. Despite all the effort Bryan had made, he could not get enough voters.

Which political parties supported Bryan in 1896?

209

Teach for Understanding

- Direct attention to the picture of President McKinley. Use the captions to guide a discussion.

  How did McKinley and Bryan campaign differently? Bryan traveled the country by train and gave exciting speeches on the topic of silver. McKinley did not travel at all. He had a front-porch campaign.

  Who won the election? McKinley

  > Conclude the discussion by asking the question on page 209. the Democratic Party, the Populists

Activity Manual

- Guide completion of pages 147–49.

when McKinley was in office and a war with Spain was making the United States nervous about the security of the Pacific, Congress voted to annex the islands.

Populism and Free Silver

Amid the hard times and the economic complexities of industrialism, silver became a seemingly simple solution for the down-and-out, a kind of patent medicine for all economic ills. In the Midwest, free silver became the battle cry for the Populist legions. Not even the major parties were immune from the growing Populist force. Lacking, however, the organizational, financial, and numerical strength of the major parties, the Populists decided to cast their lot with the more sympathetic Democratic Party in the 1896 presidential election. The result was a colorful, crucial contest—part campaign, part crusade.

The Importance of the 1896 Election

The 1896 election was a turning point in American political history, the culmination of the struggle between the past and the future, between the farm and the factory—and the factory won. The rural leadership that Populism represented was growing old with the century. For good or for bad, America's future lay amid crowded city streets.

Activity

Examine the 1896 Election Results

Display Visual 30. Read aloud the title of the map. Invite a volunteer to explain the map key and the map. Guide a discussion of the areas in which each candidate won electoral votes. Point out the names of the three territories that did not vote in the election.

83

Student Text pages 210–12
Activity Manual pages 150–51

Lesson Focus

- President McKinley dealt with the conflict between Spain and Cuba.

Objectives

- Describe events leading to the Spanish-American War
- Examine the course of the war
- Analyze the consequences of the war

Teacher's Toolkit CD

- Instructional Aid 48: *The Spanish-American War*

Review

- Invite a student to state three reasons America wanted to be involved with other nations.

> Guide a review of important terms, maps, places, and people from each previous lesson. Direct the students to find and read the corresponding entries from the Resource Treasury.

- Choose a volunteer to describe the election of 1896.

Preparation for Reading

- Generate interest as you direct the students to read the titles and examine the pictures and infograph on pages 210–12.
- Guide pronunciation of any unfamiliar words in the lesson.
- Direct the students to read the pages and complete Instructional Aid 48 in small groups.

Teach for Understanding

- Explain the meaning of the infograph on page 210.

What led President McKinley to send the USS *Maine* to Cuba? Spain reacted harshly to a rebellion against Spanish rule in Cuba. Many Americans demanded that President McKinley help the suffering Cubans. Yellow journalism awakened American emotions.

- Invite a student to read the sentences that suggest what yellow journalism does.

What is yellow journalism used for today? Answers could include that news stories use yellow journalism to promote social and political issues.

What did McKinley say that sending the USS *Maine* to Cuba would ensure? American safety in Cuba.

What did the Spanish ambassador to the United States do that angered Americans? He insulted McKinley in a letter.

What made the situation between the United States and Spain even worse? The *Maine* exploded in Havana.

What do you think caused the *Maine* to explode?

214

Spanish-American War

Almost as soon as McKinley became president, he had to deal with conflict between Spain and Cuba. Americans became concerned about their Cuban neighbors, located less than one hundred miles off the coast of Florida. Cuba had been ruled by Spain for four hundred years. For many years Cubans wanted independence. They fought to drive out the Spanish several times.

Causes

By 1895 the Spanish Empire had lost most of its American colonies. Cuba was the largest island in the Caribbean and also wanted to be free. In 1895 the Cubans rebelled against Spain for a third time.

Spain reacted harshly. Spanish troops fought the rebel soldiers and mistreated civilians. Spanish general Valeriano Weyler made the farmers leave their farms so that they could not help the rebels. In the overcrowded towns, people often lacked food. Disease killed many civilians.

Many Americans demanded that President McKinley help the suffering Cubans. Americans often favored the rebels. **Yellow journalism** awakened American emotions. Papers published stories about Spain's treatment of Cubans. Sometimes papers tried to make stories more shocking than they already were. But the horrors of Cuba rarely needed that help.

The US president responded calmly. In January 1898 he sent a ship, the **USS Maine**, to Havana, Cuba. McKinley said the ship would ensure American safety in Cuba. Then in early February, Americans learned that the Spanish ambassador, Enrique Dupuy de Lôme, had insulted McKinley in a letter. Americans were angry with Spain and its ambassador. He left the United States in disgrace.

The situation only got worse. On February 15, 1898, the *Maine* exploded in Havana. There was no proof of Spain's guilt, but Spanish troops had treated the Cubans badly and the ambassador had insulted McKinley. Many Americans believed that Spain

CAUSES LEADING TO WAR

| Civilian Oppression | De Lôme Letter | USS *Maine* Explosion |

210

Background

The Spanish-American War

The climax of American imperialism came in 1898, when the United States went to war with Spain over that nation's treatment of its colony of Cuba. Although the Cubans had intermittently revolted against the Spanish government for decades, a revolt that broke out in 1895 was unusually serious. A depression with its resulting unemployment—combined with weak, corrupt Spanish rule over the colony—provided ideal conditions for an insurrection. Bands of guerillas destroyed sugar mills, plantations, and anything else the people loyal to Spain valued. To stop the wanton destruction, Spanish troops arrested rebels and put them in barbed-wire concentration camps, where many of them died of starvation or disease. As American newspapers sensationalized the brutal Spanish suppression of the rebels, American sympathy grew.

American public opinion became inflamed with the sensationalized news reported through yellow journalism. The Spanish ambassador insulted President McKinley in a letter. Then the battleship *Maine* exploded. These events contributed to the ill feelings that Americans felt toward Spain. McKinley caved in to political pressure and gave Congress a war message. Congress demanded Spain's withdrawal from Cuba and authorized the president to use force if necessary. Spain refused, and the result was the Spanish-American War.

had blown up the American ship. They demanded consequences.

President McKinley agreed to fight to free Cuba. Congress declared that the United States should help Cuba gain its independence. On April 21, the US navy began a blockade of the island. The war had begun.

Course of the War

The United States Navy began the fight against Spain. The American navy of steam-propelled steel ships was one of the best navies in the world. Two Americans in particular had encouraged having a strong navy. Alfred Thayer Mahan wrote books about the history of the navy and taught American naval officers who studied at the Naval War College. **Theodore Roosevelt** served from April 1897 to May 1898 as assistant secretary of the navy. These men and others had prepared the navy to fight.

The United States quickly dealt with Spain's two fleets. The Spanish Pacific Fleet was based in Manila Bay in the Spanish colony of the Philippines. On May 1, American commodore **George Dewey** sunk or

captured every ship of Spain's fleet. No Americans died. Later in May, American ships trapped the other Spanish fleet in the harbor of Santiago in Cuba. The oceans were clear of Spanish attack.

Getting the army ready took a longer time than clearing the seas did. The United States Army had fought no major war since 1865. It needed more men. Volunteers and state National Guard units joined to fight, but the training and transport took time too. Finally in late June, American soldiers landed in Cuba to drive out the Spanish.

The American army first needed to capture the city of Santiago. On July 1, American forces attacked Spanish defenses outside the city. In this battle, Theodore Roosevelt famously led the **Rough Riders'** charge uphill against Spanish guns. The American forces were victorious, and Roosevelt's fame was ensured.

The rest of the war continued with success. American forces had besieged Santiago. On July 3, Americans defeated the Spanish fleet there. Two weeks later, Spain's troops in the city surrendered. In late July and August, American forces invaded the

Roosevelt was awarded the Medal of Honor for his actions at San Juan Hill. The award was given after his death.

211

- Direct attention to the picture of Theodore Roosevelt. Read the caption aloud.

What was the reaction of many Americans to the ship blowing up? They believed that Spain had blown up the ship, and they demanded consequences.

What did President McKinley agree to do? fight to free Cuba

What contributed to the United States having one of the strongest navies in the world? Americans had encouraged having a strong navy. Alfred Thayer Mahan wrote books about the history of the navy and taught American naval officers who studied at the Naval War College. Theodore Roosevelt and others had prepared the navy to fight.

Which US commodore sunk or captured every ship of Spain's fleet? George Dewey

What was the name of the group that Theodore Roosevelt led in a charge uphill against Spanish guns? the Rough Riders

Activities

Sorting Out the Spanish-American War

Divide the students into pairs. Give each student ten slips of paper. Direct the students to write an event of the Spanish-American War on each slip and then to shuffle the slips. Invite the students to trade slips and put the events in chronological order.

Display Ships

Use resources to learn about ships that were used by the United States in the war against Spain and about naval ships that are used today. Display pictures of the ships. Guide a discussion of how naval ships have changed.

Teach for Understanding

Where else did the United States intervene after defeating the Spanish forces at Santiago? Puerto Rico and Guam

What did the United States gain from the treaty with Spain? Cuba, Puerto Rico, Guam, the Philippines

How much money did the United States pay for the Philippines? twenty million dollars

What terms did the United States set for Cuban independence? The United States could intervene if it ever feared that Cuba was falling under foreign control. Also, the American navy would get a base in Cuba.

What was the outcome of Filipinos wanting independence from the United States? They lost the fight with US troops. The United States kept control of the islands.

What motive did the US have for keeping control of the Philippines? Answers should include that America feared other nations might conquer the Philippines. The US wanted a base there.

What territory did Congress vote to annex in July 1898? Hawaii

What organization was formed that opposed America gaining colonies? the Anti-Imperialist League

What arguments did the organization have against gaining colonies? It argued that ruling over nations was immoral. Any people ruled by the US government without their consent were not free.

Conclude the discussion by asking the question on page 212. The United States thought that the Philippines was too weak. The United States wanted a base in the Far East.

Activity Manual

- Guide completion of pages 150–51.

Activity

Learn About the Philippines

Locate the Philippines on a map. Discuss its location in reference to the United States.

Provide resources about the Philippines. Divide the students into groups. Direct each group to learn several facts about the Philippines. Invite each group to share what it learned.

island of Puerto Rico and defeated the Spanish. Americans also claimed the Pacific island of Guam. On August 12, 1898, Spain agreed to a ceasefire and made peace with the United States.

Consequences

A peace treaty officially ended the war. The United States gained Cuba, Puerto Rico, and Guam from Spain. Spain also gave up the Philippines, but the United States had to pay twenty million dollars for the islands. Now the United States had decisions to make. When should Cuba become an independent country? Should the Philippines gain independence? Victory brought new problems.

Congress dealt with Cuba. Before the war began, Congress passed an amendment promising Cubans their independence. Some Americans questioned whether Cuba could keep itself free. Eventually Congress said that the United States could intervene if it ever feared that an independent Cuba was falling under foreign control. Also, the American navy would get a base in Cuba. The United States refused to give Cuba independence until it agreed to these terms. In 1901 Cuba agreed.

The Philippines also wanted independence, but the United States thought that the country was too weak. European nations might try to conquer it. The United States wanted a base in

the Far East. Some Filipinos fought American troops for independence, but they lost. The United States kept control of the islands.

The United States also gained small islands during the war. Puerto Rico and Guam became US possessions. In July 1898, Congress voted to annex Hawaii as a territory. President McKinley agreed that the United States needed a secure base in the Pacific. Despite some objections, Hawaii became a possession of America.

The Spanish-American War changed the United States. By defeating the Spanish, the United States became one of the leading world powers. It gained possessions around the globe. The country had taken on an important role in the world.

Not all Americans liked the new colonies. In 1898 some Americans formed the **Anti-Imperialist League**. It opposed the United States gaining colonies and argued that ruling over nations was immoral. Any people ruled by the US government without their consent were not free. After 1898, the United States rarely expanded in size. American businesses spread around the world, but America did not control foreign lands.

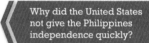
Why did the United States not give the Philippines independence quickly?

212

Background

Philippines

One major problem that Theodore Roosevelt inherited from McKinley was the situation in the Philippines. Even after the surrender of Emilio Aguinaldo and the end of the insurrection, the Filipinos were not content with American rule; they wanted independence. Roosevelt approached the Philippine problem warily. The governor of the islands, his friend and adviser William Howard Taft, tried to win the affection of the Filipinos. American leaders desired to maintain a foothold in the Pacific and feared that if the islands were granted independence too quickly, they might fall prey to another major power, such as Japan. Therefore, over a period of thirty years, the United States gradually gave the Filipinos increasing amounts of self-rule. After its liberation from Japanese occupation during World War II, the Philippines received complete independence in 1946.

Theodore Roosevelt

American Progress

After the Spanish-American War, the United States entered into the **Progressive Era**. Progressives wanted changes to improve their nation. They saw problems with possible solutions. Some Americans were concerned about living conditions of the people. Others were concerned about their morals. Some Progressives were Republicans; others were Democrats. Progressives did agree on one thing. The United States needed change, and a better-informed government would be able to make those changes.

Progressives often dealt with problems in a scientific way. Causes of problems had to be identified. If human behavior caused them, then people needed to be trained or restrained. If nature caused problems, it should be limited. Many Progressives had faith in science's ability to bring improvements.

New President

The White House saw an early change in the Progressive Era. In 1900 William McKinley was reelected with Theodore Roosevelt as his new vice president. But several months into the new term, an assassin killed President McKinley, and Theodore Roosevelt became the twenty-sixth president.

Roosevelt: A Brief Biography

Theodore Roosevelt's early life did not suggest that he would become president. The Roosevelts were a rich New York family. Theodore was often ill as a child. His parents hired private tutors and sent him on educational travels. He became healthy and well-informed.

During the 1880s, Roosevelt's life changed greatly. In 1880 he earned a degree at Harvard and was married. Two years later Roosevelt wrote a book, *The Naval War of 1812*, that showed his academic gifts. Then in 1884, his wife and mother died. That same year the man he supported for the presidency lost, hurting Roosevelt's career. Over the next two years, he spent many months on a ranch in the Dakotas.

But Roosevelt did not give up on his life or his political career. In 1886 he returned east and remarried. He also ran for mayor of

Roosevelt was born with asthma and severe nearsightedness. Few would have imagined that he would grow up to box in college, climb the Matterhorn, ranch in the Dakotas, serve as a Rough Rider, and become president.

213

Progressive Movement

Progressivism was a movement of the early twentieth century that favored achieving political and social reform through education, wider political participation, and direct government action. The Progressive movement had its roots in several nineteenth-century movements. Some Progressives, such as William Jennings Bryan, had been adherents of Populism. Others were outright Socialists. Still others were from the ranks of pro-reform Republican factions such as the Half-Breeds and the Mugwumps. Many people in the movement were members of the middle and upper classes who were shocked by the abuses of some industrialists, the corruption in government, and the plight of the poor.

The Progressives' motives varied. Many Progressives were simply moral Americans whose sense of justice was outraged. They looked at the abuses and corruption around them and concluded that something had to be done. Some of the Progressives, however, were evolutionary in their thinking. In their view, because man supposedly had been evolving and improving from a lower form of life to a higher form, he should continue to improve and progress. To these reform Darwinists, progress was a process of the natural order that could be aided by government intervention. Some Christians strongly opposed the unbiblical evolutionary view of progress but still supported Progressive reforms.

Lesson Focus

- During the Progressive Era, some Americans wanted to make changes to improve America.

Objectives
- Examine changes that Roosevelt made during his presidency

Review

- Choose a volunteer to identify the events that led to the Spanish-American War.
- Invite a volunteer to name the armed forces that Theodore Roosevelt led against the Spanish in the fight for Santiago.
- Guide a review of the consequences of the peace treaty between the United States and Spain.

Preparation for Reading

- Generate interest as you direct the students to read the titles and examine the pictures on pages 213–15.
- Guide pronunciation of any unfamiliar words in the lesson.
- Direct the students to read the pages silently to learn what Theodore Roosevelt set up to observe the nation's resources. the National Conservation Commission

Teach for Understanding

What did Progressives want during the Progressive Era? They wanted changes to improve their nation.

What did many Progressives believe had the ability to bring improvements? science

- Explain that Progressives rightly recognized the need to ensure justice. But their policies represented an overly optimistic view of human nature. They had a misplaced trust in the reliability of scientific experts. Sometimes this view led to actual injustices being perpetrated in the name of science and justice. A key example is when people use scientific theories and techniques to justify racism.

What happened several months into the new term after the election of 1900? William McKinley was assassinated, and Theodore Roosevelt became president.

What was Roosevelt's early life like? He grew up in a rich New York family. He was often ill. His parents hired private tutors and sent him on educational travels.

Where did Roosevelt receive a college degree? at Harvard

What disappointments did he face in 1884? Both his wife and his mother died. The man he supported for the presidency lost, hurting Roosevelt's career.

Teach for Understanding

What shows that Roosevelt did not give up on his life or his political career? He remarried, became the assistant secretary of the navy, became governor of New York, and in 1900 became the vice president of the United States.

What word would you use to describe Roosevelt since he did not give up easily? Possible answers include determined, steadfast.

What was Roosevelt's trust busting? Roosevelt broke up groups of companies that worked together to control an industry that harmed consumers.

What was the meat trust doing that hurt farmers? It set all the prices and tried to stop farmers from selling to any other company.

What did Roosevelt ask his attorney general to do? stop the meat companies from setting prices

What began to set meat prices again? supply and demand

What did Roosevelt encourage Congress to pass after Americans read Upton Sinclair's novel *The Jungle*? the Pure Food and Drug Act and the Meat Inspection Act

---

New York. Although he lost, Roosevelt kept trying and eventually became assistant secretary of the navy in 1896. After the Spanish-American War, he was popular. In 1899 Roosevelt became governor of New York. In 1900 he became the vice president. Theodore Roosevelt's persistence paid off.

Roosevelt as President

Roosevelt was an active president. He encouraged new laws. He traveled. Even the White House was more lively during his presidency. His six children kept a variety of pets there.

Roosevelt became famous for **trust busting**. A trust was a group of several companies working together to control an industry. For example, several railroads might jointly own a stretch of railroad. Together they could set prices favorable to themselves. Roosevelt did not try to destroy every trust. He was not opposed to big business. But he tried to stop companies that harmed consumers.

Roosevelt broke up the beef trust. This group of meat processors tried to control the meat market. Normally customers have several companies to buy from. If one company charges too much, the customer can buy from another. If prices go too high, a new company tries to bring in products. But during Roosevelt's presidency, the six

biggest meat sellers set all the prices. They tried to stop farmers from selling to any other company. Roosevelt asked his attorney general, Philander Knox, to stop the meat companies from setting prices. The attorney general of the United States helps the president to enforce the law. Roosevelt and Knox were successful. Supply and demand began to set prices again.

President Roosevelt got involved in another food case. In 1905 Upton Sinclair published a novel called *The Jungle*. It told about immigrants who worked in the meat industry. Sinclair hoped that readers would notice the poor treatment of workers. He wanted support for his political views. Instead, readers noticed the filthy meatpacking houses. Dirt and rats were mixed into ground beef. Americans were horrified that their meat might be contaminated. President Roosevelt agreed and asked Congress to pass the Pure Food and Drug Act. Congress also passed the Meat Inspection Act. Now Americans could have more confidence in their food and drugs.

President Roosevelt also tried to ensure that American public land was used well. Sometimes people lived on it. Sometimes the land was set aside. Much of the land the federal government owned was in the West. Gifford Pinchot who headed the Forest Service helped

214

Background

Protecting People and Resources

In 1906 Upton Sinclair published the novel *The Jungle*. It exposed corruption in the meatpacking industry. Later the same year, Congress passed the Pure Food and Drug Act, which allowed federal inspectors to examine slaughterhouses and meat companies that shipped across state lines. The law also forbade the use of harmful additives.

At that time, patented medicines were widely advertised and available over-the-counter or by mail. Many of them contained opium derivatives or a high percentage of alcohol. Although those medicines were often useful, they were also addictive. The Pure Food and Drug Act regulated the use of narcotics and required that the contents be listed on product labels. It also made it illegal to make claims about medicines that could not be verified.

Another issue very dear to Theodore Roosevelt's heart was conservation. As an outdoorsman, he readily responded to demands that the government protect lands for future generations to enjoy. America's first national park, Yellowstone, had become federal property in 1872. By the time Roosevelt left office in 1909, he had more than doubled the number of national parks.

Lincoln Steffens

Who: Lincoln Steffens
When: 1866–1936
Where: New York City, NY

Lincoln Steffens wrote articles exposing corruption in cities. He was born in San Francisco but wrote mainly about midwestern and eastern cities. His most famous book was called *The Shame of the Cities*. It talked about cities such as Saint Louis, Pittsburgh, and Chicago. Authors like Steffens were called muckrakers. They found the corrupt parts of society and exposed them to the light. Steffens spent his life pointing out problems and looking for solutions.

Roosevelt to care for the land. Both men wanted the American wilderness to be used for the good of the American people.

Roosevelt encouraged laws to enforce using natural resources wisely. The Reclamation Act of 1902 tried to make more land good for farming. It paid to dam western rivers so that more water would be available. Some lands were sold to fund this project. Roosevelt also set up the National Conservation Commission to observe the nation's resources. **Conservation** means using natural resources wisely. Although Roosevelt did not always

make the best decisions, he tried both to care for nature as well as benefit Americans.

Roosevelt was an ideal Progressive president. He saw many problems. He wanted many changes. From 1901 to 1909, Theodore Roosevelt stayed busy. When the election of 1908 came, he decided not to run again. When the new president took office, Roosevelt left the cities and business of America behind for an African safari.

> What were some things that Roosevelt did before becoming president?

215

Teach for Understanding

- Direct attention to the picture and the Biography box on page 215. Read aloud the informaton.

  What problem did Lincoln Steffens expose in his writing? corruption in cities

- Invite a volunteer to tell how muckraking is done today.
  Answers could include that muckraking is done through newspaper or magazine articles, newscasts, and social media.

  What did the Reclamation Act of 1902 do? It tried to make more land good for farming. It paid to dam western rivers so that more water would be available.

  What did Roosevelt set up to observe the nation's resources? the National Conservation Commission

> Conclude the discussion by asking the question on page 215. Roosevelt earned a degree at Harvard. Two years later, he published *The Naval War of 1812*. He became assistant secretary of the navy, governor of New York, and vice president of the United States.

Activity Manual

- Guide completion of pages 152–53.

Assessment
- Administer quiz.

> The quiz may be given anytime after completing this lesson.

Activity

Learn About State Conservation

Direct the students to study conservation in the state in which they live by going to the DNR (Department of Natural Resources) website or by contacting the DNR. Invite them to explain where conservation is practiced for their state. Encourage them to learn what plants and animals are endangered.

85

Student Text pages 216–19
Activity Manual pages 154–55

Lesson Focus

- The Progressive Era brought changes for people living in the cities.

Objectives

- Discuss changes in the cities during the Progressive Era
- Identify changes in voting

Review

- Choose a volunteer to tell what many Progressives believed had the ability to bring improvements.
- Invite a student to explain trust busting under President Roosevelt.
- Review what Congress passed to give Americans more confidence in the safety of their food and drugs.

Preparation for Reading

- Generate interest as you direct the students to read the titles and examine the pictures on pages 216–19.
- Guide pronunciation of any unfamiliar words in the lesson.
- Direct the students to read the pages silently to learn the name of a reform that gave voters the ability to remove officeholders from power. recall

Teach for Understanding

Why did so many people live in the cities? Cities were centers of industry. Immigrants arrived at coastal cities and remained there.

- Direct attention to the picture on 216. Invite students to read aloud the captions.
- Choose a volunteer to state the changes Progressives wanted to make in the cities as you write the changes for display.
- Choose a volunteer to suggest whether Progressives would be able to solve all of America's problems and to give a reason to support his answer.

Progressivism in the Cities

Many Americans could not leave the cities behind. Since the nation began, a larger and larger percentage of its population lived in the cities. They were centers of industry. Factory jobs were usually in a city. Immigrants arrived at coastal cities such as New York. They lived there in tenements or crowded apartment buildings. Many immigrants remained in the cities.

So many people living in the cities created several problems. Progressives had solutions. Just one street could offer many opportunities for change.

Immigrants were encouraged to learn English to "become American."

Cities introduced subways and streetcars.

People worked to end drunkenness and to stop people from wasting money on alcohol.

Christians organized outreaches to urban areas.

New laws ensured that milk and other foods were safe.

216

Background

Greeley on Urbanization

Horace Greeley observed, "We cannot all live in cities, yet nearly all seem determined to do so. Hot and cold water, baker's bread, gas, the theatre and the streetcars . . . indicate the tendency of modern taste."

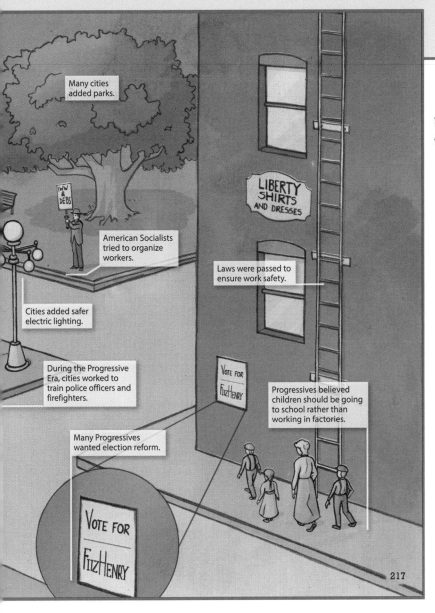

Many cities added parks.

American Socialists tried to organize workers.

Cities added safer electric lighting.

During the Progressive Era, cities worked to train police officers and firefighters.

Many Progressives wanted election reform.

LIBERTY SHIRTS AND DRESSES

Laws were passed to ensure work safety.

VOTE FOR FitzHenry

Progressives believed children should be going to school rather than working in factories.

VOTE FOR FitzHenry

217

Teach for Understanding

- Invite students to read aloud the captions on page 217.
- Choose a volunteer to state the changes Progressives wanted to make in the cities as you write the changes for display.
- Explain that the sign about American Socialists organizing workers was the type used by the Socialist Eugene V. Debs. Debs founded unions and led strikes. During a railroad strike, Pullman cars were boycotted. Strikers and unemployed ruffians destroyed engines, cars, and equipment. Because Debs refused to obey a court order to stop encouraging the railroad strike, he was sent to prison.
- Tell the students that the violence and radicalism of the union movement discredited unions for nearly half a century. Perhaps in part because of this radicalism, the government tended to side with management by providing court orders to end strikes and even troops to quell violence. Although organized labor made gains for some workers, most union goals remained unrealized until the twentieth century.

Lesson

85

Teach for Understanding

- Direct attention to the infograph and explain its meaning.
- Invite a volunteer to locate the words *initiative* and *referendum* in the Glossary and read the definitions aloud.

How could voters remove an officeholder from power after the recall was passed? If enough voters signed a petition, there would be a general election to remove the officeholder from power.

Voting

During the Progressive Era, people in urban and rural areas experienced changes in voting. Some laws expanded the number of people who could vote. Others restricted voting. New voting opportunities also came about.

Voters were sometimes frustrated by state laws. Traditionally, state laws were proposed by a member of the state legislature. If enough legislators voted yes, then the bill went to the governor's office. If the governor agreed to it, the bill was law. Members of the public had little say in creating bills. If someone wanted a new law, he could write to a legislator. Otherwise, there was not much to be done. Once legislators and the governor were in office, they could not be removed until the next election.

The initiative and referendum introduced changes to the lawmaking process. The **initiative** gave citizens of a state an opportunity to write their own laws. They could initiate, or begin, a law. Once it was written, citizens could sign it to show their approval. If enough citizens signed the initiative, two things might happen. First, the legislature might have to vote on it. Second, the initiative might go to a public vote. If the voters approved the bill, then it became a law.

The **referendum** also let citizens vote on bills. Sometimes legislatures would write a bill for the people to vote on. Another type of referendum allowed citizens to repeal, or cancel, a law that the legislature had passed. In both cases, the people of the state helped determine what the law would be.

A third reform was the **recall**. In some cases voters of a state were not happy with their officials. The voters wondered why they could vote people into office but not out. The recall fixed that inconsistency. If enough voters signed a petition, a general election could remove the officeholder from power.

INITIATIVE: citizens of a given state have the right to write laws for themselves.

REFERENDUM: citizens of a given state have the right to vote on laws proposed by their legislature or to appeal a law already signed by their legislature.

RECALL: citizens of a given state have the right to vote an official out of office before the end of his term.

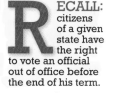

218

Suffragettes argued that all citizens should be equal and deserved an equal right to vote.

The West began much political reform. The initiative, referendum, and recall were most popular there, but they did not spread throughout the whole country. The West also introduced more voting rights for women.

The Progressive Era saw the fight for suffrage increase. After the Civil War, more women wanted the right to vote. Some Americans believed that women voters would help the country. They thought that women had superior morals to men. Maybe women voting would result in less corruption. The National American Woman Suffrage Association was formed in 1890. As western states granted women the right to vote, the nation as a whole seemed more likely to also do so.

Whether dealing with voting or other matters, Progressives were often too hopeful. They trusted that science and better laws would correct problems. They hoped to destroy corruption. They wanted children to be in school to learn. American Progressives believed that educated adults would make better voters. Better voters would not vote selfishly. The Progressives kept hoping for a perfect world and forgot that laws and science have never been able to make the world perfect.

> What new powers did voters get during the Progressive Era?

219

Teach for Understanding

- Direct attention to the pictures. Read aloud the caption.

  What organization was formed in 1890 to promote voting rights for women? the National American Woman Suffrage Association

  What did Progressives forget about making a perfect world? Laws and science have never been able to make the world perfect.

  > Conclude the discussion by asking the question on page 219. initiative, referendum, recall

Activity Manual

- Guide completion of pages 154–55.

86

Lesson Focus

- President Taft continued Roosevelt's policy of involvement in world affairs.

Objectives

- Examine William Taft's presidency
- Identify the importance of the Panama Canal

Review

- Guide a review of Progressivism in the cities.
- Identify voting changes in state general elections.

Preparation for Reading

- Generate interest as you direct the students to read the titles and examine the pictures and map on pages 220–22.
- Guide pronunciation of any unfamiliar words in the lesson.
- Direct the students to read the pages silently to learn what opened a shortcut from the Caribbean to the Pacific Ocean. the Panama Canal

Teach for Understanding

- Direct attention to the picture. Use the caption to guide a discussion.

What did William Taft do that helped prepare him to be a good president? He studied at Yale. He served as governor-general of the Philippines. He served as secretary of war under Theodore Roosevelt.

How did Congress respond when Progressives wanted to lower tariffs? Congress lowered them only slightly.

Why were Republicans unhappy with Taft over tariffs? Taft agreed with Congress about lowering tariffs only slightly.

Who was Gifford Pinchot? head of the United States Forest Service

Why did Taft fire Pinchot? Pinchot did not get along with the secretary of the interior. Pinchot wanted more conservation and the secretary did not.

How did the stronger commercial ties of the early 1900s help the United States? Buying and selling allowed the United States to influence countries that it did not officially control.

William Taft
Election of 1908 and William H. Taft

In 1908 American voters selected a new president. The Republicans listened to Roosevelt and chose **William Taft** as their candidate. The Democrats chose William Jennings Bryan for the third time. Taft easily won the election.

Taft's life seemed to have prepared him to be a good president. He was born in Ohio. His ancestors had come to the country when it was still thirteen colonies. Taft studied at Yale. After several years of government service, he received an important job. In 1900 President McKinley appointed Taft as governor-general of the Philippines. From 1901 to 1904, he helped set up a good government in that nation. After Roosevelt was reelected president in 1904, he appointed Taft to be his secretary of war. Taft's studies and career gave him experience.

Taft was not as skilled a president as Roosevelt. Not all the Republicans supported the Progressive reforms. Taft made many Americans unhappy. Progressives wanted lower tariffs. Congress lowered them only slightly, but Taft agreed with Congress. This compromise left most Republicans unhappy with Taft. The president also angered Progressive Republicans by not supporting Gifford Pinchot, head of the United States Forest Service. Pinchot and Richard Ballinger, the secretary of the interior, did not get along. Gifford Pinchot wanted more conservation, and the secretary did not. Taft eventually fired Pinchot. Progressive Republicans could not believe Taft's decision. The president failed to hold the Republican Party together.

Foreign Policy

Both Roosevelt and Taft ran a Progressive foreign policy. They thought that much of the world needed to be improved. American help, they believed, would bring improvement. Sometimes this help came with force. During the early 1900s, US policy promoted stronger **commercial** ties around the world. Buying and selling allowed the United States to influence countries that it did not officially control.

In East Asia, Roosevelt encouraged

Taft was the first president to throw the first pitch at a baseball game, the first to have an automobile, and the first to golf regularly.

He was the only president to be Chief Executive of the United States and Chief Justice of the Supreme Court.

Background

Taft and Progressivism

William Howard Taft had spent most of his career as a lawyer in the federal court system. Theodore Roosevelt had named him civil governor of the Philippines and later secretary of war, but Taft preferred the courts. His lifelong dream was to be chief justice of the Supreme Court. On Roosevelt's advice, he set aside that dream to run for president. Ultimately Taft did achieve his dream in 1921 when he left the presidency and was appointed chief justice by President Harding.

Like Roosevelt, Taft believed that government should regulate big business. But when Taft won the 1908 election over Democrat William Jennings Bryan, the course he took as president was somewhat different from Roosevelt's. He followed the advice of Republican leaders more readily, and he did not publicly push Progressive reforms. His methods and personality made him seem more casual than Roosevelt. But Taft actually initiated eighty-nine antitrust suits, compared to Roosevelt's forty-three. Taft was not as successful at communicating his successes as Roosevelt had been. People saw only Taft's mistakes. He left office a failure in the eyes of many Americans.

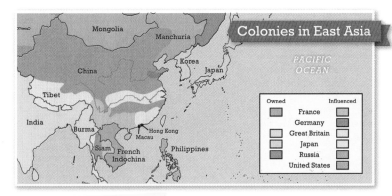

Colonies in East Asia

Map labels: Mongolia, Manchuria, China, Korea, Japan, Tibet, India, Burma, Siam, French Indochina, Macau, Hong Kong, Philippines, PACIFIC OCEAN

Map key:
Owned		Influenced
	France	
	Germany	
	Great Britain	
	Japan	
	Russia	
	United States	

the **Open Door policy**. This policy demanded that no colonial power block other countries from China. China was the oldest and largest Asian country. By the late 1800s, it was weak. European nations and Japan threatened to carve China into pieces. Secretary of State John Hay demanded an open door under McKinley. If one foreign power had rights in China, then others should too. He wanted to guarantee that each foreign nation was equal in China and that China remained independent. Americans did not want their country to gain colonies. But they wanted to do business throughout the world. The Open Door policy would allow trade.

Hay continued to support China through the Boxer Rebellion. During this conflict, Chinese rebels tried to erase foreign influence in China. Many westerners suffered injury, and some were killed. Afterward, the Chinese

government had to pay $333 million to western governments. The United States returned most of its share. It gave the money to pay for college for Chinese students. Hay and Roosevelt's administration wanted the United States and China to be friends. They hoped that if Chinese students studied at American colleges, the two countries would grow closer. American ideas could influence China.

A few years later, Roosevelt got involved in East Asia. When Japan and Russia fought a war, he served as a mediator. Roosevelt had both sides meet in New Hampshire. There, he worked out a treaty that Russia and Japan could accept. In 1906 President Roosevelt received the Nobel Peace Prize for this work.

Roosevelt also expanded the role of the United States by beginning the **Panama Canal**. In 1903 Panama was

221

Teach for Understanding

● Direct attention to the map on page 221. Invite a student to explain what the map shows and the meaning of the map key.

What was the Open Door policy? a policy that no colonial power could block other countries from China

Who demanded an Open Door policy with China under McKinley? Secretary of State John Hay

What did Hay want to accomplish with the Open Door policy with China? He wanted to guarantee that each foreign nation was equal in China and that China remained independent. The Open Door policy would allow trade.

What did Chinese rebels hope to accomplish through the Boxer Rebellion? Chinese rebels tried to erase foreign influence in China.

What impact did the rebellion have on westerners? Many westerners suffered injury and some were killed.

Why did the United States government return the money China paid for what China had done? Hay and Roosevelt's administration wanted the United States and China to be friends. The United States gave the money to pay for college for Chinese students. They hoped that if Chinese students studied at American colleges, the two countries would grow closer. American ideas could influence China.

Why did President Roosevelt receive the Nobel Peace Prize? He worked out a treaty between Japan and Russia to stop the war between the two countries.

What did Roosevelt begin building in Panama? the Panama Canal

Teach for Understanding

- Direct attention to the picture. Read aloud the caption.

What did the United Sates receive when Panama gained independence? a canal treaty

How would the Panama Canal benefit the United States? More trade would flow through the Caribbean. American merchants could make more money.

What helped show America's power around the world? the American navy

What did Taft want the United States to do in world affairs? ensure peace and prosperity in the Western Hemisphere

How did Taft fail and succeed in regard to the Republican Party? He was unable to keep the party together, and it split. But he continued Progressive ideals when he could.

>> Conclude the discussion by asking the question on page 222. China

Activity Manual

- Guide completion of pages 156–57.

---

seeking independence from Colombia. The United States wanted to build a canal. America supported Panama when the new nation declared independence. American ships blocked Colombia's access to Panama. The United States received a canal treaty when Panama gained independence.

The Great White Fleet consisted of sixteen US Navy battleships with white hulls. The fleet demonstrated that the US had become a major sea power.

The Panama Canal was hard work for the United States. The route cut through mountains and swamps. Disease-carrying mosquitoes almost stopped the work. But Roosevelt encouraged the canal. He knew that an American-controlled canal would benefit the United States. More trade would flow through the Caribbean. American merchants could make more money. The federal government spent millions of dollars to drain swamps and kill mosquitoes. Eventually the work paid off. In 1914 the Panama Canal opened a shortcut from the Caribbean to the Pacific Ocean.

The American navy helped show America's power around the world. In 1907 President Roosevelt sent the Great White Fleet of powerful new warships steaming around the globe. The journey gave the navy practical experience on the high seas. It also showed the world the power of the United States.

Roosevelt was famous for saying, "Speak softly and carry a big stick." He did not want to threaten other nations with words. Instead he wanted the world to know that the United States could take care of itself.

President Taft continued Roosevelt's policy of involvement in world affairs. He especially pushed to increase influence in the Americas. He sent marines to Nicaragua during a rebellion there. Taft also stepped into Honduran politics. When Honduras had trouble paying its debts to Britain, the United States helped. It also brought rebels and the government together to talk in 1911. Taft wanted the United States to ensure peace and prosperity in the Western Hemisphere. Although Taft's presidency saw the Republican Party split, he continued Progressive ideals when he could.

>> Which Asian country tried to remain intact while other nations carved out spheres of influence?

222

Background

Panama Canal

One of Roosevelt's favorite projects was the building of an American-controlled canal in Central America to link the Atlantic and the Pacific. Construction of the Panama Canal took approximately ten years. As many as forty thousand Americans were employed on the project at one time, despite the many hazards. The canal cost about $400 million, but its financial benefits to world shipping outweighed the cost. In August 1914—just days after World War I had broken out in Europe—the canal opened and linked ocean to ocean.

More Progressivism

Workers in America

Americans also looked to improve the workplace. Factories were often unsafe. Working hours were long. Some employers took advantage of workers. Several solutions were proposed.

The American Federation of Labor and its leader, Samuel Gompers, encouraged collective bargaining. If all the people in an industry worked together, they could get their way. For example, all the machinists could agree on a fair wage. If the factories would not pay it, then no machinists would work. Samuel Gompers ran the AFL for many years.

Many of the trade unions in other countries were Socialist. **Socialism** is a belief that emphasizes the good of a society over the good of individuals. Socialists often believe that government should control industry. They want the government to tell industry how to treat its workers. Gompers did not want the AFL to be Socialist. He thought collective bargaining was enough.

Many industrial owners did not like unions. They did not want to pay their workers more money, but they wanted their workers to work many hours each week. They did not want all their workers planning together to get more money or rights.

Anti-union men often used the government to reverse union gains. They claimed that workers planning together violated antitrust laws. These laws prevented businesses from getting too big. Men also claimed that unions were violent and dangerous.

Sometimes unions did threaten the nation's well-being. In 1892 some steelworkers in Pennsylvania went on strike. When Carnegie Steel tried to end the strike, workers fought back. Twelve people died. Carnegie Steel warned that if steel production shut down, the whole nation would suffer.

Another strike helped change America's labor movement. Employees of the Pullman train-car company went on strike in 1894. They wanted their pay restored after a cut in wages. Soon employees on the railroads went on strike. From Chicago to Saint Louis,

The Homestead Strike in Pennsylvania between the Union and the Carnegie Steel Company

223

Activity

Understand the Right-to-Work Law

Direct the students to research the Right-to-Work Law and which states follow the right-to-work principle.

Background

Dangers to Child Laborers

Dangers were a constant reality for child workers. Breaker boys could fall into the coal chutes and be crushed by the coal or choked by the dust. They kept a persistent cough from breathing the coal dust. Those who entered the mines faced death or injury from cave-ins, explosions, or asphyxiation from poisonous gases or lack of oxygen. Child workers in canneries, where they shucked oysters or peeled or sliced fruits and vegetables, risked seriously injuring fingers or hands.

Lesson Focus

- Workers suffered injustices, and black Americans struggled for equality.

Objectives

- Recognize problems related to American workers during the Progressive Era
- Examine the struggle for equality by black Americans

Review

- Guide a review of Taft's foreign policy.

Preparation for Reading

- Generate interest as you direct the students to read the titles and examine the pictures on pages 223–25.
- Guide pronunciation of any unfamiliar words in the lesson.
- Direct the students to read the pages silently to learn the meaning of Socialism. a belief that emphasizes the good of a society over the good of individuals

Teach for Understanding

What were some problems American workers faced? Factories were often unsafe; working hours were long; some employers took advantage of workers.

What did the American Federation of Labor and Samuel Gompers encourage? collective bargaining

- Invite a student to read the sentences that explain Socialism.

- Do you believe that the good of society is more important than the good of the individual?

- Explain that socialism often leads to Communism in which the government controls everything.

What was Gompers's attitude toward the AFL being Socialist? He did not want it to be Socialist. He thought collective bargaining was enough.

What was the attitude of many industrial owners toward unions? Many disliked unions.

What resulted when Andrew Carnegie tried to end a steelworkers' strike in Pennsylvania? Workers fought back. Twelve people died.

How did the Pullman train-car strike affect employees elsewhere? Soon employees on the railroads went on strike. From Chicago to Saint Louis, hundreds of trains did not run.

Teach for Understanding

- Direct attention to the picture. Use the caption to guide a discussion about segregation.

What attempt was made to end the strike? A court ordered the workers back to work.

Who was the union leader who refused to end the strike? Eugene Debs

What happened to Debs when soldiers finally broke the strike? Debs was jailed.

What did Debs become after his time in prison? a Socialist

How did some Progressives treat black Americans? They misused science in order to justify mistreating black Americans. These Progressives passed laws restricting freedom.

How did southern Democrats stop black Americans from voting? by passing laws that required literacy

In what way did laws passed in the South treat black Americans unjustly? They segregated black people and white people in everyday situations.

---

hundreds of trains did not run. A court ordered the workers back to work, but union leader Eugene Debs refused. When soldiers finally broke the strike, Debs was jailed.

After his time in prison, Debs changed American politics. He became a Socialist. For several decades, the Socialist Party gained votes in America. Debs believed that the government and industry were too close to each other. Neither cared for the workers. Many agreed with him. Some Socialist hopes eventually came to pass. Even though a Socialist did not become president, members of the party influenced American politics.

Black Americans

Another group of Americans suffered during the Progressive Era. Black

There were segregated waiting rooms at the Public Health Service Dispensary in Washington, DC.

Americans lost freedoms. Some Progressives misused science in order to justify treating black Americans badly. These Progressives passed laws restricting freedom.

In the South, Democrats worked to stop black Americans from voting. Progressivism called for good voters. To keep black American men from voting, southern states passed laws that required literacy. The laws claimed that an illiterate man could not be a good voter. Most black Americans were poor and could not enjoy a good education. And if they were illiterate, they could not vote.

Many southern states passed other laws that treated black Americans unfairly. These are often called Jim Crow laws. They segregated black people and white people in everyday situations. Schools, restaurants, and even public restrooms were segregated. In general, Jim Crow laws ensured that black Americans were treated like second-class citizens in their own country.

Black Americans worked hard to overcome this treatment. They did not agree on a unified strategy. Two men led the two main plans.

224

Extreme Progressivism

The extreme wing of the Progressive movement was the Socialists, who advocated government ownership of the major means of production and distribution. The leading Socialist of the era was Eugene Debs, former head of the American Railway Union. Debs ran for president on the Socialist ticket five times. His highest percentage of the vote came in 1912, when he won 6 percent of the total. Debs's most interesting showing, however, was in 1920, when he won nearly a million votes while in prison for opposing American involvement in World War I. The vote totals of Debs, along with a few Socialist victories in municipal elections, demonstrate that the call for radical reform was present but only among a small segment of American society.

Booker T. Washington believed black Americans should study and work hard to prove their equality.

W. E. B. Du Bois wanted black Americans to be proactive and fight to end discrimination.

Booker T. Washington fought for black American equality in the early Progressive Era. Born a slave, he worked hard for his education. Then Washington founded a school, the Tuskegee Institute, so that others could learn. Washington knew that black Americans were just as capable as white Americans. He also knew that many white people thought black Americans were less capable than white people. Some Progressives claimed that science showed that white people were better than black people. Washington wanted black Americans to study and work hard. He believed that in time they would prove their equality. He did not think it was worthwhile to fight for social equality while white Americans viewed black people as inferior.

Some black Americans wanted equality right away. They did not agree that black people should have to wait for white people to recognize the truth. **W. E. B. Du Bois** became the most famous man to argue that injustice stop immediately. Du Bois wrote and spoke, arguing his case. In 1910 a number of white and black Americans agreed to fight discrimination. They formed the NAACP. It was supposed to help bring equality to black Americans. Du Bois helped lead the organization. Neither Washington nor Du Bois had success immediately. During the Progressive Era, black Americans enjoyed little equality.

> How did groups of workers try to gain more benefits?

225

Teach for Understanding

- Direct attention to the pictures. Read the captions aloud.

  What did Booker T. Washington believe would happen in time if black people studied and worked hard? They would prove their equality.

  What did W. E. B. Du Bois believe? He believed that injustice should stop immediately.

  What organization was supposed to help bring equality to black Americans? the NAACP

  How successful were the efforts of Washington and Du Bois in gaining equality for black Americans? They were not immediately successful. Black Americans enjoyed little equality.

  > Conclude the discussion by asking the question on page 225. by forming unions and using collective bargaining

Primary Source: *Up from Slavery: An Autobiography*

- Direct attention to Activity Manual page 158. Explain that Booker T. Washington wrote about attending an institute for black Americans in his book *Up from Slavery: An Autobiography*.
- Read the introduction. Invite students to suggest some of the challenges Booker T. Washington had to overcome to go to the institute.
- Invite the students to follow along on Activity Manual page 158 as you read the excerpt. Ask a student to suggest the meaning of what Booker T. Washington is saying in the passage.

Activity Manual

- Guide completion of page 158.

Activity

Read About Booker T. Washington

Provide books about Booker T. Washington. Invite the students to read the books in their free time. Invite volunteers to share what they learn from their reading.

Lesson

88

Student Text pages 226–29
Activity Manual pages 159–60

Lesson Focus

- Progressivism continued during Woodrow Wilson's presidency.

Objectives
- Examine education in the Progressive Era
- Evaluate Woodrow Wilson's Progressive policies

Materials
- A list of local, state, or national elected representatives

Review

- Invite a student to explain problems workers faced during the Progressive Era.
- Choose a volunteer to name several solutions that were proposed to the problems that workers faced.
- Review how some Progressives caused injustices for black Americans.

Preparation for Reading

- Generate interest as you direct the students to read the titles and examine the pictures and map on pages 226–29.
- Guide pronunciation of any unfamiliar words in the lesson.
- Direct the students to read the pages silently to learn the name of the banking system Woodrow Wilson oversaw for the nation. the Federal Reserve System

Teach for Understanding

- Direct attention to the picture on page 226 and the How It Was box. Read aloud the story.

  What word might describe Alice's mother because she had lived in Ireland before coming to New York? immigrant
- Invite a student to read the sentences that show that Alice's mother's life in New York was better than in Ireland.

  What would Alice and her brother need to do in order to be successful in America? work hard and learn

  What are some things Woodrow Wilson did before becoming president of the United States? He finished a PhD, served as a professor, became president of Princeton University, and served as governor of New Jersey.
- Read aloud the caption on page 227. Guide a discussion about Woodrow Wilson.

How It Was

"Alice, here is your lunch, and don't forget your latchkey. I'm going to be late tonight cleaning at the Elting house after a party. Be sure to feed Thomas and put him to bed."

Alice pocketed the bread. "I will, Mum, but why do you have to be out late? I don't like it."

"I work so we can stay in this good apartment and eat. Back in Ireland, I lived in a cottage with six brothers and sisters. Here in New York we have three whole rooms, and you and Tommy can go to school and learn."

Alice looked around at the tiny room with a small table and three chairs. The clock on the mantle showed that class began soon.

"Must I be a maid too, Mum, when I'm grown? I like Miss Campion, our teacher. Can I be a teacher?"

"Oh, Alice, of course you can. Here in America if you work hard, you can learn and be a schoolteacher. James will have a good job too. Better than digging potatoes from the ground. Now, off with you and your brother to school!"

Alice hugged her mother and then pulled away to look into her face. "I love you, Mum."

Wilson, Democrats, and the War
Republican Split and the Election

The Republican Party split over Progressivism and lost the election of 1912. The Republican Party picked Taft as its candidate, but Roosevelt thought that Taft was not Progressive enough. He formed a new party and called it the Progressive Party. Republicans split their votes between Roosevelt and Taft. The Democrats won with just 42 percent of the national vote for their candidate, Woodrow Wilson.

Wilson

Woodrow Wilson was born in Virginia in 1856. In 1886 Wilson finished a doctorate. Over the next several years, he served as a professor at various colleges. In 1902 he became president of Princeton University. In 1910, he left that job to pursue politics. Wilson was committed to the ideas of

226

Background

Wilson and Progressivism

Woodrow Wilson was the son of a Presbyterian pastor. He was born and reared in the South. He believed that there were two sides to every issue: "a right side and a wrong side." He clung stubbornly to principles and refused to compromise. He viewed men idealistically. He believed that most people learned from experience and desired to do right. Politically, that view meant that he often underestimated his opposition, whether at home or abroad.

Effects of Progressivism on Education

What is commonly called Progressive education actually had its greatest impact in America from the 1920s to the early 1950s. The philosophy of the movement, however, is rooted firmly in the overall Progressive movement. In general, Progressive educators aimed at improving education by relating learning to the child's interests.

Progressive educators emphasized that they were teaching students, not subjects. Education, they said, should be based on experience rather than on simple memorization; therefore, activities such as laboratory experiments and field trips became part of the education process. Progressive educators de-emphasized traditional academic subjects, such

Progressives and believed that applying knowledge would solve the problems in America.

Wilson's first political job was as the governor of New Jersey. Corrupt politicians supported him at first. They thought that a college professor could not make them change. However, Woodrow Wilson helped force out corrupt politicians. He also introduced workmen's compensation for injured workers. Wilson seemed like he would make a good president.

Education in the Progressive Era

A college professor becoming a president shows the importance of education during the Progressive Era. Progressives believed that knowledge would bring improvements to the nation. Beginning with elementary schools, Americans needed to be well educated.

Throughout the nation, elementary schools tried to improve. More teachers attended teaching schools or colleges. Buildings were expanded. In general, the South had the worst schools. The southern states worked hard to change their

Wilson dropped his first name, Thomas, at age 25 and adopted his middle name, Woodrow.

Before becoming president of the United States, he was president of Princeton University.

schools. People paid more in taxes to improve their children's schools. John D. Rockefeller gave millions of dollars to improve education. Progressives brought improvements to children's schooling.

More people also went to high school and college. Cities and towns founded new high schools. It became normal for students to spend at least a few years in high school. Colleges began training high-school teachers. Many colleges encouraged careers in education.

John Dewey was a teacher who supported the rise in education. He taught both philosophy and education at the University of Chicago and at Columbia University in New York City. Dewey wanted better-educated Americans.

Dewey's ideas were controversial. He believed traditional education worked badly. He thought students memorized too much. Dewey encouraged teachers to have students learn through their own interests. As an atheist, he also opposed religious teaching in schools. Dewey's ideas are often called Progressive education. It teaches that humanity can perfect itself. During the

227

What did Progressives believe would bring improvements to the nation? knowledge

What things were done to improve elementary schools? More teachers attended teaching schools or colleges. Buildings were expanded. People paid more in taxes to improve their children's schools.

What changed in regard to high school and college? More people went to high school and college. Cities and towns founded new high schools. Colleges began training high-school teachers.

How were John Dewey's ideas about education controversial? He believed traditional education worked badly. He thought students memorized too much. He encouraged teachers to have students learn through their own interests. He opposed religious teaching in schools.

as history, and emphasized vocational education, which seemed more relevant to the student's needs.

Progressive educators rightly sought to make education interesting and to link understanding to learning. (This is not to say that many traditional educators did not want to make learning interesting or that they did not emphasize understanding.) The philosophy behind Progressive methodology, however, was problematic. John Dewey, a professor at Columbia University and the University of Chicago, was the leading representative of Progressive education and a major leader in the twentieth-century movement known as secular humanism. That philosophy denies the existence of God and affirms the goodness and perfectibility of man.

Ironically, public discontent over Progressive education was based on the Progressives' own results-oriented standard. Much of the criticism that arose in the 1950s resulted from the realization that Progressive education had done a poor job of educating America's children.

Secular Humanism in a Nutshell

Secular humanism replaces absolute standards of truth (Romans 1:8–25) and morality (Ephesians 4:17–32) with relative, pragmatic standards based on human experience (i.e., "whatever works is right"). Obviously, the Christian must reject such a system.

Teach for Understanding

- Direct attention to the map. Invite a student to explain what the map shows.

What false concept does Progressive education teach? Progressive education teaches that humanity can perfect itself.

What was the result of Progressive education spreading throughout the country? Although more Americans were educated, the country still had problems.

What ammendment did Congress pass that affected taxes? the Sixteenth Amendment

What does the Sixteenth Amendment say? Congress may tax people on their income.

Who decided how much of the money people earned had to be paid to the government? Congress

How does the government mainly pay its bills? through taxes of citizens' incomes

What changed when the Seventeenth Amendment was passed? It gave the power of electing senators to the people.

How did the Federal Reserve System work? It is controlled by a board of experts. Twelve regional banks loan money to private banks. The board oversees the regional banks and can decide to print dollar bills.

What are some examples of how Wilson was not always successful in foreign affairs? He sent troops to Mexico during a revolution. Almost no one wanted US soldiers in the country. In several Latin American countries, protests broke out against America, and Wilson eventually withdrew the troops.

What interrupted President Wilson's attempts to reform America in 1914? a war in Europe

How did the changes made by the Progressives affect the problems in America? America still had problems.

⟩⟩ Conclude the discussion by asking the question on page 229. The Republican Party split. The Democrats won with just 42 percent of the national vote for Wilson.

Twelve Federal Reserve Banks

Progressive Era, many Americans still valued memorization in teaching. Most Americans viewed religious ideas favorably. Despite this opposition, Dewey's ideas and methods spread through the country. However, even though more Americans were educated, the country still had problems.

Wilson as a Progressive

Throughout America, politicians tried to solve problems. President Wilson encouraged Congress to pass several major reforms. Some had been Progressive or Populist goals for years.

In 1913 Congress and the states changed American taxes completely. Until then the government received much of its income from tariffs. In 1909 Congress had voted to send a new amendment to the states. Over the next

four years, state after state accepted it. The Sixteenth Amendment says that Congress may tax people on their income. In 1913 Congress passed a law saying how much earned money had to be paid to the government. Since then the American government has mainly paid its bills through taxes of citizens' incomes.

The Seventeenth Amendment was added to the Constitution in 1913. The Constitution originally expected state legislators to select national senators. The Senate represented states in the federal government. The Populist Party feared that senators were being picked because they had helped businessmen. The Populists wanted senators to be directly elected by the people. Many Progressives also supported this change. The new amendment gave the power of

228

Activity Manual

- Guide completion of pages 159–60.

electing senators to the people. People hoped that senators would be elected for being good men. Some people were worried about states losing their voices in Congress.

Woodrow Wilson oversaw a new banking system for the nation. This Federal Reserve System is controlled by a board of experts. Twelve regional banks loan money to private banks. The board oversees the regional banks and can decide to print dollar bills. Wilson and other Progressives liked the idea that experts would oversee the nation's banking. They hoped that these men (and now women) would guarantee jobs for Americans.

Wilson was not always successful. In 1910 a revolution began in Mexico and continued for several years. In 1913 Victoriano Huerta was president. The United States thought that he should not be. Eventually Wilson sent troops to the city of Veracruz. Although many Mexicans did not like Huerta, almost no one wanted US soldiers in the country. In several Latin American

countries, protests broke out against America. Wilson eventually withdrew the troops. Sometimes Progressives had to learn that not everyone wanted American help.

The Great War and Progressivism

In 1914 President Wilson's attempts to reform America were interrupted by a war in Europe. The United States did not immediately join the fight, but the war distracted Americans. Progressive reforms had to be set aside for a while. However, women still wanted to vote, and many Americans wanted to ban the drinking of alcohol. Perhaps once peace came, Progressivism could continue its fight to fix problems. But one thing was certain. Even though the Progressives had made many changes, the United States still had problems.

> How did Woodrow Wilson win the election of 1912, since he won fewer than half the votes?

//// **Activity** //

Public Participation

Identify an elected representative (local, state, or national) and write a letter about an issue. Send your letter to a classmate for a response. If time allows, mail the letter to your chosen representative.

//

229

Chapter Review
Activity Manual pages 161–62

Objective
- Recall concepts and terms from Chapter 10

Materials
- A list of prepared questions with the answers

Introduction

- Concepts for the Chapter 10 Test will be taken from Activity Manual pages 147–62. You may review any or all of the concepts during this lesson. You may choose to review Chapter 10 by playing "Jump Start."

Review

Game: Jump Start

- Divide the class into two teams. Provide two "jump" chairs in the front of the room, one for each team. Instruct one student from each team to sit in his team's chair. After the question is read, the first student to stand and give the correct answer receives points for his team. Continue alternating students until all the questions have been answered. The team with the most points wins the game.

Activity Manual

- Guide completion of pages 161–62.

Lesson **90** Chapter 10 Test

Objective
- Demonstrate knowledge of concepts from Chapter 10 by taking the test

Assessment
- Administer Test 10.

Activity //

Public Participation

- Generate excitement about writing a letter to an elected representative concerning an issue as you read the Activity information aloud.
- Display the list of the names of elected officials.
- Invite the students to think of a problem in their area that needs to be solved. Direct the students to choose a person from the list to write a letter to about the problem.
- Direct the students to exchange letters and write a response to the stated issue.
- Invite volunteers to read aloud their letters and the responses to their letters.

Chapter 11

Focus

America's involvement in World War I helped end the war but had lasting effects on the American people.

Introduction

In 1914 life was good for most people in the United States, but Europe had become a "powder keg." Some European countries wanted to become more powerful and wanted to enlarge their boundaries. Some countries formed alliances. War broke out on June 28 when Austria-Hungary declared war on Serbia. Eventually much of Europe was at war.

German U-boats sunk American ships, and Germany sent a telegram to Mexico asking the country to fight against the United States in case America entered the war on the side of the Allies. The United States Congress declared war against Germany on April 6, 1917.

The Allies were weary of fighting against German forces, and they welcomed American soldiers in the fight on European soil. Eventually after many battles and great losses on both sides, the Germans had to admit defeat. German leaders met with the Allies and signed the Treaty of Versailles.

Americans had worked hard at home and overseas to help defeat the Axis Powers. It would take time for America to recover from the war.

Chapter Focus

America's involvement in World War I helped end the war but had lasting effects on the American people.

Chapter 11 Overview				
Lesson	Student Text	Activity Manual	Content	Vocabulary
91	230–33	163–65	Triple Entente Triple Alliance	nationalism
92	234–36	166	Schlieffen Plan Central Powers Battle of the Marne Allies How It Was: Away at Christmas	Battle of the Marne treason Schlieffen Plan western front
93	237–39	167–69	Eastern Front U-boat	U-boat unrestricted submarine warfare
94	240–42	170–71	Battle of Verdun Battle of Jutland Battle of the Somme Primary Source: The Zimmerman Telegram	April 6, 1917
95	243–45	172	Biography Box: General John J. Pershing American Expeditionary Force (AEF) Ferdinand Foch Meuse-Argonne Offensive	American Expeditionary Force (AEF) offensive
96	246–48	173–74	Committee on Public Information Herbert Hoover Activity: Conserving Food New Roles for Women	conserve
97	249–51	175–76	Armistice The "lost generation" Treaty of Versailles	November 11, 1918
98		177–78	Chapter Review	
99			Chapter Test	

Visit bjupress.com/resources for links to enhance the lessons.

Student Text pages 230–33
Activity Manual pages 163–65

Sinking of the *Lusitania*
1915

Treaty of Versailles
1919

1910   1914   **1915**   1917   1918   1920
War begins   America enters   Armistice
the war

Peace or Power?

The year was 1914. In the United States, life was good for most people. Nearly everyone had a job and plenty of food to eat. People everywhere—bankers, factory workers, farmers, and college students—talked about President Woodrow Wilson's recent election.

But across the ocean in Europe, life was not so peaceful. Several nations wanted to become more powerful. They wanted to enlarge their boundaries. Often this meant taking land that other countries already owned. They wanted to have the strongest armies and navies. They were all competing with each other to make and sell the best products. The people of each nation thought that their nation was the best one in Europe. Their strong patriotic feelings for their own nation were called nationalism. Some of these people would stop at nothing to advance their nation's goals.

The European Powder Keg

Germany, Russia, Austria-Hungary, and France were four of these powerful nations. Each country had a strong military force. Great Britain was also powerful. For many years the British navy was the strongest navy on the seas.

The Triple Entente

Britain wanted to stay out of the tension in Europe. It was separated from the rest of Europe by the English Channel. Britain wanted there to be a balance of power among the countries of Europe. But Britain would not be able to avoid tension for long. Several years earlier, it had made an alliance with France and Russia. An alliance is an agreement between nations to help each other if any one of them goes to war. France, Russia, and Great Britain named their alliance the Triple Entente.

231

JourneyForth

The following books are available from JourneyForth Books, a division of BJU Press, at journeyforth.com.

Understood Betsy by Dorothy Canfield Fisher

Originally published in 1916, this book is one that entertained American children during the troubled days of the first World War. When Elizabeth Ann goes to visit her Vermont relatives, she gains much more than she expected—a total life change.

The Lost Prince of Samavia by Frances Hodgson Burnett

Originally published in 1915 during World War I, this is the imaginary tale of two boys who embark on a journey across Europe to bring freedom to the war-torn country of Samavia and to help restore its rightful king.

Lesson Focus

- In 1914 Europe was a powder keg ready to ignite in war.

Objectives
- Identify the nations that made up the Triple Entente
- Recognize nations in the Triple Alliance
- Recognize events that led to war in Europe

Introduction

- Choose a student to read aloud the title of the chapter. Invite a student to give the other name for World War I. the First World War

- Invite a student to read the chapter focus aloud.

  What do you think you will learn in this chapter? the part the United States played in World War I and the effects of the war on Americans

- Direct attention to the timeline.

  When did World War I begin? 1914

  How many years did the war last until the armistice? four years

  What major event happened after the war began? the sinking of the *Lusitania*

  When did the United States enter the war? 1917

Preparation for Reading

- Generate interest as you direct the students to read the titles and examine the pictures and map on pages 230–33.

- Guide pronunciation of any unfamiliar words in the lesson.

  What does the picture on page 230 depict? a tank approaching a trench with soldiers on the ground

- Direct the students to read the pages silently to learn the names of the countries that formed the Triple Entente. France, Russia, Great Britain

Teach for Understanding

- Invite a student to locate *nationalism* in the Glossary and read aloud the definition.

  When does nationalism become a problem? when people will stop at nothing to advance their nation's goals

- Choose a volunteer to name the countries that formed the Triple Entente.

Teach for Understanding

- Direct attention to the map on page 232. Point out the alliances and the countries that formed them.

What was the Triple Alliance? an alliance between Germany, Austria-Hungary, and Italy

What was the secret agreement Italy made with France? It promised to remain neutral if another nation attacked France.

What was the situation between Serbia, Bosnia, and Austria-Hungary? Bosnia had been independent before it became part of Austria-Hungary. The Serbs thought Bosnia should belong to them.

What event happened when Archduke Francis Ferdinand, heir to the throne of Austria-Hungary, was traveling in Bosnia? He was shot and killed by a Serbian terrorist.

What was the reaction of Austria-Hungary to the assassination of the archduke? It made harsh demands on Serbia. When Serbia would not agree to all the demands, Austria-Hungary declared war on Serbia.

When did Germany declare war on Russia? when Russia was preparing its army to help Serbia

Alliances

The Triple Alliance

Germany, Austria-Hungary, and Italy had also made an alliance. They called their group the Triple Alliance. However, Italy later made a secret agreement with France. It promised to remain neutral if another nation attacked France.

Some people referred to Europe in 1914 as a powder keg. A powder keg is a small container that holds gunpowder. Gunpowder will explode the moment a spark touches it. In Europe it would take only a "spark" of a problem for the nations to explode into war. The spark came on June 28, 1914.

The Powder Keg Ignites

In 1914, Serbia was a small independent kingdom. Bosnia had been independent too, before it became part of Austria-Hungary. The Serbs, people of Serbia, thought Bosnia should belong to them. They considered Austria-Hungary their enemy.

On June 28, Archduke Francis Ferdinand was traveling in Bosnia's capital. Ferdinand was the heir to the throne of Austria-Hungary. A young man fired shots into the archduke's car. Both Ferdinand and his wife died.

The government of Austria-Hungary was outraged. The leaders learned that the young man, Gavrilo Princip, was part of a Serbian terrorist group called the Black Hand. Kaiser Wilhelm II, the ruler of Germany, urged Austria-Hungary to attack Serbia. Instead, Austria-Hungary's foreign minister sent Serbia a letter. The letter had some harsh demands. Austria-Hungary wanted Serbia to give up most of the rights it had as an independent country.

Nations Declare War

Serbia agreed to some, but not all, of Austria-Hungary's demands. That was not good enough for Austria-Hungary. It took Germany's advice and declared war on Serbia on July 28, 1914.

Serbia could not fight Austria-Hungary alone. It had to have allies. Russia prepared its army to help Serbia. When Russia's army began preparing

232

Background

Reasons for the War

Europe was in turmoil for several reasons. One reason was extreme nationalism. A devotion to and a pride in one's own nation is natural. But some countries had been building a distorted nationalism in their people in the years before the war. Germany, for example, began to believe that it had the right to build and expand no matter what the effect might be on other countries.

Imperialism and militarism also contributed to the growing tensions in Europe. Several countries had or wanted large empires. Some of them were willing to go to war to gain control of colonies or nearby territories. Several nations had built large armies to further their imperial goals or to protect possessions. Large and powerful military forces threatened weaker neighbors and caused rivals to increase their forces.

Another major reason for the eruption of World War I was the alliances of European nations. In an effort to ensure security against aggression, European nations had formed alliances to support one another militarily. Those two opposing alliances involved all the major powers of Europe, so once any of them entered a conflict, all the others were likely to be drawn in.

Heritage Studies 5

for war, Germany declared war on Russia. Shortly afterward, Germany also declared war on Russia's ally, France.

Italy had promised to side with Germany and Austria-Hungary in a war. But Italy also had a secret agreement with France. Now Italy decided to withdraw from the Triple Alliance. Later, it would join the France's side of the conflict.

As part of the Triple Entente, Britain had promised to help France and Russia. The British did not want a war. But they became angry when the Germans invaded Belgium, a small neutral country under Britain's protection. A neutral country does not take sides in a war. So the British declared war on Germany and Austria-Hungary. It seemed as though an entire continent had gone to war.

In each nation at war, the level of excitement was high. It was almost like a holiday. Crowds of people swarmed the streets. Bands played and people sang. Long lines of volunteers waited to join the army. Posters went up in every city, urging men to join. Newspapers and magazines published cartoons that mocked the enemy.

"War is a glorious thing," many people thought. "How noble to fight for one's country!" Hardly anyone expected the war to last very long.

But Sir Edward Grey, the British secretary for foreign affairs, had a different opinion. "The lamps are going out all over Europe," he told a friend. "We shall not see them lit again in our lifetime."

> Why was Europe called a powder keg in 1914?

"If I should die, think only this of me:
That there's some corner of a foreign field
That is for ever England."
—Rupert Brooke,
from "1914: The Soldier"

Brooke was a British soldier who died early in the war while on his way to serve in the Dardanelles.

233

Neutral Belgium

Neutral Belgium rejected Germany's demand to use its country as an invasion route to crush France and continue east to defeat the Russians. At the same time Britain, having treaty ties guaranteeing the neutrality of Belgium, warned Germany to call off the planned invasion by midnight of August 4 or the two countries would be at war. The German ruler, Kaiser Wilhelm II, sneered at Britain's commitment to a "scrap of paper" and ignored the ultimatum. Late that night, after a day of exhausting but vain negotiations, the British foreign minister, Sir Edward Grey, noticed the London streetlamps being extinguished, and sadly observed, "The lamps are going out all over Europe; we shall not see them lit again in our lifetime." At the stroke of twelve, world war began.

As confident German troops marched into Belgium, the words of their kaiser rang in their ears: "You will be home before the leaves have fallen from the trees." Brave Belgian and British troops, however, offered tough resistance, buying precious time for the French. By the end of August, the Germans had pushed to the gates of Paris, where their war machine ground to a halt. The French and British made valiant but costly attempts to push back the invasion. In the first month of war, the French alone lost two hundred thousand troops in battle.

Teach for Understanding

- Direct attention to the picture on page 233. Explain that World War I inspired a lot of poetry. Read aloud the quotation from the caption.

- What do you think Rupert Brooke meant? Possible answers could include that the British soldier was speaking of his loyalty to England even if he should die and be buried in a foreign land.

  Which ally of Russia's did Germany declare war against? France

  What did Italy decide to do about the conflict? Italy decided to withdraw from the Triple Alliance.

  What circumstances prompted Britain to declare war on Germany and Austria-Hungary? Germany invaded Belgium, a small neutral country under Britain's protection.

> Conclude the discussion by asking the question on page 233. Several nations wanted to become more powerful. People of each nation thought that their nation was the best one in Europe. Some of these people would stop at nothing to advance their nation's goals. In Europe, it would take only a "spark" of a problem for the nations to explode into war.

Activity Manual

- Introduce *Chapter 11 Looking Ahead* on page 164. Read the page together. Guide completion of pages 163–65.

92

Student Text pages 234–36
Activity Manual page 166

Lesson Focus

- Warfare between Allied forces and Central forces would last a long time.

Objectives

- Identify the original plan of the Central Powers to conquer the Allies
- Recognize the significance of the Battle of the Marne
- Define the *western front*
- Relate what living and fighting from trenches was like

Teacher's Toolkit CD

- Visual 31: *Trench Warfare*

Review

- Ask questions such as the following to review the previous lesson.

  Which countries formed the Triple Entente? France, Russia, Great Britain

  What was the Triple Alliance? an alliance between Germany, Austria-Hungary, and Italy

  What event caused Austria-Hungary to declare war against Serbia? A Serbian terrorist shot and killed Archduke Ferdinand who was heir to the throne of Austria-Hungary.

  What happened when Germans invaded Belgium? Britain declared war on Germany and Austria-Hungary.

Preparation for Reading

- Generate interest as you direct the students to read the titles and examine the pictures on pages 234–36.
- Guide pronunciation of any unfamiliar words in the lesson.
- Direct the students to read the pages silently to learn what the Schlieffen Plan was. The Central Powers planned to conquer the Allies quickly in the West before moving east to defeat Russia.

Teach for Understanding

- Direct attention to the picture on page 234 and the How It Was box. Read the story aloud. Guide a discussion of what it was like for a soldier to be away from home and in battle at Christmastime. Invite a student to suggest concerns that were expressed in the British officer's letter.
- What was the greatest concern that the British officer in the story had? that he might be killed and not return to his family

  Why did Germany play a greater role in the Central Powers than Austria-Hungary? The German army was larger and better trained than that of Austria-Hungary.

How It Was

A British officer sat up against the rough, muddy wall of his trench. He smoothed out the damp sheet of paper in his lap and picked up his pen.

"My dear children," he wrote. "I cannot say how sorry I am that I will not spend Christmas with you. Albert, as the tallest, you will have to hang the holly wreath on the door. Emily, be a good girl and help your mother with the Christmas pudding. And Henry, don't eat too much cake. When you go to church to sing carols, please pray. . . ." He paused and listened to a distant crackle of gunfire. "Please pray that God will bring your papa home. Love to all." He folded the letter and bowed his head.

War Begins
The Schlieffen Plan

The Great War, later called World War I, had begun. Germany and Austria-Hungary called themselves the **Central Powers**. The German army was larger and better trained than that of Austria-Hungary. The Germans did most of the actual fighting. Russia, Serbia, France, and Britain called themselves the Allied powers, or **Allies**.

The Central Powers had a plan to conquer the Allies. The plan was named the **Schlieffen Plan** after the man who thought of it. The plan called for the Germans to attack France and quickly capture the capital, Paris. Then the Germans planned to march east and defeat Russia. If the plan worked, the Germans could take Paris in about six weeks before moving east. With France defeated, the war would be almost over.

But events did not go as planned for the Germans. Before they got to Paris, they met French troops at the Marne River. The French soldiers fought fiercely. In the end, the German troops had to retreat. After the **Battle of the Marne**, the Germans realized they would not be able to use the Schlieffen Plan. The Allies were not going to be defeated quickly. Now Germany had to fight in both western and eastern Europe at the same time.

The Western Front

The Germans and the Allies began what was called the Race to the Sea. Both sides wanted to take control of

234

What was the first action the Germans were supposed to take under the Schlieffen Plan? to attack France and quickly capture Paris

Why did events not go as planned for the Germans? Germans met French troops who fought fiercely at the Marne River, and German troops had to retreat.

What did the Germans realize after the Battle of the Marne? They would not be able to use the Schlieffen Plan.

> Guide a review of important terms, maps, places, and people from each previous lesson. Direct the students to find and read the corresponding entries from the Resource Treasury.

the ports along the English Channel. If Germany could control these ports, it could prevent the British from sending help to France.

At the Belgian city of Ypres, the Allies finally stopped the German advance toward the channel. The battle lasted an entire month. Thousands of soldiers died. Today Flanders, Belgium, has fields dotted with white crosses. Many of these soldiers were buried there.

By the end of November, both sides had dug trenches. Soldiers used these trenches for protection from enemy fire. The longest trench line was called the **western front**. Two parallel trench systems snaked from the North Sea to Switzerland. The Germans occupied one trench system. The Allies settled themselves in the opposite one. On the western front, the war had reached a deadlock. Neither side was gaining ground. Many of the soldiers had hoped to be home again by Christmas. But now it seemed unlikely that the war would end soon.

Life in a Trench

Trenches were about six and a half feet deep and only wide enough for two men to stand side by side. Sometimes soldiers tried to cover the muddy ground with boards. But mud was often

"In Flanders Fields the poppies blow
Between the crosses, row on row,
That mark our place. . . .
Short days ago
We lived, felt dawn, saw sunset glow,
Loved and were loved"

—John McCrae,
from "In Flanders Fields"

McCrae was a physician and a soldier who died near the end of the war. The poppy, common in France, has become the symbol of those who died in World War I.

knee-deep on the floor of a trench. Most soldiers slept in crude dugouts cut into the trench walls. They had to go without bathing for days at a time. Lice and bad smells were problems. Rats ran around the soldiers' feet.

At the top of the trenches were parapets. Parapets were walls made of dirt, sandbags, and tangles of barbed wire. The parapets held off enemy attacks. Soldiers in the trenches fired their guns over the parapets.

Each army had a system of several trenches. There was a frontline trench with one or two support trenches behind it. Men in a support trench

235

Teach for Understanding

Why did the Germans and the Allies begin the Race to the Sea? Both sides wanted to take control of the ports along the English Channel. If Germany could control these ports, it could prevent the British from sending help to France.

What happened at the Belgian city of Ypres (EE-pruh)? The Allies stopped the German advance toward the channel.

Where are many of the thousands of soldiers who died at this battle buried? Flanders, Belgium

- Direct attention to the picture on page 235. Read aloud the quote from "In Flanders Fields." Explain that the words were taken from the poem written by a brigade doctor at the second battle at Ypres. Major John McCrae, a military doctor, was asked to perform the burial service for his friend, Lieutenant Alexis Helmer, a fellow Canadian. Many people think that later in the evening McCrae began writing the poem "In Flanders Fields."

What protected soldiers from enemy fire? trenches

What was the longest trench line that the Germans and Allies fought from during World War I? the western front

- Display Visual 31. Invite a volunteer to describe life in the trenches and the use of trenches in warfare.

Background

Violations of America's Neutrality Rights

The biggest difficulty in maintaining neutrality involved Britain's and Germany's violations of America's neutrality rights at sea. Britain was a small island nation so it was almost totally dependent on overseas trade for raw materials. Over time, Britain had developed the best and largest navy and merchant-marine fleet. The United States had benefited greatly from trade with Britain, and it did not want to lose that trade during the war. The United States wanted to continue trade with Germany too, but all sea trade with Europe was put in jeopardy by the naval strategies of Britain and Germany.

Early in the war, Britain had laid mines at the entrances to the North Sea to prevent nations from trading with Germany. However, instead of trading directly with Germany, some countries, including the United States, sent their goods to the Germans through neutral countries such as the Netherlands, Denmark, or Sweden, who resold them. Such actions angered the British, and they began to stop American ships bound for neutral nations.

Lesson

92

Teach for Understanding

- Direct attention to the picture on page 236. Read the caption aloud.

  What area would a soldier have to cross in order to attack soldiers in the opposing trenches? No Man's Land

- Invite a student to describe the Christmas Truce in 1914.

▶ Conclude the discussion by asking the question on page 236. Officers did not want their men making friends with the enemy. Calling a truce could result in a charge of treason, or betraying one's country.

Activity Manual

- Guide completion of page 166.

German and British soldiers celebrate Christmas in no man's land.

were ready to help the frontline at a moment's notice. A reserve trench was farther back. After spending time in the other trenches, men rotated to the reserve trench for rest. Soldiers could move between the trenches through narrow connecting trenches.

The land between the frontline trenches was called no man's land. This area was littered with dead bodies, barbed wire, and muddy shell holes. It was hard for soldiers to cross no man's land during an attack.

Christmas Truce

On Christmas Eve 1914, a dusting of snow covered the muddy battlefields of the western front. Lighted candles glowed along the trench lines. Some soldiers even decorated Christmas trees.

A familiar sound reached the Allies in the hushed darkness. The Germans were singing a Christmas carol in their trenches. First a few, then many more of the Allied soldiers joined in.

On Christmas Day, the guns were silent. Soldiers held signs up over their trenches saying "Merry Christmas." Men climbed over the parapets and walked out into no man's land. German soldiers in pointed caps shook hands with British soldiers in khaki berets. Some men exchanged gifts of tea, nuts, or chocolate. For just one day, the men put war aside and celebrated a holiday.

Many officers on both sides were angry with their troops. Officers did not want their men making friends with the enemy. Calling a truce could result in a charge of **treason**, or betraying one's country. After 1914, Christmas truces were forbidden.

In 1915 it became clear that the trench warfare would last a long time. The men were in mostly defensive positions. Direct attacks were too risky to be tried often. The fighting went on.

> Why were Christmas truces forbidden after 1914?

236

Background

Justified Wars

Though the Bible permits governments to wage war (Romans 13:4), the Bible favors peace when possible. When God puts the world right, it will be at peace (Isaiah 9:7). Christians have argued that nations must have righteous reasons for going to war. Defending one's nation or seeking to bring about peace are justifications for war (Numbers 10:9). In addition, because war is a result of the Fall that brings death and destruction, Christians have argued that war should be entered into only when other attempts to resolve the conflict have failed.

When wars are fought, they must be fought in a righteous manner. The force used must be proportionate, meaning that the amount of force used must not be more than is necessary to win the war and to deter future wars. The nations of Europe had decided that using gas in warfare would cause injuries and death so horrific that it was not proportionate to the aims of war. They had previously agreed in the Hague Convention of 1899 not to use gas in warfare. After World War I, these nations further resolved to avoid its use.

Since justified wars are fought to correct wrongs and bring about justice and peace, Christians have long held that those who are not fighting the war are not legitimate targets (Exodus 23:7; Matthew 7:12). They may not be targeted for killing, and their property must not be destroyed. Ships carrying war materiel were fair targets, but ships carrying noncombatants were not. This thinking is one reason why the Allied nations found unrestricted submarine warfare so reprehensible.

Activity

Reenact the Christmas Truce

Materials: tins of cookies, tea, peppermint candy, small decorated Christmas trees

Divide the students into two lines (trenches) on opposite sides of the classroom. Name one group the Allies and one group the Germans. Direct the students to begin singing "Silent Night." Choose several students from each side of the room to meet in No Man's Land between the two lines. Invite the students to share cookies, tea, and candy. Guide a discussion of what common bonds were between the soldiers that made them have a truce at Christmas. Discuss the chance the soldiers took in leaving their trenches and communicating with the enemy. Explain that the officers were concerned about soldiers committing treason.

War in Many Places
The Eastern Front

The western front was only one part of the war. Battles were also being fought in eastern Europe. The major nations fighting in the East were Russia, Austria-Hungary, and Germany. The Russians attacked the Central Powers along the borders of Germany and Austria-Hungary. The Russians had some successful battles but were repeatedly driven back.

Turkey, part of the Ottoman Empire, had joined the Central Powers early in the conflict. In 1915 the British and French launched an attack there from the Mediterranean Sea. The Allies hoped to control a water route into the Black Sea. A fleet of Allied ships sailed into a strait called the Dardanelles off the Turkish coast. They later fought on the Turkish peninsula of Gallipoli.

Turkish defenses were fierce. The Allied attacks failed, and the Allies were forced to pull back.

By May of 1915, both sides in the war had lost hundreds of thousands of men. Many thousands more were wounded. As the United States followed the war news from across the Atlantic, its people were shocked and grieved. President Wilson had declared the United States neutral. Most Americans wanted no part of the brutal European war. However, many Americans felt loyal to the Allies.

The Weapons of World War I
On Land

Machine guns had only been in use since the late 1800s. These new guns were the most important weapons of World War I. A soldier with a machine gun could fire 400–600 shots a minute.

The tank was first introduced by the Allies in this war. Tanks were armored vehicles equipped with guns. The Allies called them tanks because they wanted the Germans to think that these weapons were water carriers. But the Germans soon learned that tanks could crush anything in their paths. They could even drive over the tops of trenches.

World War I Action

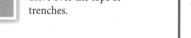

237

Review

- Invite a student to identify the Central Powers
- Choose a volunteer to explain the Schlieffen Plan and what happened to cause the Germans to realize that they could not use the plan.
- Guide a discussion of the western front and trench warfare.
- Invite a student to explain why military officers opposed the Christmas Truce.

Preparation for Reading

- Generate interest as you direct the students to read the titles and examine the pictures and map on pages 237–39.
- Guide pronunciation of any unfamiliar words in the lesson.
- Instruct the students to read the pages silently to learn which weapons were the most important in World War I. machine guns

Teach for Understanding

- Direct attention to the map on page 237. Instruct the students to use the key to locate the Central Powers, the Allied Powers and the neutral nations.

  What nation joined Germany and Austria-Hungary early in the conflict? Turkey, part of the Ottoman Empire

  What failed attacks did the British and French make in the region of Turkey? They sailed into a strait called the Dardanelles off the Turkish coast, hoping to control a water route into the Black Sea. They later fought on the Turkish peninsula of Gallipoli.

  How did Americans react to the loss of hundreds of thousands of men and the thousands of wounded in the war? People were shocked and grieved. Most Americans wanted no part of the brutal European war.

- Direct attention to Visual 32. Invite a student to describe weapons that were used during World War I.

Lesson

93

Teach for Understanding

- Direct attention to the picture on page 238. Read aloud the caption from "Dulce et Decorum Est."

- What do Owen's lines tell us about how the soldiers felt? They were exhausted, hurting, and discouraged. But they were committed to their task.

  What made it possible to carry out war in the air as well as on land? The Germans had blimps called zeppelins that were used to drop bombs. Heavy planes were also used as bombers. Fighter planes equipped with machine guns were lightweight, quick, and dangerous.

  What was a battle in the air between two opposing pilots called? a dogfight

  Who was called a "flying ace?" a pilot who shot down at least five enemy planes during the war

- Invite a student to describe U-boats and Germany's policy of unrestricted submarine warfare.

Another new weapon of World War I was poisonous gas. This chemical weapon was contained in canisters called shells. The gas spread through the air when the shell exploded. At first, only tear gas was used. Tear gas caused crying, coughing, and breathing problems, but it did not kill. Then the Germans introduced more deadly gases, such as chlorine, phosgene, and mustard gas. These gases were poisons that choked the victims and burned their skin. Mustard gas was especially difficult for soldiers to defend themselves against because it was invisible and had no odor. To protect themselves during a gas attack, soldiers wore large gas masks that covered their entire heads.

In the Air

For the first time, war was carried out in the air as well as on land. Planes were used mainly for observation early in the war. The first combat aircraft in the war were large German blimps called zeppelins. The Germans used them to drop bombs. Heavy planes were also used as bombers.

Later in the war, fighter planes were introduced. Fighter planes were lightweight, quick, and dangerous. These planes were equipped with machine guns. A Dutchman named Anthony Fokker had invented a device for airplanes. His invention allowed a machine gun to shoot between spinning propeller blades. Pilots on opposing sides tried to shoot each other down. A battle in the air between two planes was called a dogfight. A pilot who shot down at least five enemy planes during the war was called a "flying ace."

At Sea

War was also fought at sea. The Germans used submarines called **U-boats** to patrol the seas. Their main purpose was to stop British merchant

"Men marched asleep. Many had lost their boots
But limped on, blood-shod. All went lame; all blind;
Drunk with fatigue; deaf even to the hoots
Of gas-shells dropping softly behind."
—Wilfred Owen,
from "Dulce et Decorum Est"

Owen was a British soldier who was killed in action one week before the armistice.

238

Background

German Zeppelins

Count von Zeppelin flew his first aircraft in 1900. A zeppelin was made with a steel framework and was filled with hydrogen, making it lighter than the air it was traveling in. The zeppelin was made to carry civilians. As time went on, civilians could travel in gondolas beneath the elongated hydrogen-filled balloon that measured 190 meters in length (approximately 623 feet long). Later the *Hindenburg* would measure the length of three football fields.

England was not prepared when in 1915 German zeppelins were used to drop bombs on Britain. The bombing continued until England developed planes that could reach the height at which the zeppelins flew. British pilots were able to soar until the zeppelins were in target range. Then the pilots shot holes in the aircraft, causing the hydrogen to ignite and the zeppelin to crash. Technology for warfare advanced quickly during World War I. Soon zeppelins were completely replaced with fighter aircraft and bomber planes.

A German submarine torpedoed a British passenger ship, the *Lusitania*, causing the deaths of over one thousand people, including 128 Americans.

THE NEW YORK HERALD.

THE LUSITANIA IS SUNK; 1,000 PROBABLY ARE LOST

ships from bringing supplies to Britain. U-boats were equipped with torpedoes. Torpedoes were explosives that traveled underwater to their targets. When a torpedo exploded, it could badly damage or sink a ship.

German U-boats attacked any ships that came into a war zone, even if they were not warships. It was against the law to attack a neutral ship without giving it a warning and a chance to remove its passengers. People in other nations, including America, believed this policy of **unrestricted submarine warfare** was wrong.

The Sinking of the *Lusitania*

The German embassy put announcements in American newspapers. Americans traveled on British ships at their own risk. On May 7, 1915, a British passenger ship called the *Lusitania* was traveling from New York to Liverpool, England. Both American and British passengers were onboard. Suddenly a torpedo from a German U-boat struck the ship. Over one thousand people were drowned when the ship sunk. One hundred twenty-eight Americans were among those who died.

Americans were outraged. The ship had been unarmed and had carried defenseless passengers. But the Germans said that since the ship was carrying ammunition as part of its cargo, it was a fair target. President Wilson demanded that Germany apologize and stop unrestricted submarine warfare. Germany agreed to do so for a time. But some Americans were beginning to change their minds about being neutral. Many now believed the United States should become involved in the war.

> Why were Americans angered over the sinking of the *Lusitania*?

239

Activity

Make a Zeppelin or U-boat

Use resources to locate a kit or find instructions to make a model of a zeppelin or U-boat. Display the model with pictures of other zeppelins or U-boats.

Teach for Understanding

- Direct attention to the picture on page 239. Invite a student to read the headline aloud.

What announcements did the German Embassy put in American newspapers? that Americans traveled on British ships at their own risk

How did the British passenger ship, the *Lusitania*, sink? A torpedo from a German U-boat struck the ship.

What excuse did the Germans give for sinking the *Lusitania*? They said that since the ship was carrying ammunition as part of its cargo, it was a fair target.

What was President Wilson's reaction to the sinking of the ship? He demanded that Germany apologize and stop unrestricted submarine warfare.

What was changing in America's attitude toward the war? Some Americans were beginning to change their minds about being neutral. Many now believed the United States should become involved in the war.

> Conclude the discussion by asking the question on page 239. Of the people who died, one hundred twenty-eight were Americans. The ship had been unarmed and had carried defenseless passengers.

Activity Manual

- Guide completion of pages 167–69.

Assessment

- Administer quiz.

The quiz may be given anytime after completing this lesson.

Lesson Focus

- The Great War was no longer just a European war; it became America's war too.

Objectives
- Describe important European battles of World War I
- Recognize events that led to America's declaration of war
- State what the United States did to get ready for war

Teacher's Toolkit CD
- Instructional Aid 49: *Western Union Telegram*

Review

- Guide a review of the types of warfare and the weapons that were used in the Great War.
- Invite a student to tell about the sinking of the *Lusitania* and the impact it had on Americans.

Preparation for Reading

- Generate interest as you direct the students to read the titles and examine the pictures and graph on pages 240–42.
- Guide pronunciation of any unfamiliar words in the lesson.
- Direct the students to read the pages silently to discover the name of the largest sea battle. Battle of Jutland

Teach for Understanding

- Direct attention to the picture of the battle on page 240. Invite a volunteer to describe the battle scene.

  How did the Germans plan to break the deadlock on the western front? They planned to capture Verdun.

  What did Germans use to bombard Verdun's fortresses? shells, machine guns, poisonous gas

  How did the French defenders respond? They rained gunfire on the Germans. The French continued to defend Verdun for ten months and saved the city.

  How did British soldiers draw Germans away from fighting at Verdun? They attacked the Germans at a point along the Somme River.

  What did the Germans end up doing? They retreated.

- Invite a student to describe the Battle of Jutland and how it affected the course of the war.

America Enters the War
Battles and Bravery
Verdun

Early in 1916, the Germans on the western front decided it was time to break the deadlock. They planned to capture Verdun. Verdun was a French city surrounded by three rings of fortresses. But its defenses had been weakened. The French had sent some of Verdun's weapons to be used in the fighting on the front. The Germans thought that Verdun would be defeated quickly.

For two days in February, the Germans bombarded Verdun's fortresses. They used shells, machine guns, and poisonous gas. Then German foot soldiers began marching forward. They expected to find all the French defenders dead. Instead, French soldiers rained gunfire on them. The French continued to defend Verdun for ten months. Their brave efforts saved the city. But hundreds of thousands of French soldiers were killed or wounded during the **Battle of Verdun**. German losses were almost as great. Verdun was the longest battle of the war.

The Somme

In July of 1916, British soldiers tried to draw Germans away from the fighting at Verdun. They attacked the German soldiers at a point along the Somme River. The **Battle of the Somme** lasted four months. The Germans finally retreated. But even more soldiers had been killed or wounded than in the Battle of Verdun.

The Battle of Somme was fought between British and French against the Germans with trenches that stretched from the English Channel across France to the Swiss border.

Jutland

The largest sea battle happened in May of 1916. The **Battle of Jutland** was fought in the North Sea off the coast of Denmark. It was a quick and bitter battle. It lasted fewer than thirty minutes. The British lost fourteen ships, and the Germans lost eleven.

The battle did not affect the course of the war. But it did have an important result. The Germans decided that their

240

most effective strategy at sea was to use their U-boats. Once again, they resumed unrestricted submarine warfare. Two years before, the Germans had promised to stop using this type of warfare. Many Americans were angry that the Germans had broken their promise.

America's Growing Concern
Peace Without Victory?

It was now 1917, the third year of the war. The war had cost millions of lives. The nations at war had suffered heavy financial costs as well. Every country was tired of fighting. But the Allies and the Central Powers were still deadlocked. Neither side was winning.

President Wilson had won re-election in the United States. His supporters reminded Americans that "he kept us out of war." At the beginning of his second term, the president gave a speech before Congress. His message was actually directed toward the leaders of the warring nations. He encouraged the European leaders to settle for peace

without victory. But neither the Allies nor the Central Powers were willing to do that.

During February and March, German U-boats sank several US ships. President Wilson called for all American merchant ships to be armed. Americans watched the situation with growing anger and concern.

The Zimmermann Telegram

Also early in 1917, the German foreign minister, Arthur Zimmermann, sent a telegram to Mexico. Germany feared that the United States would enter the war on the side of the Allies. Zimmermann's telegram said that if this happened, Germany would reward Mexico to fight against the United States. Germany would give Texas, New Mexico, and Arizona back to Mexico.

British spies secretly got a copy of the telegram and sent the message to the United States. When Americans found out Germany was trying to make a deal with Mexico, they were outraged. President Wilson no longer wanted to talk about peace.

CAUSES LEADING AMERICA TO JOIN THE WAR

Unrestricted
Submarine Warfare + Sinking of the *Lusitania* + Zimmermann Telegram

241

Teach for Understanding

- Direct attention to the infograph on page 241. Choose a volunteer to explain the meaning.

  After President Wilson was reelected, what did he believe European leaders should do to end the war? He encouraged the European leaders to settle for peace without victory.

- Choose a volunteer to describe the Zimmermann telegram and how the message was sent to the United States.

- Invite a student to tell how President Wilson felt after he received the telegram.

Primary Source: The Zimmermann Telegram

- Direct attention to Activity Manual page 171. Invite a student to read the introduction aloud.

- Read aloud the Zimmermann telegram. Guide the students in understanding the meaning of the telegram.

Activity

Write a Telegram

Invite the students to write what President Wilson might have written to Germany after he read the intercepted Zimmermann telegram. Guide the students as they complete Instructional Aid 49.

Teach for Understanding

- Direct attention to the picture. Read aloud the caption from "Over There."

- Why do you think Americans sang songs like this one about the war? *Answers could include that singing these songs showed their patriotism; these songs made them feel hopeful and united in the cause.*

Which side would the United States fight on once it entered the war? *the Allies*

What was the state of America's army when the United States entered the war in 1917? *America did not have a large, trained army.*

What did the government do to make up for the lack of soldiers? *It used a draft system for the first time since the Civil War.*

What did America supply for the Allies? *soldiers, food, clothing, weapons, war equipment*

▶ Conclude the discussion by asking the question on page 242. *German U-boats sank several US ships, and Americans intercepted a German telegram that rewarded Mexico with Texas, New Mexico, and Arizona if the country would fight against the United States.*

Activity Manual

- Guide completion of pages 170–71.

"We'll be over, we're coming over,
And we won't come back till it's over
Over there!"

—George Cohan,
from "Over There"

Cohan was an American songwriter who wrote "Over There." It became one of America's most popular wartime songs.

America Declares War

On April 2, President Wilson went before Congress once again. He persuaded the members that America needed to make the world "safe for democracy." Then he asked for a declaration of war. Congress declared war on Germany four days later on **April 6, 1917**. The United States would enter the war on the side of the Allies.

America did not have a large trained army in 1917. So the government used a draft system for the first time since the Civil War. At first, men twenty-one years of age or older had to register for the draft. Later, men as young as eighteen had to register. The draft caused great excitement across the nation. Many Americans were eager to fight in the war. About four million Americans joined the army during World War I.

All over the United States, families said their goodbyes as soldiers headed off to training camps. The soldiers would train in the United States before boarding ships to sail to Europe. Americans also began preparing to help the Allies in Europe with war supplies. Along with soldiers, they would ship food, clothing, and weapons to the Allied nations. The Great War was no longer just a European war. It was now America's war too.

> What two events finally convinced America to declare war on Germany?

242

Background

America Prepares for War

America found itself ill prepared to answer Wilson's call to war. At the time of the war declaration, the peacetime army and National Guard numbered only 379,000 men. Remarkably, that number increased to 3.7 million by the end of the war. This rapid recruitment to meet the tremendous manpower demands of modern war was the result of a national draft through the Selective Service Act. In 1917 all men ages 21 to 30 were required to register for the draft, and in 1918 the bracket was expanded to include those 18 to 45 years old. Altogether, 2.8 million men were drafted into the army; half of that number eventually saw action.

When the recruits arrived at hastily constructed boot camps, they quickly learned just how unprepared the United States was for the war to which they were being committed. Theodore Roosevelt, an unheeded champion for military preparedness, wrote disappointedly that "the enormous majority of our men in the encampments were drilling with broomsticks or else with rudely whittled guns. . . . In the camps I saw barrels mounted on sticks on which zealous captains were endeavoring to teach their men how to ride a horse."

John J. Pershing

Who: commander of the AEF

When: 1860–1948

Where: Europe during World War I

John Joseph Pershing was born in Missouri. He attended a small school and helped on his father's farm. As a young man, he worked first as a teacher. He then trained at West Point in the 1880s and became a soldier. After his graduation, he led a regiment of African American soldiers against the Apaches and the Sioux. He often expressed appreciation for the courage of his men, earning himself the nickname "Black Jack." Pershing was known for being calm under fire. He received awards for his bravery in several conflicts before World War I. Shortly before America entered this war, Pershing lost his wife and three of his four children in a fire. Even after this great personal tragedy, he went on to command the American forces with courage and skill. For his courageous leadership during the war, he was promoted to the highest rank in the US armed forces.

US Soldiers in Europe

American soldiers marching onto French soil were a welcome sight for the Allies. These new soldiers in the war were nicknamed "doughboys." The Allies were counting on the Americans to help turn the tide of the long war.

The American army that went to fight in Europe was called the **American Expeditionary Force (AEF)**. The force was under the command of General **John J. Pershing**. Pershing worked under Marshal **Ferdinand Foch**, the commander of all the Allied troops.

Pershing did not allow American soldiers to be placed in European regiments. He kept American troops together and made sure they fought under American officers. By this time in the war, the French and British troops were weary of fighting. Many French soldiers banded together and refused orders from their officers. Some left the battlefield and never returned. Pershing did not want his soldiers to become discouraged by fighting alongside the Europeans.

243

The draft could provide the men but not the machinery of war. It took nearly a year for the nation's industry to convert to a full wartime footing. The importance of the industrial mobilization reflected the changing face of modern war. As President Wilson put it, "In the sense in which we have been wont to think of armies, there are no armies in this struggle, there are entire nations armed." All across the home front, Americans enthusiastically met the challenge to war and to win.

Lesson Focus

• American soldiers joined the war in Europe.

Objectives
• Identify the American Expeditionary Force (AEF)
• Recognize Allied military commanders
• Examine European battles

Review

• Use questions such as the following to review the previous lesson.

What was the outcome when the French defended Verdun for ten months? They saved the city.

What did the Germans use to sink several US ships? U-boats

What did Arthur Zimmermann do that angered President Wilson? He sent a telegram to Mexico to make a deal with the country.

Preparation for Reading

• Generate interest as you direct the students to read the titles and examine the pictures and map on pages 243–45.
• Guide pronunciation of any unfamiliar words in the lesson.
• Direct the students to read the pages to learn who led a new government in Russia after the czar gave up his throne. Vladimir Lenin and his party, the Bolsheviks or Communists

Teach for Understanding

• Direct attention to the picture and the Biography Box. Read the story aloud.
• Choose a student to suggest how John Joseph Pershing was suited to command American forces during the Great War.

How was Pershing rewarded for his courage and skill? He was promoted to the highest rank in the US armed forces.

Who were the "doughboys" who marched into France to help the Allies? American soldiers

What official title was given to the American army that went to fight in Europe? American Expeditionary Force (AEF)

Who commanded the AEF? General John J. Pershing

Who commanded all the Allied troops? Marshal Ferdinand Foch

Why was General Pershing careful to keep his soldiers from fighting alongside European soldiers? He did not want his soldiers to become discouraged. Many French soldiers banded together and refused orders from their officers. Some left the battlefield and never returned.

Where did the AEF first enter into major military action? along the Marne River

Lesson

95

Teach for Understanding

- Direct attention to the picture on page 244. Read aloud the words from the quotation.

What words does Binyon use to describe the soldiers' bravery? straight of limb, true of eye, steady and aglow, staunch to the end

What do you think the poem means when it says, "They fell with their faces to the foe"? Answers could include that the soldiers did not run away. They fought bravely. They were willing to die in the fight.

How did the Americans prevent the Germans from crossing the Marne River and marching on to Paris? They were stationed in the town of Château-Thierry and steadily fired on the advancing German troops.

How did American forces fare at the Battle of Belleau Wood? After three weeks of combat, 1,800 US soldiers had died and thousands more were wounded. The Americans had taken more than 1,500 German prisoners. American forces controlled Belleau Wood.

What major event happened in Russia during 1917? The Russian people forced Nicholas II to give up his throne. A new government took over under the leadership of Vladimir Lenin and his political party, the Bolsheviks or Communists.

What did Lenin promise the Russian people? bread, land, and peace .

Why would Lenin make this promise? Answers could include that Lenin wanted the people to follow his leadership and not revolt as they had done against Nicholas II.

The Second Battle of the Marne

The first major action for the AEF took place along the Marne River. This was the same river where the Allies had stopped the Germans in the early months of the war. The Germans were making another advance toward the city of Paris. American machine gunners were stationed in the French town of Château-Thierry. Their steady fire on advancing German troops kept these soldiers from crossing the Marne and marching on to Paris. Once again, the Germans had been stopped at the Marne River. This was the last major attempt by the Germans to take the city of Paris.

"They went with songs to the battle,
they were young,
Straight of limb, true of eye, steady
and aglow,
They were staunch to the end against
odds uncounted;
They fell with their faces to the foe."

—Laurence Binyon,
from "For the Fallen"

Binyon was a British poet and art scholar. He was too old to enlist in World War I, but he volunteered in a war hospital in France.

The Battle of Belleau Wood

At the same time, American troops were trying to stop the Germans in the nearby Belleau Wood. American soldiers entered the wood to attack German troops. The large number of trees made it difficult to see the enemy. The Germans used mustard gas to defend themselves. After three weeks of combat, more than 1,800 US soldiers had died, and thousands more were wounded. But the Americans had taken more than 1,500 German prisoners.

American forces now controlled Belleau Wood. They had proven that they were serious about their part in the war.

Trouble in Russia

Not all the Allied nations continued to fight in the war. At the time America joined the war, Russia was changing politically. There had been unrest in Russia for several years. During 1917, the Russian people forced their czar, Nicholas II, to give up his throne. A new government took over under the leadership of Vladimir Lenin and his political party, the Bolsheviks, also called Communists. Lenin promised the Russian people bread, land, and peace.

244

Background

Allies Hold the Line

The German commander Erich von Ludendorff knew that Germany could not prolong the war when the forces of the United States were added to those of the rest of the Allies. He decided to wage a full offensive against the British and French, forcing them to surrender before the United States could give substantial support. Germany began the British phase of the offensive in northern France and Belgium on March 20, 1918, with the heaviest artillery fire ever used. Some 6,000 German guns, answered by 2,500 British guns, pounded the front with tons of steel and explosive shells for more than four hours. Then the German infantry charged across No Man's Land. Flamethrowers, poisonous gas, hand grenades, and machine guns were used by both sides. The Germans, aided by a fog cover, successfully broke through in some places, but the drive slowed and faltered. After several days of intense battle, the British, aided by recently arrived American troops, prevented a general collapse of the line.

Having failed to break the British line, the Germans opened an attack on the French line to the south on May 27, 1918. The German assault broke the lines by May 30 and reached the Marne River, only fifty miles from Paris. But on June 2 and 3, American "doughboys" eager

American Battles

With all the hardships of war, the Russians listened to Lenin. Many Russian soldiers left the war and returned to help set up the new government. In 1918 Lenin signed a peace treaty with Germany. Russia's part in the war had officially ended. Germany now had to fight only on the western front.

The Final Battles

By this time, hundreds of thousands of American soldiers had arrived in France. Pershing commanded more than 500,000 American soldiers in an attack on the Germans at a town called Saint-Mihiel. This **offensive** was one of the strongest in the war. Tanks moved in first, followed by the AEF's foot soldiers. The French and the British also gave support from the air,

forming a force of nearly 1,500 planes. The Allies took thousands of German prisoners. The Saint-Mihiel offensive was over in four days. The Allies had won a great victory.

The last major offensive of the war began about two weeks later. It was named the **Meuse-Argonne offensive** after its location. The Allies were attacking German troops along the Meuse River and in the Argonne Forest.

Just as at Saint-Mihiel, the AEF played the major role in the attack. Once again, the Americans combined forces of tanks, foot soldiers, and airmen. The fighting went on for several weeks. Although the Allies suffered heavy losses, they refused to give up. German resistance grew weaker. Many soldiers were now also suffering from a terrible outbreak of influenza. In many cases, soldiers who had survived the long years of hardship and the strain of battle died of the flu.

The fighting finally stopped in early November of 1918. Millions of soldiers on both sides had died. Weary of the war, the Germans finally had to admit defeat.

> Why did the coming of Americans to the war front encourage the Allies?

245

Teach for Understanding

What changed about Russia's part in the war? Many Russian soldiers left the war and returned to help set up the new government. In 1918 Lenin signed a peace treaty with Germany. Russia's part in the war ended.

Who led 500,000 Americans in an offensive at Saint-Mihiel? Pershing

- Direct attention to the map on page 245. Choose a volunteer to name various locations shown on the map.

What other Allies gave air support during the Saint-Mihiel offensive? the French and the British

Who won the victory at Saint-Mihiel? the Allies

What finally led to the defeat of the Germans during the Meuse-Argonne Offensive? In spite of heavy losses, the Allies refused to give up. German resistance grew weaker. Many soldiers were suffering from a terrible outbreak of influenza. After millions of soldiers on both sides of the war had died, the Germans finally admitted defeat.

> Conclude the discussion by asking the question on page 245. The Allies were counting on the Americans to help turn the tide of the long war.

Activity Manual

- Guide completion of page 172.

for a fight poured into the gaps, halting the German drive at Château-Thierry and Belleau Wood.

Push to Victory

The largest effort by the doughboys was the American Argonne offensive that began on September 26. It was one of the costliest military campaigns in American history. One and a quarter million US troops, concentrated on a twenty-five-mile front, fought for six weeks toward the central German rail center at Sedan. The Americans suffered 117,000 casualties, including 26,000 killed in action, but the effort turned the tide. In October, the German leadership began to negotiate for peace. By early November, the kaiser fled into exile; the German lines collapsed. On November 11, 1918—at the eleventh hour of the eleventh day of the eleventh month—the Armistice was signed. The Great War was over.

Activity

Learn About Sergeant Alvin York

Use resources to learn about Sergeant York. Guide a discussion of York's background, how he became a Christian, and his exploits during World War I.

Lesson Focus

- Americans helped at home as the war continued in Europe.

Objectives

- Define the Committee on Public Information
- Examine ways that Americans supported the war
- Recognize the work of the Fuel Administration and the Food Administration
- Identify jobs American women filled

Teacher's Toolkit CD

- Visual 33: *Helping at Home*

Materials

- Three sheets of paper labeled "Meatless Day," "Wheatless Day," and "Sweetless Day" for each group of three students

Review

- Identify the Allied military leaders.
- Choose a student to describe the outcome of the Second Battle of the Marne and the Battle of Belleau Wood.
- Invite a volunteer to explain the change in Russia's government and how the country's role in the war changed.
- Guide a review of the Meuse-Argonne Offensive and how it ended.

Preparation for Reading

- Generate interest as you direct the students to read the titles and examine the pictures on pages 246–48.
- Guide pronunciation of any unfamiliar words in the lesson.
- Direct the students to read the pages silently to learn the name of the man who oversaw the Food Administration. Herbert Hoover

Teach for Understanding

- Direct attention to the picture on page 246 and read the poster and caption aloud.

  What was the attitude of most Americans at home about helping the war? Most wanted to do everything they could to help.

  What did the Committee on Public Information do? The new committee was in charge of the information given out about the war. The committee helped the American people feel more united in the cause of the war. The committee also published a large amount of propaganda about the Germans.

  What did Americans conserve to help the war effort? money, gas, food

The War at Home

World War I was fought in Europe, but Americans at home felt the effects of the war too. Though some Americans opposed the war, most were proud of the courageous young men who had gone to fight. They wanted to do everything they could to help at home.

Getting the Word Out

President Wilson created a new committee to be in charge of the information given out about the war. It was called the Committee on Public Information. The committee helped the American people feel more united in the cause of the war. Artists and writers designed posters and ads that promoted the war and urged people to support it. One famous poster from the war was a large picture of Uncle Sam pointing at the viewer. "I want you for U.S. Army," it read.

The committee also published a large amount of propaganda about the Germans. The information was meant to influence Americans to hate the enemy. Germans were called "Huns" after an ancient tribe known for their cruelty. Pictures in the ads portrayed Germans as evil and inhuman. Unfortunately, these posters and ads were hurtful to Americans of German descent. Anti-German feeling was so strong in America that German Americans sometimes feared for their safety.

Propaganda posters were designed to make a person think or feel a certain way.

Saving and Supporting

The war was expensive for the United States, just as it was for the other nations involved. The government encouraged the American people to support the war in various ways. Several new committees and boards were created to lead Americans in helping with the war.

One way that Americans helped the war effort was by **conserving**. The government encouraged people to save money, gas, and food at home. Then more of these supplies could be shipped overseas to the Allies.

246

Background

Purpose of the Wartime Agencies

The main tasks of Wilson's wartime agencies were to control prices and ensure "fair" distribution of resources. The Railroad Administration went further and actually nationalized the rail industry, outlawing all competition and running all railroads. Thankfully for advocates of free enterprise, those agencies lasted only until shortly after the war when the free market was once again allowed to function unhindered.

The Economics of War

Patriotic Americans raised money for World War I. The nationwide effort to invest in war bonds, or "Liberty Loans," reaped 17 billion dollars in revenue. Movie celebrities such as Douglas Fairbanks and Mary Pickford appeared at huge rallies to boost bond sales. Even schoolchildren saved their pennies to fill Liberty Books with 25¢ stamps captioned "Lick a Stamp and Lick the Kaiser."

The Fuel Administration was set up to help manage the use of the nation's fuel. It worked to conserve the amount of coal used in factories, homes, and businesses. Americans were also urged to have "gasless days" once a week. On these days, Americans who owned cars walked instead of driving.

The Food Administration oversaw the rationing of America's food. President Wilson chose **Herbert Hoover**, who was later a United States president, to lead this organization. Hoover encouraged Americans to have victory gardens where they grew their own food. He also asked Americans to set aside certain days as "meatless," "wheatless," and "sweetless." Conserving food allowed the government to greatly increase the amount of food it shipped to Europe. This food helped people who were hungry in other Allied nations.

Another way that people supported the war was by buying bonds. The money people spent on bonds went to help the war effort. Later the government paid these people back with interest. Calling these bonds "liberty bonds" helped people feel good about giving. They knew that the money was going toward the cause of freedom.

Many Americans joined in volunteer efforts to help the war. Women rolled bandages and knitted socks for soldiers. Some opened their homes to help care for wounded soldiers who had returned. Even children helped support the war. They could buy a savings stamp for as little as twenty-five cents to help with war costs. Schoolchildren tended victory gardens and sold the produce. Boy Scouts and Girl Scouts ran errands, passed out war propaganda, and helped sell war bonds.

Propaganda posters inspired Americans to support the war.

Working New Jobs

When a large percentage of America's men joined the military, thousands of jobs were left with no one to work them. Factories needed to

247

How did the Fuel Administration help manage the use of the nation's fuel? It worked to conserve the amount of coal used in factories, homes, and businesses. Americans were urged to have "gasless days" once a week.

What day of the week would you choose for your family to not use transportation requiring gasoline? How would your family be affected?

- Direct attention to the picture on page 247. Read the caption aloud.

- Display Visual 33. Choose a volunteer to read aloud each caption.

What were some things Herbert Hoover did as head of the Food Administration? He encouraged Americans to have victory gardens. He asked Americans to set aside certain days as "meatless," "wheatless," and "sweetless." He helped America conserve food so that it could be shipped to Europe to feed hungry people in other Allied nations.

What were liberty bonds? Americans supported the war by buying bonds. The money people spent on bonds went to help the war effort. Later the government paid these people back with interest.

What volunteer efforts did Americans join in? Women rolled bandages and knitted socks for soldiers. Some opened their homes to care for wounded soldiers who had returned.

What part did children play in supporting the war effort? They could buy a savings stamp for as little as twenty-five cents. Schoolchildren tended victory gardens and sold the produce. Boy Scouts and Girl Scouts ran errands, passed out war propaganda, and helped sell war bonds.

Activity

A Victory Garden

Invite a farmer to speak about planting a vegetable garden and to suggest what families would have planted in their garden during World War I. Invite the students to plan a victory garden. Choose students to suggest what they would plant and how they would care for the garden. Ask the students how they would use the produce.

Teach for Understanding

- Direct attention to the picture. Read aloud the caption.

  What work did American women do besides filling jobs that men had left behind? Some women worked more directly in helping with the war. A number of women became nurses. Some worked in hospitals at home, and some were shipped overseas to work on the war front. Some women enlisted in the navy as yeomen.

- Invite students to suggest some positive and some negative effects of women taking on new roles during the war.

  What happened in regard to women in the work force once the men returned from war? Many women returned to their roles in the home, and some continued to work outside the home.

  What helped women gain the right to vote after the war? the respect they earned during the war

- Why do you think it was important for American women to gain the right to vote? Answers could include that all adult citizens should be allowed to vote. Women should be able to have a say in how their country is run.

  Conclude the discussion by asking the question on page 248. Women rolled bandages and knitted socks for soldiers. Children bought savings stamps, tended victory gardens, and sold the produce. Many women took jobs in offices or factories. Some women worked more directly in helping with the war by serving as nurses at home and overseas. Some enlisted in the navy as yeomen.

Activity

Conserving Food

- Generate excitement about conserving food as you read the activity information aloud.

- Divide the students into groups of three. Distribute a set of papers with the headings "Meatless Day," "Wheatless Day," and "Sweetless Day" to each group.

- Direct each group to plan a menu for each day, avoiding meat, flour and bread, and desserts on the appropriate days.

- Allow each student to take home a menu for their family to prepare a meal during the week.

Activity Manual

- Guide completion of pages 173–74.

Women served in many roles during World War I.

produce more items for the war, such as uniforms and guns. Many people took new jobs to fill the needs in the work force.

During World War I, American women were employed in new roles. Women who had never worked outside the home now took jobs in offices or factories. Wages increased because of the shortage of workers. Many women earned a higher income than they had been able to earn before.

Some women worked more directly in helping with the war. A number of women became nurses. Some worked in hospitals at home, and some were shipped overseas to work on the war front. Some women enlisted in the navy as yeomen. They were not allowed to join the men in active service, but they could be in the reserves at home. Most of these women, nicknamed "yeomanettes," held office jobs.

When the war ended and the men returned home, many women left the work force and returned to their roles in the home. Some continued to work outside the home. An important result of the war was that women were highly respected for the part they had played. Many had accepted new responsibilities or bravely tackled new jobs. Some had even put their lives in danger to help others. The respect they earned helped American women gain the right to vote shortly after the war.

> In what ways did American women and children support the war?

Activity

Conserving Food

Label three separate sheets of paper with the headings "Meatless Day," "Wheatless Day," and "Sweetless Day." Plan a menu for each day. Be sure to avoid meat, flour and bread, and desserts on the appropriate days.

Choose one menu to take home. Ask for help to prepare the foods listed for a meal one day this week.

248

Activity

Conserving at Home

Direct the students to list ways to conserve food, water, and other resources at home. Encourage the students to practice conservation.

The End of the War
Armistice

The fighting officially ended on **November 11, 1918**. After the Meuse-Argonne offensive, the Germans agreed to an armistice. Germany was in a desperate state. Its ruler, Kaiser Wilhelm II, had fled to Holland and was about to give up his reign. The Allies had cut off supplies to Germany, and the German people were starving. Historians estimate that nearly 65 percent of Germany's forces had been wounded, taken prisoner, or killed by the end of the war. Weary German leaders met with Foch in a railroad car in a forest of France. They signed the armistice, putting an end to four years of warfare.

The armistice ended the fighting. But the war was not over yet. The leaders of the nations involved still needed to work out the details of the peace treaty. Even so, the day of the armistice was a holiday for the Allies. Allied soldiers laid down their weapons, took off their gas masks, and climbed out of their trenches. They cried and laughed and slapped each other on the back. In Allied nations around the world, people went wild with joy. They ran out into the streets, cheering, singing, dancing, and waving flags. Armistice Day became a national holiday in the United States. Later it became known as Veterans Day.

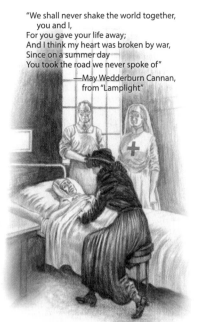

"We shall never shake the world together, you and I,
For you gave your life away;
And I think my heart was broken by war,
Since on a summer day
You took the road we never spoke of"

—May Wedderburn Cannan, from "Lamplight"

Cannan was a British nurse who served in France. Her fiancé fought in the war. He survived the war but died shortly after from influenza.

But for many families, there was sadness too. Millions of wounded were coming home. They would need special care. Many would have disabilities for the rest of their lives. And more than 115,000 American soldiers would never come home. Rows and rows of white crosses on European battlefields were silent reminders of the high cost of peace.

249

Student Text pages 249–51
Activity Manual pages 175–76

Lesson Focus

- The war ended, but Americans would feel the impact of the war for a long time.

Objectives
- Recognize November 11, 1918, as Armistice Day
- Examine the circumstances that led to the Treaty of Versailles
- Define the "lost generation"

Teacher's Toolkit CD
- Visual 34: *Armistice*

Review

What committee helped the American people feel more united in the cause of the war? the Committee on Public Information

What were Americans encouraged to conserve? money, gas, food

How did President Wilson provide for conservation of fuel? He set up the Fuel Administration.

What did Herbert Hoover oversee? the Food Administration

Preparation for Reading

- Generate interest as you direct the students to read the titles and examine the pictures on pages 249–51.
- Guide pronunciation of any unfamiliar words.
- Direct the students to read the pages silently to find out the name of the international organization that President Wilson believed could work for peace and security. the League of Nations

Teach for Understanding

- Display Visual 34. Explain that the pictures show how soldiers reacted to the news that the fighting was over.
- Direct attention to the picture of soldiers returning from World War I on page 249. Read aloud the caption and the words from "Lamplight."

- What do you think the poet meant by "You took the road we never spoke of"? The soldier was killed. She and the soldier she loved had not wanted to talk about the possibility of him being killed in the war.

When did the fighting officially end? November 11, 1918

- Invite a student to read the sentence that suggests what the armistice was.

What did world leaders still need to do after the armistice? They needed to work out the details of the peace treaty.

97

Teach for Understanding

Who were the "Big Four" at the peace conference in Paris, France? Georges Clemenceau of France, David Lloyd George of Britain, Vittorio Orlando of Italy, Woodrow Wilson of the United States

Why do you think Germany's leaders were not part of the peace discussion? Most of the Allied nations blamed Germany for the war; many wanted to see the treaty punish Germany.

Besides the Fourteen Points that Wilson formed, what international organization did Wilson want to include in the treaty? the League of Nations

What was included in the treaty in the end? It did not include most of Wilson's Fourteen Points, but it did include the League of Nations. The treaty required Germany to pay enormous costs for damages to the Allied nations. It took away large portions of Germany's territory. It forced Germany to greatly limit the number of military men and warships it could have.

Where did German leaders and Allies meet to sign the treaty? in the Hall of Mirrors at the Palace of Versailles in Paris

- Direct attention to the picture on page 250 of the signing of the treaty. Read the caption aloud.

- What world conflict followed World War I, proving that the treaty would not keep peace in the world? World War II

- Why do you think the world is unable to keep lasting peace? Answers could include that people who have not repented of their sin and trusted in Christ have sinful natures. They will continue to sin against each other. It is difficult for there to be peace when people continue to sin and resist God (James 4:1–3).

The Treaty of Versailles

Christmas came and went. In America, the celebration was a mixture of joy and sorrow. Yet many Christians thanked God for the new peace on the earth and prayed that it would last.

In January of 1919, the peace conference began in Paris, France. Leaders from many different nations gathered to discuss the peace treaty. The most important leaders at the conference were Georges Clemenceau of France, David Lloyd George of Britain, Vittorio Orlando of Italy, and Woodrow Wilson of the United States. They were known as the "Big Four."

Germany's leaders were not part of the discussion. Most of the Allied nations blamed Germany for the war. Many wanted to see the treaty punish Germany. But not all the leaders agreed on the treaty's terms.

Clemenceau wanted the treaty to be severe on Germany. He did not want the Germans ever to be a threat to other nations again. Lloyd George did not want to be quite so harsh. He wanted to decrease Germany's power, but he did not want to leave it powerless. Lloyd George saw that Communism was growing in Russia. He wanted Germany to be able to stand in the way of its growth.

President Wilson had given the treaty much thought. He had formed fourteen points that he wanted it to include. These points were meant to keep the world at peace. Wilson cared most about one of his points concerning a League of Nations. This

The "Big Four" met in France in the Hall of Mirrors to discuss and sign the peace treaty.

league would be an international organization that would work together for peace and security.

In the end, the treaty did not include most of Wilson's fourteen points, but it did include the League of Nations. The treaty also required Germany to pay enormous costs for damages to the Allied nations. It took away large portions of Germany's territory. It forced Germany to greatly

250

Background

Spiritual Effects of the War

Before the war, Americans generally had been optimistic about the prospects for world peace and the advancement of mankind. But the war had been so horrible that it led to deep pessimism and disillusionment. Progressivism, pacifism, and the hopes of the Social Gospel now seemed foolish and naive. The world was becoming more brutal and destructive, not better. Many poets, novelists, artists, philosophers, theologians, progressives, and even ordinary Americans became very pessimistic.

Christianity also stood discredited in the eyes of many Europeans. Europe was supposed to be a Christian continent. But the great nations had led their young men to barbaric slaughter. Often pastors equated service to God with fighting for the country. When the state uses religion for its own purposes, it is called civil religion. After the war many Europeans rejected not only civil religion but also true religion. Many families stopped praying together, church attendance dropped, and Christian morality was rejected.

limit the number of military men and warships it could have.

On June 28, 1919, German leaders met with the Allies in the Palace of Versailles in Paris. They signed the treaty in the Hall of Mirrors. The treaty became known as the Treaty of Versailles.

Some people, including Lloyd George and Foch, thought that the treaty was too harsh to Germany. They did not believe the treaty had settled matters in a way that would keep peace. They were concerned that Europe would have to fight another war. Time would prove them to be right.

After the Treaty

President Wilson returned to the United States. He was eager for Congress to ratify the treaty. But some congressmen were not pleased with it. They did not believe that the United States should be involved in a League of Nations. They felt that being in the league would threaten America's independence. Wilson traveled and made many speeches promoting the league. But the United States never ratified the treaty, and it never joined the League of Nations.

With the war over, most Americans wanted nothing more than for life to return to normal. But they would feel the impact of World War I for a long time to come. In the next decade, American author Ernest Hemingway wrote about the "lost generation." He was not only speaking of the young men who had died in the war. He was also referring to the war's effect on the hearts and minds of those who had lived through it. Many American young people struggled to recover a feeling of hope and purpose in life after the terrible war. More than ever, Americans needed the peace of God to keep their hearts and minds secure.

> Why did the United States never approve the Treaty of Versailles?

American heroes welcomed home

251

Teach for Understanding

- Direct attention to the picture on page 251. Read aloud the caption.

When President Wilson returned to the United States, how was the treaty received by Congress? Some congressmen were not pleased with it. The United States never ratified the treaty, and it never joined the League of Nations.

- Invite a volunteer to explain why young people were called the "lost generation" due to the impact of the war.

- Explain that America's involvement in the war helped bring World War I to an end, but the cost was great. The American people would feel the effects of the war for years to come.

> Conclude the discussion by asking the question on page 251.
> Some congressmen felt that being in the League of Nations would threaten America's independence.

Activity Manual

- Guide completion of pages 175–76.

Chapter Review
Activity Manual pages 177–78

Objective
- Recall concepts and terms from Chapter 11

Materials
- Questions on slips of paper with answers to the questions on separate slips of paper

Introduction

- Concepts for the Chapter 11 Test will be taken from Activity Manual pages 163–78. You may review any or all of the concepts during this lesson. You may choose to review Chapter 11 by playing "Mix and Match."

Review

Game: Mix and Match

- Write several questions on strips of paper. Write the answers to those questions on separate strips of paper. Place the questions in one container and the answers in another container. Mix up the papers.

- Draw a question from the container and read it aloud. Choose a student to draw an answer. The student should determine if the answer matches the question he heard. If it does match, the student receives a point for his team. If it does not match, he has the option of stating the correct answer. If he can give the correct answer, he receives a point for his team. Questions and answers that are incorrectly matched should be placed back into their respective containers before the next question is drawn. Continue until all the questions and answers have been matched correctly.

Activity Manual

- Guide completion of pages 177–78.

Lesson **99** Chapter 11 Test

Objective
- Demonstrate knowledge of concepts from Chapter 11 by taking the test

Assessment

- Administer Test 11.

Chapter 12

Introduction

The 1920s and 1930s were the best of times and the worst of times for many Americans. The Roaring '20s was a time of prosperity. Businesses grew, advertising became more influential, and America developed a consumer culture. But controversy arose between the Fundamentalists and the modernists. Christians faced serious challenges to their faith, and the Scopes Trial became a national affair. The prosperity of the 1920s came to an end when the stock market crashed in 1929. President Hoover's attempts to lead the country out of the Great Depression were unsuccessful. Under Roosevelt's New Deal, new federal programs were adopted and laws were passed in an attempt to end the Depression. His failure to end the Depression during his first term presented Roosevelt with challenges in his bid for reelection. He responded by placing blame for the Depression on the rich and the businesses. He proposed more federal programs. Although it did not end the Depression, Roosevelt's New Deal changed the role of government in the United States. Much of the New Deal remains in place today.

Chapter Focus

US citizens embraced consumer culture and a new relationship with their government during this period.

12 Roaring '20s and Depressing '30s

Focus

US citizens embraced a consumer culture and a new relationship with their government during this period.

Chapter 12 Overview				
Lesson	Student Text	Activity Manual	Content	Vocabulary
100	252–55	179–81	Changes in American culture The effects of new technology on American entertainment	conservative consumer culture
101	256–58	182–83	Fundamentalist/Modernist controversy Activity: Knowing What You Believe	agnostic liberal Fundamentalist modernist indifferentist Scopes Trial
102	259–61	184–86	Warren Harding Calvin Coolidge Primary Source: Taxation and Government	overproduction
103	262–64	187–88	Herbert Hoover and the Great Depression The stock market crash of 1929	stock
104	265–67	189–90	Franklin D. Roosevelt and the New Deal How It Was: Working for the CCC	legislation unemployment New Deal
105	268–70		Roosevelt's bid for reelection	Social Security welfare state
106	271–73	191–92	Roosevelt's second term Biography Box: Schechter Family	
107		193–94	Chapter Review	
108			Chapter Test	

Visit bjupress.com/resources for links to enhance the lessons.

Scopes trial
1925

FDR becomes president
1933

1925   **1929 1930**   **1935**
         Stock market crash

Changing Culture

After the sobering challenge of World War I, Americans were ready to return to normal. For the moment, they put aside Progressive presidents and causes. The business of America would be business. With growing business came money and time for more entertainment. The 1920s were "roaring" because people were playing music, dancing, and having fun. But hidden beneath the prosperity and fun were darker realities that could not be kept secret forever.

Consumer Culture

The combination of the factory, the assembly line, and electricity led to a variety of new products for Americans to buy. Many of these products made life easier. Electric dishwashers, washing machines, steam irons, and vacuum cleaners made housework less time-consuming. Refrigerators expanded the kinds of food that Americans could buy and eat year-round. Telephones allowed people to talk over long distances. Radios provided news and entertainment.

Many of these inventions existed prior to the 1920s. But more people were able to buy them now. And more people wanted to buy them. One reason for this change in desire was advertising. Advertising made buying appliances seem good. Sometimes it made owning these items appear necessary. Companies created brand names and advertised them across the nation. Stores such as JCPenney, Walgreens, and Woolworth had also sprung up to sell mass-produced goods to Americans.

By the 1920s, advertising and business had become significant. Some people began to look at religion through the eyes of advertising. Bruce Barton wrote a book about Jesus titled *The Man Nobody Knows*. Barton presented Jesus as a really good salesman. Barton said that Jesus'

253

Lesson Focus

- Following World War I, America became a consumer culture.

Objectives

- Describe America's consumer culture in the 1920s
- Explain the effects new technology had on American entertainment in the 1920s

Teacher's Toolkit CD

- Instructional Aid 50: *Modern Culture*

Introduction

- Invite a student to read aloud the title of the chapter and predict what the chapter will be about. a time in America called the Roaring '20s and another time called the Depressing '30s

- Invite a student to read the chapter focus aloud.

  What do you think you will learn about in this chapter? a kind of culture in America called a consumer culture and a new relationship between Americans and their government

- Direct attention to the picture on page 252.

- What do you think a consumer culture is? Answers may include that people do a lot of shopping for different products.

- Direct attention to the timeline.

  What important trial took place in 1925? the Scopes Trial

  What significant event occurred in 1929? the stock market crashed

- What do you think is meant by "the stock market crashed?" Answers may include that the value of stocks became less than when the people had bought them.

  In what year did Franklin D. Roosevelt become president? 1933

Preparation for Reading

- Generate interest as you direct the students to read the titles and examine the pictures on pages 252–55.

- Guide pronunciation of any unfamiliar words in the lesson.

- Direct the students to read the pages silently and complete Instructional Aid 50 in small groups.

Teach for Understanding

What were Americans ready for after World War I? a return to normal

JourneyForth

A No-Fuss Christmas by Susan Kirby is available from JourneyForth Books, a division of BJU Press, at journeyforth.com.

Set during the Great Depression, this heart-warming Christmas story tells of a foster girl named Sueker and her struggle to believe that nothing is too hard for God, even bringing her brother Razz to visit her at Christmas.

Teach for Understanding

What do you think Americans considered to be "normal?" Answers may include life as it was before World War I, without Progressive presidents and causes.

Why were the 1920s called the Roaring '20s? Businesses were growing, and people had money and time for entertainment. They were playing music, dancing, and having fun.

- Guide a discussion about how the variety of new products would have made life easier and allowed more leisure time.

Why did Americans now want to buy products that had been invented before the 1920s? More people were able to buy them now. Advertising made buying these items seem good, and it sometimes made owning them appear necessary.

Why do you think stores sprung up to sell mass-produced goods? Answers could include that mass-produced goods are items that can be quickly produced. This makes them readily available to stores.

- Choose a volunteer to read aloud the caption below the advertising posters on page 254. Guide a discussion about what is being advertised.

What happened when some people such as Bruce Barton looked at religion through the eye of advertising? They presented Jesus and God's Word in a way that was not biblical.

- Invite a student to read aloud the sentences that tell what Barton wrote.
- You may choose to guide the completion of Activity Manual page 181 at this point in the lesson.
- Use verses such as Romans 2:16, 3:23, 5:8, and 6:23 to guide a discussion about how Christians can use God's Word to refute Barton's statements.

What else concerned conservative Christians? The consumer culture could distract people from spiritual pursuits; people often wasted their free time.

- Choose volunteers to read aloud the glossary definitions of *conservative* and *consumer culture*. Mention that although the consumer culture concerned some conservative Christians, many gave little thought to ways in which a consumer culture can be contrary to Scripture.
- Discuss the parts of the culture that conservative Christians accepted and how they found them to be beneficial.

What difficult task did Christians living in the 1920s face? determining what parts of the modern world were helpful and what parts were harmful

message was of "a happy God, wanting His sons and daughters to be happy." Barton rejected the idea that people are sinners. He rejected the idea that Jesus had to pay the price of people's sins. He did not believe that God would judge people. Instead, he said that Christianity succeeded because Jesus was a good businessman and advertiser.

Conservative Christians rejected this picture of Jesus. It was not biblical. They also expressed some concerns about **consumer culture**. Consumer culture could distract people from spiritual pursuits. People had more leisure time. But people often wasted their free time.

Conservative Christians did not reject all modern culture. They saw the radio as an opportunity to spread the gospel. Telephones could be used by Sunday school teachers to keep up with their students throughout the week. Evangelists, Christian Bible schools, and colleges used advertising to attract people to their meetings and schools. They used

lessons on how to run a successful business or Christian organization. Christians of this time had the difficult task of figuring out what parts of the modern world were helpful and what parts were harmful.

Entertainment

New technology also transformed American entertainment. Up to this time, people had enjoyed entertainment in person. Often a family or neighbors gathered for music making or storytelling. In towns and cities, people might go to see a play, an opera, or a vaudeville show. Traveling actors and circuses would bring entertainment to people outside the city.

Advertisement posters attracted people to see live entertainment and encouraged people to watch the movie series each week at the theater.

254

Do you think the United States continues to have a consumer culture? Answers could include that American culture is still centered around buying and selling goods and services; buying is often based in peoples' wants rather than in their needs.

Do you think Christians today face the same difficult task of determining the helpful and harmful parts of the modern world? Answers could include that Christians will always have this difficult task because of living in a sinful world.

What should Christians use as their guide in determining what is helpful and what is harmful? the Bible

- Guide a discussion about how new technology transformed American entertainment during the 1920s. Choose groups to explain the effects of these changes.

The phonograph, radio, and motion pictures allowed Americans all over the country to listen to or watch the same entertainments. Now, instead of telling stories to each other, people could listen to professionals tell stories. Instead of making music together, people could listen to other people make music. This change had benefits. Not everybody could afford to go to a city to listen to an orchestra. But almost anyone could buy a phonograph record.

However, this new entertainment had some negative effects as well. Fewer people created their own music. Fewer people gathered to swap stories. They simply watched or listened to other people. Also, movies and radio programs needed to attract a large audience. Their stories needed to be something that many people would want to watch or listen to. As a result, they often did not focus on serious topics. Instead, they tended to be time wasters. Another way of attracting viewers was to appeal to sinful desires. Violence and immorality became common in movies. Some actors became movie stars. People became fascinated with the lives of movie stars, but often their lives were wicked.

These negative effects concerned conservative Christians. Pastors and evangelists warned Christians against wasting time on entertainment when they could spend that time doing some-

thing for God. They also did not want people to go to theaters instead of coming to church.

Some of these Christians wondered, however, if they could use the new entertainments to do good. Some made movies about God's creation. Others made movies that included gospel preaching. Some regularly staged dramas in their churches on Sunday to attract people to church. But other pastors warned that God had not told the church to stage plays. He told the church to preach the Word of God. The power of the gospel is presented through the preaching of the Word. It was better to trust God than to try to draw people to church with entertainment.

Many Americans, Christians included, were concerned about entertainment's effect on people's morality. Divorce became more common in the 1920s. Standards of dress and behavior that families had upheld for years were changing. Until the twenties, women wore ankle-length skirts. Now women started to wear skirts that fell just below their knees. Dancing, smoking, and drugs were also popular. Not everybody went along with these new fashions, but many did.

> **What were some helpful parts of modern culture? What parts were harmful?**

255

Lesson

100

Teach for Understanding

What did pastors and evangelists warn Christians about? wasting time on entertainment instead of using that time to do something for God; going to theaters instead of coming to church

- Guide the groups in sharing their thoughts on whether today's technology has the same effects on American culture as new technology had in the 1920s. Encourage discussion about what Ephesians 5:15–16 says about how Christians should use their time.

Did Christians agree on ways to use the new entertainments to do good? no

- Choose a volunteer to read aloud the sentences that infer that Christians did not agree on ways to use the new entertainments to do good.

What effects did entertainment have on the dress standards and behavior of many Americans? Women started to wear skirts that fell to just below their knees rather than ankle-length skirts that had been worn until the 1920s. Dancing, smoking, and drugs were also popular.

> Conclude the discussion by asking the question on page 255. See the answers on Instructional Aid 50.

Activity Manual

- Guide completion of pages 179–81.

Background

The Man Nobody Knows

The best-selling nonfiction book in 1925 and 1926 was *The Man Nobody Knows* by Bruce Barton. Barton, a successful advertiser, described Jesus Christ as "the founder of modern business," using advertising techniques to spread His message. The natural implication was that the big business of the twenties was a virtue. In the book, Barton twisted Scripture to ease the guilty conscience of a materialistic nation.

Activity

Advertise

Materials: poster paper

Give pairs of students a sheet of poster paper. Direct the partners to think of an item that would make life easier for them. Instruct them to design a poster to advertise the benefits of their item. Remind them that the poster should create a desire in others to own the item.

Lesson Focus

- Christians faced serious challenges to their faith during the 1920s.

Objectives

- Examine challenges Christians faced in the 1920s
- Analyze the significance of the Scopes Trial
- Contrast Fundamentalists and modernists
- Write about kinds of entertainment that are personally acceptable based on Scripture

Teacher's Toolkit CD

- Instructional Aid 50: *Modern Culture*

Review

- Choose a volunteer to explain what a consumer culture is and why the United States was considered to be a consumer culture during the 1920s.
- Invite a student to explain the effects new technology had on American entertainment in the 1920s.
- Use Instructional Aid 50 to guide a review of the helpful and harmful parts of America's culture during the 1920s.

Preparation for Reading

- Generate interest as you direct the students to read the titles and examine the pictures on pages 256–58.
- Guide pronunciation of any unfamiliar words in the lesson.
- Direct the students to read the pages silently to discover differences between Fundamentalists and modernists. Fundamentalists stood for the fundamental, or basic, teachings of the Bible and rejected the proposals of the modernists. Modernists thought that Christianity should be updated for the modern world. They said that Christians should accept evolution and the idea that the Bible had mistakes in it. They also said that Christians should not claim that Jesus was born of a virgin, died on the cross to pay the penalty for people's sins, and rose from the dead in His actual body. Modernists believed that Christianity was simply about following Jesus' example of doing good for others.
- Point out that modernists believed the social gospel.

> Guide a review of important terms, maps, places, and people from each previous lesson. Direct the students to find and read the corresponding entries from the Resource Treasury.

Fundamentalist/ Modernist Controversy

The United States had a long history of Christian influence. Many important Americans of the past were Christians. Many others were not. But Christianity influenced even those who were not. Many early immigrants to America were Christians seeking religious freedom. Many of those who opposed slavery did so because of Christianity. The same was true of those who wanted to see alcohol prohibited.

Christians in the 1920s faced serious challenges to their faith. The theory of evolution was a major challenge. The Bible taught that God spoke the world into existence in six days. Sin later brought suffering and death into God's good world. Evolution taught that life evolved over millions of years and that life developed only through suffering and death.

Some Americans did not want their children to be taught to disbelieve the Bible. In some places, such as Tennessee, laws were passed that did not allow teachers to teach evolution. Other people thought that the Bible should not determine what could be taught in school. The American Civil Liberties Union decided to test the law in Tennessee. Its lawyers would defend anyone who broke the law. A teacher named John T. Scopes of Dayton, Tennessee, agreed to break the law.

The **Scopes Trial** became a national affair. Reporters from all over the nation came to cover it. Three-time presidential candidate William Jennings Bryan came to argue for the prosecution. Well-known **agnostic** Clarence Darrow represented the defense.

Scopes and the ACLU lost the trial, but this case was not a victory for Christians. Darrow asked Bryan questions about the Bible and science that he could not answer. Bryan was neither a Bible scholar nor a scientist. Reporters wrote stories about how ignorant Christians were. People mocked conservative Christians so much that some thought this trial was

William Jennings Bryan was known for being a devout Christian, political crusader, and reformer.

256

Teach for Understanding

- Discuss the influence Christianity had in the United States prior to the 1920s. Include some examples of the Christian influence discussed in previous chapters.

  What major challenge did Christians in the 1920s face from outside the church? the theory of evolution

- Guide a discussion contrasting the biblical account of creation and the theory of evolution.

 What problem do Christian parents face when their children are taught something such as the theory of evolution? Answers could include that children are being taught something that is not biblical. This could result in children not believing the Bible.

  Why did the Scopes Trial take place? Some people thought that the Bible should not determine what could be taught in school. The ACLU decided to test Tennessee's law that did not allow teachers to teach evolution, and John T. Scopes agreed to break the law.

  What was the outcome of the trial? Scopes and the ACLU lost.

  Why was the outcome of the trial not a victory for Christians? Darrow asked questions about the Bible and science that Bryan could not answer.

- Invite a student to read aloud the caption for the photograph on page 256. Discuss the description of William Jennings Bryan.

Modernists believed that Christianity needed to change its teachings to survive in the modern world. They did not believe that modern people could believe the Bible was completely true.

Indifferentists believed in the truth of the Bible personally, but they opposed trying to exclude Modernists from leading in the churches, colleges, and seminaries.

Fundamentalists believed that people who changed the teachings of Christianity were creating a new religion. Fundamentalists thought Modernists should acknowledge this and stop trying to control the organizations that Christians had built.

the end of conservative Christianity. Smart people would certainly not be conservative Christians, many said.

Conservative Christians also faced challenges within the churches. Modernists within the churches did not want to be mocked. Modernists said that Christians needed to change with the times. They said Christians should accept evolution and the idea that the Bible has mistakes in it. They should not claim that Jesus was really born of a virgin or rose from the dead in His actual body. Christians should not say that Jesus died on the cross to pay the penalty for people's sins. These people said that Christianity was simply about following Jesus' example of doing good for others.

The people who wanted to make these changes were called **liberals** or **modernists**. They received this name because they wanted to update Christianity for the modern world. Conservative Christians who rejected the proposals of the modernists were called **Fundamentalists**. They received this name because they stood for the fundamental, or basic, teachings of the Bible.

Between the Fundamentalists and the modernists was a group called the **indifferentists**. The indifferentists agreed with the Fundamentalists about what the Bible taught. But they thought the Fundamentalists and the modernists should work harder to get along.

J. Gresham Machen was an important Fundamentalist. He was a professor at Princeton Seminary. Machen was one of the most capable biblical scholars of his day. He wrote books that liberals had a hard time answering.

257

Teach for Understanding

🦗 Do you think the Scopes trial has influenced the United States? Answers could include that the biblical account of creation is not taught in many public schools today. Teaching alternatives to evolution is often not permitted.

• Choose a volunteer to read aloud the glossary definition for *agnostic*.

What was Clarence Darrow's view of God? Darrow was an agnostic; he did not know if there was a God.

• Direct attention to the infograph. Guide a discussion about the challenges conservative Christians faced within the church. Include the differences in what Fundamentalists believe and what liberals believe.

Why were liberals also called modernists? They wanted to update Christianity for the modern world.

🦗 Do you think people should want to update Christianity as the modernists did? Answers could include that God's Word is perfect, and Christians should stand for its fundamental teachings. An attempt to update the foundational principles of Christianity is based on unbiblical ideas and leads to the creation of a false religion.

Why were some people called indifferentists? They did not side with the Fundamentalists or the modernists. They agreed with the Fundamentalists about what the Bible taught, but they thought the Fundamentalists and the modernists should work harder at getting along.

🦗 Do you think it is important to take a stand for what you believe? Answers could include that it is important for Christians to stand for the fundamental teachings of the Bible because God's way is perfect and the only way of salvation (John 14:6).

Why was J. Gresham Machen considered to be one of the most important Fundamentalists of his day? He was one of the most capable biblical scholars and wrote books that liberals had a hard time answering.

• Invite a student to explain Machen's view of liberals.

Background

The Scopes Trial

This famous trial in the 1920s came about through the efforts of the ACLU to challenge laws that forbade the teaching of evolution in public schools. Defense attorney Clarence Darrow, an agnostic, skillfully manipulated the proceedings to discredit the biblical account of creation. Though Scopes was found guilty and had to pay a fine, many believed the Bible had been discredited and that science provided the answers to questions such as the orgin of life. The play, *Inherit the Wind*, later made into a movie, provides a fictional and historically inaccurate account of this trial.

Fundamentalists

Baptist editor Curtis Lee Laws, in the religious newspaper *Watchman-Examiner* (July 1, 1920), coined the term *Fundamentalist*. He wrote, "We here and now move that a new word be adopted to describe the men among us who insist that the landmarks shall not be removed. *Conservatives* is too closely allied with reactionary forces in all walks of life. *Premillennialists* is too closely allied with a single doctrine and not sufficiently inclusive. *Landmarkers* has a historical disadvantage and connotes a particular group of radical conservatives. We suggest that those who still cling to the great fundamentals and who mean to do battle royal for the fundamentals shall be called *Fundamentalists*."

Teach for Understanding

How did the liberals respond to Machen's comments? They did not leave Christian churches and schools. Instead they worked with the indifferentists to take them over.

 Do you think it is okay to agree with Fundamentalists about what the Bible teaches and work in ministry with people who reject the basic teachings of the Bible and oppose the Fundamentalists? Answers could include that by working with people who reject the basic teaching of the Bible, a person shows that he does not truly agree with the Fundamentalists.

What did Fundamentalists like Machen do when the liberalists took over the schools and churches? Fundamentalists started new schools, seminaries, and churches. Machen and conservative faculty and students from Princeton Seminary started Westminister Theological Seminary to carry on the legacy of the old Princeton Seminary.

What did evangelists like Billy Sunday preach about? They called on Americans to turn from their unbelief and their sins, and they encouraged Christians to persevere in their trust in God and in His Word.

• Discuss the importance of encouraging others. Include how Christians today can encourage one another and how they can encourage unbelievers.

 Should Christians living today persevere when people oppose their belief in God and in His Word? Answers could include that Christians should continue to trust God to help them respond in a right way and to stay true to God and to His Word.

• Choose a volunteer to read aloud the sentences that tell what conservative Christians did after the Scopes Trial and after they lost their churches and schools.

What hope did the Fundamentalists have for America? They hoped that God would send another revival that would bring Americans back to Him

▶ Conclude the discussion by asking the question on page 258. They did not believe the basic truths of the Bible.

Activity Manual

• Guide completion of pages 182–83.

Activity

Knowing What You Believe

• As you read the Activity information aloud, generate excitement about knowing God's Word and using it to support decisions that you make.

• Invite students to share their paragraphs with the class.

262

Dallas Theological Seminary was one of the first to offer a four-year degree in theology.

His most famous book was called *Christianity and Liberalism*. Machen was making a point with his title. His point was that liberals were not really Christians. They had invented a brand new religion. The Fundamentalists were simply Christians who believed the basic truths that Christians had always believed. Machen said the liberals should leave Christian churches and schools. They should start their own organizations.

But the liberals did not leave. Instead they worked with the indifferentists to take over the schools and churches. Fundamentalists then left to start new schools and churches. Machen led conservative faculty and students out of Princeton. They started Westminster Theological Seminary to carry on the legacy of the old Princeton Seminary. Other seminaries and schools also began in the 1920s and 1930s to provide places for conservative Christians to study.

258

Evangelists like Billy Sunday also preached in many cities. These evangelists called on Americans to turn from their unbelief and their sins. They also provided encouragement to Christians to persevere in their trust in God and in His Word.

Conservative Christians did not die out after the Scopes Trial. They did not die out after they lost their churches and schools. They built new local churches and denominations. They built schools. They built missions organizations. They started magazines and radio programs. These new institutions took a great amount of effort and time. But the Fundamentalists had hope. Even though many Americans were turning their backs on God and the Bible, the Fundamentalists had hope that God would send another revival.

> Why did Machen say that liberals were not Christians?

Activity

Knowing What You Believe

Summarize what you believe are the fundamentals of the Christian faith that must be defended.

Write a paragraph about the kinds of entertainment that you believe are acceptable for you to take part in and what kinds are not. Give biblical reasons to support what you believe.

Activity

A Note of Encouragement

Materials: note cards

Encourage the students to think of someone who needs encouragement, such as a parent, a grandparent, a pastor, someone who is ill, or a friend. Guide the students as they write their notes.

Background

Additional Background information for this lesson is on the Teacher's Toolkit CD.

The Term *Fundamentalist* Today

Today the term *Fundamentalist* has become a slur with little specific content. In modern usage, a person can be a Muslim fundamentalist or a Hindu fundamentalist. The term is simply used for someone who radically holds to an extreme form of his or her religion, and usually the implication is that fundamentalists are intellectually backward. However, many Christians who self-identify as Fundamentalists stand in the mainstream of the orthodox Christian tradition with all its rich intellectual heritage. Along with other Christian groups, Fundamentalists insist on orthodox Christian doctrine, including the verbal inspiration of the Scripture and that church discipline (separation) be exercised toward both non-Christians who insinuate themselves into the church and toward the indifferentists who tolerate them.

Harding and Coolidge
Warren Harding

Before World War I, the Progressives had united around Woodrow Wilson. After the war, they could not unite around a candidate. Some of the issues that united them had already been turned into law. Progressives had won a constitutional amendment that banned making and selling alcohol as a beverage. They had also gained the right for women to vote.

Other issues divided Progressives. They divided over entering World War I. They divided over the League of Nations. Populist farmers believed that the Progressives had failed to help them. So Progressives and Populists divided.

The Republicans chose Warren Harding as their candidate. He promised a return to "normalcy." Americans were ready to return to a more normal life. Many Americans were weary of Progressive reforms. They did not think the reforms were good for the nation. Harding also promised to pursue policies that would help businesses grow. When businesses grew, more people had jobs. This promise sounded good to most Americans. Harding won the election of 1920.

President Harding appointed some very capable men to serve in his cabinet. For instance, his secretary of the treasury, Andrew Mellon, was respected. Mellon served Harding and the next two presidents. Mellon had Congress lower taxes. He also worked to pay off the World War I debts. His policies are credited with helping businesses prosper in the 1920s.

However, Harding also appointed close friends to serve in his cabinet. These men turned out to be corrupt. The country did not know about the corruption. But while he was on a trip to the western part of the country, President Harding died. Harding was a very popular president when he died. But then the country found out

Harding was a competent newspaperman. During his presidency, he carried a printer's rule in his pocket for good luck.

Harding's wife, Florence, burned many of his papers after his death. Historians think that she did this in hopes of preserving his reputation.

259

Lesson **102**   Student Text pages 259–61
Activity Manual pages 184–86

Lesson Focus

- Warren Harding and Calvin Coolidge served as America's presidents during the Roaring '20s.

Objectives
- Identify Warren Harding and Calvin Coolidge as America's presidents in the 1920s
- Explain Andrew Mellon's tax plan

Review

- Choose a volunteer to explain challenges that Christians faced during the 1920s.
- Invite a student to explain why the Scopes Trial took place.

What were some of the differences between the Fundamentalists and the modernists? The Fundamentalists stood for the fundamental, or basic, teachings of the Bible. The modernists wanted to update Christianity for the modern world and said that Christians should accept evolution. Modernists believed that the Bible had mistakes in it and that Christians

should not say that Jesus was born of a virgin, died on the cross to pay the penalty for people's sins, and rose from the dead in His actual body. Christianity was simply about following Jesus' example of doing good for others.

Preparation for Reading

- Generate interest as you direct the students to read the titles and examine the pictures on pages 259–61.
- Guide pronunciation of any unfamiliar words in the lesson.
- Direct the students to read the pages silently to discover the circumstances that resulted in Coolidge following Harding as president. *Harding died during his first term. Since Coolidge was Harding's vice president, he became the new president.*

Teach for Understanding

- Guide a discussion about why the Progressives could not unite around a presidential candidate after World War I.

Whom did the Republicans choose as their presidential candidate? Warren Harding

What influenced Americans to elect Harding as president? He promised a return to "normalcy" and to pursue policies that would help businesses grow, providing jobs for more people.

Why did most Americans like what Harding promised? Many Americans were weary of Progressive reforms that they did not think were good for the nation. They liked Harding's promise to pursue policies that would help businesses grow and create jobs for more people.

Who did Harding appoint to be his secretary of the treasury? Andrew Mellon

Why did Mellon serve as secretary of the treasury under Harding and the next two presidents? People respected Mellon. He had Congress lower taxes. He worked to pay off the World War I debts. His policies helped businesses prosper in the 1920s.

What happened while Harding was on a trip to the western part of the country? He died.

- Invite a student to read the captions for the picture on page 259. Guide a discussion about why Harding became one of America's least favorite presidents after his death. Include that corruption in politics demonstrates that all people are sinners and need to trust Christ to be their Savior from sin.

Lesson

102

Teach for Understanding

Was there an election to choose who would be president after Harding died? No, Calvin Coolidge became the next president because he had been Harding's vice president.

What was Coolidge known for? Coolidge was known for his honesty and for being a man of few words.

- Use the captions for the picture on page 260 to guide a discussion about Coolidge's character.

What did both Mellon and Coolidge believe the United States needed to do? pay its debts

- Choose a volunteer to use the infograph on page 261 to explain Mellon's tax plan and how Mellon followed Henry Ford's example when developing his new theory about taxes.

Which of Mellon's ideas was Coolidge happy about? lowering taxes

Why was Coolidge not happy that Mellon's idea would bring more money to the government? Coolidge worried that Congress would be tempted to spend the extra money. He thought the government spent too much money already.

- Invite a student to read aloud the paragraph that shows that Coolidge was serious about the government spending less money.

---

about the corruption. Several cabinet members had taken bribes to make themselves rich. Harding was soon one of the least popular presidents.

Calvin Coolidge

Calvin Coolidge, Harding's vice president, became the new president. Coolidge kept Harding's business-friendly policies. But Coolidge avoided scandals. Coolidge was known for his honesty. He was also known as a man of few words.

"Silent Cal" did not speak often, but he had a good sense of humor. Sometimes he would play jokes on his bodyguards by ringing for them and then hiding under his desk.

The president and the first lady had a pet raccoon named Rebecca.

A friend of Calvin Coolidge told this story: A burglar broke into the president's room while he stayed at a hotel. The president persuaded the burglar not to rob him, loaned the burglar $32, and later received the money back.

Andrew Mellon believed that the United States needed to pay its debts. Coolidge agreed. Mellon also thought the government should reduce the percentage that Americans paid in taxes. Mellon had a new theory about taxes. He pointed out that Henry Ford made more money by lowering the price of his automobiles and selling them to more people. If Ford had kept the prices high, fewer people would have bought his cars, and he would have made less money. Mellon believed the same thing would be true about taxes. If the government taxed a lower percentage of people's money, the people would have more money. If they invested that money in businesses, then businesses would make more money. In the end, the government would receive more money by lowering the percentage Americans paid in taxes.

Coolidge was happy about the idea of lowering taxes. He was not happy that Mellon's idea would bring more money to the government. Coolidge worried that Congress would be tempted to spend that extra money. He thought the government spent too much money already.

Coolidge found all sorts of ways for the government to spend less money. Government papers had often been tied together with red tape. Coolidge said that string would do just as well. The mail had been carried in blue-and-white striped sacks. Coolidge said

260

Background

Warren G. Harding

Warren G. Harding was a likable newspaper editor from the small town of Marion, Ohio. He climbed up the Ohio political ladder, eventually becoming a US senator. The political leaders in the state at that time were called the "Ohio Gang," and Harding did his share of favors for those people to achieve his political success. Harding had promised to get the country back to normal after the war. That was what the country wanted, so he was easily elected to the presidency. Once in office, Harding supported most of the popular programs of the day and big business. Unfortunately, he appointed many of his political friends who were not of the best character to important offices. Some of them used the government to promote their own gain. Although Harding may have been honest, his friends tarnished the reputation of his administration. Even though Harding was not involved in a public scandal for financial gain, he was wrong to allow the law to be disobeyed within the White House. Instead of providing firm direction, Harding allowed national affairs to drift along without guidance.

Harding's Death

President Harding was in poor health when he took a tour of Alaska in the summer of 1923, a trip that was intended to provide rest from the pressures of the presidency. On August 2, Harding was in San Francisco on his way back to Washington when he collapsed and died. The first announced cause of death was a stroke of apoplexy, but later it was changed to food poisoning from tainted seafood. After the scandals began to unfold, some people even speculated that he had committed suicide or was murdered by his wife. Harding probably died from a cerebral hemorrhage or a coronary thrombosis (although no autopsy was permitted).

Calvin Coolidge

Calvin Coolidge studied law in Massachusetts and entered politics there. He gained a reputation as a "law and order" man when, as governor of Massachusetts, he took a stand during the Boston Police Strike in 1919. He declared, "There is no right to strike against the public safety by anybody, anywhere, any time." He forced the police back to work. To a nation that feared disorder and crime, that stand won him admiration. Succeeding to the presidency after Harding's death, Coolidge was in charge when most of the Harding scandals were revealed. By firmly prosecuting the corrupt officials, Coolidge won enough support to win the presidential election of 1924. Then

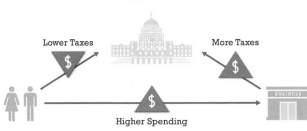

MELLON'S TAX PLAN

Lower Taxes

More Taxes

Higher Spending

that purchasing plain sacks would save money. Coolidge was careful even about how much food was served at the White House. He wanted to make sure that everyone was careful to spend government money wisely.

Coolidge sent Mellon's tax plan to Congress. Congress did not lower taxes as much as Coolidge wanted. But taxes were lowered. Mellon's predictions came true. The government brought in more money that year. Coolidge asked for lower taxes the next year as well.

Coolidge also wanted to <u>roll back</u> many of the regulations that the <u>Progressives</u> had put in place. There were still Progressives in Congress, so Coolidge did not succeed in this goal. Nonetheless, his policies helped businesses. The 1920s were, for the most part, a decade of prosperity for Americans.

There was one exception. American farmers found life difficult. They could not sell their crops for as much money as they had in the past. Farmers had

a hard time paying their loans. Some suggested that the government buy and store extra crops. Then prices would rise. Coolidge did not think the government was permitted to do this. He suggested that some Americans should move out of farming into other businesses. This solution would help stop **overproduction**.

Most Americans liked Coolidge. They liked the prosperity they enjoyed under him. He had served the remainder of Harding's term. Americans elected him for a second, and they would probably have elected him for a third. But Coolidge said, "I do not choose to run for president in 1928." He thought the precedent of presidents serving only two terms was good. He thought keeping power in the hands of one person too long was unwise.

> How did lowering the tax percentage result in bringing in more tax money?

261

he continued the basic policies that Harding had supported. Walter Lippmann, a journalist of the day, said that Coolidge had a "talent for effectively doing nothing" but that "this active inactivity suits the mood" of the country. Coolidge was credited for the prosperity in America and was enormously popular. He could have won reelection easily, but he chose not to run.

Coolidge's Inauguration

Calvin Coolidge was visiting his father in rural Vermont when President Harding died. Coolidge received the word in the middle of the night. At 2:45 a.m. on August 23, 1923, his father, a notary public, administered the oath of office by kerosene lamplight there in the farmhouse. Unfortunately, the simple ceremony was invalid because Coolidge's father was not a federal official, as required by law. So the swearing in was repeated several weeks later at the White House.

How did Congress respond to Mellon's tax plan? Congress lowered taxes but not as much as Coolidge wanted.

Why did Coolidge ask for lower taxes again the next year? Answers could include that Mellon's predictions about lowering taxes were correct. The government brought in more money the first year that the taxes were lowered.

Why was Coolidge not able to roll back many other regulations that had been put in place by the Progressives? There were still Progressives in Congress.

Which Americans found life during the 1920s difficult rather than prosperous? farmers

- Guide a discussion about why farmers found life to be difficult during the 1920s. Include how overproduction contributed to the farmers' difficulties.

Why did Americans elect Coolidge for a second term? Most Americans liked Coolidge and the prosperity they enjoyed while he served the remainder of Harding's term.

Why did Coolidge choose not to run for a third term? He thought the precedent of presidents serving only two terms was a good one. He thought that it was not wise to keep power in the hands of one person for too long.

Primary Source: Taxation and Government

- Guide the students in reading the introduction and Coolidge's speech on Taxation and Government on Activity Manual page 184. You may choose to have the students listen to a recording or view a film of Coolidge presenting the address as they silently read the text.
- Discuss the message Coolidge wanted to communicate.
- Guide the students in answering the question on the page.

> Conclude the discussion by asking the question on page 261. Lowering taxes gave the people more money to invest (spend) in businesses, so businesses made more money.

- Guide completion of pages 185–86.

- Administer quiz.

The quiz may be given anytime after completing this lesson.

103

Student Text pages 262–64
Activity Manual pages 187–88

Lesson Focus

- Hoover's plans to improve the economy during the Depression were not successful.

Objectives

- Identify Herbert Hoover and Franklin D. Roosevelt as the next two presidents of the United States after Calvin Coolidge
- Explain why the stock market crashed in 1929
- Explain why banks failed at the end of 1930
- Describe Hoover's solutions to the Depression and their effects

Review

Which two men served as president of the United States from 1920 to 1928? Warren Harding and Calvin Coolidge

Under what circumstances did Coolidge succeed Harding as president? President Harding died on a trip to the western part of the country. Coolidge was Harding's vice president, so he became the new president.

- Guide a brief review to describe Harding's and Coolidge's presidencies. Include the reasons for the popularity of both presidents and the reason that Harding became one of the least popular presidents. Also include why most Americans enjoyed prosperity during this time.
- Choose a volunteer to explain Andrew Mellon's tax plan.

Preparation for Reading

- Generate interest as you direct the students to read the titles and examine the pictures on pages 262–64.
- Guide pronunciation of any unfamiliar words in the lesson.
- Direct the students to read the pages silently to discover what event led to the Great Depression. the stock market crash of 1929

Teach for Understanding

Who was elected president after Coolidge announced he would not seek a third term? Herbert Hoover

- Invite a student to read aloud the captions for the picture on page 262.
- Why did Americans choose Hoover? Answers could include that the prosperity enjoyed under the Republican admininstrations of Harding and Coolidge led Americans to vote for Hoover. His success in leading relief and conservation efforts before the United States entered World War I, during the war, and while serving as one of Coolidge's cabinet secretaries also influenced Americans. They thought life would continue to be good under Hoover.

Herbert Hoover and the Great Depression

Herbert Hoover ran for the Republicans after Coolidge. He had worked in both the Harding and the Coolidge administrations. The prosperity that Americans had experienced under Harding and Coolidge led Americans to stick with the Republicans. However, Hoover was a more Progressive Republican. He was an engineer, and he knew how to run big projects. Hoover thought that government should work with

Herbert Hoover grew up in poverty but became a multi-millionaire. He was a successful mining engineer, traveling and locating rich mineral deposits. By the time he was thirty-five, he had left the mining firm to manage his own business affairs. As president, he donated his salary to charity.

Hoover was nominated five times for the Nobel Peace Prize.

businesses to engineer solutions to problems the nation faced.

Before the United States entered World War I, Hoover volunteered to help organize food relief for Belgians affected by the war. He made sure donated food reached the people who needed it. When the United States entered World War I, Hoover led America's food conservation effort. In 1927 the Mississippi River flooded. As one of Coolidge's cabinet secretaries, Hoover coordinated the relief effort between state officials, the Red Cross, and other volunteers. He thought that energetic, organized action could solve the problems the nation faced. But Hoover also thought that government's role was one of coordination. He did not think the government should actually do the work that businesses could do for themselves.

Americans looked at Hoover's past successes. They looked at the prosperity that Republican presidencies had overseen in the 1920s. They thought that life would continue to be good under Hoover. During this time, companies were producing new inventions. Electricity came to more and more American homes. Once a home had electricity, homeowners could buy new electric appliances. People could buy **stock** in companies that sold these appliances. And they could buy stock in other companies

---

How did Hoover think government should work with businesses to engineer solutions to problems that the nation faced? He thought the government should coordinate energetic, organized action and that businesses should do the work that they could do for themselves.

- Choose a volunteer to read aloud the glossary definition of *stock*.
- Why do you think people would want to buy stock in a company? Elicit that they would make money when stock prices went up.

What happened to the stock market in 1929? It crashed.

What caused the stock market to crash? Prices on the market had risen higher than the companies were worth.

Background

Additional Background information for this lesson is on the Teacher's Toolkit CD.

Herbert Hoover

The nation was still enjoying prosperity when the election of 1928 was held. The Republican candidate, Herbert Hoover, was swept into office by a nation satisfied with success. Hoover, a poor orphaned farm boy, had proved his abilities by becoming a wealthy mining engineer and then devoting his talents to public service. His Democratic opponent, Al Smith, was a Roman Catholic and was against Prohibition. The nation was not yet ready to vote a Catholic into the presidency or to end

that they thought would grow. But no one really knew which companies would succeed, so stock prices went up and down.

But in 1929 the stock market crashed. Crashes had happened before, and the economy had always recovered. Prices on the market had risen higher than the companies were really worth. A crash was simply bringing the stock prices back toward their real value. Then prices would slowly rise again as the value of the companies increased. And this is what happened after this crash in 1929. Few companies collapsed. Few banks failed. The stock market began to rise again. Most Americans did not own stock and were not affected at all.

Secretary of the Treasury Andrew Mellon recommended letting events take their course. He said allowing prices to fall would "purge the rottenness out of the system." But Hoover was sure that an energetic response would be best. Acting on his idea that the government should coordinate with American businesses, Hoover called business leaders to the White House. He asked them to keep

paying their employees high wages. He thought high wages were essential for a healthy economy. He asked states to spend money on public projects to keep the economy moving. In the summer of 1930, Hoover signed the Smoot–Hawley Tariff Act. He believed this tariff would protect Americans, especially American farmers, from foreign competition. Then in 1932 Hoover raised taxes in order to keep the budget balanced.

But the economy did not get better. In November banks began to fail. People began to withdraw all their money. But banks do not keep everybody's money in a vault. They loan some of that money out to others who repay it with interest. If every customer wants his money all at once, the bank will fail. When one bank fails, people start to worry. Those people might try to get their money out of their banks. If too many people withdraw their money, those banks will fail too. In December of 1930, the Bank of United States failed. Other large banks could have loaned it money to keep it from failing, but they chose not to. Now that a big bank had

HOOVER'S PLAN

263

Teach for Understanding

Do you think the stock market crash in 1929 should have caused great concern for Americans? Answers could include that it should not not have caused great concern because the economy had always recovered from previous crashes. The 1929 crash brought the worth of stocks back toward their real value, and the prices began to rise again. No companies collapsed. No banks failed. Most Americans did not own stock and were not affected at all.

Did Andrew Mellon and Hoover agree on how to respond to the crash? No, Mellon wanted to let events take their course to get rid of the rottenness in the system, but Hoover was sure that an energetic response was best.

• Invite a student to use the infograph on page 263 to explain Hoover's plan for an energetic response to the crash.

What effect did Hoover's actions have on the economy? It did not get better. Banks began to fail. In December of 1930, the Bank of the United States failed, causing people to be very worried about keeping their money in banks.

What could have prevented the Bank of the United States from failing? Other large banks could have loaned it money.

Why do you think other large banks did not loan money to the Bank of the United States? Answers could include that other banks might have feared that they would not have enough money in their vaults if their own customers wanted to withdraw all their money.

Did Hoover's policies help improve the Depression? No, his policies probably made the Depression worse.

Prohibition. Hoover was talented, but he had inherited the seeds of the impending fall from prosperity. The excesses of the twenties were about to bear the fruit of disaster. Hoover would be saddled with the responsibility for the coming Great Depression.

The Stock Market Crash

American businesses seemed to be flourishing as stock prices rose even higher in 1929. Prices reached a new height in September, but conservative investors were becoming cautious. Stock sellers found fewer buyers. Prices began to slide. By October, brokers' sell orders surpassed the orders to buy. On Thursday, October 24, a record-breaking thirteen million shares changed hands. Prices slid so low that investors lost $9 billion on that "Black Thursday." Many investors who lost all their money could not pay the stock brokers the additional money that they owed. When the investors could not pay, brokers tried desperately to sell the stock, flooding the market still more.

A panic broke out the following Tuesday when the stock exchange had orders to sell sixteen million shares. Fortunes made over a period of years vanished in minutes. Prices continued to drop until they finally reached their lowest level on November 13, 1929.

Most people expected the market to recover. Many historians deny that the crash was the primary cause for the Depression. It was only one of a number of causes that contributed to the Great Depression.

Lesson

103

WAGES / JOBS

+

FOREIGN TARIFF

+

TAXES

Teach for Understanding

- Use the infograph on page 264 to guide a discussion of the effects Hoover's policies had on the Depression.

  Why was Hoover discouraged when he faced reelection in 1932? He had always been able to take control of a situation. But nothing he did seemed to fix America's problems.

  What Democrat ran against Hoover in the election? Franklin D. Roosevelt

- Why do you think Roosevelt won the election? Answers could include that Hoover seemed beat by the Depression, but Roosevelt was upbeat. Roosevelt used the radio to speak quietly and personally to people as if he were sitting in their living rooms with them. Many people thought that he could help them.

  ▶ Conclude the discussion by asking the question on page 264. Rather than following Mellon's recommendation to let events take their course as they had in previous crashes, Hoover acted on his own idea that an energetic response would be best. However, Hoover's policies did not have the effects he thought they would. Businesses keeping higher wages resulted in businesses bringing in less money and in more Americans becoming unemployed. The Smoot–Hawley Tariff Act made prices higher for Americans and hurt businesses that exported goods. Higher taxes took money from Americans who needed it. The taxes also took money out of the economy when money needed to be going into the economy.

Activity Manual

- Guide completion of pages 187–88.

---

failed, people were more worried about keeping their money in banks.

Hoover's policies probably made the Depression worse. Businesses had agreed to Hoover's plan not to cut wages. But the businesses were now bringing in less money. If they didn't lower wages, they would have to cut jobs. The businesses tried to keep wages high, but more Americans became unemployed.

The Smoot-Hawley Tariff Act made prices higher for Americans. American companies did not face competition from other countries, so they could keep their prices higher. European countries responded by raising their own tariffs, which hurt businesses that exported goods. Many of these foreign nations owed the United States money. They had borrowed money during World War I. But their economies were having trouble too. Many of them decided not to pay the United States the money they owed. But the United States needed money.

Hoover's attempt to raise money through higher taxes hurt Americans. This policy took money from people who needed it. And it took money out of the economy when money needed

to be going into the economy. Hoover became discouraged. He had always been able to take control of a situation. But nothing he did seemed to fix America's problems.

In 1932 Hoover faced reelection. Running against him in the Democratic Party was Franklin D. Roosevelt. Hoover's and Roosevelt's ideas for how to fix the Depression were not very different. Hoover was a Progressive Republican. Roosevelt was a Progressive Democrat. But Hoover was discouraged. He seemed beat by the Depression. Roosevelt was upbeat. Roosevelt also knew how to use the radio to connect to Americans. The radio was a new tool for politicians. Many shouted as they spoke on the radio as if they were delivering a campaign speech to a large crowd. But Roosevelt spoke quietly and personally to people. Families gathered around the radio in their living rooms. Roosevelt spoke as if he were sitting there with them. Many people thought that Roosevelt could help them. They elected him to be the next president.

▸ Why did Hoover's attempts to fix the Depression fail?

Activities

How Tariffs Work

Use the following scenario to guide a discussion on how tariffs cause prices to rise.

Imagine you own an American company that makes shoes. A company from China sells the same quality shoe in America for fifteen dollars. How much would you have to sell your shoes for in order to compete? If the government decided to place a tariff on shoes made in China, the company in China would have to raise its prices in order to compete with your company. If the company in China had to raise the price for its shoes to twenty dollars, how much could you sell your shoes for now? What would happen to the price of the shoes in America? Who must pay for the increase?

Comfort

Direct students to find verses from the Bible that help people who are discouraged. Include verses such as Psalm 31:24; Psalm 46:1–3; Proverbs 18:10; John 14:27; 2 Corinthians 12:8–10; and 2 Timothy 1:7. Encourage the students to memorize some of these verses and use them to comfort someone who is discouraged.

The New Deal

In his campaign, Roosevelt promised Americans a **New Deal**. Congress was willing to work with Roosevelt and pass his New Deal **legislation**. Many congressmen believed that the Depression was a painful but brief crisis. Special action was needed to help Americans through this time.

First, President Roosevelt closed the banks for three days. He called this time a bank holiday. In those three days people's panic calmed. People stopped withdrawing all their money from the banks. Congress also passed a law that set up the Federal Deposit Insurance Corporation (FDIC). If a bank failed, the federal government would make sure that a person received up to $2,500 of all the money he had in the bank. The FDIC was also intended to stop runs on the bank. People would now leave their money in the banks because they knew they would not lose all their money if the bank failed.

Second, Roosevelt had a law passed that placed rules on businesses in the stock market. Some people thought lack of information about businesses was one reason for the stock-market crash. People did not know which businesses were wise investments and which businesses were bad investments. The law said businesses had to tell the public about how well their business was doing. The law required businesses to hire people called auditors to make sure that the businesses were telling the truth. Before this law, only people with inside knowledge could get rich. They became rich, but they hurt investors who did not have inside information. This law made trading on the stock market easier. It helped people get the information they needed to make wiser investments.

Many in Congress passed these laws because they believed the laws were necessary to get the United States through the crisis. But Roosevelt did not think the Depression was only a temporary crisis. He thought that when the United States was expanding west-

Franklin Delano Roosevelt and Theodore Roosevelt were distant cousins. Franklin Roosevelt was related to eleven other presidents.

When Roosevelt died, the New York Post listed his name at the top of the nation's war casualty list.

When Roosevelt was 39, he contracted polio. Both of his legs were paralyzed. He stood with the help of braces he wore under his pants.

265

Lesson (104)

Student Text pages 265–67
Activity Manual pages 189–90

Lesson Focus

- Congress passed Roosevelt's New Deal legislation to help Americans through the Depression.

Objectives

- Recognize that the New Deal was proposed by Franklin D. Roosevelt
- Explain the purpose of the New Deal
- Identify the Civilian Conservation Corps and the National Recovery Administration as two jobs programs begun during Roosevelt's term

Review

Who was elected to be president after Calvin Coolidge stepped down? Herbert Hoover

- Invite a student to explain why the stock market crashed in 1929.

Why did banks begin to fail at the end of 1930? People began to withdraw all their money from the banks. Some banks did not have enough money to give to these customers because they had loaned some of the customers'

---

money to other people who were supposed to repay the money with interest.

- Use the infographs on pages 263–64 to guide a review of what Hoover intended his policies to accomplish and what the actual effects of his policies were.

Preparation for Reading

- Generate interest as you direct the students to read the titles and examine the pictures on pages 265–67.
- Guide pronunciation of any unfamiliar words in the lesson.
- Direct the students to read the pages silently to discover why government leaders thought the New Deal was necessary. Many in Congress believed that the New Deal was needed to help Americans through the Depression. Roosevelt did not believe that the Depression was a temporary crisis. He thought the New Deal was necessary for the government to take an active role in making sure the economy worked.

Teach for Understanding

- Choose a student to read aloud the captions for the picture on page 265.

  What did Roosevelt promise Americans during his presidential campaign? a New Deal

- Choose a volunteer to read aloud the glossary definition for *New Deal*. Explain that the New Deal consisted of multiple programs, policies, and laws.

  What do you think the word *legislation* refers to when talking about the New Deal? Answers could include all the laws that were passed under the New Deal.

  Why was Congress willing to pass Roosevelt's New Deal legislation? Many congressmen believed that the Depression was a painful but brief crisis. Special action was needed to help Americans through this time.

  What happened when Roosevelt declared a bank holiday? He closed the banks for three days. People's panic calmed, and people stopped withdrawing all their money from the banks.

- Invite a student to explain why Congress passed a law that set up the FDIC.

  What did the law that placed rules on businesses in the stock market require businesses to do? tell the public about how well their business was doing and hire auditors to make sure that the businesses were telling the truth

- Explain that auditors examine the financial records of businesses for accuracy.

Chapter 12: Roaring '20s and Depressing '30s

Why did Congress pass the law that placed these rules on business in the stock market? Answers could include that trading on the stock market needed to be more just. All people who invested in the stock needed to be able to get information about businesses in order to make wise investments.

Teach for Understanding

Why did Roosevelt think that the Depression was not a temporary crisis? The United States had stopped expanding westward, and there was no more room for economic growth.

What did this lack of growth lead to? overproduction

What action did Roosevelt take to try to fix the problem of overproduction? He asked Congress to pass a bill that paid farmers to plant fewer crops.

- Guide a discussion about overproduction. Include how Roosevelt's bill affected the problem of overproduction and whether it helped the farmers.

- Choose a volunteer to explain the effects that the bill had on other Americans.

What other big problem did the United States face at this time? unemployment

What problem did people who were unemployed have? They wanted and needed jobs, but they could not find work.

What problems did people who did have jobs face? Their employers did not offer sufficient work hours needed for them to earn enough money to support their families.

- Invite a volunteer to explain the unemployment infograph.

Why did Roosevelt think that the government might need to start providing jobs for unemployed Americans from then on? He thought the economy had stopped growing.

---

ward, its economy still had room to grow. But now the United States was no longer expanding. There was no more room to grow. Farms and factories were producing more crops and goods. But the nation was not growing. This situation led to overproduction. For example, a farmer produces 1,000 bushels of wheat. He sells the wheat for thirty cents a bushel. The next year he produces 1,500 bushels of wheat. Other farmers produce more wheat too. But the people don't need more wheat. So the price drops to ten cents per bushel. The farmers are growing more crops and making less money.

Roosevelt thought economic growth was done now that westward expansion was done. He did not try to grow the economy. Instead, he thought that from now on the government would need to take an active role in making sure the economy worked. Roosevelt asked Congress to pass a bill that paid farmers to plant fewer crops. If fewer crops were planted, then the prices would rise. The farmers would make more money. The bill passed, but it passed after the farmers had already planted their crops. As a result the farmers plowed up their crops so they could get the money for planting less.

The farmers were happy for the money. Other Americans did not understand why the government was paying the farmers to destroy food. Some Americans starved during the Depression. The policy was most harmful to those who had the least. It raised the prices on a necessity—food—when the poor had little money to spend.

The policy also hurt sharecroppers. The owner of the farm got money for not planting some of his fields. This money did not go to the sharecropper. Sharecroppers made money from part of the sale of the crops. Now the sharecroppers grew less and earned less.

Unemployment was the other big problem facing the United States. Many people wanted and needed jobs, but they could not find work. For every ten Americans who had work, nearly two Americans could not find work. Other people had jobs, but their employers did not offer sufficient work hours needed to earn enough money to support their families.

Roosevelt thought that since the economy had stopped growing, the government might need to start providing jobs to unemployed Americans from then on. Other Americans did not agree with that idea,

EMPLOYED | UNDEREMPLOYED UNEMPLOYED

266

Background

Life in the Civilian Conservation Corps (CCC) Camps

Over three million unemployed men between the ages of 17 and 25 were employed by the CCC in efforts to help the young men and to conserve natural resources. Military men managed the camps, modeling daily routines after that of military life. The day began with reveille between 5:30 and 6:00 a.m., the raising of the American flag, roll call, and the giving of job assignments. The men worked eight to ten hours each day. They wore denim work uniforms and were given bag lunches consisting of two sandwiches and a piece of fruit. Their monthly wage was $30, $25 of which was withheld and sent home to support their families. The CCC focused on educating the men and ensuring literacy. The men also had opportunities to learn skills such as typing, welding, truck driving, stone cutting, and carpentry. Recreation was also a highlight, which included sports activities such as boxing and Ping-Pong. Other leisure-time activities included card games, reading, and listening to the radio.

How It Was

Clifford made a small hole in dark, black soil. He then placed a small sapling in the hole and spread the dirt around it. Planting hundreds of saplings with the crew of CCC men was hard work. *But at least it's work,* he thought, *and work is hard to come by.*

Being in the CCC was like being in the army, tough work and too much time between visits home. He'd even missed his little daughter's first birthday. But the money Clifford sent his family every month kept a roof over their heads and food on their table. The food here was good too. Clifford looked up at the sun rising high in the sky. The men would break for lunch soon. Sandwiches piled high with shaved ham. Apples. Cool, clear water. Clifford straightened, moved on a bit, and dug another hole. He had more trees to plant before lunch.

but they agreed that the government needed to provide some jobs until the crisis was over. One of the first programs was the Civilian Conservation Corps (CCC). The young men who worked for the CCC earned twenty-five dollars a month, which was sent to their families. They themselves would live on five dollars a month. These men built roads, bridges, and buildings for state and national parks. They also planted hundreds of trees around the country. When World War II started, the CCC built military bases. Eventually, the men of the CCC joined the military.

The CCC was a popular program. It provided work for young men, trained them for military service,

and was temporary. Other programs created more problems. The National Recovery Administration required businesses to pay workers a minimum wage. Roosevelt wanted wages to rise so that people could start to buy things again. The law also forbade businesses from competing with each other. Prices could not be lowered below a certain level. The result was that businesses made less money but had to pay higher wages. More people lost their jobs. The NRA created many other laws that had similar negative consequences.

> **How did the NRA result in lost jobs?**

267

The National Recovery Administration (NRA)

The National Recovery Administration was designed to help businesses recover from the effects of the Great Depression. The goal was to eliminate "wasteful competition" among firms. Codes were written and given to businesses. Each company was assigned a share of the national market and given annual production quotas. The codes also set maximum hours to be worked and minimum wages. An additional provision required a company to recognize a union if the majority of the employees wanted to form one.

Each firm or business that complied with the NRA codes was allowed to display the NRA's Blue Eagle seal. Rather than clutching arrows in its talons as on the Great Seal, this eagle clutched lightning bolts and a gearwheel. The NRA was soon criticized as a violation of the free enterprise system. Big businesses seemed to be favored over smaller ones, and the consumer was caught in the middle when prices went up. The Supreme Court declared the NRA unconstitutional in 1935.

Additional Background information for this lesson is on the Teacher's Toolkit CD.

Teach for Understanding

Did all Americans agree that the government should provide jobs for unemployed Americans on a permanent basis? Answers should include that some Americans agreed that the government needed to provide some jobs, but only until the crisis was over.

What were two job programs started by the government? the Civilian Conservation Corps (CCC) and the National Recovery Administration (NRA)

Who did the CCC employ? young men

How much money did the young men earn each month? thirty dollars; twenty-five dollars was sent to their families, and the young men received five dollars to live on.

What did the men who worked for the CCC do? built roads, bridges, and buildings for state and national parks; planted hundreds of trees around the country; built military bases when World War II started

- Guide the students in reading the How It Was box.

What was Clifford's job? planting saplings or small trees

Why did Clifford think being in the CCC was like being in the military? The work was hard, and he did not get to visit home often enough.

- Do you think Clifford was thankful for the work? Answers could include that he was thankful because it was difficult to find work. The work provided for his needs and the needs of his family.

What did the NRA require of businesses? that businesses pay workers a minimum wage and that businesses not lower prices below a certain level

Why did Roosevelt want workers to receive higher wages? so that people could start buying things again

- Do you think the requirements set by the NRA helped the economy? Answers could include that the requirements hurt the economy. Businesses made less money, and more people lost their jobs.

> Conclude the discussion by asking the question on page 267. Answers could include that although businesses made less money, the NRA required businesses to pay higher wages. This requirement resulted in more people losing their jobs.

Activity Manual

- Guide completion of pages 189–90.

Lesson

105

Student Text pages 268–70

Lesson Focus

- Roosevelt's attacks on the rich and on businesses and his use of a "political machine" were effective in helping him gain reelection.

Objectives

- Examine the strategies Roosevelt used to get reelected to a second term
- Explain the purpose of the Social Security Act

Review

What did the New Deal consist of? multiple programs, policies, and laws

- Invite a student to explain why Congress was willing to pass Roosevelt's New Deal legislation.

Did Roosevelt agree with how some people in Congress viewed the Depression? No, he believed that the Depression was permanent and that the government would need to take an active role in making sure the economy worked from then on.

- Guide a review of the New Deal's legislation and programs.

Preparation for Reading

- Generate interest as you direct the students to read the title and examine the pictures on pages 268–70.
- Guide pronunciation of any unfamiliar words in the lesson.
- Direct the students to read the pages silently and, in small groups, to list strategies Roosevelt used to meet the challenges of reelection.

Teach for Understanding

Was Roosevelt's New Deal effective in stopping the Depression? No, it may have made the Depression worse.

What was Roosevelt's goal for the New Deal? to provide security for ordinary Americans

- Choose a volunteer to explain what is happening in the photograph on page 268 and to explain who Wallace was.

Why did some Americans oppose Roosevelt's reelection? They thought that his programs were hurting the country and that his laws were hurting businesses that provided jobs. Since the New Deal had not fixed the crisis, they did not think it should be permanent.

Reelection

Roosevelt's New Deal did not stop the Depression. It may have made the Depression worse. But Roosevelt's goal was to provide security for ordinary Americans in the Depression. He thought that with the end of the frontier, the American economy was finished growing. The Depression was the new normal. The wealthy had enough money to help them survive through hard times. Roosevelt thought the government should provide that security for other Americans.

But not all Americans thought that Roosevelt was right. They thought his programs were hurting the country. His laws hurt businesses that provided jobs. Some people had been willing to go along with the New Deal in a crisis. But it had not fixed the crisis. And they did not think the New Deal should be permanent. These people would oppose Roosevelt's reelection.

Roosevelt was also challenged by other politicians who did not think he had gone far enough. They thought that the government should take over major businesses in the United States. One such politician proposed that the government seize the wealth of the rich and give it to other Americans. He said that the

government should give each American a certain amount of money each year. Because the Depression had made many Americans poor, these politicians gained a great deal of support.

Roosevelt was running for president again. He needed to meet these challenges. Roosevelt responded by attacking the rich. He also attacked businesses. These attacks turned the attention away from the failure of the New Deal to end the Depression. It placed the blame for the Depression elsewhere. But it also further hurt the economy. Business owners did not know what Roosevelt might do to them. Would he pass new laws that would hurt them? Would he raise taxes? The uncertainty made planning for the future difficult.

268

What did some politicians think of Roosevelt's New Deal? They did not think he had gone far enough and that the government should take over major business in the United States. One politician thought that the government should seize the wealth of the rich and give it to other Americans.

- What do you think the result would be of the government seizing the wealth of the rich and giving it to the poor? Answers could include that the rich would oppose the government, and the poor would not be motivated to work when job opportunities arose.

- Invite groups to tell strategies Roosevelt used to meet the challenges of reelection. He attacked the rich and the businesses; he remade the Democratic Party; he had Congress pass the Social Security Act; he used a political machine.

Why did Roosevelt attack the rich and the businesses? to turn attention away from the failure of the New Deal to end the Depression and to place the blame for the Depression elsewhere

What was a result of Roosevelt's attacks? The attacks further hurt the economy.

Roosevelt had another plan for winning. But his plan went far beyond winning a single election. Roosevelt wanted to remake the Democratic Party. When Roosevelt was president, both the Democratic and Republican Parties were a mixture of conservatives and Progressives. The Republicans included conservatives like Coolidge. The party also included many Progressives. Franklin Roosevelt's distant cousin, Theodore Roosevelt, had been a Progressive Republican president. The Democrats included Progressives like Franklin Roosevelt. They also included conservative Southern Democrats. Roosevelt wanted to make the Democratic Party the party of Progressives. He wanted to gain the support of Progressive Republicans. He wanted to keep Southern Democrats within the party for as long as possible. But he was willing to lose them eventually in order to make the Democrats the

party of Progressives. This change took time, but eventually Roosevelt's plan worked.

Roosevelt also gained Progressive support by proposing programs the Progressives supported. The year before the election, Roosevelt had Congress pass the Social Security Act. **Social Security** was intended to help older people who no longer had jobs. It was also designed to help people who lost their jobs. A worker and his employer would pay a tax. The money from the tax would be used to pay money to the elderly or to those without work.

Social Security was the first step toward a **welfare state**. In a welfare state, the government takes responsibility for people's welfare. Roosevelt thought Social Security was the most important of his programs. He thought that the government would need to provide for people now that the frontier had been reached and the economy had stopped growing.

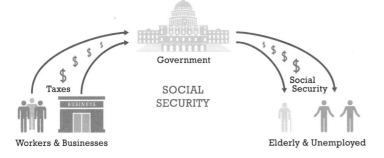

269

Background

The Social Security Act

Congress passed the Social Security Act in 1935, instituting old-age pensions and unemployment insurance for American workers. Social Security was essentially a pay-as-you-go system by which benefits were to be paid to beneficiaries from the taxes paid into the system by younger workers. The designers of this social program assumed that there would always be more workers paying in than retirees withdrawing benefits. But today the worker-to-retiree ratio is narrowing, and Social Security is beginning to pay more out to retirees than workers pay into the system.

105

Teach for Understanding

Why did Social Security secure votes for Roosevelt? People would vote for a candidate who would give them money.

What type of politics did Roosevelt use to get votes? Roosevelt used a political machine to get votes. People received help or other rewards in exchange for their votes.

• Guide a discussion about how a political machine works. Guide a second discussion about the political cartoon on page 270.

⚙ Do you think people should support or vote for a candidate based on what he gives them? Answers could include that people should vote for a candidate based on his qualifications and his willingness to do what is best for the entire nation.

▶▶ Conclude the discussion by asking the question on page 270. The attacks further hurt the economy. Businesses continued to make less money, and more people lost jobs. Not knowing what Roosevelt would do to them made it difficult for business owners to plan for the future.

Social Security also proved to be a way to secure votes. People would vote for a candidate who would give them money. Roosevelt used many New Deal agencies to gain support for himself. He also used programs to help other Progressive politicians around the country. Roosevelt made sure that New Deal agencies gave out money or assigned work projects to locations where his supporters lived. Then his supporters would urge other people to vote for him. "We'll keep help coming to you," Roosevelt's officials said. Supporters would continue to get money and work projects. People who elected Roosevelt's opponents did not receive help from the New Deal.

This type of politics had been practiced in cities for a long time. In the cities, a "political machine" was used to get votes. The "machine" was made up of a boss and his workers. The boss promised to give rewards in exchange for people's votes. The New Deal brought the corruption of the city machine to the national government. Roosevelt won reelection.

> How did Roosevelt's attacks on businesses make the Depression worse?

Political cartoon using a child's game to illustrate Roosevelt's New Deal Programs that he used to gain support for himself

270

Schechter Family

Who: Schechter family

When: the 1930s

Where: New York

The Schechters were a family of Jewish chicken butchers who were wrongly accused of selling sick chickens. The government also said that they did not follow other regulations of the National Recovery Administration. The Schechters' case went to the United States Supreme Court. The justices found that some NRA rules were absurd. The court also found the NRA itself to be unconstitutional.

Roosevelt's Second Term

Roosevelt had won a second term, but his New Deal was not secure. In his first term, the Supreme Court found that many of Roosevelt's New Deal programs were unconstitutional, including the important National Recovery Administration. The programs could not continue if they were found to be unconstitutional. Roosevelt worried that the Supreme Court might end the entire New Deal.

Roosevelt determined not to let the New Deal end. In his mind, the New Deal was not just a way to end the Depression. The Depression was the reason to get the New Deal put in place. Roosevelt thought the New Deal was necessary for the security and success of ordinary Americans whether or not

there was a Depression. He needed to get the rest of the New Deal into law before the Depression ended. And he could not have the Supreme Court declare it all unconstitutional.

Roosevelt proposed a new law to deal with the Supreme Court. Supreme Court justices serve for life unless they retire (or are impeached and removed from office). The proposal said that if a justice did not retire at age seventy, the president could add a new justice to the Supreme Court. Six of the justices were already over seventy. If they retired, Roosevelt could appoint six new justices. If they did not retire, Roosevelt could still appoint six new justices. Either way, the court would begin to support him, and Roosevelt would win. This proposal was called "court packing."

271

Student Text pages 271–73
Activity Manual pages 191–92

Lesson Focus

- During his second term, Roosevelt focused on making the New Deal permanent.

Objectives
- Examine the strategies Roosevelt used for keeping the New Deal in place
- Explain the effects of Roosevelt's strategies

Review

What did Roosevelt think the government should provide for ordinary Americans? security

Did all Americans agree with Roosevelt's New Deal? Some Americans thought his programs were hurting the country and his laws were hurting businesses that provided jobs.

- Guide a review of the strategies Roosevelt used to gain reelection. Choose a volunteer to explain the purpose of the Social Security Act and why it helped Roosevelt secure support for reelection.

Preparation for Reading

- Generate interest as you direct the students to read the titles and examine the pictures on pages 271–73.
- Guide pronunciation of any unfamiliar words in the lesson.
- Direct the students to read the pages silently to discover what supporters of the New Deal thought Roosevelt needed to do to end the Depression. spend more government money

Teach for Understanding

- Direct attention to the Biography box. Choose a volunteer to explain the information at the top of the box.

What did the government accuse the Schechters of? selling sick chickens and not following other regulations of the National Recovery Administration

What did the Supreme Court find when hearing the Schechters' case? Some of the NRA rules were absurd, and the NRA itself was unconstitutional.

What was Roosevelt's main concern at the beginning of his second term? His New Deal was not secure because the Supreme Court had found that many of the New Deal programs were unconstitutional. Programs found to be unconstitutional could not continue. Roosevelt worried that the Supreme Court might end the entire New Deal.

Why did Roosevelt want to get the rest of the New Deal into law before the Depression ended? The Depression was Roosevelt's reason to get the New Deal put in place. He also thought it was necessary for the security and success of ordinary Americans whether or not there was a Depression.

Teach for Understanding

- Invite a student to use the political cartoon on page 272 to explain how Roosevelt attempted to use court packing to deal with the Supreme Court.

Did people support the law Roosevelt proposed to gain support in the Supreme Court? No, some Americans thought that Roosevelt's New Deal programs took too much of Congress's responsibility to write laws, and it seemed as if he was trying to control the judicial branch of the government.

How did people who supported the New Deal feel about Roosevelt's plan? They felt that Roosevelt's plan went too far and spoke out against it.

What problem did the New Deal face in October 1937? The stock market fell again.

What did this event indicate? The New Deal was not making the Depression better. The economy had been getting worse for months. Americans were to experience a depression within the Great Depression.

But Congress did not pass the law. Americans could see what Roosevelt was trying to do. Even his supporters did not like his plan. The Founding Fathers had divided the government into three branches with checks and balances. New Deal programs had already made the executive branch more powerful than ever before. New Deal agencies could write regulations. Some thought the programs took too much of Congress's responsibility to write laws. Now Roosevelt seemed to be trying to control the judicial branch. Americans did not like this action. Even Supreme Court justices and Democrats who had supported the New Deal spoke out against this new plan. Roosevelt had gone too far. Congress never made Roosevelt's plan law.

But Roosevelt's plan was not really necessary. The Supreme Court would not overturn the New Deal. Four justices opposed the New Deal. Four justices supported the New Deal. One justice was a swing vote. In Roosevelt's second term, the justices came to support the New Deal. In addition, justices did retire while Roosevelt was president. He appointed justices in their place who supported the New Deal.

Even though the New Deal was safe in the Supreme Court, it faced trouble elsewhere. In October 1937, the stock market fell again. This occurrence was only an example that the economy had been getting worse months before. Americans were to experience a depression within the Great Depression.

Political cartoon using puppets to illustrate the appointing of justices who supported Roosevelt's New Deal

272

Teach for Understanding

How did Roosevelt respond to the second depression? He claimed the business leaders who did not like the New Deal conspired together and purposely caused this new depression to attack the New Deal. He asked the FBI to investigate.

What did some supporters of the New Deal think the government needed to do to end the Depression? spend more money

What did some people think led to the new depression? Roosevelt's attacks on businesses

- Invite a student to read aloud the sentences that tell the result of Roosevelt's attacks on businesses.

Did Roosevelt's decision to increase spending and get more legislation aimed at businesses help to end the Depression? no

How did the New Deal's failure to help end the Depression affect the 1938 elections? The Democrats lost seats in Congress.

What effect did the election results have on the New Deal? Conservative Democrats and Republicans in the new Congress joined together to make sure no more New Deal legislation passed.

This news was bad for Roosevelt. The Depression was the justification he had for instituting the New Deal. But if the New Deal did not make the Depression better—if it made things worse—then the New Deal would be in trouble with the voters. Roosevelt had to come up with an answer. He claimed that the business leaders who did not like the New Deal conspired together. He claimed the businesses purposely caused this new depression to attack the New Deal. He asked the FBI to investigate. Some supporters of the New Deal said that the government needed to spend more money to end the Depression. The New Deal did not go far enough.

Conservatives, and even some people who worked in the Roosevelt administration, said Roosevelt's attacks on business led to the new depression. Businesses were afraid that if they bought new equipment, Roosevelt would raise taxes on them, and then they would not be able to pay back their debts. They did not hire new workers. They just waited to see what Roosevelt would do next. The economy slipped into deeper depression since the businesses were not growing.

Roosevelt decided that more spending and more legislation aimed at businesses was needed. He got that legislation passed, but it did not help.

The Democrats lost seats in the 1938 elections for Congress. Americans were no longer confident that the New Deal was going to end the Depression. In the new Congress, conservative Democrats and Republicans joined together. They made sure no more New Deal legislation passed. Then, during World War II, Roosevelt had to work with businesses in the war effort. He stopped attacking them. After the war, America had a different president. President Truman was friendlier to businesses. After the war, businesses thrived again.

Nonetheless, much of Roosevelt's New Deal remains in place today. His policies made him one of the most controversial American presidents.

The 1920s and 1930s were the best and worst of times for many Americans. The 1920s were a time of material prosperity. But the decade was also a time when people rejected God's Word. The 1930s were hard for many Americans. Roosevelt's New Deal also radically changed the role of government in the United States.

> Why did people oppose Roosevelt's court-packing plan?

273

What was Roosevelt's relationship with businesses during World War II? Roosevelt had to work with businesses rather than attack them.

What happened to Roosevelt's New Deal? Much of it remains in place to the present time.

- Guide a discussion about why the 1920s and 1930s were the best of times and the worst of times.

What effect did Roosevelt's New Deal have on the United States? It radically changed the role of government in the United States.

>> Conclude the discussion by asking the question on page 273. People could see that Roosevelt wanted to make it so that the Supreme Court was made up of justices that would support him and the New Deal. Some people thought that Roosevelt's New Deal programs took too much of Congress's responsibility to write laws, and it seemed as if he was trying to control the judicial branch of the government.

Activity Manual

- Guide completion of pages 191–92.

Objective
- Recall concepts and terms from Chapter 12

Materials
- 3 × 5 cards

Introduction

- Concepts for the Chapter 12 Test will be taken from Activity Manual pages 179–94. You may review any or all of the concepts during this lesson. You may choose to review Chapter 12 by playing "The Best of Times, The Worst of Times."

Review

Game: The Best of Times, The Worst of Times

- Prepare an equal number of 3 × 5 (moving) cards labeled "two steps forward" and "two steps back."

- Prepare a list of questions and answers to use for review. Write the questions on strips of paper, and put them in a container.

- Place the moving cards face-down on a desk.

- Divide the class into teams. Choose one student from each team to be the mover and another student to be the speaker for giving the team's answers. Mark a starting line where the mover from each team will stand.

- Remove a question from the container and direct the question to one team. Allow the team to discuss the answer. If the team's answer is correct, choose a student from the team to select a moving card, instruct the mover to follow the directions, and mix the card back in with the others. Follow the same procedure for each team until all the questions have been answered correctly. The team whose mover is the farthest ahead from the starting line wins the game.

Activity Manual

- Guide completion of pages 193–94.

Lesson 108 Chapter 12 Test

Objective
- Demonstrate knowledge of concepts from Chapter 12 by taking the test

Assessment

- Administer Test 12.

Chapter 13

13 Rulers with Iron Fists

Focus
Unbiblical forms of government led to much suffering in the world.

Introduction

After World War I, several European governments were left with weak and indecisive governments. These countries were easy prey for dictators who made grand promises to help the people. These dictators and their governments became strong and controlling. Joseph Stalin in Russia, Benito Mussolini in Italy, and Adolf Hitler in Germany were harsh dictators.

Hirohito became the emperor of Japan in 1926. The Japanese had never been defeated in war when they attacked American ships in Pearl Harbor in 1941.

This was a dark period of history for many people. Strong men ruled nations in ways contrary to the Bible. Millions of people were harmed. Eventually the wickedness of their rule would require other nations to oppose them.

Chapter Focus

Unbiblical forms of government led to much suffering in the world.

Lesson	Student Text	Activity Manual	Content		Vocabulary	
109	274–77	195–98	Communism Joseph Stalin	Soviet Union	Communism	
110	278–80	199–201	Atheist Collective farm		atheist censor	collective farm
111	281–83	202–3	Benito Mussolini	Secret police force	Fascism	
112	284–86	204	Adolf Hitler Concentration camp der Führer	*Mein Kampf* Nuremberg Laws Swastika	concentration camp der Führer *Mein Kampf*	Nuremberg Laws swastika
113	287–89	205–6	Jews as God's special people Nuremberg Laws Biography Box: Corrie ten Boom Primary Source: German Nationalism Activity: Writing a Personal Narrative			
114	290	207	Emperor Hirohito	Showa	emperor	Showa
115	291	208	How It Was: A God or a Man?			
116		209–10	Chapter Review			
117			Chapter Test			

Chapter 13 Overview

Visit bjupress.com/resources for links to enhance the lessons.

Mussolini becomes prime minister of Italy 1922

Hitler becomes dictator of Germany 1933

1920 1925 1926 1929 1930 1935

Hirohito becomes emperor of Japan

Stalin becomes dictator of the USSR

Student Text pages 274–77
Activity Manual pages 195–98

For most of its history, the United States had tried to not get involved in the affairs of other nations. George Washington had warned against making agreements with other nations. John Quincy Adams and James Monroe developed the Monroe Doctrine, which warned European nations to not meddle in American affairs. The Spanish-American War began to draw the United States out of its isolation. America now had its own colonies on islands in the Pacific. And slowly, the United States had been drawn into World War I. After that war, many Americans wanted the United States to withdraw once again from the world stage. They did not want to join the League of Nations. They did not want to fight in other nations' wars. But powerful dictators were rising in Europe and in Asia who would soon draw the United States into a second world war.

After World War I, several European countries were left with weak, indecisive governments. Discouraged people were willing to follow anyone who might make a difference—anyone who might get their country back on its feet again. These countries were easy prey for dictators who made grand promises to help the people. However, these dictators and their governments became too strong and controlling. The leaders were harsh. The lives of people were not valuable to them. Even some of their own citizens suffered. In the years leading to World War II and throughout the war, many people lost their lives due to the actions of these men.

Stalin in Russia: The Man of Steel
Young Stalin

Joseph Stalin was born Joseph Vissarionovich Dzhugashvili in 1879. He was born in a Russian province called Georgia. The name Stalin, which he later adopted, means "man of steel."

Stalin's childhood was not a happy one. His family was poor, and his father was often drunk. Stalin had smallpox, which left his face badly scarred. At age

275

Lesson Focus

- Joseph Stalin became the dictator of the Communist Party in Russia.

Objectives
- Examine Joseph Stalin's early life
- Describe Stalin's rise to power
- State characteristics of Stalin's rule in the Soviet Union

Introduction

- Invite a student to read aloud the title of the chapter and explain what is meant by "rulers with iron fists." It will be about rulers who are very harsh.

- Invite a student to read the chapter focus aloud.

  What do you think you will learn in this chapter? how governments that go against what the Bible teaches lead to people suffering

- Explain that the picture shows the statue of a ruler. Invite a student to suggest how the people feel about life under this ruler.

- Direct attention to the timeline.

  What do all of the dates on the timeline have in common? They all show when rulers came to power.

  How many years passed from the time Mussolini became Italy's prime minister and Adolf Hitler became dictator of Germany? eleven years

  When did Hirohito become emperor of Japan? 1926

  When did Stalin become the dictator of the USSR? 1929

JourneyForth

The following books are available from JourneyForth Books, a division of BJU Press, at journeyforth.com.

Medallion by Dawn Watkins

This fantasy novel follows the adventures of Trave, a willful prince who learns the hard way that being a leader means first being a servant. Once he learns the duties of a king, he must prove he is worthy to lead his country.

Escape to Liechtenstein by Ed Dunlop

Set in Europe during World War II, this is the story of Hans and his sister Gretchen, who discover a Jewish boy hiding from Nazi troops and seek to help him to safety across the Austrian border. Other books in the Young Refugees series include *The Search for the Silver Eagle* and *The Incredible Rescues*.

Preparation for Reading

- Generate interest as you direct the students to read the title and pictures on pages 274–77.
- Guide pronunciation of any unfamiliar words in the lesson.
- Direct the students to read the pages silently to learn the name for a system of government that owns all the businesses and property. Communism

Teach for Understanding

How was it possible for dictators to rise to power in European countries after World War I? Several European countries were left with weak, indecisive governments. Discouraged people were willing to follow anyone who might make a difference—anyone who might get their country back on its feet again. These people were easy prey for dictators who made grand promises to help the people.

What name did a dictator take that meant "man of steel"? Joseph Stalin

What does the name suggest? Answers could include that Stalin would not bend or break.

Teach for Understanding

- Direct attention to the picture on page 276. Read aloud the caption.

What physical challenges did Stalin face as a child? His face was badly scarred, and his left arm was permanently disabled from an accident.

- Invite a volunteer to describe Stalin's education.

What changes took place in Russian leadership during the time Stalin was finishing school? The czar had died. The czar was succeeded by his son, Nicholas II.

How did the Russian people feel about being ruled by a czar? They wanted to have more say about how they were governed. Groups of men began to hold secret meetings and talked of revolution against the government.

What was Stalin's attitude toward these meetings and revolution? He attended the meetings and read books by some of these men with revolutionary ideas.

How did Stalin act toward the authority of the seminary where he attended? He read books that were forbidden by the school. He grew rebellious toward school authorities. He did not attend his exams and was expelled from the seminary.

- Explain that God's Word tells us that being rebellious is wrong (1 Samuel 15:23a). Scripture tells us submit to those who are over us and to obey them (Hebrews 13:17).

Who did Stalin become a devoted follower of? Vladimir Lenin

---

ten, his left arm was permanently disabled in an accident. Despite these setbacks, and with his mother's encouragement, Stalin did well in school. He went on to attend a religious seminary where he had earned a scholarship.

About the time Stalin was finishing school, changes began taking place in Russia. The czar (ZAR) had just died. He was succeeded by his son, Nicholas II. But Nicholas II was a weaker ruler than his father and less interested in politics.

All over the Russian empire, people were unhappy with rule by a czar. The Russian people wanted to have more say in how they were governed. Groups of men began to hold secret meetings. They talked of revolution, or rebellion against the government. Sometimes Stalin would attend these meetings.

Stalin read books by some of these men with revolutionary ideas. These kinds of books were forbidden by the seminary he went to. Stalin even adopted a name for himself from a political novel. He insisted that his classmates call him "Koba."

Some students liked Stalin. He had strong opinions and daring ideas that fascinated them. Others did not like him. When in a group, Stalin never wanted anyone else to take leadership. Sometimes he was defeated in debates or group discussions. He would become angry with the winner. Then he would withdraw from his friends to pout and plan revenge.

Stalin continued to read books that were forbidden by the school. He grew rebellious toward school authorities. In 1899, he did not attend his exams. He was expelled from the seminary.

Now Stalin was free to do as he pleased. He wanted to become part of the revolutionary movement. He became a devoted follower of Vladimir Lenin, the strongest leader of the movement. He wrote some of the articles that Stalin had read.

Soon Stalin was involved in political demonstrations and secret meetings. By 1901, he was writing for a political

Stalin, meaning "man of steel," was not Joseph's birth name. He adopted it in the 1910s for two purposes. It gave him an image as a tough man, and it allowed him to engage in revolutionary acts with a hidden identity.

After the death of his wife, Stalin had most of her family arrested in 1937. His brother-in-law was offered the chance to escape execution if he confessed to being a Nazi spy. He proclaimed his innocence and was executed by Stalin's orders.

Stalin was only 5'4" tall. He tried to appear taller by wearing platform shoes.

276

Background

Czarist Russia

Alexander III (1881–1894) attempted to suppress revolutionary ideas and activities. He ordered the state police and courts to intensify their efforts and demanded a strict censorship of the press. Alexander also persecuted various minority national groups, such as the Poles and the Finns. He wanted to force them to become "Russian" in language, religion, and attitude. Alexander also supported organized government massacres called pogroms, which killed thousands of Jews living in Russia, in an effort to redirect Russian anger away from his abusive rule.

The harsh policies of Alexander III were continued under his son Nicholas II (1894–1917). During his reign, popular discontent burst into revolutionary activity. Radicals and liberals of all kinds organized themselves into political parties, one of the most radical of which was the Social Democratic Party (1898). The Social Democratic Party members broke into groups. One small group called the Bolsheviks advocated change though violence. On November 7, 1917, the Bolshevik followers of Vladimir Lenin seized the government offices in St. Petersburg and arrested government leaders. Czarist Russia became a Communist state.

Bolsheviks storming the Winter Castle in Russia

newspaper. He wrote about revolution. He tried to imitate Lenin's style of writing.

In 1902 Stalin was arrested for the first time. He was sent to prison in Siberia, a very cold and isolated region in northern Russia. Over the next fifteen years, Stalin was arrested many times.

Stalin's Rise to Power

During World War I, Russia fought against Germany and Austria-Hungary. In 1917 Nicholas II was forced to resign, leaving the Russian government weak. Later that year, Lenin and his followers saw their chance to take over. These men were called Bolsheviks. The Bolshevik Revolution brought Lenin into power. He made Stalin one of the leaders in the new Russian government.

In 1922 Russia joined with other territories to become the Union of Soviet Socialist Republics (USSR). It was also called the **Soviet Union**. Soon the Bolsheviks renamed themselves Communists.

The kind of government they formed was called Communism. **Communism** is a system in which the government owns all business and property. The government makes almost all the decisions for the people. A Communist country is run by a dictator. Usually the only political party allowed under Communism is the Communist Party.

Lenin died in 1924. Stalin wanted to become the next leader of the Communist Party. He was determined to beat his rivals. One of them was Leon Trotsky. Trotsky had been second only to Lenin in authority. Stalin turned the people against Trotsky. Trotsky was forced to step down from his position. Stalin then removed the men who had helped him beat Trotsky. One by one, Stalin found ways to get rid of any man who stood in his way. On his fiftieth birthday in 1929, Stalin became the dictator.

Some people did not like the methods Stalin used to gain his power. But no one dared criticize the man of steel.

> What is Communism?

277

Teach for Understanding

In what way did Stalin imitate Lenin? He imitated Lenin's style of writing.

- Direct attention to the picture on page 277. Choose a volunteer to read aloud the caption.

Where was Stalin sent after he was arrested in 1902? prison in Siberia

What did Lenin and his followers do later in the year after Nicholas II was forced to resign? These men, called Bolsheviks, used the Bolshevik Revolution to bring Lenin into power. Lenin made Stalin one of the leaders in the new Russian government.

How did Russia become the Union of Soviet Socialist Republics (USSR)? Russia joined with other territories.

What is another name for the USSR? the Soviet Union

- Invite a volunteer to tell the new name the Bolsheviks gave themselves. Communists

- Choose a student to explain how Stalin became the dictator of the Soviet Union. After Lenin died, Stalin turned people against Trotsky who was second in authority to Lenin. Trotsky was forced to step down from his position. Stalin removed the men who helped Trotsky and found ways to get rid of anyone who stood in his way. Stalin became the dictator on his fiftieth birthday.

> Conclude the discussion by asking the question on page 277. It is a system in which the government owns all the businesses and property. The government makes almost all the decisions for the people. The government is run by a dictator. Usually the only political party that is allowed is the Communist Party.

Activity Manual

- Guide completion of pages 195–98.

110

Student Text pages 278–80
Activity Manual pages 199–201

Lesson Focus

- Joseph Stalin oppressed or eliminated anyone who stood in his way.

Objectives

- Examine collective farming under Joseph Stalin
- Identify restrictions Stalin placed on citizens
- Recognize how Stalin treated anyone who disagreed with him
- Examine Communism in light of what the Bible says

Teacher's Toolkit CD

- Visual 35: *Siberia*

Review

- Invite a volunteer to describe events that led to Joseph Stalin becoming the dictator of the Soviet Union.

  What form of government was formed by the Bolsheviks in the USSR? Communism

- Choose a student to describe Communism.

Preparation for Reading

- Generate interest as you direct the students to read the titles and examine the pictures on pages 278–80.
- Guide pronunciation of any unfamiliar words in the lesson.
- Direct the students to read the pages silently to learn the number of people who died of starvation under Stalin.
  as many as ten million people

Teach for Understanding

- Direct attention to the pictures on page 278. Read aloud the caption.

  How did Stalin plan to make the Soviet Union more industrial? He planned to increase Soviet industry by a series of Five-Year Plans. He forced people to work harder than ever before.

  Who owned the collective farms when Stalin combined individual farms? the government

  How did people oppose Stalin's plan for collective farms? by burning their livestock, grain, and farm equipment

  Where were most peasant farmers sent after they were forced off their farms? Siberia

- Read aloud the information on Visual Aid 35.

  How did Stalin's plan for increased industry impact the people of the Soviet Union? Their morale was low. Many suffered or died under Stalin's harsh working conditions. The people could not even question anything Stalin ordered.

  How did Stalin oppose writers, artists, and music composers? by censoring them

The Soviet Union Under Stalin's Rule

The Soviet Union relied mostly on farming for its income. But Stalin wanted the Soviet Union to be more industrial like the more advanced countries. One of his goals was to increase Soviet industry by a series of Five-Year Plans. He sped up production by forcing people to work harder than ever before.

Stalin combined individual farms into large **collective farms** owned by the government. Some people were angry about Stalin's plans. These people did not want to give up their rights to farm independently. Some people opposed Stalin by burning their livestock, grain, and farm equipment. Since they could not own their farms, they did not want the government to own them either.

But Stalin paid no attention to what the people wanted. He sent soldiers to the farms and forced the people to surrender at gunpoint. He sent about a million peasant families into **exile**. These people were forced to move far away from their homes. Most were sent to Siberia. Some people went to work on Siberian farms. Others were sent to prison work camps. Across the Soviet Union, as many as ten million people died of starvation as a result of Stalin's war on the farmers.

In one sense, Stalin's plans worked. Industry was increasing each year. But in another sense, his system was failing. The morale of the people was low. Many had suffered or even died under Stalin's harsh working conditions. The people had no freedom to question anything Stalin ordered.

Another group of people in the Soviet Union suffered a different kind of oppression under Stalin. Writers, artists, and music composers were not allowed to create what they wanted. Their work had to be **censored**, or changed to match what the government

Russian propaganda promoted collective farms, but many farmers were either forced into them or relocated to other parts of Russia.

278

Background

Soviet Union: Joseph Stalin

In Russia, the decades of the twenties and thirties were among the bloodiest years in human history. Stalin oversaw systematic terror and bloodshed throughout those years and became one of the bloodiest tyrants of the times.

Stalin crushed all opposition, both in and out of the Communist Party. In 1928 he ordered the destruction of all resistance to his agricultural "reforms," or collectivization, and ordered the murder of at least ten million men, women, and children. Another ten million died in Siberian slave-labor camps. Throughout the 1930s, Stalin continued to push Russia into the industrial age and fortify his own power with a chilling callousness perhaps best summarized by Stalin himself: "A single death is a tragedy; a million deaths is a statistic." Stalin also trampled any perceived threat from organized religion. Many Christians suffered and died in labor camps simply because of their loyalty to Christ.

wanted. Stalin wanted to make sure their work supported his ideas before it was published.

Under Stalin's rule, religion was also restricted. Stalin was an **atheist**. He did not believe in God. He wanted everyone else to believe as he did. Stalin closed churches of all religions. Some Christians were arrested or killed.

Stalin trusted no one. He could not tolerate anyone disagreeing with him. Over the next several years, Stalin had nearly all the former Bolsheviks in the Communist Party killed. He went on to dispose of thousands of other Communists. Anyone who seemed a threat to his authority was imprisoned. Usually prisoners were executed on some false charge. About one and a half million people were killed in four years. Others who were not killed were questioned, tortured, and starved in labor camps. People referred to those years as the Great Purge.

Stalin expected every person to spy for him. He urged neighbors and family members to tell on each other. Stalin also had his own secret-police force. People lived in constant fear of saying or doing the wrong thing—even in their own homes.

By the time World War II began, Stalin had eliminated everyone he thought was a threat to his power. At the start of World War II, Stalin fought on the same side as Hitler.

What Does the Bible Say?

Communists believed that all people should be equal. They did not think that kings or czars should rule over them. They thought that the people should rule. Communists believed that if people were freed from unjust rulers, they would be morally good.

Communists also believed that nobody should have private property. If people could have private property, then some people would have more

This propaganda poster advertises the harvest of collective farms, but in reality many people depended on bread lines for food.

279

What was Stalin in regard to religion? He was an atheist.

- Direct attention to the picture of the bread lines in the Soviet Union on page 279. Read the caption aloud.

Who did Stalin kill over the next several years of his reign? Stalin killed nearly all the former Bolsheviks in the Communist Party and thousands of other Communists; anyone who disagreed with Stalin was imprisoned and usually executed.

About how many people were killed in four years? about one and a half million people

What happened to those who were not killed? Many were questioned, tortured, and starved in labor camps.

Why did people in the Soviet Union fear saying or doing the wrong thing—even in their own homes? Stalin expected every person to spy for him. He urged neighbors and family members to tell on each other. Stalin had his own secret police force.

What did the Communists believe about people being equal and how they should be governed? They believed all people should be equal and that kings or czars should not rule over the people. The Communists believed that if people were freed from unjust rulers, they would be morally good.

Christianity During Stalin's Reign of Terror

Communism seeks to control every aspect of life. The Soviet state under both Lenin and Stalin made a strong effort to wipe out any form of Christianity within its territory. Within twenty years, the government had forced the closure of thousands of churches and schools and had killed many pastors and priests. The Soviet government's cruelty stemmed from the realization that Christian virtues (including individual responsibility) posed a threat to Communist ideas and goals. The Communists' hatred for Christianity is well illustrated by Lenin who described the idea of God as "unutterable vileness."

Pray for Persecuted Christians

Help students identify countries where Christians are persecuted today. Pray for the Christians in those nations. Guide the students as they pray for the triumph of God's purposes in our world. Pray for strength to obey His commands and to love one another as Jesus has loved. For possible information on how to pray for the persecuted church visit bjupress.com/resources.

Teach for Understanding

What did Communists believe about people owning private property? The Communists believed that nobody should have private property. The Communists thought that all property should be held in common so that everybody owned the property.

Why is the belief that says people become good when they are freed from rulers incorrect? People do not become good when they are freed from rulers. The Bible teaches that all people are sinners. Sinners need to have their hearts changed by God to become good (Ezekiel 36:26–27).

- Direct attention to the table on page 280. Invite a student to explain the meaning of the table.

Why is the idea that everyone owns all of the property a bad idea? If a person owns property, he usually takes care of it. If everyone owns a piece of property, then usually no one takes care of it. The Bible teaches us that private property is a good thing.

- Read Exodus 20:15 aloud. Explain that Exodus 20:15 gives recognition to the idea of a person owning something. Taking a person's property is forbidden.

How did Communism become a form of a dictatorship? Communists forced their ideas to work. The party ended up ruling the people. The rule of the party became the rule of the dictator. Property was actually owned by the powerful people in the party.

What did the people of Russia get in exchange for the unjust rule of a czar? the unjust rule of a dictator

> Conclude the discussion by asking the question on page 280. Communists tried to restore the perfect world that God created without admitting that the world is broken because people are sinners. They tried to restore the world without God's redemption. The Bible teaches that a person owning private property is a good thing. Communists made the great evil in the world private property instead of sin. They looked for redemption through the revolution rather than through Christ.

Activity Manual

- Guide completion of pages 199–201.

What Communism Says	What Communism Does	What the Bible Says
Man is morally good	Man is not morally good	All men are sinners
All men are equal	Some men are more equal than others	God created all men equal
Man should be free from rulers	People ruled by party, party ruled by dictator	God establishes authority
Communal ownership	Neglect by community; ownership by powerful	Individual ownership and communal care

than others, and the people would not be equal. Communists thought that all property should be held in common so that everybody owned the property. They received their name *Communist* from this belief.

The problem with Communism is that God did not make His world to work the way Communists think it should work. People do not become good when they are freed from rulers. The Bible teaches that all people are sinners (Romans 3:23). Sinners need to have their hearts changed by God to become good (Ezekiel 36:26–27).

The world does not work well without private property. If a person owns a piece of property, he usually takes care of it. But if everybody owns a piece of property, then usually nobody takes care of it. God's commandment against stealing teaches us that private property is a good thing (Exodus 20:15). And Jesus' parable about the

wise tenants seems to teach that private property is a good thing even in a fallen world (Luke 19:17–18).

When the Communists could not get their ideas to work, they tried to force them to work. The rule of the people ended up being the rule of the party for the people. And the rule of the party for the people became the rule of the dictator. Property was said to be owned by all, but it was actually owned by the powerful people in the party.

The Communists tried to restore the perfect world that God created without admitting that the world was broken because people were sinners. They tried to restore the world apart from God's redemption. In the end, the people of Russia exchanged the unjust rule of a czar for the unjust rule of a dictator.

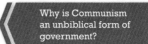
Why is Communism an unbiblical form of government?

280

Activity

Practicing Good Stewardship

Guide a discussion about having personal property. Explain that it is a blessing to be able to own property rather than everything belonging to the government. Ask the students to name some of the property that God has provided for them (pets, sports equipment, bicycles, electronic equipment, books, etc.). Point out that we belong to God and so do our possessions. Invite students to share how a person should treat God's property. Elicit that possessions should not be used in a way that is contrary to the teaching of God's Word. Explain that using the things God gives us in a responsible way is called stewardship. Encourage the students to be good stewards of the things God provides.

Mussolini in Italy: Il Duce!
Young Mussolini

Benito Mussolini was born in 1883 in Italy. His father was a tough, strong blacksmith who taught young Benito to stand up against anyone who bullied him. Italy was a constitutional monarchy, but Benito's father was a Socialist. As he worked, he often talked to Benito about politics.

Benito's mother was a schoolteacher. She was gentle and compassionate. She often worried about Benito's violent temper. Her desire was for Benito to become a teacher like herself. She persuaded his father to send him to the finest schools. Later, Benito graduated and earned a certificate to teach. He went on to teach at a school for a brief time.

Then Benito Mussolini left Italy and went to Switzerland. For months he went from job to job. He even worked in a chocolate factory. But no job satisfied him. Mussolini wanted to do something great. He wanted other people to respect him and follow him.

From his boyhood, Mussolini had been interested in politics. In Switzerland this interest continued. He spent most of his evenings in cozy little restaurants called cafés. In these places he discussed political ideas with other Europeans. Mussolini listened excitedly to their ideas about government. One idea was to have government run by ordinary working-class people. This was the same idea that Mussolini's father believed.

Mussolini returned to Italy and became involved in the Socialist Party. He wrote and edited articles for a Socialist newspaper. He stirred up workers in revolts and strikes. Once he led a violent mob in a riot through the city streets. He was even put in jail several times. Eventually, Mussolini became a leader in the Socialist Party.

After World War I began in 1914, the Socialists did not believe Italy should join the war. But Mussolini saw advantages for the nation if it joined the Allies. He thought that Italy could become a powerful nation through the

Mussolini was a violent child and was expelled from school at ten years of age for knifing a classmate.

As a young man, he carried a nickel medallion of Karl Marx in his pocket.

In 1926, a woman attempted to assassinate Mussolini from close range. She missed his head, but shot his nose. Doctors repaired his nose and his would-be assassin spent the rest of her life in an asylum.

281

Lesson Focus

- Benito Mussolini wanted total control over Italy's industry, education, and media.

Objectives
- Describe Benito Mussolini's early life
- Examine Mussolini's involvement in Socialism
- Relate Mussolini's actions as the dictator of Italy

Review

- Invite a student to describe Stalin's war on farmers.
- Identify restrictions Stalin placed on citizens.
- Choose a student to explain why Communism leads to a dictatorship.

Preparation for Reading

- Generate interest as you direct the students to read the title and examine the pictures on pages 281–83.
- Guide pronunciation of any unfamiliar words in the lesson.
- Direct the students to read the pages silently to learn why Mussolini organized his own police force. to get rid of his enemies

Teach for Understanding

- Direct attention to the picture on page 281. Read aloud the captions.

  What type of government did Italy have at the time of Benito Mussolini's birth? a constitutional monarchy

- Explain that in a constitutional monarchy, a monarch rules under a constitution. He does not make the laws.

  What was Mussolini's father in regard to politics? a Socialist

  How is Mussolini's mother described? She was a schoolteacher. She was gentle and compassionate.

  What did she desire for Mussolini? to become a teacher

  Where did Mussolini go after he taught for a short time? Switzerland

  What was Mussolini interested in? politics

  Why did Mussolini spend most of his evenings in the cafés? While in Switzerland, his interest in politics continued. He discussed political ideas with other Europeans.

  What political party did Mussolini become involved in once he returned to Italy? the Socialist Party

- Choose a volunteer to state the activities Mussolini was involved in as a member of the Socialist Party.

Teach for Understanding

- Direct attention to the pictures on page 282. Invite a student to read aloud the caption.

Why did Mussolini want Italy to join World War I in 1914? He thought that Italy could become a powerful nation through the war.

What type of men became the first Fascists in Italy? Daring men who wanted to change Italy's government. Many had been convicted of crimes. Several were former soldiers. They were tough men who sometimes used violence to reach their goals.

What did these Fascists believe? They believed that the businesses and society of the nation needed to be overseen by the government for the benefit of the nation.

What was the name of the leader of this new political party? Mussolini

What title did Mussolini choose for himself? Il Duce

Who did Mussolini's Black Shirts attack? They attacked those were were associated with Socialism. They could harm or kill anyone who did not agree with Il Duce.

How did the Black Shirts force the king to make Mussolini the prime minister of Italy? Mussolini and fifty-two thousand Black Shirts marched on Rome.

- Invite a student to name some of the helpful things Mussolini did for Italy after he came to power.

- What characteristics make a good leader besides doing helpful things? Answers could include honesty, integrity, kindness, humility, courage, responsibility, servanthood, commitment, likeability, communication, and discipline.

---

war. He lost favor with the Socialists for taking this position. But he stood firm in his views. When Italy finally joined the war with the Allies, Mussolini fought on the frontlines.

The Rise of Fascism

After the war, Mussolini met privately with a small group of men. His eyes scanned the group seated around him. They were daring men who wanted to change Italy's government. Many of them had been convicted of crimes. Several of them were former soldiers. They were tough men who sometimes used violence to reach their goals. These men would be the first **Fascists** in Italy. Fascists believed that the businesses and society of the nation needed to be overseen by the government for the benefit of the nation.

Mussolini charmed many Italians with his confident speeches. He named his political party after an ancient Roman symbol that represented power and unity, the fasces.

282

Mussolini was the leader of this new political party. He chose the title of **Il Duce** for himself. *Il Duce* means "the leader." Each man in the party wore a black shirt and a black, flat-topped hat called a fez. These men, known as Black Shirts, fought any people or groups who opposed them.

The Fascists were a terror to Italy. They attacked those who were associated with Socialism. Mussolini's Black Shirts could harm or kill anyone who did not agree with Il Duce.

In spite of all its violence, Fascism was gaining more support. Many Italians were dissatisfied with their present king. They wanted a stronger leader. Others supported the Fascist Party because they wanted to own land or keep the land they already owned. Some supported Mussolini out of fear.

In 1922 Mussolini and fifty-two thousand Black Shirts marched on Rome. The king was forced to make Mussolini the prime minister of Italy. "Duce! Duce!" shouted Mussolini's followers.

Mussolini did some helpful things for Italy after he came to power. He built roads, schools, factories, and hospitals. He provided land for farmers. He introduced new welfare benefits and sanitation programs. He even improved Italy's railroad system so that the trains ran on time.

Background

Fascism

Fascism was originally called corporatism. Mussolini, who linked Italian nationalism with socialism, organized industries into categories called syndicates. He insisted that the government plan, or coordinate, all economic activity in so-called partnership with the syndicates. The catch was that the government was the "senior partner" in such arrangements and therefore had the final say. This policy was based on the idea that government knows best. One historian described fascism as nationalizing socialism and socializing nationalism.

What Fascism Says	What Fascism Does	What the Bible Says
Government oversight of business and society	Government control of industry, education, and the media	God ordained institutions to work within their designated spheres
Loyalty to state above everything else	People live in fear and families turn on one another	Love God above all else and love your neighbor as yourself

But it did not take long for the Italian people to see what kind of ruler Mussolini was. He wanted total control over industry, education, and the media. "You must obey because you must," the schoolchildren were taught. Il Duce carefully controlled the newspapers so that only good things were printed about him.

Mussolini also organized his own secret-police force. His desire was to get rid of his enemies. This police force publicly humiliated or killed anyone who criticized Mussolini. All over Italy, people were afraid or angry. Some of them tried to fight against the government. But Mussolini's Black Shirts and secret police quickly squelched any uprising. Il Duce's reign of terror continued.

What Does the Bible Say?

Fascism teaches that people's greatest loyalty should be to the state. Their loyalty to the state should come before their loyalty to family, community, or church. Fascists also believe that their nation has better values and cultures than other nations.

The Bible teaches that God created government (Romans 13:1–7; 1 Peter 2:13–17). But God also created families and churches (Genesis 1:27–28; 2:22–24; Acts 2:47). God wants Christians to obey their government except when the government commands people to do wrong (Acts 5:29). But God does not want husbands and fathers to love the government more than their wives and children. He does not want people to love anything more than they love God.

God created a world with many different institutions. An institution is a group of people related in some way with an authority structure. Families, churches, schools, sports teams, and governments are examples of institutions. He wants each one to do what it is supposed to do in its place. He does not want one institution trying to control all the others.

> Why is Fascism an unbiblical form of government?

283

Teach for Understanding

- Direct attention to the table. Invite a student to explain the meaning of the table.

What did Mussolini want total control of? industry, education, and the media

Why did Il Duce carefully control the newspapers? so that only good things were printed about him

What did Mussolini's secret-police force do to anyone who criticized Mussolini? This police force publicly humiliated or killed anyone who criticized Mussolini.

What happened to people who tried to fight against the government? Mussolini's Black Shirts and secret police quickly squelched any uprising.

Where did Fascism teach that people's greatest loyalty should be? to the state

Who created government? God

When is it wrong to obey government? when the government commands people to do wrong

Whom does the Bible say is the most important to obey? God

> Conclude the discussion by asking the question on page 283. Fascism teaches that people's greatest loyalty should be to the state. Their loyalty to the state should come before their loyalty to family, community, or church. God wants Christians to obey their government except when the government commands people to do wrong. God does not want people to love government more than their families. God does not want people to love anything more than they love God.

Activity Manual

- Guide completion of pages 202–3.

Assessment

- Administer quiz.

> The quiz may be given anytime after completing this lesson.

112

Student Text pages 284–86
Activity Manual page 204

Lesson Focus

- Adolf Hitler achieved his goal of becoming the dictator of Germany.

Objectives

- Examine events leading to Hitler's rise to power in Germany
- Recognize Hitler's hatred of Jews and Communists
- Relate Hitler's actions as chancellor of Germany
- Identify the treatment of the Jews after Hitler became the dictator of Germany

Teacher's Toolkit CD

- Visuals 36–37: *Adolf Hitler as Chancellor; Hitler's Police*

Review

- Review Benito Mussolini's rise to power.
- Choose a volunteer to explain Italian fascism and why fascism is unbiblical.

Preparation for Reading

- Generate interest as you direct the students to read the titles and examine the pictures on pages 284–86.
- Guide pronunciation of any unfamiliar words in the lesson.
- Direct the students to read the pages silently to find out the name Adolf Hitler chose for himself. Der Führer

Teach for Understanding

- Direct attention to the picture of Hitler and read aloud the caption.

  Who did Hitler hope to imitate? Mussolini

  What was Hitler like as a boy? He was lazy and undisciplined. He did not fit in well with other children. He was often called a dreamer because he enjoyed passing the time by reading, listening to music, and drawing.

  Where did Hitler go at age eighteen? Vienna

  What happened when Hitler hoped to be accepted at the Academy of Fine Arts? He failed the entrance examinations twice.

- What may have contributed to Hitler's failing the entrance examination twice? Answers could include that he was too lazy to study and practice.

  During his time in Vienna, whom did Hitler begin to have hatred toward? the Jews

  Who did Hitler believe was a superior race of people? people of Germanic heritage

  What political party did Hitler join? The German Workers' Party

---

Hitler in Germany: Der Führer

When Mussolini was at the height of his power, he received a fan letter. It was from a young Austrian man asking for his photograph. Mussolini brushed off the request. He had more important things to do. The young Austrian's name was Adolf Hitler. He had admired Mussolini's aggressive takeover of Italy and longed to imitate him.

Young Hitler

Adolf Hitler was born in 1889 in a town in Austria-Hungary near the border of Germany. As a boy, he was a poor student. He was lazy and undisciplined. He did not fit in well with other children. He was often called a dreamer because he enjoyed passing the time by reading, listening to music, and drawing. He preferred these above other activities.

Hitler went to Vienna at the age of eighteen. There he hoped to be accepted at the Academy of Fine Arts, but he failed the entrance examinations twice. For several years he stayed in Vienna, trying to sell his paintings on the streets.

During his years in Vienna, Hitler began to hate the Jews. Perhaps he disliked them because many of them were accepted in the social circles of Vienna, while he was not. But his

hatred for them kept growing. He read books by other men who hated them. Hitler developed a belief that there was a superior race of people in the world. These people were of Germanic heritage, like himself.

Hitler Becomes Dictator

Adolf Hitler became interested in politics while he lived in Vienna. He moved to Germany in 1913 and then fought in World War I. While in the army, Hitler was sent to spy on a small political party known as the German Workers' Party. This party opposed the

Hitler had a handlebar mustache in World War I but trimmed it so that his gas mask could seal properly. He became famous for the trimmed version.

Before the Nazis rose to power, the salute with the outstretched hand was widely used by many groups, including American school children when reciting the pledge to the flag. When it was enthusiastically embraced by the Nazis, other groups discontinued its use.

284

Hitler was known for his expressive gestures when speaking.

Jews and the Communists. It supported making Germany a powerful nation. Hitler agreed with the beliefs of this party and soon joined it. The party admired Hitler's speaking skills. He had a dynamic intensity in his voice that fascinated them. By 1920, Hitler became one of the party's leaders. Soon he was in complete control.

In only a few months, the number of members in the German Workers' Party increased from one hundred to one thousand. Now Hitler wanted to make some changes in the party. He changed the party's name to the National Socialist German Workers' Party. The German word for National Socialist was shortened to **Nazi**. Hitler designed the party's flag. It was red with a white circle and a black, hooked cross called a **swastika**. The swastika became the Nazi emblem.

Hitler borrowed several ideas from Mussolini. Just as Mussolini had his Black Shirts, Hitler had his own private army, called the Storm Troopers or Brown Shirts. Hitler chose the title of **Der Führer** for himself. *Der Führer* meant "the leader" in German.

In 1923 Hitler and his Nazis tried to take over the government of Germany. But they were arrested, and Hitler was sent to prison. While in prison, he spent most of his time writing a book called *Mein Kampf*, which means "My Struggle." The book told about his hatred for the Jews and his desire to rid Germany of all of them. It described his belief in a superior German race. Hitler also wrote about his policy on foreign affairs.

Another group Hitler hated was the Communists. He did not want the Communist Party to take control of Germany. When Hitler was released from prison, he pulled the weakened Nazi Party back together. The effects of the Great Depression led struggling workers to more easily accept Hitler's ideas.

285

Teach for Understanding

What was the German Workers' Party known for? This party opposed the Jews and the Communists. It supported making Germany a powerful nation.

- Direct attention to the pictures on page 285. Read aloud the caption.

By 1920 who led the German Workers' Party after becoming one of its leaders? Hitler

What change did Hitler make as the party grew? He changed the party's name to the National Socialist German Workers' Party.

How were the words *National Socialist* shortened? The words were shortened to *Nazi*.

What was the Nazi emblem? swastika

What did Hitler call his private army? Storm Troopers or Brown Shirts

- Choose a volunteer to explain the meaning of *Der Führer*.

Why were Hitler and his Nazis imprisoned? for trying to take over the government

What did Hitler spend most of his time doing while he was in prison? He was writing a book called *Mein Kampf*.

- Invite a student to tell what Hitler wrote about in his book.

What position was Hitler appointed to in the government after he lost the election for president? chancellor

Background

Germany: Adolf Hitler

In 1923, a German war veteran sought to avenge Germany's defeat in World War I. Adolf Hitler tried to overthrow the Bavarian government in Munich. The failed coup landed him in jail. While imprisoned, he wrote his personal memoir of hatred, *Mein Kampf* ("My Struggle"), in which he set forth his ideas for a new German order. He advocated scrapping the League of Nations, ridding Germany of the "weakening" influence of democracy, uniting all Germans, and eliminating all Communists and Jews. After his release, he preached his doctrines to growing audiences of all classes. Hitler and his National Socialist German Workers' Party, or Nazi Party, came to power in Germany in 1933 when he was elected chancellor of Germany. Hitler used his new power to crush all opposition and establish himself as the *führer*. He called the Nazi regime the "Third Reich," a German empire that would last a thousand years.

Gradually, Hitler forged a police state of blind nationalism, anti-Semitism, and totalitarianism. For years, in violation of the Versailles agreements, he secretly rebuilt the German navy, army, and air force. This war machine used all the latest technological improvements and proved to be a powerful instrument in Hitler's hands.

Lesson

112

Teach for Understanding

- Direct attention to the picture on page 286 and read the caption aloud.

🐝 How do you think the children in the picture felt about being put in a concentration camp? Answers could include that they were frightened, lonely, and uncertain about their future.

Who appointed Hitler to be chancellor of Germany? President Hindenburg

- Display Visual 36. Invite a student to describe the reaction of the crowd after Hitler was made chancellor.

Who did Hitler blame for the fire in the building where the German government held its meetings? the Communists

What did Hitler send the Gestapo to do? find the enemies of the government

- Direct attention to Visual 37. Read the caption aloud.

How were the arrested people treated? They were jailed or killed without a fair trial. Many went to concentration camps.

What did Hitler order to be done to many of his own Storm Troopers? to be put to death

When did Hitler achieve his goal of becoming the dictator of Germany? in the summer of 1934

▶▶ Conclude the discussion by asking the question on page 286. The book told about Hitler's hatred for the Jews and his desire to rid Germany of them. It described his belief in a superior German race. Hitler also wrote about his policy on foreign affairs.

Activity Manual

- Guide completion of page 204.

Thousands, including children, were sent to concentration camps.

In 1932 Hitler ran for president of Germany. He lost the election, but over two hundred other Nazis won offices in the government. Despite Hitler's loss, he still gained some power. In January of 1933, President Hindenburg appointed Hitler to be the chancellor. This position made Hitler the second-highest authority in all of Germany.

Just four weeks later, on a cold snowy night in February, a mysterious thing happened. A fire started in the building where the German government held its meetings. Soon the flames were leaping from the windows. Before the fire was put out, the building was badly damaged. "The Communists are responsible for setting the fire," Hitler said. His message spread through Germany almost as quickly as the fire had spread.

After the fire, more than four thousand Communists were arrested. Hitler sent out his secret-police force, the Gestapo, to find enemies of the government. Anyone arrested was jailed or killed without a fair trial. Many went to **concentration camps**, places where people were kept as prisoners and forced to do heavy labor. Many people died at these camps. The government seemed to distrust everyone.

Hitler ordered many of his own Storm Troopers to be put to death. All the men he could think of who had ever made him angry were killed. Even so, many of them shouted, "*Heil*, Hitler!" as they died. They did not know why they were being killed. Less than a year after these murders, Hitler achieved his goal. He became the dictator of Germany in the summer of 1934.

What was Hitler's book, *Mein Kampf*, about?

286

Hitler and the Jews
The Nuremberg Laws

Adolf Hitler hated the Jewish people. He believed that he belonged to a superior race. Hitler believed that a duty of all Germans was to hate the Jewish people as much as he did. The Jews were constantly ridiculed and shunned. Sometimes they were physically harmed by German soldiers. They lost their positions in the civil service. Jewish students could no longer attend the universities. The Nazi Party boycotted Jewish shops and other businesses. Many Jews left the country to find safer places to live.

In 1935 Hitler had the legislature pass the **Nuremberg Laws**. These laws took away the Jews' freedoms as citizens of Germany. Jews could no longer vote or hold public offices. Jews could not marry other Germans. Jewish children

Corrie ten Boom

Who: Dutch Christian who sheltered Jews

When: 1892–1983

Where: Haarlem, Netherlands

Corrie ten Boom's father, a watchmaker, was a devout Christian who believed the Jews were God's chosen people. The ten Boom family began opening their home to Jews who were trying to escape Nazi persecution during World War II. As an adult daughter in the home, Corrie kept a secret room behind a false wall in her bedroom. For several years the family welcomed Jews into the home, hiding them in the secret room when Nazi searches took place. The ten Booms successfully helped hundreds of Jews to escape capture. Eventually, Corrie and her family were arrested and taken to prison. Corrie's father died in prison, and she and her sister were sent to Ravensbrück concentration camp. Corrie's sister did not survive the harsh conditions in the camp. Corrie, however, was released by mistake. After the war ended, she spent the rest of her life telling her story and the message of God's love and forgiveness.

287

Lesson Focus

- It was wrong for Hitler to attack the Jewish people whom God used to bring salvation and the gospel to the world.

Objectives

- Identify when it is right to have pride in one's nation
- Realize that it is wrong to hate people of another nation
- Relate why Hitler's hatred of the Jews was especially wicked

Teacher's Toolkit CD

- Visual 38: *Nazi Persecution of the Jews*
- Instructional Aid 51: *Personal Narrative Organizer*

Review

- Invite volunteers to give the meanings of *Nazi*, *swastika*, and *Der Führer.*
- Select a student to explain concentration camps and the Nuremberg Laws.

Preparation for Reading

- Generate interest as you direct the students to read the titles and examine the pictures on pages 287–89.
- Guide pronunciation of any unfamiliar words in the lesson.
- Direct the students to read the pages silently to learn why Hitler's hatred of the Jews was especially wicked. God chose the Jewish people to be His special people for bringing salvation through Jesus Christ and the gospel to the world.

Teach for Understanding

- Choose a student to read aloud the Biography box on page 287. Use the information to guide a discussion about Corrie ten Boom.
- Choose a volunteer to describe how Jews were treated as a result of Hitler's belief that it was a duty of all Germans to hate Jewish people as much as he did.
- How would you react if you were treated this way for being a Christian?

113

Teach for Understanding

- Invite a student to explain the freedoms of German citizens that the Nuremberg Laws took from the Jewish people.

- Direct attention to the pictures on page 288. Invite a volunteer to read aloud the captions.

  What do the people of a nation have in common? history, language, traditions, customs, and ancestry

  Why is it a good thing for people to celebrate the accomplishments of their nation? God made people and gave them the abilities to succeed in making something beautiful of His world.

  Why is it wrong to hate the people of another nation or tell lies about them? Those people are also made in God's image.

- Display Visual 38. Read the information aloud.

- What is happening in the picture? The Nazi soldier is cutting off the beard of a Jewish man.

The sign on this Jewish shop warned non-Jewish Germans not to shop there.

Jews were required to wear a yellow badge sewn onto their outer garment.

could no longer attend German schools. Jews were forbidden to ride public trains or own telephones. Many Jews were told they could no longer work. Every Jew had to wear a yellow star of David on his clothing so that everyone would know that he was Jewish.

What Does the Bible Say?

A nation is not just the country that a person lives in. A nation is a group of people who share history, language, traditions, customs, and ancestry. This concept is harder for Americans to understand because our country is made up of people from many different nations. But in Europe, many countries were made up of people from mainly one nation.

People are often proud of the customs and heritage of their nation. They celebrate the accomplishments of their nation. This is a good thing for people to do. God made people and gave them the abilities to succeed in making something beautiful of His world (Genesis 1:26–28). It is good to celebrate when a group of people succeed.

It is not good to hate the people of another nation or to tell lies about

288

Activity

Examine Dictators in the Light of Scripture

Read aloud 2 Samuel 23:3. Explain that God said that a person who rules over people must rule justly or righteously and in the fear of the Lord. Guide a discussion about dictators and how they violate what the Bible says about rulers.

What Nationalism Says	What Nationalism Does	What the Bible Says
National pride	International hatred	All men are created in God's image
One's own race is better than all others	Racial suppression	Cannot love God and hate your brother

them. Those people are also made in God's image. Their traditions may be different. But unless those traditions go against God's Word, they can be celebrated too.

Hitler's hatred of the Jews was especially wicked. God chose the Jewish people to be His special people for bringing salvation and the gospel to the world. Jesus was born a Jewish man, and He was resurrected as a Jewish man. Most of the authors of Scripture were Jewish. The apostle Paul, who brought the gospel message to the Gentiles, was a Jewish man.

It is wicked to try to persecute any group of people simply because of their ethnicity. But it was especially wicked to try to attack a people whom God had used to bring the blessings of the gospel to the world (Genesis 12:3).

How can nationalism become unbiblical?

///// **Activity** ///

Writing a Personal Narrative

Think about how life in Germany changed for Jews once Hitler rose to power. Recall how the Nuremberg Laws affected Jewish people, their families, and friends. Write a personal narrative as a fifth grader living in Germany at that time. Tell what you observed, how you felt, and what you learned. Trade your story with a friend's story. Read and compare your stories.

///

289

> **Teach for Understanding**

- Invite a student to tell why Hitler's hatred of the Jews was especially wicked.

- Direct attention to the table on page 289. Invite a student to explain the meaning of the table.

▶ Conclude the discussion by asking the question on page 289. Nationalism can become unbiblical when people hate the people of another nation or tell lies about them.

Primary Source: German Nationalism

- Direct attention to Activity Manual page 206. Direct attention to the picture and caption. Invite a student to read the caption aloud.

- Guide a discussion of the picture and caption. Explain that as people move toward Socialism or Nazism, they do not tolerate ideas contrary to their own.

// **Activity** ///

Writing a Personal Narrative

- Generate excitement about writing a personal narrative as you read the Activity information aloud.

- Distribute a copy of Instructional Aid 51 to each student. Direct the students to organize information for their personal narrative by completing the Instructional Aid.

- Direct the students to use the completed organizer to write their personal narrative on a separate piece of paper. Remind the students to write the personal narrative as though they are telling their story.

- Invite students to exchange their completed personal narratives with a friend. Encourage them to read and compare their stories.

Completing the Instructional Aid and writing the personal narrative may take more than one class period. In addition to Heritage Studies class time, students could work on their narratives as seatwork or during free time.

> **Background**

Nazi Treatment of the Jews

Within months of the Nazis coming to power, they turned Hitler's hatred of the Jews into action. Initially, they deprived Jews of citizenship and forbade their marriage to other Germans. Then, on the night of November 9, 1938, which was later called *Kristallnacht*, the Nazis severely damaged or destroyed 7,500 Jewish businesses, 155 synagogues, and numerous homes of Jews. They also killed 35 Jews. Afterward, they rounded up thirty thousand Jews and put them into concentration camps. Before long, many more Jews were sent to concentration camps and ruthlessly exterminated.

> **Activity Manual**

- Guide completion of page 205–6.

Lesson Focus

- The Japanese worshiped their emperor as if he were a god, but the Bible teaches that there is only one God.

Objectives

- Examine how the Japanese people treated Hirohito
- Identify what Hirohito was like

Review

- Invite a student to tell why it is not good to hate the people of another nation or tell lies about them.

Preparation for Reading

- Generate interest as you direct the students to read the title and examine the picture on page 290.
- Guide pronunciation of any unfamiliar words on the page.
- Direct the students to read the page silently to learn the meaning of the title "Showa" that was given to the emperor of Japan. "enlightened peace"

Teach for Understanding

How did the people of Japan think of their emperors? as gods

How did the Japanese people treat Hirohito? They carried their reverence for Hirohito to extremes. No one could touch him; they were not even allowed to look at Hirohito in public.

Why did the people give Hirohito the name Showa? The people gave him the title to represent his divinity or godlikeness; the title means "enlightened peace."

- Read aloud the table on page 290.
- Invite a student to describe what Hirohito was like.
- Direct attention to the picture on page 290. Read aloud the captions.

How did Hirohito act toward his advisors? He rarely objected to anything they recommended.

What kind of military tradition did Japan have? The nation had never been defeated in war. The soldiers were fearless and not afraid of death.

What war would be a different war for the Japanese? World War II

> Conclude the discussion by asking the question on page 290. He should not have promoted Japan's entry into World War II.

Activity Manual

- Guide completion of page 207.

Hirohito in Japan: The Showa Emperor

Before World War II, the leaders of Japan were called **emperors**. For many centuries the people of Japan thought of their emperors as gods. When **Hirohito** became emperor of Japan in 1926, he was no exception. The people carried their reverence for their emperor to extremes. No one could touch him; people were not even allowed to look at Hirohito in public. He was given the title **Showa** to represent his divinity or godlikeness. The title means "enlightened peace."

What Emperor Worship Says	What the Bible Says
Emperor is a god	One true God

Hirohito was made crown prince at age 15. He was Japan's longest ruling monarch.

Photos of Hirohito often show him wearing a uniform. Though he was not personally involved in the fighting, he wanted to show his support for Japan's military.

Hirohito was a thoughtful and reserved man. He enjoyed studying science. Hirohito realized that he was not a descendant of the sun goddess as the people believed.

Hirohito had a group of strong advisers. He rarely objected to anything they recommended. Historians still debate whether Hirohito promoted Japan's entry into World War II or whether it was mainly a decision of his advisers.

Japan was proud of its military tradition. The nation had never been defeated in a war. The soldiers were fearless and not afraid of death. But World War II would be a different war for them.

The Japanese had high hopes when they first entered World War II. In 1941 their attack on American ships in Pearl Harbor was a great victory for them. But defeating the Americans would not be as easy as the Japanese thought.

> How should Hirohito have used his power as emperor during World War II?

290

Background

Emperor Hirohito

Hirohito was born April 29, 1901, at Aoyama Palace in Tokyo, Japan. He was instated as crown prince at age 15. In 1921 he became Japan's first crown prince to travel and study abroad. At age 25, he became the emperor of Japan after his father's death. Most Japanese people regarded Hirohito as a deity. He seemed to be a gentle man who had little influence in political and military matters. But some argue that as emperor he was informed about military actions and was not totally innocent regarding Japan's policies of imperialism, which started with the penetration of Manchuria and eventually led to the attack on Pearl Harbor, Hawaii.

How It Was

Asuka stared as the emperor's car approached. She longed to see His Majesty the emperor. It was said that he was a god—god of the Empire of the Sun. One of his children, a princess, was about her own age. Did she have to bow to her father as everyone else did?

"Asuka!" her mother whispered. "Lower your eyes. He will soon be passing. You would not want him to see you gazing."

Asuka looked down at the sidewalk. She bent low from her waist as the car drove slowly by. She waited until the sound of the motor faded a little before lifting herself upright again. The crowd around her was hushed as if everyone were inside a temple.

Is it true? Asuka wondered. *Is the emperor really a god? He seems like an ordinary man.* She watched the emperor's car grow smaller and smaller in the distance.

What Does the Bible Say?

The Japanese worshiped their emperor as if he were a god. But the Bible teaches there is only one God (Exodus 20:3). The attempt for humans to become like God was at the root of the first sin (Genesis 3:5). When rulers like Pharaoh, Nebuchadnezzar, or Herod tried to rule as if they were gods, the true God showed His power over them (Exodus 9:14; Daniel 4:28–35; Acts 12:22–23).

This period of history was a dark time for many people. Nations were ruled by strong men who ruled in ways contrary to the Bible. Their rule would harm millions of people. Their wickedness would require other nations to rise up and oppose them.

How does the worship of an emperor conflict with God's Word?

291

Lesson 115 Student Text page 291
Activity Manual page 208

Lesson Focus

- Humans want to be like gods, but the Bible teaches there is only one God.

Objectives
- Compare how the Japanese worshiped the Showa to what the Bible says about worshiping one God
- Tell why this period of history was a dark time for many people

Review

- Invite a student to describe Hirohito.
- Choose a volunteer to state Hirohito's title and its meaning.

Preparation for Reading

- Generate interest as you direct the students to read the title and examine the picture on page 291.
- Direct the students to read the page silently to learn the names of some rulers in the Bible who tried to rule as if they were gods. Pharaoh, Nebuchadnezzar, Herod

Teach for Understanding

- Direct attention to the How It Was box on page 291. Read aloud the story. Invite a student to tell what happened.

  Why did Asuka wonder if the emperor was really a god? He seemed like an ordinary man.

  Why was this period of history a dark time for many people? Nations were ruled in ways contrary to the Bible. Their rule harmed millions of people.

  What would it take to change the wickedness of these dictators' rule? The rule of wicked dictators would require other nations to rise up and oppose them.

> Conclude the discussion by asking the question on page 291. The Bible teaches there is only one God.

Activity Manual

- Guide completion of page 208.

Lesson 116 Chapter Review
Activity Manual page 209–10

Objective
- Recall concepts and terms from Chapter 13

Introduction

- Concepts for the Chapter 13 Test will be taken from Activity Manual pages 195–210. You may review any or all of the concepts during this lesson. You may choose to review Chapter 13 by playing "Pair Review."

Review

Game: Pair Review

- Divide the students into pairs. Allow the students to use the Student Text for the review. Direct the students to take turns asking and answering questions about Chapter 13. Remind the students to check answers in the Student Text.

Activity Manual

- Guide completion of pages 209–10.

Lesson 117 Chapter 13 Test

Objective
- Demonstrate knowledge of concepts from Chapter 13 by taking the test

Assessment

- Administer Test 13.

Chapter 14

Introduction

Before World War II, countries around the world suffered from financial and political instability. Dictators threatened their neighbors' peace in Europe, and Japan pressed for territory in China. During this time, Germany, Italy, and Japan formed the Axis Powers and attacked other nations. World War II began when Great Britain and France declared war on Germany for invading Poland. The United States remained neutral until Japan attacked Pearl Harbor on December 7, 1941. America, Great Britain, and other Allied nations fought the Axis Powers. Churchill and Roosevelt agreed the United States would focus first on defeating Hitler, then on defeating Japan. American forces won the Battle of Midway. On D-Day, Allied forces landed in Normandy, France, creating a Western front in Europe while Soviet forces fought the Germans in Eastern Europe. Germany surrendered on May 7, 1945, ending the war in Europe. The United States used atomic bombs on Hiroshima and Nagasaki, Japan. These bombings resulted in Japan's surrender, ending World War II.

Chapter Focus

After struggling through the Great Depression, Americans were forced into a war that they determined to win.

14 The Second World War

Focus
After struggling through the Great Depression, Americans were forced into a war that they determined to win.

Lesson	Student Text	Activity Manual	Content	Vocabulary
			Chapter 14 Overview	
118	292–95	211–14	Political conditions around the world before World War II Germany's acts of aggression in Europe World War II begins	appeasement
119	296–98	215–16	Japan's acts of aggression in Asia and the Pacific The United States enters the war Primary Source: Roosevelt's Pearl Harbor Address	Axis Powers embargo
120	299–301	217–18	America's mobilization and joining in the fight against Hitler	Allies
121	302–4		Japanese domination in the Pacific Battle of Midway	atoll island hopping
122	305–8	219	How It Was: Supporting the War American support of the war Activity: Growing a Victory Garden	ration booklet
123	309–12	220–21	Biography Box: Aline Griffith Allied forces defeat Hitler and Mussolini	D-Day Holocaust
124	313–15	222	Allied forces defeat Japan	atomic bomb
125		223–24	Chapter Review	
126			Chapter Test	

Visit bjupress.com/resources for links to enhance the lessons.

Germany invades
Poland and war begins
Sept. 1

Pearl Harbor
Dec. 7

Official Japanese
surrender
Sept. 2

1940　1941　1942　1943　1944 June 6 1945 May 8 1946
D-Day　Official German
surrender

Never Such a War

As the Great Depression was ending, Americans were plunged into a bigger fight, World War II. They did not want to fight a war. However, when the war came to American soil, the country worked together to win.

The World Before the War
Europe

Before World War II, trouble shook Europe. The dictators of the Soviet Union, Italy, and Germany threatened their neighbors' peace. Most countries tried to remain democracies. Great Britain, France, Finland, Czechoslovakia, and Denmark were all fairly stable nations. But even these democracies had political groups that wanted their countries to be more like the dictatorships.

During the Spanish Civil War, one democracy fell. In the 1930s, one group of politicians wanted to change Spain. They supported Socialism. In 1936 this group of Socialists, Communists, and other similar parties won national elections. Other politicians and army leaders disagreed and joined together to overthrow the Socialist government. For the next three years, fighting shattered Spain. Joseph Stalin helped the elected leaders. Adolf Hitler and Benito Mussolini supported the military and the opposition. Eventually General Francisco Franco defeated the Socialist and Communist alliance. Franco set up a comparatively mild dictatorship.

The problems that tore Spain apart threatened other nations. In France, extreme politicians gained power. Some liked Hitler's Nazi ideas. Others supported Communism. Even in Britain many people supported the British Union of Fascists. Many Europeans approved of oppressive governments as long as they provided jobs.

Asia

During their troubles European nations held on to their Asian empires. Few Asian countries were independent. The two most important independent countries were China and Japan.

293

JourneyForth

The following books are available from JourneyForth Books, a division of BJU Press, at journeyforth.com.

A Father's Promise by Donnalynn Hess

When Nazis invade Rudi Kaplan's home city of Warsaw, Rudi must learn how to be truly brave, how to die to himself, and how to trust the God who is mightier than any army.

Gunner's Run by Rick Barry

Set in Europe during World War II, this is the story of Jim Yoder, a waist gunner on a B-24 in the United States Air Corps. When Jim finds himself on the ground trapped behind enemy lines, he must find a way to run across Nazi Germany to the safety of Allied soil. He must also learn to trust the God he once rejected.

Lesson Focus

- Germany, Italy, and the USSR threatened peace in Europe, and Japan sought to expand its territory in China.

Objectives
- Explain the state of countries around the world before World War II
- Identify the dictators of Russia, Germany, and Italy
- Analyze Germany's aggression toward other nations

Teacher's Toolkit CD
- Instructional Aid 52: *Before World War II*

Introduction

- Invite a student to read aloud the title of the chapter and predict what the chapter will be about. a second world war
- Invite a student to read the chapter focus aloud.

  What do you think you will learn about in this chapter? what forced Americans to fight the war and what they did to win it

- Direct attention to the picture on page 292.

  What is happening in the picture? American soldiers are raising the American flag.

- Explain that the illustration shows an actual event that was photographed during World War II: the flag raising on Iwo Jima. This event has also been the subject for paintings and statues.

- Direct attention to the timeline.

  When was Pearl Harbor attacked? December 7, 1941

  What event occurred on June 6, 1944? D-Day

  When do you think World War II ended? when the Japanese surrendered on September 2, 1945

  When did Germany officially surrender? May 8, 1945

Preparation for Reading

- Generate interest as you direct the students to read the titles on pages 293–95 and examine the map on page 295.
- Guide pronunciation of any unfamiliar words in the lesson.
- Direct the students to read the pages silently and complete Instructional Aid 52 in small groups.

Teach for Understanding

At the end of the 1930s, what event in American history was coming to an end? the Great Depression

Teach for Understanding

🔖 Why do you think Americans did not want a war? Answers could include that some Americans would have remembered what life was like during World War I, and the country had just suffered through the Great Depression.

• Guide a discussion about the state of countries around the world before World War II. Choose groups to explain the political conditions on the various continents and to name dictators and leaders.

🔖 Why do you think Europeans approved of oppressive governments? Answers could include that by providing jobs, oppressive governments would be meeting the needs of their people.

What problem did Chiang Kai-Shek and Mao Zedong cause in China? They opposed each other. The country suffered from their fighting.

What relationship existed between China and Japan during the 1930s? Answers could include that Japan was aggressive toward China. Japan took Manchuria from China in 1931 and then pressed for more territory in China during the remainder of the 1930s.

Why did Japan's leaders and emperor want Japan to have a strong military? They were not satisfied with conquering Chinese Manchuria; they wanted to conquer more territory.

What country did Italy take in Africa? Italy invaded and conquered Ethiopia.

• Guide the students in locating countries on the map on page 295 as you ask the following questions about Germany's pre-war expansion.

What region did Hitler take in 1936? the Rhineland, an area of France's border

Why did Germany take over Austria? Since Austrians also speak German, Hiltler claimed that the two countries should be one.

What country did Hitler threaten after taking over Austria? Czechoslovakia

Why did Hitler threaten Czechoslovakia? Many German speakers lived in Czechoslovakia's mountains. Also, a region of Czechoslovakia, the Sudetenland, bordered Germany.

Why did France and Britain give Hitler the Sudetenland rather than defend Czechoslovakia as they had promised? They thought Hitler would be satisfied with just that piece of Czechoslovakia.

China suffered from internal divisions. **Chiang Kai-shek** led the Kuomintang, or Nationalist Party. He opposed the Communists led by **Mao Zedong**. The country suffered from their fighting. Then, in 1931, Japan took Manchuria from China. This province had been part of the Chinese Empire for many years. During the remainder of the 1930s, Japan pressed for more territory in China. The Nationalists led the Chinese resistance.

Japan turned increasingly militaristic. Its leaders believed that Japan should have and use a strong military. An elected parliament ran the government, but Emperor Hirohito also had a say. Japan developed a larger and stronger military. Conquering Chinese Manchuria was not enough. Japan wanted more.

The Americas

During the 1930s, many countries in the Americas suffered from financial and political instability. In Latin America many nations had oppressive governments. Brazil, Argentina, and the Dominican Republic lacked free elections. Mexico changed between two leaders. One seemed to support Fascism. The other favored Socialism. The second leader took over foreign oil companies in Mexico. He did not want foreigners making money from Mexican oil. Although Canada enjoyed a strong democracy, it struggled during the Great Depression. The 1930s were a hard time for the Americas.

Africa

Most of Africa remained under European control. France and Britain ruled much of the continent. Ethiopia had defended its independence from Italy in 1896. But in October 1935, Italy attacked again. By the following May, Ethiopia was conquered. This victory encouraged Italy. Perhaps it was the start of a new Italian empire.

World War II Begins

During the 1930s Germany's aggression pushed the world toward war. In 1936 Hitler sent troops to the Rhineland. Germany had promised not to put troops on this area of France's border. Then, in 1938, Germany took over Austria. Since Austrians also speak German, Hitler claimed that the two countries should be one.

Soon after, Hitler threatened Czechoslovakia. Many German speakers lived in Czechoslovakia's mountains. Hitler demanded the Sudetenland, a region on the border of Germany and Czechoslovakia. France and Britain had promised to defend Czechoslovakia. Instead, they gave Hitler what he wanted. This policy was called **appeasement**, which means to submit to an enemy's demands in order to keep peace. Britain and France thought Hitler would be satisfied with a

294

Background

Pronunciations

Chiang Kai-shek (CHANG KY-SHEK)

Mao Zedong (MOU DZOO-DONG)

Hirohito (HIER o HEE to)

Nazi-Soviet Pact

If Hitler were to continue his expansion eastward, he would have to calm Soviet fears. Throughout the spring and summer of 1939, Hitler sought a nonaggression treaty with Stalin. He secretly offered Stalin a free hand to take the Baltic countries of Lithuania, Latvia, Estonia, Finland, and a slice of eastern Poland. In exchange, Hitler wanted a free hand to invade Poland from the west. Stalin agreed. The pact was based on no mutual trust, but like vultures feeding on a carcass, the tyrants' mouths were too full of flesh to be concerned with devouring each other.

Emboldened, Hitler ignored British and French threats to intervene. On September 1, 1939, sixteen hundred Luftwaffe (Nazi air force) aircraft bombed and strafed military and civilian targets while fifty-six German divisions rolled across the Polish border. Forty-eight hours after the assault began, the brave Polish defenders had suffered one

Pre-War Europe

War in Europe

During the winter of 1939–1940, the war went slowly. Germany attacked no other countries. The USSR forced the small Baltic republics to sign treaties with it. But the country of Finland refused and fought the Winter War. By March 1940, the USSR forced Finland to surrender some land.

Once spring came, Germany resumed its attacks. On April 6, 1940, it attacked Denmark and Norway. Denmark surrendered that day. Norway fought until June 10 and then surrendered.

On May 10, Germany launched attacks on the low countries and France. Belgium, Luxembourg, and the Netherlands were viewed as easy targets. Luxembourg surrendered on the same day. The Netherlands lasted until May 14. Belgium fought for two more weeks. It finally surrendered on May 28. Even France could not withstand the German military. Italy had also joined the war against France as Germany's ally. The French fought for a month and a half, but they finally surrendered on June 25. Germany seemed unstoppable. In all of Western Europe, only Britain remained to fight against Hitler.

piece of Czechoslovakia. In September 1939, he gained the Sudetenland. Only six months later German troops seized much more of the country. Appeasement had not worked.

Hitler next demanded a piece of Poland. After World War I, Germany was divided into two parts, with part of Poland between them. Hitler wanted to connect Germany, but Poland refused to give up its land. France and Britain promised to defend Poland. But in August 1939, Hitler made a deal with Stalin. Germany would take part of Poland, and the USSR would take the remainder.

On September 1, 1939, Germany invaded Poland. France and Britain determined to stop Hitler. If they did not, he would keep conquering more lands. On September 3, both nations declared war on Germany. World War II had begun. On September 17, the USSR also invaded Poland. The country was conquered on October 6.

> Which continent had the most trouble in the 1930s?

295

hundred thousand casualties, and by the end of September, Hitler's conquest was complete. By war's end, the Germans and Russians would kill six million Poles, half of them Jews.

War in Europe

On September 1, 1939, after weeks of posturing and provocation, Hitler unleashed his war machine on Poland. Hundreds of bombers soared over Poland. Divisions of armored vehicles, called panzers, and thousands of soldiers moved into the country to take control. On September 17, the Soviet Union also attacked Poland from the east. The fall of Poland was complete in October. The world had seen a new type of warfare: Germany's blitzkrieg ("lightning war").

Britain and France, knowing that Hitler had to be stopped, declared war on Germany on September 3, 1939. They rushed to prepare their armies, but little fighting took place for eight months. Then on April 9, Hitler's forces invaded Denmark and Norway. On May 10, 1940, Hitler staged another blitzkrieg, sending his forces into Belgium, the Netherlands, and Luxembourg. The Belgians and the Dutch, unable to stand against Hitler's strong armies, soon collapsed. Next, the Germans bypassed France's heavily fortified Maginot Line and moved into France through the Ardennes Forest. France eventually surrendered, Italy allied itself with Germany, and Great Britain stood alone against the Fascists.

Lesson

118

Teach for Understanding

Did the policy of appeasement satisfy Hitler? No, only six months after getting the Sudetenland, German troops seized much more of Czechoslovakia.

What land did Hitler want to take after he took much of Czechoslovakia? a piece of Poland

- Choose a volunteer to read aloud the sentences that tell why Hitler wanted a piece of Poland.

How did Hitler plan to take the part of Poland that he wanted? He made a deal with Stalin. Germany would take part of Poland, and the USSR would take the remainder.

When did World War II begin? when France and Britain declared war on Germany on September 3, 1939

Why did France and Britain declare war on Germany? France and Britain had promised to defend Poland, and they were determined to stop Hitler so that he would not keep conquering more lands.

Were France and Britain able to stop Hitler in Poland? No, Stalin kept his part of the deal he had made with Hitler. The USSR also invaded Poland, and the country was conquered.

What occurred during the winter of 1939–1940? The USSR forced the small Baltic republics to sign treaties with it and forced the country of Finland to surrender some land.

- Why do you think Germany did not attack anyone new during the winter? Answers could include that the weather was too bad.

- Invite students to name the countries Germany conquered from April 6 through June 25 of 1940. Denmark, Norway, Luxembourg, the Netherlands, Belgium, and France

After June 25, 1940, what was the only country in Western Europe that remained to fight against Hitler? Britain

> Conclude the discussion by asking the question on page 295. Europe

Activity Manual

- Guide completion of pages 211–14.

Lesson

119

Student Text pages 296–98
Activity Manual pages 215–16

Lesson Focus

- Events in Europe, the Pacific, and Asia forced the United States to enter the war.

Objectives

- Analyze efforts by the United States to remain neutral
- Identify the countries that formed the Axis Powers
- Explain why the United States declared war on Japan

Teacher's Toolkit CD

- Instructional Aid 52: *Before World War II*

Review

- Use Instructional Aid 52 to guide a review of the political conditions around the world before World War II.
- Invite students to identify the dictators of Germany, Russia, and Italy just before the war. Adolf Hitler, Joseph Stalin, and Benito Mussolini
- Guide the students in orally summarizing Germany's acts of aggression that led to World War II.

Preparation for Reading

- Generate interest as you direct the students to read the titles and examine the picture and map on pages 296–98.
- Guide pronunciation of any unfamiliar words in the lesson.
- Direct the students to read the pages silently to discover what events caused the United States to enter the war. Japan attacked the US naval base at Pearl Harbor. That same day Japan also attacked Thailand, the British colony of Malaya, and the American colony of the Philippines. Then Japan declared war on the United States.

Teach for Understanding

How did many Americans feel about the possibility of the United States becoming involved in the war in Europe? They wanted the United States to remain neutral.

Why did Americans want the United States to remain neutral? They worried that interfering would hurt the nation's economy because the United States was still suffering from the Great Depression.

During the 1930s, what action did Congress take to try to keep the United States out of the conflict? Congress passed several Neutrality Acts.

> Guide a review of important terms, maps, places, and people from each previous lesson. Direct the students to find and read the corresponding entries from the Resource Treasury.

Inching to War
Moving Toward the Fight

As Europe and the world descended into war, most Americans were happy to be far away. Many wanted the United States to remain neutral. Americans worried that interfering would hurt their nation's economy. The United States was still suffering from the Great Depression. During the 1930s, Congress passed several Neutrality Acts. These bills tried to keep Americans out of the conflict. Even so, as fighting increased in China and tensions rose in Europe, Americans began switching their views. Most sympathized with China, and most worried about Hitler and the Nazis.

After Germany invaded Poland, the United States adjusted its policies. President Franklin Roosevelt encouraged Congress to pass a cash-and-carry law. This law allowed fighting nations to buy goods from the United States. They could not buy on credit or use American ships. Congress did not want American lenders to support either side. Even so, Americans felt sympathy for Britain. After France fell, Germany bombed London and other British cities unmercifully. These attacks on civilians encouraged pro-British feelings among Americans.

At the same time, Americans turned against Japan. In September 1940, Japan joined Germany and Italy's alliance, the **Axis Powers**. Japan now threatened European colonial possessions in Asia. It also threatened American control of the Philippines. Over the next months the United States tried to stop Japan through nonmilitary means. President Roosevelt blocked the sale of oil and scrap iron to Japan. This **embargo** hurt Japan. Without oil, their ships and planes could not move. As an island nation, Japan needed cheap oil. The United States hoped that cutting off some of Japan's supplies would make Japan less aggressive.

President Roosevelt led Americans through this troubling time. He gave occasional radio addresses, called fireside chats, where he explained what was going on in the world. He also explained his decisions. Roosevelt slowly changed people's minds. He could not bring the United States into the war unless Americans supported the fight. Roosevelt encouraged American sympathy for the British. He led the nation to view Britain as an ally. In 1940 Roosevelt ran for reelection. For the first time, a president ran for a third term in office. Americans still wanted Roosevelt. He won easily.

In 1941 the war in Europe shifted. Until then Germany and the USSR had worked together. Although Hitler was a Nazi who hated Communists, he and Stalin had peacefully divided up Europe. But in June 1941, Hitler invaded the USSR. He wanted the country's natural resources. In addition,

296

How did Americans respond as fighting increased in China and tensions rose in Europe? Most Americans sympathized with China and worried about Hitler and the Nazis.

- Choose a volunteer to explain how the cash-and-carry law allowed the United States to remain neutral.

What encouraged pro-British feelings among Americans after France fell to Germany? Germany attacked British civilians by bombing London and other British cities unmercifully.

Why did Americans turn against Japan? Japan joined Germany and Italy's alliance, threatening European colonial possessions in Asia and American control of the Philippines.

What were the allied nations of Germany, Italy, and Japan called? the Axis Powers

- Invite a student to explain how the United States tried to stop Japan.
- Choose a volunteer to read aloud the glossary definition of *embargo*.
- Guide a discussion about how Roosevelt used the radio to his advantage in gaining support for the United States to enter the war.

he wanted more room for German people to spread. Hitler believed that the German people were the best in the world. He planned to destroy the people he viewed as worthless and conquer the people he thought were not as good as Germans. Stalin was shocked by Hitler's betrayal of him. But the Russians did not surrender. They worked hard to drive Hitler's armies from the USSR. They also asked the United States to send supplies. Americans were closer than ever to the war.

The Battle Begins

The situation was also getting worse in Asia. In July 1941 a new government took power in Japan. The leaders did not want to deal with American demands. President Roosevelt worked to block Japan from gaining the resources that kept its military going. He hoped that Japan would free China. Instead, the Japanese government worked out a new plan.

Japan needed American forces to leave Asia. The country wanted to capture the Dutch East Indies. These islands had oil and rubber. But in Asia the Dutch, British, and American forces worked together. Additionally, the Philippines, an American colony, lay between Japan and the Dutch East Indies. Japan decided to destroy the American navy in the Pacific.

While Japan plotted against the United States, the nations continued to negotiate. The Japanese ambassador

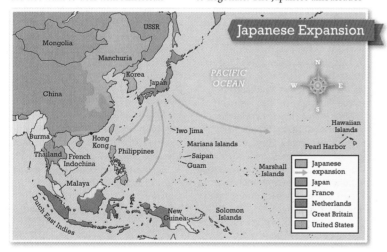

Japanese Expansion

297

Additional Background information for this lesson is on the Teacher's Toolkit CD.

Background

Hideki Tojo

Hideki Tojo was the son of an army general and a graduate of a military academy. After World War I, he became a proponent of total war. Tojo pushed the Japanese offensive in China with Emperor Hirohito's approval, and in October 1941 he brought the war party to full power when Hirohito appointed him prime minister. With the Emperor's blessing, Tojo ordered the attack on Pearl Harbor. He also directed the campaigns in the Pacific and Southeast Asia. After the Japanese surrender in 1945, Tojo was captured and tried for war crimes. Much of the blame for the war in the East was shifted from Emperor Hirohito to Tojo. Hirohito did not face trial. Tojo and six other Japanese leaders, however, were found guilty and were hanged.

Teach for Understanding

Why did Roosevelt encourage American sympathy for the British? He wanted Americans to view Britain as an ally.

What was significant about Roosevelt running for reelection in 1940? It was the first time a president ran for a third term.

Why do you think Americans still wanted Roosevelt to be president? He had led them out of the Great Depression; he worked to keep the United States neutral; in his fireside chats, he explained what was going on and explained his decisions.

What did Hitler do in June 1941 that shocked Stalin? Hitler invaded the USSR.

- Invite a student to read aloud the sentences that tell why Hitler invaded the USSR.

Do you think that Hitler viewed people the same way that God's Word teaches Christians to view others? Answers could include that God does not view some groups of people as being better than others. All people are sinners who need to trust Christ to save them from their sin. All people are made in God's image and are valuable to Him.

How did Hitler's invasion of the USSR bring Americans closer to the war? Answers could include that the Russians asked the United States to send supplies that would help them drive Hitler's armies from the USSR.

What happened to the Japanese government in July 1941? A new government took power.

- Choose a volunteer to explain the attitude of Japan's new leaders toward the United States.

- Guide the students in locating Japan, the Dutch East Indies, and the Philippines on the map on page 297 as you ask the following questions.

Why did Japan want to capture the Dutch East Indies? Japan wanted the oil and rubber that the islands had.

Why do you think Japan decided to destroy the American navy in the Pacific? American forces would be located in the Philippines, and Japan did not want the US navy to help the Dutch and British forces defend the Dutch East Indies.

Why do you think Japan allowed negotiations with the United States and regular meetings between the Japanese ambassador and American diplomats to continue while Japan plotted against the United States? Answers could include that Japan's leaders did not want the United States to know about their plans to destroy the American navy.

Teach for Understanding

Who became the new premier of Japan in October 1941?
Hideki Tojo

Why do you think Hideki Tojo wanted Japan and Hirohito to receive glory? Tojo was also a general; he was proud of his country and that Japan had never been defeated in war; he thought of Hirohito as a god.

- Guide the students in locating French Indochina, Hawaii, Thailand, Malaya, and the Philippines on the map on page 297 as you ask the following question.

  How did Japan respond when Cordell Hull demanded that Japan leave China and French Indochina? Japan moved ahead with its plans and attacked Pearl Harbor. Japan also attacked Thailand, the British colony of Malaya, and the Philippines. Then Japan officially declared war on the United States.

- Choose a volunteer to read aloud the caption for the photograph on page 298.

  Was Japan able to destroy the entire US navy? No, America's aircraft carriers were at sea and escaped without harm.

  How did Congress respond to Japan's attack? The next day, Congress declared war on Japan.

  Why did Germany and Italy declare war on the United States? They were Japan's allies.

  How did Congress respond to Germany's and Italy's declarations of war? Congress declared war on both Germany and Italy.

Why do you think many Americans were determined to win the war? Americans wanted to protect their nation, and they wanted to stop German and Japanese aggression.

How did the American people show that they backed Roosevelt's promise that with God's help, America would win? The American people supported the war effort.

What do you think Americans did to support the war effort?

Conclude the discussion by asking the question on page 298. Japan wanted American forces out of Asia so that the American forces would no longer be able to work with the Dutch and British forces there. They wanted to capture the Dutch East Indies and gain control of Asia.

Visit bjupress.com/resources for possible links to an eyewitness account of the attack on Pearl Harbor and Roosevelt's Pearl Harbor Address.

The US Pacific fleet was severely crippled when Japanese planes bombed Pearl Harbor. America's rallying cry was "Remember Pearl Harbor."

met regularly with American diplomats. Back in Tokyo, a new premier took over the government in October 1941. **Hideki Tojo** was a general who wanted Japan and its emperor, Hirohito, to receive glory. In late November, the American secretary of state, Cordell Hull, demanded that Japan leave China and French Indochina. But Japan moved ahead with its plans.

Early on December 7, 1941, Japan attacked the United States. Its target was the naval base at **Pearl Harbor** in Honolulu, Hawaii. Two waves of Japanese planes struck the American forces. The attack destroyed antiaircraft guns, planes, and warships. Fortunately for the Americans, their aircraft carriers were at sea and escaped without harm. At Pearl Harbor over three thousand Americans were killed or went missing.

Japan did not stop at Pearl Harbor. That same day the country also attacked Thailand, the British colony of Malaya, and the Philippines. Shortly after the attack, Japan officially declared war on the United States.

The United States was now at war, whether it wanted to be or not. On December 8, Congress voted to declare war on Japan. Two days later Japan's allies, Germany and Italy, both declared war on the United States. Congress replied with declarations of war on both nations.

Although few Americans wanted to go to war, they were determined to win. Japan had hoped to crush America with a surprise attack. Instead, it pushed the country to fight better than its enemies. President Roosevelt promised that with God's help, the American people would win. The nation backed his promise with support for the war effort.

> Why did Japan decide to attack the United States?

298

Primary Source: Roosevelt's Pearl Harbor Address

- Guide the students in reading Roosevelt's address on Activity Manual pages 215–16. You may choose to have the students follow the text of the speech as they listen to a recording of it.

- Explain that Roosevelt's Pearl Harbor Address is also referred to as his Declaration of War Request and his Day of Infamy Address.

Activity Manual

- Guide completion of page 215–16.

Activity

Read an Eyewitness Account

Use discretion as you read aloud an eyewitness account of the attack on Pearl Harbor. Guide a discussion of what Americans experienced at the time of the attack.

America Goes to War
Mobilization

Once the United States declared war, the country set out to win. First, the military needed to grow. Even before Pearl Harbor, the United States allowed the draft. This system enlisted men into the military. After Pearl Harbor, Congress said that every man between the ages of twenty and forty must enroll in the selective service. This organization chose men to fight. Almost ten million men were drafted during World War II. Many others volunteered to fight. Women were not drafted. But about two hundred thousand volunteered to join the military anyway.

The United States also needed to prepare war materiel. Fighting would take many ships, tanks, and planes.

Many American young men eagerly enlisted for military service after Japan's attack on Pearl Harbor.

President Roosevelt appointed men to ensure that factories had enough building materials, such as steel. Scientists and engineers worked to develop new tools to win the war. Rockets with better fuses helped target enemies. Radar alerted ships to enemy planes. New antibiotics helped American troops fight disease. Scientists also encouraged the use of DDT. This powerful chemical killed harmful insects but did not seem to harm people.

Where to Fight First?

In December 1941 President Roosevelt and his advisers had to decide where to focus their efforts. Fighting two major enemies would be hard. Should Americans focus on Japan because it had attacked them? Should they focus on Germany, which was threatening to defeat Britain? **Winston Churchill** was the British prime minister. Like Roosevelt, he encouraged his people by giving excellent speeches. Churchill and Roosevelt got along well, and they both feared Hitler. They hoped to defeat Hitler and rebuild a peaceful and cooperative world. Churchill urged Roosevelt to focus on Hitler. Roosevelt agreed to make defeating Hitler the priority. Americans would focus on Europe without forgetting about Japan. The countries fighting the Axis powers would be called the **Allies**.

299

Lesson 120

Student Text pages 299–301
Activity Manual pages 217–18

Lesson Focus

- Once the United States declared war, the country mobilized and joined the fight against Hitler.

Objectives

- Describe what the United States did to mobilize for the war
- Analyze Roosevelt's decision to make fighting Hitler the priority
- Explain how German troops were pushed out of North Africa and the USSR

Review

- Choose volunteers to explain actions taken by the United States in an effort to remain neutral.

What nations were called the Axis Powers? Germany, Italy, and Japan

Why did the United States declare war on Japan? Japan attacked the US naval base at Pearl Harbor. That same day Japan also attacked Thailand, the British colony of Malaya, and the American colony of the Philippines. Then Japan declared war on the United States.

Preparation for Reading

- Generate interest as you direct the students to read the titles and examine the pictures on pages 299–301.
- Guide pronunciation of any unfamiliar words in the lesson.
- Direct the students to read the pages silently to discover what *mobilization* refers to. It is the act of preparing and organizing the United States for war.

Teach for Understanding

What were Americans determined to do once the United States declared war? Win the war.

What did the United States need to do in order to mobilize for war? increase the size of the military and prepare war materiel

- Invite a student to read aloud the caption for the photograph on page 299.
- Guide the students in comparing the draft system before and after Pearl Harbor. Explain that before Pearl Harbor, the draft allowed the United States to enlist men into the military. To build up the military after Pearl Harbor, every man between the ages of twenty and forty was required to enroll in the selective service (compulsory military service).

 Why do you think women were not drafted? The United States did not want to make women fight in the war.

What war materiels did the United States prepare? ships, tanks, and planes

What were some new products developed by scientists and engineers? rockets with better fuses, radar, antibiotics, and DDT

- Guide the students in comparing President Roosevelt and Winston Churchill.

 Why do you think Roosevelt agreed to make defeating Hitler the priority? Answers could include that the Dutch, British, and American forces needed to work together in Asia. Germany was threatening to defeat Britain, and Roosevelt would want Britain's help in fighting Japan. Fighting two major enemies, Germany and Japan, would be hard. So the Allies decided to defeat Germany first.

 Why could the Americans not forget about Japan? Answers could include that Japan still wanted to gain control of Asia and would keep attacking Americans in Asia and the Pacific.

What were the countries fighting the Axis Powers called? Allies

Lesson

120

Teach for Understanding

Where did the Allies make their first move toward freeing Europe? in North Africa

Why did Erwin Rommel push hard to drive the British forces out of Egypt? The Axis Powers would control the Suez Canal if the British forces were gone.

- Point out the location of the Suez Canal on a world map. Point out the route to the Middle East and Asia as you explain that both the British and the Germans wanted control of the Suez Canal because it would give their country access to the oil resources in the Middle East. The canal also provided Britain a shorter route to the country's colonies in Asia rather than having to sail around the entire continent of Africa.

Who were the commanders of the Allied forces in North Africa? General Bernard Montgomery commanded the British forces. General Dwight Eisenhower and General George Patton commanded the American forces.

- Direct attention to the map on page 300 as you ask the following questions about the North African Conflict. Guide the students in following the paths of the opposing forces as you guide a discussion of the strategy used by the Allies to defeat the Germans.

Why did Hitler recall Rommel to Europe? Rommel was a brilliant general. The German effort would be hurt if he was captured by the Allies.

What did Patton do after the German army surrendered in North Africa? He continued the fight in Sicily and freed the island.

Why was it important for the Allies to gain control of Sicily? The island was a stepping stone to invading Italy.

- Guide the students in locating Sicily and Italy on the map.

North Africa

The first move toward freeing Europe took place in North Africa. At the beginning of 1942, the Germans had the advantage. Their main general, **Erwin Rommel**, pushed hard against the British forces. He hoped to drive them out of Egypt. Then the Axis powers would control the Suez Canal. Finally in late 1942, the Allies struck back.

In October 1942 the British advanced west out of Egypt. Under the command of General **Bernard Montgomery**, they forced the German troops back over the North African desert. About two weeks later, American forces surprised the Germans. Generals **Dwight Eisenhower** and **George**

Patton commanded American progress. The troops landed in western North Africa. Now Rommel faced Americans to his west and British troops to his east. To the south was more desert and to the north was the Mediterranean Sea. For months Rommel fought craftily, but the Allies were too strong. Hitler recalled Rommel to Europe. If the Allies captured this brilliant general, the German effort would be hurt. In May 1943 the German army in North Africa surrendered.

General Patton continued the fight into Sicily. This large island was a stepping stone to invading Italy and defeating Hitler's ally, Mussolini. In only thirty-eight days, Patton freed

300

Background

Women in the Military

Although men generally get the attention in accounts of the war, women made great contributions too. In fact, about 268,000 women joined the various women's auxiliary units of the service branches. The largest such unit was the Women's Army Corps (WAC), which enlisted 150,000 women. The Navy enlisted 86,000 women in its WAVES (Women Accepted for Volunteer Emergency Service) program. The Coast Guard also had a unit called the SPARS, named for the Coast Guard motto, "Semper Paratus, Always Ready," which about 10,000 women joined. The 2,000 WASPs (Women Air Service Pilots) flew new warplanes to their frontline bases for the Army Air Corps. About 20,000 women also joined the marines' auxiliary, but their unit did not have any special name or acronym.

the island. In mainland Italy, anti-Mussolini forces were encouraged. The king of Italy had been powerless to stop Mussolini. But now even Mussolini's supporters worried that siding with Hitler was a mistake. A new Italian government formed in July 1943. On September 2, 1943, Italy surrendered to the Allies. However, fighting continued in Italy. Hitler had sent many German troops into Italy to support Mussolini. They continued to fight the Allied soldiers. But the Allies were slowly pushing north and freeing the country.

A Second Front

Stalin felt that the Allies were too slow. As he fought Hitler in Eastern Europe, Stalin demanded more help from the United States and Britain. Stalin wanted them to attack Hitler more directly. He wanted an attack on occupied France. Roosevelt and Churchill were cautious. They also wanted to defeat Hitler. But they knew that a hasty attack would cost many lives. It might fail. A failed invasion of Europe would harm the Allied cause more than a wise delay.

While they planned their attack, Russian troops desperately fought the Germans. For months, Nazi troops advanced deeper into the USSR. Over the winter of 1942–1943, the key battle was for Stalingrad. This large city defended Soviet oil fields. If Hitler gained them, he would have an almost endless supply of fuel. Over the brutal Russian winter, soldiers fought house to house to save the city. Finally in early February, the Germans at Stalingrad surrendered. They could not take the city. From then on, Soviet troops steadily pushed German troops out of the USSR.

War at Sea

Protecting Allied ships was a concern for the United States. The Atlantic Ocean was full of German submarines and U-boats. Before joining the war, the United States had sold fifty destroyers to Britain in exchange for bases on British territories. After Pearl Harbor, American ships needed destroyers for defense. American shipyards worked to produce more ships. Although the Germans sunk few troop transports, many ships with supplies were torpedoed and sunk.

The Allies finally achieved greater success at defending their shipping in mid-1943. There were more Allied aircraft carriers in the Atlantic. These vessels launched aircraft that could spot and sink U-boats. Long-range aircraft could also fly farther from land. Skillful use of sonar and depth charges also helped find and destroy U-boats. As the war stretched on, the Allies eventually won the Battle of the Atlantic.

> Where did the Russians fight the Nazis to a standstill in winter?

301

Invading Mediterranean Europe

Although Hitler had lost in North Africa, he was determined to keep "Fortress Europe," the lands that he had conquered in Europe. He expected that any Allied assault would come across the English Channel into France. But the Allies under American general George Patton launched Operation Husky. First, they invaded Sicily, the large island off the tip of Italy. American troops under General Mark Clark and British troops under General Bernard Montgomery then invaded Italy at Anzio and Salerno. Working their way up the Italian coast, the Americans captured Naples in October 1943. But the push to take Rome was slowed by Germans who were entrenched in the mountains. It took the Allies four months to travel through Italy's snow-clad mountains.

Italian citizens were tired of war. They overthrew Mussolini, surrendered to the Allies, and declared war on Germany. American forces freed Rome on June 4, 1944. Fighting continued against German forces in northern Italy for another year.

Teach for Understanding

Why do you think anti-Mussolini forces in mainland Italy were encouraged when Patton freed Sicily? Now they had hope that the American or Allied forces would free them from Mussolini.

Why did fighting continue in Italy after the country had surrendered to the Allies? Hitler had sent many German troops into Italy to support Mussolini.

- Choose a volunteer to explain why Stalin was now demanding more help from the Allies as he fought Hitler in Eastern Europe. The explanation could include that Hitler had broken his deal with Stalin and had invaded the USSR.

What did Stalin want the United States and Britain to do? He wanted them to attack Hitler more directly by attacking occupied France.

- Invite a student to read aloud Churchill's and Roosevelt's response to Stalin's demand.

Why was the battle for Stalingrad the key battle in the USSR? The large city defended Soviet oil fields. After months of the Nazi troops advancing deeper into the USSR, the Russians forced the Germans to surrender at Stalingrad. From then on, Soviet troops steadily pushed German troops out of the USSR.

- Choose a volunteer to explain why American shipyards worked to produce more ships. Explanations could include that many ships were needed to fight the war, and destroyers were needed to defend other American ships.

Choose another volunteer to explain what allowed the Allies to eventually win the Battle of the Atlantic. Having more aircraft carriers in the Atlantic in mid-1943 allowed more aircraft that could spot and sink U-boats. Long-range aircraft could also fly farther from land. Skillful use of sonar and depth charges also helped find and destroy U-boats.

 Conclude the discussion by asking the question on page 301. Stalingrad

Activity Manual

- Guide completion of pages 217–18.

Assessment

- Administer quiz.

The quiz may be given anytime after completing this lesson.

Lesson Focus

- The United States military fought the Japanese in the Pacific.

Objectives

- Recognize that Allied forces were simultaneously fighting the Axis powers in Europe and in the Pacific
- Analyze Japan's dominance in the Pacific
- Explain the significance of the Allied victory at the Battle of Midway
- Analyze the Allied strategy for winning in the Pacific

Teacher's Toolkit CD

- Instructional Aid 53: *Fighting in the Pacific*

Review

- Guide a discussion about how the United States mobilized for war.

  What factors influenced Roosevelt to focus first on defeating Hitler? Fighting two major enemies would be hard. Germany was threatening to defeat Britain. Churchill urged Roosevelt to focus on Hitler.

  Where did the Allies decide to fight first against the Germans in order to free Europe? North Africa

- Choose a volunteer to explain how the Allies were able to eventually win the Battle of the Atlantic.

Preparation for Reading

- Generate interest as you direct the students to read the titles and examine the maps on pages 302–4.
- Guide pronunciation of any unfamiliar words in the lesson.
- Direct the students to read the pages silently and complete Instructional Aid 53 in pairs.

Teach for Understanding

Which Axis Power were the Allies fighting against in the Pacific? Japan

- Invite a group to name countries that were a part of the Allies.
- Choose a volunteer to explain why Japan seemed to be unstoppable after the attack on Pearl Harbor. Instruct him to include the victories that caused Japan to seem unstoppable. Guide the students in locating the victories on the map on page 303.
- Invite a group to tell why they think Japan dominated the seas.

  Who led the fight against Japan until President Roosevelt ordered him to leave the Philippines? General Douglas MacArthur

Fighting in the Pacific

Japan Advances

After the attack on Pearl Harbor, Japan seemed to be unstoppable in the Pacific. Nothing was safe from Japanese attack. The British suffered severe losses. Hong Kong, their colony in China, fell to Japan on Christmas Day, 1941. Then Singapore surrendered in February 1942. Every British colony in Southeast Asia was threatened.

The Japanese also dominated the seas. In the end of February, they fought the Battle of the Java Sea. The Japanese navy defeated four Allied militaries. The United States, Britain, the Netherlands, and Australia failed to prevent a Japanese advance. As a result, the Dutch East Indies were lost. The Allies lost a source of fuel and rubber. Japan's victory threatened even Australia with invasion.

Japan also advanced into the Philippines. On December 10, 1941, the Japanese first landed in the islands. American and Filipino troops tried to stop the Japanese conquest. By March 1942 the Philippines seemed doomed. President Roosevelt ordered General **Douglas MacArthur** to leave the islands. For months he had led the fight against Japan. When he left, General MacArthur promised, "I shall return." During the spring of 1942, the rest of the Philippines fell to the Japanese military.

Allied Resistance

The Allies refused to give up the fight. Across the seas and islands of Asia and the Pacific, American, Filipino, Australian, and other Allied soldiers kept resisting. At first they only managed to slow the Japanese advance.

In early May 1942, the United States and Australia managed to stop a Japanese advance in two days. Japan wanted to control another island, New Guinea. If it gained New Guinea, Australia would be in danger. Only a narrow strait separates the two lands. American and Australian ships raced to stop the Japanese fleet. The ships never met. For two days aircraft carriers launched planes in the Coral Sea against each other. This naval battle was the first in which the ships never met. Neither side won a clear victory, but Japan did not advance. The Allies were excited to have stopped a Japanese attack.

The Turning Point

Japan had bigger plans than New Guinea. It wanted to capture Hawaii from the United States too. To do so, it needed the island of **Midway**. This tiny **atoll** lies almost halfway between Asia and North America. Japan hoped to trick the US Navy and sink its aircraft carriers while the US military defended Midway. At the attack on Pearl Harbor, the aircraft carriers had escaped. If the United States lost its carriers, it would struggle to stop Japan.

302

What were the United States and Australia able to do in May of 1942? They managed to stop a Japanese advance.

Where did this battle take place? in the Coral Sea

- Choose a volunteer to explain why the United States and Australia fought the Battle of the Coral Sea. Point out on a world map the location of the Coral Sea and the proximity of New Guinea and Australia.

  What was significant about this naval battle? It was the first naval battle in which the ships never met. The aircraft carriers launched planes against each other.

  What was the outcome of the Battle of the Coral Sea? Neither side won a clear victory, but the Allies stopped a Japanese attack.

  What American territory did Japan want to capture? Hawaii

- Invite a student to explain Japan's strategy for capturing Hawaii. Guide the students in locating Hawaii and Midway Island on the map.

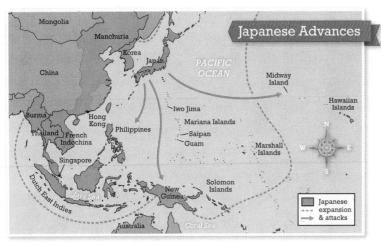

Japanese Advances

Mongolia

Manchuria

Korea

Japan

China

PACIFIC
OCEAN

Midway
Island

Burma

Hong
Kong

Iwo Jima

Hawaiian
Islands

Thailand

French
Indochina

Philippines

Mariana Islands

Saipan

Guam

Marshall
Islands

N

W   E

S

Singapore

Dutch East Indies

Java Sea

New
Guinea

Solomon
Islands

	Japanese
▨	expansion
- - -	& attacks

Australia   Coral Sea

But the American forces were ready in advance. The Japanese encoded all their communications, but the United States had broken the main navy code. The US Navy knew when and where the Japanese fleet would be.

The American fleet was not in great shape. The Japanese had four aircraft carriers, but the United States had only three. One had been badly damaged at the Coral Sea, but it still supported the fight. Aircraft already based on Midway itself would have to help attack the Japanese fleet.

Finally in early June 1942, the Japanese fleet approached Midway. Admiral **Isoroku Yamamoto** directed the operation. The American force was commanded by **Chester Nimitz**.

During the battle American aircraft struck the Japanese carriers hard. They did their job. At the end of the battle, four Japanese aircraft carriers were sunk. Only one American carrier, the *Yorktown*, was sunk. The Japanese fleet headed back, and Americans celebrated the great victory. The Battle of the Coral Sea proved Americans could stop the Japanese. The Battle of Midway proved that the Allies could win. Now the Allies needed to see if they could win an offensive.

The offensive began in August 1942 on the island of Guadalcanal. This island lay northwest of Australia. It lay in a chain of islands called the Solomon Islands. Allied forces decided that taking Guadalcanal would open a

303

Teach for Understanding

Who were the commanders of the Japanese and the American forces for the Battle of Midway? Admiral Isoroku Yamamoto directed the Japanese forces. Chester Nimitz commanded the American forces.

Who won the Battle of Midway? the Americans

- Invite a student to read aloud the paragraph that tells what information helped the United States win the battle.

Why was the Battle of Midway the turning point of the war in the Pacific? Answers could include that the battle proved that the Allies could win. The Allies then attacked and defeated the Japanese at Guadalcanal.

In what group of islands is Guadalcanal located? the Solomon Islands

- Guide the students in locating the Solomon Islands on the map on page 303. Point out the distance between Midway and the Solomon Islands.

Why did the Allied forces decide to attack Guadalcanal? The Allies wanted to open a route to free more islands captured by the Japanese.

Background

Battle of Midway

Some Japanese carriers headed toward Midway Island, an American island west of Hawaii. The Japanese hoped to attack the island base and then lure American carriers into a battle. But American naval intelligence had cracked the Japanese radio code and had advance warning. Planes from American carriers bombed the Japanese ships before the Japanese could attack Midway. The Americans sank three Japanese carriers in a few minutes, and a fourth went down the next day. The Americans' cost was also high. They lost one aircraft carrier, the *Yorktown*, and most of its planes and pilots. However, the Japanese sea offensive was stopped, and the Japanese navy had suffered a major defeat.

Additional Background information for this lesson is on the Teacher's Toolkit CD.

Breaking Code PURPLE

The United States gained a significant advantage when members of its Signal Intelligence Service (SIS) cracked a complicated Japanese code. A special machine, known as PURPLE, created the code, which was used to send diplomatic messages to various Japanese embassies.

The SIS broke PURPLE by building a copycat machine, a feat accomplished with the help of two circumstances. First, not all Japanese embassies had PURPLE machines. When Japan sent the same message to all of its embassies, American codebreakers used messages in familiar codes to help decipher transmissions in PURPLE. Second, the SIS staged an electrical failure at the Japanese embassy in Washington and sent in two agents disguised as repairmen to "fix" the problem while getting a glimpse of a real PURPLE machine.

Breaking Code PURPLE helped the United States achieve victory at critical battles such as Midway. The Japanese finally stopped using the code in 1943 when they realized that it was no longer secure.

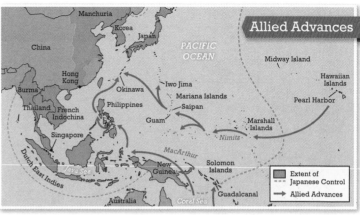

Allied Advances

Manchuria
Korea
Japan
China
PACIFIC OCEAN
Midway Island
Hong Kong
Hawaiian Islands
Burma
Okinawa
Iwo Jima
Pearl Harbor
Thailand
French Indochina
Philippines
Mariana Islands
Saipan
Guam
Marshall Islands
Singapore
Nimitz
MacArthur
Dutch East Indies
Java Sea
New Guinea
Solomon Islands
Australia
Coral Sea
Guadalcanal

Extent of Japanese Control
Allied Advances

Teach for Understanding

🔧 Was the battle for Guadalcanal an easy battle? No, the fight lasted for many months. Thousands of Allied soldiers died, but the island was eventually freed.

What did the Allies do after they freed Guadalcanal? They continued to attack Japan in neighboring islands and slowly pressed the Japanese back.

● Invite a student to read aloud the paragraph that tells what else the Allies gained during the Solomon Islands campaign.

By 1943 which Allied country provided the most men to fight in the Pacific? the United States

🔧 Why do you think the Allied forces in the Pacific consisted mainly of Americans? Answers could include that Britain was much closer to Europe than the United States and was still fighting Hitler in Europe. Other Allied countries could not establish military bases because many of their colonies in Asia and the Pacific were under Japanese control.

● Choose a volunteer to use the map on page 304 to explain the two lines of attack that the Allied forces used to fight Japan.

🔧 Do you think using two lines of attack against Japan was a good strategy? Answers could include that Britain and the United States had used a similar strategy when they defeated the Germans in North Africa. In North Africa, the Germans were forced to fight against the British to their east and the Americans to their west. In the Pacific, Japan was forced to fight Allied forces in two different areas, the islands of Southeast Asia and in the Pacific.

Why did the Allies want to establish bases on islands closer to Japan? The Allies wanted to be able to bomb Japan with land-based aircraft.

By 1943, what did the United States show the world? The United States was going to persevere, or not give up, in the fight against Japan. Americans were determined to win.

▶ Conclude the discussion by asking the question on page 304. The United States had broken the main Japanese navy code, and the US Navy knew when and where the Japanese fleet would be. American aircraft did their job, sinking four Japanese aircraft carriers and forcing the Japanese fleet to head back.

route to free more islands captured by the Japanese. The fight lasted for many months. Thousands of Allied soldiers died, but the island was eventually freed. The Allies continued to attack Japan in neighboring islands. The Japanese were slowly pressed back.

During the Solomon Islands campaign, the Allies achieved another victory. Once again American code breakers read Japanese codes. They learned where Admiral Yamamoto would be flying. By 1943 he commanded Japan's Combined Fleet. Code breakers told the American navy, which then coordinated an attack. Yamamoto was shot down, and Japan lost an important leader.

Two Lines of Attack

By 1943 the Allied forces in the Pacific were following a new strategy.

Their forces were mainly American, and American leaders commanded the offenses. In the islands of Southeast Asia, General Douglas MacArthur led a campaign to free the Philippines and advance on Japan. In the Pacific Islands, Admiral Chester Nimitz led the navy campaign. The navy worked at **island hopping**. It tried to establish bases closer and closer to Japan's home islands. The soldiers wanted to be able to bomb Japan with land-based aircraft.

The war in the Pacific showed the world American perseverance. Although fighting began badly at Pearl Harbor, the United States refused to give up. It found allies and kept fighting. Americans wanted to win the war.

◀ How did the United States defeat the Japanese at Midway?

304

Activity

Secret Code

Challenge pairs of students to create a secret code, using a combination of numbers and symbols for the letters of the alphabet. Direct the students to use their secret code to write a short message. Encourage the students to exchange and decode the messages.

How It Was

"Today I'm going to the high school," Sheila announced to her fifth-grade classmates one September morning.

Millie stared. "The high school! Why?"

"It is my brother Jimmy's birthday," Sheila said. "He just graduated in June. Now he is stationed at the Aberdeen Proving Ground, training to fight in Europe. The school cook wanted to make him a birthday cake. My parents and I are going to take the cake to him before he ships out."

Jeffrey spoke up from across the room. "My cousin is fighting in France," he said.

"I have two uncles in the navy," Emile said. "One of them knows how to fly bombers."

Millie frowned. *I wish I were old enough to go overseas and be a nurse,* she thought. *All I do is go to school every day. I'm not helping the war at all.*

"Thank you, students," Miss Hull said. "Let's all remember the brave men who are fighting to keep America safe. And don't forget the doctors and nurses who help them to be healthy. When they were in school, they said the Pledge of Allegiance just like we are about to do. Some people serve our nation by fighting. But we can serve by growing victory gardens, mailing packages, and praying for our soldiers. And you can also serve by doing your best in school. You will be our country's future leaders."

Millie stood up straight and placed her hand over her heart. She and her classmates began reciting the pledge. *Maybe I'm serving my country after all,* she thought.

305

Lesson 122

Student Text pages 305–8
Activity Manual page 219

Lesson Focus

- American civilians sacrificed, worked, and served to support the war effort.

Objectives

- List ways in which Americans at home supported the war
- Explain why certain products were rationed
- Describe the role entertainment had in supporting the war
- Plan a victory garden

Review

Although the Allies focused first on defeating Hitler in Europe, where else did they need to fight after Japan attacked Pearl Harbor? in the Pacific

At first, who dominated the seas in the Pacific? Japan

- Choose a volunteer to explain the significance of the Allied victory at the Battle of Midway.
- Choose another volunteer to explain the new strategy the Allied forces were using in the Pacific by 1943.

Preparation for Reading

- Generate interest as you direct the students to read the titles and examine the pictures on pages 305–8.
- Guide pronunciation of any unfamiliar words in the lesson.
- Direct the students to read the pages silently. Instruct pairs of students to list on paper ways in which Americans supported the war.

Teach for Understanding

- Guide the students in reading the How It Was box.
- Invite a student to read aloud Sheila's announcement to her classmates.

 Why is Sheila going to the high school? Answers could include that Sheila might be going to the high school with her parents to get the birthday cake from the school cook.

Where did Sheila and her parents need to take the cake? to the Aberdeen Proving Ground where Jimmy was training to fight in Europe

 Who had relatives fighting in the war? Jeffrey and Emile

 Why did Millie frown? Answers could include that she was sad about not being able to serve her country.

- Invite a student to read aloud what Millie thought as she began reciting the pledge.

What caused Millie to change her mind about being able to serve her country? Miss Hull suggested some ways that people at home could serve the United States.

- Guide a discussion about which of Miss Hull's suggestions the students can do to serve their country today. Include the importance of praying for the country, for national and local leaders, and for those who are serving in the military.

Teach for Understanding

- Invite pairs of students to tell ways in which Americans supported the war. People used less food and other products that were rationed. People drove less to save petroleum and rubber. People used their money to buy savings bonds. Men and women who were not in the military worked in factories. Film studios produced films that focused on the war and short films that urged Americans to buy bonds. Some entertainers traveled to encourage the troops.

- Guide a discussion about the ration booklet pictured on page 306.

  Why did the government ration some goods? The government needed to limit the amount of some goods that Americans could buy in order to increase the amount of goods that could be sent to soldiers and other Allied nations.

  What were some goods that were rationed? sugar, coffee, meat, and gasoline

  How were Americans able to obtain rationed goods? Everyone received a ration booklet with tickets. These tickets were required when buying rationed goods.

  Why did Americans have money to spend on savings bonds? There was little to buy during the war. Factories made tanks and bombs instead of cars and refrigerators. Steady work for most Americans provided the money to buy bonds.

  What did the government do with the billions of dollars that were raised through selling savings bonds? The government used the money to fight the war.

  Why did men and women who were not in the military work in the factories during the war? Millions of men who would normally work in the factories were serving in the military.

- Choose a volunteer to read aloud the caption for the propaganda poster pictured on page 306.

  Who became the symbol for working women? "Rosie the Riveter"

The Home Front
Popular Support

Most Americans supported the war effort wholeheartedly. All Americans were subject to rationing. The government worked to increase the amount of food America could send abroad. Soldiers needed goods and so did other Allied nations. Goods such as sugar, coffee, and meat were limited. Everyone received a **ration booklet** with stamps. These stamps were required when buying rationed goods.

The government also rationed gasoline. People drove less and saved petroleum and rubber. Both resources were needed to win the war.

Americans also supported the war in their spending. There was little to buy during the war. Factories made tanks and bombs instead of cars and refrigerators. Just as in World War I, Americans used their money to buy savings bonds from the United States Treasury. The government promised to repay the bonds with interest. The government raised billions of dollars to fight the war through the sale of savings bonds.

Workers Supporting the Fight

Steady work for most Americans provided the money to buy bonds. Now that the Depression had ended, most Americans had jobs. Millions of men served in the military. Their earnings helped support families back home. Other men and women worked in factories. "Rosie the Riveter" became the symbol of working women. Older men kept working instead of retiring. Much of the money earned during the war bought savings bonds or was saved in banks.

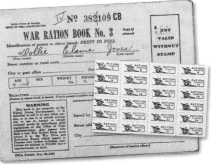

Since food was in short supply, every American was given a ration booklet with stamps for rationed items.

Propaganda posters were used to support the war effort by encouraging women to work in factories.

306

There were some problems with workers during the war. Since the late 1800s, unions had tried to make sure their workers were well paid. Even during the war they asked for more money. Factory owners said they could not pay more. Mine operators disagreed. President Roosevelt tried to get both sides to work together. He wanted workers to earn a fair wage. He also wanted factories to keep making goods to fight the war. Coal mines were important. In 1942 coal miners went on strike. Eventually the unions and the government worked out an agreement. The miners would get paid more and would keep working. Many other unions refused to strike. They thought that patriotic Americans should support the effort. Once the country was safe, the workers could demand more money.

Farmers enjoyed more prosperity during the war than before. Better seed and fertilizers helped boost their crops. In addition, any food they could grow would sell. However, getting new equipment was hard. Still, the war helped farmers financially.

Distrust at Home

Not everyone who lived in the United States was trusted to support the war. Americans worried that Japanese Americans, usually called Nisei, might betray the country. Over 110,000 Japanese Americans were taken from their homes. They were placed in internment camps. Their lives were severely restricted. They could not come and go freely. These American citizens had committed no crime. However, they were treated wrongly.

Many propaganda posters were used to attract volunteers to join the military and support the war effort.

307

Japanese American Heroes

After Pearl Harbor many people questioned the loyalty of Japanese Americans. The government discharged approximately 5,000 Japanese Americans who were in the military at the time. Some of them petitioned the government saying that they wanted to do their part to defend America. General George Marshall agreed and approved the formation of two Japanese American units. The 100th Infantry Battalion made its motto "Remember Pearl Harbor." The 442nd Infantry Regimental Combat Team had the motto "Go for Broke." By the end of the war, 33,000 Nisei were in uniform. They served with distinction in Italy and France and were among the most decorated soldiers in the war. Altogether, they were awarded 22 Medals of Honor, 53 Distinguished Service Crosses, 1 Distinguished Service Medal, 588 Silver Stars, 5,200 Bronze Stars, 22 Legions of Merit, 12 Croix de Guerre, 9,486 Purple Hearts, and 7 Presidential Unit Citations.

What problem did factory owners and mine operators face during the war? Some unions continued to ask that their workers be paid more money.

Were the unions successful in getting higher wages for the workers and miners? No, the factory owners and mine operators said they could not pay more.

- Guide a discussion about why President Roosevelt wanted to get both sides to work together.

What did the coal miners do in 1942? They went on strike.

What was the outcome of the strike? The unions and the government eventually agreed that the miners would get paid more and would keep working.

Did all unions support strikes during the war? No, many unions refused to strike. They thought that patriotic Americans should support the war effort. Once the country was safe, workers could demand more money.

Why did farmers enjoy more prosperity during the war than before it? Better seed and fertilizers helped boost their crops, and any food they could grow would sell.

- Why do you think it was hard for farmers to get new equipment during the war? Answers could include that the factories that made farm equipment and materials such as steel and rubber were being used to make items such as ships, tanks, and bombs.

Who were viewed as enemies at home? Japanese Americans (Nisei), German Americans, and Germans living legally in the United States who were not American citizens

Why were Japanese and German people in America viewed as enemies? Some Americans thought that Japanese and German people could not be trusted to support the war and that they might betray the country.

- Guide a discussion about how the Japanese and Germans living in the United States were treated. Allow the students to express their opinions about how these people were treated. Ask the students to consider how they might have viewed Japanese or German neighbors during the war.

- Discuss the messages conveyed by the propaganda posters on page 307.

Teach for Understanding

What kinds of entertainment did Americans enjoy during the war? movies or films, new music, radio dramas

Do you think Hollywood supported the war even before the United States joined the war? Yes, Hollywood told about British bravery.

What were filmgoers reminded to do? buy bonds and be frugal

Why do you think filmgoers were reminded to be frugal? Hollywood wanted to remind people to spend their money wisely and be careful in how they used different products, especially items that were rationed.

• Direct attention to the photograph on page 308.

Who entertained the troops many times? the comedian Bob Hope

What other kinds of entertainers might have traveled to perform for the troops? Answers could include people who sang songs, played musical instruments, or told stories.

How did the war bring changes to entertainment and baseball? Some actors and many baseball players were drafted to serve in the military.

Why did film, baseball, and other entertainment industries want to keep going during the war? They hoped that trying to keep life as normal as possible would keep Americans encouraged about the war.

Conclude the discussion by asking the question on page 308. Ration tickets were used to buy rationed goods. People drove less to save petroleum and rubber. People bought savings bonds. Men and women who were not serving in the military worked in factories. Film studios produced films that focused on the war and short films that urged Americans to buy bonds. Some entertainers traveled to encourage the troops.

Activity

Growing a Victory Garden

• Generate excitement about researching vegetables and planning a garden that will provide healthy food as you read the Activity information aloud.

• Invite students to share information they have about vegetables that will grow well in your area and their plans for a garden.

Activity Manual

• Guide completion of page 219.

There were also many German Americans in the United States. They were considered to be suspect. Some resident immigrants were arrested. These Germans were living legally in the United States but were not American citizens. After the war ended, these men and women were released.

Bob Hope entertained troops overseas.

Entertainment

Americans continued to enjoy entertainment during the war. Film studios produced movies. These often focused on the war. Even before the United States joined the war, Hollywood told about British bravery. Short films before the main feature urged Americans to buy bonds. Filmgoers were reminded to be frugal. Americans also enjoyed new music and radio dramas. Some entertainers traveled to encourage the troops. Comedian Bob Hope visited soldiers many times.

Of course, the war brought changes to entertainment. Some actors were drafted. The same was true for baseball. Many players served in the military. But film, baseball, and other entertainment industries found ways to keep going. They hoped that trying to keep life as normal as possible would keep Americans encouraged about the war.

> Identify ways that Americans supported the war effort.

Activity

Growing a Victory Garden

To support the war effort, many Americans grew their own kitchen gardens called victory gardens.

Research vegetables that grow well in your area. Plan a garden that will provide healthy food for your family.

308

Activities

Rationing

Instruct the students to measure and record how much of an item that was rationed during World War II (such as sugar, butter or eggs) that their family uses in a week. Compare the amount used by each family to the rationed amount allowed during World War II.

World War II Ration Recipe

Invite students to find World War II ration recipes or adjust a recipe to limit ingredients that were rationed. Encourage the students to share their recipes with the class. Invite volunteers to choose a recipe to make at home. Plan a day for the students to bring the foods they made to share with the class. Compare each recipe with similar recipes used today.

Aline Griffith

Who: World War II spy

When: 1923–present

Where: small town north of New York City

Aline Griffith grew up in a small town north of New York City. During World War II she worked in New York City and wanted to do more to help the United States. She wished she could be of some use to her country.

In 1943 she got her chance. The government organization in charge of spies, the OSS, contacted Aline. They had learned that she knew Spanish and was willing to do anything to serve the United States. The OSS hired and trained Aline as a spy. She was then sent to Spain. During the war, Spain stayed neutral. But both the Axis and the Allies sent diplomats and spies there. Aline's official job was as a clerk for a petroleum company.

Aline did much more than work as a clerk. She got to know the rich and famous people of Spain. She met diplomats from all over the world. At parties she could learn information. When she was invited to houses, she tried to learn secrets. Aline sent information back to the OSS in the United States.

After the war was over, Aline stayed in Spain. She married a Spanish nobleman and became a countess. But even then, she was willing to support her birth nation when necessary.

Many Americans were like Aline. They used their talents to serve their country and defend it. Few served as spies, but any talent could help the United States win the war.

309

Lesson **123**

Student Text pages 309–12
Activity Manual pages 220–21

Lesson Focus

- The Allies defeated Germany and Italy, ending the war in Europe.

Objectives

- Explain Eisenhower's strategy for winning the war in Europe
- Explain how the Allied Powers defeated Hitler and Mussolini
- Analyze the Holocaust

Review

- Choose volunteers to tell different ways in which Americans at home supported the war.

  Why were some goods rationed during World War II? The government needed to limit the amount of some goods that Americans could buy in order to increase the amount of goods that could be sent to soldiers and other Allied nations.

- Invite a student to identify goods that were rationed.

- Choose a volunteer to explain how the entertainment industry and the sports industry supported the war.

Preparation for Reading

- Generate interest as you direct the students to read the titles and examine the pictures on pages 309–12.
- Guide pronunciation of any unfamiliar words in the lesson.
- Direct the students to read the pages silently to discover when D-Day occurred and the significance of that day. June 6, 1944; it was the day that the Allies landed in France.

Teach for Understanding

- Direct attention to the Biography box. Choose a volunteer to explain the information at the top of the box.

  Where in the United States did Aline Griffith work during World War II? New York City

  What was the OSS? the government organization in charge of spies

- Why did the OSS contact Aline? The OSS learned that Aline knew Spanish. They wanted her to go to Spain and be a spy for the Allies.

  Was Aline willing to be a spy? Yes, she was willing to do anything to serve the United States.

  Why did the OSS send Aline to Spain? Spain was a neutral country. Both the Axis powers and the Allies sent diplomats and spies there.

  What was Aline's official job in Spain? She was a clerk for a petroleum company.

- Invite a student to explain how Aline was able gather information to send back to the OSS.

- What kind of information do you think Aline listened for while at parties and when visiting houses? Any information or secrets that would help the Allies win the war.

  Were spies the only Americans who helped the United States win the war? No, few Americans served as spies. But many Americans used their talents to serve the United States and defend it.

- Discuss ways in which the students can use their talents to serve the Lord and their country.

Lesson

123

Teach for Understanding

While Americans back home kept working to support the war, what did General Eisenhower and his advisors do? planned how to win the war

When were the Allies ready to open a second front in Europe? 1944

Who was chosen to lead all of the Allied forces in Western Europe? Eisenhower

Why do you think Eisenhower was chosen to lead all of the Allied forces? Eisenhower had already proven that he was a good leader. Eisenhower and his advisors had thought of a plan to win the war.

- Invite a student to explain Eisenhower's strategy for winning the war in Europe.

How did the Allies prevent the Germans from finding out where the invasion would occur? The Allies worked to misdirect the Germans. They encouraged the Germans to think the invasion would be just south of Belgium.

When did the Allied invasion take place? June 6, 1944, D-Day

Where did the Allied invasion actually take place? Normandy in northwestern France

- Guide a discussion about the photograph on page 310. Then guide the students in locating Normandy and Belgium on the map on page 311.

- Invite a student to read aloud the Germans' reaction when they realized the invasion was taking place at Normandy.

Where did Allied soldiers land next? in the south of France

Why were the Germans in a bad position? They could not stop Allied marches freeing Western Europe, and Russian troops were pushing hard against German forces in the East. The Nazi state was surrounded by enemies.

- Choose a volunteer to explain Hitler's response to being surrounded by Allies.

Freeing Europe
D-Day

As Americans kept working back home, General Eisenhower and his advisers planned how to win the war. Stalin continued to demand a direct attack on Germany. By 1944 the Allies were ready to open a second front in Europe. But before invading, they needed to have a good plan and a clear leader. Eisenhower became the leader of all the Allied forces fighting in Western Europe.

The plan was too big to be a secret. Eisenhower wanted to bring hundreds of thousands of men into France to drive out the Nazis. From there he hoped to march into Germany. Since Nazi pilots and spies knew that the Allies were plotting an attack, the Allies worked to misdirect the Germans. Allied intelligence workers encouraged the Germans to think the invasion would be just south of Belgium.

Instead, the invasion headed to Normandy in northwestern France. On June 6, 1944, **D-Day**, the Allies landed in France. On the first day nearly 165,000 troops came ashore. Almost 7,000 vessels provided transport and protection. The Germans were shocked. They fought back, but they could not stop the Allied advance. Almost one third of a million troops were in France within a week.

German Resistance

The Germans were in a bad position. They could not stop Allied troops landing in France. In August the Allies landed more soldiers in the south of France. The Germans could not stop Allied marches freeing Western Europe. In the East, Russian troops were pushing hard against German forces. The Nazi state was surrounded by enemies.

But Hitler refused to give up. Shortly after D-Day, Germany attacked England with loud flying bombs called V-1s.

American military landing on Omaha Beach and preparing to invade Normandy, France

310

Background

Additional Background information for this lesson is on the Teacher's Toolkit CD.

D-Day

D-Day (D, abbreviation for "day," + day) was the standard code name for the date when any military operation commenced. Operation Overlord was so large and so crucial that the D-Day of June 6, 1944, became the D-Day. Similarly, "H-hour" was the term for the precise time when an invasion was to begin.

Warning the French Resistance

On June 5, the French resistance in Normandy was warned of the Allied invasion by two secret messages broadcast over the BBC: "It's hot in Suez" and "The fairies are on the carpet." With these signals the French underground initiated sabotage operations behind enemy lines to assist the invasion.

The Pre-Invasion Attack on France

Several hours before the main D-Day amphibious assault on the Normandy coast in France, paratroopers jumped behind enemy lines. Other airborne troops landed using gliders. Both groups had orders to cut the enemy's lines of communication, secure bridges, create confusion, and prepare the way for the main assault. Many of those soldiers

Allied Advances

Axis Powers
Axis control
Neutral countries
Allied advances

The British shot many planes down, but the Germans had done much damage to England. Germany then began shooting V-2 rockets against England. These were silent and more dangerous. Nothing could stop them. In Europe, German soldiers attempted to push the Allies back. Starting in December 1944, the Germans "bulged" into Allied lines. But try as they might, the Germans could not break through. The Allied advance in the West was unstoppable.

The End of Hitler and Mussolini's Axis Powers

During April 1945 the remains of the Nazi and Fascist states crumbled. Russian troops progressed toward Berlin. American and Allied troops moved deeper into Germany. American troops also forced the Germans in Italy to surrender. On April 28, Benito Mussolini was captured by Italians opposed to his rule. They shot the dictator and displayed his dead body to the public.

By the end of April, Germany was on the verge of collapse. Russian forces had taken over much of Eastern Europe and were on Berlin's doorstep. American forces had swept south of Berlin and then met with their Russian allies. On April 30, Adolf Hitler killed himself. German forces surrendered all over Europe during the next several days. On May 7, 1945, the German government unconditionally surrendered. The European fight of World War II was over.

311

were killed or injured when their gliders crashed, and many parachutists were shot or landed in water and drowned. The survivors were widely scattered and had trouble regrouping. But they achieved their goals and made the main invasion a little easier.

Invading France

In the predawn hours of June 6, 1944, Allied paratroopers and soldiers in gliders began landing behind German lines in Normandy, France. At the same time, the largest amphibious invasion force in history moved across the English Channel toward the beaches of Normandy, twenty miles away. This was "D-Day," the day for Operation Overlord to begin. Eisenhower announced by radio, "The tide has turned. The free men of the world are marching together to victory." It marked the beginning of the end of the war in Europe.

The Allied air forces provided air protection. American soldiers landed on beaches code-named Utah and Omaha. The British landed on other nearby beaches code-named Juno, Gold, and Sword. German defenses were strong, and Allied losses were heavy. But the Allies had established a beachhead. They pushed inland yard by yard and mile by mile across some of the same ground fought over in World War I. On August 25, after a grueling three-month battle, the Allies liberated Paris.

Teach for Understanding

- Invite a student to describe the troubles Europe faced when the fighting ended.

- Why do you think the Allies did not want former Nazis to run Germany? Answers could include that the former Nazis would probably want to run Germany the way Hitler had.

  What did the Allies discover proof of after the war ended? the Holocaust

- Guide a discussion about the photograph on page 312.

  How did the Holocaust affect the Jewish population in Europe? Before the war, about nine million Jews lived in Europe. From the 1930s to 1945, the Nazis killed six million Jews.

  What proof of the Holocaust did Allied soldiers discover? the concentration (or death) camps, diaries, pictures, and the remains of many Jews

  What did the Allies want to do after they discovered proof of the Holocaust? The Allies wanted to find a way to help the Jews and other survivors of the Nazi camps.

  What did the United States and the Allies need to do before they could devote their attention to rebuilding Europe? stop Japan

  ▶▶ Conclude the discussion by asking the question on page 312. General Dwight D. Eisenhower

Activity Manual

- Guide completion of pages 220–21.

In Warsaw, Poland, Nazi soldiers had arrested Jewish families and placed them in segregated ghettos.

What Next for Europe?

The end of fighting was not the end of Europe's troubles. Almost every country had suffered from the fighting. Buildings, train tracks, bridges, and roads were destroyed. There were also problems beyond the physical destruction. Many countries lacked leaders to run governments. The Allies did not want former Nazis to run Germany. Occupied countries such as Poland and Czechoslovakia needed leaders. The Nazis had killed many of the prewar leaders.

The Allies also uncovered proof of the **Holocaust**. This tragedy was Hitler's work in destroying anyone who did not further his plan for a "perfect" world. Hitler believed that some people were not as good as others. He considered people of African descent and Roma, or gypsies, to be less valuable than other people. He thought that these people should be worked hard. Many were killed. Far worse was his view of Jewish people. Hitler thought that they were harmful to humanity and to German people in particular. He planned to destroy every Jew in Europe. Before the war, about nine million Jews lived in Europe. From the 1930s to 1945, the Nazis killed six million Jews. Most were taken to large concentration camps. Many were killed outright. Some worked hard and were then killed, or they died from ill treatment. Allied soldiers discovered the death camps and remains of many Jews. Diaries and pictures gave voice to the horror of this mass murder. The Allies needed to find a way to help the Jews and other survivors of Nazi camps. But before the United States and the Allies could devote their attention to rebuilding Europe, Japan had to be stopped.

▶ Who was the supreme Allied commander in Europe?

312

Activities

A Letter from Home

Imagine that your father, mother, brother, sister, or other relative is away fighting in the war. Write that person a letter that says what you are doing to help support the nation and the soldiers.

The Corrie ten Boom Museum

Provide a virtual tour of the Corrie ten Boom Museum.

> Visit bjupress.com/resources for possible links to the Corrie ten Boom Museum.

Background

The Holocaust

Millions of Europeans (including Communists, gypsies, people who were mentally or physically disabled, Jehovah's Witnesses, homosexuals, and members of many other groups) died in the Nazi concentration camps from the awful brutality of the Schutzstaffel, known as the SS. But the Jewish people remained Hitler's primary target. An estimated six million Jews (two-and-a-half million at the Auschwitz concentration camp alone) were methodically murdered, supposedly to save the "master race" (the Germans) from destruction.

This horrible event has become known as the Holocaust. However, many Jews prefer the term *shoah*, which means "calamity." They reject the term *holocaust* because it refers to a burnt sacrifice, and some Jews find this image objectionable.

Victory in the Pacific
Getting Close to Japan

As the Allies advanced in Europe, they had plans in the Pacific too. A key goal was getting better island bases. If American forces could get close enough, they could bomb Japan with their newest B-29 bombers. These bombers were too big for an aircraft carrier. The navy settled on Saipan as the key island.

On June 15, 1944, American forces attacked Saipan. The Japanese military was desperate to stop the Americans. Japan risked much of its fleet in the Battle of the Philippine Sea on June 19–20. The Japanese hoped to defeat an American fleet and then defend Saipan. The naval battle failed. Japan's five major aircraft carriers were no match for the nine American carriers. Americans had lost only aircraft in the battle. The Japanese forces lost three carriers and many aircraft. The American forces conquered Saipan. Japan's cities were now in bombing range.

During this time, General MacArthur advanced toward the Philippines. Finally on October 17, 1944, Allied troops landed on a Philippine island. Three days later MacArthur himself went ashore. He had promised to return, and he kept his word. But the Philippines had many islands to retake. The battle was just beginning. Once again the Japanese tried to stop the Allies at sea. In the Battle of Leyte Gulf, Allied forces won again. Japan tried a new tactic, kamikaze bombers. These skilled pilots flew explosive-filled planes into Allied ships. Kamikazes did not bring victory, but they worried the Allies. The Japanese would kill themselves to save islands far from home. What would they do when Japan was invaded?

The Allies Shift

With Saipan taken, American forces began bombing Japan's cities. Japan increasingly lacked planes and fuel to defend its skies. In the days before a raid, American planes often dropped leaflets on Japan. These leaflets warned of the bombs. They urged Japan to surrender. But most Japanese remained loyal to the emperor. The bombing did much damage and killed hundreds of thousands of Japanese citizens.

Allied forces advanced closer to Japan. They took the island of Iwo Jima in March 1945. This island allowed greater safety for American bombers flying to and from Japan. In April, Allied forces invaded Okinawa. Although not one of Japan's four major islands, Okinawa is in the same chain of islands. The battle took months. Many Japanese civilians committed suicide rather than surrender. The United States and its allies wanted to defeat Japan. But they worried how much that victory would cost. How many soldiers and civilians would die?

313

Lesson 124 **Student Text pages 313–15**
Activity Manual page 222

Lesson Focus

- The Allies defeat Japan, ending World War II.

Objectives

- Explain the Allies' strategy for fighting against Japan
- State reasons that the atomic bomb was developed
- Describe how the United States helped Japan and Europe after World War II ended

Review

Who became the leader of all the Allied forces in Western Europe in 1944? General Eisenhower

What was Eisenhower's plan for winning the war in Europe? He wanted to bring thousands of men into France to drive out the Nazis. From there he hoped to march into Germany.

- Choose a volunteer to explain how the Allies defeated Hitler and Mussolini.

What did the Allies discover after the fighting in Europe ended? proof of the Holocaust

- Invite a student to explain what the Holocaust was.

Preparation for Reading

- Generate interest as you direct the students to read the titles and examine the pictures on pages 313–15.
- Guide pronunciation of any unfamiliar words in the lesson.
- Direct the students to read the pages silently to discover two events that brought an end to World War II. The USSR declared war on Japan. The United States dropped an atomic bomb on a second Japanese city, Nagasaki.

Teach for Understanding

What was a key goal of the Allies for fighting Japan in the Pacific? The Allies wanted to get better island bases that were close enough to Japan so that American forces could bomb Japan with their newest B-29 bombers that were too big to take off from or land on an aircraft carrier.

Which island did the US Navy choose as the key island to bomb Japan from? Saipan

- Guide the students in locating Saipan and Japan on the map on page 303.

What was General MacArthur doing while Allied forces were fighting to capture Saipan? MacArthur advanced toward the Philippines.

Did MacArthur keep his promise to return to the Philippines? Yes, on October 20, 1944, he went ashore.

- Was it was easy for the Allies to retake the Philippines? No, the Philippines had many islands to retake.

What new tactic did Japan use against Allied forces? kamikaze bombers; Japanese pilots flew explosive-filled planes into Allied ships.

Were the kamikazes successful in helping Japan defend the Philippines? No, the Allied forces won.

What did American forces do after Saipan was taken? They began bombing Japan's cities.

- Do you think the United States wanted to bomb Japanese cities? No, in the days before the raid, American planes dropped leaflets that warned of the bombs and urged Japan to surrender.

- Choose a volunteer to describe the Allied advance toward Japan.

What concerned the United States and its allies about defeating Japan? how many soldiers and civilians would die

Teach for Understanding

What other option was available to the Allies by the summer of 1945? the atomic bomb

How powerful was the atomic bomb? One atomic bomb could destroy a whole city.

Why was the atomic bomb developed? It would allow American soldiers to avoid battle. Perhaps a dictator threatened by the bomb would retreat.

Why was Harry S. Truman now the president of the United States? Roosevelt had died in April 1945. Truman, Roosevelt's vice president, became president.

 As president of the United States, what decision did Truman face? whether to use the atomic bomb on Japan

- Invite a student to read aloud the paragraph that tells why the first atomic bomb was dropped on Japan.

Where in Japan was the first atomic bomb dropped? Hiroshima

Was dropping the atomic bomb on Hiroshima effective in ending the war? No, although thousands of people died, Japan refused to surrender.

What convinced Japan to surrender? The USSR declared war on Japan, and the next day the United States dropped a second atomic bomb on the city of Nagasaki, Japan.

- Use Background information to guide a discussion about the photographs on page 314.

Who took control of Japan after the war ended? the United States

- Choose a volunteer to tell what happened to Japan's political and military leaders.

Who oversaw Japan's government and reconstruction? General Douglas MacArthur

What did MacArthur encourage in Japan? greater democracy, Christianity, and peaceful industry

What kind of nation did Japan become after the war? a more peaceful and democratic nation

What countries worked together after the war to decide Europe's future? the United States, Britain, France, and the USSR

Why did the countries working with the United States make rebuilding Europe more complicated? Britain, France, and the USSR all had strongly held opinions.

- Invite a student to explain a disagreement that arose between the United States, Britain, and the USSR about Europe's future.

The Bomb

By summer 1945 another option was available. One **atomic bomb** could destroy a whole city. American laboratories developed this destructive weapon during the Manhattan Project. Beginning in 1942, scientists across the United States worked to perfect a new type of bomb. It would allow American soldiers to avoid battle. Perhaps a dictator threatened by the bomb would retreat. Finally, in the summer of 1945, the United States had two atomic bombs.

By then there was a new American president. Roosevelt had died in April 1945. **Harry S. Truman**, his vice president, became president. President Truman was ready to use the bomb if necessary. He did not want to see hundreds of thousands of Americans and Japanese dead from fighting for the Japanese islands.

On July 26, Japan was warned. Truman, Churchill, and Chiang Kai-shek demanded unconditional surrender from Japan. If not, they promised "prompt and utter destruction." Japan ignored the warning.

On August 6, 1945, the B-29 Enola Gay flew to Hiroshima, Japan. A little past 8:00 a.m., the bomb exploded in the middle of the city. Between 135,000 and 200,000 people died from the explosion and from exposure to radiation. Japan refused to surrender.

The Enola Gay

Fat Man

Atomic cloud

314

 Do you think Churchill had good reasons for opposing Stalin's idea that Eastern Europe should be left to the USSR? Answers could include that Churchill had good reasons to fear that Stalin would build a Communist empire in Eastern Europe because Stalin was a dictator. He had made a deal with Hitler before the war to gain control of other countries in Eastern Europe.

Why did most of the Allies have hope for the future? Hitler and the Nazis were defeated. Italy had a democratic government. Japan had been defeated.

What did the United States do to help the people of Europe? The United States sent food and supplies.

▶▶ Conclude the discussion by asking the question on page 315. Harry S. Truman

Activity Manual

- Guide completion of page 222.

Japan's representative signs the terms of surrender aboard the U.S.S. *Missouri*

The bombing of Hiroshima was not the end. On August 8, the USSR declared war on Japan. On August 9, the United States dropped a second bomb on the city of Nagasaki. Japan had little choice. The emperor agreed with the prime minister, and Japan surrendered. Victory had been achieved in Japan.

The Aftermath in Japan

After the war ended, the United States took control of Japan. Political and military leaders were questioned. Many were tried for war crimes. General Hideki Tojo, prime minister for most of the war, was executed. Emperor Hirohito was permitted to stay. During this uncertain time, General Douglas MacArthur oversaw Japan's government and reconstruction. He encouraged greater democracy and Christianity.

MacArthur also wanted peaceful industry to replace the making of war materiel. Japan was reshaped into a more peaceful and democratic nation.

Hope for the Future

Rebuilding Europe would be more complicated than Japan. The United States had to work with its allies to decide the continent's future. Britain, France, and the USSR all had strongly held opinions.

During the course of the war, the big three Allies, the United States, Britain, and the USSR, had met several times to plan for victory. Now they disagreed on what would become of Eastern Europe. Stalin wanted Eastern Europe left to the USSR. He would direct it. Churchill opposed that idea. He feared that Stalin would build a Communist empire in Eastern Europe.

However, in 1945 they reached a compromise. Most of the Allies felt only hope for the future. Hitler and the Nazis were defeated. Italy had a democratic government. Japan was defeated. But the people of Europe needed help, so the United States sent food and supplies. Soldiers, sailors, and airmen could go home and enjoy a civilian life. The war was over.

> Who was the US president at the end of World War II?

315

Additional Background information for this lesson is on the Teacher's Toolkit CD.

Activity Manual pages 223–24

Lesson 125

Objective
- Recall concepts and terms from Chapter 14

Teachers Toolkit CD
- Instructional Aid 54: *Victory Garden*

Materials
- A large envelope labeled "Seeds"
- 3 × 5 cards (one for each chapter review question)
- Carrots for the questions (cut from Instructional Aid 54)

Introduction

- Concepts for the Chapter 14 Test will be taken from Activity Manual pages 211–24. You may review any or all of the concepts in Chapter 14 by playing "Victory Garden."

Review

Game: Victory Garden

- Prepare a list of questions and answers to use for review.
- Prepare the "seeds" by writing review questions on the 3 × 5 cards. Place the cards in the envelope.
- Divide the class into teams. Draw a garden row for each team on a display board. Explain that students plant seeds and grow carrots by answering questions correctly.
- Direct a student to take a seed, read it aloud, and answer it. If the answer is correct, instruct him to put a carrot on his team's row. If the answer is incorrect, review the answer and put the seed back in the envelope. Alternatively, if a student gives an incorrect answer, ask the first student on another team to answer the question. Repeat the procedure for each team.
- Continue until all questions have been answered. Repeat questions or ask additional questions as needed in order for each team to have an equal number of turns and for each student to have an opportunity to answer a question.

Activity Manual

- Guide completion of pages 223–24.

Lesson 126   Chapter 14 Test

Objective
- Demonstrate knowledge of concepts from Chapter 14 by taking the test

Assessment

- Administer Test 14.

Background

Postwar Occupation of Japan

Douglas MacArthur was given the responsibility of not only presiding over the Japanese surrender but also supervising the postwar occupation of Japan. He performed his duties with the same confidence and effectiveness with which he had led his troops. The goals of the occupation were to reform Japan along democratic lines and to prevent Japan from taking aggressive military action in the future. During the six-year occupation, warmongers were removed from power. Control of the economy was expanded. The government became more involved in health and education. Suffrage was granted to women, and a new democratic constitution was written. MacArthur also issued a call for one thousand Christian missionaries and 10 million copies of the Gospel of John to be sent to Japan.

Although MacArthur worked with the Japanese government and emperor on the changes, some critics have claimed that he was trying to make the Japanese into Americans. The changes were an economic success for the Japanese, but debate continues about their overall effect.

Chapter 15

Introduction

Postwar America was a time of recovery from the loss and grief the nation had experienced during World War II. It was also a time of change. Soldiers returning from the war were ready to get on with their lives. Many families moved to the suburbs. Materialism developed in America's thriving economy. Truman proposed his Fair Deal. The civil rights of African Americans gained attention, and small steps were made toward equality. The Cold War began, and the Truman Doctrine committed the United States to fight the spread of Communism. During Eisenhower's presidency, the Saint Lawrence Seaway was built, construction of the interstate-highway system began, and Alaska and Hawaii were admitted to the union. However, the struggles for civil rights and against the spread of Communism continued. President Kennedy signed legislation designed to benefit America's poor, and he initiated the Peace Corps. The Cold War reached dangerous levels because of both the Berlin Wall and the Cuban Missile Crisis. Martin Luther King Jr. led civil rights protests until his assassination. Then President Kennedy's assassination ushered in a new era in American history.

15 Postwar America

Focus

Postwar America was an era of recovery, the Cold War, and the struggle for civil rights.

Lesson	Student Text	Activity Manual	Content	Vocabulary	
127	316–19	225–27	Changes in postwar American Harry S. Truman	G. I. Bill Fair Deal	materialism minimum wage
128	320–22	228	Civil rights movement	civil rights	discrimination
129	323–25	229–30	America's struggle against Communism Korean War Joseph McCarthy	Cold War North Atlantic Treaty Organization (NATO) Truman Doctrine	United Nations
130	326–28	231–32	Eisenhower's presidency Activity: Researching a State Capital	Federal Aid Highway Act Saint Lawrence Seaway	
131	329–31	233	The Space Race Alan Shepard Biography Box: John Glenn Changes in American culture and religious attitudes Billy Graham	National Aeronautics and Space Administration (NASA)	
132	332–34	234	John F. Kennedy Berlin Wall	Cuban Missile Crisis	Peace Corps
133	335–37	235–36	How It Was: "Whites Only" Is Gone Martin Luther King and the Birmingham protests Primary Source: A Letter from Jail Kennedy's assassination Lyndon B. Johnson	Civil Rights Bill	
134		237–38	Chapter Review		
135			Chapter Test		

Chapter 15 Overview

Visit bjupress.com/resources for links to enhance the lessons.

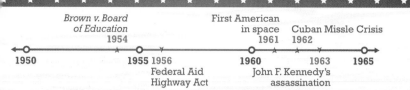

*Brown v. Board
of Education
1954*

*First American
in space
1961* Cuban Missile Crisis
1962

1950 **1955** 1956 **1960** 1963 **1965**

Federal Aid
Highway Act

John F. Kennedy's
assassination

Back to Normal Again

The second world war was over, and Americans were glad. World War II had resulted in more deaths and higher costs than any other war. Many European and Asian countries were devastated and would need years to recover. America was not dealing with physical destruction. Its economy was much healthier than other countries. But the nation had experienced loss and grief. Now Americans were ready to put war behind them and try to create a normal life again.

All over the nation, soldiers were coming home. Men who had been away for years were reunited with their families and friends. Some of the men wanted to go to college. Others began to think about finding jobs and settling down.

Many people who had worked different jobs during the war returned to their old ones. Businesses that had been producing war goods could now make other products. Americans hoped for a peaceful, prosperous future.

Historians refer to the period in the United States after World War II as postwar America. It was a time of recovery, and it was also a time of change. Americans were making new advances in technology. They were developing new attitudes. And although the world war was over, America had new battles to fight, both at home and abroad.

Changes in Postwar America
Homes and Families

Congress passed a bill to help returning soldiers get on with their lives. The **G. I. Bill** gave many benefits to veterans. Among these benefits was financial help for college. Many veterans entered universities or took night classes while working a daytime job.

The G. I. Bill also offered soldiers help with buying a house. Many young veterans decided to buy a house, get married, and start a family. The result was a shortage of houses.

317

Chapter Focus

Postwar America was an era of recovery, Cold War, and struggle for civil rights.

JourneyForth

Sherlock Jones: The Assassination Plot by Ed Dunlop is available from JourneyForth Books, a division of BJU Press, at journeyforth.com.

As you cover the John F. Kennedy assassination, students may wish to read more about dealing with a plot to assassinate a political figure. In this mystery novel, Jasper and Penny, an adventurous pair of friends, seek to rescue their state governor from an assassination plot. This is the first book in the Sherlock Jones Detective Series.

Lesson Focus

- The postwar years in America were a time of recovery and change.

Objectives
- Explain postwar changes in America
- Analyze materialism
- Explain Truman's Fair Deal

Introduction

- Invite a student to read aloud the title of the chapter and predict what the chapter will be about. America after World War II
- Invite a student to read the chapter focus aloud.

  What do you think you will learn about in this chapter? America's recovery from World War II, something called the Cold War, and America's struggle for civil rights

- Direct attention to the picture on page 316.

  What is happening in the picture? A spaceship is flying above the earth.

- Direct attention to the timeline.

  What occurred in 1954? *Brown v. Board of Education*

- Explain that the *v* is an abbreviation for *versus* which means "against." The court case of *Brown* against the *Board of Education* went all the way to the US Supreme Court. Point out that the students will learn more about this court case later in this chapter.

- Invite students to identify in order the remaining dates and events on the timeline.

Preparation for Reading

- Generate interest as you direct the students to read the titles and examine the pictures on pages 317–19.
- Guide pronunciation of any unfamiliar words in the lesson.
- Direct the students to read the pages silently to discover what soldiers did when they came home from the war. Many veterans entered universities or took night classes while working a daytime job. Many young veterans bought a house, married, and started a family.

Teach for Understanding

- Guide a discussion comparing America's recovery from World War II to the recovery in European and Asian countries.

  What were Americans ready for after World War II? to put the war behind them and try to create a normal life

Teach for Understanding

What did the soldiers who were coming home want? Some wanted to go to college. Others wanted to find jobs and settle down.

What hope did Americans have for the future? They hoped that the future would be peaceful and prosperous.

What were two ways the G. I. Bill benefited veterans? The G. I. Bill offered veterans financial help for college and help with buying a house.

- Explain that Congress had passed the G. I. Bill to help veterans move into civilian life. In addition to financial help, the G. I. Bill also helped veterans find jobs.

- Explain that this period of history was one of great missionary advance. Many soldiers who returned home after World War II later went abroad as missionaries.

  What kind of communities were created in response to a shortage of houses? suburbs

- Direct attention to the pictures on page 318. Choose a volunteer to describe the house in a suburb. Choose other volunteers to tell how the objects pictured made family life easier.

- Guide a discussion about the ethnic makeup of the suburbs, and the effects suburbs had on many cities.

  What have the children born between 1946 and 1964 come to be called? the "baby boomer" generation

- Invite a student to read aloud the sentences that tell why these children were called the "baby boomer" generation.

  What else experienced a boom after World War II? American business

  Why was there a boom in American business? American factories produced large numbers of goods for the home and family. Many Americans wanted many things. After years of living on less and doing without, they now wanted to have all the comforts of life.

  What kinds of products did Americans buy? cars, televisions, refrigerators, and other goods

---

With help from the Federal Housing Administration, builders created new suburbs. Suburbs are groups of houses located near a city. The houses in a suburb all look similar. They are affordable and popular with families. Rather than live in the city, an increasing number of couples bought houses in suburbs.

Nearly all the people who moved to suburbs were white. Many suburban neighborhoods had rules that allowed only white people to live there. This movement made a change in the makeup of America's cities. Black Americans, Jews, Hispanics, and other minority groups stayed in cities. People in these groups tended to have lower incomes than white Americans. They could not pay high taxes. Cities had less money than before to make improvements to buildings. Many inner-city neighborhoods suffered from neglect.

All over America, families were growing. During this time so many babies were born that people spoke of a "baby boom." Children born between 1946 and 1964 came to be called the "baby boomer" generation. In our country today, the baby boomer generation is still one of the largest.

Business and the Economy

Some Americans feared that the nation would go through another depression, as it did after World War I. But this did not happen. Like the baby boom, there was also a boom in American business.

American factories produced large numbers of goods for the home and the family after the war. And there were plenty of people to buy these products. Americans wanted many things. After years of living on less and doing without, they now wanted to have all the comforts of life. In the

Modern conveniences made the lives of the typical 1950s family easier.

318

Background

A Material Boom

Instead of a depression that many Americans feared would follow World War II, Americans found plenty of jobs. They kept business booming by demanding more and more material goods. They wanted new things and labor-saving devices such as dishwashers, automatic washing machines, power lawn mowers, and boats. Easy credit encouraged much spending.

Shortages and rationing of some goods during the war created high demand for them after the war. In 1944, factories had produced 100,000 planes and only 70,000 passenger cars. In 1949, only 6,000 planes were produced, but 3.7 million passenger cars rolled off assembly lines. So many goods were in demand that factories could not produce enough to satisfy the public. Waiting lists for high-demand products such as cars grew. Prices on many goods skyrocketed until the demand was met. But as more factories produced needed items, the economy became more stable.

> Additional Background information for this lesson is on the Teacher's Toolkit CD.

years after World War II, Americans bought millions of cars, televisions, refrigerators, and other goods.

Many of these goods were not new inventions. But advances in technology had improved them. Americans of the postwar era were encouraged to help the nation's economy by buying these improved goods. Some Americans felt pressure to keep up with their neighbors or to have the best of everything.

It is not wrong for people to buy things they need or things that will make life easier. But placing too much importance on having the things money can buy is called **materialism**. Some Americans had enough, but they kept buying because they wanted more and more. They placed more importance on their possessions than on spiritual things. Materialism was one of the problems that went along with America's thriving economy.

Truman's Fair Deal

President Harry Truman presented a new program to Congress. His idea, the **Fair Deal**, would build on Roosevelt's New Deal. Even though the economy was much better than it had been before the war, Truman wanted government-aid programs. Some programs he proposed were health insurance, aid for education, housing for the poor, and a higher **minimum wage** for workers. Minimum wage is

On October 5, 1947, President Truman became the first president to give a presidential address on national television. In the following election he would also become the first presidential candidate to broadcast a paid political ad.

The *S* in Harry S. Truman does not stand for a specific name. His parents gave him the initial in honor of his two grandfathers, Solomon Young and Anderson Shipp Truman.

the lowest possible pay a worker can make per hour. Truman also wanted to protect the rights of African Americans.

Americans were divided about Truman's plans. Many Americans wanted these programs. But some Americans thought that the programs would make people depend too much on the government. Truman could not get Congress to agree to all the programs he proposed. However, his speeches about the Fair Deal brought support from many Americans. Truman was reelected in 1948.

> How did the return of veterans affect American homes and families?

319

- Explain that the technological advances that had improved many goods following World War II were actually beneficial from a Christian perspective. Some of the advances provided ways people could love their neighbors. Christians could love their neighbors by using products such as cars. They could show love by offering car rides to the store, to the doctor's office, or to church.

- Read aloud Deuteronomy 6:6–20. Guide a discussion about God's abundantly providing for the Israelites. Also discuss the consequences God warns of if the Israelites would forget about Him and think that they had acquired their own wealth. Explain that having material things is not the problem: God gave Israel a good land. The problem arises when material things are valued more than God Himself or in place of God.

What was the Fair Deal? A program presented to Congress by President Truman that would build on Roosevelt's New Deal.

Why did Truman present the Fair Deal to Congress? He wanted government-aid programs.

What were some government-aid programs proposed by Truman? health insurance, aid for education, housing for the poor, and a higher minimum wage

- Invite a student to explain *minimum wage*.

What did Truman want to do for African Americans? He wanted to protect their rights.

- Choose a volunteer to explain what Americans thought about Truman's programs.

- Do you think Americans approved of Truman's presidency? Yes, he was reelected in 1948.

- Invite a student to read aloud the captions for the picture on page 319.

> Conclude the discussion by asking the question on page 319. Many young veterans returning from the war decided to buy a house, get married, and start a family. The result was a shortage of houses, and builders created suburbs near cities. Because of how many babies were born, children born between 1946 and 1964 came to be called the "baby boomer" generation.

Teach for Understanding

Why were Americans encouraged to buy the new improved goods? to help the nation's economy

What reasons did Americans have for buying new improved goods? Some Americans felt pressure to keep up with their neighbors or to have the best of everything. Other Americans had enough, but they kept buying because they wanted more and more.

What is placing too much importance on having the things money can buy called? materialism

- Why do you think materialism was one of the problems that went along with America's thriving economy? Answers may include that some people bought goods because they wanted more possessions. Some people placed more importance on their possessions than on spiritual things.

- How might people show that they place more value on the gifts God has given them than on God Himself? Answers could include that people might use the money, talents, and possessions God has given them only for themselves, so they fail to use these gifts to help build God's kingdom on earth.

> Encourage students to support their responses to higher-order questions. Provide prompts or background as needed to guide the students to the answer.

Activity Manual

- Guide completion of pages 225–27. For page 225, explain that the students will begin learning the names of the state capitals. Each of the chapters from 15 through 20 will focus on the states and capitals in a different region of the United States.

Lesson Focus

- Small steps were made toward ending discrimination and achieving equality for African Americans.

Objectives

- Demonstrate an understanding of civil rights
- Relate acts of discrimination
- Explain how some Americans worked for civil rights

Teacher's Toolkit CD

- Instructional Aid 55: *The Civil Rights Movement*

Review

What term do historians use to refer to the period in the United States after World War II? postwar America

- Choose a volunteer to explain how and why American homes and families changed after the war.
- Choose another volunteer to explain why there was a boom in American business after the war.

What was one of the problems that went along with America's boom in business and thriving economy? materialism

What is materialism? placing too much importance on having the things money can buy

- Invite a student to explain why President Truman wanted the Fair Deal and to tell some of the programs Truman proposed.

Preparation for Reading

- Generate interest as you direct the students to read the titles and examine the pictures on pages 320–22.

Guide a review of important terms, maps, places, and people from each previous lesson. Direct the students to find and read the corresponding entries from the Resource Treasury.

- Guide pronunciation of any unfamiliar words in the lesson.
- Direct the students to read the pages silently and complete Instructional Aid 55 in small groups.

Teach for Understanding

What are civil rights? the rights that are given to all US citizens by the Constitution

Why did the civil rights of black Americans gain more attention in postwar America? Black Americans were not treated as equals with white Americans.

- Choose a volunteer to read aloud the caption for the photograph on page 320, and to explain the law that is pictured.

The Civil Rights Movement
Black Americans and Injustice

As America moved into the 1950s, the **civil rights** of black Americans gained more attention. Civil rights are the rights given to all US citizens by the Constitution. Black soldiers had served bravely in World War II. Some had given their lives for their country. Yet in spite of this, black veterans were not treated as equals with white soldiers who had served. Instead, they faced the same injustices that had existed before the war.

In most southern states, Jim Crow laws were still in place. These laws kept black Americans segregated from white Americans. In many states, black people and white people could not use the same public restrooms or drinking fountains. They could not ride the same buses or attend the same schools. Restaurants, stores, hospitals, and other public places had separate areas for them. Northern states followed many of these same practices even though they were not laws.

President Truman saw this **discrimination** as a major problem in America. Discrimination is unfair treatment based on a prejudice. He did what he could to support the civil rights of black Americans. He asked Congress for laws against discrimination on trains, buses, and planes. He also wanted to ban discrimination by employers. He believed that African Americans should have the same opportunities for jobs as other citizens. He also wanted them to be able to serve alongside white Americans in the armed forces rather than in separate divisions.

Ku Klux Klan groups were still active in some states, especially in the South. The Klan still sometimes practiced lynching. Lynching was a public execution by a mob apart from a court of law. The victims were often black Americans. Truman worked to make lynching illegal across the nation. He also wanted to ban poll taxes in every state. These taxes kept African Americans from voting in some states.

Jim Crow laws kept Americans segregated.

320

Was segregation practiced only in southern states? No, many northern states followed the same practices.

- Invite students to share ways in which black Americans were discriminated against.

What is discrimination? unfair treatment based on a prejudice

What do you think prejudice is? Answers could include that prejudice is a negative attitude based on something such as a person's skin color or accent.

Was President Truman in favor of discrimination? No, he saw discrimination as a major problem in America. He did what he could to support the civil rights of black Americans.

- Choose volunteers to give examples of the laws against discrimination that Truman asked Congress for.

What organization was still active in some states and discriminated against black Americans? the Ku Klux Klan

What injustices did Truman want to make illegal throughout the United States? discrimination on trains, buses, and planes; discrimination by employers; lynching; poll taxes

How did poll taxes discriminate against African Americans? The taxes kept African Americans from voting in some states.

Small Steps Toward Equality

Truman did not see all of these civil rights laws passed during his presidency. Many Americans were just beginning to see the importance of these issues. However, America was gradually changing.

Truman appointed **William Hastie**, a black judge, to a federal court in 1949. This position was the highest a black judge had ever held in the United States. Truman also appointed a black ambassador, **Edward Dudley**, to the country of Liberia. By placing confidence in these men, Truman let the public know that black Americans could handle important government jobs as capably as white Americans.

In 1947 the manager of the Brooklyn Dodgers baseball team hired the first black player in the major leagues. **Jackie Robinson** played for the Dodgers for the next ten years. He received the Rookie of the Year award in his first season. He set records in stolen bases and kept a high batting average. He played in six World Series events. But more importantly, he overcame racial prejudice with dignity. He chose not to respond to those who harrassed him. He stayed calm and ignored the insults. Robinson's success paved the way for other black players.

Jackie Robinson became the first African American to play in the major leagues.

By the end of the 1950s, every major-league baseball team had both black and white players.

Also around this time, colleges for only white students began to open their doors to black students. Many black colleges did not have graduate programs. The Supreme Court ruled that states must provide black students the same educational opportunities that white students had. Gradually, black students were being admitted into graduate programs at white colleges.

Black Americans Work for Change

Change would take time. Many white Americans were slow to change their attitudes about racial equality. Even many Christians failed to love and respect black Americans as fellow human beings created in God's image. If change had been left entirely up to white Americans, it would have

321

Teach for Understanding

Were all the civil rights laws that Truman wanted passed during his presidency? No, America was just beginning to change.

- Invite a student to tell what steps Truman took to move America toward equality for all US citizens. Invite another student to tell what other steps moved America toward equality for all US citizens.

- Choose a volunteer to read aloud the caption for the photograph on page 321.

How did Jackie Robinson overcome racial prejudice? He chose not to respond to those who harassed him. He stayed calm and ignored the insults.

- Do you think Jackie Robinson acted wisely? Answers may include that he did act wisely. By staying calm and ignoring the insults, Robinson lessened the possibility of becoming involved in arguments that could become violent.

- Read aloud Proverbs 15:1 and 25:15.

- What does the Bible say is a wise way to respond to a person's cruel remarks to us? We should respond softly (gently) because harsh words will make others angry. A harsh response will not cause people who are hard (cruel) to change their minds, but a soft answer might.

- Discuss what the students might do if someone makes cruel remarks to them or if they see someone making cruel remarks to someone else.

- Why do you think Robinson's success paved the way for other black baseball players? Answers may include that Robinson's success in playing baseball and overcoming racial prejudice showed that black players could do well playing with white players on major-league teams.

Did change come quickly in regard to the civil rights of black Americans? No, many white Americans were slow to change their attitudes about racial equality.

- Do you think all Christians glorified God with their attitudes toward black Americans? No, many Christians failed to love and respect these Americans as fellow human beings created in God's image.

Background

Jackie Robinson

Additional Background information for this lesson is on the Teacher's Toolkit CD.

Jackie Robinson broke the color barrier in baseball in April 1947. In that year, he signed a contract to play for the Brooklyn Dodgers in return for $5,000 a year with a $3,500 bonus. In his first game against the Boston Braves, Robinson went hitless, but he scored the winning run. On a sacrifice bunt, the Braves' first baseman fielded the ball but hit Robinson in the back with it. A double by Pete Reiser drove Robinson home and allowed the Dodgers to win 5–3.

Robinson spent his entire ten-year career with the Dodgers. (Although he was traded to the New York Giants late in his career, he refused to report to the new team. The trade was later voided, and he remained a Dodger.) He amassed a career batting average of .311. He played in six World Series events, during which he amassed a batting average of .234 and stole six bases. He also played in six All Star games. He was voted Rookie of the Year in 1947. In 1949 he won the batting title with an average of .342 and was voted Most Valuable Player. He led the National League in stolen bases in both 1947 and 1949.

Teach for Understanding

In what area did an important change take place? education

🔊 Did all public schools follow a policy of "separate but equal?" No, many schools for black students could not provide the same level of education because they did not receive as much government funding as schools for white students.

- Explain that not providing the same funds for black schools and white schools was an intentional injustice of state governments.

- Choose a volunteer to explain the complaint in the *Brown v. Board of Education* case and the Supreme Court ruling.

🔊 Why do you think this case went all the way to the Supreme Court? Answers could include that the Supreme Court had already ruled that states must provide the same educational opportunities for black students and white students. But under the "separate but equal" policy, Linda Brown and other black students were not receiving the same level of education as white students.

Who spoke out for ending segregation in the schools? Thurgood Marshall

- Invite a student to read aloud the caption for the photograph on page 322.

What action did black citizens of Montgomery, Alabama, take to show their support for Rosa Parks? On December 5, 1955, nearly all of them boycotted the buses. They continued to boycott the buses for more than a year.

Which young black minister became a leader in the bus boycott and other civil rights activities? Martin Luther King Jr.

- Choose a volunteer to read aloud the sentence that tells what King believed about black Americans standing up to injustice.

- Read aloud Matthew 7:12. Explain that this verse is often referred to as the "Golden Rule."

🔊 How did the treatment of black Americans violate the "Golden Rule?" Answers should include that white Americans did not treat black Americans as they would want to be treated.

▶ Conclude the discussion by asking the question on page 322. See the answers on Instructional Aid 55. In addition, black citizens of Montgomery, Alabama showed their support for Rosa Parks by boycotting the buses for more than a year.

Activity Manual

- Guide completion of page 228.

---

happened much more slowly. But black Americans were also working for change.

One important area of change was in education. America's public schools claimed to follow a "separate but equal" policy toward black Americans. But keeping black students separated was not treating them as equal. Many schools for black students did not receive as much government funding as white schools. They were often unable to provide the same level of education. In 1954 the Supreme Court heard a case called *Brown v. Board of Education.* The parents of third-grader Linda Brown wanted her to be able to attend the all-white public school near their home. Four similar cases from different states were included in the complaint along with the Brown family's case. A black lawyer named **Thurgood Marshall** spoke out for ending segregation in the schools. The court ruled that under the Constitution black children must be able to attend the same schools as white children. All nine justices agreed on the ruling.

The following year, a black woman named **Rosa Parks** was traveling home from work on a city bus in Alabama. When the bus driver told her she had to give up her seat for a white person, she refused. Mrs. Parks was arrested. Friends raised money to keep her out of jail. But her story spread quickly in

Rosa Parks was arrested and fined for refusing to give up her seat. Her actions resulted in a bus boycott.

the black community. Black citizens of Montgomery, Alabama, decided to show their support for her. On December 5, 1955, nearly all of them stayed off the buses. This bus boycott continued for more than a year.

One young black minister became a leader in the bus boycott and other civil rights activities. He pastored a church in Montgomery, Alabama. His name was **Martin Luther King Jr.** The black community respected King. He was a highly educated man, holding a PhD from Boston University. He was also a powerful speaker and a natural leader. King believed strongly that black Americans should stand up to injustice without using violence. His courage, vision, and leadership skills made him the major force behind the civil rights movement in the years to come.

▶ How did black Americans work for change in the 1950s?

322

Background

Martin Luther King Jr.

Martin Luther King Jr. was born in Atlanta, Georgia, in 1929. He grew up only two blocks from Ebenezer Baptist Church, which his father and grandfather pastored and which he would later co-pastor with his father. He attended Morehouse College (BA, 1948), Crozier Theological Seminary (BD, 1951), and Boston University (PhD, 1955). In 1954 King became pastor of Dexter Avenue Baptist Church in Montgomery, Alabama. He joined the National Association for the Advancement of Colored People and soon became a member of its executive committee. He led a bus boycott protesting segregation on city buses and emerged as a major civil rights leader. In 1957 King was elected president of the Southern Christian Leadership Conference. He wrote five books and numerous articles. During the March on Washington, he delivered his most famous speech—"I Have a Dream." He preached "love, equality, and nonviolence," but his non-violent protests resulted in twenty-two arrests and many assaults by those who opposed his message. When he was only thirty-five, King was awarded the Nobel Peace Prize. An assassin's bullet ended his life on April 4, 1968, in Memphis, Tennessee.

Struggles Against Communism

The Cold War

While Americans were dealing with their own problems, they also had concerns about problems in other countries. In 1945, fifty world leaders had met in San Francisco. They had formed plans for a world peace-keeping organization. This organization was called the **United Nations**.

The United Nations seemed like a good idea to most people. But it was not always able to keep peace. Many different nations with differing views and goals are members of the United Nations. Trying to agree on decisions among so many nations often results in failure to accomplish anything.

Tensions arose between the United States and another nation. After World War II, the United States was the most powerful nation in the world. But another country was also powerful. That country was the Soviet Union. The United States was trying to help Europe recover from the losses of the war. America wanted to help other countries stay free like itself. But the Soviet Union had a different goal. The Soviet Union wanted to take over as many European nations as it could. It wanted to make other Communist countries like itself. Because the United States and the Soviet Union had such different goals, the tensions between them were always present. The two nations were not directly at war, but the situation between them was called the **Cold War**.

The United States and the Soviet Union were both members of the United Nations. The United Nations could not help resolve the Cold War. Any time that a free nation wanted to make a resolution against Communism, the Soviet Union could stop it. Because the countries in the United Nations could not agree on their goals, the organization could not solve the problem.

323

Lesson 129

**Student Text pages 323–25
Activity Manual pages 229–30**

Lesson Focus

- The United States began its long fight against the spread of Communism.

Objectives

- Discuss the purpose of the United Nations
- Explain what the Cold War was and the reason for it
- Differentiate America's foreign policy before and after Congress approved the Truman Doctrine
- Explain America's involvement in the Korean War

Review

What are civil rights? *rights given to all US citizens by the Constitution*

- Choose volunteers to give examples of discrimination against black Americans in the years following World War II. Choose other volunteers to explain what some Americans did to try to end discrimination and gain equality for black Americans.

Did a change in the civil rights of black Americans occur quickly? *No, many Americans were slow to change their attitudes about racial equality.*

Preparation for Reading

- Generate interest as you direct the students to read the titles and examine the pictures on pages 323–25.
- Guide pronunciation of any unfamiliar words in the lesson.
- Direct the students to read the pages silently to discover what the Cold War was. *The Cold War was a time of tension between the United States and the Soviet Union over the spread of Communism.*

Teach for Understanding

What world peace-keeping organization was formed in 1945? *the United Nations*

Has the United Nations always been able to keep peace around the world? *No, the many nations that are members of the United Nations have differing views and goals. They often do not agree on decisions and fail to accomplish anything.*

What two powerful countries did not agree with each other? *the United States and the Soviet Union*

- Invite a student use the political cartoon on page 323 to explain the differing goals of the United States and the Soviet Union. Explain that today we often refer to the Soviet Union (USSR) as "Russia." The Russia of today is no longer under a Communist dictatorship.

What did the differing goals between the United States and the Soviet Union lead to? *the Cold War; tensions that were always present between the two nations*

Did the Cold War involve actual fighting between the United States and the Soviet Union? *No, the Cold War was the situation between them.*

Why was the United Nations unable to resolve the Cold War? *Any time a free nation wanted to make a resolution against Communism, the Soviet Union could stop it.*

- Explain that the United States and the Soviet Union were permanent members of the Security Council of the United Nations (UN). The Security Council is a small group of UN members who have veto power over all UN actions. A resolution cannot be approved if even just one permanent member of the Security Council vetoes it.

What two countries were in danger of being taken over by the Communists? Greece and Turkey

How did President Truman try to prevent a Communist takeover of Greece and Turkey? He asked Congress to give military aid to both countries.

What was giving military and economic aid to countries under a Communist threat called? the Truman Doctrine

- Invite a student to explain how the Truman Doctrine affected America's foreign policy.

What organization did the United States join in 1949? the North Atlantic Treaty Organization (NATO)

What was the purpose of NATO? NATO was an alliance between the United States, Canada, and several European nations. The members agreed to provide military support for each other if attacked.

Was the Soviet Union the only country wanting to spread Communism? No, China agreed to work together with the Soviet Union for the cause of Communism. Communist North Korean invaded South Korea, sparking the Korean War.

- Choose a volunteer to use the map on page 324 to explain the actions taken by President Truman and Mao Zedong in the Korean War.

The Truman Doctrine

Greece and Turkey were two countries that were in danger of a Communist takeover. President Truman wanted to help countries like these. He believed that the United States should do its part to stop the spread of Communism. Truman asked Congress for military aid for Greece and Turkey.

Giving military and economic aid to countries under a Communist threat was called the **Truman Doctrine**. The Truman Doctrine was a change in America's foreign policy. Up to this time, the United States had usually stayed out of foreign conflicts that did not directly involve it. Now the nation was committing itself to get involved in struggles for the cause of freedom.

In 1949 the United States joined the **North Atlantic Treaty Organization** (NATO). This alliance was between the United States, Canada, and several European nations. The members agreed to provide military support for each other if attacked.

The Korean War

The Soviet Union was not the only nation trying to spread Communism. China was also a Communist nation. Shortly after World War II, a Communist dictator, Mao Zedong, had come to power in China. China and the Soviet Union signed an agreement to work together for the cause of Communism.

Communism was also gaining a foothold in Korea. Korea had been divided along the thirty-eighth parallel. North Korea was Communist, and South Korea was not. In June of 1950, North Korea invaded South Korea. This invasion sparked the Korean War.

The United Nations sent soldiers, and President Truman chose General Douglas MacArthur to lead them. Most of the soldiers were Americans. By October, the United Nations forces appeared close to victory. Then Mao Zedong's forces joined the conflict. Thousands of soldiers from Communist China poured over the border into North Korea. They pushed MacArthur's forces back into South Korea.

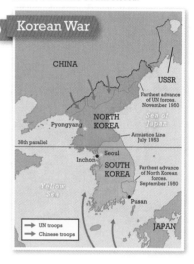

Korean War

324

Additional Background information for this lesson is on the Teacher's Toolkit CD.

NATO

In 1949 the West sought a more effective means of ensuring its defense against Soviet expansion. The solution was a regional military alliance called the North Atlantic Treaty Organization, or NATO. The alliance originally included the United States, Canada, Great Britain, France, and Italy, along with less powerful nations in the North Atlantic region. In 1952, during the Korean War, NATO added Greece and Turkey. In 1955, West Germany joined the alliance.

The Truman Doctrine: A Precedent

The Cold War changed the way Americans fought wars: presidents began to seize the initiative from Congress. The president's ability to act quickly and decisively was used as an argument for moving away from congressional leadership and toward executive leadership in fighting wars. This argument gained credence during the Cold War, when the threat of nuclear war was imminent.

After 1945, Soviet forces were taking over Eastern Europe, and President Harry Truman wanted to stop the spread

of Communism. In 1947 Truman appeared before Congress, not to ask for a declaration of war but to request economic aid for non-Communists in Greece and Turkey. He also wanted congressional approval to send Americans to train Greek and Turkish military forces. Congress agreed, and the Truman Doctrine was born. America would aid nations struggling against Communism. In this case, containment worked: America's allies in Greece and Turkey won.

The precedent for entering a war by presidential action came a few years later. In 1950, Communist North Korea invaded South Korea, and the United Nations Security Council called for a military response to North Korean aggression. Although the United Nations acted, the war was mostly an American enterprise, and General Douglas MacArthur was initially in charge. Never before had an American president committed so many troops without a congressional declaration of war.

The relative success of the Truman Doctrine led other presidents to devise "doctrines" (stated policies) concerning Communist expansion. After the Soviet invasion of Afghanistan in 1980, President Jimmy Carter outlined the Carter Doctrine, which said that the United States would resist by military force any Soviet attempt to push farther south to the Persian Gulf. In the 1980s, President Reagan announced the Reagan Doctrine, stating that America would support insurgent groups battling Communist governments in Third-World countries.

General MacArthur believed that, to win the war, the bases and supply lines in China should be bombed. But President Truman worried about expanding the war into China. He was afraid that involving China would lead to World War III. Truman wanted to keep the war in Korea. When MacArthur disagreed publicly with the president, Truman called MacArthur home.

Neither North Korea nor South Korea could gain an advantage in the fighting. Talks to end the war began, but the fighting continued for two more years. Finally the two sides signed an armistice in 1953. The boundary between North and South Korea remained about the same. But the United States had succeeded in saving South Korea from Communism.

The Korean War resulted in great losses. Nearly forty thousand American soldiers died in action. Tens of thousands more were wounded.

Joseph McCarthy

Many Americans were afraid of Communism. Some were worried that their own government might include Communist spies. In 1951 Senator **Joseph McCarthy** began investigating leaders he suspected of being Communists. He boldly accused people in the government of being disloyal to the United States.

"It's Okay—We're Hunting Communists"

People listened to McCarthy. When he accused someone, others also became suspicious of that person. Some people whom McCarthy accused lost their jobs. Then no one else wanted to hire them.

Some Americans felt threatened by McCarthy's methods. They were afraid of saying anything that might sound like criticism of the government. After a few years, the Senate determined that McCarthy had been accusing people without enough evidence.

> Why did the United States adopt the Truman Doctrine as its foreign policy?

325

Activity

Keyword Search

Direct pairs of students to do a keyword search for Communism on the Internet. Instruct them to discover facts about how Communism works and current Communist countries. Guide a discussion contrasting life in a Communist county (e.g., North Korea) and life in a capitalistic country (e.g., the United States).

Teach for Understanding

What action did General MacArthur believe was necessary to win the war? The bases and supply lines in China should be bombed.

Did Truman agree with MacArthur? No, Truman worried that expanding the war into China would lead to World War III. He wanted to keep the war in Korea.

Why did Truman call MacArthur home from Korea? MacArthur disagreed publicly with Truman.

- Invite a student to explain how the Korean War ended.

Did the boundary between North and South Korea change? No, the boundary remained the same. Korea remained divided along the thirty-eighth parallel.

Although neither side won the war, what did the United States succeed in? The United States saved South Korea from Communism.

What did Americans think about Communism? Many Americans were afraid of Communism. Some worried that there might be Communist spies in the government.

How did Joseph McCarthy respond to the idea that there might be Communist spies in the government? He began investigating leaders he suspected of being Communists. He boldly accused people in the government of being disloyal to the United States.

What effect did McCarthy's methods have on Americans? Some people became suspicious of people McCarthy accused. Some of the accused people lost their jobs, and no one else wanted to hire them. Some Americans felt threatened and were afraid of saying anything that might sound as if they were criticizing the government.

- Guide a discussion about the political cartoon on page 325.

What was the problem with McCarthy's accusations? McCarthy did not have enough evidence to support his accusations.

>> Conclude the discussion by asking the question on page 325. The United States wanted to do its part to stop the spread of Communism. It wanted to provide military and economic aid to countries under a Communist threat.

Activity Manual

- Guide completion of pages 229–30.

Assessment

- Administer quiz.

> The quiz may be given anytime after completing this lesson.

130

Student Text pages 326–28
Activity Manual page 231–32

Lesson Focus

- During his presidency, Eisenhower dealt with matters at home and continued to fight the spread of Communism overseas.

Objectives

- State benefits of the Saint Lawrence Seaway and the Federal Aid Highway Act
- Recognize that civil rights and the fight against Communism were ongoing struggles
- Identify Alaska and Hawaii as the states admitted to the United States during Eisenhower's presidency
- Explain why the United States became involved in the Vietnam War
- Report on a state capital

Teacher's Toolkit CD

- Instructional Aid 56: *State Capital Report*
- Visuals 39–40: *Saint Lawrence Seaway*; *Interstate Highway System*

Materials

- Sample of an elementary research report (from another subject area)
- Sources for researching state capitals
- Prepared list of directions for researching and writing the state capital report for each student (optional)
- Lined 4 × 6 note cards for each student

Review

Why was the United Nations formed? to keep world peace

- Choose a volunteer to explain what the Cold War was and why it occurred.

What change did the Truman Doctrine make in America's foreign policy? The Truman Doctrine committed the United States to get involved in struggles for the cause of freedom rather than follow its previous policy of usually staying out of foreign conflicts that did not directly involve it.

What caused the Korean War? North Korea invaded South Korea.

- Invite a student to explain why the United States became involved in the Korean War and the role American soldiers had in the war.

Preparation for Reading

- Generate interest as you direct the students to read the titles and examine the pictures and map on pages 326–28.
- Guide pronunciation of any unfamiliar words in the lesson.

America Under Eisenhower

The Election of 1952

In 1952 Dwight D. Eisenhower became the thirty-fourth president of the United States. Because of his popularity as a war hero, he won the election easily. His catchy campaign slogan was "I like Ike." The slogan proved true for most Americans. Eisenhower won the vote in thirty-nine of America's forty-eight states at that time. He was the first Republican president in nearly twenty years.

Dwight D. Eisenhower became one of only a handful of men to achieve the rank of Five-Star General, the highest military ranking in the country.

Eisenhower's personal skills and remarkable military experience made him such a desirable leader that both Democrats and Republicans encouraged him to run as a presidential candidate.

His popularity is reflected in the campaign slogan "I like Ike." He won two elections by a significant majority.

326

Dealing with Matters at Home
Transportation

Eisenhower dealt with several important projects during his two terms as president. One of these was the **Saint Lawrence Seaway**. In 1954 the United States and Canada agreed to work together on this project. They deepened the Saint Lawrence River and built new canals and locks. The new seaway allowed ships to travel from the Atlantic Ocean to the Great Lakes. Cities along the seaway developed into major seaports. The increased shipping helped the economies of both nations.

Another project had to do with the nation's highways. More Americans than ever before owned cars. Every day thousands of employees drove from the suburbs to the cities for work. Trucks carried supplies from city to city, sometimes traveling across the country. The military also had to be able to move troops and equipment quickly in case of war. Eisenhower saw that the nation's highway system needed to be improved.

In 1956 Congress passed the **Federal Aid Highway Act**. A major interstate-highway system would be built over the next thirteen years. The federal government would pay about 90 percent of the project's cost. This road system gradually changed America in many ways. It created new jobs and helped the economy. Rural areas became much easier to reach.

- Direct the students to read the pages silently to discover what struggles continued throughout Eisenhower's presidency. the struggle for civil rights and the fight against the spread of Communism

Teach for Understanding

Who was elected president in 1952? Dwight D. Eisenhower

What helped Eisenhower win the election? his popularity as a war hero

What were two transportation projects that Eisenhower dealt with? the Saint Lawrence Seaway and an interstate-highway system

What two countries worked together on the Saint Lawrence Seaway? the United States and Canada

- Display Visual 39. Discuss why the United States and Canada worked together on the Saint Lawrence Seaway and how the project benefited both nations.

- Invite a volunteer to explain why Eisenhower thought America's highway system needed to be improved.

What act allowed an interstate-highway system to be built? the Federal Aid Highway Act

- Why do you think the act was called the Federal Aid Highway Act? The government paid about 90 percent of the project's cost.

This highway system is still America's major way of driving from state to state. When you see a red, white, and blue shield at the roadside, you know you are using this nationwide network of highways.

Civil Rights

The struggle for civil rights was also going on throughout Eisenhower's years in office. One conflict that he faced happened in Little Rock, Arkansas. After the Supreme Court ruling in *Brown v. Board of Education*, many schools were slow to open their doors to black students. Nine black high-school students tried to enter a school in Little Rock in 1957. A mob of white students stood outside to block the doors. Even the governor of Arkansas did not support the black students. He ordered the Arkansas National Guard to help keep them out of the school.

President Eisenhower realized that the situation was dangerous. He sent federal troops to Little Rock to help the black students enter the school. The soldiers protected the students and kept order at the school for the rest of the school year. One of these nine students became the first African American to graduate from the school.

Two New States

Under President Eisenhower, two new states were added to the United States. Both states were admitted in 1959. Alaska and Hawaii are different from the other states. They are not physically attached to the rest of the states. They also have unique populations. One-fifth of Alaska's citizens are Inuits and Aleuts. Half of Hawaii's people are of Japanese, Chinese, Filipino, or Korean descent. Adding Alaska and Hawaii brought the number of states to fifty.

Fifty States

327

Activity

An Interstate Trip

Display Visual 40. Direct pairs of students to determine the location of a prominent attraction that is several states away or across the country. Locations could include Gettysburg; Washington, DC; Mount Rushmore; the Everglades; the Golden Gate Bridge, and other locations. Instruct the students to determine the most direct interstate route(s) they would need to take to travel to the locations. Allow time for the students to share their routes.

> Background information for this lesson is on the Teacher's Toolkit CD.

Lesson 130

Teach for Understanding

How did the road system benefit Americans? It created new jobs. It helped the economy. Rural areas became much easier to reach.

- Display Visual 40. Invite students to each trace a different interstate highway, telling which states the interstate passes through.

  How do you know you are traveling on an interstate highway? A red, white, and blue shield will be seen at the roadside.

- Choose a volunteer to remind the class of the Supreme Court's ruling in *Brown v. Board of Education*. Under the Constitution, black children must be able to attend the same schools as white children.

  Did all the schools in the United States immediately obey the Supreme Court's ruling? No, many schools were slow to open their doors to black students.

- Invite a student to relate the civil rights conflict that occurred in Little Rock.

- Do you think the action taken by the governor of Arkansas was legal? Answers may include that the governor's action was not legal because the Supreme Court's ruling applied to all the schools in the United States.

- Why was the situation dangerous? Answers may include that before the conflict in Little Rock occurred, white Americans who wanted segregation would sometimes act violently toward black Americans. The conflict in Little Rock could have become violent.

  What did one of the nine students achieve? The student was the first African American to graduate from the school.

- How would you have felt if you were one of the nine black students?

- Direction attention to the map on page 327.

  What two states were admitted to the United States under President Eisenhower? Alaska and Hawaii

  How are Alaska and Hawaii physically different from the other states? They are not attached to the rest of the states.

- Choose a volunteer to read aloud the sentences that explain what makes the populations of Alaska and Hawaii unique.

  How many states were there after Alaska and Hawaii were admitted to the United States? fifty

---

Chapter 15: Postwar America

130

Teach for Understanding

What was the main struggle overseas that President Eisenhower dealt with? the spread of Communism in other countries

What was one country the Communists were trying to take over? Vietnam

⚙ How was the Vietnam War similar to the Korean War? Answers could include that both Vietnam and Korea were divided into a Communist North and a free South. Just as the Korean War was between Communist North Korea and free South Korea, the Vietnam War was between Communist North Vietnam and free South Vietnam.

Who supplied military aid to North Vietnam? China and the Soviet Union

Why did the United States become involved in the war? The United States had committed itself to side with countries that were fighting Communism.

How did Eisenhower aid South Vietnam? He sent military advisors to help train the South Vietnamese Army.

⚙ Why do you think Eisenhower chose to not send American soldiers to Vietnam? Answers could include that many American soldiers had fought and died in World War II and in the Korean War. Eisenhower did not want more American soldiers to fight and die in the Vietnam War.

Did Eisenhower want the Cold War to continue? No, he thought the United States and the Soviet Union should try to ease the tensions of the Cold War.

- Choose a volunteer to relate one way Eisenhower thought the United States and the Soviet Union could ease the tensions. Choose another volunteer to relate the Soviet response to Eisenhower's Open Skies policy.

Why did the Soviet Union and the United States agree to live peacefully with each other? Neither nation wanted to start a war that might become World War III.

Conclude the discussion by asking the question on page 328. transportation projects, civil rights, and the addition of Alaska and Hawaii to the United States

Activity Manual

- Guide completion of pages 231–32.

Dealing with Matters Overseas
Vietnam

Like Truman, Eisenhower continued to fight the spread of Communism in other countries. One of these countries was Vietnam. Vietnam had been a French colony, but Communist forces were trying to take it over. The conflict turned into a war between Communist North Vietnam and free South Vietnam. Both China and the Soviet Union were giving military aid to the forces of North Vietnam.

The United States had committed itself to side with countries that were fighting Communism. Eisenhower did not want to send American soldiers to Vietnam. But he decided to send military advisers to help train the South Vietnamese Army. This was the beginning of American involvement in a long conflict that would last into the 1970s.

The Soviet Union

Eisenhower believed that the United States and the Soviet Union should try to ease the tensions of the Cold War. One thing he wanted was for each nation to be able to fly over the other's military bases. From the safety of the air, each country could make sure the other one was not building up a supply of bombs and weapons. This was called an Open Skies policy.

The Soviet Union did not want open skies. It refused to let the United States fly over its military bases. But it did agree to live peacefully with the United States. Neither nation wanted to start a war that might become World War III. So the Cold War continued.

> What matters at home did Eisenhower deal with?

Activity

Researching a State Capital

Use sources to find information about a state capital of your choice. Find out details such as the following.

- What is the city's population?
- What interests you most about its history?
- What important landmarks are located there?

- What are the city's geographical features?
- What is its ethnic makeup?
- What are its most important industries?

Follow your teacher's directions about organizing your research, writing your report, and sharing it with others.

328

Activity

Researching a State Capital

- Display the sample research report. Generate excitement about researching a state capital as you read the Activity information aloud.

- Distribute Instructional Aid 56. Explain the directions for researching and writing the report. Remind the students of the importance of recording their research sources. Give guidance as needed as the students research and write their reports.

- You may choose to allow time for the students to work on their reports while at school, or assign a specific period of time for them to complete their reports outside of the classroom.

- Allow time on several different days for the students to share their reports.

Advances and Attitudes
The Space Race

In 1957 the Soviet Union made an important scientific advance. The Russians sent a satellite, the *Sputnik*, into space. Americans did not like being behind the Russians in such an important field as space exploration. Many Americans were also afraid that the Soviet Union would use the new technology to start nuclear warfare. President Eisenhower asked Congress for more money for the American space program. The race was on between the Soviet Union and the United States. Each wanted to have the best space program and be the first to use new space technology. The space race became another way of fighting the Cold War.

In 1957 the Soviet Union sent another satellite into space with a small dog onboard. A few months later in 1958, the United States launched its first satellite, the *Explorer*. Shortly afterward, the United States created the **National Aeronautics and Space Administration** (NASA). This organization would be responsible for all of America's activity in space.

In 1961 the Russians were the first to launch a man into space. Yuri Gagarin orbited the earth one time in a spaceship. The United States sped up its own efforts to put a man in space. Less than one month later, **Alan Shepard** became the first American astronaut to enter space. Shepard was one of seven astronauts who had been specially trained by NASA for space missions. NASA named this space program Project Mercury. Shepard flew by himself in a spacecraft called *Freedom 7*. His mission lasted only about fifteen minutes. But his spacecraft flew more than three hundred miles before landing in the Atlantic Ocean.

Project Mercury was America's first manned space program including (back, left to right) Alan Shepard, Gus Grissom, and Gordon Cooper (front, left to right) Walter Schirra, Don Slaylon, John Glenn, and Scott Carpenter.

The *Sputnik* launch started the space race between the Soviet Union and the United States.

329

Lesson 131

Student Text pages 329–31
Activity Manual page 233

Lesson Focus

- By the end of the 1950s, Americans had witnessed both the beginning of the space race and the changes in their culture.

Objectives
- Explain how the space race was one way of fighting the Cold War
- Recognize changes in American culture during the 1950s
- Examine the role of Christianity in American culture in the 1950s

Teacher's Toolkit CD
- Visual 41: *Project Mercury*

Review

Who was elected president in 1952? Dwight D. Eisenhower

What were two transportation projects under President Eisenhower? the Saint Lawrence Seaway and an interstate-highway system

What allowed for the building of the interstate-highway system? Congress passed the Federal Aid Highway Act.

- Choose volunteers to describe the projects and explain their benefits.

  What states were admitted to the United States under Eisenhower? Alaska and Hawaii

  What two struggles continued into Eisenhower's presidency? civil rights and the fight against the spread of Communism

- Invite a student to describe the civil rights conflict that occurred in Little Rock, Arkansas.

- Invite another student to explain why the United States became involved in the Vietnam War.

  What was one way Eisenhower believed the United States and the Soviet Union could ease Cold War tensions? He wanted both nations to agree to an Open Skies policy.

- Choose a volunteer to explain an Open Skies policy and to tell whether both countries agreed to it.

Preparation for Reading

- Generate interest as you direct the students to read the titles and examine the pictures on pages 329–31.
- Guide pronunciation of any unfamiliar words in the lesson.
- Direct the students to read the pages silently to discover what scientific advances and cultural changes occurred during the 1950s. The space race began. The large increase in the number of homes with televisions allowed Americans to stay more aware of important events and to watch the same shows. Rock 'n' roll became popular. Christian beliefs were widely accepted and popular.

Teach for Understanding

What two countries were involved in the space race? the United States and the Soviet Union

Which country was first to send a satellite into space? the Soviet Union

- Invite students to read aloud the captions for the photographs on page 329. Discuss how the space race was another way of fighting the Cold War.

What organization was created to be responsible for America's activity in space? the National Aeronautics and Space Administration (NASA)

Who was the first man launched into space? Yuri Gagarin

What was Gagarin's mission? to orbit the earth one time

Who was the first American to enter space? Alan Shepard

What was the name of NASA's first space program? Project Mercury

What was the name of the spacecraft Shepard flew in? *Freedom 7*

- Display Visual 41. Explain that the space capsule was the only part of the spacecraft that flew in space. Point out that *Freedom 7*'s maximum speed was 5,095 miles per hour (rounded to the nearest mile). It reached an altitude of 116 miles (rounded to the nearest mile).

Who was the first American to orbit the earth? John Glenn

What was the name of Glenn's spacecraft? *Friendship 7*

How many times did Glenn orbit the earth? three

- Explain that John Glenn's mission was the third Mercury mission. Approximately two and a half months after Alan Shephard entered space, Virgil Grissom became the second American to enter space. Similar to Shephard's mission, Grissom's mission was a suborbital flight. His spacecraft was called *Liberty Bell 7*.

- Direct attention to the Biography box. Choose a volunteer to explain the information at the top of the box.

What was John Glenn's occupation before becoming an astronaut? He served as a pilot in the marines.

How many astronauts were part of Project Mercury? seven

What did all seven astronauts have in common? They were all military test pilots with at least 1,500 hours of flight time. They all had college degrees in engineering.

What other qualifications did the men need to meet in order to be selected for the Mercury Project? They had to be less than forty years old, in excellent physical condition, and shorter than five feet eleven inches tall.

What problem arose during Glenn's mission? *The Friendship 7* lost automatic control, and Glenn had to manually control the spacecraft for two of his orbits.

What position did Glenn hold after being an astronaut? He served as a US Senator from the state of Ohio.

- Do you think it is easy to become an astronaut? No, to become an astronaut requires a lot of study and hard work. Very few people are chosen to be astronauts.

What helped Americans be aware of the space missions that were being flown? the large increase in the number of homes with televisions

- Guide a discussion about other effects the increased number of televisions had on American culture.

- Why do you think Christians needed to be on their guard about how TV shows shaped their thinking? Answers may include that some TV shows could have resulted in Christians accepting or forming ideas that opposed God's Word.

- Do you think Christians today should be careful in deciding what TV shows to watch? Answers may include that Christians today should be careful because many TV shows can influence Christians to accept or form ideas that oppose God's Word.

John Glenn

Who: astronaut
When: born 1921
Where: Ohio

John Glenn grew up in New Concord, Ohio. After college he joined the Marines and served as a pilot in World War II and the Korean War. Glenn was thirty-seven when he was selected by NASA to be part of Project Mercury. All seven men chosen were military test pilots with at least 1,500 hours of flight time. They had to be less than forty years old and in excellent physical condition. They also had to be shorter than five feet eleven inches to fit comfortably into a space capsule. All the men had college degrees in engineering.

On February 20, 1962, Glenn became the first American to orbit the earth. The *Friendship 7* lost automatic control while he was in orbit. He manually controlled the craft for two of his orbits. Glenn was awarded the highest award for astronauts, the Congressional Space Medal of Honor. Later in life, Glenn served as a US senator from the state of Ohio.

The following year, another of the seven astronauts, **John Glenn**, became the first American to orbit the earth. Glenn flew a spacecraft called *Friendship 7*. He orbited the earth three times. His spacecraft reached speeds higher than seventeen thousand miles per hour during its five-hour mission.

Changes in American Culture

Entertainment and the Arts

By the end of the 1950s, many Americans were following the space race on their televisions. Over the course of the 1950s, the number of homes with televisions increased by tens of millions. Televisions helped the nation stay more aware of important news, sports, and other events. Television also provided entertainment and made Americans feel more connected. People all over the nation watched the same shows. *I Love Lucy* and *Leave It to Beaver* were popular family shows. A western called *Gunsmoke* was also a favorite with many Americans. Watching TV and talking about the shows became part of American culture. Many TV programs were clean and acceptable for families. Even so, Christians still had to

---

The Lucy Show

The television model of the ideal family received a jolt in 1960 when Lucille Ball filed for divorce from Desi Arnaz, her husband in real life as well as on television. When Ball returned to the airwaves in 1962 with *The Lucy Show*, she played a widow. In addition, actress Vivian Vance (who had played Ethel Mertz, Lucy's best friend, in the *I Love Lucy* series) played a divorcée, a characteristic that would have been frowned upon in the 1950s.

Recording Industry

New technology in the phonograph industry brought changes for postwar America. The 78 rpm records of the thirties and forties were replaced with 33⅓ rpm long-playing (LP) records in stereophonic sound for avid music lovers and with 45 rpm records that became a hit with teenagers. A new type of music, rock 'n' roll, gained popularity in the late 1950s. Broadcasted widely by radio stations, it appealed to the emerging teen culture of the 1950s by glamorizing a counterculture that challenged certain values and traditions of American society. This new style of music was often associated with rebellion and recklessness.

be on their guard about how TV shows shaped their thinking.

Music also went through changes during the 1950s. Many Americans were listening to music by the Boston Pops orchestra on their stereos. Orchestra conductor Arthur Fiedler made recordings of light classical music along with show tunes and movie themes. A new musical style called rock 'n' roll also began during this decade. At first, most Americans thought of the new music as an unusual fad. However, rock 'n' roll would permanently change popular music in America. In years to come, many Christians would develop concerns about this music style's effect on people's attitudes and morals.

Religious Attitudes

The 1950s were a time when Christianity was generally accepted and popular in America. An evangelist named **Billy Graham** began preaching and attracted huge crowds. A large percentage of Americans attended church regularly. However, not all Americans had a deep, well-taught faith. Many churches preached the gospel, but not all of them were careful to teach Bible doctrines. In addition, some Americans identified themselves as Christians to keep from being associated with Communism.

Many American families also accepted responsibilities promoted in the Bible. Women focused on rearing their children and working in their homes. Men were encouraged to be leaders and providers for the family.

American currency still bears the phrase "In God we trust," a memento to the religious growth of a bygone era.

The widespread acceptance of Christian beliefs made certain changes possible. Eisenhower wanted to make it clear that America was a "righteous" nation that in no way identified with Communism. In 1954 Eisenhower asked Congress to add the words "under God" to the pledge to the American flag. In 1956 the phrase "In God we trust" became the nation's official motto. The motto still appears on American money today.

> What were some changes in American culture in the 1950s?

331

In God We Trust

The phrase "In God We Trust" has been mandatory on currency only since 1955. It was first used, however, in 1864 and appeared consistently on American coins before 1955 with the exception of 1907–8. That exception was during the presidency of Theodore Roosevelt. He said, "It is a motto which it is indeed well to have inscribed on our great national monuments, in our temples of justice, [and] in our legislative halls. But it seems to me eminently unwise to cheapen such a motto by use on coins, just as it would be to cheapen it by use on postage stamps and advertisements." Arguing that the law did not require such a motto on currency, Roosevelt issued an executive order eliminating it in 1907. The following year, however, Congress overruled him.

Activity

An Astronaut and a Mission

Direct the students to choose an astronaut other than Alan Shepard or John Glenn. Instruct the students to research interesting facts about the astronaut and his or her space mission. Allow the students to share what they learn.

Teach for Understanding

What were some styles of music many Americans listened to during the 1950s? light classical music, show tunes, and movie themes

What new style of music became popular during the 1950s? rock 'n' roll

Why did many Christians become concerned about rock 'n' roll? Many Christians were concerned about the effect rock 'n' roll would have on people's attitudes and morals.

● Guide a discussion appropriate for your students about the effect music styles might have on people.

What was the attitude toward Christianity in America during the 1950s? Christianity was generally accepted and popular.

Whose preaching attracted large crowds? Billy Graham

Why did some Christians lack a deep, well-taught faith? Although many churches preached the Gospel, not all of them taught Bible doctrines.

Had all Americans who identified themselves as Christians actually accepted Christ as their personal Savior? No, some Americans identified themselves as Christians just to keep from being associated with Communism.

What biblical responsibilities were accepted by many families? Women focused on rearing their children and working in their homes. Men were encouraged to be leaders and providers for the family.

What changes made it clear that America did not identify with Communism? The words "under God" were added to the pledge to the American flag, and the phrase "In God we trust" became the nation's official motto.

Why do you think America's motto and the change in the pledge to the American flag clearly showed that America did not identify with Communism? Answers could include that many Communists hated Christianity.

● Choose a volunteer to read aloud the caption for the photograph on page 331.

Conclude the discussion by asking the question on page 331. The inceased number of televisions allowed Americans to be more aware of important events. New music styles, such as rock 'n' roll became popular. Some Americans identified themselves as Christians to keep from being associated with Communism.

Activity Manual

● Guide completion of page 233.

132

Lesson Focus

- President Kennedy initiated the Peace Corps and continued the fight against Communism.

Objectives

- Recognize that the election of 1960 was historically significant
- Identify the Peace Corps as a program to help people in other countries
- Identify the building of the Berlin Wall and the Cuban Missile Crisis as Cold War conflicts

Teacher's Toolkit CD

- Instructional Aid 57: *Cold War Conflicts Under Kennedy*

Review

- Choose a volunteer to explain how the space race was one way that the Cold War could be fought.

  Why were many Americans able to follow the space race on television? The number of televisions in American homes had greatly increased, allowing Americans to follow the space race and be aware of other important events.

- Invite a student to explain changes that occurred in music during the 1950s.

- Choose a volunteer to explain the concerns many Christians had about some TV programs and rock 'n' roll.

- What influence did Christianity have on American culture during the 1950s? Answers may include that because Christianity was generally accepted and popular, many Americans attended church regularly. Many American families also accepted responsibilities promoted in the Bible.

  How was it made clear that America in no way identified with Communism? "Under God" was added to the pledge to the American flag, and "In God we trust" became the nation's official motto.

Preparation for Reading

- Generate interest as you direct the students to read the titles and examine the pictures on pages 332–34.
- Guide pronunciation of any unfamiliar words in the lesson.
- Direct the students to read the pages silently and complete Instructional Aid 57 in pairs.

Teach for Understanding

Who ran against Kennedy in the presidential election of 1960? Richard Nixon

America Under Kennedy
The Election of 1960

In the election of 1960, Americans were faced with a choice between Richard Nixon and **John F. Kennedy**. Nixon, the Republican candidate, had been Eisenhower's vice president for the past eight years. Kennedy was a Democratic senator from Massachusetts.

The election was one of the closest in American history. Many thought that Kennedy, at age forty-three, was too young and inexperienced to be the

Kennedy never kept his presidential salary but rather donated it to charity and lived off inherited family wealth.

As an eleven-year-old, Jacqueline claimed the rare achievement of winning a double victory in the national junior horsemanship competition.

332

president. Some were also concerned about his Catholic beliefs. They wondered if he would rely too heavily on his church leaders when making decisions. However, the presidential debates helped Kennedy. For the first time, Americans could watch the debates on television. Kennedy's friendly personality made him more appealing to many viewers. He also supported the civil rights movement and earned the vote of most black Americans. When all the votes were counted, Kennedy had won. He was the youngest man to have been elected president of the United States.

Kennedy entered the White House in 1961 with his wife Jacqueline and their two small children. It was the first time in many years that young children had lived in the White House. Many viewed the family as a symbol of youthful American success. And many viewed Kennedy himself as a symbol of bright hope for America.

The Kennedys with their pony Macaroni

- Do you think Nixon was well qualified to be the president? Answers could include that he was qualified because he had been Eisenhower's vice president for eight years.

  What were some concerns Americans had about Kennedy becoming president? Many Americans thought that Kennedy was too young and inexperienced to be the president. Some thought that he would rely too heavily on the leaders of the Catholic church when making decisions.

  What helped Kennedy win the election? Americans could watch the debates on television. Kennedy's friendly personality made him more appealing to many viewers. His support of the civil rights movement earned the votes of most black Americans.

- Why was the 1960 presidential campaign and election considered to be historical? It was one of the closest elections in American history. It was the first time Americans could watch the candidates debate on television. John F. Kennedy was the youngest man ever to be elected president of the United States.

- Invite students to read aloud the captions for the pictures on page 332.

  How did many Americans view Kennedy and his family? Many viewed Kennedy himself as a symbol of bright hope for America. Many viewed his family as a symbol of youthful American success.

Helping the Poor

At his inauguration, Kennedy spoke about his goals for helping the poor in the United States and in other countries of the world. "If a free society cannot help the many who are poor, it cannot save the few who are rich," he said. He immediately signed new laws that he believed would benefit America's poor. The laws raised minimum wage and provided funds for housing in low-income communities.

Early in his presidency, Kennedy introduced a new program called the **Peace Corps**. He called for volunteers to go to other countries to help improve the people's way of life. Teachers, engineers, doctors, businessmen, and other skilled workers joined the Peace Corps. They traveled for short periods of time to countries in

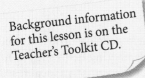

Asia, Africa, Latin America, and the Middle East. Peace Corps volunteers helped with many kinds of projects. They established schools, improved farming methods, and gave medical care. Members of the Peace Corps continue to work in many parts of the world today.

Kennedy and the Cold War
Berlin

Like the presidents before him, Kennedy continued to fight against Communism. One country where Communism continued to create problems was Germany. The eastern part of the country was controlled by the Soviet Union. The western portion had been divided among the United States, Britain, and France. Berlin, a city in East Germany, was also divided. East Berlin was Communist. West Berlin was free.

In 1961 Soviet leader Nikita Khrushchev ordered that a wall be built between East and West Berlin. Millions of East Berlin citizens had already fled to West Berlin. Khrushchev did not want any more people to leave. On August 13, 1961, workers sealed the border between East and West Berlin with a barbed-wire barrier. They eventually built a wall nearly twelve feet tall.

Conrad Schumann leaped over the barbed wire to West Germany. His jump inspired the sculpture called *Mauerspringer*, which means wall jumper.

333

Background information for this lesson is on the Teacher's Toolkit CD.

Teach for Understanding

🔖 Why do you think Kennedy was viewed as a symbol of bright hope for America? Answers may include that what Kennedy said in the televised debates caused many Americans to be hopeful about America's future.

What goals did Kennedy speak about at his inauguration? helping the poor in the United States and in other countries

- Choose a volunteer to read aloud Kennedy's statement. Choose another volunteer to tell what he thinks Kennedy meant when he made the statement. Answers may include that it is important to help the poor.

How did President Kennedy believe his goals could be met? He signed new legislation that raised the minimum wage and provided funds for housing in low-income communities. He introduced the Peace Corps.

What was the purpose of the Peace Corps? to help improve people's way of life in other countries

Who volunteered to serve in the Peace Corps? teachers, engineers, doctors, businessmen, and other skilled workers

- Invite a student to explain what volunteers did while serving in the Peace Corps.

- Direct attention to Instructional Aid 57. Choose a volunteer to name the countries in which crises occurred during Kennedy's presidency. Instruct students to read aloud the separate facts for each country.

- Invite a student to read the similarities in the two conflicts.

Who was the Soviet leader? Nikita Khrushchev

Why was the Berlin Wall built? Millions of East Berlin citizens had fled to West Berlin, and Khrushchev did not want any more people to leave.

- Guide a discussion about the photographs on page 333.

Teach for Understanding

Why did President Kennedy send soldiers to West Berlin? He wanted to make sure West Berlin stayed free.

⚙ Did control of East Berlin or West Berlin change when the crisis ended? No, East Berlin remained Communist and West Berlin remained free.

Who was the Communist leader of Cuba? Fidel Castro

Why did the United States closely watch what was happening in Cuba? The Communist country was close to the United States.

- Invite a student to explain how the United States tried to end Communism in Cuba.

What did an American spy plane discover when it was flying over Cuba? The Soviet Union had placed missiles in Cuba.

- Guide a discussion about the photograph on page 334.

What danger did the Soviet missiles present for the United States? Nuclear bombs could have been loaded on the missiles. They could have been used to destroy American cities and start a war.

Why did President Kennedy order a blockade of Cuba? to enforce his demands that the Soviets remove the missiles; so that any Soviet ship carrying weapons would be turned back before reaching Cuba

What brought an end to the Cuban Missile Crisis? Khrushchev ordered his troops in Cuba to take down the missile launching pads and return them to the Soviet Union.

⚙ Why were both the Berlin Wall conflict and the Cuban Missile Crisis dangerous situations? Both conflicts could have led to a war.

▶ Conclude the discussion by asking the question on page 334. He wanted to prevent the spread of Communism. He also wanted to keep Americans safe from the threat of Communism.

Activity Manual

- Guide completion of page 234.

President Kennedy sent troops to West Berlin. He wanted to make sure West Berlin stayed free. US soldiers tried to ensure that those from West Berlin, especially Americans in the city, would be able to enter and exit East Berlin safely. At one point the conflict reached a dangerous level, and both sides stationed tanks near the checkpoint at the border. However, the two sides avoided war, and West Berlin remained free.

Cuba

Another situation in the Cold War happened in Cuba. Cuba is an island nation located ninety miles off the coast of Florida. It had been under the rule of Communist dictator **Fidel Castro** since 1959. Many Cubans had fled to Florida. The United States watched the situation closely. It did not like having a Communist nation so close to its own country.

The United States military trained some of the Cubans who had come to Florida. Shortly after Kennedy became president, these Cuban troops returned to Cuba. They tried to take the Cuban government from the Communists. But the invasion failed.

In October of 1962, an American spy plane flying over Cuba discovered that the Soviet Union had placed missiles in Cuba. Nuclear bombs could be loaded on the missiles. If launched, the missiles could strike and destroy American cities and start a war.

President Kennedy and his advisers met secretly for several days. They discussed what to do about the **Cuban Missile Crisis**. Then Kennedy demanded that the Soviets remove the missiles. To enforce his demands, he ordered a blockade of Cuba. Any Soviet ship carrying weapons would be turned back before reaching Cuba.

The situation was tense. President Kennedy urged Khrushchev to turn his ships around. Khrushchev told Kennedy to lift the blockade. Kennedy refused and declared that the blockade would not be lifted until the missile sites in Cuba were removed.

No one knew what would happen. Many people expected war. Some Americans began building bomb shelters in their yards or basements. At last, Khrushchev ordered his troops in Cuba to take down the missile launching pads and return them to the Soviet Union. The Cuban Missile Crisis was over.

▷ Why did Kennedy intervene in Berlin and Cuba? ◁

334

Activity

Helping the Poor

Discuss how the students can help people who are in need of assistance. Organize the students in gathering items such as non-perishable foods or school supplies. Deliver the items to a local rescue shelter. Alternatively, the items may be given to the school office to divide and give to students who need assistance.

How It Was

Ruby stopped and stared at the empty space over the door of the drugstore. "Look, Mama, it's gone." She pointed. "You can see where it was 'cause the paint's brighter from bein' all covered up. The 'Whites Only' sign is gone."

Mama said nothing. When Ruby looked up at her, she was surprised to see Mama's eyes brimming with tears.

"Does that mean we can go in?" asked Ruby. "Can we sit at the tall stools? Can I order a milkshake?"

Mama wiped the back of her hand across her eyes. "I never thought I'd see the day." She squeezed Ruby's hand. "Yes, child. We can go in. We can sit wherever we want. We can order a hundred milkshakes." She tipped Ruby's chin up to look in her eyes. "This is America, child. We belong here—in the land of the free. Same as everybody else. Thank the good Lord."

Victories and Tragedies
The Birmingham Protests

In 1963 Martin Luther King Jr. led a series of protests in Birmingham, Alabama. The city still had segregation laws. It was known for racism and acts of violence against black Americans. King's group of protesters tried to use peaceful methods to oppose the city's treatment of black Americans. They marched through the city streets singing and carrying signs. They purposely sat at lunch counters where black people were not welcome. The city police arrested many black citizens, including King, and put them in jail. The police also used violent methods such as high-powered hoses and vicious dogs to break up the protests. Even school children who conducted their own march were treated violently and jailed. King wrote a powerful letter of protest from his prison cell. Finally city leaders agreed to a plan to make changes to the segregation laws.

President Kennedy was horrified at the situation in Birmingham. He believed that it was an embarrassment to the nation and to the world. Up to

335

Lesson 133

Student Text pages 335–37
Activity Manual pages 235–36

Lesson Focus

- Martin Luther King Jr. led civil rights protests in Birmingham, Alabama, and President Kennedy was assassinated.

Objectives

- Identify Martin Luther King Jr. as a leader in the civil rights movement
- Explain why there were protests in Birmingham
- Describe Kennedy's assassination and America's reaction to it

Review

What was historical about the presidential debates between Richard Nixon and John F. Kennedy? It was the first time Americans could watch presidential debates on TV.

Which candidate won the election? John F. Kennedy

What was the historical significance of Kennedy being elected president? He was the youngest man ever to have been elected president of the United States.

What program did President Kennedy introduce to improve people's way of life in other countries? the Peace Corps

What two crises brought the Cold War to a dangerous level during Kennedy's presidency? the Berlin Wall and the Cuban Missile Crisis

Preparation for Reading

- Generate interest as you direct the students to read the titles and examine the pictures on pages 335–37.
- Guide pronunciation of any unfamiliar words in the lesson.
- Direct the students to read the pages silently to discover where Birmingham is located and what a protest is. Birmingham is located in Alabama. A protest is a method of opposing something such as the way black Americans were treated in Birmingham.

Teach for Understanding

- Direct attention to the How It Was box.

  What did Ruby notice about the drugstore? The "Whites Only" sign had been taken down.

- What civil rights change had taken place? Answers may include that the drugstore now offered service to black people and white people.

- Discuss how Mama and Ruby felt about the sign being gone.

  Who was Mama thankful to for the sign being gone? the Lord

- Invite a student to tell who led a series of protests in Birmingham. Martin Luther King Jr.

- Why did King lead the protests? Answers may include that he lead the protests in response to Birmingham's segregation laws, racism, and acts of violence against black Americans; to oppose the city's treatment of black people.

- Guide a discussion of the methods used by the protesters and the response of Birmingham's police. Point out that King's group of protesters tried to use peaceful methods.

  What did King do while he was in jail? He wrote a letter of protest.

Primary Source: A Letter from Jail

- Guide the students in reading the introductory paragraph and note on Activity Manual page 235. Discuss the importance of using kind words when referring to other people.
- Guide the students in reading the excerpt of King's letter, and in answering the question at the bottom of the page.

What were some injustices that King wanted to see changed? Answers may include that he wanted black Americans to have a chance to escape poverty, black children to go to the same amusement parks as white children, motels and other businesses to accept black customers equally with white customers, and black women to be treated with respect.

How did the city leaders respond to the protests? They agreed to a plan to make changes to the segregation laws.

Teach for Understanding

How did President Kennedy respond to the protests? In a televised speech, Kennedy announced that he was going to ask the federal government to make laws against segregation nationwide.

Why were nationwide laws against segregation needed? Up to this time, the segregation laws had been left up to the states.

- Invite a student to describe what is happening in the photograph on page 336.

What did King want for America? He wanted all Americans to get along and live together peacefully. He wanted them to be equally free.

What word has been used to describe the marches that King led? peaceful

- Discuss why it was important for the protests to be peaceful.

What enraged black Americans and white Americans alike? Four young girls were killed by the bombing of a black church in Birmingham.

Why did it take months for civil rights to change in Birmingham? Segregation laws had been in place for a long time, and some people did not want to change.

What changes did occur? "Whites Only" and "Blacks Only" signs were removed from public places. Restaurants and businesses began opening their doors to black Americans. And the Civil Rights Bill was slowly making its way through the lawmaking process.

Who had asked Congress for civil rights legislation? President Kennedy

Did President Kennedy see the Civil Rights Bill become law? No, he was killed before the bill became law.

this time, the segregation laws had been left up to the states. In June of 1963, Kennedy made a speech on television. He announced that he was going to ask the federal government to make laws against segregation nationwide.

After his release from prison, Martin Luther King Jr. continued to hold peaceful marches in support of civil rights. His most famous speech was delivered during a march in Washington, DC. "I have a dream," he said, "that . . . one day right there in Alabama little black boys and black girls will be able to join hands with little white boys and white girls as sisters and brothers." His speech ended with a triumphant plea to "let freedom ring" from every part of the United States.

Only one month after this speech, a bomb exploded at a black church in Birmingham. Four young girls were killed. The bombing outraged black and white Americans alike around the nation.

Segregation laws had been in place for a long time, and some people did not want to change. But slowly, over several months, change did come to Birmingham, Alabama. "Whites Only" and "Blacks Only" signs were removed from public places. Restaurants and businesses began opening their doors to black Americans. And the **Civil Rights Bill** was slowly making its way through the lawmaking process.

A President Is Killed

President Kennedy did not live to see the Civil Rights Bill become law. On November 22, 1963, the president and his wife were on a tour in Dallas, Texas. They were riding through the streets in an open car. Suddenly shots rang out, and President Kennedy was struck by several bullets. He died at the hospital a few hours later.

336

Background

Scene of the Assassination

Vice President Lyndon Johnson was in Dallas with Kennedy, riding two cars behind the president, when the assassination occurred. Texas governor John Connally was riding in the front seat of the car bearing President and Mrs. Kennedy, and he was was wounded in the shooting.

National Mourning

For four days after the assassination, the nation watched almost continuous television coverage of the events surrounding Kennedy's assassination and his funeral. Scenes of mourners filing through the Capitol Rotunda, where the body lay in state, and of his flag-draped coffin moving through the streets of Washington, DC, on a horse-drawn caisson created great emotion for the nation. Perhaps one of the most memorable photos of the funeral was that of little John ("John-John") Kennedy saluting his father's casket as it passed.

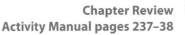

The assassin was a man named Lee Harvey Oswald. Oswald was a former US marine with ties to the Soviet Union. But he was never brought to trial. Two days after he killed the president, he too was killed. A civilian gunman shot him as the police were taking him to prison. Oswald's motive for the assassination will never be clear.

Shocked Americans watched as the president's death was announced on television. Only a few hours after Kennedy died, Vice President **Lyndon B. Johnson** was sworn in to take his place. A couple days later, hundreds of thousands of people lined up to file past the flag-draped casket at the Capitol Building. The entire nation grieved the loss of its president.

Moments before Kennedy was assassinated while driving through Dallas, Texas

Family mourning Kennedy

Recovering Again

On November 25, 1963, President Kennedy was laid to rest in Arlington National Cemetery. Millions of Americans watched on television. After years spent recovering from their losses in World War II, Americans now had to recover from another great tragedy. But America would never really be the same. In many ways, the death of President Kennedy ushered in an entirely new era in American history.

> What victory resulted from the Birmingham protests?

337

Chapter Review
Activity Manual pages 237–38

Objective
- Recall concepts and terms from Chapter 15

Teachers Toolkit CD
- Instructional Aid 58: *Space Race*

Materials
- 3 × 5 cards

Introduction

- Concepts for the Chapter 15 Test will be taken from Activity Manual pages 225–38. You may review any or all of the concepts during this lesson. You may choose to review Chapter 15 by playing "Space Race."

Review

Game: Space Race

- Cut the space capsules from Instructional Aid 58, and attach the capsules to one side of a display board.
- Prepare a list of questions and answers to use for review. Write the questions on the 3 × 5 cards, and place them face down on a desk.
- Divide the class into teams. Assign each team a space capsule.
- Direct the first player to choose a question, read it aloud, and then give the answer. If a correct answer is given, instruct the student to move his team's space capsule a specified distance across the display board. If an incorrect answer is given, review the answer and mix the card back in with the unanswered questions. Alternatively, if a student gives an incorrect answer, you may ask the first student on the other team to answer the question. Continue rotating teams and players until all the questions have been answered. The team whose space capsule has traveled the farthest wins the game.

Activity Manual

- Guide completion of pages 237–38.

Teach for Understanding

Who assassinated President Kennedy? Lee Harvey Oswald

Does anyone know Oswald's motive for killing Kennedy? No one will ever know. Two days after Oswald killed the president, he was killed by a civilian gunman.

Who was sworn in as president after Kennedy died? Lyndon B. Johnson

- Guide a discussion about the photographs on page 337. Explain that they show only two of the many scenes that Americans watched on television in the days following Kennedy's death.

How did Kennedy's death affect Americans? Americans were shocked. They grieved, and they needed time to recover from the tragedy.

> Conclude the discussion by asking the question on page 337. The Civil Rights Bill became law.

Activity Manual

- Guide completion of pages 235–36.

Lesson 135 **Chapter 15 Test**

Objective
- Demonstrate knowledge of concepts from Chapter 15 by taking the test

Assessment

- Administer Test 15.

Chapter 16

Introduction

Shortly after the assassination of John F. Kennedy, Lyndon B. Johnson took the oath to be president of the United States. Johnson promised to create a Great Society if he was reelected. Johnson continued the Vietnam War. During his presidency, liberalism split between the old liberals and the New Left. This divide created a counterculture.

Richard Nixon was elected president of the United States in 1968. Martin Luther King Jr. was shot the same year. The economy struggled. Nixon created the Environmental Protection Agency. In 1973 the Supreme Court made abortion legal. The Vietnam War ended, but the Cold War continued. Nixon resigned because of the Watergate scandal. Gerald R. Ford became the next president. He inherited a large government deficit. Vietnam and Cambodia fell to the Communists during Ford's presidency.

Americans elected Jimmy Carter president in 1979. Carter claimed to be conservative, but many of his policies were liberal. By the end of Carter's presidency, Americans believed their nation was in decline.

16 The Rise of the Counterculture

Focus
New ideas about how Americans should live raised new problems for the country.

Chapter 16 Overview

Lesson	Student Text	Activity Manual	Content		Vocabulary	
136	338–41	239–42	Lyndon Johnson Civil Rights Act of 1964 Primary Source: Address on Voting Rights Act	Voting Rights Act of 1965	Civil Rights Act of 1964 filibuster Voting Rights Act of 1965	
137	342–44	243	The Great Society War on Poverty	War in Vietnam Tet Offensive	Great Society War on Poverty	Tet Offensive
138	345–47	244–45	The New Left Counterculture Malcom X	Stokely Carmichael Betty Friedan Feminist movement	counterculture feminist movement New Left	
139	348–51	246–47	Richard Nixon Michael Collins, Neil Armstrong, and Buzz Aldrin Poverty and the economy Environmental Protection Agency *Roe v. Wade* How It Was: Apollo 11	Silent majority	currency Environmental Protection Agency inflation silent majority	
140	352–55	248	Vietnam War The Cold War Biography Box: Billy Graham	Watergate	Visit bjupress.com/resources for links to enhance the lessons.	
141	356–58	249	Gerald R. Ford	Activity: Creating a Budget	deficit	
142	359–61	250	Jimmy Carter	Rising oil prices	shah	
143		251–52	Chapter Review			
144			Chapter Test			

Civil Rights Act
1964

Nixon resigns
1974

1960   1965   1970   1973   1975

Voting Rights Act

Roe v. Wade

Lyndon Johnson Takes Charge

Lyndon Johnson was riding in a convertible several cars behind John F. Kennedy when shots rang out and killed the president. Immediately a Secret Service agent pushed Johnson to the floor of the car. He knelt on Johnson to shield him from any further shots. The agent shouted for the driver to speed away.

Within a few hours Johnson learned that Kennedy was dead. Johnson was now the president of the United States. When a president is killed, the vice president becomes the president. Johnson took the oath of office before leaving Texas. He wanted Americans to see that the American government remained strong.

After Kennedy's funeral, Johnson spoke to the American people. He stood before a special session of Congress to give his speech. He said that the country should honor Kennedy. He said Kennedy would be honored best by Congress passing the bills that Kennedy

had wanted passed. Johnson said the most important of these bills was the Civil Rights Bill.

Johnson's Path to the White House

Kennedy had sent Congress several important bills. But he had not been able to get Congress to pass them. Lyndon Johnson knew how to get those bills passed.

Before he had become president, Lyndon Johnson had spent much of his life in Congress. From the time he was young, Lyndon Johnson wanted to eventually become president of the United States. He had a plan for how to achieve his goal. He would become a representative in the House of Representatives. Then he would become a US senator. Finally, he would become the president.

When Franklin Roosevelt was president, Johnson came to Washington as a representative. Roosevelt had

339

Chapter Focus

New ideas about how Americans should live raised new problems for the country.

Lesson Focus

- President Johnson served as a liberal president during a time of protests and social injustices in America.

Objectives
- Understand the meaning of the Civil Rights Act of 1964
- Examine the meaning of the Voting Rights Act of 1965

Teacher's Toolkit CD
- Instructional Aid 59: *President Johnson Takes Charge*
- Visual 42: *Address on the Voting Rights Act*

Introduction

- Invite a student to read aloud the title of the chapter and predict what the chapter will be about. the counterculture
- Invite a student to read the chapter focus aloud.

  What do you think you will learn in this chapter? that new ideas about how Americans should live caused new problems for the country

  What do you see in the picture? people protesting

- Direct attention to the timeline.

  What legislation was passed in 1964? the Civil Rights Act

  When was the Voting Rights Act passed? 1965

  How many years passed from the date of the Civil Rights Act to the date Nixon resigned? ten years

Preparation for Reading

- Generate interest as you direct the students to read the titles and examine the pictures on pages 338–41.
- Guide pronunciation of any unfamiliar words in the lesson.
- Direct the students to read the pages and complete Instructional Aid 59 in small groups.

Teach for Understanding

What tragic event caused Lyndon Johnson to become president of the United States? President Kennedy died after being shot.

Where did Johnson spend most of his political career before becoming president? Before he became president, Lyndon Johnson had spent most of his political career in Congress.

- Direct attention to the picture on page 340. Read aloud the captions.

What did Johnson do to be elected as a senator from Texas? Texas was a conservative state so Johnson ran for the Senate as a conservative. When Johnson did not have enough votes to win, he contacted an influential man who added several hundred fake votes to the tally sheet to help Johnson win the election. Johnson stopped his opponent from proving the cheating by appealing to a friend in Washington to stop the court case.

How can we know that Johnson was not a true conservative? He had won the election as a New Deal liberal, but Texas was a conservative state. So Johnson ran for the Senate as a conservative. When Johnson was in the Senate, he would talk like a conservative with the conservatives, and he would talk like a liberal with the liberals.

What results from having a leader who keeps changing his political views in order to succeed politically? Answers could include that people might not trust the political leader. People would not know what he believes.

Who would filibuster in order to delay a bill or prevent a bill from being passed? senators

- Invite a student to explain how senators filibuster a bill.

promised to bring the benefits of the New Deal to the voters of Johnson's district in Texas. Johnson said he was the biggest Roosevelt supporter. So the Texan people sent him to Washington.

After more than eleven years as a representative, Johnson became a US senator for Texas. Even though he had won the election as a New Deal liberal, Texas was a conservative state. So Johnson ran for the Senate as a conservative. Still not having enough votes to win, Johnson contacted an influential man who added several hundred fake votes to the tally sheet to

help Johnson win the election. When Johnson's opponent was about to prove this cheating in court, Johnson appealed to a friend in Washington to stop the court case.

Once in the Senate, Johnson worked his way up to the position of majority leader. The majority leader runs the Senate. Johnson was known for getting legislation passed. He knew how to persuade senators to pass the bills he wanted passed. He would talk like a conservative with the conservatives, and he would talk like a liberal with the liberals. He also knew the rules of the Senate better than most senators. He used his knowledge of Senate rules to get his bills passed and to get bills he opposed blocked.

The Civil Rights Bill

Kennedy's Civil Rights Bill was stalled in Congress. Southern Democrats and Johnson knew how to stop these bills. Johnson had been a southern Democratic senator himself. He had even worked to stop other civil rights bills.

He knew the southern Democrats would try to keep the bill backed up in committee. If the bill made it out of committee, they would **filibuster** it. *Filibuster* meant that senators would speak for a long time to delay the bill. Sometimes they would speak so long that they stopped the vote on the bill. A bill could pass with a simple

Lyndon B. Johnson was a descendant of the Johnson family for whom Johnson City, Texas, is named. The family settled in the area as farmers and ranchers during the Civil War.

Because of Kennedy's assassination, Johnson had to take the presidential oath in an unusual way. He was the first President to be sworn in by a woman, Federal District Judge Sarah Hughes. The event took place aboard Air Force One, though not while in flight.

Johnson was known to give gifts frequently. Among those gifts, an electric toothbrush stamped with the presidential seal was common. When asked why he gave that, he replied, "I want people to think of me right away when they wake up and right before they go to bed."

340

The Civil Rights Act of 1964

This act established fairer procedures for voter registration, forbade racial discrimination in public buildings such as restaurants and stores, promoted the desegregation of public schools, authorized withholding federal funds from projects or institutions that discriminated against minorities, and created the Equal Opportunity Commission to ensure that job seekers did not encounter discrimination.

Brown v. the Board of Education

In 1954 the Supreme Court made one of the most significant decisions of the twentieth century. The ruling in the *Brown v. Board of Education* cases said that segregating children by race in public schools was in violation of the Equal Protection Clause of the Fourteenth Amendment. Although the Supreme Court decision did not fully desegregate public schools immediately, it did give support for racial equality and helped to promote equal rights.

By 1964 there were still some schools that were not fully desegregated. At that time, some black parents requested to send their children to an all-white school. The white citizens of the town discriminated against them for their request. This was only one of the injustices that black Americans faced during the 1960s.

majority vote. But a vote of two-thirds of the senators was necessary to end a filibuster. It was difficult to get enough votes to end filibusters against civil rights bills.

But Johnson worked to get the votes. Republicans favored civil rights, but they had concerns about federal regulation of private businesses. The bill was adjusted to meet some of these concerns. Then northern Democrats joined with Republicans to pass the **Civil Rights Act of 1964**.

Just days after Congress passed the Civil Rights Act, police arrested three civil rights workers in Mississippi and led the workers into a Ku Klux Klan ambush. All three workers were killed. Even after the murderers had been found, the state would not bring them to court. As a result, charges had to be filed in a federal court. The United States Supreme Court had to insist that the trial take place. Seven of the murderers were eventually convicted.

The conviction was unusual. It was not common for whites who murdered black people to be convicted. Sadly, the murder of black people who resisted segregation was common.

Murder was not the only weapon used to fight the Civil Rights Act. In one town, some black parents signed a request to allow their students to attend an all-white school. The white students were receiving a better education than the black students were. These parents wanted their children to have a good education. But once the parents' request became known, stores would not sell food to those families. Banks would not allow them to keep accounts. White business owners would no longer hire them.

The Fourteenth Amendment to the Constitution affirmed black citizens' right to vote. But some states had created ways to keep black people from voting. For instance, in an Alabama county, new voters needed to have existing voters testify to their good character. A person could testify only a certain number of times. Many white voters refused to help, so black citizens who wished to vote had difficulty finding someone to testify for them. These state laws continued to keep black people off the voting roles. Sometimes election officials would simply break the law and not allow black people to register to vote. Other times, black people who tried to register were beaten.

In response to these injustices and the murder of three voting-rights advocates in Selma, Alabama, Lyndon Johnson pressed Congress to pass the **Voting Rights Act of 1965**. This act removed barriers designed to keep black citizens from voting. It raised hopes among black Americans that they would soon enjoy equal opportunity.

> What injustices led to the Civil Rights and Voting Rights Acts?

341

The Voting Rights Act of 1965

President Johnson encouraged Congress to pass the Voting Rights Act of 1965, which sent federal officials into states to help register black Americans to vote and outlawed literacy tests for voters. Such tests were often administered only to black Americans to prevent their voting. This measure augmented the provisions of the Twenty-fourth Amendment, ratified in January 1964, which outlawed the use of poll taxes, similarly used to prevent black suffrage. The intent of both the amendment and the Voting Rights Act was to help black Americans receive equal treatment by giving them a greater political voice.

Activity

Martin Luther King Jr.'s Speech

Locate a copy of King's "I Have a Dream" speech. Read aloud the conclusion to King's speech. Guide a discussion of the speech.

Teach for Understanding

What helped pass the Civil Rights Act of 1964? Johnson worked to get the votes. The bill was adjusted to meet Republican concerns about federal regulation of private businesses. Northern Democrats joined with Republicans to pass the bill.

- Guide a discussion of how the Civil Rights Act of 1964 did not stop racial injustice.

In what ways were black citizens kept off the voting roles? State laws continued to keep black people off the voting roles by saying that existing voters had to testify to the good character of black people, but black citizens had difficulty finding someone to testify for them. Sometimes election officials would simply break the law and not register black people. Other times, black people who tried to register to vote were beaten.

What was Johnson's response to these injustices? Lyndon Johnson pressed for Congress to pass the Voting Rights Act of 1965.

- Display Visual 42. Explain that some people believe Johnson's speech to Congress to pass the Voting Rights Act of 1965 was his greatest speech.

Primary Source: Address on the Voting Rights Act

- Direct attention to Activity Manual page 242.
- Read aloud the introduction and the excerpt from President Johnson's address to Congress prior to the passing of the Voting Rights Act.
- Discuss the excerpt.

> Conclude the discussion by asking the question on page 341. Civil rights workers were killed. Stores would not sell food to families if black parents requested to send their children to white schools. Banks would not allow these parents to keep accounts. White customers would no longer hire them for work. In addition, Southern states created ways to keep black people off the voting roles.

Activity Manual

- Guide completion of pages 239–42.

Lesson Focus

- President Johnson oversaw the war on poverty and the war in Vietnam.

Objectives

- Identify the national program led by President Johnson to eliminate poverty
- Recognize the informal name for Johnson's program to end poverty
- Identify the name of the failed attack by the North Vietnamese on South Vietnam

Teacher's Toolkit CD

- Visual 43: *World Map: Vietnam*

Review

- Invite a student to explain why senators filibuster.
- Choose a volunteer to state ways opposition was shown to the Civil Rights Act of 1964.
- Invite a student to tell the name of legislation that removed the barriers that kept black people from voting.

Preparation for Reading

- Generate interest as you direct the students to read the titles and examine the pictures on pages 342–44.
- Guide pronunciation of any unfamiliar words in the lesson.
- Direct the students to read the pages silently to learn what Communists launched in an effort to sweep through South Vietnam. the Tet Offensive

Teach for Understanding

- Direct attention to the picture. Read aloud the caption.

  What did Johnson promise to do if he was reelected? He would create a Great Society.

  What did Johnson announce after his reelection? an unconditional war on poverty in America

  Where did President Johnson plan to get money to fight the war on poverty? Johnson thought the government could use the money from the strong economy.

  What is a reason that the poor did not receive the kind of help that would have reduced poverty in America? Because of the accusation of blaming the poor, poor people did not receive the best kind of help.

  What do both liberals and conservatives say is one of the major reasons that poor people stay poor? the breakup of the family

  What did Johnson ask Congress to do in his war on poverty? to pass a series of bills to create new programs to help the poor

Wars
War on Poverty

Johnson served the last year of John F. Kennedy's term as president. To remain president, Johnson had to run for election in 1964. Johnson promised that he would create a **Great Society** that would attack poverty if he were elected. After his election, Johnson announced an "unconditional **war on poverty** in America."

People in poverty lack the necessities of life. At this time, the American economy was strong. Johnson thought the government could use the money from this strong economy to end poverty. One of Johnson's men thought that poverty could be eliminated in ten years.

Johnson had people study the problem of poverty. One study said that opposition to black civil rights had damaged black families. The report said that children in families without both a father and a mother often stayed poor. It was important for fathers and mothers to be married. It was important for them to stay married. Later studies would find the same to be true of white families as well. The report concluded that the government should find ways to support the rebuilding of the family in America.

But when the report became public, it was accused of blaming the poor for the problem of poverty. Critics of the report argued that poor people have

President Lyndon Johnson visiting with Tom Fletcher on the porch of Fletcher's cabin. As part of his war on poverty, Johnson listens to Fletcher's descriptions of various problems in Martin County, Kentucky, in 1964.

different values from middle-class people. Middle-class people might think it is important for fathers and mothers to remain married. But the critics said poor people might believe differently. The critics said that no one should judge the poor for believing differently.

Both liberals and conservatives today agree that the breakup of the family is one of the major reasons that poor people stay poor. But because of the accusation of blaming the poor, poor people did not receive the best kind of help. They did not receive the help that would have reduced poverty in America.

Instead, Johnson pressed Congress to pass a series of bills to create new programs to help the poor. One of these programs was Medicare. Medicare

342

Background

War on Poverty

In his first State of the Union message, Johnson declared a "war on poverty." Through the newly formed Office of Economic Opportunity (OEO), the government attacked poverty through job-training and job-placement programs; Head Start (a preschool program for children in poor families); and Volunteers in Service to American (VISTA), a sort of domestic Peace Corps in which thousands of enthusiastic young people volunteered to work in government programs helping the poor. The programs of the war on poverty did succeed in raising thousands of people above the poverty level (although the general economic prosperity of the Johnson years might have had much to do with that success).

Christians and Societal Problems

Proverbs 22:3 says that wise people foresee calamity and avoid it. Johnson's Great Society, rather than helping people out of poverty, gave people incentives to not work. In the end, many of Johnson's programs had the unintentional effect of trapping people in poverty. However, God expects His people to help the poor, and He promises to bless

provided government medical insurance for older Americans. But within a decade, older Americans were still spending the same amount of their own money on healthcare. Many doctors would not take Medicare patients. The government paid doctors very little. It also required doctors to fill out lots of forms to receive payment. As a result, the benefits received from medicare were limited.

Another program provided federal money to school districts. The money was intended to help the poor get a better education. But the money was spent ineffectively. The program was not helping the poor as Johnson had intended it to.

These kinds of problems repeated themselves throughout Johnson's war on poverty. The government could not end poverty. Many of Johnson's programs actually made poverty worse. Conservatives and liberals disagreed about the solution. They wanted the government to manage healthcare for all Americans. They also said that more money needed to be spent on schools. Conservatives argued that government programs were now part of the problem.

War in Vietnam

The war on poverty was not Johnson's only war. At the same time, Americans were fighting Communists in Vietnam.

Americans went to Vietnam to stop the spread of Communism. Many people feared that just as one domino knocks down the next, one country after another would fall to Communism if the United States did not fight.

When Johnson became president, a war was under way in Vietnam between the Communists in the North and the democratic Vietnamese in the South. The United States already had soldiers in Vietnam. These soldiers did not fight. They trained the South Vietnamese to fight the Communists.

Johnson slowly sent more and more American soldiers to Vietnam. American soldiers began to participate in the fighting. But Johnson was slow to reveal to the American people how

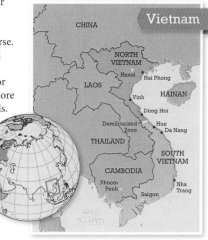

343

What program did the government pass to help older Americans? Medicare

What were some problems with Medicare? Older Americans were still spending the same amount of their own money on healthcare. Many doctors did not take Medicare patients. The state paid doctors very little. It required doctors to fill out lots of forms to receive payment.

How effective was the program that gave federal money to schools? The money that was intended to help the poor get a better education was being spent in other ways.

How successful was Johnson's war on poverty? Many of Johnson's programs actually made poverty worse.

- Direct attention to the map on page 343. Invite the students to use the locator map to find Vietnam.
- Display Visual 43. Locate Vietnam on the map. Invite a student to name the countries surrounding Vietnam.

When Johnson became president, what groups were at war with each other in Vietnam? the Communists in the North and the democratic Vietnamese in the South

What role did American soldiers play in Vietnam? At first the American soldiers trained the South Vietnamese to fight the Communists. But as Johnson sent more and more American soldiers to Vietnam, the American soldiers began to participate in the fighting.

those who do (Psalm 41:1; Proverbs 19:17). Christians should give money, seek opportunities to spend time with the poor, and help them develop skills to earn a living. Christians who do this will see that sin often lies at the root of societal problems, and they may have opportunities to share the gospel.

What is the Difference Between Medicare and Medicaid?

Everyone over age 65 (younger if disabled) qualifies for Medicare, an insurance program that is run by the federal government, regardless of income.

All ages qualify for Medicaid. It is income based. No monthly premiums or co-pays are required. It is state administered with federal regulation.

Discover How God Feels About the Poor

Locate Bible verses about the poor. Read the following verses aloud: Deuteronomy 15:11; Proverbs 19:17; Proverbs 22:9. Guide a discussion of what the verses say about helping the poor.

Teach for Understanding

- Direct attention to the picture. Read the caption aloud.

What did Johnson want people to think about himself and his opponent regarding Vietnam at the time of his reelection? He wanted people to think that his opponent was for war and that he was for peace.

Why did Johnson not want Americans and Congress to think of Vietnam as a big war? He wanted Congress to pass programs for his war on poverty. If Congress realized that Vietnam would be a long and expensive war, then Congress would not pass the war on poverty bills.

After Johnson was re-elected, what did he want the American public to think about the Vietnam War? that all was going well

What was the Tet Offensive? The Communists launched an attack in an attempt to sweep through South Vietnam and conquer it.

What was its outcome? The Tet Offensive failed. The Communists were driven back. Americans knew that the war would not be over quickly. It turned many Americans against the war.

Conclude the discussion by asking the question on page 344. the rebuilding of the family

Activity Manual

- Guide completion of page 243.

Guide a review of important terms, maps, places, and people from each previous lesson. Direct the students to find and read the corresponding entries from the Resource Treasury.

---

deeply the United States was involved in Vietnam.

Johnson was up for election in 1964. Johnson did not want Americans to know that he was getting the country more involved in Vietnam. He wanted people to think that his opponent was for war and that he was for peace.

After he was elected president, Johnson did not want Americans to think of Vietnam as a big war. He wanted Congress to pass programs for his war on poverty. These programs were expensive. If Congress realized that Vietnam would be a long and expensive war, then Congress would not pass the war on poverty bills.

After Johnson was elected, the war became more visible to Americans. But Johnson did not share with the American people the difficulties the United States faced in fighting this war. He wanted the public to think that all was going well.

But in January 1968 the Communists launched an attack called the **Tet Offensive**. They thought they could finally sweep through South Vietnam. They thought they could conquer it. But the Tet Offensive failed. The Communists were driven back. However, Americans now knew that the war would not be over quickly.

Vietnamese soldiers advance along a street towards a building attacked by Viet Cong soldiers during the Tet Offensive in Saigon, Vietnam, in 1968.

The Tet Offensive turned many Americans against the war. Americans began to wonder if the United States was really winning the war. Johnson was not known for always telling the truth. He had not told all of the truth about Vietnam. Some people wondered if the United States was winning at all.

Some Americans argued that the United States should not be fighting Communism. They did not think that Communism was bad. It certainly was not worth fighting against. These people began to protest the war. Other Americans did not want Communism to spread, but they did not think the war in Vietnam was a good idea.

What is important for reducing poverty?

344

Background

The Tet Offensive

Support for the war changed dramatically after the Communists launched the Tet Offensive in January 1968. During the South Vietnamese celebration of Tet, the lunar new year (January 30), the Viet Cong infiltrated the major cities in the South. They smuggled in arms by carrying them into the cities in coffins during funeral processions. On the first day of the new year, 60,000 Viet Cong troops launched attacks on nearly every major city and strategic point in South Vietnam. One force even captured part of the US Embassy for a time. In the weeks that followed the attacks, American and South Vietnamese forces drove back the enemy, recapturing what had been lost and inflicting massive casualties on the enemy.

Militarily, the Tet Offensive was a major failure for the Communists, but it had a dramatic effect on the American public. Television newscasts emphasized only the negative aspects—the suddenness of the attack and the heavy losses—leading many Americans to believe that the Tet Offensive was a Communist victory. The US government, to some extent, reaped what it had sown. Having misled the American people and media about the course of the war, the government now faced the wrath of a public who wanted to know how things could come so close to disaster so suddenly. After the Tet Offensive, many Americans were no longer looking to win the war; they only wanted a way out.

Culture in the 1960s–'70s

The New Left

The war in Vietnam was an effort to protect the freedom of the Vietnamese from Communist dictators. Liberals were in favor of liberty. Conservatives supported liberty too. But conservatives were divided about whether the United States should get involved in foreign wars.

At this time liberalism split between the old liberals and the **New Left**. The New Left formed among college students and some professors. It claimed that Western civilization was unjust and needed to be swept away. The New Left said that the old liberals and the conservatives were all alike. People in both groups held power in government and culture. The New Left wanted to get rid of those who had authority.

The Vietnam War was the focus of many protests. The New Left denied that the United States was protecting freedoms in the war. The New Left said the United States was killing innocent people. The members thought that Communism and Marxism were better than American capitalism. The New Left opposed American efforts to fight Communism.

Counterculture

The New Left protested American life by creating a **counterculture**. The members would not participate in the culture of most Americans. Instead the New Left created a culture to oppose American culture. Both men and women grew their hair long. They wore an unusual style of clothing. They sometimes spoke with crude and foul language. They wanted to provoke people. People who dressed and acted this way were often called hippies.

The counterculture had its own music too: rock 'n' roll. Rock music first emerged in the 1950s, but it became the music of the counterculture in the 1960s. It often celebrated rebellion against authority. These authorities included both the government and parents. The music also celebrated drugs and immorality.

345

Countering the Counterculture

The Bible teaches that people are born corrupt (Psalm 58:3; Romans 5:12), and forsaking possessions or breaking restrictions does nothing to free people from the power of sin. Solving people's problems requires changing their sinful natures through the power of God in salvation (2 Corinthians 5:17).

Activity

Vietnam

Use resources to discover facts about Vietnam today. Ask the students to choose one of the following topics to research: climate, economy, education, government, people, religion. Invite students to share what they learn.

Lesson Focus

- The New Left created a counterculture, and Betty Friedan launched the feminist movement.

Objectives
- Identify groups that the liberals split between during the 1960s
- Identify who said that black people should use force to gain power over white people
- Identify how the New Left protested the establishment
- Identify the founder of the feminist movement

Review

- Invite a student to explain President Johnson's war on poverty and whether it was effective.
- Choose a volunteer to describe Johnson's handling of the Vietnam War.

Preparation for Reading

- Generate interest as you direct the students to read the titles and examine the pictures on pages 345–47.
- Guide pronunciation of any unfamiliar words in the lesson.
- Direct the students to read the pages silently to learn what the New Left thought was better than American capitalism. Communism and Marxism

Teach for Understanding

- Direct attention to the picture. Invite a student to read aloud the signs and suggest what the people are protesting.

  In what way did liberalism split during the time when Americans were divided over involvement in the Vietnam War? Liberalism split between the old liberals and the New Left.

  Who formed the New Left? college students and some professors

  Which groups did the New Left say were all alike? the old liberals and the conservatives

  What did the New Left want to do to the old liberals and conservatives? The New Left wanted to get rid of those who had authority in the government and in the culture.

- Invite a student to describe the counterculture.

Teach for Understanding

What were some things that the counterculture did to oppose the Vietnam War? Protesters filled sidewalks and streets to protest the war. Sometimes protesters took over college administration buildings. Others broke into government offices and stole or destroyed government papers.

What type of warfare did some people in the New Left use? guerilla warfare

How successful was the use of violence in accomplishing New Left purposes? The use of violence did not accomplish their purposes.

- Direct attention to the picture and read aloud the caption.

How did civil rights leaders feel about the race riots in American cities? Civil rights leaders opposed race riots. Martin Luther King Jr. said that protests should be nonviolent.

How were King and his supporters treated when they marched in protest against segregation and injustice? They were beaten and jailed.

How did King and his supporters act when they were beaten and jailed? They did not fight back.

Who said that black Americans were superior to white people and that black people should gain power over white Americans by force? Malcolm X and Stokely Carmichael

---

People in the counterculture said drugs like marijuana, LSD, and heroin gave people insight into life. They said drugs promoted love instead of war. But these drugs were addictive. In reality, drug addiction ruined people's lives.

Violence

The counterculture opposed the Vietnam War. It called for peace instead of war. Protesters would fill sidewalks and streets. Sometimes protesters took over college administration buildings. Others broke into government offices and stole or destroyed government papers.

Some in the New Left did not think peaceful protests would work. They believed that only violence would topple those in control of the US government. They planned to wage guerilla warfare against the United States government. They set bombs at places such as police stations. They even planted a bomb at the Pentagon. These violent groups never attracted as many followers as other protests. In the end, they failed to accomplish their purposes.

Race riots in American cities produced more violence at this time. Civil rights leaders such as Martin Luther King Jr. opposed race riots. King

said that protests against segregation and injustice should be nonviolent. When King and his supporters marched, they often suffered violence. They were beaten and jailed. But they did not fight back. As a result American views about segregation began to change. They saw the injustices black people faced, and they began to call for these injustices to cease. The civil rights and voting rights laws were passed. King and many other black Americans wanted to be a part of American culture. Civil rights laws would help them.

Malcolm X and **Stokely Carmichael** declared that black people should remain separate from white people. They said that black people were superior to white people and should gain power over white people. And they should take this power by force.

A building burns during a race riot in Detroit, Michigan, in 1967.

346

Background

Challenges on the Home Front

As the war continued, political activists who strongly opposed the war gained increasing public attention. A "New Left" emerged. On the one hand, the New Left was energized by moral concerns. They were active in seeking to advance civil rights for black Americans and to reduce poverty. They also raised moral objections to the way Americans fought in Vietnam. Yet they ignored clear evidence that the Vietnamese Communists had killed thousands of civilians and placed thousands more in labor camps. By burning flags and draft cards, fleeing the country to avoid the draft, and participating in anti-war demonstrations, the New Left seemed anti-American even to many liberals.

The antiwar movement was an outpouring of a radical change in thinking and morals among American young people. But in many ways it was the bitter fruit of their parents' vain search for happiness through hard work and material wealth. The counterculture looked for happiness by throwing off respect for authority and turning to drugs and immorality.

Feminism and the Search for Happiness

Betty Freidan opened *The Feminine Mystique* with a paragraph that raises the same issues raised by Solomon in Ecclesiastes:

"The problem lay buried, unspoken, for many years in the minds of American women. It was a strange stirring, a sense of dissatisfaction, a yearning that women suffered in the middle of the twentieth century in the United States. Each suburban wife struggled with it alone. As she made the beds, shopped for groceries, matched slipcover material, ate peanut butter sandwiches with her children, chauffeured Cub Scouts and Brownies, lay beside her husband at night—she was afraid to ask even of herself the silent question—'Is this all?'"

Historian Claire Bond Potter comments: "What Friedan describes is a set of feelings that women can't put into words. That they are prosperous, they have children, they have husbands. In other words, they have everything that they have been told by commercial culture that they're supposed to want, and yet they're still unhappy and they don't know why."

Americans saw the results of this violence as race riots erupted in cities like Los Angeles, Chicago, and Detroit. Martin Luther King Jr. argued that the rioters did not represent the majority of black Americans. He was right. In fact, the rioters often harmed black businesses and neighborhoods. Nonetheless, the news coverage given to these new spokesmen and riots fueled the conflict.

Betty Friedan leads a feminist march in the 1960s.

Feminism

For many Americans the 1950s and early 1960s were a prosperous time. Americans were living the American dream. They had nice houses and nice cars. They could buy modern gadgets that made life easier. But as Ecclesiastes teaches, prosperity without God does not satisfy. Many Americans were not satisfied despite all they owned.

People pointed to various causes for their dissatisfaction. For example, **Betty Friedan** argued that American women were dissatisfied because they were trapped in the role of homemaker. She launched the **feminist movement**.

Feminists pushed for easier divorce laws to free women from unwanted marriages. They said that the role of housewife was demeaning to women and denied them the opportunity to reach their full potential. They pressed for more women to work outside the home and to work the same jobs that men worked. The feminists did point out some ways that women were being treated unjustly by men. They pressed for changes that would correct these injustices. Sadly, many feminists also came to support abortion rights.

But many American women did not view easy divorce and pressure to work as an improvement. They wanted to stay home, raise their children, and love their husbands. They did not like pressure from feminists to free themselves from marriage and family. Christian Americans especially realized the great wrong of killing unborn children. Christians believe it is not right to kill a child so that the mother can lead the life she wants.

> What actions of the New Left were contrary to the Bible?

347

Teach for Understanding

What did Martin Luther King Jr. argue about rioters? King argued that the rioters did not represent the majority of black Americans.

- **Direct attention to the picture on page 347. Read aloud the caption.**

Why were many Americans dissatisfied despite living in a prosperous time? Prosperity without God does not satisfy.

What did Betty Friedan argue about the satisfaction of women? She argued that American women were dissatisfied because they were oppressed by men.

Where does real satisfaction come from? It is a gift from God (Ecclesiastes 2:24–26).

- **Choose a student to describe the feminist movement.**

How did many American women feel about feminism in spite of the feminists pointing out injustices toward women? Many American women did not view easy divorce and pressure to work as an improvement. Christian Americans especially realized the great wrong of killing unborn children.

Conclude the discussion by asking the question on page 347. Protestors showed rebellion by taking over college administration buildings. Others broke into government offices and stole or destroyed government papers. Some used guerrilla warfare against the United States government.

Activity Manual

- Guide completion of pages 244–45.

Activities

Learn About Young People Coming to Christ

Explain that evangelists, pastors, Sunday School teachers, and youth workers were busy teaching God's Word in the 1960s and 1970s, a time that was marked by war and turmoil. Christian workers saw young people become Christians or rededicate their lives to Christ. Some "baby boomers" headed off to Christian colleges. The greatest hope for American young people is found in dedicated faith in Jesus Christ as Savior.

Invite an evangelist, missionary, or youth pastor to speak about reaching young people for Christ today.

The Virtuous Woman

Read Proverbs 31:10–31. Discuss how the Bible describes a woman who fears the Lord. Compare the virtuous woman with the feminist movement.

Student Text pages 348–51
Activity Manual pages 246–47

Lesson Focus

- Nixon's presidency faced many difficulties.

Objectives

- Describe the economy under President Nixon
- Identify the purpose for the Environmental Protection Agency
- Evaluate the *Roe v. Wade* Supreme Court ruling
- Determine whether Nixon's presidency was conservative

Review

- Invite a student to explain the New Left and the counterculture.
- Invite a student to explain what many American women felt toward feminism.

Preparation for Reading

- Generate interest as you direct the students to read the title and examine the pictures on pages 348–51.
- Guide pronunciation of any unfamiliar words in the lesson.
- Direct the students to read the pages silently to learn the result of a program began by Kennedy that triumphed during Johnson's first year as president. Americans landed on the moon.

Teach for Understanding

- Direct attention to the picture and the How It Was box. Read aloud the story. Invite volunteers to explain what they think it would be like to actually step on the moon.

Who ran against Johnson for the Democratic nomination in 1968? Eugene McCarthy, Robert Kennedy, and George Wallace

What candidate formed the American party? George Wallace

Why did Johnson declare in March of 1968 that he would not run for reelection? Johnson could see that he was unpopular.

Who joined the race when Johnson withdrew? Hubert Humphrey

How It Was

It was July 16, 1969. All over America, people gazed at their televisions as three astronauts climbed into the spacecraft. *Apollo 11* lifted off, and the astronauts fired the engines to escape earth's gravity. *Apollo 11* was headed to the moon!

The rocket took three days to reach the moon. Commander Neil Armstrong finally found a safe landing spot when the lunar module, the *Eagle*, was almost out of fuel.

"We copy you down, *Eagle*," came the message from Mission Control in Texas.

"Tranquility Base here," Armstrong said. "The *Eagle* has landed." Americans were on the moon!

Six hours after landing, Armstrong stepped out onto the moon. "That's one small step for a man, one giant leap for mankind," he said.

The astronauts left an American flag on the moon. They also left a plaque inscribed with the names of the *Apollo 11* astronauts and President Nixon, along with one simple statement: "We came in peace for all mankind."

Nixon and the Silent Majority

1968 Election

Going into the election, the Democratic Party was deeply divided. The current president, Johnson, was a Democrat. He was responsible for expanding the war in Vietnam. But an increasing number of Democrats now opposed the war. Eugene McCarthy, a senator, ran against Johnson as an antiwar Democrat. Robert Kennedy, John F. Kennedy's brother, also joined the race.

Since the end of Reconstruction, the southern states had been firmly Democratic. But Johnson had become a supporter of the civil rights movement. Johnson found himself challenged by George Wallace, a man who still believed in segregation. He split away to form the American Party.

Johnson could see that he was unpopular even in parts of his own party. He declared in March 1968 that he would not run for reelection. When Johnson made this decision, his vice president, Hubert Humphrey,

348

Background

Nixon and the Silent Majority

In a speech during his first year in office, Richard Nixon appealed to "the great silent majority of . . . Americans" for support. With the term *silent majority*, the president affirmed the belief that most Americans were not violent radicals wholly discontent with peace and order. Nixon claimed that he represented the interests of that silent majority and that his administration would represent their values. Many writers called Nixon's statement an appeal to "Middle America," the views of the dominant middle class.

joined the race. The Democrats chose Humphrey as their candidate.

The year 1968 was a difficult one for Americans. In April 1968 a gunman shot Martin Luther King Jr. as he stood on a balcony outside his hotel room. Then in June a gunman shot Robert Kennedy as he was leaving a campaign stop. Americans began to wonder what was happening to their country. National leaders were gunned down. Rioters burned American cities and looted businesses. The war in Vietnam seemed endless. And the economy was not doing as well as it had been at the beginning of the decade.

The Republicans chose Richard Nixon as their candidate. He had been Eisenhower's vice president. Nixon appealed to what he called the **"silent majority."** He knew that most Americans were not represented by the protesters seen on television. He promised to represent this "silent majority." He promised to find a way to end the war in Vietnam. But he also said the United States would not just run away. It would secure "peace with honor." Nixon won the election.

Nixon's presidency would face many difficulties, but in his first year, the United States saw the triumph of a program begun by Kennedy and Johnson. Americans landed men on the moon. Astronaut **Michael Collins** piloted the command module, *Columbia*. As it neared the moon,

Neil Armstrong and his copilot, **Buzz Aldrin,** took a separate lunar module to the moon's surface. The astronauts spent two and a half hours walking on the moon. They took photographs and set up research equipment. With television cameras in place, the world was able to watch this milestone in history.

Poverty and the Economy

Nixon did not approve of Johnson's War on Poverty. Nixon knew that the program was expensive and was not working well. Conservatives were especially concerned that welfare affected American families unfairly.

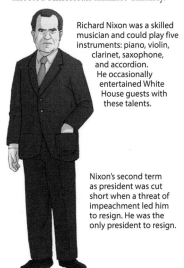

Richard Nixon was a skilled musician and could play five instruments: piano, violin, clarinet, saxophone, and accordion. He occasionally entertained White House guests with these talents.

Nixon's second term as president was cut short when a threat of impeachment led him to resign. He was the only president to resign.

349

Teach for Understanding

What two fatal events happened in April and June in 1968? A gunman shot Martin Luther King Jr.; a gunman shot Robert Kennedy.

What was the economy like by the 1970s? The economy was not doing as well as it had been at the beginning of the decade.

Who did the Republicans choose for their candidate during this difficult time in 1968? Richard Nixon

Which group of people did Nixon appeal to? the silent majority

What is meant by the "silent majority"? Nixon was referring to most Americans who were not represented by the protesters seen on television.

What did Nixon promise about the Vietnam War? He promised to find a way to end the war in Vietnam

• Direct attention to the picture. Read aloud the information.

What was the first triumph in Nixon's presidency? Americans landed men on the moon.

How did Nixon feel about Johnson's war on poverty? Nixon did not approve.

Activity

Lunar Landing Display
Use resources to learn more about the first landing on the moon. Display information and pictures.

Teach for Understanding

What was an example of how welfare only helped some families in need? Unmarried women with children received money from the government, but poor families with two parents did not.

How did Nixon deal with Johnson's poverty programs? Nixon expanded many of the poverty programs that Johnson had started.

What are some ways that help people defeat poverty in their lives? Answers could include getting an education, working hard, and using resources wisely.

- Direct attention to the infograph. Read aloud the caption. Discuss inflation.

What effect did Nixon's freeze on prices and wages have on the economy? The freeze did not halt inflation.

Did the economy improve when Congress passed Nixon's budget to spend a lot of money? The government spending did not improve the economy.

As inflation increases, the purchasing power of money decreases.

For example, unmarried women with children received money from the government, but poor families with two parents did not.

Nixon came up with a new plan. In his plan, every poor family would receive a certain amount of money from the government. Liberals opposed Nixon's plan. They said he was not giving out enough money. Conservatives also opposed Nixon's plan. They said it would grow the power of the national government. Liberals and conservatives together defeated Nixon's plan. Nixon ended up expanding many of the poverty programs that Johnson had started.

By the 1970s, the economy was slowing down again. People were losing their jobs. **Inflation** was also becoming a problem. Inflation is when there is more **currency** per person. This makes money worth less, and the prices for goods rise. When prices rise, the same amount of money will not buy as many goods.

Some people wanted the government to stop inflation. Nixon had said earlier that the government should not interfere with the wages that businesses pay their workers. It should not interfere with the prices that they set. He had said such meddling never helped the economy. But now he thought that something must be done. He issued an executive order that prices and wages would be frozen for three months. He found that his earlier idea was correct. The freeze did not halt inflation.

Nixon had also said earlier that more government spending would not fix the economy. But with a reelection looming, he believed he needed to try something. He presented to Congress a budget in which the federal government spent a great deal of money. He thought spending money might help the economy. Again, Nixon's earlier idea was correct. The government spending did not improve the economy. The American economy would struggle throughout the 1970s.

The Environment

In the 1970s, many Americans began to be concerned about pollution.

350

Background

The Environmental Protection Agency

During the 1970s, a growing number of people voiced concern about the effects of industrial development on the environment. Beginning in the 1960s, the environmental movement—composed of disparate groups including pantheists, Communists, and antihuman organizations—began to sound warnings about industrial pollution of the water and air, particularly pollution caused by automobiles. Under pressure from these groups, Congress passed a number of laws that regulated pollution. In 1970, Congress established the Environmental Protection Agency to oversee and coordinate environmental regulations. The main acts to combat pollution were the Clean Air Act (1970, amended 1977) and the Clean Water Act (1977).

Those actions helped reduce pollution of the environment, but they also increased demands on the nation's energy resources. Many industries, for example, began to switch their power sources from highly pollutant coal to oil, further straining American oil resources. Likewise, regulations to reduce air pollution by cars required adding emission-control devices, which reduced pollution but also lowered fuel efficiency.

Polluted air and polluted water were real concerns. For instance, in the late 1960s parts of a polluted Lake Erie caught fire. Some parts of the lake were considered dead. Waste from sewers and industrial plants flowed into the water. Plants and animals could not survive in the polluted water.

Many conservatives agreed that pollution was a problem. They wanted to limit pollution. But they were suspicious of environmentalists who were liberals. Conservatives feared that these environmentalists were claiming that some problems were worse than they really were. For example, environmentalists incorrectly warned that the world had too many people and that the population would lead to worldwide starvation. The environmentalists said that conserving nature was not enough. They called for a revolution that would change the way people lived. Some environmentalists thought it might be necessary to halt economic growth to save the environment. But such changes would harm many people.

Nixon responded by creating the **Environmental Protection Agency**. This agency would research environmental problems. It would also create rules to try to solve these problems. Congress passed laws to limit the pollution of air and water.

Roe v. Wade

In 1973 the Supreme Court claimed the Constitution provided a right to privacy. The court said that this right to privacy made the killing of unborn babies legal. This decision was known as *Roe v. Wade*. Many Christians were heartbroken. Never before had America allowed murder to take place on such a large scale. This decision revealed that Americans had stooped to a very low point in their evaluation of human life.

At the time, important Democrats and Republicans opposed abortion. But feminism and the New Left came to control the Democratic Party. The Democratic Party gradually became almost entirely pro-abortion. Republicans attracted conservative Christians to their party by opposing abortion.

Pro-life protestors

What did President Nixon do about poverty?

351

Activity

Inflation

Discuss how families could survive during times of inflation, job loss, or other financial difficulties. Include ideas such as putting aside money for "a rainy day" and finding ways to use less money and other resources.

Teach for Understanding

What happened that showed that polluted water was a real concern? A part of polluted Lake Erie caught fire. Plants and animals could not survive in the polluted water.

Why did conservatives fear the environmentalists? They were suspicious of environmentalists who were liberals. Conservatives feared that these environmentalists were claiming that some problems were worse than they really were.

What was Nixon's response to the growing concerns about polluting the environment? He created the Environmental Protection Agency.

What was the job of the Environmental Protection Agency? The agency would research environmental problems. It would create rules to try to solve these problems.

● Direct attention to the picture on page 351. Read aloud the signs in the picture.

In 1973 what did the Supreme Court claim was legal because of the Constitutional right to privacy? abortion, the killing of unborn humans

What was the decision called? *Roe v. Wade*

● Read Psalm 139:16–17 and Exodus 20:13. Discuss the *Roe v. Wade* decision in light of Scripture. Explain that the students will be evaluationg this decision in the Activity Manual.

Was President Nixon a conservative president? Answers could include that Nixon was not conservative when he increased government spending.

Conclude the discussion by asking the question on page 253. Nixon expanded many of the poverty programs that Johnson had started.

Activity Manual

● Guide completion of pages 246–47.

Lesson

140

Student Text pages 352–55
Activity Manual page 248

Lesson Focus

- The Vietnam War came to an end, and Nixon resigned the presidency.

Objectives
- Examine events that led to the end of the Vietnam War
- Identify the circumstances of the Cold War
- Relate events leading to Watergate and the end of Nixon's presidency

Review

- Invite a student to explain how Nixon handled the economy and whether his ideas were successful.
- Invite a student to describe Nixon's way of handling poverty and whether he was able to end poverty.
- Invite a student to explain what Nixon did to protect the environment.

Preparation for Reading

- Generate interest as you direct the students to read the titles and examine the pictures on pages 352–55.
- Guide pronunciation of any unfamiliar words in the lesson.
- Direct the students to read the pages silently to find out what replaced the Republic of China after it was removed from the United Nations. the Communist People's Republic of China

Teach for Understanding

- Direct attention to the pictures. Read aloud the captions.

  During Nixon's presidency what did most Americans think about the war in Vietnam? Most Americans thought the war in Vietnam was a big mistake.

  What were the problems with the way Americans were fighting the war? In the course of fighting, villages would be destroyed. Many Vietnamese people suffered. American soldiers were frustrated because they could not tell the difference between the friendly Vietnamese and the Communists. Sometimes the villages were traps for the soldiers.

  What happened in My Lai? American soldiers killed almost everybody in the village even though there were no Communists present.

- Explain that these men had been in the field much longer than was normal for soldiers. They had seen many people die. The soldiers were stressed when they reached My Lai. The Viet Cong had infiltrated villages before and had pretended to be villagers, so there were some reasons that the soldiers started fighting. But in the end, they were just killing people that they should have been protecting.

356

The End of the Vietnam War and the End of Nixon's Presidency
Vietnam War

The Vietnam War was one of Richard Nixon's biggest challenges. Opposition to the war had grown. Now even a portion of the Democratic Party opposed the war. Some senators were part of this strong opposition. Most Americans thought that the war in Vietnam was a big mistake.

Nixon believed that the United States needed to end the war. But Nixon knew he could not end it right away. The United States needed to be seen as strong around the world. Otherwise other nations would think they could attack the United States or its allies.

In the months before Nixon was sworn in as president, a new general took charge of the war. He changed the way the war was being fought.

The previous general had soldiers sweep through areas to clear them of Vietnamese Communists. Often they would fight with Communists in Vietnamese villages. In the course of the fighting, the village would be destroyed. Many Vietnamese people suffered even though the United States was there to defend these Vietnamese. American soldiers were often frustrated because there was no way to tell the difference between the friendly Vietnamese and the Communists. Sometimes the soldiers found villages to be traps.

In March of 1968 one unit of American soldiers entered the village of My Lai. They killed almost everybody in the village even though there were no Communists present. The army tried to cover up the massacre. But when the news came out, Americans were angered. This massacre deepened opposition to the war.

People crossing from Laos into South Vietnam were helped by South Vietnam forces and protected by American tanks and artillery.

A young American marine carries an elderly woman during the Vietnam War.

352

Background

Public Perception of My Lai

In response to the My Lai massacre, the military convicted only one man, William Calley. Second Lieutenant Calley had directed his men to sweep through My Lai and kill the villagers. One of the soldiers in his command testified that Calley killed some villagers himself. These villagers were not military targets; they were unarmed civilians.

Americans in general were appalled that American troops could commit such a slaughter, but for a variety of reasons a large segment of the population sympathized with Calley. Many believed that the army was making him a scapegoat to cover for other officers or that the antiwar movement was persecuting him in anger over the whole war effort. And many agreed that Calley was guilty but were angry that no one else was convicted.

From a Christian perspective, the massacre of hundreds of civilians simply cannot be excused. Christians must be careful not to let their political concerns override the Bible's moral teaching.

Vietnam War

The new general changed the way Americans fought the war. He did not have soldiers hunt for the Communists. Americans now provided security to villages and towns against the Communists. They found the supply routes the Communists were using and began to destroy them.

Nixon also decided that the United States should have the South Vietnamese do more of the fighting. The United States gave the South Vietnamese weapons and equipment. The South Vietnamese military was built up. Now the United States could begin to bring its soldiers home. Nixon did this gradually throughout his first term as president.

After he was reelected in 1972, Nixon made a final push toward

peace. But the peace talks with the North Vietnamese Communists went nowhere. Nixon ended the talks and began a massive bombing campaign. He bombed military buildings and equipment in North Vietnam. This strategy brought the North Vietnamese back to the peace talks. On January 27, 1973, the United States signed a peace agreement with the North Vietnamese. According to the agreement, the North Vietnamese had to return American prisoners of war. The United States agreed to pull out of Vietnam. The United States promised South Vietnam that it would continue to supply it with military equipment and supplies.

The Cold War

Nixon also wanted to bring about a thaw in the Cold War. The Soviet Union and China were the two major Communist nations. Nixon wanted to make both friendlier toward the United States.

The United States did not recognize Communist China as the true government of China. The United States said that the Republic of China was the true government of China. Previously, the Communists had seized all of mainland China. The Republic of China kept only the island of Taiwan. The Republic of China also held an important place in the United Nations.

Nixon was the first US president to visit Communist China. He wanted

353

How did a new general change how the Americans fought the war? He did not have soldiers hunt for the Communists. Americans now provided security to villages and towns against the Communists. They found the supply routes the Communists were using and began to destroy them.

How did the United States help the Vietnamese do more of the fighting? The United States built up the South Vietnamese military by giving them weapons and equipment.

- Direct attention to the map. Choose a volunteer to explain the meaning of the key. Invite the students to locate areas on the map that are described in the key.

What did Nixon do to make peace with the North Vietnamese? He made peace talks.

What did Nixon do when peace talks with the North Vietnamese were going nowhere? Nixon ended the peace talks and began a massive bombing campaign.

What resulted from the bombing? The North Vietnamese came back to the peace talks. The United States signed a peace agreement with the North Vietnamese.

What agreements were made by the United States and the North Vietnamese? The North Vietnamese agreed to return American prisoners of war. The United States agreed to pull out of Vietnam. The United States agreed to continue to supply South Vietnam with military equipment and supplies.

Which two Communist nations did Nixon want to make more friendly toward the United States? China and Russia

- What do you think is the most important reason that Nixon wanted China and Russia to be more friendly with the United States? Answers could include that Nixon wanted to reduce the threat of war from China and Russia toward the United States.

Activity

Honor Vietnam Veterans

Many Vietnam veterans returned home discouraged after fighting an unpopular war. Invite relatives of students who fought in Vietnam to a special lunch or program to honor them. Decorate with American flags and streamers. Write notes of gratitude to the Vietnam veterans for their military service.

Lesson

140

Teach for Understanding

● Direct attention to the picture. Read aloud the caption.

Why did Nixon visit Communist China? He wanted the United States and China to trade goods. He thought trade would make China less likely to go to war with the United States because China's economy needed the trade.

What did the United States have to admit in order to trade? The United States had to say that Communists had set up a true government.

After the Republic of China was removed from the United Nations, what nation replaced it? the Communist People's Republic of China

What did the treaties that the United States signed with the Soviet Union put limits on? The treaties limited the number of missiles each nation could have. They also limited the missile defenses that each nation could have.

Who did Richard Nixon run against in the 1972 election? George McGovern

What dirty tricks did Nixon have his supporters play in order for Nixon to win the election? He had supporters write letters to news magazines. These letters made false charges against people who opposed him.

Who were the "plumbers"? The people in the White House that Nixon gave permission to in order for them to break the law to help him get reelected. The "plumbers" spied on the Democratic Party's headquarters in the Watergate Hotel.

What did Nixon do when he found out the "plumbers" had been caught? He tried to cover it up.

President Nixon visiting the Great Wall of China. The Secretary of State William P. Rogers is on his left.

the United States and China to trade goods. He thought trade would make China less likely to go to war with the United States because China's economy needed the trade. But in order to trade, the United States had to say that the Communists had set up a true government. The Republic of China was removed from the United Nations, and the Communist People's Republic of China took its place in the United Nations. However, the United States did tell the Republic of China that it would defend Taiwan from invasion by the Communist Chinese.

Nixon also signed treaties with the Soviet Union. These treaties limited the number of missiles each nation could have. They also limited the missile defenses that each nation could have.

Watergate

In the 1972 election, Richard Nixon ran against George McGovern. McGovern was a Democrat who supported the New Left. McGovern was far too radical for most of the nation. Nixon won reelection overwhelmingly. He lost only Massachusetts and Washington, DC.

But Nixon was worried that his opponents would play dirty tricks on him to steal the election. So Nixon played dirty tricks himself. He had supporters write letters to news magazines. These letters made false charges against people who opposed him. He also gave some people in the White House permission to break the law to help him get reelected. This group called themselves the "plumbers."

354

Background

Nixon Diplomacy with the Soviet Union

At least in part because of his overtures to China, Nixon was able to win some concessions from the Soviet Union. Through the influence of Nixon and Henry Kissinger, his secretary of state, the United States entered a period of detente (day TAHNT), a relaxation of the tension that had existed between the two nations since World War II. In the Strategic Arms Limitations Talks (SALT), the United States and the USSR agreed to limit the number of missiles and warheads each nation had. Nixon also arranged the sale of large amounts of grain to the Soviets. Americans watched in surprise as Nixon, the former anti-Communist "cold warrior," did more to improve relations between the United States and Communist nations than any other president. Under Nixon, the United States government actively sought to develop friendly relationships with repressive Communist regimes.

Billy Graham

What: evangelist
When: 1918 to the present
Where: North Carolina

In the 1960s and '70s, Billy Graham was America's best-known evangelist. He had become close friends with both Lyndon Johnson and Richard Nixon. Initially, he supported the Vietnam War, but later he began to doubt its wisdom. He also strongly supported Nixon during the Watergate affair until it became obvious that Nixon had lied. Graham later said he should have stayed out of politics. His main mission was to preach the gospel. Graham attracted many people to listen to his preaching. Many people responded to his appeals to receive the gospel. Nevertheless, a number of Christian leaders were concerned about Graham's ministry because he was willing to partner with those who denied the gospel. Still, Billy Graham remains one of the most significant religious figures of the 20th century.

The "plumbers" decided to spy on the Democratic Party's headquarters. These headquarters were in the Watergate Hotel. But their break-in was sloppy. They were caught. No one knows if Nixon knew about the spy operation before it happened. But when Nixon found out it had gone wrong, he tried to cover it up.

Nixon was reelected by a wide margin. But reporters and Congress began to investigate Nixon's cover-up. Nixon fiercely opposed their investigation. But his lies came to light anyway.

The House of Representatives determined that Nixon had acted as a criminal. He tried to stop justice from taking place by not giving Congress the records that it had a right to demand. The House of Representatives moved to impeach the president. Nixon resigned from the presidency, however, before the House actually voted to impeach him.

> What change in strategy improved American fighting in Vietnam?

355

Billy Graham

The first full-time evangelist for Youth for Christ was Billy Graham, who gained national fame after receiving positive attention by the press during his 1949 Los Angeles crusade. Graham also became the center of the major post–World War II dispute in Fundamentalist Christianity. In 1957 Graham accepted the sponsorship of liberal Protestants in a New York City crusade. Graham and his supporters claimed that such a move would help bring Fundamentalism into the mainstream of public life and allow it to build bridges to liberal Christianity. However, some Christian leaders refused to associate with Graham because of this issue. Having come through the fierce struggles with modernism in the 1920s, staunchly Fundamentalist Christians would not compromise their faith by joining with religious liberals. Protestants who accepted Graham's cooperation with liberal churches adopted the label "new evangelicals." Those who rejected Graham's actions kept the name "Fundamentalist."

Activity

The Billy Graham Library

Visit the Billy Graham Library website. Visit bjupress.com/resources for a possible link to the website. Discover activities and exhibits at the library.

Teach for Understanding

- Invite students to share what they know about Billy Graham.
- Direct attention to the Biography box and read aloud the information.
- Choose a volunteer to state two things that Billy Graham changed his mind about and why his views changed.
- Invite a student to tell what Billy Graham realized he should have done rather than getting involved in political matters. preach the gospel

  What was the result of Graham's preaching the gospel? Many people received the gospel.

  After reelection, how did Nixon act when reporters and Congress began to investigate his cover up? He fiercely opposed their investigation.

  What did Nixon refuse to give to Congress? records that they had a right to demand

  What action did the House of Representatives take? It moved to impeach the president.

  What did Nixon do before they could vote to impeach him? He resigned.

- Direct attention to the political cartoon. Invite a student to explain the meaning of the cartoon.

> Conclude the discussion by asking the question on page 355. Americans provided security to villages and towns against the Communists. They found the supply routes the Communists were using and began to destroy them.

Activity Manual

- Guide completion of page 248.

Lesson Focus

- Gerald Ford became president at a very difficult time.

Objectives
- Relate how Gerald Ford became president
- Describe the economic challenges Ford faced as president
- Examine the Communist takeover of Vietnam and Cambodia
- Create a budget

Teacher's Toolkit CD
- Instructional Aid 60: *Creating a Budget*
- Visual 43: *World Map: Vietnam*

Review

- Choose a volunteer to explain what the peace agreement between the United States and the North Vietnamese required of each country.
- Ask a student to relate what Nixon did to "thaw" the Cold War with China and with the Soviet Union.
- Invite a student to explain how Nixon's presidency ended.

Preparation for Reading

- Generate interest as you direct the students to read the titles and examine the pictures on pages 356–58.
- Guide pronunciation of any unfamiliar words in the lesson.
- Direct the students to read the pages silently to learn what is meant by a government deficit. A government deficit occurs when the government is spending far more money than it is bringing in by taxes.

Teach for Understanding

- Direct attention to the picture. Read aloud the caption.

How did Gerald Ford become president of the United States? President Nixon's vice president had resigned. Nixon nominated Gerald Ford to be the new vice president, and Congress approved Ford by a majority vote. In a little less than a year later, Nixon resigned. Ford became the president of the United States.

Why was this a very difficult time for Ford to become president? Never before had the vice president and president resigned in scandal.

Why did Ford come under sharp criticism after being so well liked by both Democrats and Republicans? He pardoned Nixon.

Why was Ford willing to take criticism? to do what was best for the nation

- Do you think Ford did or did not do the right thing when he pardoned Nixon? Why

Gerald Ford was more than a politician. He was a national football champion in college, a forest ranger, and serviceman on a Navy aircraft carrier in World War II.

When he took the presidency after Nixon's resignation, Ford said, "I assume the Presidency under extraordinary circumstances. . . . This is an hour of history that troubles our minds and hurts our hearts."

Gerald R. Ford
Becoming President

When Nixon resigned, **Gerald R. Ford** became president. Ford became president in a different way than ever had been done before. He had served in the House of Representatives for twenty-five years. He was the leader of the Republican minority in the House.

But before Richard Nixon resigned the presidency, his vice president resigned. The vice president had accepted large bribes while serving as governor of Maryland. He had also avoided paying some of his taxes.

The Twenty-Fifth Amendment to the Constitution tells Americans how to replace a vice president. The president nominates a new vice president. Congress must approve the nomination by majority votes. Ford was approved by a majority vote.

In a little less than a year later, Nixon resigned. Ford became the president of the United States. He became president at a very difficult time. Never before had the vice president and president resigned in scandal. Ford stepped into his new office with humility. He also showed great ability to take charge quickly as president. He made the transition smoothly, which took great skill, though it was not widely noticed at the time.

Ford was well liked by both Republicans and Democrats. But he came under sharp criticism when he pardoned Nixon. The pardon covered any crimes Nixon "committed or may have committed" while president. Ford knew he would be criticized for pardoning Nixon. But he also knew that the investigations and trials would stretch on for years. He thought this long process would only further hurt and divide the nation. Ford was willing to take the criticism to do what he thought was best for the nation.

356

The Economy

When Ford became president, the American economy was struggling. The government was spending far more money than it was bringing in by taxes. This situation is called a **deficit**. In addition, prices were rising, but Americans' paychecks were not increasing. In fact, the number of people losing their jobs was increasing too.

At first Ford proposed a tax increase. He thought increased taxes would help the government reduce the deficit. He also thought higher taxes would stop prices from rising.

But some of Ford's advisers told him that he should cut the amount of money the government spent. They also said he should cut taxes. If he cut taxes, people would have more money to spend, and the economy would improve.

Congress did pass a tax cut, but it was far smaller than Ford had wanted. Congress also refused to make any further cuts in spending. The economy did not improve.

Vietnam

The United States had made promises to South Vietnam before leaving the country. Nixon had promised that the United States would continue to send supplies to South Vietnam. The

South Vietnamese needed barbed wire, sand bags, and other supplies.

President Ford went to Congress to ask for the money to send these supplies. But Congress refused to spend more money on Vietnam. South Vietnam fell to the Communists.

The fall came quickly. The Americans still had an embassy in the capital city of Saigon. American businessmen worked in South Vietnam. Many South Vietnamese had worked for the Americans during the war.

Soon the North Vietnamese were about to take the city of Saigon. Americans and those who worked for them came flooding to the US embassy. They were looking for a way of escape. Helicopters from US Navy ships landed on the US embassy roof all day long. The helicopters took South Vietnamese and American people to the safety of

US troops delivering supplies to the South Vietnamese

357

What was the economy like for Americans when Gerald Ford became president? The American economy was struggling. The government was spending far more money than it was bringing in by taxes, creating a deficit. Prices were rising, but Americans' paychecks were not increasing. The number of people losing their jobs was increasing.

What did some of Ford's advisors tell him to do about the economy? The advisors told him that he should cut the amount of money the government spent. They said he should also cut taxes.

How did Congress react to these recommendations? Congress passed a tax cut that was smaller than Ford had wanted. Congress refused to make any further cuts in spending.

What was the outcome in regard to improving the economy? The economy did not improve.

What had Nixon promised to South Vietnam? The United States would continue to send supplies to South Vietnam.

- Direct attention to the picture. Read aloud the caption.

What were some of the supplies that the South Vietnamese needed? barbed wire, sand bags, and other supplies

Why was President Ford unable to continue sending supplies to the South Vietnamese? Congress refused to spend more money on Vietnam.

What happened to South Vietnam? It fell to the Communists.

Where did the United States still have an embassy in Vietnam? in Saigon, the capital city

- Display Visual 43. Locate Saigon on the map.

What did the American businessmen and the South Vietnamese who worked for American businessmen do when Saigon was about to be taken by the North Vietnamese? They came flooding to the US Embassy.

Ford's Effort to Whip Inflation

When Gerald Ford took office, Nixon's wage and price controls had failed to stop inflation. Inflation reached a record 12.2 percent in 1974.

Ford could do little directly to solve the main cause of the problem. The Federal Reserve, an independent government agency created in 1913, controlled the supply of money. When more money is in circulation, prices rise.

At first, Ford pushed for a voluntary anti-inflation crusade, called WIN ("Whip Inflation Now"). The plan urged consumers to stop buying high-priced goods. It asked workers not to seek wage increases. But workers and businesses believed they were the victims of inflation rather than the cause of it, so they ignored WIN. The economic recession grew worse when the Federal Reserve raised interest rates (a tool it uses to limit the amount of money in circulation). Sales of new products fell. The number of people out of work climbed above 9 percent.

Ford then asked Congress for spending cuts and for a tax cut. Liberal Democrats, who controlled Congress, approved the tax cut, but they spent more and more money on new programs. Ford vetoed sixty-six bills in an effort to hold down the growth of government. But inflation continued to increase.

Teach for Understanding

What made it possible for many people at the US embassy in Saigon to escape? Helicopters from US Navy ships landed on the US embassy roof all day long. The helicopters took South Vietnamese and American people to the safety of American ships.

What happened to the people left behind when there was no more time to rescue them? Many Vietnamese fled in small boats.

- Direct attention to the pictures. Invite a student to read aloud the captions.

What happened to opponents of Communism in Vietnam? Over a million opponents were sent to brutal "reeducation camps."

What happened to opponents of Communism in Cambodia after the Communists took over? Two million Cambodians were killed.

- What did the Communist actions show about the New Left's thinking that the Communists were better than the Americans? Answers could include that the ideas of the New Left were contrary to what God teaches about loving our neighbor as ourselves. The Communists broke God's commandment to not murder when they took the lives of millions of people.

> **Conclude the discussion by asking the question on page 358.** Ford knew that the trials would stretch on for years. He thought this long process would only further hurt and divide the nation. He wanted to do what was best for the nation.

Activity Manual

- Guide completion of page 249.

Activity

Creating a Budget

- Generate excitement about creating a budget as you read aloud the Activity information on page 358.
- Distribute Instructional Aid 60. Guide the students as they complete the organizer. Explain that they should first write down income and expenses for every week. Then they can add other expenses or income that they think of.
- Invite students to share their responses to the questions on the instructional aid.

> You may suggest income amounts as well as expense amounts that a student might incur.

People board an American helicopter as Saigon is about to fall to North Vietnamese troops.

Fearing for their lives, many South Vietnamese fled in small boats.

American ships. But many people were left behind. There was not time to get everybody out who wanted out. Many Vietnamese fled in small boats. They hoped to be picked up by ships and resettled in other nations.

The New Left had protested the war. It had supported the Communists as being better than the Americans. But now the Communists had taken all of Vietnam. They were also able to take over the government of neighboring Cambodia. In Vietnam over a million opponents to Communism were sent to brutal "reeducation camps." In addition, around two million Cambodians were killed as the Communists purged their opponents from the population. It was difficult to say that the Communists were better.

> Why did Ford pardon Nixon?

Activity

Creating a Budget

List your sources of income, such as an allowance or any money you earn on a regular basis each month. Review your spending habits over the past month. Record your monthly income and your expenses. Ask yourself whether your expenses are greater than your income. Decide how to adjust your budget so that there is not a deficit. If your income is greater than your expenses, plan how you will use the surplus.

358

President Carter is the only president from Georgia and the first to be born in a hospital.

Carter is well-known for growing up on a peanut farm. There was even a giant peanut-shaped balloon at the parade on his Inauguration Day.

Because his role as president required so much reading, Carter took a speed-reading course. He increased his reading speed to 2,000 words per minute and was able to read three to four books per week.

Jimmy Carter
The Election of 1976

In 1976 Ford chose to run for another term as president. His opponent was former Georgia governor **Jimmy Carter**. Carter had a big smile. He said that he was a born-again Southern Baptist. And he promised Americans that he would never lie to them. This integrity was what Americans were looking for after the Nixon years.

Carter was also a tough campaigner. He worked hard, but it was difficult for Americans to determine what he really believed. He would speak like a liberal to liberals and like a conservative to conservatives.

Ford's campaign stumbled, especially when he said in a debate that he did not think Eastern Europe was under Soviet domination. Everybody, including Ford, knew that it was. Ford lost people's trust as a leader.

Domestic Affairs

When Carter first became president, people thought that he might actually be a conservative. He canceled some government projects. He said that they were not needed. They were just ways for congressmen to send money back to the districts that elected them. He also tried to reduce the amount of money that the government spent. And even though he had promised to promote government healthcare in the campaign, as president he found that government healthcare would be too expensive.

But at other times Carter governed more as a liberal. He increased spending on welfare, and he worked with Congress to pass sharp tax increases to fund Social Security.

Because he sometimes seemed conservative and sometimes seemed

359

Background

The Carter Style

Jimmy Carter became president of the United States professing his desire to be a "people's president" with an open, honest, and compassionate administration. He appointed record numbers of women and minorities to government positions. But not all his "healing" gestures were appreciated. When he granted amnesty to draft dodgers who fled the country to avoid fighting in Vietnam, Carter felt the wrath of veterans who had loyally fulfilled their obligation and fought in the war.

Carter was a compulsive worker who tried to micromanage every aspect of the government. As a result, he was often bogged down by details that could have been delegated to subordinates. Carter did not like to bargain with Congress, so some people viewed him as aloof and humorless. That view, along with Carter's "outsider" status in Washington, made it hard for him to work with Congress, despite large Democratic majorities in both houses. These flaws eventually damaged Carter's career, causing Americans to become disenchanted with his policies and adding to the public perception of him as an ineffective leader.

Lesson Focus

- By the end of Jimmy Carter's presidency, Americans believed that their nation was in decline.

Objectives
- Identify who won the presidency in 1976
- Relate Carter's handling of foreign affairs
- Recognize that Americans struggled with discouragement about their nation

Review

What did Gerald Ford do that he thought was best for the nation even though it brought criticism to himself? He pardoned Nixon.

What is created when a government spends more money than it brings in by taxes? a deficit

What eventually happened in Vietnam and Cambodia? The Communists took over. In Vietnam, over a million opponents to Communism were sent to "reeducation camps." In Cambodia, around two million Cambodians were killed as the Communists purged their opponents from the population.

Preparation for Reading

- Generate interest as you direct the students to read the title and examine the picture on pages 359–61.
- Guide pronunciation of any unfamiliar words on the pages.
- Direct the students to read the pages silently to discover the name of the person who backed a revolution against Iran. Ayatollah Khomeini

Teach for Understanding

- Direct attention to the picture on page 359. Read aloud the captions.

Who won the election of 1976 against Gerald Ford? Jimmy Carter

What did Carter do in his handling of domestic affairs that made him appear conservative? Carter canceled some government projects. He tried to reduce the amount of money the government spent. He decided government healthcare would be too expensive.

In what ways was Carter liberal? He increased spending on welfare. He worked with Congress to pass sharp tax increases to fund Social Security.

Teach for Understanding

- Invite a student to explain why Carter did not have a good working relationship with Congress.

  How did inflation affect Americans? The amount of money people earned would buy less and less.

  What was employment like at this time? Unemployment was up. Fewer people had jobs.

  How did high oil prices effect Americans by the end of Carter's presidency? Cars would line up at gas stations to get gas before it ran out.

- Direct attention to the picture on page 360. Read aloud the caption.

  What did Carter say would be the basis for how the United States related to other nations? human rights, whether citizens were treated badly

  What countries did Carter press to improve the treatment of its citizens? the Soviet Union, Latin American allies, and Iran

- Direct attention to the picture on page 361. Read aloud the caption.

  What resulted in countries where Carter pressed for improvement in the treatment of citizens? There was little improvement in the Soviet Union. When Latin America and Iran began to improve the treatment of their citizens, the revolutionary groups used new-found freedoms to gain more power.

  What happened in countries of allies where Carter hesitated to support their governments? Without American support, the governments of American allies fell. Soviet-backed governments were put in place.

  What changed Iran from being an American ally to becoming an enemy of America? A radical Muslim leader, Ayatollah Khomeini, backed a revolution against the ruler of Iran. Carter did not intervene, and Khomeini's forces seized Iran.

- Invite a student to locate Iran on a map or globe. Explain that Iran remains a threat to Israel and the United States.

  What did Americans believe about their nation by the end of Carter's presidency? Americans believed that their nation was in decline.

  How was the United States affected by many new ideas about how Americans should live? Many of the new ideas raised new problems for the country.

   Conclude the discussion by asking the question on page 361. Carter hesitated to support U.S. allies.

Activity Manual

- Guide completion of page 250.

---

liberal, Carter received criticism from both sides. In addition, Carter did not have a good working relationship with Congress. He would announce policies that he wanted Congress to pass without talking to the men in Congress whose help he would need in order to see the policies passed. Or he would oppose a bill in Congress and simply let congressmen find out by reading the newspaper. As a result, congressmen did not want to work with Carter.

The United States faced several challenges at this time. Inflation was going up. The amount of money people earned was buying less and less. Unemployment was also up. Fewer people had jobs. In addition, the price of oil was sharply up.

Carter proposed solving the oil problem in several ways. He suggested raising taxes on cars that used a lot of gas. He also wanted a tax on gasoline to reduce the amount of oil being used. Later, Carter asked Americans to save gas by limiting the number of miles they drove every week. He asked them to obey the speed limit to save gas. He said the government would set the example in conserving energy by keeping its buildings warmer in the summer and cooler in the winter.

By the end of his presidency, cars would line up at gas stations to get gas before it ran out. Americans were feeling bad about the direction of their country. Carter made a speech to the nation. He said there was a "crisis of the spirit of our country." He asked Americans to "say something good about our country."

Foreign Affairs

President Carter announced early on that human rights were very important. They would be the basis for how the United States related to other nations. The United States would not support countries that treated its citizens badly. Both conservatives and liberals were encouraged at first.

Carter pressed the Soviet Union to improve its treatment of its citizens. But this talk produced little change. Carter also pressed US allies in Latin America to improve the treatment of their citizens. He

Long lines of cars at service stations during the gasoline rationing of the 1970s

---

Background

Pronunciation

Ayatollah Khomeini (eye-ah-toh-LAH hoh-may-NEE)

Carter and Energy

From 1973 to 1977, the cost of imported oil for the nation skyrocketed from $8 billion to $40 billion a year. Carter devised a program that he believed would end dependence on foreign oil. His program included nationwide conservation. He created the Department of Energy to help American companies find new oil fields and develop alternative energy sources. He proposed deregulation and an end to price controls on gas and oil. Carter wanted to tax profits on oil and then use that revenue to fund his government programs.

Carter's plans were set back when Muslim radicals took over Iran. They cut oil production in 1979. This created an energy crisis similar to the 1973 oil embargo.

Carter believed that using nuclear power might help solve the energy crisis. He faced opposition from conservatives who feared a massive monopoly run by the federal government. He also faced opposition from liberals who feared the potential hazards of nuclear waste and nuclear accidents.

US President Jimmy Carter, Israeli Prime Minister Menachem Begin, and Egyptian President Anwar al-Sadat at the Camp David Accords where peace was made between Israel and Egypt. This peace agreement was the greatest foreign policy achievement of Carter's presidency.

did the same with Iran. These efforts backfired. When countries began to improve the treatment of their citizens, the revolutionary groups used new-found freedoms to gain more power. These groups were often supported by the Soviet Union. But Carter hesitated to help US allies stop the revolutionary groups. He said the human rights records of the allies did not rise to his standards. Without American support, the governments of American allies fell. Soviet-backed governments were put in place. The human rights records of these new governments were often far worse than the original governments.

These policies were most disastrous in Iran. Iran was an important ally for the United States because it bordered the Soviet Union. It gave the United States a good location from which to keep an eye on the Soviets.

But a radical Muslim leader, Ayatollah Khomeini, backed a revolution against the ruler of Iran. Carter could not decide whether to support his ally, the **shah**. He thought about supporting Khomeini. Carter wondered if Khomeini would support human rights in Iran. As Carter hesitated, Khomeini's forces were able to seize Iran. Since that time Iran has not been an ally of the United States. It has become an enemy. It has promoted terrorism in the Middle East. It uses terrorist groups to oppose American allies, such as Saudi Arabia and Israel.

By the end of Carter's presidency, Americans believed that their nation was in decline. They thought that life would be worse for their children than it had been for them. As the 1970s drew to an end, many Americans were discouraged. They did not know that the new decade would bring changes that would lift the spirit of the nation as a whole.

What was a major flaw in Carter's foreign policy?

361

Those fears seemed justified on March 28, 1979. The failure of the cooling system at the Three Mile Island nuclear power plant near Harrisburg, Pennsylvania, released radioactive steam and contaminated a nearby stream. The accident prompted increased antinuclear protests and hampered the building of more nuclear power plants.

Carter and Foreign Affairs

Carter tried to pursue a foreign policy based on fairness and morality, much as Woodrow Wilson had tried to do. The cornerstone of Carter's foreign policy was the defense of human rights, protecting people from government oppression. While Carter's goals were laudable, the United States could influence only friendly nations concerning human rights. Communist nations, among the worst violators of human rights, were impervious to Carter's pressures and continued to brutally oppress their people.

Objective
- Recall concepts and terms from Chapter 16

Materials
- Folded pieces of paper with both a question and its answer written on the inside of each to be used as "ballots."
- A container for each team to be the "ballot box."

Introduction

- Concepts for the Chapter 16 Test will be taken from Activity Manual pages 239–52. You may review any or all of the concepts during this lesson. You may choose to review Chapter 16 by playing "Cast Your Ballot."

Review

Game: Cast Your Ballot

- Divide the students into teams. Choose a volunteer from each team to "run for president." Label a "ballot box" for each team with a name of its candidate.
- Invite a student from the first team to select a ballot and hand it to you. Read the question. If the player answers correctly, he may cast his "ballot" in the "ballot box" for his team's candidate. Rotate teams and players until all the questions have been asked. Make sure all the teams have the same number of turns. The team who receives the most votes for its candidate is the winner.

Activity Manual

- Guide completion of pages 251–52.

Lesson **144** **Chapter 16 Test**

Objective
- Demonstrate knowledge of concepts from Chapter 16 by taking the test

Assessment
- Administer Test 16.

Chapter 17

Introduction

The 1980s would prove to be a decade of both strength and challenge for the United States. America faced the Cold War and the Iran hostage crisis. The election of Ronald Reagan as president brought new hope to America. Reagan signed the Economic Recovery Act. He promoted his Strategic Defense Initiative (SDI) for a strong national defense. Reagan met with Mikhail Gorbachev in an effort to avoid nuclear war.

Reagan's second term in office was marked by the Iran-Contra Affair. In Reagan, Christians found a leader who would support them on moral issues. The 1980s were a decade of many scientific advances. The Cold War ended when Reagan and Gorbachev signed the Intermediate-Range Nuclear Forces (INF) Treaty and the Berlin Wall was torn down.

Chapter Focus

During his presidency in the 1980s, Ronald Reagan strengthened America and helped end the Cold War.

17 — A Time of Strength and Challenge

Focus

During his presidency in the 1980s, Ronald Reagan strengthened America and helped end the Cold War.

Lesson	Student Text	Activity Manual	Content		Vocabulary
			Chapter 17 Overview		
145	362–65	253–56	Summer Olympic Games boycott Iran hostage crisis	Election of 1980 Ronald Reagan	hostages Iran hostage crisis
146	366–68	257	Reaganomics Economic Recovery Act	Sandra Day O'Connor Assassination Attempt	Economic Recovery Act
147	369–71	258–59	Strategic Defense Initiative (SDI) Activity: Participating in a Summit		Reagan Doctrine Strategic Defense Initiative
148	372–74	260	Election of 1984 Biography Box: Nancy Reagan	Iran-Contra Affair	
149	375–77	261	How It Was: Space Shuttle Dreams Space Shuttle Program *Challenger*	Technology Jarvik Heart Magnetic resonance imaging	*Challenger*
150	378–79	262	Mikhail Gorbachev Berlin Wall Intermediate-Range Nuclear Forces (INF) Treaty The fall of the Berlin Wall Primary Source: Tear Down this Wall		Intermediate-Range Nuclear Forces (INF) Treaty
151		263–64	Chapter Review		
152			Chapter Test		

Visit bjupress.com/resources for links to enhance the lessons.

Iran releases
American hostages
1981

Challenger
explosion
1986

Fall of the
Berlin Wall
1989

1980   1985   1987   1990
         Geneva Summit   INF treaty

America in the Eighties

The United States was ready to enter a new decade. The 1970s had been a period where America lacked strong, consistent leadership. But that situation was about to change. Americans would choose a new president in 1980. They would keep that president for two terms. His leadership would provide great stability for the nation.

Americans entering the 1980s wanted to see freedom increase around the world. They hoped to win victory in the Cold War. They planned to continue defending other nations from Communism.

America also had challenges to face in the 1980s. Some challenges were negative. The nation was in debt. Problems continued to arise in peace-keeping efforts. But Americans also faced positive challenges. There was new progress to make in technology. And there were new heights to climb in science and medicine. The 1980s would prove to be a decade of both strength and challenge for the United States.

International Tensions
The Cold War Continues

For many Americans, the 1980s began with disappointing news. America had been angered by the Soviet Union's invasion of Afghanistan at the end of 1979. On January 14, 1980, President Carter made an announcement. The Soviet Union must withdraw from Afghanistan. If it did not withdraw, the United States would boycott the Summer Olympic Games in Moscow. None of the US athletes would compete in the games.

The boycott of the Olympics had support from Congress. The American people in general supported the boycott. Many other nations, such as Canada, West Germany, and Israel, also chose to boycott the games. However, many American athletes and fans were disappointed about staying home from the Olympics.

The conflict continued for another nine years. The Soviet Union did not withdraw from Afghanistan. In 1984

363

JourneyForth

The following books are available from JourneyForth Books, a division of BJU Press, at journeyforth.com.

What About Cimmaron? by Lauraine Snelling

Set in Washington State in 1980, this historical fiction book tells the story of Sarah's search for her horse after the Mount Saint Helen's volcano erupts.

Children of the Storm by Natasha Vins

This autobiographical book tells the story of Natasha's upbringing in the Soviet Union during the Cold War. Natasha's father, Georgi Vins, was a leader in the underground church. Natasha witnessed firsthand the hardships involved in being faithful to Christ. Her book recounts her struggle to decide whether to conform to the Communist ideals she was taught in school or to embrace the Christ her parents served.

Lesson Focus

- The United States faced positive and negative challenges in the 1980s.

Objectives
- Recognize Soviet aggression
- Name Ronald Reagan as the winner of the 1980 presidential election
- Identify the country that took Americans hostage

Introduction

- Invite a student to read aloud the title of the chapter and predict what the chapter will be about. the strength and challenges of America

- Invite a student to read the chapter focus aloud.

    What do you think you will learn in this chapter? how President Reagan made America stronger and worked to end the Cold War

- Direct attention to the timeline.

- What does the first event on the timeline suggest? Answers could include that America was having problems with Iran; Iran captured some Americans.

    What event happened in 1986? The *Challenger* exploded.

- Invite a volunteer to tell whether he has heard of the *Challenger* and what he knows about the *Challenger*.

    What happened in 1989? the fall of the Berlin Wall

- Direct attention to the picture of people at the Berlin Wall. Invite a student to tell what he thinks the picture means.

Preparation for Reading

- Generate interest as you direct the students to read the titles and examine the pictures on pages 362–65.

- Guide pronunciation of any unfamiliar words in the lesson.

- Direct the students to read the pages silently to learn what the United States did in 1980 when the Soviet Union did not withdraw from Afghanistan. The United States boycotted the Summer Olympic Games.

Teach for Understanding

- Invite a student to tell some of the negative challenges America faced in the 1980s.

- Discuss the positive challenges America faced.

    What country did the Soviet Union invade? Afghanistan

    What did the United States do when the Soviet Union refused to withdraw from Afghanistan? The United States boycotted the Summer Olympic Games that were held in Moscow.

Teach for Understanding

How long did the conflict continue in Afghanistan after the United States boycotted the Olympic Summer Games? nine years

What did the Soviet Union do in regard to the 1984 games? The Soviet Union refused to send athletes to the 1984 games that were held in Los Angeles.

What event caused the shah of Iran to flee the country? Islamic forces had risen to power in Iran. The shah was forced to flee the country when the people revolted.

- Explain that the word *shah* was a term used for a monarch or king who had inherited the throne in Iran.

What happened in Iran after President Carter welcomed the shah to the United States to receive medical treatment? Some radical students in Iran wanted to get back at America for helping the shah. These students took more than sixty Americans from the US embassy as hostages.

- Choose a volunteer to describe the attempt by the United States to rescue the hostages.

Why did the Iran hostage crisis cause many Americans to lose confidence in President Carter and his foreign policy? They thought that the failure to rescue the hostages made America look weak in the eyes of the world.

Who were the two candidates in the presidential election of 1980? Jimmy Carter, Ronald Reagan

What was Reagan's political background? He had served as the governor of California.

---

the Olympic Games were held in Los Angeles. The Soviet Union refused to send athletes to the 1984 games. The Olympic boycotts of the 1980s were just one sign that the Cold War was far from over.

The Iran Hostage Crisis

Another problem arose between America and the country of Iran. At this time, Iran was an ally with America against the Soviet Union. Islamic forces had risen to power in Iran. Iran's leader, the shah, was forced to flee the country when the people revolted. President Carter welcomed the shah to the United States to receive medical treatment. Some radical students in Iran wanted to get back at America for supporting the shah, who was a brutal ruler. In late 1979, they took more than sixty Americans from the US embassy as **hostages**.

At first, President Carter tried to make deals with Iran to free the hostages. But his efforts failed. In April of 1980, the United States attempted to rescue the hostages. However, thick dust clouds over the desert created problems for the helicopters. Some of them had equipment failures. The rescue mission had to

be canceled. On the return flight, a helicopter collided with a transport plane. Eight servicemen were killed.

Americans watched the news broadcasts with growing concern. Many Americans lost confidence in President Carter and his foreign policy. They thought that the failure to rescue the hostages made America look weak in the eyes of the world. For many Americans, the **Iran hostage crisis** was proof that America needed new leadership.

The Election of 1980

November brought another presidential election. Jimmy Carter's major opponent was Republican **Ronald Reagan**. Reagan had served as the governor of California. He had also been an actor and was a highly

Iranian students held 52 Americans hostage in Iran for 444 days.

364

Background

The Iran Hostage Crisis

On November 4, 1979, a group of radical students with connections to Khomeini stormed the US embassy in Iran and took sixty-six Americans hostage.

President Carter responded by freezing Iran's assets in America. Then he stopped the importation of Iranian oil to the United States. He made some attempts at secret talks, but the Iranians demanded conditions that the United States could not accept. Carter set no deadlines, nor did he authorize any military actions. By Christmas, Carter was considering a rescue attempt, and the attempt took place in April of 1980. But a dust storm damaged several of the rescue helicopters, and the mission was canceled. In returning from the staging ground in Iran, a helicopter collided with a transport plane, killing eight soldiers. This failure only added to America's feelings of frustration and humiliation.

The situation changed when neighboring Iraq invaded Iran in September 1980. The two countries locked horns in a deadly eight-year war. More than three hundred thousand people were killed. Khomeini offered to release the American hostages on three conditions. Carter must free Iranian assets, promise never to interfere in Iranian affairs, and return the shah's wealth. Since the United States had no legal access to the shah's money, it refused. The crisis did not end until the day of

Ronald Reagan's love for jelly beans was no secret. A crystal jar of jelly beans always sat on the table during his cabinet meetings. A new flavor, blueberry, was created so that he could celebrate events with red, white, and blue jelly beans.

His sense of humor was apparent just days after an assassination attempt. While recovering from the surgery that removed the bullet, he told his wife, "Honey, I forgot to duck."

Iran hostages back on American soil

WELCOME BACK TO FREEDOM

skilled speaker. The American people responded well to his optimism and his conservative views. Reagan won the election by a landslide in the Electoral College. He also won the popular vote. At sixty-nine, Reagan became the oldest man in the nation's history to be elected president.

Release of the Hostages

Up to his last day as president, Carter continued working for the release of the hostages in Iran. However, Iran did not release the hostages until Reagan's inauguration was taking place on January 20, 1981. The hostages boarded a plane in Iran while the new president was giving his inaugural speech. Later that day, President Reagan announced that the hostages were free and on their way home. The hostages had been in captivity for 444 days. Across the nation, Americans celebrated. Church bells rang. Signs and banners proclaimed thanks to God. People wept, sang, and cheered as the hostages rejoined their families.

President Reagan's inauguration day was a joyful day in United States history. American hope ran high. Americans celebrated freedom, and they looked forward to what they might accomplish under their new leader.

> How did the Iran hostage crisis affect Carter's chance at reelection?

President Reagan's inauguration. On January 21, 1981, after 444 days in captivity, the American hostages were set free.

Activity

Reagan's Jelly Beans

Materials: jelly beans

Invite students to use resources to learn the brand of jelly beans Ronald Reagan liked that are still sold today. Discover the three flavors of jelly beans that were served at Reagan's inauguration. Discover Reagan's favorite flavor of jelly bean. Find out what the US government authorized the president of the Herman Goelitz Candy Company to develop. Invite students to enjoy jelly beans as they share what they learned.

Teach for Understanding

- Direct attention to the pictures on pages 364–65. Invite a student to read aloud the captions. Explain that the original 66 hostages were American diplomats, embassy employees, and citizens. Some hostages were released soon after being taken. This left 52 American diplomats who were held for 444 days.

  What were the election results? Reagan won the election by a landslide in the Electoral College. He also won the popular vote.

- What made Reagan's inauguration day a joyful time in America? The hostages were released. American hope ran high. Americans looked forward to what they might accomplish under their new leader.

> Conclude the discussion by asking the question on page 365. Many Americans lost confidence in President Carter and his foreign policy. For many Americans, the Iran hostage crisis was proof that America needed new leadership.

Activity Manual

- Guide completion of pages 253–56.

Lesson

146

Student Text pages 366–68
Activity Manual page 257

Lesson Focus

- President Reagan worked to make improvements in America.

Objectives

- Identify the name for Reagan's economic goals
- Analyze whether Sandra Day O'Connor was a conservative
- Recognize who made the assassination attempt on President Reagan

Review

- Invite a student to explain how the Cold War continued between the Soviet Union and the United States.
- Choose a volunteer to describe the Iran hostage crisis.

Preparation for Reading

- Generate interest as you direct the students to read the titles and examine the pictures on pages 366–68
- Guide pronunciation of any unfamiliar words in the lesson.
- Direct the students to read the pages silently to learn who made an assassination attempt on President Reagan's life. John Hinckley Jr.

Teach for Understanding

- Direct attention to the infograph on page 366. Invite a student to explain the meaning of the graph.

  What was the financial state in America when Reagan became president? The country was in debt. Taxes were high, and many people were unemployed.

- Choose volunteers to state goals that Reagan set for his presidency.

  What did Reagan's opponents call his plans? Reaganomics

  What did the Economic Recovery Act do for Americans? The act lowered income taxes by 25 percent.

> Guide a review of important terms, maps, places, and people from each previous lesson. Direct the students to find and read the corresponding entries from the Resource Treasury.

The Reagan Era Begins

As president, Reagan quickly earned the nickname "the Great Communicator." Whenever he spoke to the American people, he was convincing, clear, and seemed sincere. His optimism made him appealing to America's young people. He inspired trust. Although he had opponents, he was admired and respected by a large number of Americans.

"Reaganomics"

President Reagan believed it was important to improve America's economy. The country was in debt. Taxes were high, and many people were unemployed. Reagan's new policies made the greatest changes in the economy since Roosevelt's New Deal. Reagan set several goals for his presidency. He wanted to help the government cut back on its spending. He also wanted to reduce the amount Americans paid in income taxes. And he wanted the government to have less control over business so that the people could make their own decisions. Allowing people more freedom with money would encourage businesses to grow. New jobs would be created. Reagan also believed his policies would stop inflation.

Reagan's opponents referred to his plans as "Reaganomics." They thought Reagan would only create more problems for the country. But Reagan moved forward with his program anyway. In 1981 he signed the **Economic Recovery Tax Act**. The act lowered income taxes by 25 percent. This was the largest tax cut in American history.

For a short time, the American economy struggled. But then it began to grow again. Over the eight years President Reagan was in office, he saw nearly all of his economic goals succeed. Taxes and interest rates dropped. Inflation almost disappeared. However, the government did not stop spending. Money went out much faster than it came in. The national debt continued to climb.

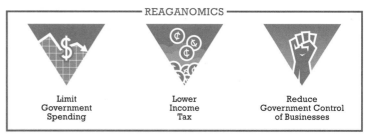

REAGANOMICS

Limit Government Spending — Lower Income Tax — Reduce Government Control of Businesses

366

Background

Reagan and Tax Cuts

Reagan focused on making more products available by lowering taxes and reducing regulations on businesses and investors. Businesses would then have more money to make products, and individuals would have more money to invest. The improved economic benefits would then "trickle down" to the average consumer.

Reagan called his solution supply-side economics. He argued that tax cuts actually increased tax revenues.

In 1981, Congress passed the first part of Reagan's plan. It cut inheritance and gift taxes, corporate taxes, and income taxes. The Economic Recovery Tax Act of 1981 included the largest income tax cut in American history—25 percent reduction over three years for each taxpayer. To help balance the budget, the president hoped to cut the size of the government bureaucracy. He also wanted to reduce increases in federal spending in almost every area except the military. But the House of Representatives was not interested in reducing spending. When Reagan pushed for cuts, Democrats accused him of being hard-hearted and wanting to hurt the poor.

Sandra Day O'Connor made history as the first woman to be a Supreme Court justice.

Sandra Day O'Connor grew up on a ranch learning the value of hard work. She was a diligent student and excelled in school, graduating third in her class in law school. Even so, O'Connor faced challenges finding a job since many offices turned her away saying, "We don't hire women."

Supreme Court Justices

President Reagan made changes in the Supreme Court. When he became president, one of the justices was ready to retire. Reagan appointed **Sandra Day O'Connor** to fill the opening. O'Connor became the first female justice on the Supreme Court. O'Connor had been an Arizona state senator. She was considered conservative in her views. However, she did not always vote as a conservative. Sometimes her vote swung court decisions in favor of the liberals. Christians were especially disappointed in her vote to uphold the Court's earlier decision *Roe v. Wade*. This decision had made abortion legal in 1973. Reagan had hoped to overturn the decision during his presidency.

Reagan replaced many liberal judges with conservative ones. He later named William Rehnquist chief justice. During his time in office, Reagan appointed two other justices to the court. Antonin Scalia joined the Supreme Court in 1986, and Anthony Kennedy was appointed in 1987. Scalia would maintain a conservative voting record on many of the issues brought before the court in the following decades. Reagan also appointed more than eighty judges to the nation's federal courts.

Assassination Attempt

During Reagan's first year as president, an attempt was made on his life. On March 30, 1981, Reagan was leaving a hotel in Washington, DC, after making a speech. A mentally ill man named John Hinckley Jr. fired several shots at the president. Reagan's Secret Service agents acted quickly and bravely. One of them pushed the president into the waiting limousine. Another turned and faced the gunman, taking a bullet aimed at Reagan. As the car rushed away, the agents discovered that Reagan had also been hit.

367

Teach for Understanding

- Direct attention to the picture on page 367. Read aloud the captions.

  What made it possible for President Reagan to appoint Sandra Day O'Connor to the Supreme Court? One of the justices was ready to retire.

  What was O'Connor's political background? She had been an Arizona state senator.

- Was O'Connor a conservative or a liberal justice? Answers should include that she was conservative in her views. However, she did not always vote as a conservative. Sometimes her vote swung court decisions in favor of the liberals.

  In what way did O'Connor disappoint Christians? She voted to uphold the Court's earlier decision in *Roe v. Wade* that had made abortion legal.

- Why is abortion wrong? Abortion kills an unborn person (Psalm 139:13–16). All people are created in the image of God. God forbids murder (Exodus 20:13).

  What justice did Reagan appoint that maintained a conservative voting record on many issues in the following decades? Antonin Scalia

  Who made an assassination attempt on President Reagan? John Hinckley Jr.

  How did the Secret Service agents respond? They acted quickly and bravely. One of them pushed the president into the waiting limousine. Another turned and faced the gunman, taking a bullet aimed at Reagan.

Before tax reforms passed, the country fell into a deep recession and Reagan agreed to tax increases on some products, such as cigarettes and airline tickets, to ease worries that the government was not earning enough money. Otherwise, he called on Americans to "stay the course" he had proposed. The recession lifted.

In 1983, the United States entered its longest period of continuous economic growth. Inflation almost disappeared. Jobs were abundant. Tax revenues almost doubled, just as Reagan had predicted. But Congress continued to spend money faster than it came in. Government debt mounted to record levels. America's long-term prosperity was threatened.

Lesson

146

Teach for Understanding

- Direct attention to the pictures on page 368. Read aloud the captions.

  What happened to Reagan once the limousine reached the hospital? Doctors performed surgery and removed a bullet from the president's lung.

- Invite a student to explain the changes the Secret Service agents made in the way they protected the president.

  ▶▶ Conclude the discussion by asking the question on page 368. Taxes and interest rates dropped, and inflation almost disappeared.

Activity Manual

- Guide completion of page 257.

President Reagan looks at a photo of his supporters during recovery from being shot.

Nicknamed "the Great Communicator," Reagan knew how to speak with dignity, sincerity, and humor.

The limousine sped to the hospital. Doctors immediately performed surgery. They removed a bullet from the president's lung. After two weeks of recovery, Reagan was able to return to the White House. His Secret Service agent recovered as well. However, his press secretary, who had also been hit, was disabled for life.

A few weeks after the shooting, Reagan felt well enough to make a speech to Congress about the Economic Recovery Tax Act. He took time to thank the American people for their compassion and prayers. He then quoted from a letter he had received from a second grader named Peter Sweeney. "I hope you get well quick or you might have to make a speech in your pajamas," the boy had written. As usual, Reagan could look at a difficult experience with humor.

The assassination attempt caused Secret Service agents to make changes in the way they protected the president. They tightened security whenever he entered and exited events. They used metal detectors to screen people for guns. Reagan also began wearing bulletproof vests under his clothing in public.

Like every life, the president's life is in God's hands. No life will end before the day God has appointed for it to end. However, along with trusting God, a nation can show respect for its God-given leaders by acting responsibly to protect them.

> How did Reagan's policies change America's economy?

368

America and Other Nations

National Defense

President Reagan wanted the government to spend less money in almost every area. But one thing he wanted to spend more money on was national defense. He believed that America needed a strong military. Military power would give the nation confidence in relations with other countries. Military strength was especially important because of the threat of nuclear war with the Soviet Union.

Reagan decided that the military should develop B-1 bomber aircraft. A program to build these types of planes had been canceled under President Carter. Now Reagan approved funds for the air force to start it again.

He also promoted a missile program called the **Strategic Defense Initiative** (**SDI**). His opponents nicknamed the program "Star Wars." Reagan called for missile defense from both the ground and space. Scientists were studying ways to destroy missiles in space before they reached their targets on the ground. The plan would mean developing costly new technology. Some in Congress thought Reagan's plan was too expensive. But Reagan did not back down. He believed that these programs would help the United States show its strength to other nations. He continued his efforts to build up the US military throughout his presidency.

Lebanon

As a member of the United Nations, the United States sometimes sent its military to keep peace in other

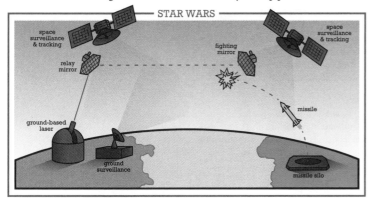

STAR WARS

space surveillance & tracking

space surveillance & tracking

fighting mirror

relay mirror

missile

ground-based laser

ground surveillance

missile silo

369

Lesson Focus

- Reagan strengthened the United States military.

Objectives

- Identify President Reagan's strategy for helping anti-Communist movements in other countries
- Examine the United States' involvement with other countries
- Participate in a mock summit

Teacher's Toolkit CD

- Instructional Aids 61–62: *America and Other Nations*; *Summit*
- Visual 44: *The B-1B*

Review

- Choose a volunteer to state several goals Reagan had for his presidency.
- Invite a student to tell what the Economic Recovery Act did for Americans.

  Who was the first woman to be a justice on the Supreme Court? Sandra Day O'Connor

  Who made an assassination attempt on President Reagan? John Hinckley Jr.

Preparation for Reading

- Generate interest as you direct the students to read the titles and examine the pictures on pages 369–71.
- Guide pronunciation of any unfamiliar words in the lesson.
- Direct the students to read the pages and complete Instructional Aid 61 in small groups.

Teach for Understanding

Where did President Reagan want the United States to spend more money? national defense

What type of planes did Reagan approve funds for the air force to start building? B-1 bombers

- Display Visual 44. Read the caption aloud. Explain that when Reagan restarted the B-1 bomber program. The long-range bomber became the B-1B.

What missile program did Reagan promote? the Strategic Defense Initiative (SDI)

- Invite a student to explain the meaning of the graphic on page 369.

Teach for Understanding

Why did the United States send 1,800 marines to Beirut? As a member of the United Nations, the United States sometimes sent its military to keep peace in other countries. The UN agreed to help Lebanon end the fighting there.

- Ask a group to explain what happened to the US Marine barracks in Beirut.

- Choose another group to tell how the United States responded to the attack in Beirut.

- Direct attention to Instructional Aid 61B. Invite a student to explain the meaning of the map.

What was the government like in Grenada? In the 1970s, a government with ties to Cuba came to power. Cuba was trying to help turn Grenada into a Communist country.

- Invite a group to describe the conflict in Grenada.

- Choose another group to explain America's response to the conflict.

countries. The city of Beirut, Lebanon, was the location of one of these peace-keeping missions. Lebanon had been involved in civil war. The UN agreed to help the war-torn nation end the fighting. America sent about 1,800 marines to Beirut. France, Italy, and Great Britain also sent soldiers.

One October morning in 1983, a terrorist drove a truck into the US Marine barracks in Beirut. The truck was carrying explosives. The bombs destroyed an entire four-story building. More than two hundred American marines and other service members were killed.

Americans were angered at the terrible and unjust loss of life. President Reagan pulled the rest of the troops out of Lebanon. America later learned that a Muslim terrorist group from Iran was behind the attack. America was just beginning to understand the threat of Islamic terrorism in the Middle East. The nation saw firsthand how deadly it could be.

Grenada

Grenada is a small island nation in the Caribbean. In the 1970s, a government with ties to Cuba came to power. Cuba was trying to help turn Grenada into a

Communist country. Reagan watched events in Grenada with concern.

Grenada had a medical college with several hundred American students. When civil war broke out, Grenada's president was killed. President Reagan began to fear for the safety of the American students. He also wanted to avoid a Communist takeover of Grenada. Several nearby Caribbean nations asked the United States to get involved.

On October 25, 1983, United States forces invaded Grenada in a surprise attack. Several thousand troops took part in the invasion. Special Caribbean forces helped too. In only a few weeks, Americans had overthrown the government of Grenada. They restored peace until a new election could be held. About six hundred American students were rescued.

Grenada Invasion

370

President Ronald Reagan and General Mikhail Gorbachev at the first Geneva Summit

The Soviet Union

America continued to have a tense relationship with the Soviet Union. Reagan publicly condemned the nation, calling it "the evil empire." He believed it was wrong for the Soviets to spread Communism to other nations. Like other presidents before him, Reagan had a strict policy against Communism. His strategy was called the **Reagan Doctrine.** The United States was committed to helping anti-Communist movements in other nations.

The US military buildup, and especially the "Star Wars" program, made Soviet leaders nervous. The Soviets had fallen behind the United States in their development of technology. They knew that they were unable to match American strength in this area. The Soviets also worried about Reagan's decision to place more missiles in Western Europe.

All through Reagan's first term as president, the Soviet government was going through upheaval. The nation had several changes in leaders. Three of its leaders died in a three-year period.

Finally, in 1985 a new leader named **Mikhail Gorbachev** came to power. Gorbachev was the first Soviet leader who was willing to meet with Reagan. At their first **summit** in Geneva, Switzerland, they talked about the problem of the Cold War. Gorbachev wanted Reagan to get rid of his SDI program. Reagan refused. However, both leaders saw the importance of avoiding nuclear war.

Nothing was resolved at the meeting known as the Geneva Summit. But many Americans were encouraged by the fact that the two leaders had talked. Perhaps they were one step closer to ending the Cold War.

> **Why did Reagan believe a strong military was important?**

///// **Activity** //////////////////////////

Participating in a Summit

Imagine that you are the leader of a powerful nation. Write three goals for your nation.

Meet with a leader from another nation. Discuss your goals, and then listen to his or her goals. What problems might develop between your two nations if you both pursue your goals? How could these problems be avoided? Write your ideas in a summit report.

//////////////////////////////////////

371

Teach for Understanding

What was the continuing relationship like between the United States and the Soviet Union? It was tense.

What did Reagan call the Soviet Union? the evil empire

Why do you think Reagan referred to the Soviet Union that way? Answers could include that he believed that it was wrong for the Soviets to spread Communism to other nations. The Soviet Union had previously invaded Afghanistan and refused to withdraw.

What was the name of Reagan's strategy to help anti-Communist movements in other nations? the Reagan Doctrine

- Invite a group to tell what the Soviet government was going through.
- Ask a group to describe Reagan's response to the tense relationship between the United States and the Soviet Union.
- Direct attention to the picture on page 371. Invite a student to read aloud the caption.

> Conclude the discussion by asking the question on page 371. Military power would give the nation confidence in relations with other countries. Military strength was especially important because of the threat of nuclear war with the Soviet Union.

Activity Manual

- Guide completion of pages 258–59.

Assessment

- Administer quiz.

The quiz may be given any time after completing this lesson.

Activity //

Participating in a Summit

- Generate excitement about participating in a summit as you read the Activity information on page 371 aloud.
- Divide the students into pairs. Suggest the names of two countries that will meet for a summit.
- Distribute a copy of Instructional Aid 62 to each student. Ask each pair to decide which person is the leader of which country. Direct each student to record the name of his country on the instructional aid.
- Direct the students to write three goals they have for their country.
- Invite the pairs to hold summits and record information on the instructional aid.
- Direct the students to use the information to write a summary of the summit.
- Choose volunteers to read their completed summaries aloud.

Lesson Focus

- Reagan remained a popular president throughout his second term.

Objectives

- Recognize why the United States bombed Libya
- Examine the Iran-Contra Affair
- Identify ways Reagan supported Christians on moral issues

Review

- Review what Reagan did to strengthen the United States' military defense.
- Choose volunteers to explain the conflict of the following countries and how the United States responded: Lebanon, Grenada, the Soviet Union.

Preparation for Reading

- Generate interest as you direct the students to read the titles and examine the pictures on pages 372–74.
- Guide pronunciation of any unfamiliar words in the lesson.
- Direct the students to read the pages silently to discover what Reagan promised to continue in his second term. *his economic and military policies*

Teach for Understanding

What candidate opposed Reagan in 1984? *Walter Mondale*

How many states did Reagan win on election night? *forty-nine of the fifty states*

How did a majority of Americans feel about Reagan's second term? *They felt hopeful about the future.*

Why was it necessary for the United States to send planes into Libya on a bombing mission? *Terrorism in Western Europe was linked to Libya. Some Americans were killed in these attacks.*

- Direct attention to the picture on page 372. Read aloud the caption.

- Why did Libyan terrorism stop for a long time after US planes bombed several Libyan military targets? *Answers could include that these air strikes proved that the United States could respond strongly to terrorism threats.*

In what Latin American country was a Communist group setting up government? *Nicaragua*

Why did President Reagan give permission for the US government to aid the Contras? *The Contras were fighting against the Communists. This action was consistent with the Reagan Doctrine.*

An American tactical fighter wing F-111 aircraft used in Libyan strikes

A Second Term for Reagan
The Election of 1984

Reagan was easily reelected in the election of 1984. The Democratic candidate was Carter's former vice president, Walter Mondale. Mondale chose Geraldine Ferraro as his running mate. She was the first female vice-presidential candidate for a major party.

On election night, Reagan won forty-nine of the fifty states. He received 525 electoral votes—the highest number any president had ever earned. Reagan promised to continue his economic and military policies during his second term. A majority of Americans had been pleased with Reagan's first term. They felt hopeful about the future.

Problems in Libya

Reagan continued to deal with the terrorism threat in the Middle East. Americans were still shocked and angry over the terrorist attack in Lebanon. Reagan knew he must take strong action to combat this threat in other places.

In the early 1980s the leader of Libya, Muammar al-Qaddafi, was a threat. Several acts of terrorism in Western Europe were linked to Libya. Some Americans were killed in these attacks. Reagan responded by sending planes to Libya in 1986. The planes bombed several Libyan military targets. These air strikes proved that the United States could respond strongly to terrorism threats. After this bombing raid, Libyan terrorism stopped for a long time.

The Iran-Contra Affair

The Cold War continued during Reagan's second term. Reagan's dealings in one part of this war received much criticism. A Communist group was setting up government in the Latin American country of Nicaragua. Reagan feared that Communism would spread to other Latin American countries. He gave permission for the government to aid the Contras, a group fighting against the Communists. This action was consistent with the Reagan Doctrine. However, many Americans feared becoming involved in another conflict like the Vietnam War.

372

Background

Iran-Contra Affair

An underground newspaper in faraway Beirut reported that the Reagan administration had traded arms to Iran in exchange for the release of American hostages in Lebanon. As the story unfolded, it revealed that members of the White House National Security Council (NSC)—principally chief John Poindexter, his aide US Marine Lt. Col. Oliver North, and CIA director William Casey—had set up secret arms sales to Iran. At the time, Iran was locked in a costly war with neighboring Iraq and needed missiles and military spare parts. Because of strategic interests in Iran, the covert operation was aimed at cultivating a moderate successor to the aging Ayatollah Khomeini. In addition, the United States hoped that the arms deal would encourage Iran to help gain the release of American hostages in Lebanon who were held by terrorists loyal to Khomeini.

Investigations into what happened to the money from the arms sales to Iran thickened the plot. The money, funneled through Swiss banks, was used to supply the Nicaraguan Contras battling the Communist Sandinistas, giving the whole matter the name Iran-Contra Affair.

Nancy Reagan

Who: First Lady; wife of Ronald Reagan

When: 1921–2016

Where: New York and California

Born in New York City, Nancy Robbins grew up in Maryland with her aunt and uncle after her parents' divorce. She was later adopted by her stepfather, taking his surname of Davis. During her brief acting career, she met fellow actor Ronald Reagan. They married in 1952 and had two children. Nancy Reagan also became stepmother to the two children from Reagan's previous marriage. Mrs. Reagan served behind the scenes, rearing her children and supporting her husband's role as governor of California.

As the First Lady, Nancy Reagan campaigned for drug awareness. She targeted young people with the advice to "just say no" when offered drugs. Partly as a result of her efforts, Reagan signed an anti-drug abuse bill into law in 1986. Even after leaving the White House, she worked tirelessly in support of drug-prevention programs in schools.

The Reagans were famous for the love and loyalty they displayed in their marriage. When the former president was diagnosed with Alzheimer's disease, Mrs. Reagan cared for him until his death in 2004. After his death, she continued to support Republican causes. She also accepted several awards in her husband's honor. Mrs. Reagan passed away in 2016.

Some disturbing facts came to light about the Contras. They used unnecessary violence and did not respect human rights. Congress decided that the United States should no longer help them. In 1987 Congress discovered that government officials had sold weapons to Iran in exchange for some American hostages. Some of the money from the sale had been given to the Contras. The situation was called the **Iran-Contra Affair.**

Reagan claimed that he had not known about the money given to the Contras. Members of his administration were tried. Some of them were convicted of doing wrong. They had to leave their jobs.

Reagan was never proved guilty of any wrong. However, many Americans

373

Teach for Understanding

• Direct attention to the picture and the Biography Box on page 373. Read aloud the information. Discuss how Mrs. Reagan worked to improve America.

Why do you think Mrs. Reagan worked tirelessly to support drug-prevention programs in schools? Answers could include that Mrs. Reagan wanted students to understand that drug use was harmful. She wanted students to do well in school and to be successful in life.

What disturbing facts came to light about the Contras? They used unnecessary violence and did not respect human rights.

What did Congress decide? They decided that the United States should no longer help the Contras.

What did Congress discover in 1987? Government officials had sold weapons to Iran, and some of the money had been given to the Contras.

What happened to some members of Reagan's administration? They were tried. Some of them were convicted of doing wrong. They had to leave their jobs.

What do you think President Reagan should have done if he had knowledge about the government officials selling weapons to Iran and then giving the money to the Contras? Answers could include that he should have stopped the officials from helping the Contras.

The support to the Contras came at a time when Congress, under the provisions of a law known as the Boland Amendment, had cut off military aid to the Contras. The Reagan Administration was already embarrassed over the disclosures of the Iranian arms sales, which were essentially an attempt to pay ransom to kidnappers, contrary to long-stated policy. The administration faced a Democrat-controlled Congress that was eager to pin criminal charges on the president's men for supplying funds to the Contras. The matter raised questions about Reagan's management of the White House. On March 4, 1987, in a speech to the nation, the president took responsibility for the actions of those who served in his administration. Reagan denounced the methods used to accomplish what many had viewed as laudable goals of freeing hostages in Iran and supporting anti-Communist forces in Nicaragua.

Throughout 1987, investigations and congressional hearings continued to bring to light details of the Iran-Contra affair. The White House insisted that the Boland Amendment did not apply to the NSC; congressional investigators disagreed. Eventually, North and Poindexter were tried and convicted on lesser criminal charges. William Casey died shortly after the hearings began, so he was never tried. When the dust of dispute settled, North's indictments were eventually overturned on a technicality in 1990.

Teach for Understanding

- Direct attention to the picture on page 374. Explain that as Reagan struggled to preserve moral values in America, the culture continued to move in the other direction.

What impact did Reagan have on Christians and conservatives in America? *Christians benefited. Many Christian organizations grew stronger during Reagan's presidency. Conservative news shows and publications gained more respect. Evangelical Christians enjoyed more influence in America than they had experienced in a long time.*

What should Christians remember even when Christian influence in a culture is strong? *Christians must obey Jesus' command to seek first the kingdom of God.*

- Explain that it is good for a Christian to be politically involved. A Christian should be motivated by love for his neighbor, even if that neighbor is his political enemy. Elections do not bring lasting solutions to problems. The people of a nation and a culture of eroding morals can be transformed only by the gospel.

> Conclude the discussion by asking the question on page 374. *Reagan opposed abortion. He wanted laws to limit the use of drugs and alcohol. He wanted public schools to be allowed to lead students in prayer. He communicated respect for the Bible.*

Activity Manual

- Guide completion of page 260.

---

thought he should have known what his administration was doing. He lost some of his support through the Iran-Contra Affair. Even so, many Americans still trusted him. He remained a popular president throughout his second term.

Support for Morality

American Christians had become concerned about the direction of their country in the 1960s and 1970s. Drug use, immorality, and rebellion against authority had become more common. The Supreme Court had made abortion legal. And it had made it illegal for public schools to lead students in prayer and Bible reading.

Christians found a leader in Reagan who would support them on moral issues. He opposed abortion. He believed the Constitution granted every living person the right to life, including unborn children. He also wanted laws to limit the use of drugs and alcohol. He warned that abuse of these products harmed the human body. He wanted public schools to be allowed to lead students in prayer. Throughout his presidency, Reagan communicated respect for the Bible. He declared 1983 "the Year of the Bible" and encouraged all Americans to examine its message.

Christians in America benefited from having a leader who showed respect for God's commands. Many Christian organizations grew stronger during Reagan's presidency. Conservative news shows and publications gained more respect. During the Reagan years, evangelical Christians enjoyed more influence in America than they had experienced in a long time.

However, this influence came with dangers as well. Some Christians began to value political power more than being true to their faith. Some were willing to do wrong to gain that power. And some Christians saw other Americans only as political enemies instead of people who needed the gospel. Even when Christian influence in a culture is strong, Christians must obey Jesus' command to seek first the kingdom of God.

> On what moral issues did Reagan take a strong stand?

374

Background

Prayer in Public Schools

Many people believe that a Supreme Court decision in 1962 made it illegal to pray in a public school. However, the decision was in response to teachers and administrators leading students in a public prayer. The Supreme Court ruled that this action violated the US Constitution's First Amendment that prohibits a state from establishing a religion. The public prayers essentially grouped all students into the same religion. Although the Supreme Court's decision removed the school-led prayers, it did not remove the right to pray in schools. Students of any religion still enjoy the First Amendment right to free speech—even speech of a religious nature.

How It Was

Jeremy stared at the picture of a rocket on his bedroom wall. He had always wanted to be an astronaut, but now? Now he wasn't so sure.

"Still working on that science report, Jeremy?" Mom asked from the doorway.

Jeremy nodded. "Mom, I don't know if I want to do my report on space exploration anymore. And I might even want to take down that picture."

Mom sighed. She sat on the bed beside him. "Jeremy, I know you're upset about the space shuttle. We all are. Tragedy has a way of shaking up our dreams." She too looked at the rocket picture. "But, Jeremy, every dream comes with its own risks. If no one were willing to take those risks, no dream would ever come true."

"So you think I should leave the picture up?"

"Yes, Jeremy. We must go on dreaming—and trust God."

Science and Technology

The 1980s had many scientific advances. Americans made important progress in astronomy, technology, and medicine. Along with the successes, there were also some tragic failures. But Americans continued working to understand and use God's creation.

The Space-Shuttle Program

NASA launched the first space shuttle on April 12, 1981. The space shuttle looked more like a plane than the earlier spaceships did. Space shuttles were launched by powerful rockets. After completing a space mission, they were designed to glide back to earth and land safely on a runway.

The first space shuttle, *Columbia*, flew several successful missions. Then NASA launched a second shuttle, the **Challenger**. The *Challenger* also had several successful flights. Then on its tenth flight, on January 28, 1986, the shuttle exploded just seconds after lifting off. All seven of its crew members were killed. One of the crew members, Christa McAuliffe, was a high-school teacher. She had hoped to communicate with students from space.

375

Activity

Honoring Christa McAuliffe

Use resources to learn several ways Christa McAuliffe was honored after she was killed in the *Challenger* explosion.

Student Text pages 375–77
Activity Manual page 261

Lesson Focus

- Americans made advances in science and technology along with some tragic failures.

Objectives
- Recognize the space shuttle program
- Acknowledge advances in medicine

Teacher's Toolkit CD
- Instructional Aid 63: *Science and Technology*
- Visual 45: *The* Challenger

Review

- Choose a volunteer to explain why the United States bombed Libya.
- Invite a student to describe the Iran-Contra Affair.
- Review Reagan's support for morality in America.

Preparation for Reading

- Generate interest as you direct the students to read the titles and examine the pictures on pages 375–77.
- Guide pronunciation of any unfamiliar words in the lesson.
- Direct the students to read the pages silently and complete Instructional Aid 63 in small groups.

Teach for Understanding

- Direct attention to the picture and the How It Was box. Read aloud the story. Discuss the meaning of the story.

  How would you describe the space shuttle? The space shuttle looked more like a plane than earlier spaceships did. Space shuttles were launched by powerful rockets. After completing a space mission, they were designed to glide back to earth and land safely on a runway.

- Invite a student to explain events surrounding the January 28, 1986, launch of the *Challenger*.
- Display Visual 45. Direct attention to the crew of the *Challenger* and the shuttle launch.

Teach for Understanding

What effect did the *Challenger* explosion have on future shuttle flights? The space shuttle program was put on hold for the next several years.

• Invite a student to explain what NASA discovered about the explosion of the *Challenger*.

What continued to make great progress in the 1980s? technology

🔧 What was a reason so many people were able to own personal computers by the end of the 1980s? Answers could include that personal computers became much more affordable.

• Direct attention to the picture. Invite a student to tell how computers have changed.

What advances in entertainment came about through developments in technology? video games, music videos

What did some people object to in the music videos? Some people objected to the offensive content often found in these videos.

In what ways did Americans allow music videos to influence them? They allowed music videos to influence the way they dressed, acted, and thought.

🔧 What are some appropriate ways to enjoy music? Answers could include learning to play an instrument, attending concerts, listening to recordings of music, or singing in a choir.

President Reagan addressed the nation on television that evening. "I want to say something to the schoolchildren of America who were watching the live coverage of the shuttle's takeoff. I know it's hard to understand, but sometimes painful things like this happen. It's all part of the process of exploration and discovery. It's all part of taking a chance and expanding man's horizons. The future doesn't belong to the faint-hearted; it belongs to the brave. The *Challenger* crew was pulling us into the future, and we'll continue to follow them."

NASA investigated the explosion. The scientists discovered that the cold weather had caused thin rubber rings in the rocket booster to fail. The space-shuttle program was put on hold for the next several years.

The Personal Computer

Technology made great progress in the 1980s. The personal computer became much more affordable. By the end of the decade, many people had computers in their homes. Jobs that had been done with paper and pencil or typewriters could now be done on computers. Schools also opened computer labs and began teaching students how to use computers.

Technology and Culture

Developments in technology brought lasting changes to American culture during the 1980s. The entertainment industry relied more on technology than ever before. Video games became widely popular. People could play games on their personal computers or at arcades. Video games had a powerful appeal to children and teens. Just like today, parents and teachers warned against the dangers of wasting too much time playing the games.

Music videos became popular in the 1980s. Instead of just listening to music, people watched videos of the performers. An entire television network was devoted to music videos, especially for rock music. Some people objected to the offensive content often found in these videos. Yet many young Americans allowed music videos to influence the way they dressed, acted, and thought.

The bulky monitor of the 1980s personal computer was eventually replaced with a flat screen monitor on today's personal computer.

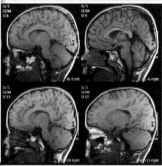

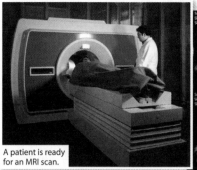

A patient is ready for an MRI scan.

Images from an MRI scan show organs and other structures in the human body.

149

Some people thought that new technology was corrupting America's youth. But the technology itself was not wrong. Sinful thoughts and behavior come from hearts that do not love God. Creators of games and videos knew that exciting technology appealed to young people. These creators often took advantage of this appeal for wrong purposes. Games and videos could have been a means of teaching what is true and right, but they often taught just the opposite.

Medicine

The 1980s saw some important advances in medicine. One of these was the development of the artificial heart. Experiments had been going on for years. Finally an engineer named Robert Jarvik designed a heart that worked with the help of a large air-pumping machine. In 1983 a medical team placed the Jarvik heart in a patient named Barney Clark. Clark lived for 112 days with the heart. The brief success was an important first step.

Another medical advance was a type of test called magnetic resonance imaging (MRI). MRI was invented in the 1970s, but the test was not widely used until the 1980s. During an MRI test, a patient is placed inside a large scanning machine. MRI uses a magnetic field and radio waves to create images. An MRI scan can produce detailed pictures of a person's organs, tissues, and bones. Today doctors use MRI scans to learn more about injuries, find cancer, or diagnose diseases.

What effects did new technology have on the culture, especially among young people?

377

Teach for Understanding

What is it that actually causes human corruption? Sinful thoughts and behavior come from hearts that do not love God. Creators of games and videos took advantage of the technology's appeal to young people for wrong purposes.

What could the creators of games and videos have done instead of using technology for the wrong purposes? They could have taught what was true and right.

- Explain that some music videos were labeled as Christian. Some of these music videos contained rock music, and the performers dressed and acted in ways like many offensive rock performers acted. Remind the students that the Bible teaches us not to conform to the ways of the world (Romans 12:1–3).

What were two important advancements in medicine that were used in the 1980s? the artificial heart and magnetic resonance imaging (MRI)

- Direct attention to the pictures on page 377. Read aloud the captions.

How do doctors use MRI scans today? to learn more about injuries, find cancer, or diagnose diseases

What advancements in medicine would you like to see in your lifetime? Answers will vary.

Conclude the discussion by asking the question on page 377. Technology allowed people to spend a lot of time playing video games. Instead of just listening to music, people watched videos of the performers. Young people were influenced in the way they dressed, acted, and thought.

Activity Manual

- Guide completion of page 261.

Lesson Focus

- Reagan worked to end Communism and protect the world from nuclear war.

Objectives

- Identify what Reagan wanted Gorbachev to do when Reagan went to West Germany
- Explain what the Intermediate-Range Nuclear Forces (INF) Treaty did

Teacher's Toolkit CD

- Visual 46: *Tearing Down the Wall*

Review

- Invite students to identify advances in technology during the 1980s.
- Choose a volunteer to describe how technology affected the culture in America.
- Ask a student to name two advances in medicine during the 1980s.

Preparation for Reading

- Generate interest as you direct the students to read the titles and examine the pictures on pages 378–79.
- Guide pronunciation of any unfamiliar words in the lesson.
- Instruct the students to read the pages silently to learn what influenced Gorbachev to reach an agreement with Reagan. The Soviet economy was struggling. The Soviets could not develop missiles as quickly as the Americans could.

Teach for Understanding

- Direct attention to the picture on page 378. Choose a volunteer to read aloud the caption.

  What did President Reagan and Gorbachev talk about at the Iceland meeting in 1986? the possibility of getting rid of all nuclear weapons

  What did Gorbachev want Reagan to give up? the SDI program

- Why do you think Gorbachev wanted Reagan to give up the SDI program? Answers could include that Gorbachev may have seen the program as more advanced than the systems that the Soviet Union had.

  Why did Reagan and Gorbachev fail to make an agreement? Reagan believed that it was important to have a defense system in place. He would not sacrifice safety for an agreement with the Soviet Union.

- Discuss changes Gorbachev made in the Soviet Union.

  When Reagan went to West Germany, what did he want Gorbachev to do? tear down the Berlin Wall

The Cold War Ends
Reagan and Gorbachev

President Reagan met with Soviet leader Gorbachev again in Iceland in 1986. They talked about the possibility of getting rid of all nuclear weapons. The two leaders came close to reaching an agreement. But Gorbachev still wanted Reagan to give up SDI. Reagan believed that it was important to have a defense system in place. He would not sacrifice safety for an agreement with the Soviet Union.

Gorbachev had begun making changes in the Soviet Union. For the first time since the Communist government began, he allowed greater freedom of speech in the country. People in the Soviet Union could express discontent with the Communist system. Gorbachev also began making economic reforms. He limited governmental control of trade. Eventually he allowed some private ownership of businesses. He loosened control of some of the countries in Eastern Europe that wanted independence. All these reforms were great changes for the Soviet Union. All the changes moved the country in the direction of greater freedom.

"Tear Down This Wall!"

Less than one year after the Iceland summit, Reagan visited West Germany. Since 1961 the Berlin Wall had been a symbol of Communism. President Reagan made a speech at the Brandenburg Gate, part of the wall between East and West Berlin. Reagan challenged Gorbachev to open up East Berlin. "Mr. Gorbachev," he said, "tear down this wall!" The crowd burst into applause, and the line became famous.

Reagan giving his "Tear down this wall!" speech at the Brandenburg Gate near the Berlin Wall

378

Background

The Berlin Wall

John F. Kennedy had several dangerous confrontations with the Soviets. Thousands of East Germans—mostly professionals—were escaping into the free city of West Berlin. As a result, in 1961 the Soviet dictator, Khrushchev, ordered a wall to be built around West Berlin. Guards had orders to shoot anyone who tried to escape across the Berlin Wall.

Kennedy responded by sending more troops to West Berlin. In 1963 he made a dramatic visit to the Berlin Wall. Thousands of Berliners lit candles to show their support of freedom. Kennedy expressed his support by saying in German, "Ich bin ein Berliner." ("I am a Berliner.") Despite Kennedy's actions, the wall remained a blow to the free world.

Activities

Reagan Library Tour

Visit www.bjupress.com/resources for a possible link to a Reagan Library video tour.

Reagan Activity Book

Use resources to compile an activity book about Ronald Reagan. Create a cover and an introduction for your book. Include a drawing of Reagan to color, a timeline of his life, a list of the places he lived, a crossword puzzle or acrostic using information in the book, and any interesting facts about his life.

An Agreement at Last

In December of 1987, Reagan and Gorbachev at last reached an agreement. This time the summit was on American soil in Washington, DC. The Soviet economy was struggling. Gorbachev knew that money problems would keep the country behind the United States. The Soviets could not develop missiles as quickly as the Americans could.

The treaty the two men signed was called the **Intermediate-Range Nuclear Forces (INF) Treaty.** During the next three years, both the Soviet Union

Reagan's piece of the Berlin Wall is decorated with a large butterfly on its western side, symbolizing freedom.

and the United States would get rid of certain types of missiles. This treaty marked the first time that both sides had agreed to reduce their number of nuclear weapons. It was a major victory in the Cold War.

The Fall of the Berlin Wall

It was not until nearly two years later in 1989 that the Berlin Wall came down. Following an announcement on East German television, Germans on both sides stormed the wall. Many brought hammers and picks to chip away pieces of stone. Others swarmed through the checkpoints to join family and friends on the other side of the border. East and West Germans celebrated a freedom that had been lost for more than forty years.

Reagan's presidency had ended by this time. But in 1990 Reagan was presented with a piece of the wall. Today the nine-and-a-half-foot-tall concrete slab is on display at the Ronald Reagan Presidential Library and Museum. Reagan's commitment to talks with Gorbachev had played a key role in ending the Cold War. He will be remembered as a president who worked hard to end Communism, to strengthen America, and to protect the world from nuclear war.

> How did Reagan help to end the Cold War?

379

Teach for Understanding

Where did Reagan and Gorbachev meet in December of 1987? Washington, DC

What treaty did Reagan and Gorbachev sign? the Intermediate-Range Nuclear Forces (INF) Treaty

Why was this a major victory in the Cold War? This treaty marked the first time that both sides had agreed to reduce their number of nuclear weapons.

When did the Berlin Wall come down? 1989

- Choose a volunteer to explain German reactions to the announcement on East German television.
- Display Visual 46. Read aloud the caption.
- Direct attention to the picture on page 379. Choose a student to read the caption aloud.

How is President Reagan remembered? He is remembered as a president who worked hard to end Communism, to strengthen America, and to protect the world from nuclear war.

Primary Source: Tear Down this Wall

- Direct attention to Activity Manual page 262.

Chapter 17: A Time of Strength and Challenge

- Read aloud the introduction and the excerpt from President Reagan's speech at the Brandenburg Gate in Berlin.
- Discuss the meaning of the excerpt.

> Conclude the discussion by asking the question on page 379. Reagan met with Gorbachev to sign a treaty that would get rid of certain types of missiles. Reagan was successful in getting Gorbachev to tear down the Berlin Wall.

Activity Manual

- Guide completion of page 262.

Lesson **151** Activity Manual pages 263–64

Objective
- Recall concepts and terms from Chapter 17

Materials
- A list of prepared questions and answers

Introduction

- Concepts for the Chapter 17 Test will be taken from Activity Manual pages 253–64. You may review any or all of the concepts during this lesson. You may choose to review Chapter 17 by playing "Tear Down This Wall."
- Create a display. Draw rectangles to create a wall with the same number of sections as review questions.

Review

Game: Tear Down This Wall

- Ask volunteers the prepared questions. After answering questions correctly, the students may remove or erase rectangles to help tear down the "wall."

Activity Manual

- Guide completion of pages 263–64.

Lesson **152** Chapter 17 Test

Objective
- Demonstrate knowledge of concepts from Chapter 17 by taking the test

Assessment
- Administer Test 17.

Chapter 18

George H. W. Bush followed Ronald Reagan as president of the United States. Bush signed a bill to help Americans with disabilities. He also signed bills to protect the environment. President Bush broke his word and raised taxes in order to balance the budget. Americans worried about crime and morals, and they feared for the future of the nation. Bush dealt with foreign conflicts. The United States went to war in Operation Desert Storm to free Kuwait.

Bill Clinton won the election of 1992. As president, he failed to bring healthcare reform to America. He supported gun control, and his vice president reduced the number of unneeded government rules and employees. Talk show hosts spoke out about Clinton's liberal policies. Clinton promoted peace in warring nations. Technology seemed to change daily.

Scandals plagued Clinton's second term. He succeeded in helping to bring peace to Northern Ireland. He promoted international trade. America experienced domestic and international terrorism. By the end of Clinton's presidency, Americans enjoyed prosperity and saw one last Clinton scandal, which blew over just as previous ones had.

18 Leader of the Free World

Focus

During the 1990s Americans enjoyed advances in technology as the nation dealt with problems abroad and at home.

Chapter 18 Overview

Lesson	Student Text	Activity Manual	Content		Vocabulary	
153	380–83	265–67	George H. W. Bush Americans with Disabilites Act	Oil Pollution Act Clean Air Act	Americans with Disabilites Act Clean Air Act	Oil Pollution
154	384–86	268–70	Manuel Noriega Boris Yeltsin Tiananmen Square Primary Source: State of the Union Address	Saddam Hussein Operation Desert Storm	Operation Desert Storm Tiananmen Square	
155	387–89	271	Recession North American Free Trade Agreement (NAFTA)	Bill Clinton	North American Free Trade Agreement (NAFTA) recession	
156	390–92	272–73	Healthcare reform Gun control	Government reform Newt Gingrich		
157	393–96	274–75	Biography Box: Bill Gates Personal computers Microsoft Cable News Network	Michael Jordan O. J. Simpson 1996 Olympic Games		
158	397–99	276–77	Clinton scandals Balkan Peninsula Conflict	Northern Ireland NAFTA	perjury scandal	World Trade Organization
159	400–403	278	How It Was: Y2K Bug *Exxon Valdez* disaster Kyoto Protocol	1993 World Trade Center bombing Oklahoma City bombing Activity: Presenting a News Story	Kyoto Protocol pardon World Trade Center	
160		279–80	Chapter Review			
161			Chapter Test			

Visit bjupress.com/resources for links to enhance the lessons.

Strengths and Problems

As the 1980s came to an end, America was the clear leader of the free world. Communism was collapsing in many parts of the world. The United States seemed to be winning the Cold War. Its economy had also improved. Inflation had slowed. Low taxes and interest rates made goods and housing more affordable.

However, Americans had concerns too. Conservatives worried about poor morals. More people used illegal drugs. Disease connected to immoral behavior became widespread. Liberals worried too. They thought that Reagan was too hard on the poor. Many Americans noticed that the government spent more money than it earned. What was the solution? Spending less, taxing more?

A New President
Life and Career

As President Reagan's term ended in 1988, Americans chose a new leader. Many wanted someone to carry on Reagan's policies. **George H. W. Bush**

was the leading candidate to replace Reagan. Bush's life showed both patriotism and ability. Bush grew up in Connecticut. In 1942 he graduated from high school and joined the military. During World War II, Bush served as a pilot. After the war, he attended college and then made a fortune in the Texas oil industry. Then in 1966, Bush entered politics.

Over the next fourteen years, Bush showed much political talent. He served as a member of Congress, an ambassador to the United Nations, and an envoy to China. He was a leader in the Republican Party and called for Nixon to resign. Finally in 1980, he was elected vice president. These experiences prepared Bush to lead the nation.

Campaign for the White House

In August 1988 Bush became the Republican candidate for president. Bush promised to continue Reagan's policies. However, he promised a "kinder, gentler nation." Most famously

381

Timeline

Gulf War 1990–91

Clinton Elected/Inaugurated 1992/93

Bush Elected/Inaugurated 2000/2001

1990 — 1991 — 1995 — 1996 — 2000

Fall of the USSR

Atlanta Olympics

Chapter Focus

During the 1990s, Americans enjoyed advances in technology as the nation dealt with problems abroad and at home.

Lesson Focus

- Americans had concerns about their country in the 1990s.

Objectives

- Identify experiences that prepared George H. W. Bush for the White House
- Examine legislation Congress passed

Teacher's Toolkit CD

- Instructional Aid 64: *George H. W. Bush Era*

Introduction

- Invite a student to read aloud the title of the chapter and predict what the chapter will be about. It will be about the United States being the leader of the free world.

- How would you define the free world? Answers could include countries that are not run by dictators. Countries in the free world are more democratic. People can own property and make a profit.

- Invite a student to read the chapter focus aloud.

  What do you think you will learn in this chapter? about advances in technology and problems abroad and at home

  What do you see in the picture? a US Olympian with his hand raised in victory and waving an American flag after winning a race

- Direct attention to the timeline.

  What event happened during 1990 and 1991? the Gulf War

  What event happened one year later? the fall of the USSR

  When were the Olympics in Atlanta, Georgia? 1996

Preparation for Reading

- Generate interest as you direct the students to read the titles and examine the pictures on pages 380–83.

- Guide pronunciation of any unfamiliar words in the lesson.

- Direct the students to read the pages silently and complete Instructional Aid 64 in small groups.

Teach for Understanding

- Invite a student to name some of the strengths America had as the 1980s came to an end.

- Choose a volunteer to state concerns Americans had by the end of the 1980s.

- Invite a student to describe Bush's political experience that helped prepare him to be the president.

  What did George H. W. Bush promise about Reagan's policies and the kind of nation he would create? to continue Reagan's policies and to have a "kinder, gentler nation"

Lesson

153

Teach for Understanding

- Direct attention to the picture of George H. W. Bush. Read aloud the caption.

  What promise did Bush make about taxes? "Read my lips: no new taxes."

- Invite different groups to name the legislation Bush and Congress agreed on and to give a brief description of each.

- Use the Background information to discuss the passing of the Americans with Disabilities Act.

- Explain that Christians have a responsibility to care for the creation that God made. Because it is made by God and because God has blessed mankind with rulership over the created world, polluting and destroying the world is wrong.

- What are some ways people can care for God's creation?

  Answers could include preventing forest fires by putting out campfires, avoiding the use of harmful chemicals that could run into streams and ponds, replanting trees in areas where they are harvested, and obeying laws about hunting, fishing, and trapping.

- Explain the dangers of environmental alarmism and of environmental views that see humanity as a blight upon the earth. Humans are not lately-evolved invaders that have upset the environmental balance but are instead created image-bearers of God and made to rule over the creation.

---

he also promised, "Read my lips: no new taxes." Americans were happy that taxes would not rise. Bush chose Dan Quayle from Indiana as his running mate.

In the general election Bush faced a strong challenger, Michael Dukakis. As governor of Massachusetts, Dukakis had improved many things. At one point, polls suggested that almost six of every ten voters would choose Dukakis. But Bush fought hard. He pointed out that Dukakis had raised taxes in Massachusetts. Bush wanted Americans who liked Reagan's ideas for low taxes to reject a Democratic candidate. In December 1988 Bush won far more than half the country's votes.

Congress

Democrats did better in elections for Congress. They controlled both houses. President Bush tried to work with them. Congress and the president agreed on a few major bills.

In 1990 President Bush signed the **Americans with Disabilities Act**. This bill helps many Americans. For example, public buildings must be accessible to people who cannot walk. Signs must have Braille lettering for the

George Herbert Walker Bush joined the Navy during WWII. He was the youngest commissioned pilot at the time. While flying over the Pacific Ocean on one of his 58 combat missions, he was shot down by the Japanese. A US submarine rescued him, and he later received the Distinguished Flying Cross for his bravery.

blind. This law helped President Bush fulfill his promise to make the United States a "kinder, gentler nation."

During this time, many Americans were concerned about the environment. Scientists warned that tree cutting and man-made chemicals were damaging the earth. Some results were invisible. The ozone layer protects the earth from solar radiation, but chemicals were destroying this layer. During the late 1980s and early 1990s, American manufacturers reduced the amount of ozone-destroying chemicals they made. But Americans still worried about other damage.

In 1989 an accident showed how easily the environment could be harmed. An oil tanker, the *Exxon Valdez*, spilled millions of gallons of oil near Alaska. Miles of coastline were polluted. Pictures of dying bald eagles, seals, and other wildlife horrified Americans. As a result of the accident, Congress passed an **Oil Pollution Act**.

President Bush also asked Congress to help keep the air clean. The **Clean Air Act** of 1990 was their response. It attempted to decrease acid rain. Acid

382

Background

Americans with Disabilities Act

President Bush lost some public support by first opposing and then finally signing the Americans with Disabilities Act. This legislation prohibited job discrimination based on disabilities. It also required local governments and businesses to improve and alter their accommodations (e.g., provide special parking places for the disabled and install ramps for wheelchairs) for the disabled. When Bush opposed the legislation as an intrusion by the federal government on local governments and private citizens, the bill's supporters labeled him as uncompassionate. When he finally gave in and signed the bill, he angered those who opposed the new costs and invited a potential flood of lawsuits (which did not materialize).

The Search for Clean Air and Water

The publication of Rachel Carson's book *Silent Spring* (1962) launched the modern environmentalist movement, a concern about humanity's relationship to the environment. That book contained inaccurate information and alarmed Americans by exaggerating the harmful effects of pesticides, such as DDT. Nevertheless, there were real environmental problems that needed to be addressed. Under President Johnson, the government spent billions of dollars to clean up lakes and rivers. His

rain damages stone buildings and bodies of water. The act also limited the amount of pollution that cars could emit.

These bills show some of the concern Americans felt for the environment. Not all Americans wanted new laws. Some thought that the government cared more for the environment than for people. They feared that the laws would cost too much. But many Americans believed that a healthy environment would help keep people healthy too.

American Life

During President Bush's time in office, Americans enjoyed much prosperity. However, people had concerns. Paying the national debt was one. Other concerns were the problems with the rise of crime and immorality.

Economy

President Bush inherited years of deficits from the government spending more money than it made. During the Reagan administration, the government spent more than it earned and borrowed millions of dollars to pay the deficit. Americans accepted this spending because the nation was fighting the Cold War and the economy was slowly recovering. But now President Bush and Congress wanted to stop spending more than the government earned. However, they did not agree on what should be cut. At the same time, the economy got worse, and the government earned less from taxes than it had planned.

To balance the budget, President Bush broke his promise. Congress said it could not balance the budget without more tax money. If the budget remained unbalanced, some government departments would be unable to run. In 1990 President Bush agreed to raise taxes. Americans were angry. They focused on the rising taxes and not on government spending. Bush had promised "no new taxes." Now Americans wondered if Bush had lied about other things in order to be elected president.

Morality

Americans also worried about crime and morals. Drugs and gun violence seemed to plague the nation. The national news reported increased drug use. New York City suffered from increased robberies and muggings. In 1992 rioting shook the nation's second largest city, Los Angeles. For six days people burned buildings, looted, and murdered. The rioting began after police officers were declared not guilty of violence against a black man who was suspected of using illegal drugs and who tried to escape arrest. During the riot, more than fifty people died. Although most cities were safe, stories of violence appeared on television screens across the country. Americans feared for the future of the nation.

> What major promise did President Bush break?

383

Teach for Understanding

Why were some Americans against the new laws? Some thought that the government cared more for the environment than for people. They feared that the laws would cost too much.

How did many Americans feel about protecting the environment? Many Americans believed that a healthy environment would help keep people healthy too.

What helped to create the national debt that Bush inherited when he became president? The government spent more money than it made. During the Reagan administration, the government spent more than it earned and borrowed millions of dollars to pay the deficit.

When the economy got worse, what was the impact on the government? The government earned less from taxes than it had planned.

What did President Bush do in an effort to balance the budget? He agreed to raise taxes.

How did Americans feel about Bush breaking his word by raising taxes? Americans were angry. They wondered if Bush had lied about other things in order to be elected.

 What would help reduce the national debt? Answers could include cutting spending, budgeting extra money to pay off the national debt, and preventing money from being wasted.

- Choose a group to describe some things that were happening in the United States that caused Americans to be worried about crime and morals.

What did Americans fear in regard to their country? They feared for the future of the nation.

> Conclude the discussion by asking the question on page 383. "Read my lips: no new taxes."

Activity Manual

- Guide completion of pages 265–67.

---

wife, "Lady Bird" Johnson, led a crusade to beautify America. However, cities and states retained primary responsibility for regulating their own industries and pollution.

April 22, 1970, witnessed a nationwide protest called "Earth Day." It encouraged the federal government to step in and work for clean air and water. That year, Congress established the Environmental Protection Agency (EPA) to oversee environmental regulations. The Clean Air Act of 1970 (amended in 1977 and 1990) regulated air pollution. The Water Pollution Control Act (1972) and the Clean Water Act (1977) regulated water pollution.

Activities

Learning about Clean Water

Contact the water supplier in your area for information about water purification at their facility. Guide a discussion of how water is made clean enough to drink. Go on a tour of the water facility if possible.

Watching the National Debt Grow

Visit bjupress.com/resources to find a possible link to the National Debt Clock. Notice the various categories of debt. Invite the students to watch the numbers grow in real time before their very eyes.

Lesson

154

Student Text pages 384–86
Activity Manual pages 268–70

Lesson Focus

- The United States was involved in international affairs.

Objectives

- Identify the leader in Panama who surrendered to US forces
- Recognize who opposed a Communist coup in the USSR
- Analyze the crisis in the Middle East and the US involvement

Teacher's Toolkit CD

- Visuals 47–48: *Panama; Tiananmen Square*

Review

- Choose a volunteer to describe legislation Bush and Congress were able to pass.

> Guide a review of important terms, maps, places, and people from each previous lesson. Direct the students to find and read the corresponding entries from the Resource Treasury.

- Invite a student to describe the cause for increased national debt and what Bush did in an effort to balance the budget.

Preparation for Reading

- Generate interest as you direct the students to read the titles and examine the map and picture on pages 384–86.
- Guide pronunciation of any unfamiliar words in the lesson.
- Direct the students to read the pages silently to learn where thousands of Chinese citizens gathered to demand more freedom. Tiananmen Square

Teach for Understanding

- Display Visual 47. Invite a student to locate Panama and explain its location in regard to North America.

  Who was the corrupt leader in Panama? Manuel Noriega

  What tactics did Noriega use? He stayed in power by force. He faked election results, violently silenced his opponents, and smuggled drugs to earn money.

  What specific reason influenced Bush to stop Noriega? American soldiers in Panama were ill-treated.

  What did Noriega do two weeks after American troops entered Panama? He surrendered to American forces.

  What happened to Noriega once he was in the United States? He was tried for drug smuggling and other crimes.

- Invite students to name countries that abandoned Communism.

  What did President Bush encourage the Soviet premier, Mikhail Gorbachev, to promote? more democracy

---

The United States and the World

Noriega

Early in his presidency, Bush dealt with a minor threat. For years the United States had influenced the Central American country of Panama. Americans controlled the Panama Canal. Americans wanted a friendly leader in Panama. But the leader in the late 1980s was corrupt. **Manuel Noriega** stayed in power by force. He faked election results, violently silenced his opponents, and smuggled drugs to earn money. Some of these drugs ended up on American streets.

The situation became worse in 1989. Noriega ignored election results. The actual winner was attacked and beaten, and Americans heard about the violence. President Bush wanted to stop Noriega. When some American soldiers in Panama were ill-treated, Bush had a specific reason to act.

On December 20, 1989, American troops entered Panama. Two weeks later, Noriega surrendered to American forces. He was tried in the United States for drug smuggling and other crimes. President Bush showed the world that the United States would fight criminals and dictators who threatened peace.

Communism

Eastern Europe

The Cold War was ending in Eastern Europe. The United States had opposed Communism for over forty years. Changes were finally being seen.

A shocking change was the opening of the Berlin Wall on November 9, 1989. Travel between the two parts of Germany increased. Eventually the Wall itself was torn down. On October 3, 1990, both parts of Germany reunited to form one country.

Other Eastern European countries also turned to democracy. Even before the Berlin Wall fell, both Poland and Hungary set up non-Communist governments. In Czechoslovakia, Communism collapsed in late 1989. This peaceful change was called the Velvet Revolution. Bulgaria also switched from Communism to democracy. Only in Romania did the Communist leader resist. Over one thousand Romanians died before the dictator was captured and executed.

The USSR

The United States cheered these victories against Communism. But the USSR still existed. President Bush encouraged the Soviet premier, Mikhail Gorbachev, to promote more democracy. Democracy came in steps.

In the spring of 1989, the USSR allowed more freedom. There were some democratic elections. People hoped for more freedom of speech. The non-Russian parts of the USSR continued their push for freedom.

384

Background

Panama

Panama's drug-dealing leader, General Manuel Noriega, had become an embarrassment to the US government. Reagan had tried unsuccessfully to remove him peacefully. In December of 1989, Noriega went too far. His troops killed a US Marine and attacked an American couple. Then he declared war on the United States.

In the early morning hours of December 20, Bush launched Operation Just Cause. Within days, American troops had crushed Noriega's forces and captured Noriega. There were few American casualties. Noriega was the first foreign head of state to be captured and tried in a US court. He was convicted in 1992 of drug trafficking and sentenced to forty years in prison.

The USSR Divided

Finally in August 1991, the USSR collapsed. Some Communist leaders staged a coup. They locked up Gorbachev because he gave too many freedoms. They announced that they would run the USSR. **Boris Yeltsin** opposed the coup. He was the new leader of the Russian "republic" inside the USSR. The coup collapsed within days. Its leaders freed Gorbachev. On December 25, 1991, Gorbachev resigned as leader of the USSR. The Soviet Union divided into fifteen separate nations. The Cold War was over.

China

Communism did not collapse all over the world. Cuba, China, Vietnam, and North Korea remained the most influential Communist nations. China treated protesters harshly. In 1989 thousands of Chinese citizens

demanded more freedom. They gathered in a large square in the capital, Beijing. After about six weeks, the Chinese government reacted. Tanks rolled into **Tiananmen Square**. At least 200 protestors died, and thousands were injured on June 4, 1989. Many others were imprisoned. Unlike Eastern Europe, China would not gain democracy. President Bush condemned China's actions. He promised not to sell weapons to the Chinese government.

The Middle East

As the Cold War faded, the Soviet Union no longer existed, but war loomed in the Middle East. **Saddam Hussein** had led Iraq since 1979. Although he acted as a dictator, the United States often supported Hussein during the 1980s. During that decade,

385

Teach for Understanding

- Invite a student to explain the Communist coup in the USSR and what happened to the Soviet Union once it was disbanded.
- Direct attention to the map. Choose a volunteer to explain the meaning of the map.

What happened in China when thousands of Chinese citizens met in Tiananmen Square to demand more freedom? After about six weeks, the Chinese government reacted. Tanks rolled into the square. At least 200 protestors died, and thousands were injured. Many others were imprisoned.

- Display Visual 48. Choose a volunteer to describe what is happening in the pictures.

When President Bush condemned China's actions, what did he promise in regard to the Chinese government? President Bush promised not to sell weapons to the Chinese government.

Who was Saddam Hussein? He had led Iraq since 1979.

The USSR

Changes were taking place in the Soviet Union. As the "evil empire" began to break apart, Bush continued to support Gorbachev. Bush spoke with Gorbachev about creating a "new world order." They negotiated a Strategic Arms Reduction Treaty (START). Shortly after this, members of the Red Army, KGB, and Communist party attempted to remove Gorbachev from power. The revolt did not succeed, but it did seriously damage Gorbachev's reputation as a capable leader. Soon he was replaced by Boris Yeltsin, who favored dissolving the Soviet Union. Over the next several months, Bush cautiously observed these events from a distance. He did communicate to Gorbachev and then Yeltsin that the United States would support the nation's democratic movement. This move was made final on Christmas Day 1991. On that day, the Soviet Union ceased to exist.

- Direct attention to the picture on page 386. Read aloud the caption.

  What was Hussein's attitude toward Iran during the 1980s? He opposed Iran.

  What country did Saddam become increasingly hostile toward? Israel

  Where did Hussein launch an attack in August of 1990 that threatened the world economy? Kuwait

  Why did Hussein attack Kuwait? He wanted the oil that Kuwait had.

  What other country did Hussein threaten to attack? Saudi Arabia

  Who led the world's response to this threat? the United States

  What did the United Nations tell Saddam Hussein? to withdraw from Kuwait

  Fearing war, what did the United States and other nations do? They sent military forces to the Persian Gulf and Saudi Arabia.

  Who did President Bush assign to lead the Joint Chiefs of Staff? General Colin Powell

  Who was in charge of the troops on the ground? General Norman Schwarzkopf

- Choose a volunteer to describe Operation Desert Storm.

Primary Source: State of the Union Address

- Direct attention to Activity Manual page 268.
- Read aloud the introduction and the excerpt from President Bush's address to Congress at the time of the Middle Eastern Crisis.
- Discuss the meaning of the excerpt.

  ▶ Conclude the discussion by asking the question on page 386. Saddam Hussein was an enemy of the United States. He became hostile toward Israel, an American ally. The attack on Kuwait threatened the world economy.

Activity Manual

- Guide completion of pages 268–70.

---

he opposed Iran, an enemy of the United States. But by 1990, the United States did not want Hussein as a friend. He became increasingly hostile toward Israel, an American ally. Then in early August 1990, Saddam Hussein attacked Kuwait.

This attack threatened the world economy. Kuwait is only a small country between Iraq and Saudi Arabia, but it is rich in oil. Hussein wanted that oil. He also threatened to attack Saudi Arabia, a large country with even more oil than Kuwait. If Hussein controlled the oil from Iraq, Kuwait, and Saudi Arabia, he could cut the world off from those energy supplies.

USAF military aircraft fly over burning oil fields in Kuwait during Operation Desert Storm, 1991

The United States led the world's response to this threat. The United States worked together with the United Nations to act against Iraq. The UN told Hussein to withdraw from Kuwait by January 15, 1991. Fearing war, the United States sent military forces to the Persian Gulf and Saudi Arabia. Many other nations also sent troops.

President Bush assigned competent men to plan for war. General Colin Powell led the Joint Chiefs of Staff who advised the president on all military affairs. General Norman Schwarzkopf was in charge on the ground. He directed the coalition forces against Hussein's forces.

The battle to free Kuwait took place in February 1991. After Hussein refused to retreat in January, coalition forces began a bombing campaign. On February 24, ground troops advanced into Kuwait and Iraq. One hundred hours later, President Bush announced a ceasefire. Kuwait was free, and the Iraqi troops were retreating in disarray.

This short Gulf War, **Operation Desert Storm**, made Bush popular. The United States had easily won a war. It had freed a little country from an invasion. Americans were pleased that their country was leading the world. It seemed like the long, expensive Cold War had resulted in complete victory for the United States.

> Why did the United States lead the alliance against Saddam Hussein?

386

Background

Storm in the Desert

The United Nations overwhelmingly passed a resolution authorizing the use of military force to push the Iraqis out of Kuwait if they did not withdraw voluntarily by January 15, 1991. It did not, however, authorize the removal of Hussein from power or the invasion of Iraq itself. The allies (the United States, Kuwait, Saudi Arabia, Egypt, Great Britain, France, and several other nations) gathered a force of 700,000 in Saudi Arabia. Before launching a military attack, the allies exhausted every possible diplomatic effort to get the Iraqis to withdraw. Finally, on January 12, 1991, Congress voted to authorize Bush to use force if necessary to get Iraq out of Kuwait.

The January deadline became a line in the sand as the Iraqi forces defiantly dug in. On January 16, Bush ordered a massive military assault on Iraqi military targets. Code-named Operation Desert Storm, the liberation of Kuwait began. The allied commander, American general Norman Schwarzkopf, told his forces, "Now you must be the thunder and lightning of Desert Storm."

The war began with more than five weeks of massive, around-the-clock bombing and air strikes on military targets in Iraq and Kuwait. Allied cruise missiles, bombers, and fighters, including the new stealth

Election 1992

The Problem

Despite winning the Gulf War, Bush struggled to gain support for reelection. Americans were concerned about the economy. The nation was suffering a **recession**. A recession is a decline in the economy. Unemployment rose. The government struggled to spend only what it brought in. These two problems left many Americans questioning whether they should reelect Bush.

When Bush tried to save money, it seemed to make matters worse. Since the Cold War was over, the secretary of defense decided to save money in the military. He proposed closing bases around the country. This angered many Americans. Some feared that the United States would be too weak. Others worried about the people who would lose their jobs. With so many people already out of work, it seemed like the situation would only be worse. Even though closing the bases saved money for the government, many Americans were unhappy about it.

The **North American Free Trade Agreement (NAFTA)** also hurt Bush. This treaty promised to let trade occur openly between the United States, Canada, and Mexico. Americans were afraid that jobs would be lost to Mexicans. President Bush said that free trade would help the nation. Factory workers especially did not agree.

NAFTA was an agreement to allow free trade between Canada, Mexico, and the United States.

People's opinions about President Bush were not always based on facts. The economy began improving again in 1992. But many Americans did not notice. They remembered that Bush had raised taxes after promising not to. He closed bases and put thousands out of work. He was supporting NAFTA, a trade agreement that might cost some Americans their jobs. As the election drew closer, President Bush faced difficult challenges.

The Candidates

In the spring of 1992, most Americans were wondering who would be running for president. President Bush was the Republican choice. The Democrats struggled to decide on a candidate. By April it seemed likely that **Bill Clinton**, the governor of Arkansas,

387

---

fighters, pounded enemy installations. Enjoying almost complete air superiority, the US-led forces destroyed much of Iraq's military capability—communications networks, airfields, bridges, roads, chemical-weapons plants, and missile launch sites. Then the attacks targeted Iraq's ground forces, demolishing tanks and artillery and relentlessly pounding Hussein's entrenched legions.

The 100-Hour War

The second stage of the war was a ground attack on the Iraqis. On February 24, a coalition of American, Arab, and British troops assaulted enemy positions in southern Kuwait, pinning down the Iraqis, who thought this attack was the main thrust. But while the attack was raging, American and British forces supported by French units moved into southern Iraq west of Kuwait. With amazing speed, armored and infantry forces flanked the Iraqi lines, encircling and entrapping the main Iraqi force in Kuwait and southern Iraq. Dispirited by the weeks of bombing and virtually surrounded, thousands of Iraqi soldiers deserted and surrendered to the coalition army. Some Iraqi units fought fiercely but, with the lines of communication severed, ineffectively. The allies destroyed them piecemeal. On February 27, hours after the ground war began, Bush told America, "Kuwait is liberated."

Chapter 18: Leader of the Free World

Lesson Focus

- President Bush failed in his struggle to gain reelection.

Objectives
- Identify the meaning of NAFTA
- Recognize that Bill Clinton defeated Bush and Ross Perot in the presidential race

Review

- Invite a student to describe the defeat of Manuel Noriega in Panama.
- Review how the USSR was disbanded.
- Choose a volunteer to describe the Chinese government's treatment of protestors.
- Review the conflict with Saddam Hussein.

Preparation for Reading

- Generate interest as you direct the students to read the title and examine the pictures on pages 387–89.
- Guide pronunciation of any unfamiliar words in the lesson.
- Direct the students to read the pages silently to learn what the North American Free Trade Agreement (NAFTA) promised. to let trade occur openly between the United States, Canada, and Mexico

Teach for Understanding

- Direct attention to the picture on page 387. Read aloud the caption.

  What impact did the recession have on the economy? The economy was in a decline. Unemployment rose. The government struggled to spend only what it brought in.

  How did many Americans feel about Bush being re-elected as president? They questioned whether Bush should be president for four more years.

  Why were some Americans upset about closing military bases to save money? Some feared that the United States would be too weak. Others worried about the people who would lose their jobs.

  What did factory workers fear about the North American Free Trade Agreement? They were afraid that jobs would be lost to Mexicans.

- Choose a volunteer to describe some of the difficult challenges President Bush faced as the election drew closer.

Teach for Understanding

Who were the candidates in the 1992 presidential election? Bush was the Republican choice. Bill Clinton was the Democratic candidate. Ross Perot also ran.

• Direct attention to the pictures of the candidates on page 388.

🖎 Why do you think Ross Perot dropped out of the presidential race even though the early summer polls suggested that he could defeat both Bush and Clinton? Answers could include that he did not want to be the president. He may have thought he could not win the election. He did not want to keep spending money on his campaign. Campaigning may have affected his family and his personal life.

• Invite a student to identify accusations against Clinton.

How did the accusations affect people's attitudes toward Clinton? Despite the accusations, Clinton remained popular.

What happened at the Republican National Convention that seemed to help Bush in his campaign? Reagan spoke and supported Bush's campaign.

would be the party's choice. But there was also a third candidate for president.

This third candidate, Ross Perot, seemed an unlikely president. He had never been elected to a government post before. But he was a highly successful businessman. Like many Americans, he wanted the nation to be economically strong. He opposed allowing the government to spend more than it earned. Unlike most Americans, he had millions of dollars to spend on running for president.

Perot was not sure if he wanted to be president. In late February, he mentioned in a television interview that he might run. This news excited many Americans. Perot said that if he knew he had enough supporters, he would join the race. Across America thousands of people worked to raise support for Perot. They ensured that his name would be on the ballot even though he was not running with a

major political party. The early summer polls suggested that Perot could defeat both Bush and Clinton. But in July, Perot stopped running.

Over the summer, Bill Clinton's chances at winning kept improving. Early on, he was accused of scandals. Some people suggested that he was not faithful to his wife, Hillary. Others said that he had run away from the country so that he would not have to fight in Vietnam. They pointed out that he had smoked marijuana when he was younger. Despite these accusations, Clinton remained popular. With his wife and daughter, Clinton toured the country. He assured Americans that he understood how hard life could be.

President Bush struggled to regain the public's favor. The Republican National Convention in mid-August helped somewhat. President Reagan spoke and supported Bush's campaign. But the next week, a major hurricane

Ross Perot, Bill Clinton, and George H. W. Bush at a 1992 presidential debate

388

Background

Ross Perot

Complicating the campaign was an unusual third-party candidate. Billionaire Ross Perot financed his own campaign for the presidency. A small, folksy man with the spirit and blunt speaking of a Texas maverick, Perot promised to put an end to "politics as usual" and to trim the budget deficit. He made a virtue of the fact that he was no politician. Many Americans—put off by the candidates of the major parties and what they saw as dirty Washington politics—warmed to a candidate who was a true outsider. Even his wealth, which might have offended some voters, made Perot seem independent and self-sufficient. No special interests could "buy" him in return for their financial support.

The campaign was confusing. Perot dropped out of the race and then returned. Bush focused on Clinton's moral failings and tried, unsuccessfully, to label him as just another "tax-and-spend" liberal like those Reagan vanquished. Responding to the recession that followed the Gulf War, Clinton shrewdly made the economy his central issue.

Clinton defeated Bush by only a plurality, 43 to 37 percent. But in the Electoral College, he won by a landslide of 370 to 168. Although he did not have a majority of voters behind him, Clinton became the new president.

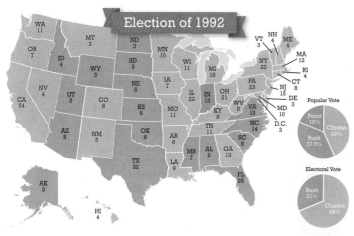

Election of 1992

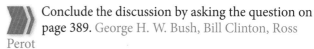

hit Florida. Hurricane Andrew devastated the state. Although the federal government sent help, millions of people suffered. President Bush was blamed for not helping faster. Americans questioned how much he cared about their struggles.

The campaign went from bad to worse for Bush. In early October, Ross Perot decided to rejoin the race. The president had to work to keep from losing voters to Perot.

Then in late October, a debate seemed to seal the election. An audience member asked the three candidates how the recession affected them. Perot pointed out facts about the national debt. Bush suggested that he cared even though it had not personally affected him. But Clinton asked the audience member how it affected her. Then he talked about how it affected his state of Arkansas. And he promised that he would change the economy to help working Americans. Although he did not say how it affected himself personally, Clinton won the debate. He presented himself as a leader who cared about the American people.

When the election took place in early November, the results were no surprise. Bill Clinton won the most votes, 43%. George Bush gained 37.5%. Perot took the rest. After twelve years of Republican presidents, the nation now had a Democratic one.

> Who were the three candidates for president in 1992?

389

Teach for Understanding

- Direct attention to the map and charts on page 389 and invite a volunteer to explain their meaning. Explain that the number on each state represents the number of electoral votes each state has.

What events happened after the convention that worked against Bush's bid for reelection? Hurricane Andrew caused millions of people to suffer. President Bush was blamed for not helping faster. Perot rejoined the race for president. Then Bill Clinton won the debate.

Who won the election? Clinton won the election with 43% of the votes.

What effect did a third candidate have on the election? Some of the votes that might have gone to Bush or to Clinton went to Perot.

What was the difference in the percentage of votes between Bush and Clinton? Clinton had 2.5% more votes than Bush.

>> Conclude the discussion by asking the question on page 389. George H. W. Bush, Bill Clinton, Ross Perot

Activity Manual

- Guide completion of page 271.

Activity

Voting for Choices

Lead the class to vote between two lunch favorites such as a piece of pizza or a hamburger. Record the votes for each. Have the students vote again, but add a third choice such as a taco. If the votes are split three ways, explain that when there are three choices, the votes are split three ways rather than two. Sometimes that makes it difficult to get a majority of votes for one particular choice. Try the experiment again, choosing among three favorite colors.

156

Student Text pages 390–92
Activity Manual pages 272–73

Lesson Focus

- After Bill Clinton became president, he made many changes in America and faced challenges abroad.

Objectives
- Recognize the Republican leader who fought Clinton's ideas
- Examine how Clinton promoted peace abroad

Review

- Ask questions such as the following to review the previous lesson.

What treaty promised to let trade occur openly between the United States, Canada, and Mexico? the North American Free Trade Agreement (NAFTA)

Who were the candidates in the election of 1992? Bush, Clinton, Perot

What happened after the Republican National Convention that hurt Bush's chance of winning the election? President Bush was blamed for not helping faster when Hurricane Andrew hit Florida. In late October, Bill Clinton won the debate.

Preparation for Reading

- Generate interest as you direct the students to read the titles and examine the pictures on pages 390–92.
- Guide pronunciation of any unfamiliar words in the lesson.
- Direct the students to read the pages silently to learn which bill regarding domestic policies Clinton could not get support for. a governmental healthcare program

Teach for Understanding

- Direct attention to the picture on page 390 and read aloud the captions.

What was confusing about the healthcare plan that Mrs. Clinton worked on? The details were confusing. No one seemed certain how the government would run the program.

How did Republicans feel about the healthcare plan? They opposed the plan. They called it "Hillarycare," and said it was doomed to fail.

What happened to the bill in Congress? Congress would not support the bill.

What did Clinton's gun control bill require gun sellers to do? a background check on purchasers

Who did President Clinton assign to "reinvent government"? Vice President Al Gore

Bill Clinton, born William Jefferson Blythe III, was named after his father who died in a car accident three months before Bill's birth. His mother later remarried. In high school, Bill changed his name to Clinton after his stepfather.

Clinton was often chosen for leadership positions during high school and college. At age 17 he was sent to the American Legion's Boy Nation as the elected representative of Arkansas. While in Washington, DC, he met President John F. Kennedy. Later Clinton was inspired to pursue work in public service himself.

President Clinton
Domestic Policies

Once he was president, Clinton set out to make many changes in the United States.

Healthcare

One of Clinton's key goals was healthcare reform. Americans spent large sums of money on medicine and doctors. Poorer Americans struggled to afford healthcare. President Clinton wanted a better system. His wife and some advisors worked on a plan. Hillary Clinton led the team as they worked on their proposal for most of 1993.

When the plan was eventually announced in the fall, few people liked it. The plan demanded that employers provide insurance. But the details were confusing. No one seemed certain how the government would run the program. Republicans opposed the plan. They called it "Hillarycare" and said it was doomed to fail. Although Democrats controlled Congress, President Clinton could not get support for the bill. Mrs. Clinton's popularity declined.

Gun Control

President Clinton also supported more gun control. Many Americans did not believe the federal government should make more rules for purchasing guns. They said that the Second Amendment's right to keep and bear arms would be worn away. Others felt that it was too easy for criminals to get guns. The bill that Clinton supported required that gun sellers do a background check on purchasers. Congress passed the bill, and President Clinton signed it.

Government Reform

President Clinton wanted the government to run more smoothly. He assigned his vice president, Al Gore, to "reinvent government." People had complained for years that the government was too big and complicated. Rules covered every action that a government employee took. Gore noticed that many government

390

Background

"Contract with America"

As the 1994 congressional elections approached, Republicans in the House of Representatives issued what they called a "Contract with America." House Republicans laid out ten popular bills they promised to bring up for a vote—if they were elected—in their first hundred days in office. This legislation included such issues as term limits and a balanced federal budget. Displeasure with the Clinton healthcare plan; the opposition to Democratic policies, amplified by talk radio; the efforts of the Religious Right; and the Contract with America all contributed to a stunning repudiation of the president in the fall elections. The Republicans captured control of both houses of Congress for the first time since Eisenhower's first term. Some Republicans confidently predicted that Clinton would be a one-term president like George H. W. Bush. But as those opponents would soon learn, the president was only down, not out.

Big government is harmful to the good of society.

organizations had too many employees. All these employees cost taxpayer dollars. Gore tried to reduce the number of unnecessary rules and workers. He reduced the number of federal employees by about 350,000. Although the government was not completely reinvented, it was improved.

Midterms

Two years into Clinton's term as president, Americans elected a new Congress. The battle over that election showed Clinton how people felt about his presidency. Many people were unhappy.

Two issues, abortion and government size, were reasons why Americans were unhappy. Many felt that Clinton was too approving of abortion. He praised *Roe v. Wade*. He allowed American money to pay for abortions in foreign countries. Many Americans did not approve of abortion

at all. Conservatives also thought the government was still too powerful. "Hillarycare" showed that Clinton approved of more government programs. Some Republicans wanted an extreme solution. They believed that Congress members should serve no more than twelve years. These Republicans hoped that term limits would prevent Congress members from trying to give the government more power.

Talk radio programs revealed the unhappiness many Americans felt. In the late 1980s, conservative talk show hosts became popular. The most popular was Rush Limbaugh. On his radio show, he gave his opinion of the government. Listeners could call in to agree or disagree. During the first two years of Clinton's presidency, Limbaugh continually attacked the president's positions. Millions of Americans listened to him.

In 1993 and 1994, Congress usually supported the president. Both the House and the Senate were controlled by Democrats. But as the election of 1994 heated up, a congressman from Georgia opposed Clinton. **Newt Gingrich** led Republicans in fighting Clinton's ideas. Gingrich called for a "Contract with America." This contract promised to deliver good government. It claimed it would cut taxes and provide for hard-working Americans.

391

- Direct attention to the picture on page 391. Choose a volunteer to read the caption aloud and explain the meaning of the cartoon.

What did Al Gore do to change government? He tried to reduce the number of unnecessary rules and workers.

What did the election of a new Congress show about Clinton's popularity after his two years in office? that many people were unhappy

What was Clinton's attitude about abortion? He praised *Roe v. Wade*. He allowed American money to pay for abortions in foreign countries.

How did many Americans feel toward abortion? Many Americans did not approve of abortion at all.

What did conservatives think about the government? They thought it was too powerful.

What part did talk show programs play regarding how many Americans felt? Talk show programs revealed the unhappiness many Americans felt.

What congressman led the Republicans to fight Clinton's ideas? Newt Gingrich

What did Gingrich's "Contract with America" promise? It promised to deliver good government. It claimed it would cut taxes and provide for hard-working Americans.

Lesson

156

Teach for Understanding

- Direct attention to the cartoon of Gingrich's "Contract with America" on page 392. Explain that the cartoon suggests that if Americans voted for a Republican Congress, Congress would deliver good government.

What position did Gingrich hold after Republicans gained control of both houses of Congress? the Speaker of the House

In what ways did President Clinton change his policies after the election that put Republicans in control of Congress? He focused more on policies that would be agreeable to both parties instead of focusing on strongly Democratic ideals.

What happened when Clinton and Congress could not agree on a balanced budget? Parts of the government shut down for almost thirty days.

What eventually happened regarding the budget? Both sides agreed to a balanced budget.

What were some problems that Clinton helped to solve in the Americas? Clinton sent troops to Haiti to keep the peace. He had the United States loan money to Mexico to help keep the country stable.

What was Clinton's relationship to Asian nations? He ended a trade embargo with Vietnam. He encouraged American ties with China.

In what ways did Clinton promote peace in warring nations? He wanted Israel to have peace with its neighbors. He urged warring groups in Northern Ireland to resolve their differences.

> Conclude the discussion by asking the question on page 392. Possible answers include that Clinton wanted government to run smoothly. Clinton also wanted to put Democratic ideals in place.

Activity Manual

- Guide completion of pages 272–73.

Assessment

- Administer quiz.

The quiz may be given anytime after completing this lesson.

Americans responded to Gingrich in the election. Republicans gained control of both houses of Congress. Newt Gingrich became the new Speaker of the House. President Clinton changed his policies after the election. He focused more on policies that would be agreeable to both parties instead of focusing on strongly Democratic ideals.

However, Clinton and the Republican Congress still had some deep disagreements. In late 1995 and early 1996, the two sides could not agree on a budget. Parts of the government shut down for almost thirty days. The American public was unhappy. Both Clinton and Gingrich fell in popularity. Eventually, both sides agreed on a balanced budget.

Foreign Affairs

President Clinton also faced challenges abroad. Although the Cold War was over, the world continued to have problems. The United States was a major superpower in the world, and many people hoped that it would use its wealth and power to solve problems.

In the Americas, Clinton tried to help neighboring countries. He demanded that unelected government officials in Haiti resign. In 1994 the elected Haitian president returned to power. Clinton sent troops to Haiti to help keep the peace. He also had the United States loan Mexico twenty billion dollars in 1995. The money helped keep Mexico stable. Over the next few years, Mexico repaid the debt with interest.

Clinton encouraged closer trading ties with Asian nations. He ended a trade embargo with Vietnam. Americans remembered the cruelty and torture their soldiers had suffered from the Communist Vietnamese, but Clinton argued that Vietnam had changed. He claimed that more trade would help turn it into a freer nation. Clinton also encouraged American ties with China.

Finally, Clinton promoted peace in warring nations. He wanted Israel to have peace with its neighbors. He also urged warring groups in Northern Ireland to resolve their differences.

> What did President Clinton want to do with government besides making it larger?

392

Student Text pages 393–96
Activity Manual pages 274–75

Bill Gates

Who: Inventor and Businessman

When: 1955–present

Where: Washington State

William Gates III grew up in the state of Washington. Computers interested him in high school. In 1973 he left home to attend Harvard University.

Gates showed great ability to program computers. He left college in 1975 after starting a programming company. For four years his new company, Microsoft, was based in New Mexico. Then in 1979 it moved close to Seattle, Washington.

Over the next decades, Microsoft dominated the programming world. By the 1990s, Microsoft programs ran the majority of American computers.

Gates is also a generous philanthropist. Because of Microsoft's success, Gates became rich. Beginning in 1995, he was the wealthiest man in the United States. Like Andrew Carnegie and John D. Rockefeller, Gates has tried to use his money to help other people.

Life in the 1990s: Progress
Technology

Life in the United States during the 1990s was full of endless progress. Technology seemed to change daily. Americans learned to interact with each other and the world differently during the decade.

One change was the continued growth of television. The 1990s saw the explosion of cable television. Unlike network television, customers had to pay to receive cable channels. These provided news or shows twenty-four hours a day. Channels became devoted to specific themes. An American could watch a cable channel with food shows all day long. Other channels provided shows focused mainly on teenagers.

News channels also became increasingly popular. The Cable News Network (CNN) gained popularity during the Gulf War. Its live coverage kept Americans glued to their screens. Later in the decade, two other news channels began. Fox News offered a more conservative perspective. Microsoft National Broadcasting

393

Lesson Focus

- Progress in the 1990s made Americans feel pleased with their country.

Objectives
- Identify improvements in technology
- Evaluate the economy and crime during the 1990s

Review

- Use questions such as the following to review the previous lesson.

How did President Clinton feel about gun control? He supported more gun control.

What did Al Gore do to try to improve government? He reduced the number of unnecessary rules and workers.

How did Americans show Clinton that they were unhappy with his presidency? They elected a new Congress.

Who became the new Speaker of the House? Newt Gingrich

What did Clinton do to help keep peace in Haiti? He sent troops there.

Preparation for Reading

- Generate interest as you direct the students to read the titles and examine the pictures on pages 393–96.
- Guide pronunciation of any unfamiliar words in the lesson.
- Direct the students to read the pages silently to learn the name of the company that made computers easier to use. Microsoft

Teach for Understanding

- Direct attention to the Biography Box on page 393. Read aloud the biography.

What did Bill Gates have a great ability to do? program computers

- Invite a student to tell the name of the company Gates founded and how successful it was.

What helped to make television grow? the explosion of cable television

- Choose a student to name several of the cable networks and identify which one was more conservative.

Activity

Creating a Technology Timeline

Use resources to make a pictorial timeline of the development of technology. Students may choose to trace the progression of television from the old black-and-white television to cable, satellite, and wireless television today. You may choose to do a pictorial timeline of the changes in telephone or computer technology.

Teach for Understanding

- Direct attention to the pictures of technology devices on page 394. Invite a student to name the devices.

  How was cable news coverage different than the old broadcast stations' news coverage? Cable channels allowed more stories to be covered, and Americans could always watch something happening.

  Who helped to create a world wide web to make it easier to access information? Tim Berners-Lee

  What did browsers allow computer users to do? access informaton on the Internet and share information with others

  What company helped Americans use computers easily? Microsoft

- Invite a student to name some things Americans could do on the computer.

Company (MSNBC) tried to be unbiased. Since Americans wanted news whenever they turned their televisions on, channels had to provide more coverage. The old broadcast stations gave news only in the morning and evening. Cable channels allowed more stories to be covered, and Americans could always watch something happening.

A second change was the rise of personal computers. Until the 1990s, personal computers were very expensive. Although the Internet contained a large amount of information, it was difficult for the average person to access. But a programmer named Tim Berners-Lee developed a specific programming language to create a worldwide web that could be used more easily. Soon people created browsers, programs that allow computer users to access information on the Internet and share information with others.

At the same time, a company called Microsoft made computers easier to use. Millions of Americans began purchasing personal computers. They could send electronic messages, called *emails*, to each other. Companies began creating webpages. Even the government created webpages.

The changes to American life were immense. Before computers, information was most easily available in libraries. Searching for a phone number required a phone book. Even typing a school assignment required hours at a typewriter, and mistakes could not be easily corrected.

The personal computer, the cell phone, and the Nintendo Game Boy grew in popularity in the 1990s.

394

A third major change was the introduction of cell phones. A few cell phones had been available since the 1980s. They were as large as bricks and had a short battery life. They could only send and receive calls. In the 1990s, newer cell phones were developed. They became increasingly lighter. Some even let users send text messages to other cell phone users. These early cell phones were expensive to buy and use. But as they became less expensive, cell phones permitted Americans to be increasingly connected to each other.

Technology also affected American lives in smaller ways. Toymakers began using computer chips in toys. Computer chips could even allow toys to interact with a child. Computers affected all of American life.

Sports

Perhaps the biggest sports story of the decade was that of Michael Jordan and the Chicago Bulls. From 1991 to 1993, the Bulls won three consecutive championships. Then Jordan retired. But only two years later, he rejoined the team. The Bulls then won three more championships in a row. Americans everywhere cheered for Jordan and the Bulls.

Americans were also excited to host the Olympic Games in 1996. Atlanta, Georgia, welcomed thousands of the world's best athletes. The United States' Olympic Team performed well in many sports. At the end of the games, America had more medals than any other country.

Five-time MVP Michael Jordan (left) led the Chicago Bulls to victory in six NBA championships.

The '96 Olympics brought the US women's gymnastics team (above) their first ever team gold medal.

Michael Johnson (above) set world and Olympic records in the 400 and 200 meter races respectively, becoming the first man to win gold in both events.

395

Teach for Understanding

What were the first cell phones like? They were as large as bricks and had a short battery life. They could only send and receive calls.

What could cell phone users do on the new cell phones that they could not do on the old ones? send text messages to other cell phone users

In what way did technology affect toys? Toymakers began using computer chips in toys. Computer chips could even allow toys to interact with a child.

• Direct attention to the pictures on page 395. Read aloud the captions.

What player helped the Chicago Bulls win three championships in a row twice? Michael Jordan

How did American teams do at the 1996 Olympic Games in Atlanta, Georgia? The American teams performed well in many sports. America won more medals than any other country.

- Direct attention to the pictures on page 396. Read aloud the captions.

  What famous American football player was tried for murder? O. J. Simpson

  What was the outcome of his trial? He was found not guilty.

- Explain that the outcome of the trial removed the charges against O. J. Simpson.

- What do the events in O. J. Simpson's life suggest? Even successful athletes do not have perfect lives.

- Choose a student to describe what contributed to a strong economy during the 1990s.

  What did the major bill Congress passed do to help attack crime? It increased the size of many police departments. If a person committed three serious felonies, he or she could be imprisoned for life.

- What do you believe happens when the government does not punish criminals and the size of a police department is decreased? Crime could increase. There would not be enough officers to take care of the crimes in a community.

- Choose a student to name reasons that Americans were pleased with their country.

  ▶ Conclude the discussion by asking the question on page 396. Atlanta

- Guide completion of pages 274–75.

During his trial, O. J. Simpson tries on gloves similar to those connected to the murder of his ex-wife and her friend.

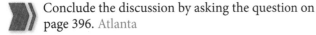

O. J. Simpson led the NFL in rushing yards for four years at the height of his career.

One sad sports story also gained much attention. O. J. Simpson was a famous American football player. In 1994 his ex-wife and her friend were murdered. Simpson was arrested for the murder and put on trial. Televisions, radios, and newspapers broadcasted the details of the case for months. Millions of Americans followed the story. Simpson was eventually found not guilty, but the trial showed America's interest in celebrities. Famous people made news.

The Economy and Crime

During the 1990s, the economy grew consistently. Year after year, unemployment remained low. New industries, such as technology, helped provide jobs. American companies led the world in many fields. Companies sold products internationally, and the profits benefited the nation.

During the decade, Alan Greenspan received praise for much of the economic growth. He led the Federal Reserve Bank. Because he set the interest rate at which the government loaned money, he was credited with encouraging a strong economy.

President Clinton also promoted an attack on crimes. Congress passed a major bill in 1994. It increased the size of many police departments. If a person committed three felonies, he or she could be imprisoned for life. Local governments also tried to be more effective in policing. They wanted to stop small crime. People hoped that if small crime stopped, major crime would stop as well. Crime did decrease during the decade.

All in all, the United States seemed to prosper in the 1990s. People had jobs. Crime in the cities slowly decreased. Technology became cheaper and better. Americans were pleased with their country.

> What American city hosted the 1996 summer Olympics?

396

"The Comeback Kid"

Throughout his career, Bill Clinton was called "the comeback kid." After his defeat in the 1980 Arkansas governor's race, he came back to recapture that office two years later. After allegations of sexual immorality led to his defeat in the 1992 New Hampshire presidential primary, he rebounded to capture the Democratic nomination. Faced with embarrassing defeats involving his healthcare plan and the congressional elections, Clinton began another comeback.

The success of Clinton's comeback became evident in the 1996 presidential election. The Republicans nominated Senate Majority Leader Bob Dole of Kansas. Dole was a decorated World War II veteran with a conservative voting record. He was also an experienced legislator with a thorough knowledge of Washington politics. Ross Perot was on the ballot again with his Reform Party, splitting the votes of Clinton opponents.

Clinton cruised to reelection. Although he failed again to get a majority of the popular vote, he had 49 percent to Dole's 41 percent and Perot's 8 percent. In the Electoral College, the president swamped Dole 379–159. But the Republicans retained control of Congress and maintained their hold on the majority of governors' chairs. Bill Clinton "came back," but his party remained in the minority in Congress.

Problems at Home and Abroad

Election 1996

Americans voted in a presidential election in 1996. Clinton enjoyed high popularity throughout the campaign. He won 49.2% of the popular vote. The Republicans selected Senator Bob Dole of Kansas. He gained 40% of the vote. Ross Perot ran once again and got less than 10%. Although Clinton won the presidency, the Republicans kept both houses of Congress.

Scandals

President Clinton won reelection easily, but his second term offered new troubles. Several **scandals** arose. One even threatened his position.

The first scandal suggested that China bought influence with the White House. Reporters connected the Chinese Embassy to donations supporting President Clinton. Vice President Gore was involved in a similar scandal. He had attended an illegal fundraiser. Clinton and Gore both denied knowledge of wrongdoing. Nothing was ever proven, but many Americans wondered what Clinton and Gore had actually known.

At the same time a woman named Paula Jones tried to sue President Clinton. She claimed that he had behaved improperly toward her before he was president. The lawsuit was eventually dismissed. But people wondered what had really happened.

During the course of the lawsuit, another problem arose. President Clinton was accused of having an improper relationship with an intern. Clinton denied the affair. He even testified under oath that he had done nothing wrong.

Eventually the truth came out. President Clinton had lied. Many Americans believed that this scandal was more than just a marriage problem. Since he did not keep his marriage promises to his wife, and since he had lied under oath, could he be trusted to keep his oath of office? Some people wanted him to be punished for **perjury**.

Congress investigated Clinton's behavior and impeached him. If a president commits certain crimes, the House of Representatives can impeach him. The Senate then puts him on trial. A convicted president would lose his

397

Lesson 158

Student Text pages 397–99
Activity Manual pages 276–77

Lesson Focus

- President Clinton remained in office in spite of accusations of improper behavior.

Objectives

- Recognize scandals involving President Clinton
- Examine Clinton's foreign accomplishments
- Relate how international trade grew during Clinton's time in office

Teacher's Toolkit CD

- Visual 49: *Conflict in Northern Ireland*

Introduction

- Invite a student to tell how technology changed everyday life for Americans.
- Choose a student to explain why Americans were pleased with their country in the 1990s.

Preparation for Reading

- Generate interest as you direct the students to read the titles and examine the picture and map on pages 397–99.
- Guide pronunciation of any unfamiliar words on the page.
- Divide the students in pairs. Direct the students to read the pages and describe on a half sheet of paper what NAFTA, GATT, and the World Trade Organization were.

Teach for Understanding

- Direct attention to the picture on page 397. Invite a student to explain the meaning of the newspaper headline.

After Clinton won the election of 1996, which political party kept both houses of Congress? Republican

What scandals did Clinton face after his reelection? A scandal suggested that China bought influence with the White House. Reporters connected the Chinese Embassy to donations supporting President Clinton. In addition, Vice President Gore had attended an illegal fundraiser. Then Paula Jones claimed that Clinton had behaved improperly toward her before he was president. President Clinton was accused of having an improper relationship with an intern and then lied under oath.

What is it called when someone lies under oath? perjury

After Congress investigated Clinton's behavior, what action did they take? They impeached him.

What is an impeachment? a formal accusation of wrongdoing

What does the Senate do after an impeachment? The Senate puts the person on trial.

What would result if a president was found guilty? A convicted president would lose office.

Chapter 18: Leader of the Free World   Lesson 158 • 401

Lesson

158

Teach for Understanding

What was the outcome of Clinton's impeachment? The Senate found Clinton not guilty of perjury.

What consequences did Clinton face? He was unable to push for all the legislation he wanted. He had to pay a fine for being in contempt of court. He paid Paula Jones $850,000.

What did many Americans believe about Clinton's wrongdoings? They believed that his wrongdoings were personal. They thought that a fault in his personal life should not count against his professional life.

What did conservative Americans think Clinton's moral failing and his lie made him? an untrustworthy man

How is a country's government affected when its people no longer care about a leader having virtue? Answers could include that the country will have bad leaders.

• Direct attention to the map of the Balkan Peninsula. Explain that there is some disagreement about what countries make up the Balkan Peninsula. Most people accept the countries or part of the countries of Albania, Bosnia and Herzegovina, Bulgaria, Croatia, Kosovo, Macedonia, Montenegro, Romania, Serbia and Slovenia as part of the Balkans. Areas in Turkey and Greece are also considered to be part of the Balkans. Guide students in locating the countries that make up the Balkans.

What groups of people were fighting each other in countries now known as Croatia, Bosnia and Herzegovina, Serbia, and Montenegro? Catholic Croats, Muslim Bosniaks, and Orthodox Serbians

Where did these groups meet in 1995 and agree to a peace treaty? Dayton, Ohio

How did the United States help keep the peace? by stationing American troops in Bosnia to keep the peace

Why did the United States and NATO bomb Serbian forces four years later? Serbians were accused of fighting Muslim Kosovars in a region of Serbia.

How successful was Clinton's effort to work out a solution for the Balkans? He could not bring lasting peace to the region.

---

office. The Senate found Clinton not guilty of perjury. Senate Democrats did not believe that Clinton's failings were serious enough to remove him from office.

Clinton kept the presidency, but he faced consequences. He was unable to push for all the legislation he wanted. In addition, he had to pay a fine for being in contempt of court for showing disrespect to the court's authority. He also paid Paula Jones $850,000.

Many Americans cared little about Clinton's behavior. They believed that his wrongdoings were personal. They thought that a fault in his personal life should not count against his professional life.

However, many conservative Americans disagreed. They thought that a moral failing followed by a lie showed that Clinton was untrustworthy. Some Americans worried for the nation's future. They believed a healthy democracy needed virtue. If voters did not care about virtue, the nation would have bad leaders.

Clinton's Foreign Accomplishments

Yugoslavia's Successors

During the 1990s, the Balkan Peninsula suffered from constant warfare.

After Communism collapsed, so did the country of Yugoslavia. Its people followed different religions. They spoke different languages, making it difficult to communicate with one another. Many people hated each other.

The biggest problems occurred in the countries now called Croatia, Bosnia and Herzegovina, Serbia, and Montenegro. Here Catholic Croats, Muslim Bosniaks, and Orthodox Serbians all fought each other. In 1995 all three groups met in Dayton, Ohio. They agreed to a peace treaty. Clinton agreed to station American troops in Bosnia to keep the peace.

Four years later, the United States intervened again. Serbians were accused of fighting Muslim Kosovars in a region of Serbia. The United States and NATO bombed Serbian forces to end the fighting. Although Clinton tried to work out a solution for the Balkans, he could not bring lasting peace to the region.

Balkan Peninsula

Background

The Balkan Conflict

The fierce ethnic and religious divisions of the Balkans had long been an explosion waiting to happen. Catholics, Muslims, and Orthodox Christians there competed fiercely with each other. The Serbs and the Croats were (and still are) the dominant ethnic groups, with several other smaller groups. Some fifty years of cruel Communist oppression after World War II enforced a relative peace in the region. When Communism fell in most of the area in the 1980s and 1990s, however, conflict broke out again. The nation of Yugoslavia became the focus of the trouble as it splintered into several different nations.

The United States became involved first in Bosnia, located in the center of the former Yugoslavia. Bosnia embodied all the conflicts in the region. While other countries were predominantly Croat or Serb, Bosnia's population had both Croats and Serbs. In addition, Bosnia had one of the largest Muslim populations in the Balkans. In 1992, civil war broke out—a war furthered by Croatia in the west and what was left of Yugoslavia in the east.

Northern Ireland

President Clinton is credited for helping settle the conflict in Northern Ireland. For decades, Northern Ireland was torn by violence. Nationalists, mainly Catholic, wanted Northern Ireland to unite with the rest of Ireland. Loyalists, mainly Protestant, wanted to remain part of the United Kingdom. Both sides committed acts of violence. Bombings and assassinations happened regularly. Nationalists even bombed cities in England.

President Clinton visited both Ireland and Northern Ireland three times. He encouraged leaders from both sides to talk. On Good Friday 1998 they came to an agreement. They would stop fighting and work together. The peace that President Clinton pushed for has lasted since he left office.

Trade

A lasting part of President Clinton's legacy is the growth of international trade. Clinton wanted Americans to be part of a global system. He succeeded.

NAFTA

The North American Free Trade Agreement (NAFTA) was a major battle for Clinton. Although President Bush had supported it, not all Republicans agreed with it. Bush had overseen the writing of the agreement. In 1993 Clinton had to get it approved by Congress.

The battle was hard. Americans feared that jobs would be lost to Mexico. Clinton promised that the deal would benefit Americans. When Congress voted, both parties split with some members of each party refusing to support the deal. However, the deal received enough support from each party to pass.

GATT

President Clinton also urged Congress to vote for an expansion of the General Agreement on Tariffs and Trade (GATT). This agreement set rules on trading between nations. It was expanding to become the **World Trade Organization**. Once again, Congress listened to Clinton. In 1994 the Senate accepted the treaty.

China

Throughout his presidency, Clinton pushed for closer ties with China. For years, opponents had argued against granting a permanent normal trade relation to China. They noted that China was not a free land. But Clinton persuaded Congress that the status would benefit both the United States and China. In 2000 Clinton signed a bill normalizing trade with China.

> How did Clinton's scandals affect his presidency?

399

Teach for Understanding

What was the cause of the conflict in Northern Ireland? Nationalists, mainly Catholic, wanted Northern Ireland to unite with the rest of Ireland. Loyalists, mainly Protestant, wanted to remain part of the United Kingdom.

- Display Visual 49. Choose a volunteer to locate Northern Ireland.
- Invite a student to identify the countries shown in red that make up the United Kingdom.
- Choose a volunteer to explain the meaning of the flags.

What was the conflict like? Both sides committed acts of violence. Bombings and assassinations happened regularly.

How did Clinton intervene in the conflict? Clinton visited both Ireland and Northern Ireland three times. He encouraged the leaders from both sides to talk, which led to an agreement to stop fighting and work together.

How successful was Clinton's intervention? The peace that Clinton pushed for has lasted since he left office.

What controversial agreement was approved by Congress to make Americans part of a global trade system? the North American Free Trade Agreement (NAFTA)

What did the General Agreement on Tariffs and Trade (GATT) do? The agreement set rules on trading between nations.

What did the GATT grow to become once Congress voted to expand it? the World Trade Organization

What did Clinton do in spite of opposition to granting permanent normal trade relation to China? Clinton persuaded Congress that the status would benefit the United States and China. Clinton signed a bill normalizing trade with China.

> Conclude the discussion by asking the question on page 399. He kept the presidency but faced consequences. He was unable to push for all the legislation he wanted.

Activity Manual

- Guide completion of pages 276–77.

At first, Clinton did not send soldiers to Bosnia, but he did provide air support for the United Nations' efforts to keep the peace. Furthermore, American diplomats took a leading role in trying to negotiate a peaceful settlement in the area. Finally, all the parties met together at Wright Patterson Air Force Base in Dayton, Ohio, and hammered out the Dayton Accords. That fragile agreement fashioned Bosnia into a confederation in which the Serbs, Croats, and Muslims shared power. To enact the agreement, the United Nations worked with NATO. The UN was responsible for the civil duties; NATO took on the burden of the military duties. As part of the peacekeeping efforts, Clinton sent American troops to Bosnia. An uneasy peace settled over the bitterly divided nation.

The creation of new nations in the Balkans reduced Yugoslavia to a federal union of two small states, Serbia and Montenegro. Even in the shrunken Yugoslavia, the province of Kosovo became the scene of ethnic clashes. Most of the people in the province were Albanian Muslims, but a large minority were Serbs, who were nominally Christian.

Lesson Focus

- There were terrorist attacks at home and abroad during the Clinton presidency.

Objectives

- Recognize the Clinton administration's attitude toward the environment
- Relate domestic and international terrorist acts

Teacher's Toolkit CD

- Instructional Aid 65: *Writing and Presenting a News Story*

Materials

- Resources for writing and presenting a news story; optional 18 × 24 inch posterboards

Review

- Review the troubles that Clinton presented after his reelection.
- Invite a student to describe Clinton's attempts to keep peace in the Balkans and in Northern Ireland.
- Discuss legislation that changed American trade.

Preparation for Reading

- Generate interest as you direct the students to read the titles and examine the pictures on pages 400–403.
- Guide pronunciation of any unfamiliar words.
- Direct the students to read the pages silently to discover what agreement by major countries was designed to slash the amount of carbon dioxide they emit. Kyoto Protocol

Teach for Understanding

- Direct attention to the picture and the How It Was box on page 400. Read aloud the story.
- Use the Background information about the Y2K bug to discuss the reason for Tyler's fears.
- Invite a student to tell how Tyler's dad responded to Tyler's fears.

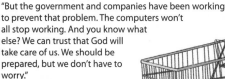

How It Was

"Dad, shouldn't we get more food?" Tyler asked as he stood with his father in the grocery store.

His dad looked at the shopping cart. "We have pizza, chips, dip, and ice cream for New Year 2000 party. Your mom has all the normal shopping done. Is there anything else we're missing?"

"Well, do you think we have enough food at home?" Tyler asked.

"Remember, your mom and Emily already went grocery shopping today. You and I got everything on the list. We just need to pick up some flowers."

"Okay, Dad. As long as you think that we will be okay and not run out of food."

Tyler's dad paused and looked at him. "Tyler, what's going on? What are you worried about?"

"Well, you know my friend Mariah's family? They have a lot of canned food and water because they said that the stores might run out of food if all the computers break."

"I know a lot of people are worried about that," Dad said. "But the government and companies have been working to prevent that problem. The computers won't all stop working. And you know what else? We can trust that God will take care of us. We should be prepared, but we don't have to worry."

"Do you really think so, Dad?"

"Yes, Tyler," Dad said. "Remember, Jesus told us not to worry because He loves us and cares for us."

"Okay, well that's good."

"C'mon, let's go choose the flowers," Dad said.

400

Background

Y2K Bug

American people feared that a computer glitch might happen when December 31, 1999, changed to January 1, 2000. They thought the computers that controlled technology would read the date incorrectly. People called it the Y2K bug. Y2K stands for the "Year 2000."

Fearing what may happen with computers, some Americans prepared by storing extra food, water, batteries, and fuel. They feared there would be transportation and banking problems. They wondered how Y2K would affect national security. But when the year 2000 came, people realized that very few problems occurred because of the millenium bug.

Other Issues in the 1990s
Environment

President Clinton worked to further environmental protection. He tried to prevent more oil drilling. Clinton would not let companies drill any new wells off American coasts. He also stopped oil companies from drilling in the far north of Alaska. Environmentalists feared that drilling in the Arctic National Wildlife Refuge would endanger the animals living there. They also worried that piping the oil out would risk spills like the *Exxon Valdez* disaster.

Vice President Gore was probably most connected in the public mind with the environment. He helped bring attention to the idea of climate change.

Some scientists had warned for decades of something called the greenhouse effect. They said that humans were putting gases, especially carbon dioxide, into the air at too high a rate. These gases would remain in the atmosphere and trap heat on earth. The whole planet would slowly overheat. They warned that icecaps would melt, and oceans would rise. For most of the 1990s, this idea was called global warming. It was occasionally called climate change.

Gore wanted the United States to sign the **Kyoto Protocol**, named after a Japanese city. In the agreement, many major countries agreed to significantly reduce the amount of carbon dioxide they emit.

Many Americans did not approve of the Kyoto Protocol. It seemed to threaten the economy. It required the United States to use significantly less coal and oil. These fuels were major sources of energy. Americans noticed that the agreement applied to only some nations. Others could keep using the inexpensive fuels. Americans wondered how the Kyoto Protocol would help if only a few countries participated. President Clinton decided never to ask Congress to vote on the agreement.

Terrorism
Domestic Terrorism

Throughout Clinton's term, the United States suffered several terrorist attacks. Although most were planned by non-Americans, two of the worst were planned by American citizens.

On April 19, 1995, a federal office building in Oklahoma City was blown up. The bombing killed 168 people. Many more were injured. Americans wondered why someone would attack people at work. The bombers were

401

Teach for Understanding

How did Clinton further environmental protection? He tried to prevent more oil drilling by not allowing companies to drill new wells off American coasts.

What did Gore help bring attention to? climate change

• Invite a student to explain what climate change means.

What agreement did Vice President Gore want the United States to sign? Kyoto Protocol

Why was the Kyoto Protocol never voted on by Congress? President Clinton never asked Congress to vote on the agreement because he thought that it would not pass.

Where was a federal building blown up? Oklahoma City

How many people lost their lives when the federal building was blown up in Oklahoma City? 168 people

1995 Oklahoma City bombing

1993 World Trade Center bombing

Teach for Understanding

- Direct attention to the pictures on page 402. Read aloud the captions.

  What other terrorists attack was carried out by an American? A bomb killed one person and injured over one hundred more during the 1996 Olympic games.

  When was the bomber finally identified? 2 years later in 1998

 How many years passed from the time of the bombing until the bomber was caught? about seven years

- Invite a student to read the sentence that suggests what the bomber believed about white supremacy.

  What international terrorism happened in New York City in 1993? The World Trade Center was bombed by Middle Eastern Muslim terrorists.

  What terrorist attacks occurred abroad? Nineteen American airmen died when terrorists bombed a building in Saudi Arabia. American embassies in Kenya and Tanzania were bombed. Over 200 people died in Kenya, and eleven died in Tanzania.

Teach for Understanding

What attack occurred in Yemen? The USS *Cole* was bombed, and seventeen sailors were killed.

Who designed these attacks? radical Muslims

 Why do you think that Americans thought Clinton was a good president? Answers could include that his years as president were filled with prosperity. The president always seemed like a kind man.

What scandal erupted at the end of Clinton's presidency? Clinton issued 140 pardons. Americans questioned Clinton's motives. Some people suggested that he gave pardons in exchange for monetary donations to causes that benefited him.

⟫ Conclude the discussion by asking the question on page 403. climate change

Activity Manual

- Guide completion of page 278.

soon captured. Both men expressed anti-government views. They believed that the federal government threatened the freedom of the American people. Americans were horrified at the mass murder. One bomber was executed, and the other was sentenced to life in prison.

Another attack occurred in Atlanta during the 1996 Olympic games. A bomb killed one person and injured over one hundred other people. The police had no reliable suspects for months. Finally in 1998, they identified the bomber. He appeared to support white supremacy. He thought that white people were superior to other ethnicities. He fled into the North Carolina woods and was not captured until 2003.

International Terrorism

International terrorists also attacked the United States. Sometimes they attacked in the country. Other times, they attacked Americans overseas.

Early in Clinton's presidency, the **World Trade Center** in New York City was bombed. Middle Eastern Muslim terrorists wanted to destroy the buildings. On February 26, 1993, they bombed the North Tower. The building didn't collapse, but six people died. Americans were shocked that terrorists could be so successful in the United States. Clinton promised to discover how and why the bombing took place. He assured Americans that the government would work to keep them safe.

Three more attacks killed Americans abroad. In June of 1996, terrorists bombed a building in Saudi Arabia that housed American airmen. Nineteen died. Then in August of 1997, American embassies in Kenya and Tanzania were bombed. Over 200

402

people died in Kenya, and eleven died in Tanzania. As Clinton's presidency ended, the USS *Cole* was bombed in Yemen in October of 2000. Seventeen sailors were killed.

Like the World Trade Center bombing, radical Muslims planned these three attacks. Few Americans worried about the attacks. The attacks seemed to be directed at military and government targets. For the most part, they happened far away. In each case, President Clinton promised that the perpetrators would be punished.

Clinton's years in office ended with one last scandal. On the last day of his presidency, Clinton issued 140 **pardons**. A pardon is a presidential action that forgives people for crimes they have committed. Americans questioned Clinton's motives. Some people suggested that he gave pardons in exchange for monetary donations to causes that benefited him. But in the end, the pardon scandal, like Clinton's other scandals, blew over.

Conclusion

As President Clinton's term was ending in late 2000, Americans reflected on his time in office. They liked him. His eight years were filled with financial prosperity. The president always seemed like a kind man, even though Americans knew that Clinton was not always a good man. But they thought he was a good president.

The conviction and courage seen in the Persian Gulf showed American character in action. The determined spirit that contributed to this victory for world peace and justice is the same spirit that gave Americans the ability to meet tough challenges at home. Americans are steadfast and resourceful. If they could selflessly confront the evil for the sake of good in a land so far away, then surely they could make this land all that it should be.

> What issue did Vice President Gore work with most?

//// **Activity** //

Presenting a News Story

Decide on the topic for a news story. Ideas include a school event, a field trip, or a new pet. Report on local, state, national, or world news. Write the details of your news story in a script or make cue cards. Record the newscast or present the news story live.

///

403

Activity //

Presenting a News Story

- Generate excitement about presenting a news story as you read aloud the Activity information on page 403.
- Distribute a copy of Instructional Aid 65 to each student. Read the information together. Explain the organizer and the type of information the student needs to complete the page. Use resources for further information about developing a news story.
- (Note that when a student is reporting on a news event, he may complete the organizer at home to get information from a televised or written news story.)
- Encourage the students to read through their completed news story several times and make adjustments before presenting the news report orally.
- (Note: Students may choose to use cue cards for another person to hold for them when they present their news story. These can be made by writing with a black marker on posterboard.)

> Completing the instructional aid and writing the news story may take more than one class period. Students may work on the news report as seatwork or during free time.

Objective
- Recall concepts and terms from Chapter 18

Materials
- Indoor basketball hoop and foam basketball

Introduction

- Concepts for the Chapter 18 Test will be taken from Activity Manual pages 265–80. You may review any or all of the concepts during this lesson. You may choose to review Chapter 18 by playing "Basketball."

Review

- Divide the class into two teams and assign a name for each team. Write team names for display. Each team should choose a spokesperson. Give the teams time to create six questions from pages 380–403 in the Student Text. They should record the questions with the correct answers.
- The teams will take turns asking each other a question. The team may discuss the answer to a question, but the final answer should come from the team's spokesperson. If the team answers correctly, it receives two points. Write the score for display. If desired, the team may also get a chance to make a "basket" by shooting a foam ball into the indoor basketball hoop. Continue playing until all the questions have been asked. Total the scores and declare which team is the winner.

Activity Manual

- Guide completion of pages 279–80.

Lesson **161**   **Chapter 18 Test**

Objective
- Demonstrate knowledge of concepts from Chapter 18 by taking the test

Assessment

- Administer Test 18.

Chapter 19

Introduction

George W. Bush served two terms as president of the United States from 2000 to 2008. He promoted faith-based initiatives, education reform, tax cuts, and Social Security and Medicare reforms. Bush opposed killing unborn humans for stem cell research. Congress gave Bush permission to use force against terrorists after attacks against the United States on September 11, 2001. Another disaster occurred when Hurricane Katrina slammed the Gulf Coast in 2005, causing extreme damage to New Orleans. President Bush wanted to end malaria in Africa and develop the continent's great potential to grow economically. The Federal Reserve System used government money to help rescue the American economy during a large financial crisis in 2008. President Bush openly declared his faith in Jesus Christ and demonstrated that Christian beliefs should shape important decisions in America.

Chapter Focus

The United States met challenges from Islamic terrorism and tried to improve people's lives at home and around the world.

19   A New Millennium

Focus

The United States met challenges from Islamic terrorism and tried to improve people's lives at home and around the world.

Visit bjupress.com/resources for links to enhance the lessons.

Sept. 11 attack
2001

Hurricane
Katrina

2000

2003
Iraq War begins

2005

Elections, Taxes, and Schools

Election

In the election of 2000, Bill Clinton's vice president, Al Gore, ran for president as the Democratic candidate. Republicans chose former president George H. W. Bush's son, George W. Bush, as their candidate.

Al Gore had been involved in politics for a long time. The economy had done well under Clinton. Voting for Gore looked like an opportunity to continue the prosperity of the Clinton years.

George W. Bush had been a successful governor of the large state of Texas. He had worked with Texas Democrats to pass conservative policies. He campaigned under the banner of "**compassionate conservatism**." For Bush, compassionate conservatism involved four major issues. First, as governor of Texas, Bush had worked to improve education. He believed good education was the best way to help those in poverty. Well-educated

children could move out of poverty. He thought the existing education policies hurt children.

Second, Bush believed that the government should not take over the roles of other institutions. The family, the church, and the community all have important roles to play. Bush wanted the government to help, not replace, these other institutions.

Third, Bush argued that all Americans would benefit from a tax cut. Finally, Bush said that both Social Security and Medicare needed to be reformed.

COMPASSIONATE CONSERVATISM

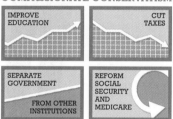

IMPROVE EDUCATION

CUT TAXES

SEPARATE GOVERNMENT FROM OTHER INSTITUTIONS

REFORM SOCIAL SECURITY AND MEDICARE

405

Lesson Focus

- George W. Bush sought to have compassionate conservatism during his presidency.

Objectives
- Identify who won the 2000 presidential election
- Recognize the issues of compassionate conservatism

Teacher's Toolkit CD
- Visual 50: *Election 2000*
- Instructional Aid 66: *Compassionate Conservatism*

Introduction

- Invite a student to read aloud the title of the chapter and predict what the chapter will be about. a new time in history

- Why do you think the chapter is called "A New Millennium"? Answers could include that *millennium* refers to one thousand. Every time one thousand years pass, a new millennium begins.

- Invite a student to read the chapter focus aloud.

  What do you think you will learn in this chapter? how the United States dealt with terrorism and helped Americans and others have better lives

  What do you see in the picture? President Bush with a firefighter and a bullhorn

- Direct attention to the timeline.

  How many years after the attack on September 11, 2001, did the United States go to war with Iraq? two years

  What natural disaster occurred in 2005? Hurricane Katrina

Preparation for Reading

- Generate interest as you direct the students to read the titles and examine the pictures on pages 404–7.

- Guide pronunciation of any unfamiliar words in the lesson.

- Direct the students to read the pages and complete Instructional Aid 66 in small groups.

Teach for Understanding

Who were the candidates in the election of 2000? Al Gore and George W. Bush

- Invite a volunteer to describe each candidate's political experience.

  What did Bush call the policy that he campaigned under? compassionate conservatism

- Direct attention to the graphic on page 405. Invite a group to name the issues of compassionate conservatism.

Teach for Understanding

- Direct attention to the picture of George W. Bush on page 406. Invite a volunteer to read aloud the captions.

  What state was key in the presidential election? *Florida*
  How was Bush declared the winner in Florida? *Recounts in three counties were not completed on time. Bush was declared the winner. Gore sued to have the recounts go beyond the deadline. The Supreme Court ruled that counting votes by different standards in different counties was unconstitutional. It ruled that the declaration of Bush's victory should stand.*

- Display Visual 50. Invite the students to locate their home state to identify how their state voted. Direct the students to use the map key to discover the percentage of popular votes and electoral votes each candidate received nationally.

- Explain that one of the electors who should have voted for Gore refrained from casting an electoral vote.

- Why did Bush win the election even though Al Gore had a higher percentage of the popular vote? *Answers could include that Bush won the most electoral votes.*

- Invite a group to give details about the tax cut Bush wanted for Americans.

The election between Bush and Gore was very close. It was not decided the night of the election. The key state was Florida. Whoever won Florida won the election. Because the vote was so close, the votes had to be recounted. Bush still won the election, but he won Florida by only 327 votes after this first recount. Gore asked for recounts in four specific counties that voted for Democrats. When the recounts in three counties were not completed by the deadline, Bush was declared the winner. Gore sued. He said that the recounts should be allowed to proceed beyond the deadline set by the law. The case went all the way to the Supreme Court. The Supreme Court ruled against how the recount was done. It said that counting votes by different standards in different counties was unconstitutional. It ruled that the declaration of Bush's victory should stand.

Tax Cuts

The American economy had been strong during much of President Clinton's presidency. But as President Bush came into office, it was starting to slow down again.

Bush believed that Americans should be able to keep more of their money. He thought this would help the economy. Businesses that paid lower taxes would be able to pay for more workers. Jobs would increase. Lower taxes would also let American individuals use more of their money.

Bush's critics argued that the tax cuts increased inequality. It allowed rich people to stay rich. It prevented the government from taxing the rich to give to the poor.

Bush's defenders said that greater equality did nobody good if everybody was worse off. They claimed that cutting everybody's taxes and growing the economy would help everybody. They also said equality was the wrong measure for success. There will never be a time when everyone has equal

George W. Bush received a Master's degree of Business Administration from Harvard. He is the only president to earn this degree.

Bush painted as a hobby. His subject matter ranged from dogs and cats to portraits.

George W. Bush is the only president to have played Little League Baseball. Before serving as the governor of Texas, George W. Bush was part owner of a Major League Baseball team called the Texas Rangers. In 2001, Bush threw out a first pitch at Yankee Stadium in New York City. He threw a strike.

406

Background

The Candidates Compared

Bush and Gore differed significantly on some issues. Governor Bush was pro-life, for example, and Vice President Gore was pro-choice. But both candidates tried to appeal to the undecided, middle-of-the-road voters. Both wanted tax cuts, but of a different nature. Gore wanted tax cuts for select groups, but Bush favored cuts for all taxpayers. Many of the dominant issues focused more on personality. The Gore team tried to portray Bush as an "intellectual lightweight" who was incapable of handling the job of president. The Bush forces responded by highlighting the vice president's numerous exaggerations, including his remarks suggesting that he had played a role in inventing the Internet.

Popular Vote vs. Electoral College

Gore became the first candidate since Grover Cleveland in 1888 to win the popular vote but lose in the Electoral College.

amounts of wealth, so improvement of life is the better measure of success.

The economy improved in the years after the tax cuts. However, in Bush's final year as president, the country experienced a financial crisis.

Education Reform

One of President Bush's main goals was to improve American public schools. He believed that it was wrong to advance students to the next grade when they did not know how to do the math or read for their grade level. Bush believed that low expectations were harmful to students. Setting the standard too low was a way of looking down on students as if they could not do better. But Bush thought they could do better.

He knew that students who cannot read well or do math are unlikely to do well in college. They are unlikely to get jobs that pay well. Some schools did not do a good job teaching students these skills. Too often these were schools that poor children attended.

President Bush did not think spending more money would solve this problem. He had another plan. He called it **No Child Left Behind**. Students would be tested each year in reading and math. Schools that had many students do poorly on the tests would face pressure to change. Parents would be given the option to send their children to better schools.

President George W. Bush stops for a question from Tez Taylor, age 9, during a bill signing ceremony for the No Child Left Behind Act.

Liberals did not like the program. They said that more money should be spent on education. Many conservatives were also concerned about Bush's program. Conservatives had long been concerned about keeping education a local and state matter. They pointed out that the Constitution does not support a national department of education. They were also concerned that public school education favors liberal ideas. They thought that greater control by the national government would increase the liberal ideas in public schools.

But conservatives liked the idea that teachers and schools should be able to show that they teach students well. Conservatives also supported giving parents greater choice about which schools they send their children to.

> What are the four issues of compassionate conservatism?

407

Teach for Understanding

Why did Bush believe it was wrong to advance students to the next grade when they did not know how to do the math or read for their grade level? Setting the standard too low was a way of looking down on students as if they could not do better.

- Choose a group to tell about the changes Bush made in education.

▶ Conclude the discussion by asking the question on page 407. to improve education, to have the government help (not replace) other institutions, to cut taxes, and to reform Social Security and Medicare

Activity Manual

- Guide completion of pages 281–83.

Lesson

163

Student Text pages 408–9
Activity Manual page 284

Lesson Focus

- President Bush restricted embryonic stem cell research.

Objectives
- Examine Bush's policies regarding embryonic stem cell research

Review

- Invite a student to tell what President Bush believed about faith-based initiatives.

Preparation for Reading

- Generate interest as you direct the students to read the titles and examine the pictures on pages 408–9.
- Guide pronunciation of any unfamiliar words in the lesson.
- Direct the students to read the pages silently to learn how research could be done without killing human embryos. Scientists figured out how to take adult cells and turn them into stem cells.

Teach for Understanding

- Direct attention to the picture on page 408. Read aloud the caption.

What is a human embryo? It is a baby in its first eight weeks of development.

How did the Clinton administration get around the fact that the government could not pay for research that involved destroying human embryos? It let private groups destroy embryos. Once the embryos were killed, the government paid for scientists to do experiments with them.

What did scientists say they could do with stem cells from embryos that were killed? Scientists said that embryonic stem cells could be used to treat diseases like diabetes or Alzheimer's.

What did President Bush believe about killing a baby? He believed it was wrong.

- Invite a student to read what Bush later wrote about human life.

> Guide a review of important terms, maps, places, and people from each previous lesson. Direct the students to find and read the corresponding entries from the Resource Treasury.

Embryonic Stem Cell Research

The US government has laws about scientific research. The government was not allowed to pay for research that involved destroying **human embryos**. A human embryo is a baby in its first eight weeks of development. But the Clinton administration had decided that it could get around the law. It let private groups destroy embryos. Once the embryos were killed, the government paid for scientists to do experiments with them.

Now that he was president, Bush needed to decide what to do. Scientists said their research could heal people. The embryos had cells called stem cells. A **stem cell** can grow into different kinds of cells, such as nerve cells or muscle cells. Scientists said that embryonic stem cells could be used to treat diseases like diabetes or Alzheimer's.

Curing disease is a good thing. But to get the embryonic stem cells, the embryo had to be killed. Bush believed that killing a baby was wrong, even if the baby was still an embryo. Bush later wrote, "My faith and conscience led me to conclude that human life is sacred. God created man in His image and therefore every person has value in His eyes." Bush believed that just because something could be done did not mean it should be done. There were moral lines that science should not cross. Killing human embryos crossed those lines. It crossed those lines even when done in the hope of a cure for serious diseases.

Yet Bush wanted to see these cures happen. Many people with serious diseases asked him to allow this research. Family members of people with serious diseases asked him to allow this research. Bush and his advisors came up with a compromise. Some embryos had already been destroyed. Bush thought that was wrong. But since

Parents with their children attend George W. Bush's news conference after Bush vetoed a stem cell bill.

408

Background

Justice and Moral Judgments

Most people in the West would agree that a government is responsible to defend its people, but they do not always agree about a second responsibility of government: promoting morality and discouraging its opposite. But promoting a particular vision of morality is impossible to avoid because justice always requires moral judgments. As one writer puts it, "Laws represent in part the moral aspirations of a given society."[1] That's obvious when we're talking about laws against murder and theft. It's obvious when we talk about laws against racism. In the civil rights era, America woke up to (at least some of) its moral obligations to African Americans, a group it had first enslaved and then relegated to second-class citizenship. Civil rights laws helped teach America that racism was wrong not just in formal, legal ways, but also in personal ones.

But the right and moral way is not always so easy to see. It can't be found in popular slogans, even slogans as respected as ones about "freedom" or "equality." We must always ask, "Equality in what respect? Freedom to do what?" Edmund Burke says, "The effect of liberty to individuals is, that they may do what they please: we ought to see what

1. Carl R. Trueman, *The Creedal Imperative* (Wheaton: Crossway, 2012), 178.

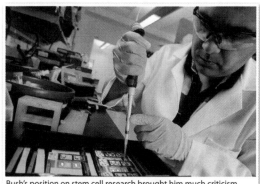
Bush's position on stem cell research brought him much criticism.

to know whether a scientist is acting rightly or wrongly. For President Bush, the most important fact was that all humans are created in God's image, so even unborn humans should not be killed.

Bush's opponents claimed that his position hurt people with serious diseases. If he did not allow these embryos were already destroyed, Bush agreed that the government could pay for research on their stem cells. The government would not pay for research done on embryos destroyed after that point.

Many people were concerned that Bush had opened the door to using embryos for the sake of research. But most of the criticism came from people who did not think Bush went far enough. They said that Bush was opposed to science. They did not like the idea of religious or moral guidelines limiting what scientists should do. But just because something can be done does not mean that it should be done. People use science to figure out what can be done. But science cannot tell us what should be done. People need information from outside of science

more of this research, sick people might not get the cures they needed. But no one knew if research on embryos would bring the cures that people wanted. On the other hand, killing an embryo did end a human life. It was good to try to find cures for diseases, but it was not good to kill other humans to do so. Instead, scientists needed to look for cures that did not involve killing embryos.

By the end of Bush's presidency, scientists had figured out how to take adult cells and turn them into stem cells. Now research for cures could be done safely. No humans would be killed in the process of this research.

> **Why is killing an embryo for research wrong?**

409

Teach for Understanding

- Direct attention to the picture on page 409. Invite a student to read the caption aloud.

  What decision did President Bush make that concerned many people about his opening the door to using embryos for the sake of research? Bush agreed that the government could pay for research done on stem cells of embryos that were already destroyed.

  What did scientists learn to do that made it so that no humans would be killed in the process of stem cell research? Scientists figured out how to take adult cells and turn them into stem cells.

> Conclude the discussion by asking the question on page 409. An embryo is a human. The Bible teaches that humans are made in the image of God. God's Word says that murdering a person is wrong.

Activity Manual

- Explain that without the wisdom that comes from God, people end up doing evil (Proverbs 1:7; 3:5–7). Tell the students they will look at God's Word and come to conclusions about religious and moral guidelines limiting what scientists do.
- Guide completion of page 284.

it will please them to do, before we risk congratulations, which may soon be turned into complaints."[2]

It will always be this way because God's image-bearers are moral creatures. We have a drive to shape the world with our moral visions. God, in fact, despite being all too aware of the evil that rulers are capable of, says He has sent rulers "for the punishment of evildoers, and for the praise of them that do well" (1 Peter 2:14; cf. Romans 13:3). Even modern secular societies will never escape the moral purpose of government, no matter how often they insist that they are worldview-neutral. As Solomon says, "Righteousness exalteth a nation: but sin is a reproach to any people" (Proverbs 14:34).

2. Edmund Burke, *Reflections on the Revolution in France* (London: Printed for J. Dodsley in Pall-Mall, 1791), 9.

164

Lesson Focus

- Bush encouraged religious groups to help solve problems in communities.

Objective

- Identify Bush's attitude toward faith-based initiatives

Review

- Choose a volunteer to describe the election for president in 2000.
- Invite a student to explain what President Bush meant by compassionate conservatism.

Preparation for Reading

- Generate interest as you direct the students to read the title and examine the picture on page 410.
- Guide pronunciation of any unfamiliar words in the lesson.
- Direct the student to read the page to learn what Bush believed weakened communities. rebellion created by the New Left

Teach for Understanding

- Direct attention to the picture on page 410. Read aloud the caption.

What were President Bush's reasons for believing that many community problems were best solved by religious groups? Some prisoners responded to the gospel in prison. Christians connected prisoners to mentors. The mentors provided prisoners work after they were freed. These prisoners were less likely to end up back in prison.

How did Bush feel about government money going to only non-religious groups? He argued that it was wrong to exclude religious groups.

What objection did Progressive critics make when Bush made it so religious groups could receive money? They said this change went against the separation of church and state.

What was Bush's response to the critics? He said the government was not giving money to share the gospel but for religious groups to do community work.

▶▶ Conclude the discussion by asking the question on page 410. They wanted to remain independent of the government.

Activity Manual

- Guide completion of page 285.

Faith-Based Initiatives

Long before he was a governor or president, Bush worked for a group that helped inner-city youth. What he saw convinced him that the New Left hurt poor communities.

The New Left rebelled against authority. It rebelled against parents, religion, and local community leaders. It weakened the values that hold communities together. It did this with the books they wrote, the entertainments they produced, and the laws they pushed to have passed.

Families, churches, and communities were weakened by this rebellion. The government stepped in to prevent bad consequences from this rebellion. But government involvement brought its own problems.

President Bush believed that government programs were not the best solution for many community problems. He believed that these problems were best solved by religious and community groups. He pointed to the work of Christian ministries in prisons. Some prisoners responded to the gospel in prison. Christians also connected the prisoners with mentors. The mentors provided prisoners work after they were freed. These prisoners were less likely to end up back in prison.

The government already gave money to various groups to help

Men meet to talk and pray with prisoners at a minimum security prison near Houston, Texas.

solve problems in communities. But the money could be given to only non-religious groups. Bush argued that it was wrong to exclude religious groups. He helped change the rules so that religious groups could receive government money.

Progressive critics said that President Bush's change went against the separation of church and state. Bush responded that it did not. The government was not paying religious groups to share the gospel. It was giving money for community work. Religious Americans appreciated the support the president gave their work. They were glad that the president recognized the importance of churches and religious groups. But some of them did not want government money. They wanted to remain independent of the government.

> Why did some religious groups not want to accept government money?

410

Background

Personal Faith Expressed Publicly in the White House

Bush personally made religion a more prominent issue. He was unashamed to share his faith in Christ, and he embraced a greater role for evangelical Christians. He enlisted pastors, both white pastors and pastors of other ethnicities, to help administer social programs that put into practice his "compassionate conservatism." Such faith-based initiatives became an important part of his domestic program to combat problems in the inner cities. But some conservative Christians questioned the wisdom of those initiatives. They worried about government involvement in their programs.

How It Was

Kayla's father turned up the volume on the television. It was the evening of September 11, 2001, and President Bush was preparing to speak. Kayla leaned against her mother's shoulder. It had been a strange day. Her teacher had dismissed class early when they learned about the terrorist attacks. When Kayla's mother picked her up from school, Kayla could tell she had been crying. "Mom," said Kayla, "is our country going to be okay?"

Mom was quiet for a moment before answering. "Honey, I'm not sure what's going to happen. All I know is that God is still God. He's still in control, and we must trust Him."

Now the president was saying something that caught her attention. He said, "Tonight I ask for your prayers for all those who grieve, for the children whose worlds have been shattered."

"Dad?" asked Kayla. "Can we pray right now?"

Dad turned off the television. "Yes, Kayla. Praying is the very best thing we can do—right now."

September 11

On a clear September morning in 2001, a plane struck the North Tower of the New York World Trade Center's Twin Towers. People did not know what to make of the news. People questioned whether it was an accident or an attack. But an hour later, a second plane struck the South Tower. This was clearly no accident. Thirty minutes later, a third plane crashed into the **Pentagon** in Washington, DC. The Pentagon is the headquarters of the US Department of Defense. It was clear that someone was attacking the United States.

President Bush was visiting an elementary school when the planes hit the World Trade Center. Bush knew that two planes hitting the World Trade Center was not an accident. This was an act of terrorism. No one knew who was behind the attack or what it meant. It might mean war on the United States. As President Bush sped toward his plane, Air Force One, he learned about the third plane hitting the Pentagon. The Secret Service decided that it was too dangerous to fly the president to Washington, DC. Instead Air Force One flew to military bases in Louisiana

411

Background

God's Providence and September 11

Confronted with the horrible events of September 11, 2001, many Americans asked why it had happened. On one level, the answer is that evil men motivated by false religion chose to attack the United States. But the question for the Christian is deeper because God rules over all that happens. Not even sin happens if God does not choose to permit it (Genesis 45:5–8). The Bible reveals that God has purposes for good even in permitting evil (Genesis 50:20). Often it is impossible to discern these reasons without special revelation. Nevertheless, Luke 13:1–5 provides an answer that can be applied to the September 11 attacks. In that passage, Jesus instructed His listeners about how to respond to two disasters that had occurred. Jesus said they should not conclude that the people who suffered in these disasters were worse sinners than themselves. Instead the listeners should realize that death is the consequence that all sinners face. Disasters should cause people to realize that they must repent of their sins and turn to Christ. God may have had many purposes for allowing the September 11 tragedy, but surely one of them was to cause people to reflect on their need for salvation.

Lesson Focus

- President Bush comforted Americans after the attacks on September 11.

Objectives

- Examine events of September 11, 2001
- Identify the forces behind the attacks on September 11

Teacher's Toolkit CD

- Instructional Aid 67: *September 11*

Review

- Invite a student to tell how President Bush tried to help faith-based groups solve community problems.
- Choose a volunteer to explain Bush's beliefs about embryonic stem cell research and what changed about the way scientists did stem cell research.

Preparation for Reading

- Generate interest as you direct the students to read the titles and examine the pictures on pages 411–14.
- Guide pronunciation of any unfamiliar words in the lesson.
- Direct the students to read the pages and complete Instructional Aid 67 in small groups.

Teach for Understanding

- Direct attention to the How It Was box on page 411. Read aloud the story.
- Choose a volunteer to name the disaster President Bush was preparing to speak about.

  Why was Kayla's mom not able to say that the country would be okay? She was not sure what would happen.

  What comfort was Kayla's mom able to give? She said that God was still in control, and they needed to trust Him.

  What did President Bush ask people to do? to pray for those who were grieving and for the children whose worlds had been shattered

- Choose different groups to describe the events on September 11.

- What was it about the attack on the Pentagon that made it very clear that the United States was under attack? Answers could include that the Pentagon is the headquarters of the US Department of Defense.

Teach for Understanding

- Direct attention to the pictures on page 412. Read aloud the captions.

Where did the Secret Service decide to fly President Bush on Air Force One? military bases in Louisiana and Nebraska

- Direct attention to the Biography box on page 413. Read aloud the information.

What type of person was Todd Beamer? He had a Christian background. He seemed to be a brave person.

Why did Todd Beamer and the people on the fourth hijacked plane decide to take action? They learned that the three other hijacked planes had been crashed into buildings.

What did the passengers on this hijacked plane decide to do? fight back against the hijackers

What did Todd Beamer do before he took action? He prayed the Lord's Prayer and recited Psalm 23.

What happened to the plane? It crashed into an empty field in Pennsylvania.

Why did the actions of the passengers probably save many lives? Their actions may have prevented the plane from crashing into the White House or the Capitol.

What happened just before the last hijacked plane crashed? The South Tower of the World Trade Center collapsed. Almost half an hour later, the North Tower collapsed.

Who was responsible for killing 2,977 people on September 11? nineteen terrorists

and Nebraska. The president ordered the air force to shoot down any other hijacked planes. The secretary of transportation ordered all civilian aircraft to land.

There was one more hijacked airplane still in the air. Before September 11, people in a hijacked airplane usually did whatever the hijackers asked them to do. They thought the best way to stay alive was to cooperate until the hijackers landed. Then the hijackers were given what they wanted in exchange for letting the passengers go free. But as these passengers called family and friends on their cell phones, they learned that three other hijacked planes had been crashed into buildings, killing more people. These passengers decided to fight back against the hijackers. During their struggle, the plane crashed into an empty field in Pennsylvania. Many

people believe that the hijackers were targeting either the White House or the Capitol building. Though none of the passengers survived, their attempt to regain control of the plane may have saved many lives. Only minutes before the last hijacked plane crashed, the South Tower of the World Trade Center collapsed. Almost half an hour later, the North Tower also collapsed.

The Twin Towers were 110 stories tall. Tens of thousands of people worked in the Twin Towers. Many could not escape before the buildings collapsed. Many firefighters and police officers were also in the Twin Towers trying to help people when the towers collapsed.

Nineteen terrorists killed 2,977 people on September 11. People died at the World Trade Center, at the Pentagon, and in the plane that crashed in Pennsylvania. The attacks struck at

Terrorists flew two planes into the Twin Towers of the World Trade Center, and a third flew into the Pentagon.

Dust and debris covered much of the surrounding area after the towers collapsed.

Background

The Rise of Muslim Terrorist Groups

A fundamental part of Islamic teaching is the need to spread the Islamic faith around the world. Muslims saw their religion and the territory it controlled grow for centuries. But European colonial expansion in Asia and Africa rolled back Muslim power and influence in the world. This reversal in power and territorial control created a theological problem for Muslims. Lost territory meant parts of the world were no longer being ruled according to what they saw as true religion. The decadence of Western popular culture, especially in dress, music, and movies, only served to exacerbate this sense of loss. The establishment of Israel in 1948 as an independent state was another instance of land being removed from Islamic control. In the Gulf War, Arab nations called on the United States and other Western powers for protection against Saddam Hussein. American soldiers remained stationed in Saudi Arabia, the home of Islam's most holy sites. The presence of non-Muslim Americans at these holy sites further angered some Muslims. Terrorist groups arose to oppose the United States and any Muslims considered to be less faithful.

the heart of the nation's economy and at the headquarters of the nation's military.

Americans were stunned with shock and grief. All over the nation, people watched news coverage on their televisions and tried to understand. Who had planned these horrible attacks, and why? Who was the enemy?

On the evening of September 11, President Bush spoke to the grieving nation from the White House. President Bush assured Americans that the economy would keep going on September 12. He also told Americans that the United States would find out who had committed these terrorist acts. The United States would not allow another country to protect the terrorists.

On September 14, President Bush visited **Ground Zero**. This was the name given to the ruins of the Twin Towers. Rescue workers were clearing away rubble. They still hoped to find survivors. President Bush climbed atop a crushed fire truck. With a bullhorn in hand, Bush spoke to the rescue workers. "I can hear you," he said. "The rest of the world hears you, and the people who knocked these buildings down will hear all of us soon."

That same day Congress gave the president authority to use force against the terrorists. He could also use

Todd Beamer

Who: United Flight 93 passenger

When: 1968–2001

Where: New Jersey

Todd Beamer grew up in a Christian family and attended a Christian high school and college. On September 11, 2001, he was on United Flight 93 for business travel when it was hijacked by terrorists. When he and several other passengers made phone calls, they learned that other hijacked planes had been crashed into the Pentagon and the Twin Towers. Beamer and several other passengers and flight attendants decided to take the plane back. He prayed the Lord's Prayer and recited Psalm 23 before telling the group, "Let's roll." The courageous, selfless action of Beamer and the other passengers kept the hijacked plane from striking its target.

413

Teach for Understanding

What did President Bush assure the American people of when he spoke on September 11? He assured Americans that the economy would keep going on September 12. He also told Americans that the United States would find out who committed these terrorist acts.

Why did President Bush visit Ground Zero on September 14? Answers could include that he wanted to speak to rescue workers and other Americans to let them know that he and the world were aware of the sorrow and anger people were feeling. He wanted the people who knocked the buildings down to know that they would not get away with what they did.

What did Congress give permission for the president to do in addition to using force against the terrorists? Congress gave the president authority to use force against any nation that protected the terrorists.

Lesson

165

Teach for Understanding

- Direct attention to the pictures on page 414. Invite a student to read aloud the captions.

  What was the name of the Muslim group that the terrorists were part of? al-Qaeda

  Who was the leader of al-Qaeda? Osama bin Laden

  In what country was the al-Qaeda base located? Afghanistan

- What was a reason that bin Laden opposed the United States? Saudi Arabia had asked the United States to oppose Saddam Hussein in 1992. Because Saudi Arabia is home to Islam's two most holy cities, bin Laden thought it was wrong for US soldiers to defend Saudi Arabia.

Primary Source: Address to the Nation

- Direct attention to Activity Manual page 286.
- Read aloud President Bush's address to the American people after the terrorist attacks on September 11, 2001.
- Discuss the excerpt.

  Conclude the discussion by asking the question on page 414. Bin Laden opposed the United States. Previous terrorist attacks had killed Americans in other parts of the world, but the terrorists wanted to attack the United States itself.

Activity Manual

- Guide completion of pages 286–87.

Assessment

- Administer quiz.

The quiz may be given any time after completing this lesson.

Investigators search the Flight 93 crash site in a meadow in Pennsylvania on September 12, 2001.

The USS *Cole* after a terrorist attack at Aden Harbor off the coast of Yemen

Osama bin Laden

military force against any nation that protected the terrorists.

The FBI investigated the hijackings. They learned who the nineteen terrorists were. The terrorists were part of a radical Muslim group called **al-Qaeda**. Al-Qaeda was led by **Osama bin Laden**. Its base was in Afghanistan, a mountainous country that lies between Iran and Pakistan.

Bin Laden opposed the United States because Saudi Arabia asked the United States to oppose Saddam Hussein in 1992. Saddam Hussein ruled Iraq. He had invaded Kuwait. The Saudis did not want him to invade Saudi Arabia. Bin Laden was angry that Saudi Arabia had asked the United States for help. Saudi Arabia is the home of Islam's two most holy cities. Bin Laden believed that only Muslims

should defend Saudi Arabia. He thought it was wrong for the soldiers of the United States, an unbelieving nation, to defend Saudi Arabia.

The CIA had been watching bin Laden for five years. They knew his terrorists wanted to attack Americans. In 1993 al-Qaeda terrorists exploded a truck bomb at the World Trade Center. In 1998 al-Qaeda bombed US embassies in Kenya and Tanzania. In 2000 a small boat filled with explosives blew a hole in the USS *Cole*. The USS *Cole* was a navy ship anchored off the coast of Yemen. Each of these attacks killed people. Now al-Qaeda had attacked the United States itself.

> Why did Islamic terrorists attack the United States on September 11, 2001?

414

Background

The War on Terror

US intelligence experts learned that the nineteen hijackers on September 11, 2001, were members of an international terrorist network called al-Qaeda, led by Osama bin Laden, a wealthy Saudi. The organization was linked to several other terrorist attacks. Al-Qaeda members trained for terrorist activities in bases in Afghanistan, where the Taliban government protected them. Osama bin Laden financed and commanded al-Qaeda's worldwide network.

The US war against terrorism began both at home and in foreign countries. President Bush warned that the war would be neither short nor conventional.

Bush's first task was to assemble a multinational coalition to oust the Taliban from Afghanistan. On October 7, those allied forces invaded Afghanistan, using "smart" weapons to minimize military and civilian casualties. The coalition received help from the anti-Taliban Northern Alliance in Afghanistan and from Pakistani volunteers. In only two months, Taliban forces fled into the mountains on the Afghan-Pakistani border. Afghan leaders of several anti-Taliban factions met in Germany in December and signed a peace agreement. They established a temporary government and began working to rebuild their country.

Middle East

War in Afghanistan

On October 6, Bush gave the order for the US military to respond to the September 11 attack. The **Taliban**, a fierce Islamic group, ruled Afghanistan. They allowed Osama bin Laden to train terrorists in Afghanistan. President Bush decided that there should be no safe place for terrorists to train.

The American and British militaries dropped bombs on al-Qaeda terrorist training camps. They bombed Taliban military sites. The Americans also dropped food and other supplies to the people of Afghanistan. The United States was fighting against the Taliban and al-Qaeda. But Bush wanted the Afghans to know the United States was also fighting for them. Many Afghans did not like the Taliban.

The bombs were just the beginning. Bush wanted to put an end to Taliban rule. He did not want al-Qaeda to be able to plan attacks from a safe place.

The CIA was already working with Afghans in the north. This Northern Alliance was already fighting against the Taliban. After a couple of weeks, American special forces arrived. They fought with the Northern Alliance against the Taliban. In one case, American special forces rode horseback alongside Northern Alliance fighters. They captured the important city of Mazar-i-Sharif. Riding to battle on a horse was not common for the modern soldier. But the Americans also had modern weapons. They could use GPS, which used satellites to pinpoint a location, and laser guidance to direct American missiles and bombs.

415

To protect Americans at home, Bush created the Office of Homeland Security. It later became a cabinet-level department. Congress also overwhelmingly passed the Patriot Act, an act it hoped would make it easier for law enforcement officials and the courts to catch, convict, and imprison terrorists. Most Americans agreed with Bush's practical, common-sense approach. But critics complained that the government, in its zeal to protect citizens from terrorism, had gone too far and was infringing on the rights of Americans. The Supreme Court later declared some provisions of the Patriot Act unconstitutional.

The Work of the Office of Homeland Security

The Office of Homeland Security was responsible for US borders, transportation (especially at airports), chemical and biological attacks, and preparations for emergencies. To screen for potential terrorists, Americans accepted longer delays and lines for check-in at airports.

A New Type of Enemy

Muslim extremists did not follow conventional rules of war. They resorted to suicide bombings, targeted innocent civilians, and even threatened to use weapons of mass destruction such as biological or chemical weapons.

Lesson Focus

- Terrorists could no longer use Afghanistan as a safe haven to plan attacks against the United States.

Objectives
- Recognize why the United States dropped bombs in Afghanistan
- Examine events of the war in Afghanistan
- Identify a major goal President Bush achieved in regard to Afghanistan

Review

- Guide a review of the previous lesson by asking questions such as the following.

  What buildings did terrorists attack on September 11, 2001? the Twin Towers and the Pentagon

  Where did Bush speak to rescue workers on September 14? Ground Zero

  What Muslim group were the hijackers part of? al-Qaeda

  Who was al-Qaeda's leader? Osama bin Laden

Preparation for Reading

- Generate interest as you direct the students to read the titles and examine the map and pictures on pages 415–17.
- Guide pronunciation of any unfamiliar words in the lesson.
- Direct the students to read the pages silently to learn where the Taliban and the al-Qaeda fighters fled when Afghanistan was no longer safe for them. Pakistan

Teach for Understanding

What order did Bush give to the military? Bush gave the order to respond to the September 11 attack.

- Invite the students to locate Afghanistan on the map on page 415.

  What fierce Islamic group ruled Afghanistan? the Taliban

  What did President Bush decide about terrorists training in Afghanistan? There should be no safe place for terrorists to train.

  How did the American and British militaries respond to terrorists training in Afghanistan? They dropped bombs on al-Qaeda terrorist training camps. They bombed Taliban military sites. The Americans also dropped food and other supplies to the people of Afghanistan.

  In one case, what mode of transportation did the American special forces and the Northern Alliance fighters use? horses

  What city did they capture? Mazar-i-Sharif

  What modern weapons did Americans use? GPS and laser guidance to direct American missiles and bombs

Lesson

166

Teach for Understanding

- Direct attention to the pictures on page 416. Choose a volunteer to identify what is depicted in each picture.

⚙ Why did the United States need a leader who could unite tribes in Afghanistan? Answers could include that the tribes sometimes fought each other. The tribes in southern Afghanistan did not trust the Northern Alliance.

Who did the Afghan tribes elect to lead them in the fight against the Taliban? Hamid Karzai

After the Taliban collapsed, what did the United States do instead of fighting a war? The United States sent aid to Afghanistan. The United States and its allies built roads. They supplied drinking water. They brought materials for schools. They improved healthcare.

What type of government did President Bush hope would be established in Afghanistan? a democracy

Where did the Taliban, the al-Qaeda fighters, and most likely bin Laden flee after being pushed from power? Pakistan

What group in Pakistan supported the Taliban? some members of the Pakistani spy service

What did some people believe the Pakistani spies were helping the Taliban to plan? new attacks on Afghanistan

---

Afghanistan is made up of many different tribes. These tribes may unite in the face of a common enemy. They also sometimes fight against each other. The tribes in southern Afghanistan did not trust the Northern Alliance. Afghanistan needed a leader who could unite the tribes. The United States suggested Hamid Karzai. Karzai was a military leader from the south. He spoke multiple languages and had earned a university degree. He had served in the Afghan government before the war. He was presented to the representatives of the Afghan tribes. The tribes elected Karzai as their leader.

The Taliban quickly collapsed. The United States turned from fighting a war to sending in aid. The United States and its allies built roads. They supplied drinking water. They brought materials for schools. They improved healthcare.

President Bush also wanted to turn Afghanistan into a democracy.

At first, all of these efforts seemed to succeed. It did not seem as though many soldiers were necessary now. The Taliban had been pushed from power. But the failure to capture Osama bin Laden was a major disappointment. The Americans thought that he had fled across the border to Pakistan. That was where other Taliban and al-Qaeda fighters had gone.

Pakistan was supposed to be an ally of the United States. But Pakistan would not let the United States follow al-Qaeda into Pakistan. Some members of the Pakistani spy service supported the Taliban. Many people believe that Pakistani spies helped the Taliban plan new attacks on Afghanistan.

In 2005 Taliban fighters began to attack the people who were

US special forces and members of the Northern Alliance ride on horseback during Operation Enduring Freedom.

US soldiers about to enter a building in Afghanistan in search of members of al-Qaeda and the Taliban

US soldiers distributing food, toys, and shoes to the Afghan people in 2004

416

MQ-1 Predator unmanned aircraft

The Taliban opposed education for girls. After American forces liberated Afghanistan from the Taliban, Afghan girls had the opportunity to receive education.

constructing new roads and buildings. They killed government officials, school teachers, and others.

The Taliban also won back support from some of the Afghan people. Karzai's government and the local governments were too corrupt. The Afghan people were willing to see them replaced by someone else.

The Taliban grew stronger, and the fighting increased. President Bush sent more troops to Afganistan in 2006. They fought the Taliban, and they continued to help rebuild the country. But they still could not go into Pakistan to defeat the Taliban. The Pakistani military did some fighting against the Taliban. But eventually, they pulled the military out of Taliban areas in western Pakistan.

The United States could not send soldiers into Pakistan. But it could fly unmanned aerial vehicles (UAVs) over those regions. UAVs are often called drones. These drones were like airplanes, but there was no pilot inside. Instead, the drone was flown by pilots on the ground. The drones had cameras so that the pilots could see what was happening. The drones could be used to spy on the Taliban. Many drones also had missiles. These could be used to kill Taliban leaders.

The war in Afghanistan continued after President Bush finished his two terms as president. President Bush did succeed with one major goal. Al-Qaeda could no longer use Afghanistan as a safe place to plan attacks against the United States.

> Why did the United States go to war in Afghanistan?

417

Teach for Understanding

- Direct attention to the pictures on page 417. Read aloud the captions.

  What kind of attacks did the Taliban make in Afghanistan? The Taliban attacked people who were constructing new roads and buildings. They killed government officials, school teachers, and others.

- Why was it so difficult for the United States to defeat the Taliban? Answers could include that Pakistan would not allow the United States to send soldiers into Pakistan.

  What did the United States use in an effort to defeat the Taliban? The United States flew unmanned aerial vehicles (UAVs) over regions in Pakistan. Cameras on the drones allowed the pilots to spy on the Taliban. Many drones had missiles that could be used to kill Taliban leaders.

  Which of President Bush's major goals for Afghanistan was successful? Al-Qaeda could no longer use Afghanistan as a safe place to plan attacks against the United States.

  > Conclude the discussion by asking the question on page 417. The Taliban ruled Afghanistan and allowed bin Laden to train terrorists in Afghanistan.

Activity Manual

- Guide completion of page 288.

Lesson

167

Student Text pages 418–20
Activity Manual page 289

Lesson Focus

- The United States and its allies invaded Iraq.

Objectives

- Understand events leading toward the invasion of Iraq
- Recognize mistakes American leaders made while overseeing Iraq
- Identify the major groups of people in Iraq
- Examine opposition to the war in Iraq

Review

- Invite a student to identify the terrorist group that ruled Afghanistan.
- Review the events of the war in Afghanistan.
- Choose a student to state the major goal Bush had for Afghanistan.

Preparation for Reading

- Generate interest as you direct the students to read the titles and examine the pictures on pages 418–20.
- Guide pronunciation of any unfamiliar words in the lesson.
- Direct the student to read the pages to learn which fighters in northern Iraq fought with the United States against Saddam Hussein. Kurdish fighters

Teach for Understanding

- Direct attention to the picture of Colin Powell on page 418. Explain that Powell became the secretary of state.

  What requirement was placed on Iraq after the Gulf War of 1992? Saddam Hussein was required to destroy his weapons of mass destruction.

  What responsibility did the United Nations have in regard to Iraq? It had to make sure that Iraq did not make more weapons of mass destruction.

  What did Hussein do in 1998? He forced the weapons inspectors out of Iraq.

- What concerns did Bush have about Hussein? Answers could include that Bush was concerned that Saddam Hussein would support terrorists. There was a possibility that weapons of mass destruction were hidden in Iraq.

  What did President Bush believe an invasion of Iraq would accomplish? It would eliminate a threat to the United States. It would be an opportunity to create a democracy in the Middle East.

  Who did the CIA and US special forces connect with? the Kurds

War in Iraq

In 2002 the Bush administration shifted attention to Iraq. After the Gulf War of 1992, Saddam Hussein was required to destroy his weapons of mass destruction. These included chemical and biological weapons. Many of these were destroyed. The United Nations had the responsibility to make sure that Iraq did not make more weapons of mass destruction. But in 1998, Hussein forced the weapons inspectors out of Iraq. No one knew if Hussein had destroyed all of the weapons. No one knew if he had created more weapons.

After September 11, Bush was concerned that Saddam Hussein would support terrorists. This concern was shared widely among American congressmen. Leaders of nations around the world also shared this concern.

The Americans brought a proposal to the United Nations. The proposal demanded that Hussein demonstrate that he did not have any weapons of mass destruction. He had to open his country to weapons inspectors from the United Nations. If he did not do this, he would face consequences. Hussein did not cooperate.

Bush concluded that Hussein was hiding weapons of mass destruction. Several other nations agreed. If Hussein was not hiding anything, why would he not allow inspectors to do their job?

Secretary of State Colin Powell speaking to the United Nations about possible weapons hidden in Iraq

The United States and its allies decided to invade Iraq. President Bush believed this invasion would eliminate a threat to the United States. It would also be an opportunity to create a democracy in the Middle East. Bush thought that democracies would stand in opposition to Islamic terrorism.

On March 20, 2003, the United States and its allies invaded Iraq. The war began with heavy bombing of Iraqi military and government buildings. Special forces from the United States, the United Kingdom, and Poland gained control of oil rigs. They also secured a port through which oil flowed. In the first Gulf War, Hussein had set the oil fields on fire, so seizing control of the port and rigs would prevent another fire. The CIA and US special forces also connected with Kurdish fighters in northern Iraq. The Kurds would fight with the United

418

Crowds gathered as US Marines pulled down a statue of Saddam Hussein.

States against Hussein. Troops began to fight their way up from southern Iraq to Baghdad. Baghdad was the capital city of Iraq. By April 9, the Americans had captured Baghdad. The marines helped the Iraqis topple a statue of Saddam Hussein.

The United States and its allies had defeated the Iraqi military. Saddam Hussein and other government officials had gone into hiding. But this created new problems. No one was left to make sure the basic functions of government continued. Iraqi police no longer continued to work. There were not enough American soldiers to keep order.

At this point the American leaders overseeing Iraq made three mistakes. The first mistake was the decision that they did not need to send more soldiers to keep order. The Iraqi people would support the Americans if the Americans could keep them safe. But if the Americans could not keep them safe, Iraqis would not support the Americans. More soldiers were needed to protect Iraqis, but the United States didn't send more.

The second mistake was that American leaders said members of Saddam Hussein's Ba'ath party could not serve in the new Iraqi government. Many Iraqis were part of the Ba'ath party. They were not part of the Ba'ath party because they liked Hussein. They joined the party because they wanted a job. The order that removed members of the Ba'ath party from government jobs hurt ordinary Iraqis. Iraqis in certain positions, such as school teachers, were fired. Many ordinary Iraqis who might have supported the Americans turned against them instead.

The third mistake was that American leaders disbanded the Iraqi military instead of appointing new leaders for the Iraqi army. Many Iraqi soldiers took their weapons and went home. They ended up fighting against Americans. The Americans faced other challenges in Iraq. Iraq is a country with three major groups of people. In the north are the **Kurds**. Though they

419

Teach for Understanding

- Direct attention to the picture on page 419. Read aloud the caption.

What city did Americans capture? Baghdad

By the time the Iraqi military was defeated, what had Hussein and his government done? They had gone into hiding.

What new problems did the lack of both a military and a government create? No one was left to make sure the basic functions of government continued. Iraqi police no longer worked. There were not enough American soldiers to keep order.

What mistakes did the American leaders make while overseeing Iraq? They did not provide enough soldiers to protect Iraqis. They removed all members of the Ba'ath party from government jobs. They disbanded the Iraqi military instead of appointing new leaders for the Iraqi army.

Why was it important to provide enough soldiers to protect Iraqis? The Iraqi people would support the Americans if the Americans could keep them safe. Otherwise they would not support the Americans.

What did many ordinary Iraqi people do once the members of the Ba'ath party were removed from government jobs? They turned against the Americans.

After the US military neglected to appoint new Iraqi military leaders, what did many Iraqi soldiers do? They ended up fighting against Americans.

Lesson

167

Teach for Understanding

- Direct attention to the picture on page 420. Invite a student to read aloud the caption.

  What are the three major groups of people in Iraq? the Kurds, the Sunni Muslims, and the Shia Muslims

- Explain that Shia Muslims are sometimes called *Shiite*.

  What concern did these groups of people have about a new government in Iraq? Each group worried that the others would control the new government of Iraq.

  Which group began to fight the Americans? the Sunnis

  What other group attacked Americans and their allies? Shia fighters

  What did Shia leaders who received support from Iran hope to claim? part of Iraq

  Which groups fought each other for the control of Iraq? Sunni and Shia Muslims

  What factors contributed to increased opposition in the United States to the war in Iraq? Violence increased in Iraq. No weapons of mass destruction were found. People thought President Bush had lied to get the United States to go to war.

» Conclude the discussion by asking the question on page 420. President Bush and others believed that Saddam Hussein was hiding weapons of mass destruction.

Activity Manual

- Guide completion of page 289.

---

are predominately Muslim, the Kurds are not Arabs. Hussein killed many of the Kurds while he was in power. The **Sunni** and the **Shia** Muslims make up the other two groups in Iraq. These two groups are ancient divisions within Islam. Saddam Hussein was Sunni. The majority of Iraqis are Shia. Each of these groups worried that the others would control the new Iraqi government.

Roadside bombs were a continual threat to US troops traveling through Iraq.

The Kurdish area in the north stayed relatively peaceful. The Sunnis had the most to lose after Saddam's fall. Sunnis began to fight the Americans. Fighters would make homemade bombs and hide them beside roads the US military used. They would ambush soldiers on patrol. Al-Qaeda fighters also came to Iraq to fight against the Americans and their allies. By 2004 Shia fighters had begun to attack the Americans and their allies. Shia leaders had support from Iran and saw an opportunity to claim at least part of Iraq for themselves. The Iraqis were not happy with the lack of progress in rebuilding Iraq. Many supported this uprising, and Sunni and Shia Muslims fought each other for control of Iraq.

As the violence increased in Iraq, opposition to the war increased in the United States. In addition, investigators did not find weapons of mass destruction in Iraq. They found that Hussein did have a program to develop weapons of mass destruction. He had laboratories that were working on producing the necessary ingredients for biological weapons. But nothing was ready to be turned into weapons.

President Bush's opponents claimed that Bush lied to get the United States to go to war. This was an unfair charge. Many people had believed Hussein had those weapons. Congressmen from both parties believed it. European allies and UN weapons inspectors also believed it. But the weapons were not there. Americans seemed to be losing the war. Invading Iraq seemed to many Americans to be a bad mistake.

> Why did the United States go to war in Iraq?

420

A Helping Hand
Troop Surge in Iraq

The Iraq War continued year after year. The violence increased year after year. Many Americans wanted to see the United States leave Iraq. President Bush was not willing to consider this. If the United States went home, it would be leaving Iraq worse off than before the war. Bush wanted to make the United States safer from terrorists. If the soldiers left, Iraq would be a safe space from which terrorists could plan attacks. Bush was not willing to give up on his vision of seeing the Iraqis have their own democracy.

Bush thought about changing the way the United States fought the war. Bush's advisors noted that in a certain part of Iraq, the commanding officer had defeated his opponents. He had kept them from retaking his territory. He began to rebuild the area. Another commanding officer saw similar results. He put his men out on foot patrols. This let them meet Iraqi people. The American soldiers could let the Iraqis know that they were there to help. In these areas, the Iraqis began to support the Americans.

President Bush believed the United States should follow this plan in the whole country. This was the best chance the United States had for success. But it meant putting many more soldiers in Iraq. Bush faced opposition even in

US soldiers were able to interact with local children during a food distribution mission.

his own party. Many people thought the United States should be bringing the troops home. They did not want to send more soldiers. But Bush was determined not to lose Iraq.

He sent the troops. When the Iraqi people saw that the Americans were living among them and providing protection for them, they began to provide more support. They could now tell the Americans where terrorists were hiding without fear of being killed in return. Tribal leaders who had sided with al-Qaeda to ensure that they were protected from other groups now turned against al-Qaeda. They gave their support to the United States. The tide of the war had turned.

Hurricane Katrina

Bush also faced challenges at home. In August 2005 **Hurricane Katrina** hit the Gulf Coast. It was one of the deadliest and most destructive hurricanes ever to strike the United

421

Lesson **168** Student Text pages 421–23
Activity Manual pages 290–91

Lesson Focus

- George W. Bush dealt with problems in Iraq, at home, and in Africa.

Objectives
- Recognize what caused the Iraqi people to give their support to the United States
- Explain the problem with Social Security and how Congress responded to the problem
- Identify what Bush wanted for Africa
- Make an infograph

Materials
- Note cards
- Samples of infographs
- Poster board for each student
- Resources about malaria

Teacher's Toolkit CD
- Visual 51: *Hurricane Katrina*

Review

- Invite a student to explain the events that led to the invasion of Iraq.
- Choose a volunteer to state mistakes American leaders made while overseeing Iraq.
- Guide a review of the major groups of people living in Iraq.
- Invite a student to explain American opposition to the war in Iraq.

Preparation for Reading

- Generate interest as you direct the students to read the titles and examine the pictures on pages 421–23.
- Guide pronunciation of any unfamiliar words in the lesson.
- Direct the students to read the pages to learn the name of the state that had relief plans in place when Hurricane Katrina struck. Mississippi

Teach for Understanding

- Direct attention to the picture on page 421. Read aloud the caption.

  Why was President Bush unwilling to bring US troops home from Iraq? Bush wanted to make the United States safer from terrorists. If the soldiers left, Iraq would be a safe space from which terrorists could plan attacks. Bush was not willing to give up on his vision of seeing the Iraqis have their own democracy.

- Invite a student to describe how the Iraqi people responded when an American officer put his soldiers out on foot patrol.

  What storm hit the Gulf Coast in 2005? Hurricane Katrina

Teach for Understanding

- Direct attention to the picture on page 422. Read aloud the caption.

- Display Visual 51. Explain that the storm covered a very large area. Direct attention to the eye of the storm. Explain that it is calm in the eye of a hurricane. The winds rotate around the eye.

What city was hit especially hard by Hurricane Katrina? New Orleans

What caused the city to be plunged under water? New Orleans is below sea level. When the levees broke, the city was plunged under water.

- Direct attention to the graphic on page 422. Ask the students to find sea level and to notice how New Orleans is situated below sea level.

What kept many people from evacuating before the storm hit? The mayor waited too long after federal officials urged an order of evacuation.

How did the Federal Emergency Management Agency respond? It had trouble knowing what was going on. It did not provide aid quickly or to the places that needed it most.

Why was President Bush unable to send the military to help in New Orleans? The governor of Louisiana repeatedly rejected granting the president this authority.

- Why do you think the governor rejected help? Possible answers could include that he believed he could manage the crisis himself. He may have feared criticism for the lack of handling the situation correctly. He did not want US government intervention.

States. New Orleans was especially hard hit. New Orleans is below sea level. The levees, or flood walls, that hold back the water broke. Much of the city was plunged under water.

Federal officials had urged the mayor of New Orleans to order an evacuation of the city before the storm hit. But the mayor waited too long. Many people did not evacuate.

The Federal Emergency Management Agency was supposed to provide relief after the hurricane. But it had trouble knowing what was going on. It did not provide aid quickly or to the places that needed it most.

The disaster also resulted in a breakdown of law and order. Many people participated in looting New Orleans. President Bush wanted to send in the US military to help maintain law and order. He wanted the military to help with the relief effort. But by law, the president cannot send the US military into a state to provide for law and order unless the governor allows for it. The governor of Louisiana repeatedly rejected granting the president this authority.

The relief efforts in Mississippi went much better. The state of Mississippi had relief plans in place. Officials in Mississippi were able to respond effectively to the crisis.

Most Americans remember Hurricane Katrina not only as a natural disaster but as a disaster in the government response as well. The systems in place to offer help in times of disaster broke down.

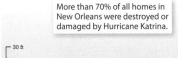
More than 70% of all homes in New Orleans were destroyed or damaged by Hurricane Katrina.

422

Background

New Orleans

New Orleans, Louisiana, sits at the delta of the Mississippi River, making it a central part of the economy. Tourism is also another major part of the economy. French buildings and creole food attract many people. Creole cooking combines foods from European, African, Caribbean, and American cultures.

Bush's Opponent in the 2004 Election

Although John Kerry was a decorated Vietnam veteran, he opposed the war when he returned home, and that opposition to the Vietnam War hurt him among veterans in the 2004 election. Kerry also seemed indecisive. After voting for the Iraq War, he later opposed measures necessary for fighting it. His effort to defend his actions—"I actually did vote for the 87 billion dollars [for the war in Iraq] before I voted against it"—only cemented his image as a "flip-flopper."

Activities

Learning about Hurricanes

Materials: Resources about hurricanes

Social Security

George W. Bush was elected to his second term. One of the problems that he wanted to fix was Social Security.

Social Security was part of the New Deal. People who retire receive Social Security checks. This provides them some money after they stop working. The people who are working now pay taxes on what they earn. This tax money pays for the people who are retired.

That system worked well as long as there were more people working than there were people retired. But now more and more people were retiring. Eventually, the Social Security program would run out of money.

Bush wanted to make changes to how Social Security worked. He did not want high taxes to pay for Social Security in the future. He did not want young Americans to pay into Social Security and get nothing back. But Congress wasn't willing to act. Changing Social Security could be controversial. Congress decided to wait.

Africa

President Bush believed that Africa had great potential. But it had not grown economically like other parts of the world. Part of the problem was disease. Sick people have a hard time working. One common disease that keeps Africans from working is **malaria**. Malaria is spread by mosquitoes. Almost 10 percent of Africans will die from malaria.

Bush knew that nobody needed to die from malaria. Medicines can help people who become sick. Sleeping under a mosquito net can prevent people from being bitten. Insecticides can kill the mosquitoes that carry the disease. Bush believed that the United States could help eliminate malaria in Africa.

He also believed that African nations were the best ones to design programs that worked. He brought the United States alongside these African nations to lend a helping hand.

> Why does sickness keep some nations poor?

Activity

Making an Infographic

Create an infograph about malaria. You might show the life cycle of the malaria parasite and how the disease is spread by the female Anopheles mosquito. You could prepare an infograph on the prevention of malaria or an infograph that shows where malaria is present in the world. Be creative as you think of an idea for your own infograph.

423

Provide information about hurricanes. Direct the students to work in small groups to learn what causes hurricanes. Challenge them to learn about other hurricanes that have hit the United States. Invite different groups to share several facts that they learned.

Fixing Social Security

Explain that President George W. Bush knew that Social Security would one day run out of money. He wanted younger workers to be able to pay into a retirement savings account rather than into Social Security so that these younger workers would have money in retirement, but he did not gain enough support to make a change in Social Security. Invite students to decide whether Bush's plan would be a good idea and to give reasons for their answers.

What government program did Bush want to fix? Social Security

What is the purpose of Social Security? It is intended to provide some money to employees after they stop working.

- Explain that Social Security pays money to the retired, to the elderly, to the disabled, and to some families that have had a parent or a spouse die.

What condition is necessary for Social Security to work? more people working than there are people retired or drawing Social Security

What would happen if there were more people receiving Social Security than there were people working and paying Social Security taxes? Eventually the Social Security program would run out of money.

What was the response by Congress to changing Social Security as Bush wanted? Congress was not willing to act. Congress decided to wait.

What did President Bush believe about Africa's potential? Africa had great potential.

What was true of Africa's economy? Africa had not grown economically like other parts of the world.

What was a common disease in Africa? malaria

How is malaria spread? by mosquitoes

What were some things that could prevent people from dying from malaria? medicines to treat the illness, mosquito nets to prevent mosquito bites, insecticides to kill mosquitoes

Who did Bush believe were the best ones to design programs to help Africa? African nations

 Conclude the discussion by asking the question on page 423. Sick people have a hard time working.

Activity Manual

- Guide completion of pages 290–91.

Activity

Making an Infographic

- Generate excitement about making an infograph as you read aloud the Activity information on page 423. Direct attention to the suggestions for an infograph about malaria.

- Direct the students to explore resources about malaria and to choose information they want to include in their posters. Sources of information may be recorded on note cards. Remind the students to include a title and attractive illustrations. Encourage the students to plan their poster on a separate piece of paper before making the poster. Display the posters.

169

Student Text pages 424–25
Activity Manual page 292

Lesson Focus

- Several factors contributed to a financial crisis in America.

Objectives

- Recognize factors that hurt the American economy
- Explain Bush's response to the financial crisis

Review

- Review what caused the Iraqi people to give their support to the United States.
- Invite a student to explain the problem with Social Security and how Congress responded to the problem.
- Choose a volunteer to identify what Bush wanted for Africa.

Preparation for Reading

- Generate interest as you direct the students to read the titles and examine the pictures on pages 424–25.
- Guide pronunciation of any unfamiliar words in the lesson.
- Direct the student to read the pages to learn what it is called when the government does not own the businesses. free market

Teach for Understanding

- Direct attention to the picture. Read aloud the caption.

  What were two businesses that used the internet? Amazon.com and Pets.com

- Which of these businesses was successful? Amazon.com

  What enabled the owners of these new businesses to become wealthy? People bought lots of stock in these new businesses.

  How was the economy hurt by some of these businesses? Some of these businesses failed and went out of business. Many investors lost their money.

- Why did Bush press Congress to pass tax cuts? Answers could include that he believed that tax cuts would help people and businesses have more money to spend, which would help the economy.

  What mistake did banks make when they made house loans? The banks gave loans to many people who could not afford to pay the money back.

  What was the outcome of loaning money to peple who could not pay the money back? The banks lost money. Some banks collapsed.

Financial Crisis

When George W. Bush became president in 2001, the economy was slowing down again. During the 1990s, many people had begun to use the Internet. Businesses sprang up to take advantage of the Internet. For instance, Amazon.com started to sell books online. Another business, Pets.com, sold pet supplies online. Many other Internet businesses started during this time as well.

The owners of these new businesses became wealthy because people bought lots of stock in these new businesses. The stock market rose to new heights.

Some of these businesses, like Amazon, became very successful. But many more, like Pets.com, failed. They had not figured out how to make the business profitable. The people who bought stock in these failing companies were not getting money back on their investment. They sold their stock. Many of these companies went out of business, and many investors lost their money. This hurt the American economy.

President Bush pressed Congress to pass tax cuts. These tax cuts reduced taxes on all Americans. They also reduced taxes on small businesses. Bush sent tax cut proposals to Congress in 2002 and 2003. These also passed. In 2003 the economy began to improve.

The economy continued to grow through the rest of Bush's two terms as president. But by the end of Bush's presidency, it became clear that some of this growth was caused by unwise investments.

Banks took back houses when owners were unable to make the payments.

During this time, banks made unwise loans and economic decisions. To encourage people to buy houses, the banks gave loans to many people who could not afford to pay the money back. Then the banks lost money when people could not repay the loans. Some banks even collapsed

424

- Direct attention to the graph on page 425. Invite a student to name the events that affected the economy.

  Who did Bush's advisors agree would lend money to intervene in the financial crisis? the Federal Reserve System

  What did Congress do when the intervention by the Federal Reserve System failed to solve the problem? Congress passed a bill that allowed the government to buy stocks of banks in trouble.

  What happened when the government bought the stocks of banks in trouble? The government became part owner of these banks.

- Do you think it was right for the government to become part owners of these banks? Possible answers could include that it was not right because the American economy is built on a free market where the government does not own businesses.

  Why did Bush go against his belief in the free market to bail out the banks? He was afraid that if the banks failed, all Americans would be hurt by the effect on the economy.

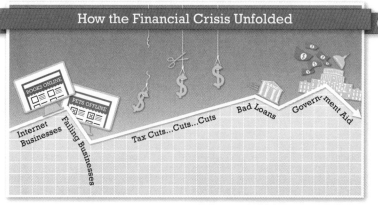

How the Financial Crisis Unfolded

Internet Businesses · Failing Businesses · Tax Cuts...Cuts...Cuts · Bad Loans · Govern-ment Aid

because of these unwise decisions. President Bush's advisors recommended that he use the **Federal Reserve System** to intervene, but this did not solve the problem.

Finally, Congress passed a bill that allowed the government to buy stocks of banks in trouble. The money from the stocks gave the banks the money they needed, but the government also became part owner of these banks.

President Bush was a supporter of the **free market**. A free market is one in which the government does not own the businesses. It lets business leaders run their own businesses. Bush said that he did not like bailing out the big banks. But he was afraid that if the

banks failed, all Americans would be hurt by the effect on the economy.

The Bush presidency was a significant time for Americans. The United States came under attack from Islamic terrorists and responded with wars in Afghanistan and Iraq. A conservative president held office for eight years. Many conservatives wished Bush had done more to shrink the growth of government. Nonetheless, Bush did cut taxes. He also demonstrated that Christian beliefs should shape important decisions on matters such as embryonic stem cell research.

> Why is it unwise for the government to give money to failing banks?

425

Conclude the discussion by asking the question on page 425.
America is built on a free market. The government was not designed to own businesses. The money the government gave to failing banks put the nation in greater debt.

Activity Manual

• Guide completion of page 292.

Objective
• Recall concepts and terms from Chapter 19

Materials
• Questions on slips of paper and answers to the questions on separate slips of paper

Introduction

• Concepts for the Chapter 19 Test will be taken from Activity Manual pages 281–94. You may review any or all of the concepts during this lesson. You may choose to review Chapter 19 by playing "Mix and Match."

Review

Game: Mix and Match

• Write several questions on strips of paper. Write the answers to those questions on separate strips of paper. Place the questions in one container and the answers in another container. Mix up the papers.

• Draw a question from the container and read it aloud. Choose a student to draw an answer. The student should determine if the answer matches the question he heard. If the student correctly recognizes it does match, he receives a point for his team. If it does not match, he has the option of stating the correct answer. If he can give the correct answer, he receives a point for his team. Questions and answers that are incorrectly matched should be placed back into their respective containers before the next question is drawn. Continue until all the questions and answers have been matched correctly.

Activity Manual

• Guide completion of pages 293–94.

Lesson **171** Chapter 19 Test

Objective
• Demonstrate knowledge of concepts from Chapter 19 by taking the test

Assessment

• Administer Test 19.

20 Change Sweeps the Nation

Focus

During the Obama presidency, the United States experienced much change.

Introduction

A desire for change and a downturn in the United States' economy led to Barack Obama defeating John McCain in the 2008 general election. The economy was the most urgent problem Obama faced. Despite opposition, government programs, including the Stimulus, were set up. Obama signed the Affordable Care Act, and he faced the challenges of ending the Iraq War and the war in Afghanistan. His presidency was complicated by the Arab Spring. Domestically, Americans continued to struggle with racism and gun violence. The Democrats did well in the 2012 general election, and Obama was reelected. America experienced a shift in religious identity, and an increased use of technology caused concern about the ease of stealing and using private information. Foreign policy in the Middle East became more complicated, and Obama faced problems in Europe as Russia tried to regain influence, especially in Ukraine. Finally, Americans remained divided over moral issues such as the environment, gay rights, and abortion. Christians in the United States are able to serve God in every part of life, knowing that pleasing God is of primary importance, regardless of whether the surrounding culture supports or opposes God's way.

Lesson	Student Text	Activity Manual	Content	Vocabulary	
172	426–30	295–99	The 2008 election Primary Source: A Speech on Race John McCain Joe Biden Barack Obama	maverick	
173	431–33	300	Obama's domestic programs	Affordable Care Act domestic program inaugurate	Stimulus tax revenue Tea Party Movement
174	434–37	301–2	How It Was: Hearing bin Laden was dead Foreign affairs during Obama's first term Iraq War Hamid Karzai Afghanistan Muammar al-Qaddafi	Arab Spring embassy militant	Navy SEALs Nobel Peace Prize
175	438–40	303	Gun violence The 2012 election Racial issues		
176	441–43	304	America's shift in religious identity Advances in technology	hacker secularization	viral whistleblower
177	444–47	305	Biography Box: Nancy Writebol Vladimir Putin Foreign policy during Obama's second term Ukraine Middle East	Islamic State	
178	448–51	306	Environment Abortion Gay Rights Activity: Presenting a Speech	Clean Power Plan greenhouse gases	green energy
179		307–8	Chapter Review		
180			Chapter Test		

Visit bjupress.com/resources for links to enhance the lessons.

Signing the
Affordable Care Act
March 23, 2010

Death of the American
ambassador to Libya
September 11, 2012

2005   November 4, 2008   **2010**   May 2, 2011   **2015**
Election of   Death of bin Laden
President Obama

As George W. Bush's presidency ended, Americans wanted some sort of change. They were tired of the war. They wanted a stronger economy. Since Bush could not run for reelection and his vice president would not run, the election of 2008 would bring change to the White House, no matter who was elected.

Election of 2008
The Candidates
Republican

The Republican Party had several potential candidates. Senator John McCain was an early favorite. McCain had the reputation of being a **maverick**. He did not always follow common Republican ideals. He even encouraged a way for illegal immigrants to become citizens. McCain was also a strong supporter of the war in Iraq. Rudy Giuliani, the former mayor of New York City, also wanted to become the Republican candidate. He had a good record of running the city. Mitt Romney and Mike Huckabee also ran for the nomination. Romney

had been governor of Massachusetts, and Huckabee had been governor of Arkansas. Romney brought a record of working well with a Democratic legislature, and Huckabee appealed to conservative Christians.

As the campaign ran, it narrowed to Romney versus McCain. Although Romney had a good record as governor, McCain had more experience in national government. By the beginning of March 2008, McCain was the Republican's candidate.

Democrat

The Democrats had fewer strong candidates. Their race quickly narrowed to two. Hillary Clinton was a senator from New York. She promised to bring both her experience as a senator and her experience as the wife of former president Bill Clinton. Senator **Barack Obama** of Illinois was the youngest of all the major candidates. He gained fame for a speech he gave in 2004. Either candidate's victory would make history. Hillary Clinton would be the first female president. Barack Obama

427

Chapter Focus

During the Obama presidency, the United States experienced much change.

Lesson   **172**   **Student Text pages 426–30**
Activity Manual pages 295–99

Lesson Focus

- Barack Obama campaigned against John McCain and won the presidential election of 2008.

Objectives
- Name the presidential candidates in the 2008 general election
- Examine the political strengths of Barack Obama and John McCain
- State campaign promises made by Barack Obama
- Explain why the 2008 general election was historic

Teacher's Toolkit CD
- Instructional Aid 68: *A Presidential Election*

Introduction

- Invite a student to read aloud the title of the chapter and predict what the chapter will be about. a time of change in America

- Invite a student to read the chapter focus aloud.

  What do you think you will learn about in this chapter? changes that occurred in the United States during Obama's presidency

- Direct attention to the picture on page 426.

- What do you think the picture illustrates? Answers could include that the picture illustrates the excitement Americans felt over the changes that would occur during Obama's presidency.

- Direct attention to the timeline.

  When was Obama elected president? November 4, 2008

  What happened on September 11, 2012? The American ambassador to Libya died.

- Invite students to identify the remaining dates and events in order on the timeline.

Preparation for Reading

- Generate interest as you direct the students to read the titles and examine the pictures on pages 426–30.

- Guide pronunciation of any unfamiliar words in the lesson.

- Direct the students to read the pages silently and complete Instructional Aid 68 in small groups.

Teach for Understanding

What did Americans want as George W. Bush's presidency ended? change

Would the election of 2008 bring change? Yes, it would bring change to the White House because Bush could not run for reelection and his vice president would not run.

- Why could Bush not run for reelection? Answers should include that he had already served two terms as president.

- Invite students to name the potential Republican and Democratic candidates for president in 2008.

- Choose a volunteer to read aloud the glossary definition of *maverick* and tell how it relates to John McCain. He did not always follow common Republican ideals. He supported whatever he believed to be right even if the Republican Party did not.

> If potential candidates for president are currently campaigning for president, you may choose to have students name those candidates.

Lesson

172

Teach for Understanding

- Direct attention to the pictures of the presidential candidates on page 428. Invite a student to name each candidate and the candidate's political party. Invite another student to name the two Republican candidates that remained after the number of candidates narrowed.

- Choose volunteers to read aloud the sentences that tell what areas of government the two potential Republican candidates and the potential Democratic candidates had served in.

  Why would both of the potential Democratic candidates make history if elected president? Hillary Clinton would be the first female president. Barack Obama would be the first African American president.

- What issues helped Obama take the lead among the Democrats? Answers could include that Obama gained the support of younger voters and African Americans because he was both young and African American. His opposition to the Iraq War gained him the support of anti-war voters. He also promised to close the American prison in Guantanamo Bay, Cuba.

- Invite a student to tell which potential candidates were chosen to be the Republican and Democratic candidates for president. Explain that primaries and caucuses are held for Americans to select one candidate from each political party to run for the office of president.

  What strength did Barack Obama offer American voters? He gave many Americans hope that the American dream still worked.

  What was the basis for the hope that the American dream still worked? Obama's life and career

- What do you think the American dream is? Answers may include that every American who works hard can be successful in whatever he or she chooses to do.

  What encouraged Americans to hope that the nation would improve, and that the lives of poor Americans would become easier? Obama's promise to improve the economy. Like many Democrats, Obama said that people with more money should pay higher taxes than people with less money had to pay. He claimed that voting for him would help bring an increase in jobs.

 McCain

 Giuliani

 Clinton

 Obama

 Romney

 Huckabee

would be the first African American president.

Obama eventually took the lead among the Democrats. Younger voters and African Americans strongly supported Obama. He was also able to gain anti-war voters. Clinton had voted in favor of the Iraq War as a senator, but Obama had always opposed it. He also promised to close the American prison in Guantanamo Bay, Cuba. This prison held suspected terrorists without trial. Despite these advantages, it took Obama until early June to clinch the nomination. By then McCain had enjoyed several months of unifying the Republicans behind him.

428

The General Election

The Candidates

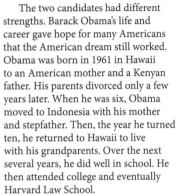

The two candidates had different strengths. Barack Obama's life and career gave hope for many Americans that the American dream still worked. Obama was born in 1961 in Hawaii to an American mother and a Kenyan father. His parents divorced only a few years later. When he was six, Obama moved to Indonesia with his mother and stepfather. Then, the year he turned ten, he returned to Hawaii to live with his grandparents. Over the next several years, he did well in school. He then attended college and eventually Harvard Law School.

After law school, Obama's life continued to go smoothly. He married a fellow lawyer, Michelle Robinson. Obama taught law at the University of Chicago. He was also elected to serve in the Illinois State Senate. Then, in 2004, he was elected as a United States senator.

Obama encouraged people to hope that the nation would improve. He

Heritage Studies 5

promised to improve the economy. Like many Democrats, Obama said that people with more money should pay higher taxes than people with less money had to pay. He gave hope that the lives of poor Americans would become easier. He claimed that voting for him would help bring an increase of jobs. He strongly opposed the war in Iraq. Obama wanted to bring American troops out of that conflict. He also wanted an end to involvement in Afghanistan. Although Obama acknowledged that fighting the Taliban was not wrong, he wanted Americans to hope for peace and justice. He also promised that he would make healthcare affordable for all Americans. Going to the doctor was very expensive. Having a serious illness could leave someone bankrupt. Obama said that "in the wealthiest nation on Earth, no one should go broke just because they get sick."

In addition, Obama's candidacy offered the hope that Americans could move beyond the issue of racism. If a black man could be elected president, then perhaps the Civil Rights Movement had finally won. Americans of every ethnicity hoped that individuals would be judged by their actions, not their skin color.

John McCain offered a different strength to voters. He offered experience. Both his father and his grandfather served as admirals in the navy. McCain himself served as a naval pilot during the Vietnam War. In 1967 he was shot down over North Vietnam and then captured. For five and half years, he was tortured and mistreated. Finally in 1973, he was released. After a few more years serving in the navy, McCain ran for Congress.

After winning a seat in the House in 1982, McCain diligently served in Congress. Both as a representative and then as a senator, McCain had a good reputation. He was generally conservative, but not always. He supported whatever he believed to be right, even if the Republican Party did not. But in the election of 2008, McCain

In 1990 twenty-eight-year-old Barack Obama was elected the first black president of the Harvard Law Review. It is considered the most prestigious student position at Harvard Law School.

President Obama wears only gray or blue suits. This is to save his decision-making energy for more important decisions than fashion.

President Obama is an avid basketball player, but an injury in 2010 resulted in twelve stitches in his upper lip. He has since taken up golf.

429

Teach for Understanding

- Discuss why Americans could hope for a peaceful and just nation.

  What hope did Obama's candidacy offer regarding racial issues? His candidacy offered the hope that Americans could move beyond the issue of racism, and that individuals would be judged by their actions rather than by their skin color.

- Choose volunteers to read aloud the captions about Barack Obama on page 429.

Primary Source: A Speech on Race

- Guide the students in reading the information and excerpt from Barack Obama's speech on Activity Manual page 297. Discuss the excerpt as you guide the students in answering the questions. Proverbs 16:1–11 may be useful in helping the students formulate an answer for the third question.

  What strength did John McCain offer American voters? the strength of experience

- Guide a discussion about how McCain had gained his experience. In addition to McCain's many years of serving in Congress, include that his naval experience and the naval influence of his father and grandfather might have helped McCain gain experience in leadership. His experience as a prisoner in Vietnam might have helped him to persevere when facing opposition.

Teach for Understanding

Who seemed to have a better understanding of foreign policy? McCain

🔧 Do you think it is important for a president to have a good understanding of foreign policy? Answers may include that a good understanding of foreign policy is important because a president needs to be able to work effectively with other nations and to deal with difficult foreign issues.

- Invite a student to name the running mate for each candidate.

- Guide a discussion about why it was hard to predict the outcome of the election in late August and early September.

What caused the campaigns to change in mid-September? The stock market began a major decline. One large bank went bankrupt and several others seemed likely to collapse. Car manufacturers General Motors and Chrysler also faced bankruptcy.

🔧 Why did the Republican Party lose favor among Americans? Answers could include that people blamed Bush's Republican government for the economic downturn.

How did Obama use the economic downturn to his advantage? Obama pointed out that the economy had done well under the last Democratic president. Obama promised that he and the Democrats would bring back American prosperity.

- Invite a student to tell who was elected president on November 4, 2008.

What was historical about the election? Americans voted in record numbers. And in record numbers, they voted for Obama. Obama would be the first African American president of the United States.

- Direct attention to the "Election of 2008" map on page 430. Choose volunteers to name which states were won by which candidate. Discuss the difference between the popular vote and the electoral vote. Remind the students that the president is elected indirectly through the Electoral College. Explain that the victorious candidate is not technically elected to office until the Electoral College votes and its ballots are counted by the Senate. To win, a candidate must gain at least 270 of those votes.

▶ Conclude the discussion by asking the question on page 430. to improve the economy, to end the war in Iraq and the war in Afghanistan, to make healthcare affordable for all Americans, and to bring back American prosperity

Activity Manual

- Guide completion of pages 295–99.

Election of 2008

was the choice of Republicans and the voters who valued years of committed service. He also seemed to understand foreign policy better than Obama.

The Election

In late August and early September, the results were hard to predict. Obama enjoyed a lead among young Americans and minority voters. His campaign used social media effectively. But at the end of August 2008, McCain made a huge announcement when he introduced his running mate, Sarah Palin. She was the governor of Alaska. Unlike McCain, Palin appealed to many conservative Americans. It seemed possible that McCain and Palin could defeat Obama and his running mate, **Joe Biden**.

But in mid-September, the campaigns changed. The stock market began a major decline. Banks had loaned money unwisely. One large bank went bankrupt and several others seemed likely to collapse. Car manufacturers General Motors and Chrysler also faced bankruptcy. As Bush's government struggled to save the economy, the Republican Party lost favor. Obama pointed out that the economy had done well under Bill Clinton, the last Democratic president. Obama promised that he and the Democrats would bring back American prosperity.

On November 4, 2008, Americans made history. They voted in record numbers. And in record numbers they voted for Obama. An African American would be the next president of the United States.

What promises were made by Obama?

430

Obama's Domestic Front
Getting Started

In preparation for taking office, President-elect Obama began planning his cabinet. These people would advise him on major issues. The biggest domestic problem was the economy. Obama chose Timothy Geithner as secretary of the treasury. In foreign affairs, Americans were still fighting in the Middle East. Obama kept President Bush's secretary of defense, Robert Gates. Obama asked Hillary Clinton to serve as his secretary of state. Finally, in late January 2009, Barack Obama was **inaugurated** as president of the United States.

Keeping the Economy Going

The economy was the most immediate problem. Millions of Americans were out of work. Others were working only part-time. Many could not pay their house payments. They feared losing their homes. President Obama continued Bush's policy of improving the economy through government spending.

The government set up two major programs to help Americans keep their houses. One helped people who were behind on their payments. The second helped people who were in danger of falling behind. Judges were allowed to make house payments more affordable. Despite these helps, many Americans still lost their houses.

Obama continued Bush's actions to rescue car manufacturers. Few Americans were buying new cars. The American government spent billions to help General Motors and Chrysler survive bankruptcy.

Houses   Manufacturing   Cars

Another program helped all car manufacturers. A person could trade in a used car for a discount toward a new car. The government paid the difference. This policy would help the car companies and put more fuel-efficient cars on the road.

The biggest government program was called the **Stimulus**. Congress agreed to spend almost $800 billion to help the economy. The money was used in a number of ways. Some of it provided unemployment benefits. This money gave some income to unemployed people looking for work. The government also gave tax credits to many Americans. Obama hoped that people who paid less in taxes would spend that money. More money in circulation helps businesses grow and hire more workers. The government also spent money on roads, water mains, and other utilities. The Stimulus included many programs. All were designed to improve American life and the economy.

431

Invite a student to contrast the strengths of Barack Obama and John McCain.

What were some of the promises Obama made during his campaign? to improve the economy, to end the war in Iraq and the war in Afghanistan, to make healthcare affordable for all Americans, and to bring back American prosperity

Which candidate was elected president? Barack Obama

Why was the election of 2008 historical? Americans voted in record numbers. And in record numbers, they voted for Obama. Obama would be the first African American president of the United States.

Preparation for Reading

- Generate interest as you direct the students to read the titles and examine the pictures on pages 431–33.
- Guide pronunciation of any unfamiliar words in the lesson.
- Direct the students to read the pages silently to discover the most immediate problem Barack Obama faced at the beginning of his presidency. the economy

Teach for Understanding

- Choose a volunteer to read aloud the glossary definition of *inaugurate*. Discuss the definition as needed.

How did people refer to Barack Obama before he was inaugurated as president of the United States? President-elect

Why was he called President-elect Obama? He had already been elected president, but had not yet been inaugurated.

What was a task that Obama worked on while waiting to be inaugurated? He began planning his cabinet.

What is the president's cabinet? A group of people who advise the president on major issues.

When was Barack Obama inaugurated as president of the United States? in late January 2009

- Explain that presidents are inaugurated at noon on January 20 in the year following the election because the Twentieth Amendment to the Constitution states that "the terms of the President and the Vice President shall end at noon on the 20th day of January." If January 20 falls on a Sunday, the inauguration ceremony takes place on January 21.

What problems did Americans face in the struggling economy? Millions of Americans were out of work. Others were working only part-time. Many could not pay their house payments.

What policy for improving the economy did Obama continue? Bush's policy of improving the economy through government spending

---

Lesson **173**   Student Text pages 431–33
Activity Manual page 300

Lesson Focus

- When he assumed the presidency, Obama continued Bush's policy of improving the economy through government spending.

Objectives

- Recognize that the economy was the most immediate domestic problem when Barack Obama assumed the presidency
- Describe government programs intended to improve the economy
- Explain why some Americans opposed Obama's programs

Review

Who were the Democratic and Republican candidates for president in the 2008 general election? Barack Obama was the Democratic candidate. John McCain was the Republican candidate.

Guide a review of important terms, maps, places, and people from each previous lesson. Direct the students to find and read the corresponding entries from the Resource Treasury.

- Direct attention to the icons on page 431. Invite students to describe government programs that were intended to help homeowners and car manufacturers.

  What was the biggest government program called? the Stimulus

  What was the Stimulus designed to do? improve American life and the economy

Teach for Understanding

- Choose a volunteer to read aloud the glossary definition of *Stimulus*. Use the infograph on page 432 to guide a discussion about some of the programs and incentives included in the Stimulus. Explain that although the original Stimulus approved by Congress totaled almost $800 billion, increases over the next few years raised the cost of the Stimulus to approximately $830 billion.

- Review the glossary definitions for *recession* and *deficit*.

  Why did Americans question the Stimulus and Obama's other responses to the recession? People knew that the nation was struggling financially. But they wondered how the government would pay for all these expenses. Some asked if Americans were just buying relief now and passing the bill to the next generation. Others doubted if short-term government spending could provide long-term benefits.

- Discuss the wisdom of planning programs that required large deficits, knowing that the government would need to borrow money to pay for the expenses.

  What would pay back the debts? tax revenue

- Invite a student to read aloud the glossary definition of *tax revenue*.

- Where would the tax revenue come from? Answers should include taxes paid by the American people.

  What was Obama's main domestic program? better national healthcare

- Choose a volunteer to read aloud the glossary definition of *domestic program*.

- Why was the program for better national healthcare a domestic program? It was a government program that dealt with an issue, healthcare, within America's border.

- Discuss why Obama made better national healthcare his main domestic program.

- Why did it take more than a year for Congress to plan and pass a national healthcare bill? Answers may include that many questions needed to be answered. The bill was long and complicated.

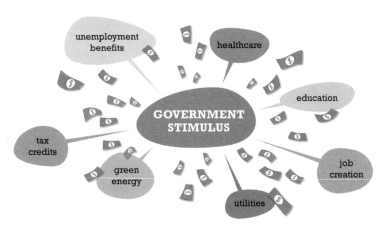

Some Americans questioned the Stimulus and Obama's other responses to the recession. People knew that the nation was struggling financially. But they wondered how the government would pay for all these expenses. Obama's plans required large deficits. The government would have to borrow money until the economy began recovering. At that point, **tax revenue** would begin to pay back the debts. Some asked if Americans were just buying relief now and passing the bill to the next generation. Others doubted if short-term government spending could provide long-term benefits.

Healthcare

As Obama dealt with the recession, he kept working on his main **domestic program**, better national healthcare. Many Americans lacked affordable healthcare. Obama wanted every American to have access to doctors and medicine. He also wanted to keep costs down. The planning and passing of a bill to make this happen took more than a year.

Early in his presidency, Obama encouraged Congress to come up with a plan. Planning was a difficult process. Who would pay? Could people keep their current insurance? Was it the government's role to provide healthcare? Since Democrats controlled both houses, Obama's request was easier to fulfill. Despite this advantage, a final bill was not submitted to the president until late March 2010. He signed it.

432

Background

Inauguration Day: The Official Date

The Founding Fathers designed the first presidential inauguration to take place on March 4, 1789, which was the same day the Constitution went into effect. March 4 continued to be Inauguration Day until 1933, when the crisis of the Great Depression led to a change. Americans wanted quick action from a new president and from Congress, so Congress adopted the Twentieth Amendment, which changed the inauguration date to January 20. President Franklin D. Roosevelt was the first president to be inaugurated under the new amendment on January 20, 1937.

The **Affordable Care Act**, sometimes called Obamacare, was long and complicated. However, the basic facts were straightforward. Businesses with fifty or more full-time employees had to provide insurance. If someone's company did not provide insurance, he would have to buy it for himself. The federal government would help people purchase insurance. If someone did not buy insurance, he would have to pay extra taxes to the government. Congress planned to pay for this system with more taxes. They also claimed that forcing everyone to get insurance would help keep rates lower.

Opposition to Obama's Plans

Not all Americans liked Obama's plans. In the past, Republicans in Congress would fight against a Democratic president to keep his goals in check. But the Republicans had suffered poor election results in 2008, so the Democrats dominated both houses of Congress. Although they did not like all of Obama's proposals, Republicans had no clear strategy to oppose them.

But Americans across the nation soon joined in opposition. In late February, the **Tea Party movement** first became active. Despite its name, the movement was not a political party. Instead it took its name from the Boston Tea Party in 1773 when Bostonians protested tea taxes imposed by the British Empire. Supporters of the Tea Party movement were upset with Obama's plans to help some homeowners keep their houses. They wondered why people losing their houses should receive tax money. Over the course of the year, the Tea Party movement grew. It protested growing government expenses and taxes. It opposed the government reworking of insurance. Most people associated with the movement wanted fewer taxes.

The Tea Party movement was somewhat successful. It could not stop the Affordable Care Act from becoming law. However, it influenced elections in 2010. That year Democrats lost their House majority. Republicans held sixty-three more seats after the election. President Obama no longer had a House that would pass whatever bills he wanted. In the Senate, the Republicans gained seats, but the Democrats kept the majority.

Despite these losses, Obama had much to be happy about. The economy had not collapsed. Millions of Americans were still out of work, but things were slowly improving. Most importantly, his healthcare reform had been achieved.

> In 2010 how did some Americans show their response to Obama's policies?

433

Activity

A President's Inauguration

View all or part of a video of the inauguration of the current president of the United States. Discuss the contents of the president's inaugural address.

Teach for Understanding

What was the final national healthcare bill called? the Affordable Care Act; Obamacare

- Invite a student to read aloud the glossary definition of *Affordable Care Act*.

What kind of coverage did the Affordable Care Act give low income Americans? Medicaid

- Guide a discussion about the basic facts of the Affordable Care Act. Point out that tax revenue is needed to pay for this healthcare program.

Were all Americans in favor of Obama's plans? No, the Republicans did not like all of Obama's proposals. The Tea Party movement protested the growing government expenses and taxes. The movement also opposed the government reworking of health insurance.

Why were the Republicans in Congress not able to keep Obama's goals in check? The Democrats dominated both houses of Congress. The Republicans had no clear strategy to oppose Obama's proposals.

- Guide a discussion comparing the Tea Party movement to the Boston Tea Party.

In what way was the Tea Party movement successful? The Tea Party movement influenced elections in 2010. That year Democrats lost their House majority. President Obama no longer had a House that would pass whatever bill he wanted. The Democrats kept a much smaller majority in the Senate.

After two years in office, what could President Obama be happy about? The economy was slowly improving, and his healthcare reform had been achieved.

> Conclude the discussion by asking the question on page 433. Americans elected Republicans who opposed Obama's policies in Congress. The Democrats lost their majority in the House and had a much smaller majority in the Senate.

Activity Manual

- Guide completion of page 300.

Lesson Focus

- Obama faced challenges in the Middle East and the Arab world.

Objectives

- Relate Obama's actions in Iraq and Afghanistan to promises he made while campaigning for president
- Recognize that Osama bin Laden's death was a major victory for the United States
- Explain the Arab Spring and why Obama chose to support it

Review

What was the most immediate domestic problem Obama faced when he became president? *the economy*

- Invite students to describe government programs that were intended to improve the economy.

What program was Obama's main domestic program? *better national healthcare; the Affordable Care Act*

- Choose a volunteer to explain why some Americans opposed Obama's plans.

Preparation for Reading

- Generate interest as you direct the students to read the titles and examine the pictures on pages 434–37.
- Guide pronunciation of any unfamiliar words in the lesson.
- Direct the students to read the pages silently to discover what area of the world presented President Obama with major international problems. *the Middle East and the Arab world*

Teach for Understanding

Who did Obama choose to be secretary of state? *Hillary Clinton*

Why was Clinton chosen to be secretary of state? *to help build stronger relations with foreign nations*

Why was Obama awarded the Nobel Peace Prize? *The Nobel organization claimed that Obama encouraged better international relations.*

What had always been President Obama's position on the Iraq War? *He had opposed the war before it had even begun. As a candidate, he promised to end it.*

Did Obama keep his promise to end the Iraq War? *Yes, the last combat troops left Iraq by the end of August 2010.*

How It Was

Mackenzie was walking with her best friend in the warm, spring sunlight. "Daniela," she said, "my parents saw on the news that bin Laden was killed. Are we safer now? What did he do?"

"Do you remember Miss Olivarez talking about the airplanes crashing into the buildings and the field on September 11?"

Mackenzie nodded. "So he did that?"

"Yes, and Americans have been trying to find him ever since! My dad says that when he was serving in Afghanistan, they always wanted to get bin Laden. Now he's finally caught. President Obama was talking about it on TV. We finally caught him after ten years."

"Wow," Mackenzie said. "My mom always says to keep working at a problem. I'm glad that the military didn't give up."

Foreign Affairs

From the election on, foreign affairs played a major role in Obama's presidency. He chose Hillary Clinton as secretary of state to help build stronger relations with foreign nations. Many people claimed that Bush had caused the United States to lose friends. Obama wanted to work together with other nations.

Obama received early praise for his work. In October 2009 he was awarded a **Nobel Peace Prize**. The Nobel organization claimed that Obama encouraged better international relations, but many Americans questioned whether Obama had deserved the prize so quickly.

Iraq War

President Obama wanted to end the Iraq War. He had opposed the war before it had even begun. As a candidate, he promised to end it. Once in office, Obama set out to withdraw American troops from Iraq.

Withdrawing troops took a long time. In February 2009 Obama promised to remove all combat troops by the end of August 2010. During that time, Americans would provide security while Iraq rebuilt the Iraqi army. Iraq did not become peaceful during those eighteen months. However, the last combat troops left Iraq by the end of August 2010.

434

Background

Osama bin Laden

Osama bin Laden was born in 1957 in Saudi Arabia to a Syrian mother and a Yemeni father. Because his father had numerous wives, Osama was one of about fifty children and of relatively low status in the family. His father owned a construction company with close ties to the Saudi royal family and became a billionaire through his contracts with the Saudis. Osama bin Laden was heavily influenced by radical Wahhabi Muslim teachings, which insisted on returning to strict observance of Islam.

When the Soviet Union invaded Afghanistan, bin Laden supported the mujahideen (guerilla fighters). He set up numerous Islamic schools in Afghanistan and Pakistan. Many recruits for radical Islam came from these schools, and many later joined his terrorist network known as al-Qaeda. He also opposed the Saudis' permitting US military bases on Saudi soil from which the United States conducted the war that pushed the Iraqi military from Kuwait. The Saudis expelled bin Laden in 1991 and revoked his citizenship in 1994 because he allegedly was plotting the overthrow of the Saudi royal family.

But not all American troops were gone from Iraq. About 50,000 American troops remained as advisors. They were not there to fight. In December 2011 these troops also left. The only American forces in Iraq were those guarding the American **embassy**.

The withdrawal of troops from Iraq did not mean the country was peaceful. Violence continued between Sunni and Shia Muslims and between Arabs and Kurds. But political pressure influenced the withdrawal so that Obama could run for reelection having kept a major promise.

Afghanistan

The situation in Afghanistan also presented Obama with difficulties. When campaigning, he had promised to end the Afghanistan War. In 2009 violence still ravaged the country. An early withdrawal might push the country into complete chaos.

Obama tried to stabilize the country. During 2009 he promised to send tens of thousands of additional troops to Afghanistan. He hoped to enforce peace. This plan did not work.

Afghanistan continued to be torn apart by problems. The various tribes did not work well with each other. The president, **Hamid Karzai**, was accused of corruption. In addition, Karzai wanted to negotiate with the Taliban.

But the Americans viewed the Taliban as their enemy because it had protected Osama bin Laden. Many American soldiers were killed by Taliban fighters and allies. All in all, Afghanistan enjoyed little peace and stability.

Obama did enjoy one major victory in the area. Early in the morning of May 2, 2011, Osama bin Laden was killed. A group of **Navy SEALs** entered bin Laden's hiding place in Pakistan. He died in the fight. For almost a decade, the United States had tried to bring bin Laden to justice. Now the mastermind behind the 9/11 terrorist attacks was

435

Osama bin Laden was purported to have been behind the 1993 World Trade Center bombing, the 1998 bombings of US embassies in Kenya and Tanzania, and the 2000 bombing of the USS *Cole*, as well as other attacks on US troops and facilities in the Middle East. In 1998 he called for all Americans and Jews, including women and children, to be killed. Then he plotted the infamous September 11, 2001, attacks that resulted in planes crashing into the World Trade Center, the Pentagon, and a field in Pennsylvania.

It was a primary objective of United States forces to capture or kill Osama bin Laden in the war against the Taliban in Afghanistan. Shortly after 1:00 a.m. (Pakistan time) on May 2, 2011, a team of Navy SEALs, acting on intelligence reports, raided bin Laden's compound in Abbottabad, Pakistan. Bin Laden was shot and killed. His body and documents were brought back to Afghanistan, and he was buried at sea within twenty-four hours.

Did all American troops leave Iraq in August 2010? No, about 50,000 American troops remained as advisors. Other American forces remained to guard the American embassy.

Was there a peaceful Iraq when American troops were removed? No, violence continued between Sunni and Shia Muslims and between Arabs and Kurds.

- Discuss how political pressure influenced the withdrawal of American troops from Iraq.

What other war had Obama promised to end? the Afghanistan War

- Guide a discussion about the difficulties Obama faced in trying to end the Afghanistan War. Explain that the photograph on page 435 shows US Army soldiers and Afghan National Army soldiers on a combined patrol in an Afghan village.

What was one major victory in Afghanistan that Obama enjoyed? Osama bin Laden was killed.

Why did the United States want bin Laden brought to justice? Bin Laden was the mastermind behind the 9/11 terrorist attacks.

- Besides being a major victory for the United States, why do you think bin Laden's death was front-page news in many newspapers? Answers could include that bin Laden had masterminded the 9/11 terrorist attacks and was responsible for the death of many American soldiers. Americans had tried for almost a decade to bring bin Laden to justice.

- How long is a decade? ten years

- Invite a student to read aloud the glossary definition of *Navy SEALs*.

- Why do you think Navy SEALs were sent on the mission to find bin Laden? Answers may include that Navy SEALs are specially trained for this kind of operation.

- Direct attention to the How It Was box on page 434.

What terrorist attacks were masterminded by bin Laden? Airplanes crashed into buildings and a field on September 11.

- Explain that these attacks took place on American soil.

- Why could Mackenzie and Daniela feel safer now that bin Laden was dead? Answers could include that bin Laden could no longer plan terrorist attacks against the United States.

- Do you think Mackenzie's mom gives good advice when she says to keep working on a problem? Answers could include that it is good advice. Continuing to work on a problem often leads to solving it.

Lesson

174

Teach for Understanding

🔧 Why do you think President Obama's approval rose in the polls after bin Laden's death? *Answers could include that bin Laden's death was a major victory for the United States. Obama's rising approval in the polls showed that Americans approved of how Obama handled the situation.*

What group of people did Obama try to reach out to at the beginning of his presidency? *Muslims*

What issues in the Middle East was Obama concerned about? *Iraq, Israel, nuclear weapons, and lack of democracy*

Why did democracy become a major crisis of the Middle East? *Many nations in the region had dictatorial leaders. Crowds in many of these countries protested.*

Where did the wave of protests begin? *Tunisia*

● Guide the students in finding Tunisia on the map on page 436. Then guide them in locating Egypt, Yemen, Syria, Libya, and Bahrain.

What was this wave of conflict in these Arab nations called? *the Arab Spring*

In addition to the hope of springtime, what hope did the Arab Spring bring? *the hope that the uprisings would bring democracy and freedom to the Arab world*

Why did Obama choose to support the protests? *He wanted democracy in Arab nations, not dictatorship.*

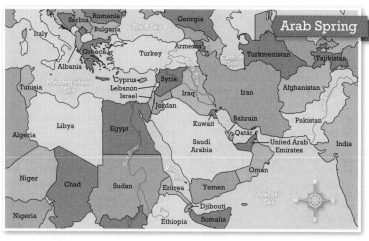

Arab Spring

dead. President Obama experienced rising approval in polls after bin Laden's death.

The Arab Spring

In addition to inherited wars, Obama's presidency was complicated by other Middle Eastern turmoil. At the beginning of his presidency, Obama tried to reach out to Muslims. In early 2009 he spoke at a university in Cairo, Egypt. He mentioned Iraq, Israel, nuclear weapons, and lack of democracy as concerns. The issue of democracy became a major crisis for the Middle East.

Starting in early 2011, many Arab nations in North Africa and the Middle East experienced conflict. The situation began in Tunisia in December 2010. Crowds protested the country's dictatorial president. The next month, he fled to exile. Many nations across the region had similar dictatorial leaders. Egypt, Yemen, Syria, Libya, and Bahrain all erupted in protests.

This wave of unrest is called the **Arab Spring**. Most of the protests grew in the spring. The name also reflects the hope of springtime. Perhaps the uprisings would bring democracy and freedom to the Arab world.

President Obama had difficult choices to make. He had criticized President Bush for interfering in other nations' affairs. However, Obama wanted democracy and not dictatorship. He chose to support the protests.

436

Yemen protesters demanding the removal of the president

Violence and instability soon followed. Obama wanted Hosni Mubarak, the president of Egypt, to step down. Mubarak resigned, but the new Egyptian government failed to bring peace. Rival groups rioted, Christians were attacked, tourism declined, and Egypt suffered. In Yemen, the president also stepped down. His departure did not bring stability. In Bahrain, the government jailed protesters and treated them harshly.

Libya collapsed into civil war. The long-time dictator, **Muammar al-Qaddafi**, fought armed protesters. As the country split, the United Nations allowed a no-fly zone. Other nations could prevent Qaddafi from using his planes against the people of Libya. Fighting raged all summer and into the fall. Finally in October of 2011, revolutionaries killed Qaddafi.

His death did not bring peace. The nation would not reunify. Some Libyans wanted a Muslim country with some freedom of religion. Others wanted a country that rigorously followed Islamic law. A year after Qaddafi's death, the country was still in turmoil. On September 11, 2012, the American ambassador to Libya was killed by Islamic **militants**. Americans criticized both President Obama and Secretary of State Hillary Clinton for failing to protect the ambassador. The Arab Spring had brought Obama more trouble than hope. He found that democracy did not grow easily in new ground.

Other Foreign Affairs

President Obama generally enjoyed good foreign relations during his first term as president. He encouraged the United States to build stronger ties with Asian nations. He and Clinton tried to reset American-Russian relations. Obama stopped George W. Bush's plans to put missiles in Eastern Europe. This decision had angered Russia. Obama also removed sanctions and trade limitations that Bush had placed on Russia. With the exception of the Middle East and the Arab world, Obama had few major international problems.

How successful was Obama in bringing peace to the Middle East?

437

Teach for Understanding

- Invite a student to read aloud the caption for the photograph on page 437. Discuss the violence and instability that resulted from the protests.

  Did the Arab Spring bring the democracy and freedom that Obama had hoped for? No, it brought Obama more trouble than hope.

- Why do you think democracy did not grow easily in the Arab world? Answers could include that the protests did not unify Arab nations. Some people wanted freedom of religion. Others, including Islamic militants, wanted their countries to follow Islamic law.

- Choose a volunteer to read aloud the glossary definition of *militant*.

- Why do you think Islamic militants killed the American ambassador to Libya? Answers could include that the militants were violently protesting America and democracy.

- Do you think Islamic militants would have been involved in the protests in other Arab countries? Answers could include that militants would probably have protested in other Arab countries. Those countries may also have had Islamic militants who wanted the countries to rigorously follow Islamic law.

- Invite a student to describe President Obama's foreign relations during his first term as president.

  Conclude the discussion by asking the question on page 437. Obama was not very successful in bringing peace to the Middle East. His only success was in keeping his promise to pull American troops out of Iraq. However, countries in the Middle East still experienced conflict.

Activity Manual

- Guide completion of pages 301–2.

Assessment

- Administer quiz.

The quiz may be given anytime after completing this lesson.

Lesson

175

Student Text pages 438–40
Activity Manual page 303

Lesson Focus

- Americans faced problems of gun violence and racism, and they reelected President Obama.

Objectives
- Identify gun violence and racism as domestic issues during Obama's presidency
- Explain why Americans could not agree on a solution for gun violence
- Recognize that African Americans suffered more disadvantages than other racial groups
- Relate that President Obama was reelected in 2012

Review

- Discuss whether President Obama was able to fulfill his campaign promises to end the Iraq War and the Afghanistan War.

  What was the one major victory the United States achieved in Afghanistan? Osama bin Laden was killed.

- Choose a volunteer to explain what the Arab Spring was and why it occurred.

  Why did President Obama choose to support the protests? He wanted democracy in Arab nations, not dictatorship.

Preparation for Reading

- Generate interest as you direct the students to read the titles and examine the map on pages 438–40.
- Guide pronunciation of any unfamiliar words in the lesson.
- Direct the students to read the pages silently to discover two domestic issues Americans faced during Obama's presidency. gun violence and racial issues

Teach for Understanding

- Use the map on page 439 to guide a discussion appropriate for your class about incidents of gun violence in the United States.

  What did some people want immediately following each attack? more gun control

Create a safe environment for the students as you discuss gun violence and racism. Remind students to listen and respond respectfully when differing opinions are expressed.

Domestic Affairs

Violence was not only a problem overseas. In the United States, violence drew people's attention. Americans struggled to identify the root problems and come up with solutions.

Gun Violence

In 2009 two shootings took place in military settings. In June an American convert to Islam attacked a military recruiting office in Little Rock, Arkansas. One soldier died and another was injured. The shooter declared that he wanted to fight people who fought Muslims. Only five months later, an army major killed thirteen people and injured many more when he opened fire inside Fort Hood in Texas. Once again, the shooter claimed Islamic beliefs motivated his attacks.

Over the next few years, other attacks troubled the country. A member of Congress was shot in January 2011. Gabby Giffords from Arizona was meeting the people she represented. A man killed six people and left more wounded. Giffords survived but suffered long-term damage. The next year, a man killed and injured many people at a movie theater in Colorado in July 2012. Then in December 2012, a man killed many children at an elementary school.

Americans questioned how these horrible attacks could happen. Immediately following each attack,

people called for more gun control. Because some of these shooters suffered from mental illnesses, many people wondered if there should be more laws about who could own a gun. But some Americans doubted that more gun control was the right answer. Gun control laws already existed. Perhaps these laws needed to be better enforced. People also called for better treatment for mental illnesses.

Racial Issues

Americans also worried about issues of racism. Although all humans belong to the same race, superficial differences often separate people. Skin color, accent, and culture divide Americans into different groups. Treating a person differently because of these characteristics shows racial prejudice.

African Americans had often suffered more disadvantages than other racial groups in the country. They had been more likely to be imprisoned, to grow up in single-parent families, and to receive lower wages. Most Americans recognized this problem. However, solving it presented a challenge. Some people called for African Americans to try harder to better themselves. Others claimed African Americans were treated differently no matter how hard they tried.

President Obama's election helped Americans believe that the country

438

- Discuss the differing opinions regarding gun control.

  How many races do all humans belong to? one

  What often separates people? racial prejudice; treating a person differently because of differences in skin color, accent, and culture

  What disadvantages were African Americans more likely to experience than other racial groups? African Americans were more likely to be imprisoned, to grow up in single-parent families, and to receive lower wages.

- Guide the students in completing Activity Manual page 303. Discuss varying opinions about racism as needed, emphasizing the biblical point of view.

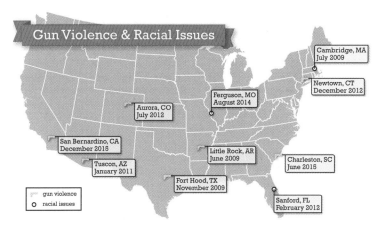

Gun Violence & Racial Issues

Cambridge, MA
July 2009

Newtown, CT
December 2012

Ferguson, MO
August 2014

Aurora, CO
July 2012

San Bernardino, CA
December 2015

Little Rock, AR
June 2009

Charleston, SC
June 2015

Tuscon, AZ
January 2011

Fort Hood, TX
November 2009

Sanford, FL
February 2012

gun violence
racial issues

What effect did Americans hope President Obama's election would have on racism? Americans believed that Obama's election could help the country overcome racial prejudices. They hoped that he could bring more harmony between different groups of Americans.

• Use the map on page 439 to guide a discussion appropriate for your class about the occurrence of racial issues in the United States.

could overcome racial prejudices. They hoped that he could bring more harmony between different groups of Americans. Obama worked to do so. For example, in early 2009, he tried to calm an odd situation.

A Harvard professor was arrested in his own house. When the professor returned from a trip, his front door would not open. After he and his driver broke the door open, police showed up. A neighbor had suspected that the two African American men were thieves. A police officer arrested Professor Gates for disorderly conduct and protesting his being questioned. Although charges were soon dropped, he was angry. He felt that racial prejudice had led to his arrest. President Obama invited both

Professor Gates and the police officer to Washington to talk.

Although Gates's arrest caused no long-term harm, other incidents did. In 2012 an unarmed seventeen-year-old African American was shot and killed in a fight with a neighborhood watch volunteer. Americans debated who was to blame. The volunteer had been following the teen. The two began to fight when the teen confronted the volunteer for following him. Many Americans believed that the volunteer suspected the teen merely for being black. But when the shooter was tried for murder, he was found not guilty.

Also troubling was the shooting of a young man in Ferguson, Missouri, in 2014. A police officer responded to a

439

Lesson

175

Teach for Understanding

Did Obama's election help Americans overcome racism? No, the country remained divided on the issue.

Who opposed President Obama in the 2012 election? Mitt Romney

Who won the election? President Obama

 Why do you think Obama and the Democrats did well in the election? Answers could include that people were confident in Obama's presidency. They liked his health-care and military policies.

 Why do you think that some people urged President Obama to push for progressive reforms? Answers may include that Obama's winning by almost five million votes gave some people hope that Americans would like progressive reforms. They had hope that Congress would pass progressive reforms because Democrats gained seats in both the House and the Senate.

> Conclude the discussion by asking the question on page 440. gun violence and racism

Activity Manual

• Guide completion of page 303.

---

drugstore theft and stopped a suspect. Their interaction became violent, and the eighteen-year old was shot after grabbing the officer's gun. Video footage from the store later showed that he was the thief. The incident caused problems. People were concerned about police treatment of African Americans and demanded a thorough investigation. They asked how a non-violent theft could end with the thief shot and killed. Defenders of the police officer claimed that racism was not part of the story. A man stole, disobeyed a police officer, attacked him, and was shot. Both sides seemed to have some truth to their arguments. The officer was attacked. However, the Ferguson police department showed evidence of racism. The city of Ferguson suffered weeks of violence and rioting from those angry about the young man's death.

Americans struggled to deal with the issues of racism. Each of these cases divided the country. Some blamed long-term racism for high rates of poverty and crime among African Americans. Others noted that African Americans were often punished more harshly than other Americans for similar crimes. Despite the electing of an African American president, racism still bothered the United States.

Elections of 2012

As the United States considered problems at home and abroad, national elections were held in 2012. President Obama ran for reelection against Mitt Romney. Americans also voted in Congressional elections.

Media presented the election as a vote of confidence in Obama's presidency. If people liked his healthcare and military policies, they should vote for him. They should also support Democrats running for Congress.

However, Romney attracted much support. He was a successful businessman. He had also served as a successful governor of Massachusetts. In spite of this history, he was less popular than Obama for almost the entire campaign.

Obama and the Democrats did well in the November election. The president won reelection by almost five million votes. Democrats gained seats in both the House and the Senate. Although the Republicans still controlled the House, the Democrats enjoyed their victory. Some urged President Obama to push for progressive or liberal reforms.

> What were two problems facing Americans at home?

440

444

Heritage Studies 5

Life in the United States
Religion

A major shift in religious identity took place during Obama's presidency. Fewer Americans associated themselves with any religion. In 2014 almost one in four Americans answered "none" when asked about their religion.

This trend was linked to the increasing **secularization** of American life. *Secular* typically means not religious. For most of its history, the United States was an extremely religious nation. The Constitution ensured freedom of religion. Even people with little personal belief associated with religious groups. In the early twenty-first century, that was changing quickly. Fewer Americans claimed a religion, especially among the younger generation.

Two facts seemed to create this trend. First, fewer Americans held to religious beliefs. Many people claimed to be atheists. Others said they were agnostics. Second, people were more open about their beliefs. Previously, many people would rarely attend religious services, but would still claim to belong to a religious group. By the 2010s, this habit was dying. Those who claimed a religion were increasingly likely to actually attend services. Those who did not attend were not as likely to claim a religion.

Technology

During Obama's presidency, Americans continued to use technology more and in new ways. Some of the biggest growth was in the rise of social media. This term describes programs that let people interact online. When running for president, Obama used social media skillfully to raise awareness of his campaign. His promises of hope and change were especially attractive to younger voters. They were also the voters most likely to use new online tools. Websites let people declare their support for Obama. He also raised a lot of money from online donations.

Social media changed how people learned news and interacted with the world. Stories that spread quickly online were called "**viral**." If someone was filmed doing something good or bad, the video might be shared millions of times online. A person might become famous or infamous for something they thought only their closest friends would see.

Rising Internet use also changed the world of sales. Shopping malls lost customers to online sales. By searching online, customers

441

Lesson **176**
Student Text pages 441–43
Activity Manual page 304

Lesson Focus

- During Obama's presidency, fewer Americans associated themselves with any religion, and the use of technology grew.

Objectives
- Explain the secularization of American life
- Relate positive and negative effects of the changing digital world
- Recognize information as possibly the most valuable resource in the early twenty-first century

Review

What were two significant domestic issues during Obama's presidency? gun violence and racism

- Choose a volunteer to explain why Americans could not agree on a solution for gun violence.

What racial group was more often affected by racism than other racial groups in America? African Americans

- Choose a volunteer to tell disadvantages African Americans suffered, and why solving this racial issue was a challenge for Americans.

What was the outcome of the 2012 presidential election? President Obama was reelected.

Preparation for Reading

- Generate interest as you direct the students to read the titles and examine the pictures on pages 441–43.
- Guide pronunciation of any unfamiliar words in the lesson.
- Direct the students to read the pages silently to discover what was likely the most valuable resource in the early twenty-first century. information

Teach for Understanding

- Invite a student to read aloud the glossary definition of *secularization*.

What trend was linked to the secularization of American life? Fewer Americans claimed a religion.

How did the shift in religious identity differ from most of America's history? For most of its history, the United States was an extremely religious nation. Even people with little personal belief associated with religious groups.

What ensures Americans' freedom of religion? the Constitution

What two facts seemed to create the shift in religious identity? Fewer Americans held to religious beliefs. People were more open about their beliefs.

What area of technology experienced some of the biggest growth? social media

- Discuss how Obama used social media when campaigning for president.
- Use the social media icons on page 441 to guide a discussion appropriate for your class about about how social media allows people to interact online.

How did rising Internet use affect the world of sales? Malls lost customers and stores closed because people could find better deals online.

Teach for Understanding

What technology encouraged the trends of social media and Internet purchases? smartphones

Why did Americans increasingly buy smartphones? Smartphones allowed users to access the Internet. They allowed users to be online at all times.

- Invite students to tell positive and negative consequences of the changing technology.

What was a major concern of rising Internet use during the 2010s? the theft and use of private information

What facts could a thief try to learn when stealing a person's private information? Answers could include a person's date of birth, social security number, and bank and credit card account numbers.

- Explain that illegal use of a person's private information by another person is called "identity theft."

Are only individual people harmed if information is stolen? No, companies and governments can also be harmed.

What were people who took information from the government called? whistleblowers and hackers

- Choose volunteers to read aloud the glossary definitions of *whistleblower* and *hacker*.

---

could find better deals than in stores. Even sales of videos and music changed. People bought much of their music and videos online. Video rental stores closed across the nation.

The rise of smartphones helped encourage these trends of social media and Internet purchases. Until about 2008, most Americans preferred basic mobile phones to smartphones. However, Americans increasingly bought smartphones. These allowed the user to access the Internet. By allowing users to be online at all times, smartphones changed how people interacted with the world.

The changing digital world had both positive and negative consequences. For example, workers complained that they were expected to answer work emails even in the evening and on weekends. Scientists were concerned that interacting with people mainly through electronic media left people less able to communicate successfully in person. But there were also some positive effects. Fundraising websites allowed strangers to help each other. Apps helped consumers find better deals while shopping. The Internet provides easy and fast access for information. As with any technology, smartphones could be used for good or ill.

Hacking

Rising Internet use made information easier to get to. This knowledge could benefit people. However, private information could be stolen more easily. The theft and use of private information was a major concern during the 2010s.

The most common worry was that someone's identity would be stolen. If a thief could get key facts about a person, he might set up false credit card accounts in that person's name. He might spend a lot of money and leave the individual with high debt. Companies went to great expense to prevent their customers' data from being stolen.

Companies might also be embarrassed if their own information was stolen. In one case, criminals attacked a major film company's computers online. They stole all the information. They then released computer viruses to destroy the company's computers. While this attack harmed few people's privacy, it reminded Americans how vulnerable their information was.

Even the American government was unable to protect its information completely. Both **whistleblowers** and **hackers** took information from the government. Whistleblowers use information to let the public know about problems. Hackers steal to benefit themselves. The government tried to block both types of lost information.

In 2010 a soldier named Bradley Manning released millions of secret

442

military files to the public. Shortly after that, he was arrested. Manning believed that the government had done wrong things. He thought that only public exposure would force a change. Manning was sentenced to thirty-five years in prison for releasing the information.

Three years later, more government files were released. The perpetrator was Edward Snowden, a man who had access to top-secret files through his job as a security expert. He released them because he believed the government was behaving immorally. Rather than be arrested, he traveled abroad and then announced what he had done. Snowden then traveled to Russia, which would not allow the United States to arrest him.

In 2015 the government announced another loss of information. This time someone had stolen files about government employees, but the stolen information was not put online. News sources stated that China was behind the theft, but the government did not accuse anyone.

Information seemed to be the most valuable resource in the early twenty-first century.

> What are some ways that computers could help or harm Americans?

Teach for Understanding

- Use the political cartoon on page 443 to further discuss whistleblowers and hackers. Explain that whistleblowers and hackers might also take information from individuals and companies. Point out that people have developed technological ways to protect information and to help prevent other people from being harmed if their information has been stolen.

- Explain that technology and the devices it makes, such as computers and smartphones, are tools that can be used for good or for evil. Because humans are sinful, they often use technological tools to sin. Christians should use technological tools in a way that is honoring and pleasing to God.

- Discuss ways that Christians can use technological tools to honor and please God.

> Conclude the discussion by asking the question on page 443. Computers made it easier for people to interact with each other through social media. Computers also made it easier for people to learn information and to shop. However, computers also made it easier for private information to be stolen.

Activity Manual

- Guide completion of page 304.

177

Student Text pages 444–47
Activity Manual page 305

Lesson Focus

- Obama faced serious problems in the Middle East and in Europe.

Objectives

- Identify the Middle East and Eastern Europe as regions where Obama faced serious problems
- Explain why the Middle East was important to the United States
- Describe the Islamic State
- Explain the problem Obama faced with Russia in Ukraine

Materials

- A map of the countries in Africa

Review

- Choose volunteers to define *secularization* and explain the trend that was linked to it.
- Invite students to relate positive and negative effects of the changing digital world.

What seemed to be the most valuable resource in the early twenty-first century? information

Preparation for Reading

- Generate interest as you direct the students to read the titles and examine the pictures on pages 444–47.
- Guide pronunciation of any unfamiliar words in the lesson.
- Direct the students to read the pages silently to discover what areas of the world presented President Obama with serious problems. the Middle East and Eastern Europe

Teach for Understanding

- Direct attention to the Biography box. Choose a volunteer to explain the information at the top of the box. Choose another volunteer to locate Liberia on the map of Africa.

What was the Writebols' occupation? They were missionaries.

When did the Writebols move to Liberia? in 2013

What happened to Nancy Writebol in July 2014? She became ill with the Ebola virus.

- Explain that although Ebola is a virus, it is not spread like other viruses such as a cold or the flu. Ebola is spread through body fluids.

- Why do you think Nancy was taken to the United States for treatment? Answers could include that she was seriously ill and would receive better treatment in the United States than in Africa.

Nancy Writebol

Who: Nancy Writebol
When: 1955–
Where: Liberia, Africa

Nancy Writebol and her husband David were missionaries. David ran a local organization, and Nancy helped coordinate missionaries coming and going on the field. In 2013 they moved to a new missionary job in Liberia.

The next year, Nancy briefly became known by Americans when she became ill with the Ebola virus. This dangerous virus sickened and killed many people in West Africa. Liberia had many cases. Nancy stayed in the country and even volunteered to help at a hospital that treated Ebola patients.

In July 2014 she became ill. But Nancy did not give up hope. She was taken to the United States for intensive treatment. After weeks of illness, she recovered. Her faithful service as a Christian was shared in the news to millions of Americans.

After she recovered, Nancy kept serving God. In 2015 she returned to Liberia. Her goal was to bring God glory by caring for the needy and sharing the Gospel.

Foreign Policy Part II

While American culture changed, President Obama faced serious problems overseas. Syria's civil war threatened to spread to Iraq. Iran wanted nuclear weapons. And in Eastern Europe, Russia seemed ready to take over Ukraine.

Syria

Obama's problems with Syria dated back to the Arab Spring. In 2011 the Syrians rebelled against President Bashar

al Assad. Both Assad and his father before him seemed to be little more than dictators. Despite this, many Syrians did not rebel. The country was divided among religious groups. Some preferred Assad to the rule of a rival group.

The situation became more complicated for Obama. He had promised that if Assad used chemical weapons, the United States would try to stop him. In August 2013 there was evidence that Assad had used chemicals

444

Why did Nancy return to Liberia after she recovered? She wanted to bring God glory by caring for the needy and sharing the gospel.

- Choose a volunteer to explain why this part of the chapter is titled "Foreign Policy Part II." It tells about America's foreign policy during Obama's second term.

When did Obama's problems with Syria begin? during the Arab Spring

What caused the civil war in Syria? The country was divided among religious groups. Some preferred the dictatorial rule of President Bashar al Assad to the rule of a rival group.

- Discuss what complicated the situation in Syria in August 2013.

against Syrians. However, Obama did not launch attacks. Most Americans did not want to get involved in another Middle Eastern war. Congress did not support the idea. The Assad government finally agreed to destroy their chemical weapons. The civil war continued.

ISIS

In 2014 the situation became even more complicated. In Iraq, the Sunnis, Shias, and Kurds were not working well together. The Sunnis felt that the government was being run to benefit the Shias. After President Obama pulled out Americans troops, a rebel group emerged in both Syria and Iraq.

This new group called itself the **Islamic State**, and many people began to refer to it as ISIS. It claimed the authority to govern all Muslims across the world. It quickly captured cities in both Syria and Iraq. It even captured Iraq's third largest city, Mosul. It treated non-Muslims harshly. Christians were killed or enslaved. The situation in the Middle East seemed to be getting worse.

President Obama was faced with difficult choices. One option was to do nothing. Some Americans supported this position. They said that problems so far from home were not their problems. But many Americans were unhappy to see cruelty taking place anywhere. Obama could send troops to fight the Islamic State. But few Americans wanted soldiers fighting in Iraq. Obama had promised that he would end the Iraq War. Finally, Obama tried to help the legal government of Iraq. Not everyone was happy. Some Americans pointed out that the legal government had let the Islamic State come to power in the first place. Despite these criticisms, Obama sent some troops to advise the Iraqi government. He also allowed bombing ISIS. These actions slowed the rapid advance of ISIS, but they did not bring peace.

Kobani was a key battleground between ISIS and Syrian Kurds.

445

What complicated the situtation in Iraq during 2014? The Sunnis, Shias, and Kurds were not working well together. The Sunnis felt that the government was being run to benefit the Shias.

What rebel group emerged in both Syria and Iraq after President Obama pulled American troops out of Iraq? the Islamic State (ISIS)

- Invite a student to read aloud the glossary definition of *Islamic State.*

Which Islamic group formed the Islamic State? the Sunnis

What authority did the Islamic State claim? the authority to govern all Muslims across the world

- Discuss the options President Obama considered for dealing with the Islamic State. Include the opinions of Americans regarding the options.

How did Obama help the Iraqi government? He sent some troops to advise the Iraqi government. He also allowed bombing ISIS.

- Choose a volunteer to read aloud the caption for the photograph on page 445.

Did Obama's actions in Iraq bring peace to the area? No, his actions only slowed the advance of ISIS.

177

Teach for Understanding

What Middle Eastern country did President Obama try to develop peace with? Iran

Why were the United States and Iran enemies? Iran had wanted to build nuclear weapons.

Did all Americans agree that Obama should make a deal with Iran? No, few Americans trusted the Iranian government. Iran had lied in the past, and many Americans feared that Iran was lying again.

● Discuss why Obama decided that the United States should trust Iran.

Why do Americans strive for peace in the Middle East? It is located where Africa, Asia, and Europe meet. It contains vast supplies of oil. It is the birthplace of three of the world's major religions: Judaism, Christianity, and Islam. Many Americans want Israel to survive.

● Discuss why many Americans want Israel to survive.

Did countries in the Middle East agree with President Obama's deal with Iran? No, both Israel and Sunni Arab nations disagreed with his opinion.

● Why do you think Israel disagreed with Obama's opinion? Answers could include that Iran and other Islamic nations had threatened Israel in the past. The deal would not provide more security for Israel.

● Why do you think Sunni Arab nations disagreed with Obama's opinion? Answers could include that Sunni Arab nations wanted to take control of Israel because many Muslims lived there.

What country presented Obama with military problems in Europe? Russia

What was Russia trying to do in Europe? regain influence

Who was the Russian leader at the time? Vladimir Putin

Iran

President Obama also attempted to develop peace with Iran. Since 1979, the United States and Iran had been enemies. Iran had wanted to build nuclear weapons since the 1980s. Obama wanted to make a deal with Iran.

Once again, he faced challenges at home. Few Americans trusted the Iranian government. It had lied in the past. Most Republicans feared that Iran was lying again. Many Democrats agreed with the Republicans. But Obama decided that the United States had no better option than trusting Iran. Iran influenced Assad in Syria, terrorists in Lebanon, and the Shias in Iraq. Obama wanted to encourage broader peace throughout the region. He hoped that establishing friendlier ties with Iran would build peace in the Middle East.

Peace in the Middle East

Americans have been involved in encouraging peace in the Middle East since World War II. There are several reasons that so much energy is spent on this area of the world. It is located where Africa, Asia, and Europe meet. Also, it contains vast supplies of oil. It is the birthplace of three of the world's major religions: Judaism, Christianity, and Islam. Because of these facts, war in the Middle East affects the rest of

the world. In recent history, Islamic terrorists have even launched attacks on Americans.

In addition, many Americans want the nation of Israel to survive. After World War II, Israel was founded as a home for Jews. Its population is largely Jewish, but many Muslims and Christians also live there. Several nations, including Syria and Iran, have threatened Israel in the past. American presidents usually work hard to help keep Israel safe.

President Obama did not always get along with Israel. He often disagreed with its leaders. However, he stated that he wanted Israel to be safe. He said that the deal with Iran would help provide more security for Israel. But both Israel and Sunni Arab nations disagreed with his opinion.

Russia

President Obama also faced military problems in Europe. After the end of the Cold War, Russia seemed less threatening. Nations that had escaped the Soviet Union became friendly with the United States. By the 2000s, Russia began trying to regain influence. A new leader, **Vladimir Putin**, attempted to make sure that Russia was the most important influence in Eastern Europe.

Putin's actions centered on the large nation of Ukraine. In the early 2010s,

446

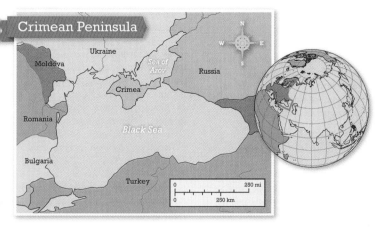

Crimean Peninsula

Ukraine • Moldova • Russia • Sea of Azov • Crimea • Romania • Black Sea • Bulgaria • Turkey

0 — 250 mi
0 — 250 km

Ukraine struggled financially and politically. Its president wanted Ukraine to have stronger ties with Russia. Many Ukrainians also wanted to be friendlier with the United States and Western European nations. In early 2014, riots and fighting forced Ukraine's president to step down. A new government that was much friendlier to the West formed.

In the south of Ukraine, the Crimean Peninsula was friendlier to Russia. In the spring of 2014, the province voted to join Russia. The Ukrainian government protested that the vote was illegal. But Russia began to govern Crimea. In addition, it encouraged rebels in eastern Ukraine to fight the nation's government.

The situation in Ukraine left Obama in a bad situation. He encouraged the original rebellion against the pro-Russian president. But he refused to help the government when Russia took Crimea. He sent little help to the Ukrainian government. Even when rebels shot down a passenger plane in 2014, the United States did not give much more help to Ukraine. The situation did not reflect well on President Obama.

> Why does the distant Middle East matter to the United States?

447

Teach for Understanding

In what Eastern European nation did Putin want to gain a strong influence? Ukraine

● Direct attention to the Crimean Peninsula map on page 447. Choose a volunteer to give an opinion of why Putin might have wanted a strong influence in Ukraine.

Did many Ukrainians want to have stronger ties with Russia? No, many Ukrainians wanted to be friendlier with the United States and Western European nations.

Why was Russia able to gain control of Crimea? The Crimean Peninsula was friendlier to Russia. The province voted to join Russia.

Did Russia stop trying to gain influence in Ukraine? No, Russia encouraged rebels in eastern Ukraine to fight the nation's government.

● Discuss President Obama's response to the situations in Ukraine and Crimea.

▶ Conclude the discussion by asking the question on page 447. The Middle East is located where Africa, Asia, and Europe meet. It contains vast supplies of oil. It is the birthplace of Judaism, Christianity, and Islam. Many Americans want Israel to survive.

Activity Manual

● Guide completion of pages 305.

178

Student Text pages 448–51
Activity Manual page 306

Lesson Focus

- During Obama's presidency, Americans remained divided over environmental issues, gay rights, and abortion.

Objectives

- Recognize the environment, gay rights, and abortion as moral issues that separated Americans
- Evaluate environmental issues, gay rights, and abortion in light of God's Word
- Present a speech about a moral issue

Materials

- Sources for researching current issues
- Prepared list of speech topics (optional)
- Prepared list of directions for preparing the speech for each student

Review

What areas of the world presented President Obama with serious problems? the Middle East and Eastern Europe

- Invite a student to explain why the Middle East is important to the United States.

What do many people call the Islamic State? ISIS

- Review what the Islamic State is. Choose a volunteer to explain the authority claimed by the Islamic State.
- Choose a volunteer to review Russia's actions in Ukraine, and Obama's response to the situtaion.

Preparation for Reading

- Generate interest as you direct the students to read the titles and examine the pictures on pages 448–51.
- Guide pronunciation of any unfamiliar words in the lesson.
- Direct the students to read the pages silently to discover some issues that Americans were divided on. the environment, gay rights, and abortion

Teach for Understanding

- Guide the students in completing Activity Manual page 306 as you teach the lesson.

What kind of issues are the environment, gay rights, and abortion? moral issues

- What do you think moral issues are? Answers could include that moral issues are issues that have to do with what is right or wrong.

Create a safe environment for the students as you discuss the issues in this lesson. Remind the students to listen and respond respectfully when differing opinions are expressed.

Moral Issues

During Obama's presidency, Americans divided over some key issues that people on both sides viewed as morally important. People who believed differently were viewed as wrong, not just mistaken. These issues tended to divide along political lines.

Environment

The issue of climate change created problems. There were some basic questions to be answered. Was the earth warming? If it was, were people responsible for that warming? Could anything be done to stop the problematic changes?

A majority of scientists claimed to have definite answers. Yes, the world was warming. Yes, it was a result of human actions, especially burning coal. Yes, radical changes in human behavior could decrease the change. These scientists had grim warnings. Unless people produced fewer **greenhouse gases**, the earth would warm. The icecaps would melt. Extreme weather would plague the world. Crops would fail, and people would die.

A major hurricane was cited as an example of climate change in action. In October 2012 Hurricane Sandy landed in New Jersey. Its wind and rain caused much damage. New York City had to shut its airports and subway. Many people's homes were flooded. Although no one could prove that Sandy was a result of climate change, news stories said that climate change would bring more storms like it.

For many Americans, this dire forecast demanded action. They believed that the government should make new laws that protected the

Windmills generate green energy, but power plants use fossil fuels to generate energy.

448

- Invite a student to read aloud questions that were raised because of climate change. Explain that the issue of the earth warming is often referred to as "global warming."

How did many scientists answer the questions people asked? Many scientists said the world was warming as a result of human actions. Radical changes in human behavior could decrease the change.

- Choose a volunteer to read aloud the glossary definition of *greenhouse gas*. Choose another volunteer to describe the climate inside a greenhouse.
- Invite a student to read aloud the warnings given by the scientists.
- Guide the students in presenting the contrasting views on actions that should be taken to combat global warming.

environment. Coal-fired power plants emit large amounts of carbon. Many Americans wanted these carbon emissions reduced. They hoped that renewable energy such as wind and solar power would replace coal and oil.

Other Americans questioned the need for such drastic action. Some noticed that not all scientists agreed on climate change. Perhaps the facts were not completely settled. Some Americans pointed out that over the earth's history, there had been both warmer and cooler periods of time. These climate changes happened long before people burned coal and oil to provide electricity. Other people considered the costs. Energy prices would rise if coal and oil were used less. Poorer Americans would struggle to pay to heat their homes. Those least able to bear the costs would have the hardest time.

Despite these concerns, President Obama encouraged more "**green energy**" use. This term refers both to using energy smarter and to using renewable energy. In the Stimulus, he included green energy projects. People received tax breaks for making their houses more energy-efficient. Businesses could buy solar panels and get money back. By 2015, Obama's opposition to coal was working. Coal provided only a third of American electricity. It used to provide one half. He introduced a **Clean Power Plan** in 2015. This plan worked to

further reduce coal use. The rise of green energy left Americans feeling somewhat better about the climate change problem. They did not all agree on what was occurring in the climate, but at least they were trying to make the world a cleaner, better place.

Gay Rights

Another issue that troubled Americans was gay rights. During his time as president, Obama encouraged the growth of gay rights. He said that men should be able to marry men and that women should be able to marry women. When Obama first took office, many Americans disagreed with this view. By 2015, many agreed.

Americans who disagreed faced problems. Many believed that God designed marriage to be between a man and a woman. They trusted that His plan benefited humanity. These Americans did not support gay marriage. They thought that it would harm society. For example, children in families where there is a same-sex marriage are denied having both a father and a mother. But in 2015, the Supreme Court ruled in favor of gay marriage. It had redefined marriage.

Five justices voted in favor of gay marriage, but the other four justices voted against it and pointed out that this change threatened religious liberties. Some Christians who owned bakeries, flower shops, or photo studios

449

Teach for Understanding

- Choose a volunteer to read aloud the glossary definition of *green energy*.
- Invite a student to read aloud the caption for the photographs on page 448. Guide the students in contrasting the kinds of energy being used in the photographs.

What did President Obama do to encourage more green energy use? He included green energy projects in the Stimulus.

Did Obama's incentives for using green energy work? Yes, by 2015, coal provided only a third of American electricity. It used to provide one half.

- Choose a volunteer to read aloud the glossary definition of *Clean Power Plan*.

What did the Clean Power Plan achieve? It further reduced coal use.

- Discuss how Americans felt about the rise of green energy. Remind the students that God has given people dominion over all the earth (Genesis 1:26–28). Discuss the importance of being good stewards of all that God has given to us, including the earth.

What was President Obama's view on gay rights? He encouraged the growth of gay rights. He said that men should be able to marry men and that women should be able to marry women.

What did Americans think about Obama's view on gay marriage? At first, many Americans disagreed with his view. But by 2015, many agreed.

- Why do you think many Americans changed their views about gay marriage? Answers could include that they did not believe that God set up marriage to occur only between a man and a woman.
- Discuss why Americans who disagreed with Obama did not support gay marriage.

What did the four justices who voted against gay marriage point out about the Supreme Court's ruling? They said that the ruling threatened religious liberties.

- Do you think that religious liberties were threatened? Answers could include that religious liberties were threatened because some Christian business owners were sued and fined for refusing to participate in same-sex weddings.

Background

Christians and the Environment

Environmental concerns have increased in recent years. Conservatives typically minimize the issue, while liberals tend to be concerned about it. Christians should view the world as part of God's revelation. It communicates that God exists, that He is a powerful Creator, and that He is good toward the righteous and unrighteous alike (Psalm 19:1–6; Romans 1:20; Acts 14:17). God has commanded all people to exercise good and wise dominion over the world. Because of sin, the world groans and decays (Romans 8:19–22), and humanity's work at exercising dominion is hindered by the fallen world (Genesis 3:17). People should use the world's resources. But in doing so, they should act in a way that tends and cares for the earth that has been entrusted to them. Christians especially should use the world's resources for the benefit of others and in a wise way that respects God's creation (Genesis 1:26–28). Christians thinking through climate change need to decide whether climate change is part of a natural cycle or whether it is caused by humans. If the latter, they need to decide whether attempts to reverse global warming will actually work or whether they might do more harm than good.

Teach for Understanding

- Choose a volunteer to read aloud other questions that were raised when the Supreme Court redefined marriage.

- Should Christians violate their beliefs because of legal rulings made by the courts? Answers could include that Christians should not violate their beliefs. It is more important to obey God's law than human law. But Christians should obey all laws that do not oppose God's law.

  What other issue raised questions in America? abortion

- What is abortion? the killing of unborn babies

  When did abortion become legal? in 1973

- Why did some states try to limit abortion? Answers could include that states with laws limiting abortions were trying to help Americans.

  Did all Americans support limits on abortion? No, many Americans supported the limits, but others wanted few or no limits.

  What was President Obama's view on abortion? He generally supported it.

- Invite students to tell how Obama supported abortion.

- Do you think Christians should support abortion? Answers should include that Christians should not support abortion because unborn babies are people who have been created in God's image and should not be killed.

  What effect did the issues of the environment, gay rights, and abortion have on politics in the United States? These three issues widened political divisions so that Democrats and Republicans often found it hard to work together.

- Use the political cartoon on page 450 to guide a discussion about the widening political divisions.

  Was Obama able to keep his promise to unite Americans? No, political divisions between Americans deepened.

  When will people be able to better judge the influences from Obama's presidency? Why? Influences from Obama's presidency will be better judged in the future. Events that happened long ago are easier to judge than events that happened recently.

  Can Americans know what will happen in the future? Answers should include that only God knows what will happen in the future.

- Use the last paragraph to encourage the students to confidently serve God regardless of what the future brings.

  ⟫ Conclude the discussion by asking the question on page 451. Americans do not agree on moral problems, so they cannot unite to solve them.

Activity Manual

- Guide completion of page 306.

were sued for not participating in a same-sex wedding. These businesses served all other customers, but refused to participate in same-sex weddings. Many of these business owners lost their court cases and were fined.

This change in the United States raised other questions. Could religious schools continue to teach their views of marriage? Would schools and business owners come under more pressure to violate their beliefs on these issues? These questions remained unanswered.

Abortion

Abortion also raised questions. Since 1973, abortion had been legal throughout the nation. However, some states tried to limit abortion.

Laws limiting abortion claimed to help Americans. Some called for women to receive counseling. Others said that a woman had to wait a certain amount of time before an abortion to ensure that she was not making a rash decision.

Although many Americans supported these limits, not everyone did. Some Americans believed that any limitation of abortion deprived a woman of her freedom. They wanted few or no limits on abortion.

President Obama generally supported abortion. He permitted American money to pay for abortions in other countries. His healthcare program allowed the federal government to help pay for some abortions. Also, when a major provider

450

Background

Responding to Cultural Marginalization

Americans tend to fight for their liberties. When American Christians have their religious liberties threatened, their first response might be to fight back. It might be to get angry.

There is an appropriate appeal to the protections guaranteed to Christians by the Constitution and by law. The apostle Paul appealed to Roman law numerous times to avoid unjust proceedings.

But Christians cannot become angry or bitter. They do not have a *right* to be in the majority or to avoid persecution. Jesus said, "Blessed are ye, when men shall revile you, and persecute you, and shall say all manner of evil against you falsely, for my sake. Rejoice, and be exceeding glad: for great is your reward in heaven: for so persecuted they the prophets which were before you" (Matthew 5:11–12). The Bible praises Christians who were persecuted, saying, "Ye . . . took joyfully the spoiling of your goods, knowing in yourselves that ye have in heaven a better and an enduring substance" (Hebrews 10:34). Christians are to follow Christ in loving their enemies. Following Christ and loving others is far more important than a job or a house or even a reputation.

of abortions was accused of violating federal law about abortions, his administration supported the provider before all the facts were known.

These three issues widened political divisions in the United States. Republicans generally opposed abortion and gay marriage. They often questioned the science behind climate change and whether humans were to blame. Democrats tended to support abortion and gay marriage. Democrats typically believed that climate change was happening and that it was due, in part, to human action. With these deep divisions, Democrats and Republicans often found it hard to work with each other.

Obama's presidency saw this division deepen. When running for president, he promised to unite Americans. But that job may have been more than a president could do.

Conclusion

The closer a person is to history, the harder it is to judge what is most significant. The events of the American Revolution passed so long ago that historians find it easier to judge what was most influential. But events in the past decade are close. People will eventually be able to better judge what influences from the Obama years mattered most. Will Americans continue to become less religious? Will the nation remain ineffective in foreign wars? Will President Obama's healthcare plan work? Time will tell.

Despite this uncertainty, the world is not without hope. People have always been flawed. God uses men and women with flaws to bring good changes. Christians can confidently serve God. Nothing done for Him is in vain.

> Why do Americans not unite to solve moral problems?

//// **Activity** //

Presenting a Speech

Speeches are a major part of politics, but everyone in life needs to verbally present an argument at one time or another. Pick a topic (e.g., Caring for Human Life, Caring for the Environment,

Immigration in American Life), research it, write a brief outline, and present a short speech. The speech can be either persuasive or informative.

//

451

Activity //

Presenting a Speech

- Generate excitement about presenting a speech as you read the Activity information aloud.

- Explain the directions for preparing and presenting the speech. Remind the students of the importance of recording their research sources. Guide the students in choosing appropriate topics by assigning each student a topic or by allowing each student to choose a topic from a prepared list. Give guidance as needed as the students prepare and present their speeches.

- You may choose to allow time for the students to work on their speeches while at school, or assign a specific period of time for them to prepare their speeches outside of the classroom.

- Allow time on several different days for the students to present their speeches.

Objective
- Recall concepts and terms from Chapter 20

Introduction
- Concepts for the Chapter 20 Test will be taken from Activity Manual pages 295–308. You may review any or all of the concepts during this lesson. You may choose to review Chapter 20 by playing "Q and A."

Review

Game: "Q and A"
- Divide the students into two teams. Direct the teams to write down questions from the chapter to ask the other team. Alternate having one team ask the other team a question. Award points for correct answers. The team with the most points at the end of the game wins.

Activity Manual
- Guide completion of pages 307–8.

Lesson **180** Chapter 20 Test

Objective
- Demonstrate knowledge of concepts from Chapter 20 by taking the test

Assessment
- Administer Test 20.

Appendix

Explaining the Gospel

One of the greatest desires of Christian teachers is to lead children to faith in the Savior. God has called you to present the gospel to your students so that they may repent and trust Christ, thereby being acceptable to God through Christ.

Relying on the Holy Spirit, you should take advantage of the opportunities that arise for presenting the good news of Jesus Christ. Ask questions to personally apply the Ten Commandments to your students (e.g., What is sin? Have *you* ever told a lie or taken something that wasn't yours? Are *you* a sinner?). You may also ask questions to discern the child's sincerity or to reveal any misunderstanding he might have (e.g., What is the gospel? What does it mean to repent? Can you do anything to save yourself?). Read verses from your Bible. You may find the following outline helpful, especially when dealing individually with a child.

1. I have sinned (Romans 3:23).

- Sin is disobeying God's Word (1 John 3:4). I break the Ten Commandments (Exodus 20:2–17) by loving other people or things more than I love God, worshiping other things or people, using God's name lightly, disobeying and dishonoring my parents, lying, stealing, cheating, thinking harmful and sinful thoughts, or wanting something that belongs to somebody else.
- Therefore, I am a sinner (Psalm 51:5, 58:3; Jeremiah 17:9).
- God is holy and must punish me for my sin (Isaiah 6:3; Romans 6:23).
- God hates sin, and there is nothing that I can do to get rid of my sin by myself (Titus 3:5; Romans 3:20, 28). I cannot make myself become a good person.

2. Jesus died for me (Romans 5:8).

- God loves me even though I am a sinner.
- He sent His Son, Jesus Christ, to die on the cross for me. Christ is sinless and did not deserve death. Because of His love for me, Christ took my sin on Himself and was punished in my place (1 Peter 2:24*a*; 1 Corinthians 15:3; John 1:29).
- God accepted Christ's death as the perfect substitution for the punishment of my sin (2 Corinthians 5:21).
- Three days later, God raised Jesus from the dead. Jesus is alive today and offers salvation to all. This is the gospel of Jesus Christ: He died on the cross for our sins according to the Scriptures, and He rose again the third day according to the Scriptures (1 Corinthians 15:1–4; 2 Peter 3:9; 1 Timothy 2:4).

3. I need to put my trust in Jesus (Romans 10:9–10, 13–14*a*).

- I must repent (turn away from my sin) and trust only Jesus Christ for salvation (Mark 1:15).
- If I repent and believe in what Jesus has done, I am putting my trust in Jesus.
- Everyone who trusts in Jesus is forgiven of sin (Acts 2:21) and will live forever with God (John 3:16). I am given His righteousness and become a new creation, with Christ living in me (2 Corinthians 5:21; Colossians 1:27).

If a child shows genuine interest and readiness, ask, "Are you ready to put your trust in Jesus and depend on only Christ for salvation?" If he says yes, then ask him to talk to God about this. Perhaps he will pray something like the following:

> God, I know that I've sinned against You and that You hate sin, but that You also love me. I believe that Jesus died to pay for my sin and that He rose from the dead, so I put my trust in Jesus to forgive me and give me a home with You forever. In Jesus' name I pray. Amen.

Show the child how to know from God's Word whether he is forgiven and in God's family (1 John 5:12–13; John 3:18). Encourage the child to follow Jesus by obeying Him each day. Tell him that whenever he sins, he will be forgiven as soon as he confesses those sins to God (1 John 1:9).

Student Text Index

Mexico, 137, 187, 392
Miami, 102
middle class, 54, 342
middle colonies, 47, 59–61
Middle East, 23
Midway, Battle of, 302–3
Midwest, 14, 129, 134
migrated, 12
militants, 437
military, 369
militia, 70
mill girls, 133
minimum wage, 319
mining towns, 176
Minuit, Peter, 33
minutemen, 77–78
Mississippi River, 108
Missouri Compromise, 114–15
modernists, 257
Monroe Doctrine, 113
Monroe, James, 113–14, 129
Montcalm, Louis Joseph de, 72
Montenegro, 398
Montgomery, Bernard, 300
Moody, Dwight L., 205
morality, 255
Morris, Robert, 80
Morse, Samuel, 131
MRI, 377
munitions, 153
music, 203, 331, 345, 376
Muslim, 23, 27, 33, 37, 61, 370, 398, 402–3, 414, 419–20, 436–38, 445–46
Mussolini, Benito, 281–82
mustard gas, 238

N

NAACP, 225
Nagasaki, 315
National Aeronautics and Space Administration (NASA), 329, 375
National American Woman Suffrage Association, 219
national bank, 122
nationalism, 231
Nationalist Party, 294
National Recovery Administration, 271
National Recovery System, 267
National Republican Party, 120
National Road, 129
Native Americans, 109
Navajos, 7–8, 20
Navy SEALs, 435
Nazi, 285–87, 312
negotiate, 154
Netherlands, 33, 39, 83
Nettleton, Asahel, 127

Neutrality Acts, 296
New Deal, 265, 268, 270–73, 366, 423
New England, 43–44, 47, 53, 56–57, 59, 62, 65, 70
New England Primer, 58
New Left, 345–46, 358, 410
New Netherland, 33, 49
New Orleans, 108
newspapers, 203
New World, 17, 51–53
Nez Perce, 13–14, 181
Nicaragua, 222
Nicholas II (czar), 244
Nimitz, Chester, 303–4
Niña, 27
ninety-five theses, 31
Nisei, 307
Nixon, Richard, 332, 349–50, 352–55
Nobel Peace Prize, 221, 434
No Child Left Behind, 407
no man's land, 236
Noriega, Manuel, 384
Normandy, 310
North Africa, 300
North American Free Trade Agreement (NAFTA), 387, 399
North Atlantic Treaty Organization (NATO), 324
Northeast, 16, 18–19, 69
Northern Ireland, 399
Northwest Passage, 32
Nova Scotia, 70
nullify, 121
Nuremberg Laws, 287

O

Obama, Barack, 427–31, 434, 440, 444–45, 448, 450
O'Connor, Sandra Day, 367
offensive, 245
Oglethorpe, James, 52
Ohio River valley, 70, 72
oil, 186
Oil Polution Act, 382
Okinawa, 313
Oklahoma Territory, 125
"Old Ironsides," 111
Olmecs, 5
Open Door policy, 221
Open Skies policy, 328
Operation Desert Storm, 386
orally, 20
Oregon Territory, 135
Orlando, Vittorio, 250
Oswald, Lee Harvey, 337
Ottoman Empire, 23
overproduction, 261

P

pacifism, 71
Palin, Sarah, 430
pamphlet, 61
Panama, 222, 384
Panama Canal, 221–22
parapets, 235
pardons, 403
Parks, Rosa, 322
Parliament, 72
Paris, 74
patent, 188
Patriots, 74, 78–79, 82, 84
Patton, George, 300
peace, 37, 41, 88–90, 103–4, 149, 154, 181, 222, 229, 231, 241, 244, 249–51, 293–94, 323, 344, 346, 349, 353, 369–70, 384, 392, 398–99, 403, 429, 435, 437, 445–46
Peace Corps, 333
Peace of Paris, 90
Pearl Harbor, 290, 298–99
Penn, William, 50–51, 72
Pentagon, 411
perjury, 397
Perot, Ross, 388–89
Perry, Oliver Hazard, 111
Pershing, John J., 243
personal computer, 376, 394
Philadelphia, 50, 61, 81–82
philanthropist, 194
Philippines, 72, 211
phonograph, 189
photography, 198
Pilgrims, 17, 39–42
Pinchot, Gifford, 214, 220
Pinckney, Eliza, 63
Pinta, 27
Pitcalm, John, 78
Pitt, William, 72
Plains of Abraham, 72
planes, 238
plantations, 63
plumbers, 354–55
Plymouth, 17, 40, 42, 47
Plymouth Colony, 42–43, 47–48
Pocahontas, 37, 139
poisonous gas, 238, 240
Poland, 295
political machine, 270
political parties, 103, 105, 112, 142
Polk, James, 135–37
pollution, 350–51
Pope, John, 150
Populist Party, 228
Portugal, 23, 26, 28
postal service, 130

potlatch, 11
powder keg, 232
Powell, Colin, 386
power plants, 189
Powhatan, 36–37
Prescott, Samuel, 78
prime minister, 74
Princeton, 66
Princeton Theological Seminary, 204
Proclamation of 1763, 73
Progressive Era, 213, 218–19, 224–25, 227–28
Project Mercury, 329
proprietary colonies, 53
Providence, 49
Prussia, 72
public library, 61
pueblo, 5, 7–8, 19
Puerto Rico, 212
Pullman, George, 190
Puritans, 39, 44–45, 48–49, 56–57
Putin, Vladimir, 446

Q

Qaddafi, Muammar al-, 437
Qaeda al-, 414–17, 421
quadrant, 24
Quakers, 50, 59, 71
Quayle, Dan, 382
Quebec, 32, 72

R

Race to the Sea, 234
ranchers, 182
rationalism, 126
ration book, 306
railroads, 130, 180, 186, 190
Reagan Doctrine, 371
Reagan, Nancy, 373
Reagan, Ronald, 364–68, 371–74, 378–79, 381
Reaganomics, 366
realism, 201
reaper, 134, 177
recall, 218
recession, 387
Reclamation Act of 1902, 215
Reconstruction, 161, 163, 165, 167, 170, 172, 174
Reconstruction Act of 1867, 166–67
referendum, 218
religion, 19, 410
repeal, 74
representative government, 51
republican government, 93

Teacher's Edition Index

Student Text Photo Credits

Chapter 1

4 ©iStockphoto.com/Brian_Brockman; **8** © Ejkrouse | Dreamstime.com; **9t** Nativestock/Getty Images; **9b** "Basketry tray, Santa Barbara Mission, early 1800s"/Wikimedia Commons/Public Domain; **15** © Niday Picture Library / Alamy; **19t** © Dja65 | Dreamstime.com; **19b**, **20** Werner Forman/Contributor/Universal Images Group/Getty Images

Chapter 2

29 World Digital Library/Public Domain; **34l** "Castello-PlanOriginal"/Wikimedia Commons/Public Domain; **34r** ©iStockphoto.com/amriphoto; **38** Courtesy Preservation Virginia; **42** Photo courtesy Plimoth Plantation © 2015

Chapter 3

51 ©iStock.com/vgoodrich; **58** © North Wind Picture Archives/Alamy

Chapter 4

74 "Proof sheet of one-penny stamps submitted for approval to Commissioners of Stamps by engraver. 10 May 1765"/Wikimedia Commons/Public Domain; **83t** ©iStockphoto.com/LPETTET; **83b** ©iStockphoto.com/Maher; **89** "Surrender of Lord Cornwallis"/Wikimedia Commons/Public Domain

Chapter 5

94 © North Wind Picture Archives / Alamy; **108** Courtesy American Philosophical Society

Chapter 6

125 SuperStock; **131** ilbusca/E+/Getty Images; **133l** Geoff Brightling/Dorling Kindersley/Getty Images; **133r** Dorling Kindersley/Getty Images

Chapter 7

146 Library of Congress; **148** "Scott-anaconda"/Library of Congress/Wikimedia Commons; **155** Library of Congress; **157** "1st Minnesota at Gettysburg" by Don Toiani/Courtesy of the National Guard/Wikimedia Commons/CC-BY-2.0; **158** "ShirleysWhiteHouseVicksburg1863"/Wikimedia Commons/Public Domain; **159** Public Domain; **160** National Geographic/SuperStock; **161** Library of Congress

Chapter 8

169tl Wikimedia Commons/LOC/Public Domain; **169bl** Buyenlarge/Archive Photos/Getty Images; **169tc** Getty Images/ullstein bild; **169bc**, **169tr** Wikimedia Commons/LOC/Public Domain; **169br** Buyenlarge/Archive Photos/Getty Images; **171t** Public Domain; **171b** The New York Historical Society/Archive Photos/Getty Images; **173** © CORBIS

Chapter 9

187 Public Domain; **193** Chicago History Museum/Contributor/Archive Photos/Getty Images; **194** Library of Congress; **195** © Ferenz | Dreamstime.com; **196** Copyright Bettmann/Corbis/AP Images; **197** The Art Archive at Art Resource, NY; **199t**, **199b** The Museum of the City of New York / Art Resource, NY; **200** © Sueddeutsche Zeitung Photo/Alamy; **202l** "John Singer Sargent - Miss Beatrice Townsend"/Wikimedia Commons/Public Domain; **202r** Courtesy National Gallery of Art, Washington; **203l** © The Metropolitan Museum of Art. Image source: Art Resource, NY; **203r** Rago Arts/Bigstock.com

Chapter 10

219t Photo 12/Getty Images; **219bl** Buyenlarge/Getty Images; **219br** © Bettmann/CORBIS; **222** U.S. Navy/Public Domain; **223** LOC/Public Domain; **224** ©Everett Historical/Shutterstock

Chapter 11

236 "Illustrated London News - Christmas Truce 1914"/Wikimedia Commons/Public Domain; **239** Hulton Archive/Getty Images; **240** Public Domain; **246** "Unclesamwantyou"/Wikimedia Commons/Public Domain; **247l**, **247r** Public Domain; **248** Hulton Collection/Hulton Archive/Getty Images; **250** Universal Images Group/Getty Images; **251** Paul Thompson/FPG/Archive Photos/Getty Images

Chapter 12

254l ©Everett Collection/Alamy Stock Photo; **254r** Seattle Children's Theatre (presents) Flight" a living newspaper play LCCN98518444"/Wikimedia Commons/Public Domain; **256** Hulton Archive/Staff/Getty Images; **258** Dallas Theological Seminary; **268l** ©Richard Levine / Alamy Stock Photo; **268r** AP Photo/CH; **270** © CORBIS; **272** Fotosearch/Archive Photos/Getty Images

Chapter 13

277 SuperStock; **278l** Heritage Images/Contributor/Hulton Archive/Getty Images; **278r** Sovfoto/Contributor/Universal Images Group/Getty Images; **279l** Fine Art Images/Superstock; **279r** © Bettmann/CORBIS; **282** Keystone/Staff/Hulton Archive/Getty Images; **285** National Archives; **286** Sovfoto/Contributor/Universal Images Group/Getty Images; **288l** Anthony Potter Collection/Contributor/Archive Photos/Getty Images; **288tr** Hulton Archive/Getty Images; **288r** Galerie Bilderwelt/Contributor/Hulton Archive/Getty Images

Teacher's Notes

472

How to Use the Teacher's Toolkit CD

Contents

The Teacher's Toolkit CD contains the following materials:

- Activity Manual Answer Key
- Background Information
- Instructional Aids
- Instructional Aids Answer Key
- Interactive Visuals
- Visuals
- Quizzes
- Quizzes Answer Key
- Materials List
- Rubrics

Getting Started

Viewing the Teacher's Toolkit CD materials requires Adobe® Reader® 9.0 or higher. The most recent version of Adobe Reader may be downloaded at no charge from the Adobe website at www.adobe.com. An Internet connection is required to download Reader.

Windows

Insert the CD. The CD is designed to start automatically if your computer is set to allow it. If it does not start automatically, click "Run" if given the option. You may also choose to open the folder to view the CD's files and double-click "Startup.exe" to start the CD. Read and accept the license agreement to begin using the Teacher's Toolkit materials. Navigate within the CD using the bookmarks on the left side of the screen.

Mac

Insert the CD, click on the CD icon, and open the file "main.pdf" to begin using the Teacher's Toolkit CD materials.

Minimum System Requirements

Processor (CPU): Pentium 4
Operating System: Windows XP; Mac OS Leopard (version 10.5)
RAM: 256 MB
Display: 1024 × 768
Application: Adobe Reader 9.0

Additional Help

Additional usage information can be found on the CD. For further assistance, call BJU Press Customer Service at 1-800-845-5731.